Focus th Word

IDEAS AND RESOURCES FOR A
LIVING LITURGY FOR EVERY SUNDAY OF THE YEAR

SUSAN SAYERS

Illustrated by
Arthur Baker

Kevin Mayhew

This edition first published in
Great Britain in 1989 by

KEVIN MAYHEW LTD
Rattlesden
Bury St Edmunds
Suffolk IP30 0SZ

ISBN 0 86209 095 4

Cover design by Robert Williams
Cover drawing by Juliette Clarke

Printed and bound in Great Britain by
Redwood Burn Limited, Trowbridge, Wiltshire

Contents

ORDINARY TIME	Year A	Year B	Year C
Second Sunday in Ordinary Time	54	149	238
Third Sunday in Ordinary Time	55	150	239
Fourth Sunday in Ordinary Time	56	152	240
Fifth Sunday in Ordinary Time	58	153	241
Sixth Sunday in Ordinary Time	59	155	243
Seventh Sunday in Ordinary Time	60	156	244
Eighth Sunday in Ordinary Time	62	158	245
Ninth Sunday in Ordinary Time	64	159	247
Tenth Sunday in Ordinary Time	65	160	248
Eleventh Sunday in Ordinary Time	67	162	249
Twelfth Sunday in Ordinary Time	69	163	251
Thirteenth Sunday in Ordinary Time	71	165	252
Fourteenth Sunday in Ordinary Time	72	166	254
Fifteenth Sunday in Ordinary Time	73	167	255
Sixteenth Sunday in Ordinary Time	75	169	256
Seventeenth Sunday in Ordinary Time	76	171	258
Eighteenth Sunday in Ordinary Time	77	172	259
Nineteenth Sunday in Ordinary Time	79	173	261
Twentieth Sunday in Ordinary Time	80	175	262
Twenty-First Sunday in Ordinary Time	82	176	264
Twenty-Second Sunday in Ordinary Time	83	177	265
Twenty-Third Sunday in Ordinary Time	85	179	266
Twenty-Fourth Sunday in Ordinary Time	87	180	268
Twenty-Fifth Sunday in Ordinary Time	88	182	270
Twenty-Sixth Sunday in Ordinary Time	90	183	271
Twenty-Seventh Sunday in Ordinary Time	91	184	273
Twenty-Eighth Sunday in Ordinary Time	92	186	274
Twenty-Ninth Sunday in Ordinary Time	94	187	275
Thirtieth Sunday in Ordinary Time	95	188	277
Thirty-First Sunday in Ordinary Time	96	190	278
Thirty-Second Sunday in Ordinary Time	97	191	280
Thirty-Third Sunday in Ordinary Time	99	193	281
Our Lord Jesus Christ, Universal King (Last Sunday in Ordinary Time)	100	194	282

How to use this book

This book is intended as a resource for a parish and the individuals and groups within it. It focuses attention on the theme of each Sunday, exploring it in terms of the Penitential Rite, Bidding Prayers and readings for the day.

There are suggestions, too, for less usual expressions of worship, which are the mark of a living, growing Church. Drama, mime and dance are well within the capability of many congregations and can be used most effectively in the context of worship.

The ideas, even the prayers offered, are not meant to be exhaustive. You might, for example, "borrow" the sentiments and content of the intentions of the Bidding Prayers, but leave the exact wording to the reader (or deacon).

It is hoped that this resource book will help to encourage the members of Christ's body to share in their preparation and celebration of worship, even the very young, so that their Christian response is enriched and deepened, so that our liturgy comes alive.

Group Preparation

The worshipping community will be richer for shared preparation of the Word, ready for the Sunday celebration.

Groups are best kept fairly small, varied in age, and, to avoid cliques and to spread gifts and talents, it may be wise to shuffle members round regularly.

Begin with silence, to concentrate attention and focus on Christ, who is present at each group. After some prayer, read the following Sunday's readings aloud.

The ideas on the readings in this book are intended to start discussion, suggest links with the theme, and stimulate thought. For each season of the Church year questions are included as a way to focus attention on particular issues arising from the readings. Use them as a springboard and then dive in.

It may be valuable to make notes of any suggestions or queries which emerge, so they can be referred to the community as a whole.

Finish with silence and praise, and avoid running over time.

Prayer of the Faithful

No mass-produced form for the intercessions will be right for an individual parish with its own particular needs and form of expression.

At the same time, it is sometimes difficult for a group to work out the expression of needs in a vacuum. Accordingly, I have written suggested prayers quite fully, growing out of the week's theme. The best way to use these is to read them through and see if they trigger any particular needs of the parish. Then change and simplify them according to who is going to be present.

Children

If your community offers Sunday "lessons" for the children, the teachers or catechists should meet regularly to prepare their material and decide on the aim of each lesson. Once a month is probably enough to prepare the next four or five lessons, and a different team member may be given responsibility for each week.

The children's work in this book links closely with the week's theme and readings, so that the whole family of Christ will be sharing the Word and focusing their attention on particular areas through the Church's year.

They can, of course, be adapted to suit the age and needs of each class. The teachers should also prepare for the readings at their own level, so that the children will benefit from these thoughts and insights, too.

The children may have produced a display or model. It is important, not just for them, but also for the whole congregation, that the work is seen and shared. Often the directness of the children's work can trigger new understanding among adults.

Drama and Dance

Many of the Old Testament and Gospel readings can be brought to life, movingly presented through dance, mime and drama.

The drama group needs to study the reading prayerfully before discussing how best to stage it. The freshness of original ideas may be most effective, but here are a few suggestions to start you off:

- have a narrator to read, and simply mime what he says. Anyone not involved in the action at any one time freezes in his last position, like "statues";

- give individuals their words to say, and work on making these part of the narration;

- have one or two instruments (guitar and percussion, for instance, or organ) to play quietly as a background to the reading, giving extra time between sentences for mimed action;

- use a few materials as props and costumes. They need not be elaborate, just enough to aid imagination;

- use all corners of the building and involve the congregation as members of the crowd;

- use live or taped music and depict not only the actions, through mime, but also the atmosphere and feelings, through dance. Keep it natural and simple, but controlled.

Involvement

Within every parish the gifts are many and varied, and can be developed and used in worship.

Musically there may be the raw material for a rock or folk group, orchestra or recorder group.

There may be *dancers*, of all weights and ages; for in

liturgical dance reverence and gracefulness are much more important than how high you can kick!

The *Bidding Prayers* may sometimes be prepared and led by a particular organisation, or those living in a particular street, and suggestions are given in this book to help prepare them.

There may be many who are *artistically inclined*, and could, as a team, decorate the church or prepare a teaching display board on each of the seasons and work of the church. For the building can also be a witness to visitors, who may be touched or moved by the care and love it shows, and we cannot afford to waste any opportunity for bringing others to Christ.

Music

Sometimes instrumental music can be an alternative to singing a hymn, or an aid to prayer and meditation during communion or between the readings. This may be an opportunity for a group of musicians in the parish to contribute to the worship; for parishes where such talent is thin on the ground, taped music is a very valuable resource.

Accordingly, there are suggested pieces of music for each Sunday, chosen to reflect the theme of the week. They are mostly well-known pieces which should be widely available. They are only suggestions: having prepared the readings, other ideas may spring to mind.

In the same way, particular hymns are suggested for certain days. They are not the obvious choices, such as 'O come, O come, Emmanuel' during Advent, for instance, since these can be easily found and chosen from a comprehensive hymn book such as *Hymns Old and New*. Instead, hymns have been selected which seem very appropriate for the theme of the day, but which may not normally be considered.

The following references have been used throughout the book:

BSOS	Best of Songs of the Spirit
MSOS	More Songs of the Spirit
MWTP	Many Ways to Praise
ONE	Hymns Old & New (Enlarged)
SONL	Songs of New Life
SOS 3	Songs of the Spirit, 3

Year of Matthew : A

ADVENT

1st Sunday of Advent

Theme
Prepare for God's coming

The ancient stories and prophecies of the Old Testament speak of a time when both natural and political violence will be past, as God's great purpose for the world is accomplished. That time is fast approaching: we must put our lives in order to be ready for the Saviour's coming.

Penitential Rite

Give us strength to grow in love,
Lord, have mercy. **Lord, have mercy.**

Give us light to see our sin,
Christ, have mercy. **Christ, have mercy.**

Give us grace to be prepared,
Lord, have mercy. **Lord, have mercy.**

Notes on the Readings

Isaiah 2:1-5

All around him the prophet sees people turning their backs on God and adding miseries, burdens and insecurities to their quality of life as a result. Political unrest, hostile attitudes and violence abound.

Yet in this vision Isaiah sees beyond the immediate, depressing troubles to a time when God's purpose is accomplished, and he is Lord and sovereign over all nations. With a loving God accepted into each heart, the whole fabric of society will be charged with joy and peace, so that war at last becomes irrelevant.

Does this sound too good to be true in our own unsettled and violent world? Isaiah is not an idle dreamer: this is not a pipe-dream but a 'vision' or 'showing' of God-filled reality. When, in the Lord's Prayer, we say: 'may your kingdom come', this is what we are praying about. But how soon the kingdom comes, depends entirely on us.

If we all use our lives in being instruments for God to work through, then his influence will spread rapidly throughout our areas of living and working, and many will start living by Christ's way of love. If we all wait for someone else to start working full-time for God, can we really ever pray the Lord's Prayer again?

Romans 13:11-14

We are physical beings and our bodies are very important. Through them we can express our loving and caring, our thoughts and feelings, sorrows and joys. They are also survival machines; physical, mental and spiritual cravings are built in so that we are alerted to provide what is necessary for continued life.

All this is sensible and good. We should 'listen' to our bodies, sometimes, so that we can provide them with the food, rest or exercise they need. They are God-given, and precious.

On the other hand, we should not become 'addicted' to them, in the sense that their satisfaction is all-important. Of course, the advertising world and media will try to convince us that it is.

But as Christians we know that life is more than the body, and if we are to be ready when Christ comes, we must discipline ourselves and instead of indulging every craving for immediate satisfaction, set our eyes on the far more deeply satisfying joy of living in tune with our body's creator and sustainer, God himself.

Matthew 24:37-44

Jesus' teaching about the second coming gives us ample warning, if we will listen. People are always inclined to think that disasters may happen to others but won't happen to them. We also tend to tell ourselves that there will be plenty of opportunity to prepare ourselves for death later on – when the children are off our hands, for instance, or once the decorating is finished, or when the ironing is out of the way.

Jesus tells his disciples quite clearly that we will not know when the Son of Man comes until it is too late to start preparing. There is only one time when we can prepare to make sure we are ready when he comes: that time is now.

Bidding Prayers

Celebrant　My brothers and sisters, in the knowledge that God our Father is here present, let us pray.

Reader　For the Church of Christ and its mission to the world; that it may alert all sinners to repentance, and bring many to the joy of living in your love.
Pause
Lord, our Father: **hear us as we pray.**

For the whole created world and its peoples; that no evil may thwart your will, but that rather your kingdom may be established and your will fulfilled.
Pause
Lord, our Father: **hear us as we pray.**

For all who suffer – mentally, physically and spiritually; for those who see no further than immediate, material comforts, and do not realise their spiritual poverty.
Pause
Lord, our Father: **hear us as we pray.**

For this parish and all who serve our community; that we may strive each day to align our lives with the life of Christ who saves us from our sin.
Pause
Lord, our Father: **hear us as we pray.**

Celebrant　Father, trusting in your mercy, we lay these prayers before you, through Jesus Christ, our Lord. **Amen.**

Ideas for Adults

The Old Testament reading can be dramatised using different voices. Where a phrase is marked 'All' why not have everybody joining in? The other parts are read by small groups of men and women.

Men: The vision of Isaiah, son of Amoz,
concerning Judah and Jerusalem.
Women: In the days to come
the mountain of the Temple of the Lord
shall tower above the mountains   *crescendo*
Both: and be lifted higher than the hills.
Men: All the nations will stream to it,
Women: peoples without number will come to it;
and they will say:
All: 'Come, let us go up to the mountain of the Lord,
to the temple of the God of Jacob
that he may teach us his ways
so that we may walk in his paths:
since the Law will go out from Zion,
and the oracle of the Lord from Jerusalem.'
Men: He will wield authority over the nations   *f*
Women: and adjudicate between many peoples,
Men: these will hammer their swords into ploughshares,
their spears into sickles.
Both: Nation will not lift sword against nation,
there will be no more training for war.   *p*
All: House of Jacob, come,
let us walk in the light of the Lord.   *crescendo*

Ideas for Children

Explain that Advent means 'coming' and that in the weeks before Christmas we are preparing ourselves for the coming of Jesus. Tell them that as well as coming as a baby at Christmas time, 1,986 years ago (or however many years ago it is), he will come again one day with glory and power. We don't know when it will be, so we must be ready for him. (With older children, read today's Gospel.) How can we get ready for Jesus?

Have written on a chart or blackboard:
1. We must get to know him by reading about him and talking to him every day.
2. We must try to be kinder and more loving.

Show the children a good selection of Bible story books which will be lent to them each week. If you do not have a church library for children this is a good time to start one. Have them sign for each book they borrow, and appoint two older children to be in charge each week. Then help the children make their own book of prayers to use every day. Give out cardboard covers with 'My Book of Prayers' on the front. This can be coloured and decorated. Inside have eight pages. On the first page have written:

Dear Father,
I want to get
to know you better,
so that I
can love you more.
Please help me.
Amen.

They can all read this out as a prayer together, and sing I *have a friend (MWTP)*.

Suggest that they say this prayer every day, and read at least one Bible story book during the week.

Music
Recorded Music

The end of the Lloyd Webber *Requiem* (with the boy's voice sustained)

'Live' Music

I was glad when they said *(ONE, 261)*
There will be signs *(ONE, 544)*
They shall hammer their swords into ploughshares *(SONL, 55)*

2nd Sunday of Advent

Theme
Repent, for the kingdom of heaven is near

The only way to prepare for the Saviour's coming is through thorough self-examination and repentance. This complete break with sin will open the way for growth and fruit, which will eventually encompass the whole of creation in a kingdom of peace, safety and fulfilment.

Penitential Rite

Remove all our obstacles to your love,
Lord, have mercy. **Lord, have mercy.**

Break down all our barriers to your love,
Christ, have mercy. **Christ, have mercy.**

Uproot the sins we have grown used to,
Lord, have mercy. **Lord, have mercy.**

Notes on the Readings

Isaiah 11:1-10

Authority brings not only power, but also responsibility. Government brings both in large quantities; unfortunately, possessing power often provides plenty of opportunity and temptation for avoiding responsibilities.

This passage gives an idea of what government can be like if it springs out of an allegiance to God, as supreme Lord: at its best, government can become the instrument for God's caring, just and merciful nature. But we are quite mistaken if we assume that any political ideology will do this automatically. A government's capacity for doing God's will is dependent on those within it and it is important to pray that they may be receptive to God's truth, wisdom, justice and compassion. The more we make ourselves right with God, the nearer our world will be enabled to come to a God-filled kingdom of peace and love.

Romans 15:4-9

In case we start despairing of any real change happening in areas of darkness, Paul reminds us, as well as the Christians in Rome, that scripture teaches us much about hope; many have been blessed who have struggled on in spite of setbacks, and refused to give up.

With us, too, there will be an inner peace and joyfulness if we persevere in spreading the respect and tolerance of Christian care through our society. We have Christ's example of involved friendship; as we follow it, more people will be attracted to the God who can save them, and the world will be a better place: more caring, less violent, and in tune with its creator.

Matthew 3:1-12

We have a strong instinct for survival. Once we see a real possibility of a winnower approaching we will make pretty certain that we shall be among the wheat and not the chaff. No doubt at the end of time, vast numbers will come to a late repentance at the first glimpse of the son of man actually coming in glory.

The sight of John the Baptist, with the clothing and life-style of a holy man, impressed upon his contemporaries an urgency to prepare themselves for the coming Messiah; and even the complacent, who assumed spiritual birth-rights, were shocked into making a confession of their sin. John warns them that the extent of their repentance will not be hidden: for thorough repentance is bound to burst into fruit before long.

Perhaps it seems that the urgency is lacking for repentance in our lives, because we see no immediate threat of extinction.

It is worth remembering that with the coming of Christ, a new and final age was begun. We, who have seen him, have far less excuse to be unprepared or to have frittered our lives away without reference to the good news he brought. From us, to whom much has been given, much will be expected. And whether at death, or at the end of the world, we shall meet him face to face. Perhaps we should start taking repentance seriously straight away.

Bidding Prayers

Celebrant As children of our caring,
heavenly Father, let us pray.

Reader For all Christians throughout the world;
that they may simply and wholeheartedly
follow Christ, so that their lives
witness to the beauty
and peace of his kingdom.
Pause
Father of love: **remake our lives.**

For all world leaders, governments
and their advisers;
that they may be inspired to lead
their people wisely and fairly,
with understanding and sensitivity.
Pause
Father of love: **remake our lives.**

For all those who feel trapped
by the emotional, financial or
political circumstances of their lives;
that in Christ they may find
freedom and vitality.
Pause
Father of love: **remake our lives.**

For our own families and loved ones,
especially any from whom
we are separated;
that we may learn to see Christ
in each face, and serve him
in caring for each other.
Pause
Father of love: **remake our lives.**

Celebrant Father of all time and place
accept these prayers through
Jesus Christ. **Amen.**

Ideas for Adults

In the Old Testament reading have flute, recorder, guitar or keyboard playing softly in the background from 'The wolf lives with the lamb' until 'as the waters swell the sea.' Alternatively, this section could be read by a young, clear voice in contrast to an older voice in the first half and last few lines.

Ideas for Children

Continue the library exchange and give a short time to discussing what the children have learnt about Jesus during the week. Then tell them the story of John the Baptist, if possible against the background of slides showing the bare mountainous region he lived in, and the river Jordan. (The local Christian resource centre may be able to help here. And if a parish visit to the Holy Land is ever planned, ask for some specifically teaching slides to be brought back for future reference.) Point out that Advent is a good time to be 'washed' from all our nastiness, grumpiness, disobedience, bad temper etc.

In the next page of their prayer book ask them to write an 'I am sorry' prayer, asking God the Father to forgive them, and help them live more lovingly in future.

Music
Recorded Music

Mendelssohn – *Calm Sea and Prosperous Voyage*   Op 27

'Live' Music

Amazing grace *(ONE, 36)*
From the depths of sin and sadness *(ONE, 155)*
Lead us, heavenly Father *(ONE, 298)*
Lord Jesus think on me *(ONE, 327)*
Sprinkling song (SONL, 81)

3rd Sunday of Advent

Theme
Take heart; the Lord is very near

As the coming of Jesus, both at Christmas, and at the end of all things, grows closer, we need not be fearful but rejoice. For he has promised to bring life where it is barren, like water to a desert. Let us wait patiently in this great hope so that we recognise him when he comes.

Penitential Rite

Where we are barren, you can bring life,
Lord, have mercy. **Lord, have mercy.**

Where we are blind, you can bring sight,
Christ, have mercy. **Christ, have mercy.**

Where we are scattered, you can make whole,
Lord, have mercy. **Lord, have mercy.**

Notes on the Readings

Isaiah 35:1-6, 10

Isaiah recognises that all human systems are fallible and liable to be weak or corrupt. None can ever be totally satisfying for man, who craves a profound peace and fulfilment. However, the good news is that the craving can be satisfied, for the world's creator and powerful sustainer is a God of goodness and love, a God of 'resurrection' or bringing-to-life, as he demonstrated personally in Christ.

This means that no area of apparent bleakness or despair is beyond the touch of God's life-giving refreshment. Even the most appalling human errors, the most enervating disease, the harshest bitterness or deepest depression can be transformed, made whole and renewed by God's power.

So we have a great deal to rejoice about; and as we catch the excitement of what that power can do, let us make sure that we bring it everywhere we go, getting it to the heart of the worst problems, so that God's saving power is not blocked by human obstacles.

James 5:7-10

James gives very practical advice about living life Christ's way, and here he commends us to be patient, like farmers waiting for seeds to grow. They have no doubt that, having planted the grain, they will eventually reap a harvest, but it would be pretty pointless standing round in the field all day expecting them to sprout immediately.

Spiritually, though, we often do this. Having recognised God's power and a problem, we put the two together and then grumble at God for taking so long over sorting things out. James suggests we calm down, and trust that all will be accomplished; instead of complaining about things to God and each other we shall then be able to rest in his love, confident and stable in the knowledge that all things are in his good hands.

Matthew 11:2-11

The Old Testament had been a gradual unfolding of God's character and purpose, and there had been plenty of time for people to form fairly rigid ideas of the Messiah they were expecting.

John the Baptist, too, had been preaching about the coming Messiah as one who would judge, and sort out the good from the bad in awesome justice. So he is rather perplexed and surprised at the way Jesus is behaving, and begins to wonder if he might even have been mistaken in thinking him to be the promised Messiah. It is a sobering thought that even one as open to God's will as John could doubt Jesus' authority, due to preconceived ideas.

We often find that God works through the most unlikely people and places, and must be on our guard against rejecting his presence because it is not where we expected to find it.

Jesus sets John's mind at rest by pointing to his own 'good fruit'; if the sick are healed, and the blind are given sight, then the evidence is there – God's saving love is at work. We have to make up our own minds as to whether or not we accept the evidence.

Bidding Prayers

Celebrant   Trusting in the promise of God our Father
              to be faithful, let us approach him
              with our cares and concerns.

Reader   Let us pray for all Christians
           who are imprisoned or persecuted
           because of their faith;
           for the lapsed and the doubting;

for the newly-converted
and for all godparents;
that they may know the sovereignty
of God in all areas of life.
Pause
Father, you are our hope:
you are the hope of the world.

Let us pray for the world
of commerce and trade;
for the advertising companies,
for those working for television,
radio or the press;
that these may be channels
for enlightenment and discernment,
and instruments for good
in our society.
Pause
Father, you are our hope:
you are the hope of the world.

Let us pray for the malnourished
and the starving, for those
whose land no longer supports them;
for the diseased and the crippled;
that all people may be inspired
to care for one another,
to share the world's resources
and work towards unity
and mutual trust.
Pause
Father, you are our hope:
you are the hope of the world.

Let us pray for ourselves and our families
as we prepare for Christmas;
that we may grow in patience and faith,
and that our material preparations
may not blind us to God's love,
but rather be infused by it so that
he is central in our celebrations.
Pause
Father, you are our hope:
you are the hope of the world.

Celebrant   Lord, we ask you to hear these prayers
              for the sake of Jesus, our Saviour. **Amen.**

Ideas for Adults

1. A reading of the Isaiah prophecy can be accompanied by music (guitar and recorder or flute) or by shakers and handbells like this:

(shakers)   Let the wilderness and the dry-lands exult.
              Let the wasteland rejoice and bloom;
(bells in slow   let it bring forth flowers like the jonquil,
peal)   let it rejoice and sing for joy.
(bells peal twice)
(with shakers)   The glory of Lebanon is bestowed on it,
(one bell joins in) the splendour of Carmel and Sharon;
(two bells)   they shall see the glory of the Lord,
              the splendour of our God.
(bells peal once)
(shakers)   Strengthen all weary hands *(one bell rings once)*,
(shakers)   steady all trembling knees *(one bell rings once)*
              and say to all faint hearts,
(all bells peal   'Courage! Do not be afraid.
throughout)   Look, your God is coming,
              vengeance is coming,
              the retribution of God;
              he is coming to save you.'

(shakers) Then the eyes of the blind shall be opened,
the ears of the deaf unsealed,
then the lame shall leap like a deer
and the tongues of the dumb sing for joy;
(bells peal for those the Lord has ransomed shall return.
throughout) They will come to Zion shouting for joy,
everlasting joy on their faces;
joy and gladness will go with them
(bells emphasise
words) and sorrow and lament be ended.
(Final slow peal. Shakers finish)

If no bells are available, use glasses with different levels of water, tapped with a fork. This is simple but very effective.

2. The Gospel is effective if parts are taken and the words spoken by them. Have John sending his disciples in mime as the gospel reader begins. Then they ask Jesus the question and Jesus replies. They leave, and Jesus then walks down among the congregation who are the crowd. Have people ready to answer 'No' and 'Yes' where appropriate.

At 'he is the one of whom scripture says' have someone bring up a 'scroll' from which the words are read. Then the scroll is rolled up again as Jesus addresses the people for the last sentence.

Ideas for Children

Continue the library exchange and have a short discussion about what the children have discovered about Jesus. They will now have seen evidence of him healing, giving sight etc.

If you have Bibles available (such as the *Good News*) suitable for children, help them all to find the Isaiah reading. Explain that this was written long before Jesus lived, and then read it with them, asking them to see if it reminds them of anything they have been reading. Who did these things?

Then tell them about John the Baptist being put in prison, and sending his followers to ask if Jesus really was the man they had been waiting for. Spread out all the books and pictures of Jesus, so they can seen how Jesus was fulfilling Isaiah's prophecy.

In the next page of their prayer books, write an act of faith:

Jesus, I believe
you really are
the Son of God.
I have seen you . . .

Have some small pictures ready to colour, cut out, and stick on to the page. Sing: *Jesus is my friend ; All the people ; Who is this man? (MWTP)*.

Music
Recorded Music

Brahms – *Variations on a theme of Haydn* (St. Anthony Chorale) Op 56

'Live' Music

Come to the waters *(SONL, 86)*
Comfort, joy, strength and meaning *(SONL, 68)*
He's got the whole world in his hand *(ONE, 209)*
If God is for us *(ONE, 231)*
Man of Galilee *(ONE, 343)*

4th Sunday of Advent

Theme
God is with us

God's great sign of love is that he is carried through a human pregnancy and born into a human family which is descended from David. His mother, Mary, is chosen for this unique privilege and responsibility. In this way Isaiah's prophecy is quite literally fulfilled: God is personally among us, to save us from our sin.

Penitential Rite

We have wandered from your pathway,
Lord, have mercy. **Lord, have mercy.**

We have shut our ears to your voice,
Christ, have mercy. **Christ, have mercy.**

We have avoided committing ourselves entirely to you,
Lord, have mercy. **Lord, have mercy.**

Notes on the Readings

Isaiah 7:10-14

In the face of crisis, Ahab is shaking like a leaf, and Isaiah tells him that such terror suggests he doesn't really trust in God. As an act of faith he is urged to ask God for a sign, but Ahab prefers not to stick his neck out, excusing his lack of faith by arguing that you shouldn't put God to the test anyway.

God's response is the affirmation that a new royal child of his own making will be established to put things in order and rectify the wrongs of weak and sinful humanity. With the birth of Jesus this prophecy is to be stunningly fulfilled at nothing less than the cost of God's own Son.

God is supremely trustworthy; even in times of crisis and panic his power and faithfulness stand like rock. We need not be afraid for he is with us.

Romans 1:1-7

Paul establishes quite firmly that Jesus Christ was both human and divine. The family into which he was born a son was descended from David, thus making Jesus a definite member of the Jewish race, God's chosen people. However, his resurrection proved beyond doubt what those who kept company with him had already realised: that Jesus was also the Son of God himself, and all the spiritual life and grace of the Church comes through him. Jesus is therefore 'available' in a far freer, more abundant way than a merely human person could be, and all nations – the Romans and ourselves included – are called to belong to Jesus and receive the grace and truth of his life.

Matthew 1:18-25

Matthew realises that the prophecy in Isaiah has been fulfilled in a way beyond all expectations. God has indeed given his sign, and intervened in his created order of life at this crucial stage of man's redemption. Matthew shows Joseph, an honourable and considerate man, agonising over how best to cope with the extraordinary and unexpected situation in which he finds himself.

In his dream he is addressed as 'Joseph, son of David' which perhaps alerts him to there being a good reason for God's plan; it is in this way that Jesus will be both the Son of God and son of David as foretold by the prophets.

We can learn a great deal from the way Joseph deliberates, comes to a sensible decision and then promptly does what, in the world's eyes, is foolish in order to obey his Lord. He has now left himself wide open to gossip and shame for improper conduct of which he was innocent, and the accusations must have been particularly hard to accept for one respected as a man of honour.

We may be asked by God to be fools for Christ's sake. It will never be an easy thing to do. But it is the only right thing to do; and, after all, surely no one's opinion of us matters as much as God's.

Bidding Prayers

Celebrant   My brothers and sisters in Christ,
let us bring before God our Father
the cares and concerns of our hearts.

Reader   We bring to his love all those called
to serve Christ in his Church;
that they may not flinch
from responding to their calling,
but rather abandon themselves
to his guidance and protection.
Pause
Lord, let your will be done: **be with us this day.**

We bring to his love all who hold
positions of authority throughout
our world; that they may be filled
with integrity and a sense of
responsibility towards those
who depend on them; and that they
may be strengthened to stand firm
in what is right,
even if is unpopular.
Pause
Lord, let your will be done: **be with us this day.**

We bring to his love those who have been
rejected or abandoned by their families
or society; those who are constantly
ridiculed, criticised or badly treated;
that God's love may break down prejudice,
disperse hatred and build
bridges of reconciliation.
Pause
Lord, let your will be done: **be with us this day.**

We bring to his love the friends
and neighbours we meet regularly;
the members of this worshipping community;
the inhabitants of this town/city/village;
that our daily care of one another
may nurture strong growth
of Christian love in our society
Pause
Lord, let your will be done: **be with us this day.**

Celebrant   Now, Father, in silence we bring you
our own particular, personal concerns.
We ask you to accept our prayers
through Christ Jesus, our Saviour. **Amen.**

Ideas for Children

Talk about all the things they are doing ready for Christmas, and remind them of what they have been doing to prepare themselves for Jesus:

 – finding out more of Jesus' life,
 – talking to him,
 – trying to be more kind and loving.

Tell or read the story of Mary and Joseph getting ready for Jesus, their journey to Bethlehem, and why they had to go there. Older children may like to find the Isaiah prophecy in the Bible, and link it with the Christmas story.

In the last page of their books, have a picture of the nativity (from old Christmas cards) to stick in, and write beside it: Jesus, I love you. Encourage them to use these prayer books at home regularly.

Now help the children to make a small crib to put up in their homes, with a candle to light. Below is a pop-up version to try. The children will need scissors and colouring pencils. Perhaps the finished cribs could be blessed in church.

Music
Recorded Music

Handel – *Messiah: The trumpet shall sound*

'Live' Music

Emmanuel *(SONL, 15)*
The angel Gabriel *(ONE, 516)*
Through the mountains *(ONE, 569)*
When Mary listened *(ONE, 611)*
Where are you bound *(ONE, 614)*

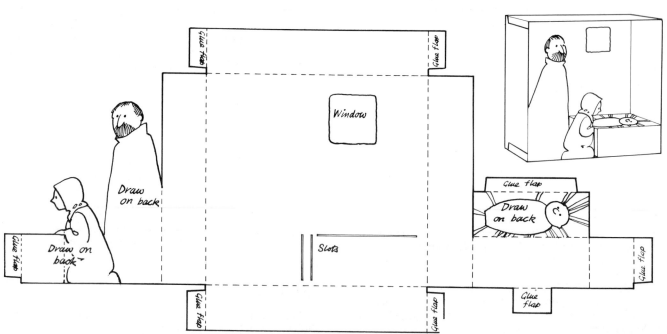

CHRISTMASTIDE

Christmas

Questions for Discussion Groups
1. What difference has Christ's coming made to your life?
2. How can we show Christ to the world in this parish/city/country?

Christmas Day
Mass at Midnight

Theme

Jesus, our Saviour, is born

The God who made the world confines himself willingly and generously within the form of man whom he has created. The humility of such an act is a measure of God's love for us.

Penitential Rite

As we stumble towards your light,
   Lord, have mercy. **Lord, have mercy.**

As we marvel at your humility,
   Christ, have mercy. **Christ, have mercy.**

As we relinquish our future to you,
   Lord, have mercy. **Lord, have mercy.**

Notes on the Readings

Isaiah 9:2-7

This great prophecy of healing and restoration is fulfilled in the incarnation. Nothing can disperse darkness but light, and now that light has come in the universal sign of hope – a new baby.

   With Christ being born, hope springs up, for the darkness can never win or overcome us anymore. No wonder it is an occasion for rapturous delight and gladness – nothing can ever be quite the same again.

Titus 2:11-14

Steadily the Good News seeps into the whole world from one ordinary stable, until everyone will know the hope bursting from God's plan to save his people.

   And, when Christ comes again in glory, all the work which has been going on 'back stage' will become clear and emerge into a splendid and everlasting joy.

Luke 2:1-14

Cataclysmic though this event was, it was worked out in terms of inns and travellers, stables and shepherds – just the ordinary, everyday things among unremarkable people. It was as if God let himself in by a side door, quietly and unobtrusively, just as he often does to many hearts in every generation.

   But once we find him there, the pleasure and excited gladness of what his presence means opens our lives to a richness we can hardly believe, and, like the angels and shepherds, there is great rejoicing.

Bidding Prayers

Celebrant My brothers and sisters, as we gather to worship the Christ child, born tonight, let us trustingly pray to our heavenly Father.

Reader For all Christians celebrating this great feast all over the world, in all climates and at all times as our planet turns.
Pause
Light of ages: **be born in our hearts.**

For all areas of darkness where God's light is desperately needed to bring peace, understanding, sensitivity and compassion.
Pause
Light of ages: **be born in our hearts.**

For those who this night are hungry, cold or homeless; for all who are separated from their loved ones; all who find the festivities of Christmas emphasising their isolation and misery.
Pause
Light of ages: **be born in our hearts.**

For our homes, families, neighbours and friends; for all children and young babies.
Pause
Light of ages: **be born in our hearts.**

Celebrant Father, in thankfulness we praise you, and ask you to accept these prayers through your Son. **Amen.**

Ideas for Adults

Instead of beginning the Mass straightaway, arrange for people to gather some time before so as to keep vigil together. The time can be spent singing carols, praying together in silence or with recorded music in the background. A duplicated sheet of short meditations could be provided, and the opportunity used for singing some of the less known carols – hymns for Christmas which explore the wonder of the incarnation.

Music

'Live' Music

Oh Mary, when our God chose you *(ONE, 407)*
The shepherd in the hills *(ONE, 546)*

The Nativity of the Lord (Mass During the Day)

Theme
Christ our Saviour is born

At a particular time in history, eternal God breaks into human existence to transform and redeem it. In the darkness of night, God's majestic glory becomes a vulnerable, newborn baby; creator of all is entirely dependent on those he has created. Such is the measure of his infinite love.

Penitential Rite

Where our minds are closed, open them,
    Lord, have mercy. **Lord, have mercy.**

Where our hearts are stone, melt them,
    Christ, have mercy. **Christ, have mercy.**

Where our lives are empty, fill them,
    Lord, have mercy. **Lord, have mercy.**

Notes on the Readings

Isaiah 52:7-10

In the midst of human guilt, misery, disillusion, frailty and fear is the profound desire to be sorted out and saved from the evil in and around us, rescued from all that traps and enslaves us, so that our goodness and wholeness can be fully realised. Now, at last, we are to be saved. God himself is coming to rescue us, and we shall be free. O come, let us adore him.

Hebrews 1:1-6

There is no more waiting, because God intervened and broke into human life at an actual, historical date; his son is Jesus, the child born in Bethlehem. Having lived as man amongst our sin but unsullied by it, he has destroyed the power of evil and is therefore worthy of all praise – even the praise of angels.

John 1:1-18

John expresses the 'now-ness' of God's Word which is always present even from before the beginning of creation; indeed, creation itself was achieved through him. And now he is present in the tangible form of man, with power to gather into the Godhead our humanity so that we who believe in him can become children of God by his grace.

Bidding Prayers

Celebrant   Companions in Christ, let us pray
       to our heavenly Father,
       the God of all mercy and love.

Reader   Let us pray for the world-wide
       Christian community, that unceasing
       prayer and praise may be offered
       as our planet turns through night and day;
       that every individual member of Christ
       may be strengthened, encouraged,
       and bear good fruit.
Pause

Hear us, Father: **we trust in you.**

Let us pray for the direction
and guidance of our world;
that in all areas of discussion,
negotiation, policy-making and reform,
Christ may be present, touching our lives
and wills with his peace.
Pause

Hear us, Father: **we trust in you.**

Let us pray for all those whose
Christmas celebrations will be affected
by war, homelessness, pain or separation
from loved ones; that in all their troubles
they may know that Christ's human birth
confirms his immense love for us
and his desire to share our suffering.
Pause

Hear us, Father: **we trust in you.**

Let us pray for our homes and families;
that Christ may be born in them,
and live among us, to deepen and extend
our love, one for another.
Pause

Hear us, Father: **we trust in you.**

Celebrant   Father, with thanks and joy we offer
       these prayers through Jesus our Saviour. **Amen.**

Ideas for Adults

The Isaiah reading can be dramatised using a group of voices: light, medium and dark. A flute or guitar can be played quietly in the background.

Light:	How beautiful on the mountains are the feet	
	of one who brings good news.	*slow*
Solo dark:	who heralds peace	
Solo medium:	brings happiness	*crescendo*
Solo light:	proclaims salvation	
Light:	and tells Zion,	
All:	'Your God is King!'	*ff*
Solo dark:	Listen	
Dark:	Your watchmen raise their voices,	*p*
Light:	they shout for joy together,	<
Medium:	for they see the Lord (*pause*) face-to-face,	
	as he returns to Zion.	
All:	Break into shouts of joy together,	*f*
	you ruins of Jerusalem;	
Light:	for the Lord is consoling his people,	
Medium:	redeeming Jerusalem.	
Dark:	The Lord bares his holy arm	*p*
	in the sight of all the nations	
All:	and all the ends of the earth shall see . . .	<
	. . . the salvation of our God.	*ff*

Church Decoration

Banners for pillars can be made from richly coloured materials with black paper silhouettes tacked on to them. Have different layers of paper, and to make a three-dimensional

effect, curve the paper and only fasten to the background at the sides. Extras like straw, palm trees or feathery wings can be made by curling the paper. Roll strips round a pencil or 'stroke' a strip with a ruler until it curls. Here are some suggestions for themes:

– Shepherds
– Bethlehem, city under the stars
– Angels

Offertory procession

At the offertory, the people can bring to the altar gifts which they have bought or made for a relief organisation, such as simple children's clothes, blankets, books and pencils etc. They will then be seen as being a direct result of our love for Jesus, and the giving of presents is fixed firmly in the context of showing Christ's love to others.

Ideas for Children

It is important that the children contribute to the family worship at some point in the festival. They may present a Nativity tableau or simple Nativity play during the Mass, either instead of a homily or during Communion. They may have practised a special carol which they can sing during the Mass.

Many churches find the Christingle symbolism helpful. Others ask the children to wrap up a present for another child and bring it up to the crib as an offering. These are then given to those in children's homes or to any local area of need.

Elderly residents in nursing homes love to hear children singing, too. If cards are made and distributed at the same time, the children will be providing a most valuable ministry.

Leaflets providing an outline of Christingle, using the traditional orange (as the world) and candle (as the light of Christ) can be obtained from The Children's Society, Old Town Hall, Kennington Road, London SE11 4QD.

Music
Recorded Music

J.S. Bach – *Christmas Oratorio*
Britten – *A Ceremony of Carols*

'Live' Music

Oh, how good is the Lord *(ONE, 396)*
The bakerwoman *(ONE, 517)*

The Holy Family of Jesus, Mary and Joseph

Theme
At Christmas, Jesus became a member of a family

That holy family of Mary, Joseph and Jesus is an example and inspiration for all families. The qualities of mutual respect and understanding, affection and security which we see there are the qualities which provide the best conditions for children to grow and develop, emotionally and spiritually. The effects of a good, stable and accepting life spread out into the whole of our society.

Penitential Rite

For our lack of consideration at home,
   Lord, have mercy. **Lord, have mercy.**

For our lack of respect, one for another,
   Christ, have mercy. **Christ, have mercy.**

For our lack of patience and forgiveness,
   Lord, have mercy. **Lord, have mercy.**

Notes on the Readings

Ecclesiasticus 3:2-6, 12-14

Based on the commandment: 'Honour your father and your mother', these guidelines for respectful care of parents are full of gentleness and compassion. We are sometimes in danger of dismissing the elderly and frail in our society; this robs them of their dignity, and the young of a most valuable resource of wisdom and experience.

Certainly our rapidly-changing fashions mean that the methods of old and young may be different, but the universal, human qualities of life (such as perseverance in suffering, or coping with failure and success) do not change, and we can learn from those who, through living longer, have had more practice.

Colossians 3:12-21

In an effort to avoid hypocrisy, and nurture individuality, we sometimes discard the self-discipline and control which are vital in sustaining a stable, peaceful atmosphere in our homes.

Our values, as Christians, are simply not the same as those around us; we have to recognise that being a Christian family will mean conflict with the current expectations in behaviour, possessions and obedience. There may be resentment about this, especially among children.

But if we do uphold and live by the values urged here, our families and homes will be welcome anchors in a shifting, unsettled society. People should be able to notice a quality about us by which they are impressed: 'see how these Christians love each other.'

Matthew 2:13-5, 19-23

The obedience to God's commands within the Holy Family is absolute. Right from the start of Jesus' life on earth he is subject to the evils of the world and exposed to danger because of them. How easily could God's plan of salvation have been thwarted almost before it was begun, without the wholehearted compliance of Joseph and Mary.

We are never taken out of areas where God plans to work through us for good. Instead he provides us with guidance, help and strength, so long as we keep listening to him, and obey his will, even if we cannot immediately see the necessity for acting as he wishes. In time it will all be made plain. Meanwhile, we must allow ourselves to be led, or we may be thwarting God's purpose in some way.

Bidding Prayers

Celebrant   My brothers and sisters in Christ,
              let us come to God our Father
              with our burdens and cares.

Reader   Let us ask him to bless our Christian
           family, both in this parish
           and in the world; that we may witness
           to his life-giving presence
           by the kind of lives we lead,
           and the work we do.
           Pause
           Father, live among us: **live in our lives.**

           Let us ask him to bless the leaders
           of each country and each community;
           that we may not wander as sheep
           without a shepherd, but rather be led
           and directed by God in the way of love.
           Pause
           Father, live among us: **live in our lives.**

           Let us ask him to bless all
           children at risk; all those born
           prematurely; those with brain damage
           or deformity, and for their families;
           that where much is demanded,
           much strength may be given.
           Pause
           Father, live among us: **live in our lives.**

           Let us ask him to bless our own homes
           and our relationships with our parents,
           brothers and sisters, and children;
           that we may learn to see and
           experience Christ in each other,
           and cheerfully love and serve
           with generosity of spirit.
           Pause
           Father, live among us: **live in our lives.**

Celebrant   Heavenly Father, we ask you to accept
              these prayers for the sake of Jesus,
              your Son. **Amen.**

Ideas for Adults

Have a complete family offering the gifts and introducing
the Bidding Prayers.

Church Decoration

Relief organisations will supply photographs and posters
for you to put up today, either on the walls or pillars. It is
important that several different countries are represented.

Ideas for Children

Bring along a family of bears or dolls and have them sitting
round the central table, having a meal with a doll's tea-set.
Talk with the children about what a family is, what times
the family gets together, and what they enjoy about living
in a group like this.

Have a large sheet of paper or blackboard, and together
make up a prayer to thank God for our families, putting
in the things they appreciate – family parties, meals, special
jokes, cuddles, outings, holidays, bedtime stories, cooking,
comfort if you're sad etc. Then say this prayer all together.

In groups read or tell the story of the escape into Egypt.
Help them to see how they supported each other in times

of danger. Make a banner showing the escape to Egypt.
This can be carried into church and presented at the offering of gifts. You will need a sheet of coloured sugar paper,
a bamboo cane, sellotape, black and silver paper,
templates, glue and pens.

Music
Recorded Music

Vivaldi – *The Four Seasons :· Spring*

'Live' Music

Bind us together, Lord *(ONE, 62)*
God is love: his the care *(ONE, 178)*
Lord of all hopefulness *(ONE, 329)*
The family of Christ *(SONL, 94)*

Solemnity of Mary, Mother of God

Theme
Through Mary, God was born as man

Mary is Christ's mother, and since we are, through grace,
co-heirs with him, she is spiritually our mother too. Supported by her prayers and encouraged by her example we
can be helped towards responding positively to God.

Penitential Rite

We need to pray with more fervour,
  Lord, have mercy. **Lord, have mercy.**

We need to obey you with more humility,
  Christ, have mercy. **Christ, have mercy.**

We need to accept you with more commitment,
  Lord, have mercy. **Lord, have mercy.**

Notes on the Readings

Numbers 6:22-27

Light is a remarkable symbol of God's love. Whatever it
shines on is transformed and stands out brightly; it suggests
the warmth and power of the sun, the safety of daytime
and the confidence of clear vision. The firm promise of the
source of light entering our lives emerges through the
prophecies of the Old Testament.

Galatians 4:4-7

Finally the true light came into the world, born of a woman
and subject to the Law, so therefore truly bound as man
by physical, religious and political restrictions imposed by
his birth. But this was necessary; he could not have redeemed us from any other position. Through him the light
has shone on us, and we have been brought back from
where we were held fast by our sin. Not only are we set
free, but we are also made inheritors of all God's richness
and abundance.

Luke 2:16-21

Mary was chosen to accomplish this astounding act of generous love. Throughout her life she had many secrets and treasures to store. With eyes open she watched the plan of her Lord unfolding; with a loving acceptance of God's will, regardless of her personal happiness or safety. This special relationship with God makes her able to pray for us as our spiritual mother.

Bidding Prayers

Celebrant Let us pray to the Father, trusting
in his power and love.

Reader We bring to his love all those
who have committed their lives to Christ
in lay and ordained ministries;
that they may grow into spiritual maturity,
and live always as freed sons
and daughters of God.
Pause
Abba, Father: **you have set us free.**

We bring to his love the world
and its problems, mistakes and errors
of judgement; that in every society
the Lord's light may shine,
and bring his peace.
Pause
Abba, Father: **you have set us free.**

We bring to his love the deaf,
the blind and the partially sighted,
all those who are chronically ill
and all who tend them;
that they may be constantly upheld
by the tenderness of God's care.
Pause
Abba, Father: **you have set us free.**

We bring to his love our own mothers,
all foster mothers, and all those
in labour now; that they may be blessed
and strengthened.
Pause
Abba, Father: **you have set us free.**

Celebrant Father, we bring these prayers
through Jesus Christ, our Saviour. **Amen.**

Ideas for Children

Talk about when we have been given an important or responsible job to do – looking after a pet, drying up the best china, taking a younger child to school, for instance. How do we feel?
– Nervous? Anxious? Excited? Proud? Happy?
(perhaps many mixed feelings)
Why do you think you were chosen?
– Because you were thought sensible enough?
– Because the person who chose you was sure you
could do it well?
Now show them a picture or statue of Mary. Explain that she was given a very important job by God. What was it? How do you think she felt? What did her job involve?
– washing swaddling clothes
– cooking
– cuddling and comforting Jesus
– getting him ready for school, etc.
Give the children some plasticine, and let them make a model of Mary helping Jesus (or Jesus helping Mary) in one of their everyday jobs.

Music
Recorded Music

Grieg – *Peer Gynt Suite: Solveig's lament*

'Live' Music

At Bethlehem she bore her son *(ONE,47)*
Oh Mary, gentle one *(ONE, 406)*
Oh Mary, when our God chose you *(ONE, 407)*

2nd Sunday after Christmas

Theme
The Word becomes flesh

In Christ's birth the eternal Word, present from before all time and all created things, breaks into the immediate human world. Through him, we are called to share in the vast plan of God's glory.

Penitential Rite

Clear our lives of cluttered restlessness,
  Lord, have mercy. **Lord, have mercy.**

Quieten our clamour and constant noise,
  Christ, have mercy. **Christ, have mercy.**

Make us sensitive and receptive,
  Lord, have mercy. **Lord, have mercy.**

Notes on the Readings

Sirach 24:1-4, 12-16

As creatures of time it is difficult for us to imagine the timeless, eternal nature of God. It is quite possible for him to be present and in charge of the first swirling origins of our galaxy, and at the same time choose you, personally, to fulfil part of his plan. He is far greater than our brains can encompass, and the true Master of the Universe is, thankfully, utterly good and loving. His wisdom, or personality, has taken root within the creation, and we are part of that plant.

Ephesians 1:3-6, 15-18

This is an immense privilege, for it means that, though God is fully aware of all that is mean and selfish in us, he still loves us enough to allow us to participate in his plan. We can so easily mess it all up, block it with obstacles, clutter it with divisions or slow it down with distractions.

But God does not give up on us. Every time we are sorry for our blundering he forgives us, takes us on again as responsible partners, and will work through us in ways we may not even realise.

In the face of such treatment, we are inspired to stay close to God in prayer, Bible reading and sacramental worship so that our spiritual perception will be heightened.

John 1:1-18

The awesome daring of God chills us as we realise the risk he was taking; indeed, many for whom he came failed to recognise him, and would not receive him. As in the Holman Hunt picture, there are so many overgrown doors which remain firmly shut against Christ, even though he would bring light into the darkness. But if we do receive him – what then?

It will mean that we have opened our door to the cataclysmic power which brought volcanoes, stars, glaciers and brains into being; the power of life itself. We must not be surprised, then, if it leads to radical change in our behaviour and develops gifts we had hardly noticed before.

The incarnation allows us first-hand experience of God's powerful love, if we will only receive it. The offer is there: we have only to accept.

Bidding Prayers

Celebrant Fellow pilgrims, let us quieten our hearts
and pray to our loving Father.

Reader Let us pray for those who work to spread
the Good News of God's saving love;
especially for those undergoing
hardship, danger or persecution;
that they may stand firm in the
knowledge of Christ's victory over evil.
Pause
Lord, we love you: **help us spread your love.**

Let us pray for all those in our world
who do not know God's love;
for those who put their faith
in human systems or material possessions;
for those whom we have failed
by inadequate Christian example.
Pause
Lord, we love you: **help us spread your love.**

Let us pray for all those addicted
to drugs, solvent abuse, alcohol,
violence or gambling; those experiencing
drugs for the first time today;
that their cravings may be re-directed
to the only real, lasting source
of peace and fulfilment –
Jesus, the Son of God.
Pause
Lord, we love you: **help us spread your love.**

Let us pray for the strengthening
of this community in mutual care
and affection; that behaving as sons
and daughters of light we may draw
others to share the great
happiness of God's presence.
Pause
Lord, we love you: **help us spread your love.**

Celebrant Father, almighty and ever-present,
we commend our prayers to your mercy,
through Christ our Lord. **Amen.**

Ideas for Adults

Dance of the Word made flesh

Into the centre of the church strides an albed figure, holding a lit candle. From four different directions in the church small groups of dancers come towards him when the horns begin, as if being drawn by his light into existence. They stretch their arms out towards the light and move, hesitatingly at first, until they are all grouped round the central figure like this:

Slowly, he turns round in a circle, facing each group in order. As he faces each one he extends his candle outwards, and that group starts busily working. The first group mime building skills, such as chopping wood, hammering, brick laying etc. The second group mime food preparation, such as stirring, kneading dough, tossing pancakes etc. The third group mimes clothes-making, such as sewing, weaving, knitting etc. The fourth group mimes farming – cutting corn, milking, picking fruit etc. The idea is of everyone being involved in their own business, and while they are occupied, the central figure walks away and watches them from the distance.

Then, as the music changes to an oboe solo, he walks back to them. They freeze in their postions watching him, while he extends one arm in greeting. Slowly and deliberately they turn their heads away from him (with the cellos) group by group, and then one member from each group looks at him again, gets up and walks up to him, kneeling before him.

He raises these four to their feet and they bring out candles which have been tucked in their belts. They light these from the main candle and hold them high, facing out from the central figure as the music reaches a crescendo and joyfully move in a 'step, together, wait' sequence round the central figure, four steps one way, then four steps the other way.

Finally, as the groups resume their own, inward-looking 'busy-ness', the central five move down the centre and out into the world, one arm stretched out holding the candle, the other stretched   out towards the central figure.

Fade the music as it comes to a natural fall.
The music for this dance is the beginning of the fourth movement of Dvorak's '*From the New World*' Symphony.

Ideas for Children

Show the children Holman Hunt's 'Light of the World' picture and help them to notice the fact that the door hasn't been opened for a long time; that there is no handle on the outside; that Jesus is holding a lantern.

Now read with them John 1:1-12. Use the *Good News* version and read it slowly and clearly, explaining it where necessary. Then sing a prayer of commitment and acceptance such as 'Jesus loves me, alleluia, and I love him, alleluia' or 'Jesus, we love you' (Good Morning, Jesus).

Let the children make lanterns from jam jars, string, night-lights and sticky tape. These can be lit and carried in a procession of light to the sanctuary, where they remain burning for the rest of the Mass.

Music
Recorded Music

Sibelius – *Finlandia*

'Live' Music

Come, follow me *(SONL, 20)*
Life pervading, all containing *(SONL, 46)*
Lord of the universe *(ONE, 330)*
The King of glory comes *(ONE, 527)*

The Epiphany of the Lord

Theme
Jesus, the Light, is shown to the world

In fulfilment of old prophecies the promised Messiah is now revealed to those of all nations, symbolised by the three wise men. The offering of their gifts foreshadows the time when all nations will be drawn to acknowledge the omnipotence of God.

Penitential Rite

For our wasted opportunities,
Lord, have mercy. **Lord, have mercy.**

For hindering the spread of your kingdom,
Christ, have mercy. **Christ, have mercy.**

For our unwillingness to be changed,
Lord, have mercy. **Lord, have mercy.**

Notes on the Readings

Isaiah 60:1-6

When we talk of God speaking through his prophets it is passages like this which spring to mind. For here, in a bleak landscape of decay and despondency, the unlikely vision is bright and accurate: we are aware of God's personal voice piercing the gloom and pointing with conviction and authority to a certain future of hope. All his tender compassion, loving forgiveness and generous sharing are in evidence; and now, the prophecy is fulfilled.

Ephesians 3:2-3a, 5-6

In every generation, every stage of his plan, God speaks in visions through a few who have the gift of prophecy. Prophecy did not finish when Jesus had come; it will never finish until the end of time, the completion of God's purpose.

The next stage of enlightenment after the incarnation and resurrection was the opening-up of all races to the Good News. This could not happen until the light had been shed first on the chosen people. From there it spreads outwards until it reaches all nations, with none excluded.

Matthew 2:1-12

Right at the beginning of Christ's life on earth people are drawn to his presence to worship him, just as the prophecy in Isaiah foreshows. First come representatives of the Jewish people – the shepherds on whom the brightness of heaven had shone to direct their way.

Then, one or two years later, come representatives of nations far away and with different cultures and religions. They, too, are given a sign, and a guide: the star. This was a sign which was significant in their own culture, for God always starts leading us from where we are at the moment; he will use all kinds of incidents and experiences we are naturally involved with in order to draw us to himself.

We must learn from him in this, and check that newcomers to worship or fringe members of the church are always met with love at the point they start from, and are never expected or required to have 'arrived' when they are just setting out.

Bidding Prayers

Celebrant Companions in Christ, the glory of God
is all about us. With thankful and
adoring hearts, let us pray.

Reader We bring to the Lord all those involved
with teaching the Christian faith;
our schools and catechism classes;
missionaries (especially any missionary
work closely connected with the parish).
Pause
Father of light: **shine in the darkness.**

We bring to the Lord all peoples
of our earth with their different
cultures, philosophies and traditions;
multi-racial communities, especially
those experiencing problems
with integration and harmony.
Pause
Father of light: **shine in the darkness.**

We bring to the Lord all newborn babies,
especially those who are unwanted
or abandoned; all those who are elderly
and approaching death, especially
those who are frightened.
Pause
Father of light: **shine in the darkness.**

We bring to the Lord our own parish,
its programme for education and outreach,
its availability to those who do not
yet know the richness of God's love;
its areas of stagnation;
its potential for growth.
Pause
Father of light: **shine in the darkness.**

Celebrant Heavenly Father, we ask you to accept
these prayers through Christ,
our Saviour. **Amen.**

Ideas for Children

Tell or read the story of the wise men, with their gifts

displayed on the table. If possible, have something of real gold, a thurible with incense burning, and some anointing oil. Talk about these things, and how we use them in our worship (or way of showing the "worth") of our God. How can we give God a present?

Wrap each child in Christmas wrapping paper and give each a label to write and decorate, thread on wool and hang round his neck. At the offering of gifts, let the 'presents' walk up to give themselves. The labels can be collected and blessed before they are returned to the children.

Music
Recorded Music

Prokofiev — *Romeo and Juliet: Act 1*

'Live' Music

Do you know that the Lord walks on earth? *(ONE, 124)*
Forth in the peace of Christ we go *(ONE, 147)*
In Christ there is no east or west *(ONE, 244)*
Let all the world in every corner sing *(ONE, 302)*

The Baptism of the Lord

Theme
'This is my Son, the Beloved'

At his baptism by John, Jesus was anointed by God with the power of his Spirit before beginning his ministry among men to heal, restore and liberate. The promised Messiah had come, and men would now see the character of God revealed in human word and action.

Penitential Rite

Perverse and stubborn, we come to you,
  Lord, have mercy. **Lord, have mercy.**

Mean and selfish, we come to you,
  Christ, have mercy. **Christ, have mercy.**

Arrogant and vain, we come to you,
  Lord, have mercy. **Lord, have mercy.**

Notes on the Readings

Isaiah 42:1-4, 6-7

The prophet must have been very close to the mind of God, for the character and actions of the chosen servant he describes are remarkable in their breadth, capacity for mercy, compassion and lack of vengeance, in spite of the general climate of opinion at the time he was writing.

Jesus, having studied this passage from childhood, began to see how he must indeed be the fulfilment of this prophecy.

Holy men and women of all ages and all regions have always shared this ability to understand the divine character in some way which is nothing to do with knowing facts about him, or observing rules and rituals. Their understanding grows like a plant that is rooted in him; by keeping constantly in his company through prayer and meditation, they 'soak up' his essence, and it shows.

He has invited us to this close companionship. If we accept, he will transform us in the same way, however unpromising the material!

Acts 10:34-38

This was a giant step for Peter to take. It could not have happened unless he had been a close companion of the risen Christ, willing to be led by him, even if that meant changing his mind, admitting error and abandoning previous principles. (All these things are often considered weakness and foolishness by the world).

It is impossible to live in the world but remain uncontaminated by its evils if we rely on our own physical and mental strength. But then, we don't have to. God does not charge for the use of his power; he holds no entrance examinations or suitability assessments. He does not even require references, and takes no notice of them, even if we have them.

The reason for this is that he calls us from exactly where we are at the moment, to rely entirely on him for everything. In fact, of course, we do rely entirely on him, since he is the Lord of all power and all life; but mostly we assume that these basic things just happen, and jog along fairly smoothly without any reference to God.

Once we accept God's over-all power, and acknowledge his Lordship in all areas of life, we are tapping a limitless supply of power which can renew the whole face of the earth.

Matthew 3:13-17

It comes as a surprise to find how obedient Jesus was to the religious Law and customs. He, after all, had no need to be washed of sin, for he was sinless, so why did he insist on John baptising him?

In sending his Son into the world, God showed his desire to be completely identified in love with the creatures he had made. And now, at the point of baptism, he again shows full identification with the people; he is not above us but alongside us; in our sin and repentance as well as our odd moments of sanctity.

He also needed to be seen to be anointed by God, just as David had been anointed by Samuel. In their culture this expressed God's choosing; his setting apart of someone for a special task.

As Jesus came up from the water, God expressed his confirmation of love and power, both for Jesus himself, and for those whose spiritual eyes were open to understand.

Bidding Prayers

Celebrant My companions in Christ, let us pray together for the needs of the Church and the world.

Reader We bring to the Lord all who preach and teach the Christian message of salvation, and for those who hear it; that through God's Spirit its reality, truth and hope may take root and grow.
  Pause
  Father, fill us all: **fill us with your life.**

  We bring to the Lord our stewardship of the world's resources; all discussions and councils where far-reaching decisions are made concerning government,

conservation, International Aid
programmes, methods of harnessing power,
and fighting disease;
that the generous will of God may
prevail over human greed and prejudice.
Pause
Father, fill us all: **fill us with your life.**

We bring to the Lord all who are
apathetic, mentally exhausted or aimlessly
wandering through life; all who are
eaten up with jealousy, poisoned by hate
or weighed down with guilt;
that they may feel and know the warmth
and depth of God's love,
and his yearning for their peace.
Pause
Father, fill us all: **fill us with your life.**

We bring to the Lord ourselves,
our friends and all we shall meet
during this week, however briefly;
that we may be so full of Christ's love,
that others may see it and be drawn
towards their Saviour.
Pause
Father, fill us all: **fill us with your life.**

Celebrant In thankfulness for all our blessings
we ask you, Father, to hear our prayers
through Christ our Lord. **Amen.**

Ideas for Adults

The Isaiah passage is effective when read chorally. Voices should be grouped into light, medium and dark.

All:	Thus says the Lord:	*f*
Medium:	Here is my servant whom I uphold,	
Light:	my chosen one in whom my soul delights.	*mp*
Dark:	I have endowed him with my spirit	
All:	that he may bring true justice to the nations.	*f*
One light:	He does not cry out	
One medium:	or shout aloud	
One dark:	or make his voice heard in the streets.	
Dark:	He does not break the crushed reed,	*p*
Light:	nor quench the wavering flame.	
Medium:	Faithfully he brings	*slowly*
All:	true justice:	
One light:	he will neither waver,	
Another light:	nor be crushed	
All:	until true justice is established on earth	<
Dark:	for the islands are awaiting his law.	
All:	I, the Lord, have called you	*mp*
Medium:	to serve the cause of right	
Light:	I have taken you by the hand and formed you;	
All:	I have appointed you as covenant of the people and	*f*
	light of the nations,	*ff*
One dark:	to open the eyes of the blind,	
One medium:	to free captives from prison	
All:	and those who live in darkness from the dungeon.	

Church Decoration

The font can receive special treatment today, with white flowers all around it, set on mirrors with pebbles and shells to suggest water.

Ideas for Children

If you have any pictures of the Jordan, show these first, so that the children realise it is a real place and can identify more easily with events there.

Also have a large baking tray, some earth or sand, metal foil, stones and twigs, and plasticine. Explain that you are all going to make a model of the Jordan and then let the children help assemble it. With the foil make a trough which can be filled with water for the river. Plasticine models of

people can also be made, one of whom is John, and one Jesus. The rest are the crowds. Make a dove too.

Then tell the story of Jesus' baptism, moving the models as you do so. Rattle a sheet of thick card as God's voice speaks.

Give the children cards to fill and colour, like this:

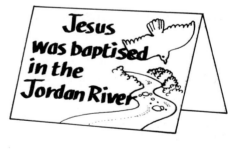

Music
Recorded Music

Smetana – *The Moldau*

'Live' Music

Dear Lord and Father of mankind *(ONE, 116)*
Oh come to the water *(SONL, 67)*
The Spirit lives to set us free *(ONE, 547)*

LENT

Lent

Questions for Discussion Groups
1. Is any kind of 'fasting' or self-discipline still valuable today?
2. In what ways are we afraid of Christ transforming us?

Ash Wednesday

Theme
Be reconciled to God

We are to turn our backs on sin and reject it; we are to turn towards God and accept him. Lent is the time to take a long, hard look at our lives so that where necessary they can be reshaped and re-directed.

At baptism, turning towards God has begun, but our human sin and weakness mean that we must constantly examine our consciences, repent and re-affirm our commitment to Christ.

Penitential Rite

This is expressed today by the distribution of ashes. As an alternative to the antiphons the *Pie Jesu* from the Lloyd Webber *Requiem* may be sung or played.

Notes on the Readings

Joel 2:12-18

It is so easy, while life flows smoothly along, to become complacent, almost without realising it. Although we may deplore the jolts and tragedies that make open sores in our well-ordered lives, they may sometimes do us a great service.

Whenever our timetable is disrupted, it challenges us about whose order really underpins our life; every time material possessions are lost or stolen we are challenged as to where our real treasure is on which our hearts are fixed.

These challenges are very good for us, and provide marvellous opportunities for relinquishing another layer of independence from God and committing ourselves to him more deeply.

From time to time this needs to be a great communal act of repentance and re-commitment. There may be potential within the whole parish which is not being realised; needs which are not being met; opportunities which are not being taken.

The way forward in all Christian communities is through thorough, heart-searching repentance. This alone can open the way to God's forgiveness, leading to stronger, more vigorous growth, and lots more fruit.

2 Corinthians 5:20-6:2

If we repent thoroughly we shall be reconciled to God, and all that separates us from him will be swept away. That will enable us to become increasingly like him, and our characters will be more loving, open-hearted, compassionate and strong.

Matthew 6:1-6, 16-18

True repentance is humbling. It is quite possible to give the appearance of one who is living a useful, Christian life, when there has been no genuine repentance at all – merely a reshuffling of vanities. Some people can be quite as proud, mean and obstinate about church flower arranging, giving money to the poor, or saying prayers, as other people are about buying extravagant clothes, pushing into queues or refusing to give help where it is needed.

So no amount of outward acts can make us right with God, however busy or dedicated we may appear. Our first, fundamental task, is to acknowledge and confess all the things which hurt God, other people or God's world, and which drive his love from our hearts. Then, when we are truly sorry and have hidden nothing from him, he will be able to act in our lives and use us to help establish the kingdom of heaven on earth.

Bidding Prayers

Celebrant My brothers and sisters let us bring our needs and cares to the mercy of our heavenly Father.

Reader Let us pray for the deepening of prayerfulness among all Christians; for firmer faith and more receptiveness to God's will.
Pause
Father of mercy: **we turn to you for our help.**

Let us pray for our world, especially for areas of degradation and moral decay; that there may be turning away from self-indulgence to self-discipline; from deception to integrity; from lawlessness to ordered peace.
Pause
Father of mercy: **we turn to you for our help.**

Let us pray for those who have been damaged or injured through violent abuse, or terrorism; for all victims of war and rebellion, and for those who are responsible.
Pause
Father of mercy: **we turn to you for our help.**

Let us pray for God's strength in our own lives, especially in those areas we know to be weak and open to temptation; that we may rely more and more on his power, so that we live in him and he in us.
Pause
Father of mercy: **we turn to you for our help.**

Celebrant Father, hear the prayers of your people for the sake of Christ Jesus. **Amen.**

Ideas for Children

It is important for the children to take part in the distribution of ashes along with the rest of God's family. Provide each child with a duplicated sheet for colouring, which can be worked on during the homily.

Music

Recorded Music

Music from Taizé – *Jesus, remember me* (Vol. I)

'Live' Music

From the depths of sin and sadness *(ONE, 155)*
Lord, have mercy *(ONE, 323)*
Lord, when I turn my back on you *(SONL, 40)*
My God, accept my heart this day *(ONE, 355)*
Our hearts were made for you, Lord *(SONL, 36)*

1st Sunday of Lent

Theme
Christ has overcome evil

Man and woman spoilt God's perfect creation by falling into temptation and disobeying their creator. As fellow members of the human race we are all guilty of sin, but through Christ Jesus we are given the strength and grace to resist temptation just as he did.

Penitential Rite

Powerless without you, we turn to you now,
   Lord, have mercy. **Lord, have mercy.**

Wilful and selfish, we turn to you now,
   Christ, have mercy. **Christ, have mercy.**

Longing to love you more, we turn to you now,
   Lord, have mercy. **Lord, have mercy.**

Notes on the Readings

Genesis 2:7-9; 3:1-7

Nakedness always suggests vulnerability; in our clothes we can, to some extent, choose the image we present to the world, but naked we are just ourselves, as at birth and death. This is why we usually need a relationship of trust before we are at ease being naked in company; yet where this happens, as in family groups, for instance, there is no doubt that the nakedness points to a special, trusting relationship there.

When Adam and Eve were suddenly embarrassed by their nakedness it showed that their special, trusting relationship with their creator had been damaged and spoilt. They knew they had been disobedient and they were ashamed; much as we find it hard to meet people's eyes directly if we know we have wronged them in some way.

Romans 5:12-19

In one sense, Jesus came so that we could once more stand naked before God, without trying to hide any part of our bodies or characters; so confident in his love that, as children, we could have a secure relationship with him based on love and acceptance.

The only way this could be done was for the profound disobedience to be reversed. Someone had to go through all the temptations but still resist the urge to disobey God's will, whatever happened.

Someone did it. What happened to that person was the agony of betrayal, torture and crucifixion, resulting in death. But it was, in another way, life; for Jesus went right through to the farthest edge of human temptation and suffering and yet still remained absolutely obedient. He hung naked before his heavenly father at that moment of human death, and in so doing won back for us the long lost relationship with God that Adam and Eve had been created to enjoy.

Matthew 4:1-11

In today's Gospel we see some of the main temptations Jesus had to resist. They were, naturally, aimed at the weakest areas, and they all had just enough relationship with good sense to make them dangerous. After all, if someone approached us proposing a brutal act of murder we should not find that very hard to resist; but if we are persuaded that a dishonest act is going to harm no one and will benefit those we love, then the moral issues blur and it is much harder to see and resist temptation.

As with Adam and Eve, hunger is used, and the great advantage of immediate, dramatic results. 'You will be like gods,' Adam and Eve were persuaded. Jesus, knowing he had power, was urged to behave like a man-god, pandering to our craving for excitement and grandeur, but ignoring our real needs.

In resisting these temptations Jesus was abandoning any possibility of a peaceful end to his life; instead he kept the door wide open for our salvation.

Bidding Prayers

Celebrant   Followers of the Way of Christ, let us
         bring to the Lord the needs of our times.

Reader   We pray for God's blessing on all
      who confess belief in him; that they
      may witness powerfully to his unselfish
      love and humility by the way they act
      and the lives they lead.
      Pause
      Father, lead us: **free us from all that is evil.**

      We pray for God's blessing on all
      who administer justice; those working
      in Law Courts, all who are serving
      on juries and those who make Laws; that
      they may be given insight and integrity.
      Pause
      Father, lead us: **free us from all that is evil.**

      We pray for God's blessing on all those
      in prison or on probation; on those
      living in acute poverty; or in
      refugee camps; on all who are working
      among them to heal, redirect, support
      and encourage.
      Pause
      Father, lead us: **free us from all that is evil.**

      We pray for God's blessing on us
      during this Lent as we examine
      our lives and draw closer to him;
      that through our self-discipline and
      prayer we may enter God's stillness,
      and know his will for us.
      Pause
      Father, lead us: **free us from all that is evil.**

Celebrant   In silence we bring to the Lord
         our individual concerns. Father,
         accept these prayers through
         Jesus Christ our Lord. **Amen.**

Ideas for Adults

Have a large frame of wood knocked up (about 6' x 8') and stick lining paper all over it. Paint brick markings on it and through the week have all parish groups to write on it the sins that separate us off from God.

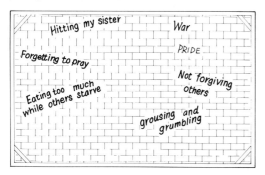

Just before the Penitential Rite, put the wall of sin between the people and the altar. Directly after communal confession, have a group of people representing *all* ages, to burst through the wall and tear off all the lining paper. Now we are not 'cut off' any more – a symbol of how God's forgiveness demolishes our sin and reconciles us to him.

Ideas for Children

Tell the children the story of Adam and Eve explaining that it was their disobedience which cut them off from the happy life they had before with God. Then help them make a large collage picture of the garden with the tree of knowledge in the middle. Make sure all the other trees have lovely fruit as well as this one; there was, after all, no actual need for them to eat its fruit. Use lots of bright materials, or colours cut from magazine pages, and write on the picture 'Adam and Eve did not do as God told them. That spoilt things.'

Then give them two large twigs each and make them into a simple cross. This is another tree of life. Help them to see how Jesus did obey, even though it meant he was killed. Because he obeyed, he put everything right again. So now, if we do wrong, we can be completely forgiven, all because of Jesus.

Use a prayer of penitence and thanks for forgiveness.

> Heavenly Father,
> we are very sorry
> that we have hurt you
> and each other
> and spoilt your world.
> Thank you for sending Jesus
> to put things right.
> Please forgive us
> because of his goodness.
>   Amen.

Music
Recorded Music

Mozart – *Oboe quartet in F major K370*

'Live' Music

Alleluia . . .By your Spirit we will sing *(SONL, 18)*
Fear not, for I have redeemed you *(ONE, 136)*
Lord Jesus Christ, you have come to us *(ONE, 326)*
Lord, let me know *(SONL, 2)*
Oh, Lord, all the world belongs to you *(ONE, 403)*

2nd Sunday of Lent

Theme
This is my Son . . . listen to him

When Jesus was transfigured in the presence of Peter, James and John, they had a vision of the glory which had always been there from the beginning. Whenever we are called by God to suffer, or launch out into unknown waters for his sake, we need not be afraid, for we are placing our lives into nothing less than the hands of the glorious all-powerful God.

Penitential Rite

We have not trusted you enough,
    Lord, have mercy. **Lord, have mercy.**

We have not listened to your voice,
    Christ, have mercy. **Christ, have mercy.**

We have not recognised your power,
    Lord, have mercy. **Lord, have mercy.**

Notes on the Readings

Genesis 12:1-4a

Abram's obedience is so simply told that it sounds quite easy. In fact, it must have been a great upheaval and a move which was no doubt ridiculed as senseless by many; why did he want to uproot everything and wander off, leaving all his security behind, for goodness' sake?

Obviously Abram was not like a reed in the wind, easily persuaded by anybody. So he must have recognised that this calling, though unusual and unexpected, was nonetheless full of authority. He sensed the greatness of God, and bowed before it, committing his future security and welfare to God's protection.

If we say that we acknowledge God's greatness, then we must show it to be true in the way we willingly submit to changes, new directions, dangerous or unpleasant undertakings, without grumbling about what we have had to give up.

Whenever we are called forward we shall have to leave something behind. But God will be going with us, so we shall end up not poorer, but richer.

2 Timothy 1:8-10

Paul has first-hand experience of this paradox. He knows that any hardships he encounters are abundantly worthwhile and far outweighed by the new life brought about through Jesus. Freely given, and quite unearned, God's grace is poured out liberally and is well able to support and sustain us through whatever we are called to endure. So we can afford to worry far less, and confidently step out into a future filled with love.

Matthew 17:1-9

Jesus was quite probably transfigured like this whenever he became rapt in prayer, but normally he sought out lonely places and prayed privately. On this occasion he allowed three of his closest followers to witness his godliness, and the sight stunned and strengthened them with its intense purity, and unblemished loveliness.

Sometimes, when we are deeply touched by a glorious sunset, or our children singing their best, for instance, we glimpse a reflection of God's glory. If we can train our senses to see it in all kinds of small, everyday occurrences we shall be richer, more thankful and happier people.

For our God is so great, so full of purity and perfection that we need not hold ourselves back in lavishing all our worship on him. We have within us an instinctive need and longing to lavish worth and adoration on something or someone.

Here, in Christ, we find the true object for all the love we long to give. We were made for it, that is why worshipping God brings such peace and joy.

Bidding Prayers

Celebrant My brothers and sisters, knowing
that our Father loves us, let us
come to him with our prayers.

Reader Let us pray for more courage
among all Christians;
that they may stand up against
evil and injustice wherever they find it,
trusting in God's power
and without thought for personal safety.
Pause
Lord, speak in our hearts: **and we will listen.**

Let us pray for those countries at war;
those between whom there is distrust
and suspicion; that peace may never
be dismissed as impossible,
but acknowledged as the only real
victory and striven for
by all those in positions of power.
Pause
Lord, speak in our hearts: **and we will listen.**

Let us pray for those who are living
through a personal crisis at the
moment; those who do not know which way
to turn for the best;
that God's will may be made very clear
to them, so they are guided
and comforted by his strength
and all-seeing love.
Pause
Lord, speak in our hearts: **and we will listen.**

Let us pray for our own lives,
and those of our families;
that we may all know what work
God is calling us to do, and
trust him enough to obey his will.
Pause
Lord, speak in our hearts: **and we will listen.**

Celebrant Father, your glory fills the world,
and so we entrust our cares to you,
through Christ our Lord. **Amen.**

Ideas for Adults

Dance of the Transfiguration

Use two songs as the music for this: *Near the heart of Jesus* and *Abba I belong to you*. Clothing of the crowd can be anything brightly coloured, but Jesus, and the dancers on the mountain expressing his glory should all wear white. Start at the back of the church.

WORDS	ACTION
Near the heart of Jesus here we start with Jesus loving as friends of Jesus tirelessly	*Jesus walks slowly forward and stops. Two or three come across from other areas to join him. He extends his arms to them and they to each other.*
Near the mind of Jesus here we find what Jesus wills for the friends of Jesus constantly	*Jesus walks slowly forward. Others come, one brings a stool on which Jesus sits and teaches them as they group, settle and listen to him.*
Near the feet of Jesus here we meet with Jesus guiding the friends of Jesus patiently	*Jesus stands, beckons, and moves forward, talking and guiding them through imaginary obstacles, checking the last person.*
Near the arms of Jesus here the calm of Jesus comforts the friends of Jesus ceaselessly	*A crying child runs down from front to meet the group. Jesus lifts him and cuddles him, and puts his arm around another in the group.*
Music only (one verse)	*The group wave to Jesus as they return to the back, except for Peter, James and John, who go with Jesus. He settles them down to watch near the front.*
Abba I belong to you Abba I belong to you Abba I belong to you Our Father who art in heaven	*As this begins he moves forward to the centre front and kneels in prayer, facing the congregation head bowed.*
hallowed be thy name Thy Kingdom come, thy will be done	*Slowly raises head to look upwards slowly stands up*
on earth as it is in heaven	*raises his hands. A group of dancers in white join him, three on either side, moving to the chant of 'Abba I belong to you' in a set sequence: Step, together, step and turn. Transfer of weight, swaying.*
Give us this day our daily bread	*Jesus lowers arms to 'asking' with palms up,*
and forgive us our trespasses	*kneels on one knee and bows head*
as we forgive those who trespass against us and lead us not into temptation	*stands as if lifting something from the ground as he does so, palms up walks three steps slowly forward and stops,*
but deliver us from evil for thine is the kingdom the power and the glory	*steps back with one foot and brings arms up as if to shield his face, then flings open his arms in praise as he is spotlighted in brightness.*
for ever and ever. Amen. Amen. Amen.	*The dancers work their way back to the sides, the light fades and Jesus slowly returns to his friends who kneel at his feet. He raises them and they all walk, arm in arm, to the back of the church.*

Ideas for Children

Have lots of candles, fruit, flowers and glass in a beautiful arrangement, with quiet music playing as the children come in.

Point out the way the light and beauty is reflected in the glass. Talk about the lovely things in our world which reflect God's glory in this way – sunny days, rain drops, snowflakes, spring flowers, animals, cobwebs etc. – and thank him for them in a prayer or song.

Then tell them how one day, Jesus showed his glory, the glory of God, not as a reflection but directly. Tell the story of the transfiguration as music plays in the background, explaining that God is full of glory like that all the time, even if we only see it sometimes.

Give each child a card folded like this:

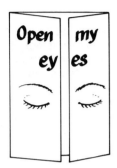 

Have the eyes and words already on it. Let them fill the centre with all kinds of lovely things, either drawn, or cut out and stuck on.

Music
Recorded Music

Brahms: *Symphony No. 1: final movement*

'Live' Music

Forward in faith *(ONE, 151)*
God is love: his the care *(ONE, 178)*
Immortal, invisible *(ONE, 242)*
I watch the sunrise *(ONE, 262)*
Lead us, heavenly Father, lead us *(ONE, 298)*

3rd Sunday of Lent

Theme
The living water of Christ

Physically, our bodies are dependent on water: without it we die. Spiritually, our life depends on the grace and presence of Christ, so he is like spiritual 'water' which refreshes, quenches our 'thirst' or longing, and gives us health and vitality; without it we are bound to die spiritually.

Penitential Rite

You know all we have ever done,
  Lord, have mercy. **Lord, have mercy.**

You see all we could become,
  Christ, have mercy. **Christ, have mercy.**

Through you our healing is begun,
  Lord, have mercy. **Lord, have mercy.**

Notes on the Readings

Exodus 17:3-7

Moses was responsible for the welfare of these people whom he had led out of slavery in Egypt. Those responsible are inevitably on the receiving end of criticism, complaints and grumbles.

When this happens life can be very miserable, and we may start wondering how on earth we are to cope, and whether we might even be beaten down by it all, especially when we can understand the grievances but simply have no more resources left to help.

When God calls us to lead others he calls us to work hand in hand with him, and not to try to manage on our own. When problems arise or needs are expressed, we, like Moses, have to appeal to the Lord. We won't be demeaning ourselves by admitting frankly to him that we have reached the end of our tether, and can't do any more without his help.

And every single time we approach him as Moses did, God acts by providing the necessary resources, be they patience and a sense of humour or money and equipment. Whatever is needed for eternal life and spiritual growth he will always provide if we ask.

Romans 5:1-2, 5-8

We do not have to wait to be saints before working alongside God in this way. If that were the case God would have very few labourers around! But since we do not earn his love by doing a certain number of heroic deeds or good turns, we can enjoy belonging to him straight away, happy in the knowledge that he loved us enough to die for us even when we were still sinners.

John 4:5-42

The new life, with all its vitality, freedom and peace, is available to everyone of every nationality, not just the chosen race to whom and through whom it was first brought.

In this intriguing story of the Samaritan woman at Jacob's well we see how Jesus saw his ministry of salvation as fulfilling the Law to the extent that it overflowed into all the world, like a spring constantly bubbling up to revitalise and refresh.

The woman is in turn shocked, amused and impressed by what Jesus says. She is drawn to question him about the issues which worry her and make her angry, until gradually she is led to see that all these wranglings are submerged in the greater significance of God's eventual purpose for his creation, just as the water drawn from her well is only temporally satisfying compared with Christ's 'living' water. As she dashes off to tell her friends about his strange, compelling personality, it is as if she has filled her jar at his well, and this brings others back to the water's source – Christ himself.

That is what we must do: introduce others to Christ by the water we have drawn, but aim to bring them to draw water themselves eventually – to believe because of their own experience rather than just our witness.

Bidding Prayers

Celebrant Remembering that we are God's people
  and belong to him, let us offer
  him our prayers.

Reader For the spreading of God's Good News
  among the affluent and the poor,
  the thirsting and the apathetic,
  the well-educated and the illiterate;
  that the Church may bother with

every individual and work enthusiastically
in the strength of Christ.
Pause
Living water: **well up within us now.**

For the reawakening of conscience
among those whose standards have slipped
and those who have become disillusioned;
that moral decay may be halted
and healed in our society.
Pause
Living water: **well up within us now.**

For those who are dying of thirst
and hunger; those who are in acute pain
or have undergone surgery;
that though all else is blurred
and confused by their distress,
yet they may sense God's personal
tender love as he enfolds them
in his arms.
Pause
Living water: **well up within us now.**

For a more loving atmosphere
in our homes and personal relationships;
that we may embark on the kind
of costly love we see in Jesus,
and work at increasing our care
and affection especially for those
we tend to dislike.
Pause
Living water: **well up within us now.**

Celebrant Christ is among us, and through him
we offer these prayers to our heavenly
Father. **Amen.**

Church Decoration

Have an arrangement of boulders and rocks and sand round
a shallow dish or tray of water. Beside the water place an
earthenware jug or waterpot. A hint like this often makes
people more receptive to the readings.

Ideas for Children

Talk about being thirsty – perhaps after running about on
a hot day, when your mouth feels dry like dust, and you're
gasping for a drink. The children may have seen news re-
ports where people are desperate for water. Explain how
our bodies need water to live. Then pour some cold, clear
water from a jug into a glass. How refreshing it sounds! At
this point you could sing the 'Water!' song from 'Many Ways
to Praise', and thank God for the gift of water.

Now read or tell the story of the Samaritan woman and
Jesus. If possible have a large picture of women collecting
water from a well, so they can see how it is done, and what
heavy work it is.

Bring out the point that with their water you get thirsty
again, but with the kind of water Jesus was talking about,
your thirst would be quenched forever. What did Jesus
mean? He meant that we will be happy and comfortable
even when life is difficult, if we
have his Spirit living in us.

Give each child a paper cup
to decorate with stickers.
Write on it 'Jesus is living
water'. They can drink water
from their cups at home, and
be reminded of Jesus'
spiritual water.

Music
Recorded Music

Debussy – *La Mer*

'Live' Music

As earth that is dry *(SONL, 86)*
If you are thirsting *(SONL, 83)*
Oh come to the water *(SONL, 67)*
The Lord's my shepherd *(ONE, 533)*
There is a river *(ONE, 541)*

4th Sunday of Lent

Theme
Christ, the anointed King

When David was anointed by Samuel he was set apart as
the chosen leader of God's people. Had Samuel not looked
with God's vision, the wrong person may have been chosen.
Jesus is the anointed, chosen Messiah, but if we are spiritually blind we shall fail to recognise him.

Penitential Rite

Open our eyes to see things your way,
    Lord, have mercy. **Lord, have mercy.**

Open our ears to hear you speak,
    Christ, have mercy. **Christ, have mercy.**

Open our hearts to recognise your presence,
    Lord, have mercy. **Lord, have mercy.**

Notes on the Readings

1 Samuel 16:1, 6-7, 10-13

The choice of this king was crucial and, as often happens,
God had a particular person in mind for the job. But whether
or not his will would be done depended on Samuel's readiness to comply with God's instructions even if that meant
waiving his independent judgement. Fortunately Samuel
stayed close to God and refused to anoint anyone until he
felt God's firm assurance that this was the right man.

If we ever find that setbacks make it impossible to
achieve some work we know God desires to have done,
we must not make a bodged job with what seems to be
available; we must wait for clear guidance – the proper
solution may be somewhere else, quite unexpected. The
important thing is to stay listening, as God will show his
way forward soon enough.

Also, we must bear in mind that outward appearances
count for little in God's eyes, so he often rejects and
chooses in ways which take us by surprise. Perhaps judging
by appearances would be a useful thing for us to give up
during Lent.

Ephesians 5:8-14

The light Christ brings into our lives is really 'enlightenment' for it means that, in his presence, right and wrong
become clearer, and we can see how to act for good rather
than evil.

One of the most alarming things about evil is that quite
often we have simply no idea how destructive our well-
meant behaviour can be. Without Christ it is not at all
obvious and we desperately need his guidance, his light,
to show up the areas of our characters which may seem all
right to us, but which are causing others distress or blocking

God's work. If we really want God to work in us then we must earnestly pray for his light. When it shines we can be sure of one thing – we shall not like what it shows at all, as it will be bound to touch raw nerves. We must pray bravely, then, in the knowledge that, even if it hurts to put right, we shall be stronger, more useful Christians once God has been let in to heal.

John 9:1-41

This story beautifully illustrates spiritual and physical blindness, as we watch the way the blind man's restored sight brings with it great spiritual insight, while the myopic vision of those peering closely at the Mosaic Law, fails to see anything broader or more far-reaching.

We see, by and large, what we want or expect to see, and no more. Most of us are fairly unobservant until some startling event causes us to look more carefully. This startling event really set everyone going. Something in them wanted to believe that the man's sight must point to a great power at work – possibly the power of God himself. But pulling against that is the doubt: that this is too good, too incredibly simple, to be true.

What about all the rules and regulations they had worked on for years? What about the different expectations they had about the true Messiah? Could this man Jesus really be the chosen one they taught the people about? If he were, it would mean that they had to abandon their authority and start again at the bottom, learning instead of teaching, giving up cherished pedantry. The challenge was simply too great: they decided to shut the light out instead, and call it darkness. Sadly, there are Christians who sometimes do the same. We are all sometimes guilty of it.

Yet what exuberant freedom the blind man has, as he abandons himself to Christ. His healing seems to liberate not only his eyes, but his wit and humour, confidence and enthusiam as well. In acknowledging Christ as his Lord he is made totally whole.

Bidding Prayers

Celebrant Christ is here among us and cares for us all. Let us therefore pray.

Reader For the needs of his Church as it works within the world to reconcile humanity with its creator;
that Christians may speak in words the world understands, advising wisely, counselling lovingly and welcoming wholeheartedly.
Pause
Lord, guide us: **for you are our shepherd.**

For the needs of each community and country on this planet;
that wherever feelings have boiled over and are out of control,
the calm reassurance of Christ may restore harmony and goodwill among enemies and the unforgiving.
Pause
Lord, guide us: **for you are our shepherd.**

For those attending hospitals and clinics, those in residential homes and all in intensive care units;
for their relatives, and the staff who look after them;
that they may be sustained, strengthened, and brought to wholeness by the healing God of love.

Pause
Lord, guide us: **for you are our shepherd.**

For the needs of this parish and our city/town; for all who lead lonely, unhappy lives, all whose marriages are crumbling, all who cannot cope with the demands of young children or elderly relatives; that as members of Christ we may be shown where we can help and be given courage to act.
Pause
Lord, guide us: **for you are our shepherd.**

Celebrant Loving Father, we bring you these prayers through Christ our Lord, and through him we offer ourselves to be used in your service. **Amen.**

Ideas for Adults

There is such a lot of dialogue in today's Gospel that it can easily be dramatised, with the actors speaking and miming their parts. A few simple costumes add to the performance – and they need only be pieces of material, sheets, towels etc. You will need:
a narrator
the blind man
a group of disciples
Jesus
neighbours
Pharisees
the man's parents

Ideas for Children

The Gospel of today is very well told in the Palm Tree version called 'The Man Born Blind'. Before you read it, ask the children to shut their eyes for a minute (or blindfold them) while they try to do an ordinary task like putting their shoes and socks on. Talk about how difficult it is for blind people to go shopping, cook or even walk along pavements where bikes have been left about.

When you have read the story, ask them if they can think of anyone else in it who was 'blind' apart from Abner. Remind them of the 2nd Sunday of Lent's card (Open my eyes to see your glory). Then let them make these masks to make the point of seeing God's way.

Music
Recorded Music

Handel – *Zadok the Priest*

'Live' Music

Amazing grace *(ONE, 36)*
Colours of day *(ONE, 87)*
I want to build my life *(ONE, 260)*
Take my hands and make them as your own *(ONE, 509)*

5th Sunday of Lent

Theme
Christ is the Resurrection

Christ has power to bring new life wherever we are spiritually dead. His life is stronger even than the physical death of our bodies, for if we are filled with his life-giving grace, we shall experience a fundamentally new existence which does not finish at the grave, but lasts for ever.

Penitential Rite

Wherever our prayer has become mechanical,
   Lord, have mercy. **Lord, have mercy.**

Wherever our worship has become stagnant,
   Christ, have mercy. **Christ, have mercy.**

Wherever good relationships have turned sour,
   Lord, have mercy. **Lord, have mercy.**

Notes on the Readings

Ezekial 37:12-14

When hope finishes, it is as if a candle gutters and dies; as if a heart misses a beat and stops. Carcasses remain, and many people's lives are littered with carcasses: their hopes are dead, and fester to rank bitterness. What chance is there of bringing such people back to life?

Often their despair is treated with drugs which may affect the outward symptoms, but if the cause is deep-seated anger and bitterness, because hopes have been dashed, the despair and depression cannot be cured by drugs alone.

This prophecy points to the only lasting and complete wholeness: the Spirit of God can awaken new life in the deadest, most hardened, and seemingly hopeless situations. Nothing is too dead or beyond his life-giving breath.

We who know Christ must work tirelessly to open the floodgates for that life to pour in; wedge a foot of love in the door to keep it open in those who are in danger of closing it completely; and constantly clear away all that clutters and blocks his love in our own lives.

Romans 8:8-11

Once Christ lives in us we shall be alive in four dimensions, as it were. He will give us the grace to embrace life with a fullness and generosity which is unfettered by self-interest or prejudice. And even death does not mark an end, but an entrance to the complete fullness of eternal life lived out for ever in the presence and kingdom of the risen Christ.

John 11:1-45

Jesus deliberately chose to wait until his close friend had actually died before coming to heal him. The pathos and overwhelming sadness and loss of a loved one comes through this account very powerfully. Jesus feels it to the quick, even though he knows that Lazarus will rise again. It is right and important that we feel able to mourn; squashing our human grief firmly out of sight in an effort to be brave can actually damage us emotionally and create long-term problems of adjustment. Yet at the same time, beneath the pain of grief, is the quiet reassurance that Jesus is here, Jesus loves, and Jesus cancels death.

When he raised Lazarus to life, all those who witnessed the event could see that God's care and love did not finish with the pulse, and was stronger than physical death. Even then, not everyone believed. We are each of us shown evidence of God's love in action: whether we believe or not is a personal decision which no one else can make for us.

Bidding Prayers

Celebrant   In the presence of God, the giver of all life, let us lift our hearts and pray.

Reader   For all assistant priests, deacons and ordinands, all students of theology and their teachers;
that as they are trained for ministry they may grow in wisdom and humility, and be increasingly filled with the life of Christ.
Pause
Lord, breathe into us: **that we may live.**

For all areas of bureaucracy which frustrate and delay the course of useful action; for areas where anarchy threatens to undermine stability; all areas of political corruption; that whatever is good may flourish and grow, so that evil may be overcome and rendered powerless.
Pause
Lord, breathe into us: **that we may live.**

For all who are engaged or newly married; for those coping with family problems, difficult circumstances or bereavement; that they may lean on the loving presence of Christ who dispels all fear and brings life and peace.
Pause
Lord, breath on us: **that we may live.**

Celebrant   Father, we thank you for your constant love, and offer these prayers for the sake of your Son, Jesus. **Amen.**

Ideas for Children

Tell the children the story in today's Gospel using an overhead projector or cereal packet 'television'. Explain that God not only brings life, he actually is life. You could sing *Lord of the Dance* which expresses this idea.

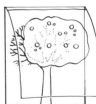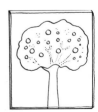

Greaseproof paper

Then let the children cut out, colour and staple together these two pictures to show the effect of God's love.

Music
Recorded Music

Mahler – *Symphony No. 1: final movement*

'Live' Music

Father, you are living in us now *(SONL, 65)*
Jerusalem the golden *(ONE, 273)*
Love divine all loves excelling *(ONE, 337)*
My song is love unknown *(ONE, 363)*
Take me, Lord *(SONL, 92)*

HOLY WEEK

Looking ahead

Through Holy Week and Easter we shall be seeing how we, creatures of clay, have been given the light of undying hope through Christ.

A rather unusual, but powerful preparation for this is to meet as a group some time this week to dig clay from the ground, knead it and mould it into a small bowl, and fill it with oil and a wick. It is not difficult, and the working hands become part of the prayer.

As the group works, either have silence, or taped music (from Taizé, perhaps.) Give instruction beforehand and work, if possible, in a circle. Have bowls of soapy water available.

Instructions

1. Any sticky mud can be moulded, and as the bowls will not be fired, there is no need to use first class clay. But many areas have a good supply quite near the surface.
2. Knead thoroughly, moistening with water as necessary. It will gradually become more pliable.
3. Make a lump into a ball, push in your thumb, and widen the dent bit by bit by pressing your thumb on the inside and first finger on the outside.
4. Decorate the outside using a small twig or spent match. The finished bowl should be large enough to hold a night light or a floating wick.
5. Leave the bowls to dry out slowly in an airy place. They will be ready to use for Holy Saturday.

Passion Sunday (Palm Sunday)

Theme

Hosanna to Jesus, our King!

As Prince of Peace, Jesus enters Jerusalem, and the people acclaim him as Lord. At the heart of our rejoicing is the pain of what he is bound to suffer in redeeming us through unflinching love. Yet we still certainly rejoice, for we know him to have won the victory; he is our everlasting Lord and King.

Penitential Rite

Keep us from falling into temptation,
   Lord, have mercy. **Lord, have mercy.**

Help us to worship in spirit and in truth,
   Christ, have mercy. **Christ, have mercy.**

Re-form us till our lives reflect your life,
   Lord, have mercy. **Lord, have mercy.**

Notes on the Readings

Isaiah 50:4-7
Philippians 2:6-11
Matthew 26:14-27, 66

The crucifixion was not an isolated act, but more like the final piece in a jigsaw which makes the whole picture clear. The long line of prophecies had already wrestled with the unpalatable and harsh truth that a suffering servant, mocked and cruelly treated, was the only way to win over the evil of the world. The sufferer would remain unsullied and unresentful, knowing that God's spiritual power of good surpasses all that man can devise to damage the body, no matter how warped or sadistic he may be.

If victory is regarded as a matter of who can torture and kill most enemies, then evil has the victory and our world is lost.

But the prophecies point to a different way of looking at victory altogether, which Christ was to explain by his perfect sacrifice. Full victory has to do with an eternal, everlasting life; neither mankind nor the powers of evil have potency to obliterate this. For God, in the person of Jesus, has travelled through the darkest, bleakest terrors of evil with his purity and perfect goodness.

Victory, then, belongs to goodness, and we, catching hold of Christ's spirit, can be drawn up with him into the life that evil cannot overcome.

No wonder we acclaim him and worship him, reverencing even his name; for in all the turbulent violence and destruction of our world, Christ on the cross, agonised yet forgiving, marks the only victory worth having and he offers it to us for nothing. We need run away no more; we need make no more excuses or pretend that the evil is not there. It is there, powerful and chaotic; but Christ has met it head on and his love has won.

Bidding Prayers

Celebrant   Fellow pilgrims, as we welcome Jesus and hail him as our King, let us offer to God our Father in prayer the deep concerns and needs of the Church and the world.

Reader   We bring to his love all who are baptised, and especially those who have lost their faith or stopped praying; that they may be brought back through Christ's love, and put into contact with those who can guide and reassure them.
Pause
Father Almighty:
   we pledge ourselves to your service.

We bring to his love every meeting, demonstration, convention and all large crowds; that they may be peaceful and ordered, inspiring those present for good rather than inciting them to violence.
Pause
Father Almighty:
   we pledge ourselves to your service.

We bring to his love those suffering from incurable or life-threatening diseases; those who need medical care but are either too poor or live too far away to receive it; that we may be more ready to help with our time, money and influence, so that unnecessary suffering and death are avoided.
Pause
Father Almighty:
   we pledge ourselves to your service.

We bring to his love our own loved ones, the members of our families, our friends and especially those from whom we are separated, either by distance or death, and all who are missing from their homes; that God's powerful love may protect us from all that is evil.
Pause

Father Almighty:
we pledge ourselves to your service.

Celebrant Merciful Father, we know that you hold
all life in your hand; please hear
our prayers through Jesus our Redeemer. **Amen.**

Ideas for Adults

If anyone owns a donkey, look into the possibility of using
it in the procession, and try to go round a route where the
procession is likely to be seen. Encourage everyone to
bring greenery, and use hymns which everyone knows:
there is little worse than a witness of mumbling, solemn-
faced, book-peering Christians trailing round. Our involvement in the triumphal entry of Jesus should show in clothes,
singing and faces!

The Passion

Throughout the Passion parts can be taken by different
people, with the congregation joining in as the crowd.

Ideas for Children

Encourage the children to bring large leaves or branches
to wave in the procession, or colourful streamers. They may
also join in the crowd sections of the gospel if they are in
church at this point.

If not, read 'Jesus on a Donkey' (Palm Tree Bible Stories)
which tells the story of Jesus entering Jerusalem and then
help the children make a model of that ride. Use a large
tray as the base, with hills of crumpled paper under a green
towel. The track is a strip of brown or beige material. Houses
can be made from white paper like this:

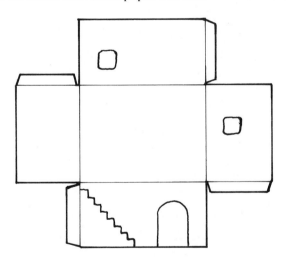

and palm trees from green paper like this:

Have a farmyard model of a donkey and make plasticene
figures, waving real leaves. Pieces of material cut out can
be laid on the path in front of Jesus.

Display the finished model where the rest of the congregation can see it.

Music
Recorded Music

Bach – St. Matthew's Passion

'Live' Music

Hosanna! *(ONE, 219)*
How lovely on the mountains *(ONE, 223)*

Holy Thursday
Evening Mass of the Lord's Supper

Theme
Christ fills the Passover with new meaning

God's lasting covenant with his people had always been
celebrated as giving them freedom from slavery in Egypt.
Now, in Jesus' institution of the eucharistic sacrament, there
is a new covenant – God's promise to give us freedom from
the slavery of sin.

The essence of the covenant is loving service, which
Jesus shows by example when he, the master, washes his
servants' feet. If we are to follow him, we too must freely
and joyfully expend our lives in the service of the world.

Penitential Rite

In your generosity we see our selfishness,
Lord, have mercy. **Lord, have mercy.**

In your humility we see our pride,
Christ, have mercy. **Christ, have mercy.**

In your loving service we see our unconcern,
Lord, have mercy. **Lord, have mercy.**

Notes on the Readings

Exodus 12:1-8, 11-14

The profound significance of this occasion is marked by the ritual and the reordering of the calendar. (Every time we write the date we have a similar reminder of God's great act of Incarnation.)

The instructions are highly practical for a meal before a journey, and often the fulfilment of God's will depends on people obeying his instructions, however odd or irrelevant they may seem. For the chosen people, this sets them apart and protects them from the destroying plague in Egypt.

1 Corinthians 11:23-26

It is no accident that the Last Supper was a celebration of Passover. The symbolism would now be given new meaning, and the new covenant marks the next stage in God's relationship with his people.

And just as the people of Israel were instructed to celebrate Passover as a festival every year, so we are instructed to celebrate the Eucharist regularly until the second coming.

John 13:1-15

There is only a thin dividing line between self-respect and arrogance. 'No self-respecting person would allow himself to be treated like that', we often hear, and we may instinctively shy away from being helped if we feel it is an insult to our independence or ability. Peter was offended by Jesus' behaviour: perhaps he felt that Jesus was degrading himself by doing a servant's job, and he wanted no part in it. It didn't seem right for a Lord and Master to be washing feet. How would we feel if a Cardinal came to the parish and started cleaning everyone's shoes!

Jesus again uses a physical act to explain the love he was telling them about. In the act of feet washing, in which they were involved, they could see that this love was not an emotional feeling or vague affection. It meant renouncing all right to rank and privileges, and serving reverently wherever there may be needs.

Those in need are not always the most attractive or pleasant people to deal with; they may smell, insult us, inject themselves with heroin or sleep around irresponsibly. They may encompass all the values we reject. But none of this matters, for we are not asked to like, or fall in love with one another – only to love one another. That involves the will, practical care, generosity and commitment. And we may well find that this leads to deeper, warmer friendships than we had believed possible.

Bidding Prayers

Celebrant   We belong to the body of Christ. In his name let us pray to the Father for the Church and for the world.

Reader   Let us pray for all Christian leaders of all denominations; for a breaking down of the barriers which divide the Church; for the healing of old wounds, for forgiveness and an openness among all Christians to the Holy Spirit which alone can make us one.
Pause
Lord of love: **teach us to care.**

Let us pray for the inner city areas where there is poverty, overcrowding and neglect; for areas of high rise flats where many feel isolated; for areas of depression and high unemployment; that mankind, working hand in hand with God, may bring to the world the freshness and vitality which springs from hope and caring love.
Pause
Lord of love: **teach us to care.**

Let us pray for all who are trapped by handicap, illness or addiction; all who feel unwanted or rejected; that they may experience as a living reality the liberation of Christ's accepting love.
Pause
Lord of love: **teach us to care.**

Let us pray for the areas of our own lives which need to be remade in Christ; for any trying or difficult relationships, anyone we tend to criticise or despise; that God's uncompromising love may inspire us to give without limits and without exceptions.
Pause
Lord of love: **teach us to care.**

Celebrant   Father, we ask you to accept these prayers through Jesus Christ, and use us for your glory. **Amen.**

Ideas for Adults

1. Encourage everyone to bring a bell and ring it during the Gloria.
2. Have representatives of all age groups and ways of life among those whose feet are to be washed. It is better to have different people each year.

Ideas for Children

If the children can be involved with the celebrations in church today, that is lovely. It is helpful to provide a duplicated picture for each child to colour in during the homily: a simple line-drawing of Jesus breaking the bread, or washing the disciples' feet, for instance.

Music
Recorded Music

Bach – St. John's Passion

'Live' Music

A new commandment *(ONE, 39)*
Love is his word *(ONE, 338)*
Take this and eat it *(SONL, 77)*
This is my body *(ONE, 556)*

Good Friday

Theme

Jesus lays down his life for us

Christ's great love does not even draw back from the act of death, a death in which the shame and guilt of the whole world was carried by one who was entirely innocent and sinless. Through that total sacrifice God redeems or buys back his lost people. If we are grafted on to him we too shall be able to give our lives away in service and receive through him the victory of abundant, everlasting life.

Penitential Rite

This is expressed today through the veneration of the cross and the silence of repentance at the beginning of the liturgy.

Notes on the Readings

Isaiah 52:13-53:12

Today we stand, with those closest to Jesus, at the foot of the cross. We witness the physical, mental and spiritual anguish of a man undergoing the punishment of crucifixion. The punishment is harsh, cruel and deadly. Torment is ugly and disfiguring: there is nothing beautiful about it.

Then comes the stunning realisation that the punishment his wracked body receives is our own punishment. Our selfishness, pride and disobedience; our mean and unkind behaviour cause terrible misery and work against the will and plan of God. That behaviour is condemned and our punishment is death.

Yet here is Christ, taking our place and submitting to the death sentence for us. One thing blazes out from the cross, then: that there is no doubt of Christ's love for us, for 'through his wounds we are healed'. His death pays our debt and therefore saves us.

Hebrews 4:14-16; 5:7-9

In one sense Christianity is a very materialistic religion, for our salvation is in no way based on abstract ideals. Jesus Christ was a real, flesh-and-blood human being who knew all about tiredness, coldness, weakness, sorrow, excitement, anger and affection. There is nothing in the human condition in which our God does not participate, so we can be sure he will listen eagerly when we cry to him in our need; he will always respond with mercy and tenderness.

John 18:1-19, 42

Dare we pledge ourselves to Christ's way? When we read the account of his crucifixion the example it shows is so daunting. It is relatively easy to say 'use me, Lord' in the safety and fellowship of worship, and certainly this is the right beginning.

But we are bound, as indeed Jesus was, to recoil from the horrors of physical torture, emotional taunting and ridicule, or the call to submit obediently without gaining anyone's approval or praise. When we feel very much alone, and the God-given task weighs heavily and seems to be doing no one any immediate good; when we are tired and mocked for taking it seriously – these are the times we are truly offering ourselves for God's use. Such times must be expected and not resented, for they are the moments when we have the privilege of identifying with the suffering Christ. They are the times when others can be drawn to the strange freedom which owes nothing to comfort or a substantial bank balance, and everything to repentance, forgiveness and love.

Bidding Prayers

The general intercessions are used today. To aid prayer some slides may be projected, which focus attention on each intention. Alternatively a spotlight behind a large cross can make the shadow of the cross stretch over the people.

Ideas for Adults

The different sections of the Isaiah reading can be read by different voices. This will emphasise the different stages of the meditation and bring out the development of the prophet's message. Experiment with the group of readers to decide which voices are most appropriate for each section.

Ideas for Children

While older children can actively participate in the drama and liturgy of Good Friday and gain much from its richness, younger children may find it all too overwhelming and distressing.

It is probably better for them to have a separate liturgy to walk the Way of the Cross, and a suggested timetable for this is:

10.00 a.m.	Introduction with brief talk (what happened on Good Friday) prayer and a song. Some Stations of the Cross may be used.
10.25 a.m.	Begin activities
10.45 a.m.	Break; drink and hot cross bun
11.00 a.m.	Resume and complete activities
11.20 a.m.	Gather for short litany, and a song and blessing
11.30 a.m.	End

Another possibility is that they prepare a dramatic presentation which may be used as part of the adults' liturgy.

Music
Recorded Music

Faure – *Requiem-Agnus Dei*

'Live' Music

Life pervading, all containing (SONL, 46)
Lord Jesus, think on me (ONE, 327)
Man of Galilee (ONE, 343)
My people (SONL, 85)

EASTER

Holy Saturday
The Easter Vigil

Theme
The night of Resurrection

According to his promise, and in accomplishment of his great, saving work, Christ passes through death into new and everlasting life. And we can share that life as, in baptism, we die to sin and rise to a new existence, powered and charged with his Spirit.

Liturgy

This night is the most significant and important in the whole liturgical year; the central point of Christianity and the focus of all the Church's belief and teaching.

The worship therefore deserves particular thought and planning, worthy of such a great and special occasion.

The liturgy provides an abundance of powerful symbolism which can heighten our understanding of the pascal mystery we are celebrating. It is worth using these symbols to the full, so that they are caught and experienced by the whole community.

There is a fund of ideas in *Focus on Holy Week* which will ensure that the vigil is as meaningful as possible.

Notes on the Readings

Genesis 1:1-2:2
Genesis 22:1-18
Exodus 14:15-15:1
Isaiah 54:5-14
Isaiah 55:1-11
Baruch 3:9-15, 32-4:4
Ezekiel 36:16-28

From the very beginning of matter God has been in charge. He chose to fashion the universe, and through his will and command it was created with all its potential for life and variety. Even as it was being formed, God's plans for its direction and purpose were fully developed. Gradually through history we can see that plan unfolding, as a tentative, halting progress, often spoiled but repaired; often wounded but healed; often wandering but led back to the source of creation, by the creator himself who loves what he has made.

These readings take us in a time-capsule through some of the main events in that revealed plan, so that we begin to see God's patient, guiding presence, which gradually leads to the point of intervention at the act of God becoming man: creator and created merge in the person of Jesus.

A selection of ideas for the presentation of Readings is given in *Focus the Word* (*Year of Luke*).

Romans 6:3-11

When we repent of all that blunts us as God's instruments, all that destroys and damages, all that prevents growth and peace – we are on the way to cancelling these sins. But in order for them to die, we must 'die' to ourselves, because suicide is devoid of hope and marks despair. In baptism we symbolically die to all that is evil in us, knowing that we cleave to Christ and that therefore the death will actually bring us a fuller, richer life than we had before, because it will be rooted in a force of goodness – Christ himself.

Matthew 28:1-10

When Jesus was born at Bethlehem he couldn't tell people the good news himself; it was conveyed to the shepherds by angels, who told them not to be afraid, but directed them to the stable where they would find him.

We know from human experience that birth and death both involve helplessness and vulnerability, and in many ways death is a kind of birth. Now, at this 'resurrection-birth' the angels are here again, calming the women's fears and directing them to where Jesus can be found. Just as the shepherds fell down and worshipped the baby in the manger, so both the Marys fall down and worship at the feet of the risen Christ. In both cases there is a great wonder, and immense joy.

Whenever we are confronted with the tragedy of death, and the terrible aching sense of loss, this account of the resurrection can help us to see all death in the light of eternal (or unending) life; Jesus has achieved this by breaking through the wall of death and rising to new life which lasts for ever. Since that victory, death is no longer the end for our loved ones, and angels direct us, too, to where we can find them still: in Christ.

Ideas for Adults

The clay pots can be used with night lights or small candles in them.

Ideas for Children

It may be that many families will make a point of worshipping together at the Easter Vigil, especially if it includes a variety of imaginative presentation and involvement.

However, many young children are likely to miss the celebrations. It may be worth considering whether the renewal of baptismal vows, with the lighting of each person's candle and the sprinkling of water, could not be incorporated into the Easter Day Mass, so that even the youngest members of the family can participate.

Music
Recorded Music

Haydn – *Creation*
Elgar – *Dream of Gerontius*
Mahler – *Symphony* No. 8

'Live' Music

Blessed be God for ever (SONL, 27)
He is Lord (ONE, 206)
They go out full of tears (ONE, 552)
Whom do you seek (SONL, 30)

Easter

Questions for Discussion Groups
1. Has the resurrection really affected our attitude to death?
2. In what ways is Jesus 'different' after the resurrection? Are there any differences in his followers at this stage?

Easter Sunday
(Mass of the Day)

Theme
He is risen!

Having passed through death to life, Christ has won the victory over everything evil and destructive. Full of glory and power, he enables us to bring hope and joy of resurrection into the world's problems and tragedies. With God, nothing is impossible.

Penitential Rite

In our weakness, strengthen us,
Lord, have mercy. **Lord, have mercy.**

In our apathy, revitalise us,
Christ, have mercy. **Christ, have mercy.**

In our joylessness, set us dancing,
Lord, have mercy. **Lord, have mercy.**

Notes on the Readings

Acts 10:34, 37-43

Peter's witness to the resurrection of Jesus is unequivocal and full of conviction, for he has actually seen Christ alive after his crucifixion, and has even eaten and drunk with him. You don't eat and drink with an allegorical character or a vision. There is no doubt about what Peter is saying: Jesus' new life is real and complete. So to believe in Jesus as the living Lord is not something for the gullible and naive, since they are the only ones crazy enough to believe such an impossible tale. The belief is based on the evidence of hard-headed, working men who had themselves taken quite a lot of convincing. Of course it is impossible in purely human terms. That does not mean we need to remould the facts to fit human possibility; it means that we need to acknowledge that God is altogether 'bigger' than the human experience. We are not the god – he is.

Colossians 3:1-4 or Corinthians 5:6-8

There is no way we can half die with Christ if we are to be brought back to true life with him. It simply cannot be done, though often we pretend it can. We submit bits of ourselves but hang on to other bits with a grip of steel. Perhaps we are frightened we may lose our identity along with our companionable sins. Danger and insecurity yawn before us if we contemplate really radical changes in our giving and our life style.

And we are right to count the cost first, for there is no doubt that there will certainly be risks and hardships. Living in Christ is rarely comfortable and never settled; it is full of the unexpected, of constant rethinking, challenge and change. It never allows us to get fixed in a rut or creep into holes when danger threatens.

But then, Christ never promised us a rose garden on the world's terms. We are to look instead for the heavenly things which belong with life in Christ. These treasures – such qualities as truth, joy, compassion and serenity – pour out in profusion, last through all affliction and satisfy as nothing material can. It is infinitely worth taking the risk, and giving ourselves away.

John 20:1-9

Although Jesus had explained to his disciples that he must die and then rise from the dead, they had not grasped what he meant. The terrible events of Friday had bludgeoned their hope into despair, because Jesus' torture and death were so horrifyingly real. No one in his right mind could hold out hope after the lifeless body was lowered from the gallows, and even the sun had darkened and the earth shuddered at the killing of this man.

So of course, on Sunday morning, the absence of Jesus' body suggested to them that it had been taken away, rather than that the impossible had happened. Gradually, as they saw the cloths left in their place, as one may leave night-clothes, having got up from sleep, the disciples began to wonder, and then were convinced that when Jesus had spoken of rising from the dead, he had meant exactly that. He really was more powerful even than death; suddenly all his teaching fell into place, and they saw that he was, indeed, God's Son who had fulfilled all the Messianic prophecies. Even death could not hold him, for he was the Lord of life.

Bidding Prayers

Celebrant In the joy of this Easter morning let us pray to the God who loves us so completely.

Reader For all who have been called by Christ to serve the world as his followers; that initial enthusiasm may not die but deepen, to set us all on fire with his love.
Pause
Lord of life: **transform us all.**

For a fairer distribution of the world's resources, so that life and hope are brought to the starving and homeless; for all places where fear and violence rule, that peace and justice may be restored.
Pause
Lord of life: **transform us all.**

For those who feel they are wasting their lives, for those under pressure at home or work, for all who feel lost, uncertain or worthless; that God's living power may stabilise, heal and rebuild them.
Pause
Lord of life: **transform us all.**

For ourselves, our friends and relatives, and any difficulties or problems that may be known to us; that in all our troubles we may open ourselves to the healing life of Christ, which has power to bring hope.
Pause
Lord of life: **transform us all.**

Celebrant In silence we praise you, Father,
for your abundant blessings, and
ask you to hear these prayers
for the sake of Jesus Christ. **Amen.**

Ideas for Adults

Unleavened bread for today can be baked by one of the
congregation, and home-made wine (provided it is suitable) can be used. The makers bring their gifts to the altar.

This recipe makes a soft bread which is not too crumbly:

Ingredients	
1lb wholemeal flour	¼ pt milk
pinch of salt	2 oz butter

1. Mix flour and salt together, and make a well in the centre.
2. Warm the milk and butter to blood heat, and gradually
   add to the flour.
3. Knead well for 2 minutes.
4. Divide the dough into 24 pieces and flatten each piece
   to a circle, about ¼ inch thick.
5. Cook each one in a frying pan over a gentle heat until
   speckled brown.
6. Wrap in a clean cloth until needed.

Ideas for Children

Read the first part of '*Jesus is Risen*' (Palm Tree Bible Stories)
or tell the story in your own words, acting it out with plasticine models on a tray with a stone 'cave' built on it in a
garden.

Sing one of the Easter songs together and give each child
a margarine tub with oasis in it, a selection of Spring flowers
and a tall white candle.

Help them make an arrangement of joy at Jesus being
alive forever. When they have finished, light all the candles,
and let the children carry them in procession into the church
near the altar.

Music
Recorded Music

Handel – *Messiah: Hallelujah Chorus*
Beethoven – *Symphony No. 6: Thanksgiving after the storm*

'Live' Music

At the name of Jesus *(ONE, 50)*
Go in peace, to be Christ's body *(SONL, 45)*
Let the mountains dance and sing *(SONL, 4)*
The Lord is risen today *(SONL, 58)*
The Spirit lives to set us free *(ONE, 547)*
This joyful Eastertide *(ONE, 565)*

2nd Sunday of Easter

Theme
Happy are those who do not see, yet believe

Having been an eye-witness to the crucifixion, Thomas was
not prepared to believe that Jesus could really be alive
unless he became an eye-witness to this as well. From the
early Church down to our own time many believe without
seeing the physical presence, but knowing the reality of
Christ's presence spiritually. It makes for great joy and
enthusiasm, fervour and commitment, inspiring us to live
more caring and less selfish lives.

Penitential Rite

We fail to see you through eyes of faith,
  Lord, have mercy. **Lord, have mercy.**

We do not notice you standing near us,
  Christ, have mercy. **Christ, have mercy.**

We do not recognise your face in those around us,
  Lord, have mercy. **Lord, have mercy.**

Notes on the Readings

Acts 2:42-47

We cannot help but be impressed by this community of
Christians. It is as if the Spirit of Christ has broken so
powerfully into their lives that the usual petty jealousies
and quarrels of human groups are jettisoned as they concentrate on something of much greater importance.

If we look at our own parish we may see different behaviour. The important thing is to remember that all behaviour develops from what we believe. If we really believe
that Jesus is alive, here among us, that will show in our
attitude to worship, our reverence, our discipline and our
generosity.

If we really believe that Jesus was a figure fixed in history
and God isn't too bothered about our immediate problems,
but expects us to carry on working where he left off, then
that will show, too. We shall start working in our own
strength, becoming defensive and aggressive, tired and
disheartened, critical and resentful.

Yet every time we hear the words: 'Peace be with you'
it reminds us that Christ is here among us. We can reach
out and touch him as we share his peace with our
neighbours. And with the living Christ among us, we can
cast aside our wranglings and differences, and enjoy living
together in love. Apart from anything else, it is far more fun!

1 Peter 1:3-9

Peter's letter is very encouraging, particularly for any who
are finding life difficult. He assures us that any patience
or perseverance we practise during rough patches of our
lives will be kept in heaven, and form part of the glory that
will be revealed at the end of time.

It may look as if we are failures in the world's eyes; we
may be hounded by false values, or feel as if we are bashing
our heads against a brick wall as we try to bring up our
children as Christians in a materialistic and pagan world,
hold an unstable marriage together, or cope positively with
unemployment or illness.

It is how we respond to these challenges and trials which
will make the lasting treasure. Instead of trying to act inde-
pendently of God we can trust him and use his grace of
forgiveness, his patience, his perseverance and his
strength. Then we will be building something beautiful with

and for God, whether the world sees it or not. The thrill of being privileged to work with God like this takes much of the sting our of the suffering, and an incongruous joy well up even among the tears.

John 20:19-31

Thomas was not with the other disciples when they were joined by Jesus. Perhaps he needed to sort things out in his mind alone after the death of his leader and friend. It cannot have come as a surprise to Thomas that Jesus would be killed; he had expected it earlier when they returned to Bethany to visit Lazarus' grave. Thomas had been prepared to die with him.

So if Thomas thought of Jesus as a great prophet, and a remarkable man, then an era of his life was now over, and he would have to sort out the rest of his life, trying his best to follow the example of his dead teacher. The prospect would be daunting in its difficulty and loneliness.

He must have had niggling questions about those strange sayings of Jesus concerning new life, and rising again. But Thomas was too dedicated to his human teacher to insult him by believing fairy stories – Jesus being alive again was simply too 'good' to be true: he preferred Jesus to be human, noble and dead.

When he did meet the risen Christ, his amazed acclamation of faith shows what had happened. Thomas had swapped a human teacher for the human Son of the all-powerful God; Christ was not only to be loved and listened to, but actually worshipped. It is not idolatry for us to worship Christ, although he has a human face. For his resurrection proves him also to be divine.

Bidding Prayers

Celebrant Brothers and sisters in Christ, our fellowship is rooted in the love God has for us all. Let us pray to him now.

Reader For the deepening of faith among all Christians; that we may be so convinced of Christ's closeness to us that we spend every minute of the rest of our lives in the joy and security of knowing that our God is alive and in charge.
Pause
Christ is risen from the dead: **our God reigns!**

For the spreading of the Good News throughout the world, so that wherever important decisions are made and policies planned, people may work, in harmony with their creator, for goodness, peace and reconciliation.
Pause
Christ is risen from the dead: **our God reigns!**

For the healing and repairing of broken lives, for vision and enlightenment among those whose hearts are darkened by fear or hatred; that God's living Spirit, let loose in the world, may anoint and soothe, pacify and recharge.
Pause
Christ is risen from the dead: **our God reigns!**

For a more loving atmosphere in our homes and our parish; more care and concern for each other; more willingness to forgive, understand and respect those with whom we live.

Pause
Christ has risen from the dead: **our God reigns!**

Celebrant Father, coming together with thanks and praise to worship you, we ask you to accept these prayers for the sake of Jesus Christ. **Amen.**

Ideas for Children

Begin by passing round a 'feeling' bag with a couple of objects inside it, such as a sieve and a marble, for instance. Each child has a turn to feel the bag and guess what the objects are, but the guesses aren't shared until everyone has had a go.

Then each one says: 'I believe there's a . . . in the bag'. Take the objects out to see who's right, and talk about how they didn't know for sure what was there until they saw it, but they could believe it by using clues, such as what it felt like.

Display a large sign: 'I believe Jesus is God's Son.'
How do we know?
Have we actually seen him?
What clues do we use, then?

Talk about the record of his friends in the Bible, the way Jesus helps us to be kind when we feel like being nasty, (so long as we ask him); the way he helps us through sad or painful times; and the happy feeling we have when we enjoy the lovely world with him.

Then read the Thomas section of 'Jesus is risen' and give the children a picture of this to colour, with Thomas's prayer on it. Encourage them to use this prayer themselves in church or at home.

Dance of the Resurrection

Have a group of dancers walking slowly in a highly organised procession, all in step, with their formation strictly kept. Heads are bowed and they are all wearing black cloaks. It should have the atmosphere of a funeral procession.

When they reach the centre front, a line of twelve children, who have been standing in front of the altar, turn to face the procession and, all together, lift up large card brightly coloured letters, which read:
JESUS IS ALIVE
Suddenly the music becomes joyful, the dancers throw off their black cloaks and dance together or separately to the music. If some can put up brightly coloured sunshades or umbrellas, so much the better. Their clothes should be colourful as well. The children sway their letters in time to the music. The dance finishes with a great shout of 'Alleluia!' New Orleans jazz music is best for this.

Music
Recorded Music

Corelli – *Concerto Grosso in G minor Op 6, No. 8*

'Live' Music

Sing to the mountains (*ONE, 495*)
The King of love my shepherd is (*ONE, 528*)
Walk with me, oh my Lord (*ONE, 582*)
Without seeing you, we love you (*SONL, 13*)

3rd Sunday of Easter

Theme
Christ is the fulfilment of the Scriptures

All the prophecies of the Old Testament culminate in the person of Jesus, whose resurrection holds all the evidence together and enables us to see God's supremacy both in life and death. The wonder of this spreads light and joy among his followers, as they grow closer to him, through the breaking of bread.

Penitential Rite

For our prejudices and preconceived ideas,
Lord, have mercy. **Lord, have mercy.**

For our lack of flexibility,
Christ, have mercy. **Christ, have mercy.**

For the time we have wasted,
Lord, have mercy. **Lord, have mercy.**

Notes on the Readings

Acts 2:14, 22-28

Peter, speaking in the fresh power of the Spirit released at Pentecost, has just discovered the key to all kinds of half-answered questions, which now form a complete picture that unifies past, present and future. It is rather like the 'Gestalt' psychology of suddenly realising what a structure is, as a whole, though it can't be grasped from looking at its separate components.

All the gathered memories of Jesus' ministry, all the snippets of prophecy, all the disparate puzzles, searchings and misunderstandings are focused, by the resurrection, into a new understanding of God and his love for the world. The disciples have found the pearl of great price, and it is so valuable that they cannot keep quiet about it.

1 Peter 1:17-21

Until Christ came to live among us in person we could not know God or hope and believe in him in quite the same way, because he had not yet been revealed to the world.

But Jesus changed all that, for in him we see the power and love of God acted out in human terms that we can understand.

Having acknowledged God as our Father, through seeing and listening to Jesus, we must be careful to act out our faith scrupulously as we journey through life to our heavenly home; not following meticulous rules of conduct, but living closely with Christ who will save us from evil.

Luke 24:13-35

The two disciples had been full of expectation. As Jesus' ministry progressed they had begun to see that he was not only a great prophet but possibly the Messiah himself. Now, at last, the Roman occupation would become a thing of the past, and Israel would once more be free and powerful.

The nails hammered into Jesus' body on Good Friday had hammered into their fervent hopes and dreams. No angel came to save him from death and when he died, so did their illusions.

Now Jesus approaches them, not abandoning them for having got it wrong, but working to redirect, explain and enlighten. Never mind if they didn't recognise him during the learning – they listened and began to think more openly, to broaden their expectations until, at the breaking of bread, things fell into place and they were filled with tremendous joy. So much so, that they raced back to Jerusalem straight away in the dark, though it was seven miles away and they had already done the journey once!

Sometimes, when we keep company with Jesus, we grasp part of what he is and teaches, but our egocentricity leads us off at a tangent. And when we start off in a wrong direction we can go alarmingly fast. Eventually our precious dreams and visions will crash, and we are bound to be hurt and jarred.

Christ will not abandon us for our foolishness. Through many and varied means he will teach and explain, and it is vital that we listen, even if we don't recognise it as Christ who is speaking. Then we shall grow in awareness and understanding, until we see Jesus revealed somehow in our lives, assuring us of his reality and closeness. Set on the right road again we shall be full of his joy and excitement.

Bidding Prayers

Celebrant Fellow pilgrims, as we journey along the Way of Christ, let us pray to the Father for the Church and for the world.

Reader For all who preach the word of God in this city/parish and throughout every country; that their message may be bright with the living Spirit of Jesus, and those who hear them may listen, understand and encounter Christ.
Pause
Lord, our Father: **help us to see you more clearly.**

For all involved in communication in our world – those working in radio, television and the press; solicitors, social workers, and all those in advisory services; that misunderstandings and grievances may be cleared up and all communications grounded in sincerity, honesty and open-mindedness.
Pause
Lord, our Father: **help us to see you more clearly.**

For the elderly and infirm, who are having to accept a loss of independence; for all with mental or physical disabilities which cause isolation and rejection; for all who are blind to the needs around them; that we may see what Christ would have us do in our lives.
Pause
Lord, our Father: **help us to see you more clearly.**

For a deepening of our own commitment to the service of Christ; for a greater receptiveness to his calling; for a more profound conviction of his real presence among us.
Pause
Lord, our Father: **help us to see you more clearly.**

Celebrant Father, in silence, we adore you and open ourselves to your healing love. Accept us, and our prayers, dear Father, for the sake of Jesus, the Christ. **Amen.**

Ideas for Children

Read the Emmaus section of 'Jesus is Risen' which captures the atmosphere very well. Talk about the story with the children:

- why do they think the disciples couldn't believe Jesus had risen?
- do they sometimes wonder if it is all true, and then later feel certain of Jesus being with them?
- talk about having expectations (for Christmas presents, for instance) which make us feel let down when they are not what we had in mind.
- when have they been surprised by God acting in their lives?

Teachers can give great encouragement in faith by being prepared to talk about some of their own surprises and disappointments; the children are then brought into contact with a real, living faith, rather than history. Help the children make this pop-up scene of Jesus breaking bread.

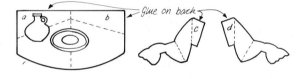

Music
Recorded Music

Grieg – *Peer Gynt Suite: Morning*

'Live' Music

Jesus himself drew near (*ONE, 277*)
Let all mortal flesh (*ONE, 300*)
Open your ears, O Christian people (*ONE, 422*)
We are the Easter people (*ONE, 586*)

4th Sunday of Easter

Theme
The good shepherd, who gave his life for us, is risen

Just as a good shepherd leads and cares for his sheep, and is prepared to die to keep them safe, so Christ leads and cares for us, even to the extent of dying for us. Although we have wandered off he draws us back, by paying off our debts for us, so that we may live in the joy of his peace.

Penitential Rite

We have wandered away from you,
Lord, have mercy. **Lord, have mercy.**

We have fulfilled our wills instead of yours,
Christ, have mercy. **Christ, have mercy.**

We have turned away from your love,
Lord, have mercy. **Lord, have mercy.**

or 'Come, Spirit come' *(See 6th Sunday of Easter page 46.)*

Notes on the Readings

Acts 2:14, 36-41

The image of a sandwich board wearer urging the High Street shoppers to repent has really become a joke, and I doubt if the message has any meaning at all for most.

The trouble is that the message of repentance is an answer to a question; unless the question has been asked first it will be meaningless. It's like '9 W', which means very little until you know the question: 'Does your name begin with a V, Mr. Wagner?' Then all is made clear!

You cannot tell people to be sorry before they know they are guilty. Peter's hearers were 'cut to the heart' when Peter's words and behaviour made them realise what they had unwittingly allowed to happen – they had helped to kill the god they worshipped. As the full horror dawned on them they longed to do something, anything to try to put things right.

The answer is to repent or, in other words, feel such sorrow for their sin that they are led to die to their old selves and be reborn through baptism into the new life of Christ. No new life can begin at all until there is sorrow for sin. No sorrow for sin can begin at all until we see, in Christ's light, our own infested darkness.

1 Peter 2:20-25

People often talk loosely of the cross they have to bear, when they mean one of the many hardships which are simply part of being human. But that cannot be what Jesus meant by taking up our crosses and following him. For him and us it signified a willingness to face and undergo persecution and death if necessary even when we are not guilty of what our accusers claim. And that, as Peter says, is where the merit lies, as far as God is concerned.

We are able to take as our example and prototype Christ, the suffering servant, who did not condemn or retaliate or even defend himself; instead he trusted in an eternal defence against which death is a powerless weapon. Drawing together the two aspects of purification symbolised by the scapegoat and sacrificed goat of the Jewish people, Jesus is both sent off into the wilderness, laden with our sin, and also offered as a pure victim as he dies a sinless death. He is therefore the complete atonement for reconciling us to God, for he is both human and divine.

John 10:1-10

Anyone who has walked along behind sheep will realise what Jesus meant when he talked so often of humans as sheep. They scuttle out of immediate danger and immediately start eating, as if nothing had happened. Seconds later they see danger catching up with them again so there is another short-lived scuttle, as they follow each other however foolishly they are led.

Hence the need for a really trustworthy shepherd, for sheep are woefully in need of a responsible leader. (Of course, the shepherds in Israel always lead, rather than drive the sheep, as in Britain.)

Some of those posing as the good shepherd can be very convincing, so that we sheep are sometimes coaxed into trusting them.

Bidding Prayers

Celebrant   My brothers and sisters in Christ, as we gather in the great hope of our risen Lord, let us pray to the Father who has shown us such generous love.

Reader   For unity among all who follow Christ, the good shepherd, that in keeping our eyes fixed on him we may be inspired to break down barriers, to forgive and be reconciled, through the healing force of accepting love.

Pause

Good shepherd: **lead us all.**

For all who hold positions of responsibility and leadership, both internationally and in our own community; that they themselves may be led by God's Spirit to make wise decisions and help create a humane and caring world.

Pause

Good shepherd: **lead us all.**

For all who incite others to antisocial or criminal behaviour; for all drug pushers and those involved in drugs traffic; that they may be transformed and made whole; for the weak, lonely, young and depressed who are so vulnerable to their temptations; that they may be given help and strength to resist the pressures around them.

Pause

Good shepherd: **lead us all.**

For all the families represented here today, their hopes and sorrows, difficulties and celebrations; that all our relationships may be bathed in the love of Christ, full of tenderness and compassion.

Pause

Good shepherd: **lead us all.**

Celebrant   Father, we bring you our cares and concerns, and ask you to hear these prayers through Jesus Christ. **Amen.**

Ideas for Adults

If there are any photographers (or snapshot-takers) in the parish, they could start compiling a collection of photographs for use in exhibitions and displays.

Today, for instance, a lovely display of sheep, shepherds and crowds of people could be shown, with short quotations and prayers. During the week this kind of display can become a useful starting point for prayer and a help to visitors.

Ideas for Children

Have a green sheet of paper on the table with some farmyard models of sheep and lambs, a sheepdog and a shepherd. (Britain Toys make a good one.) Talk with the children about what a shepherd's job involves. Some of them may have watched sheep being moved from one pasture to another. What would happen to the sheep if there was no shepherd? Talk about the way they stray into danger, and other ways they are vulnerable.

Now build a model of a sheep fold, or pen, which is used in the country Jesus lived in. Make it from small stones or from plasticine which has been given a stone pattern. The shepherd lay in the doorway to sleep, so he was the door! That kept the sheep all safe inside.

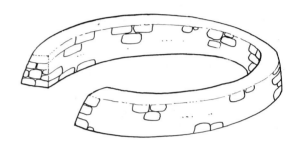

Next read the first part of today's Gospel, and help them understand that Jesus is the Good Shepherd and we are the sheep and lambs.

Then help the children to make sheep headgear on which is written: 'The Lord is my shepherd'. Perhaps they could process, bleating, into church and kneel for a moment of silence in front of the altar before joining their families.

Tie at back of head

White socks

Music
Recorded Music

Faure – *Pavane*

'Live' Music

Good shepherd (SONL, 12)
He's got the whole world (ONE, 209)
Oh Lord, my God, when I in awesome wonder (ONE, 404)
Oh the love of my Lord (ONE, 430)

5th Sunday of Easter

Theme
Christ is our route to the Father

To have seen Christ is to have seen God, our Father, and he will lead us in the way of truth and life; for we have been chosen as his people in order to serve the world with all the care and devotion of God himself. Living in Christ we shall be shown where the needs are, and be given the means to provide help.

Penitential Rite

We need to know you more clearly,
    Lord, have mercy. **Lord, have mercy.**

We need to love you more wholeheartedly,
    Christ, have mercy. **Christ, have mercy.**

We need to follow you more closely,
    Lord, have mercy. **Lord, have mercy.**

Notes on the Readings

Acts 6:1-7

As the young Church grew there were bound to be new difficulties about administration and organising practical help. The recognition of this takes the form of a complaint – much better that complaints should be voiced early on and sorted out, than that they should fester in tight-lipped silence.

Once out in the open, the complaints become an opportunity for development, and the decision is made to give the non-Jewish community greater authority and more participation in the running of the Church.

We need to be prepared to listen when there are complaints in our parishes and homes, without immediately bridling and gathering our arguments for defence, though this will probably be the instinctive reaction. It may help to visualise reconciliation in our mind's eye, when there seem sharp divisions of opinion, and arrange for everyone concerned to gather in silence before God. Then the complaints will certainly be used by him and may lead, not only to reconciliation, but also to rich growth and far-reaching developments.

1 Peter 2:4-9

Peter explains the role of Christ's followers in terms of the children of Israel who were the chosen race, set apart for God's purpose. Then, the temple containing the ark of the covenant represented the dwelling place of the Almighty. Now that God has revealed himself in the person of Jesus, the temple housing his presence is built of living stones – the followers of Christ. By grace they have become the chosen race, which is no longer bound to any ethnic group but has widened to embrace those from all nations who acknowledge Jesus as Lord.

There are times when it comes as a nasty shock to find that people, whom perhaps we love dearly, are stumbling over the very rock which provides our own foundation. It can be very tempting to try to kick that rock away, for it seems to stand in the way of a precious relationship.

Of course, it cannot be discarded, for Jesus is the vital centre of salvation, without whom there is no hope or life or healing. Instead, we are to offer ourselves as a sacrifice so that through our lives being grounded in Christ, even the most cynical, the most unexpected, are drawn to experience the security and joy of living in Jesus.

John 14:1-12

Placed at the point after the Last Supper and before the crucifixion, these words of Jesus are particularly poignant and significant. The disciples were being asked to bend their minds round the impossible truth that God the creator was one with this man, with whom they spent so much time. Certainly they had seen him perform some startling acts of healing; certainly his teaching had an unprecedented authority which helped them understand the scriptures in a more meaningful way than ever before.

But the final acknowledgement would have to be a leap of faith, as it always must be for us all. There is considerable evidence, and there are many signposts, but because in human terms the incarnation and resurrection are impossibilities, the step of faith has to be taken. There will always be some who cannot believe, even when faced with overwhelming evidence, and we are all likely to have times of severe doubting.

It is worth remembering that we can pray for the faith to believe, strange as that may seem. We can admit that we are not certain even of God's existence, but we long to be able to believe. It was Saint Theresa who prayed 'I do not long to love you, but I long to long to love you'.

Bidding Prayers

Celebrant Chosen by God to be members of his body,
let us gather our cares and concerns
and bring them before our heavenly Father,
who loves us.

Reader We pray for the many individuals who
comprise the body of Christ, with all
their varied ministries; and especially
for those who are unsure of God's purpose
for their service, that his will
may be made obvious and they may
be given courage to accept his call.
Pause
Lord, nourish us: **that we may bear fruit.**

We pray for the world and its areas
of conflict, political unrest, decadence
and deceit; that Christ, the Lord of all
truth and life, may lead mankind to
desire justice, peace and integrity.
Pause
Lord, nourish us: **that we may bear fruit.**

We pray for the bereaved and all
who mourn; for those who have recently
miscarried or given birth to a still-
born baby; for those who feel uncared
for and unloved; for those who must
watch their children die
from lack of food.
Pause
Lord, nourish us: **that we may bear fruit.**

We pray for a deeper trust in God
among all of us here; that we may
spend our life in getting to know
him better, so that we reflect his light
more and more brightly and can be of
more use to him in serving his world.
Pause
Lord, nourish us: **that we may bear fruit.**

Celebrant Merciful Father, we ask you to accept
our prayers for the sake of Christ,
our Lord. **Amen.**

Ideas for Children

Working on the theme of Jesus being 'The Way', begin by setting up two model villages, built by the children in lego or building bricks, in different parts of the room.

When they are finished, sit down with the children between the villages and talk about how the people could get from one to the other. They would need a road, with signs saying 'THIS WAY' whenever other roads branched off. Otherwise they would get lost. (Draw some roads in chalk.)

Explain that Jesus called himself the 'Way'. If we follow him we shall not get lost, and he will direct us to heaven. Let each child make a signpost out of card, a lolly stick, glue and a blob of plasticine. Arrange all the signs at intervals along the road, and sing 'Keep me travelling along with you' or 'Forward in faith'.

Music
Recorded Music

Vaughan Williams – *Fantasia on Greensleeves*

'Live' Music

Forward in faith *(ONE, 151)*
Lead us, heavenly Father, lead us *(ONE, 298)*
Listen, let your heart keep seeking *(SONL, 26)*
Loving shepherd of thy sheep *(ONE, 340)*
Make me a channel of your peace *(ONE, 342)*
Near the heart of Jesus *(SONL, 29)*

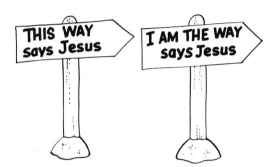

6th Sunday of Easter

Theme
Anyone who loves Jesus will be loved by the Father

Although Jesus was going back to heaven, his Spirit would be released and poured out on all who believed. Beginning with his disciples in Jerusalem it would spread to those of other races and other lands, filling those who received it with effervescent hope.

Penitential Rite

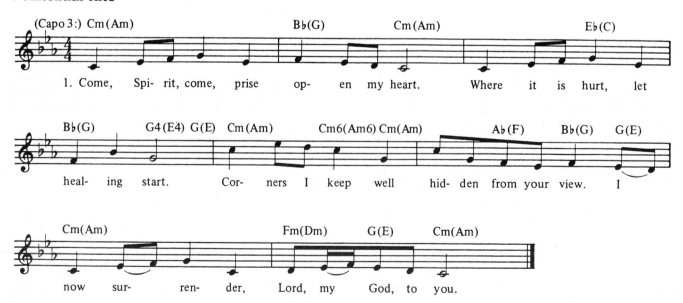

2. Come, Spirit, come, take charge of my mind.
   Show me the darkness that you find.
   Help me to trust you, even with my shame,
   till I freely acknowledge where I am to blame.

3. Come, Spirit, come, bring life to my soul.
   Your forgiveness makes me whole.
   Then from the pain and stress of sin set free
   I am dazed by the awesome love you have for me.

Notes on the Readings

Acts 8:5-8, 14-17

Philip has been commissioned by the Church leaders, and following Saul's persecution of Christians, he goes straight to the Samaritans, taking the Good News to foreigners and showing, by his behaviour and works of healing, evidence of God's holy Spirit just as Jesus had promised.

The Samaritans were generally detested by the Jews; the division was deep and rooted in history. Yet Philip's work is greatly blessed, and when the two apostles, Peter and John, are sent down to lay hands on the new believers, a bond of love is established which must have been thought impossible.

We must *never* accept any barriers or rifts, whether political or religious, as being beyond hope. With God's Spirit of love burning in us and all who have committed their lives to him, the most unexpected links can be forged, wounds healed and rigid attitudes softened. Before we know it, the impossible starts to happen and the resurrection victory of love over death is yet again revealed.

It happens in marriages, family feuds, nationally and internationally. But for it to start happening we must constantly draw all our life, strength and energy from the living Spirit of God.

1 Peter 3:15-18

It can be extremely irritating, when we are feeling in a self-pitying mood, to watch others who have more reason than us to complain, enjoying life and obviously happy! We resent their happiness and challenge it. The way they reply can either turn us off them for good or help us to see a way out of our own depresssion.

Seeing it that way round may illustrate why our reply, as Christians, to those who challenge us is so important. We must not condemn their present position, nor take offence at the resentment in their voice, nor shrug off the responsibility of giving a proper answer through embarrassment or the fear of causing offence. At least one part of anyone's reason for challenging our hope is the need for help, subconscious though this may be. We cannot let them down.

If, in the end, we suffer because of standing up for what we believe – so what? Jesus did, after all, and his suffering led to eternal life. So will ours, if we walk with him.

John 14:15-21

Walking with Christ entails keeping his Commandments. We are so used to love being described as an emotion that the idea of loving by command is alien to many. In fact, its very paradox points us towards the kind of loving Jesus meant: love that involves the will. We can choose whether to follow him or not, but having chosen, we cannot love God and our neighbour when we feel like it, only if the neighbour is attractive and only if he treats us well in return.

We cannot separate God from love or love from God; and if we are living in Christ, it should show. When people meet us and work with us, they should be able to see there the same love that God has for his world – a welcoming, accepting, loyal and compassionate care which reaches outwards, encourages and brings with it a sense of security, warmth and joy. If only we would let him, God could make us real, working instruments of a love like that.

Bidding Prayers

Celebrant Fellow travellers of the Way, let us pray in the Spirit of Christ for the Church and the world, remembering God's love for us.

Reader For all those involved in missionary work, both at home and abroad; for industrial chaplains, chaplains in the armed forces, in schools and hospitals; that through meeting them, those to whom they minister may encounter Christ.

Pause

Father Almighty: **pour on us your love.**

For all meetings between heads of government, all international events in commerce, sport and culture; all those involved with travel and tourism; that wherever people of different backgrounds meet, there may be courtesy and respect, friendliness and trust.

Pause

Father Almighty: **pour on us your love.**

For all whose bodies, minds or emotions are crippled or deformed; for those addicted to violence or poisoned by emotionally damaging videos and films; that God's values of goodness, purity and love may suffuse our society and liberate it from all that is evil.

Pause

Father Almighty: **pour on us your love.**

For the friendships and relationships we have had through our lives; that wherever there is hurt there may be healing, and wherever there is estrangement there may be reconciliation. In silence we bring the individual names of any who have hurt us, or those we love, to the healing power of God.

Pause

Father Almighty: **pour on us your love.**

Celebrant Father of mercy, look compassionately on your children, and hear us as we pray through Christ. **Amen.**

Ideas for Adults

On one day this week arrange to meet up before dawn so as to praise God as the sun rises. Go to a place which is either a local beauty spot or, if there are none nearby, a sportsfield, the top of a car park or anywhere which has a good view of the sky. Music from a group of instrumentalists helps, but is not essential. The collective experience of praying outside and so early in the day forges strong bonds of unity, so it is an excellent time to link up with Christians of other denominations.

A simple communal breakfast is a good way to finish.

Ideas for Children

Today is a good opportunity to look at the very beginnings of the Church as it was spread to the Samaritans by Philip. Refer to a large map as you tell the children how Saul tried to stamp out this new-fangled Christianity while it was still in Jerusalem, but the Christians, who scattered to escape prison, spread the news everywhere they went. So instead of dying out, it grew.

Point out that the Jews and Samaritans didn't like each other but Philip still told them about Jesus (who was Jewish). And the Spirit of Jesus in Philip made people better and changed many believers into kinder, more loving people.

Peter and John travelled out from Jerusalem to lay hands on them so they would receive the Holy Spirit too.

We are needed by Jesus to help spread the Good News at home, at school, at football, at dancing – wherever we are we can work for Jesus by being loving, forgiving and kind, by talking and listening to God, and by thanking and praising him.

Have a very large globe cut out from green and blue paper with string to hang from the ceiling so it can turn. Let each child write 'God loves you' anywhere on it (younger ones can draw and cut out a happy face) until the world is full of the Good News. Then set it spinning while you all sing 'Shout aloud for Jesus' (Good Morning, Jesus).

Music

Recorded Music

Rachmaninov – *Piano concerto No. 2: Adagio sostenuto*

'Live' Music

Christ is our king, let the whole world rejoice *(ONE, 84)*
Farmer, farmer *(SONL, 37)*
Follow Christ and love the world *(ONE, 144)*
Peace, perfect peace *(ONE, 445)*
Walk, walk in love *(SONL, 44)*

7th Sunday of Easter

Theme
Pray constantly

Through prayer we can communicate directly with God our Father, and from the way Jesus prayed we can learn how to approach him. For in prayer Jesus trustfully poured out his concerns and cares. This kind of prayer was used by the disciples after the Ascension. Such close contact with God provides the strength to accept all suffering.

Penitential Rite

For the times we have forgotten to thank you,
  Lord, have mercy. **Lord, have mercy.**

For the times we have not asked for your help,
  Christ, have mercy. **Christ, have mercy.**

For the times we have prayed with lips, but not hearts,
  Lord, have mercy. **Lord, have mercy.**

Notes on the Readings

Acts 1:12-14

The Ascension marked the end of Jesus' earthly life, but the apostles, the women and Jesus' family had different feelings from the misery, disappointment and hopelessness following Jesus' death on Good Friday. That, too, had been an end.

But now, in the light of the resurrection, the apostles understood more about Jesus' constant presence, whether they could actually see him or not. They had become accustomed to finding him there among them when they were praying; they knew that he would keep his word and remain with them always.

So they were able to go back, calmly but full of expectation, keeping 'tuned in' to him continually by praying. In this way they would be prepared to receive his life, or Spirit; so that, through them, Christ could continue to work within the world.

If we are to receive his life, then we, too, must prepare for him by being constantly in his presence through our prayer. It need not be words; it is more like a continual awareness of our life, our work, our leisure and our relationships all depending on his love and taking place within it.

1 Peter 4:13-16

Living close to the Spirit of Jesus is bound to make us unpopular in the world's eyes from time to time. Christ's way of living is a loving, caring and forgiving way, which is bound to make us vulnerable. We shall at some time be misunderstood, used and criticized, let down and rejected, and it will hurt. All lovers take these risks with their partners; if Christians are loving in a wider sphere, then the hurt will be wider as well.

That would make a pretty awful advertisement for prospective Christians, if it were the whole story, but of course it is not the whole story. Not only are we privileged to share suffering with the all-giving Christ, but also we share his glory, his peace and his joy. Suffering for Christ, then, it not anything to be ashamed of or to resent, but rather a cause for thanks; it proves we have become part of his body and will therefore share in his glory too.

John 17:1-11

When Jesus wrestles with burdens and problems he never does it alone. Always we read of his many hours of prayer in a solitary place where he could communicate with his heavenly Father. All his ministry was under-girded with the strength of this prayerfulness.

If we find ourselves having sleepless nights worrying about something, we ought to follow Jesus' example and worry it through with God instead of keeping it to ourselves. The difference is amazing. Instead of going round and round in circles with no glimpse of a solution anywhere, the whole process becomes manageable and productive. We may still spend sleepless hours thinking, but they are no longer chaotic and tense. Solutions may spring to mind which we had not even considered. (God, after all, can see the whole picture, not just the little section our human eyes are aware of.)

Bidding Prayers

Celebrant   My brothers and sisters in Christ,
          following his example of constant prayer,
          let us pray to the Father in faith and
          share with him our cares and concerns.

Reader   For all monks and nuns in contemplative,
          nursing or teaching orders; for those in
          seminaries, both teachers and students;
          that there may be a constant flow
          of prayerfulness as the world
          spins through time.
        Pause
        Lord, hear us: **hear us as we plead.**

For all places of noise and bustle,
such as rail and air terminals, crowded
shopping areas, factories, schools at
change of lesson, quarries, mines and
docks; that amongst the noise there may
be the inner tranquility of peace
which pulses from God's love.

Pause

Lord, hear us: **hear us as we plead.**

For anyone in need of warmth, shelter,
food or comfort at the moment; any
who feel abandoned or rejected;
any who are too exhausted, too ill
or too terrified to be able to pray
for themselves; that the collected
prayer of the Church may ease
their burdens, calm their fears,
and give them strength.

Pause

Lord, hear us: **hear us as we plead.**

For ourselves; for those beside,
and around us; for each member of
our family; that we may deepen our
prayer life so that we live more closely
with God, and are more ready to serve
him in serving those in need.

Pause

Lord, hear us: **hear us as we plead.**

Celebrant   Father Almighty, take us by the hand
and lead us in your ways of peace
and love; we ask you to hear our prayers
for the sake of Jesus Christ. **Amen.**

Ideas for Adults

During the Bidding Prayers, have white flowers scattered
on the ground at each of the intentions, to be symbols of
those who are being prayed for. These are then gathered
up into a basket, and brought up when the gifts are offered.
They can then be arranged near votive candles.

Ideas for Children

If you have access to a toy walkie-talkie set, this would be
ideal. Otherwise, yoghurt pots and string can be used. First
talk about how we can keep in touch with people when
they are in different places, for example:

  radio
  telephone
  radar
  letters.

Talk about when these aids are used for space travel, dock-
ing a ship, in aeroplanes or at other times when it would
be dangerous to act without the guidance of someone who
can see better than we can.

  Link this with what prayer is – it is keeping in touch with
God, who understands and can see clearly, even if we can't.
Help the children make yoghurt pot telephones. Write on
them: 'Don't forget to keep in touch with God'.

Music

Recorded Music

Telemann – *Viola concerto in G*

'Live' Music

Father, into your hands *(SONL, 23)*
Father, I place into your hands *(ONE, 133)*
I ask your blessing, Lord *(ONE, 229)*
Lord of all hopefulness *(ONE, 329)*

The Ascension of the Lord

Theme
Jesus Christ ascends into heaven

The ascension marks the end of Jesus' historical, physical
life, and the beginning of a far-reaching, all-pervasive presence unlimited by time or location. We who believe are
given his promise that we shall one day share his glory.

Penitential Rite

Our faith is often so weak and thin,
    Lord, have mercy. **Lord, have mercy.**

We do not allow you to reign in our lives,
    Christ, have mercy. **Christ, have mercy.**

There are times we forget your promise of hope,
    Lord, have mercy. **Lord, have mercy.**

Notes on the Readings

Acts 1:1-11

Even after the resurrection the apostles were still hankering
after an immediate, physical kingdom where power would
be restored to Israel. The breadth of Christ's kingdom could
not become apparent to them until they had received the
Holy Spirit; they could not yet grasp the idea of salvation for
everyone, regardless of their language, their country of birth,
their hair style or their eating habits. Christ's ascension
would set him free from all material or historical boundaries
so that his living Spirit could be spread throughout the
whole world.

Ephesians 1:17-23

When we look at the incredible details of Jesus' life – his
teaching and signs, his death and resurrection – we cannot
fail to be impressed by the power illustrated there. Thankfully it is a loving power; some of the 'star wars' sagas hint at
the terror and devastation that would result from a similarly
powerful force of evil. Though fiction, all such stories, both
ancient and modern, depict an instinctive human terror of
evil taken to the ultimate.

  As Christians we are privileged to see glimpses of goodness taken to the ultimate. It is revealed in the person of
Jesus, who, through complete unselfishness, has brought
mankind into a new relationship with the seat of power –
God himself.

  His great, universal, cosmic presence draws all things towards the splendid all-glorious harmony of completion. We
have been chosen to work in harness with him to achieve it.

Matthew 28:16-20

Perhaps the most significant part of Christ's ascension is the
commissioning of his closest friends to go and make disciples of all the nations. It was a commission which could only

come from one who was divine, with full authority over everything, seen and invisible. In his body, Jesus ministered to those living in and around Galilee; in his spiritual body (which includes us) he would be ministering to every person in every country. That is what mission is all about.

We may not need to travel very far before we meet people who do not yet know Jesus. They may be lost, or searching among the dustbins for spiritual food, when there is a meal served up specially for them. It is both our duty and our joy to bring these people to Christ; to introduce them to Christ by our caring behaviour, our forgiveness, open-heartedness and joy.

Bidding Prayers

Celebrant Trusting in Christ's victory over all evil, let us pray to the Father for the needs of the Church and the world.

Reader For all who witness to Christ in spite of danger and persecution; all who work to bring others to Christ; that in God's strength they may be blessed, encouraged, and bear much fruit.
Pause
King of glory: **reign in our hearts.**

For those who have never received the Good News of God's saving love; for those areas where violence and terrorism make normal life impossible; that the Spirit of Jesus, the Prince of Peace, may filter through to increase love and understanding, respect and goodwill.
Pause
King of glory: **reign in our hearts.**

For ourselves and those with whom we live and work; for particular areas of need known to us personally; that in everything we do, and every minute we live, God may be glorified and his will be accomplished.
Pause
King of glory: **reign in our hearts.**

Celebrant Father, trusting in your great love for us we bring you these prayers through Christ Jesus, our Lord. **Amen.**

Ideas for Children

Many churches and schools celebrate Mass specially planned for children, when they have the opportunity to take an active role in the readings, psalms, bidding prayers and serving.

Perhaps the church or chapel could be decorated by the children on the theme of Christ, reigning in glory, with different groups or classes producing posters showing God's glory in the seas and oceans, stars and planets, hills and mountains, animals and birds, people, and in Jesus.

Music
Recorded Music

Shostakovich – *Symphony* No. 5
Beethoven – *Symphony* No. 7

'Live' Music

Glorify the Lord *(SONL, 17)*
Live in the Spirit of your maker *(ONE, 314)*
Praise, my soul, the king of heaven *(ONE, 449)*
You shall cross the barren desert *(ONE, 627)*

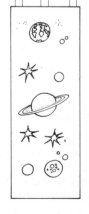

Pentecost

Questions for Discussion Groups
1. What evidence of the Holy Spirit do you see among Christians today – including your own life this week?
2. If the Holy Spirit leads us into all truth, how is it we so often disagree?

Pentecost Sunday

Theme
The Church receives God's Holy Spirit

Coming first to the apostles as they waited in prayer, the Holy Spirit has continued to be poured out on Christ's followers ever since. If we open ourselves to receive it, the body of Christ will be charged with his life.

Penitential Rite

Use the song 'The Story of Love' (SONL, 76)

Notes on the Readings

Acts 2:1-11

The apostles had been commissioned to tell all people everywhere about Jesus; the magnificent sign of being understood by everyone without a language barrier serves to encapsulate this task of the apostles and all their successors.

As time passes initial fervour usually fades, but since this fervour is occasioned by the power of a living God, it continues to burst out in every generation of believers. People still find their lives drastically transformed through an encounter with Christ; many still find the Spirit so real and invigorating that sacrifices are undertaken with joyful serenity; unpleasant and dangerous work is gladly undertaken; individuals stand firm to witness in a corrupt society, and countless numbers spread love and peace daily among those around them.

There is still much to be done. But, living in the Spirit, we can work as harvesters and take part in establishing God's kingdom on earth.

1 Corinthians 12:3-7, 12-13

We should not undervalue ourselves, because God values us very highly, and has particular jobs for us to do. If we spend a lot of time in his company it will become clear where he needs us to work. Do we always consult God about our subject choices at school, career prospects, job applications, use of spare time, organisation of our daily routine, choice of marriage partner, finances or house hunting – the list is endless. Yet if we really want to be part of God's body we cannot take all these decisions on our own and then just offer him the scraps that are left.

God wants to use our lives, our places of work, our homes, our illnesses and our travel; it is so easy to block his Spirit carelessly, without even noticing, and the world suffers as a result.

John 20:19-23

Wherever people come together to focus their hope on their Lord, and submerge their own selfishness in their longing to be part of him, Jesus stands among them and his presence is powerfully experienced in a wave of joy. Although at such times Christians are aware of their unworthiness, Christ's presence does not give rise to an inward groan of despair as one might expect when he is so loving and we have let him down so often.

Instead there is a sense of contentment and tranquility; a light-heartedness as all problems are seen in the context of someone who is loving, forgiving, and in full control. Faces relax and eyes soften; many feel great warmth of affection for those around them; many feel very close to loved ones who have died, as if the barrier of death is no longer there.

Such cherished times bind Christians together in the life of our Lord, and it is from such experiences of a real presence that all mission must spring. With the peace of God in us (which is, as Paul knew, quite beyond reasoned understanding) we shall be literally 'inspired' or 'breathed into' by the life of Jesus, so that we shall be able to bring him to each room we visit and each person we meet.

Bidding Prayers

Celebrant We have been chosen as members of Christ's body. Let us then pray in his Spirit to our heavenly Father who cherishes this world.

Reader For every Christian; that each may be more receptive to the Holy Spirit, until every worshipping community is charged with the vitality and enthusiasm of the living Christ.
Pause
Father of love: **let your Spirit live in us now.**

For all those in prison, all criminals and all who are trying to go straight after completing their sentences; for those trying to keep off drugs or alcohol; that they may be filled with God's strength and hope, undergirded with his love and encouraged by Christian support.
Pause
Father of love: **let your Spirit live in us now.**

For a deepening of our own faith, more understanding of God's will, a clearer insight into where the needs are, and a greater desire to give our lives away in serving others.
Pause
Father of love: **let your Spirit live in us now.**

Celebrant Father, in grateful thanks for all your blessings in our lives, we relinquish our wills to yours, and ask you to accept these prayers through Christ our Lord. **Amen.**

Ideas for Adults

Have everyone in the church holding hands in an unbroken chain during the Creed or one of the hymns.

Church Decoration

Pillars and walls can be decorated with fabric to represent the fruits of the Spirit. Different groups from parish organisations can work on each, and their preparations used as prayerful times of spiritual offering.

Instead of being displayed straight away, the finished collages can be offered with the gifts and hung in place then.

Ideas for Children

Tell the children what happened at Pentecost, emphasising that Jesus' friends were keeping in touch with him through prayer, so they were prepared when his life, or Spirit, came to them so powerfully. Explain that we need to keep in touch with him, too, if we want him to live in us.

Talk about qualities the Holy Spirit gives us – love, joy, peace etc. Then help the children to make long streamers out of orange, red and yellow, with these qualities drawn or printed on them. As the children come into church they dance round the aisles waving the streamers and twirling them so they look like fire.

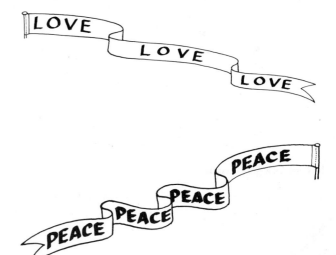

Music
Recorded Music

Sibelius – *Symphony No. 6*

'Live' Music

Lay your hands gently upon us *(ONE, 295)*
Lord of my life *(SONL, 21)*
Spirit of the living God *(ONE, 501)*
The Spirit of the Lord is with us *(ONE, 549)*
Veni, Sancte Spiritus *(SONL, 24)*

The Most Holy Trinity

Theme

God is Father, Son and Holy Spirit

The qualities of God are revealed in the three persons of the Trinity, and in us too when we found our lives on him. Filled with his life, the Christian community will be enabled to show the love of God, the grace of Jesus and the fellowship of the Holy Spirit.

Penitential Rite

1. With love the fight a-gainst fear is won, we will break down the bar-ri-ers,

one by one, as the Fa-ther in the Spi-rit and the Spi-rit in the Son, may the

Chorus

Trin-i-ty in un-it-y make us one. Lord, have mer-cy up-on us.

2. With faith the healing is begun,
   we will break down the barriers, one by one,
   as the Father in the Spirit, and the Spirit in the Son,
   may the Trinity in unity make us one.
   Christ, have mercy upon us.

3. With hope the work for peace is done,
   we will break down the barriers, one by one,
   as the Father in the Spirit, and the Spirit in the Son,
   may the Trinity in unity make us one.
   Lord, have mercy upon us.

Notes on the Readings

Exodus 34:4-6, 8-9

Both the people and their priests, left to themselves, had abandoned the high demands of God and created their own man-made religion which was pleasantly self-indulgent, good fun, and did not expect too much arduous self-discipline.

Moses acts as mediator between his wayward people and the God who has chosen them. It is encouraging to find that the chosen people are displayed in all their weak-willed and obstinate behaviour, in spite of their high calling: they are never shown as a super-race with whom we could not identify.

As Moses approaches God on behalf of the people, God shows him a glimpse of his glory – the characteristics of an all-loving, merciful and compassionate creator.

God will divulge more and more of his nature to us as we show him, by our commitment, loyalty and reverence, that we want to see him.

2 Corinthians 13:11-13

Wherever we live lovingly and peacefully together, God will be there, since he is love and peace. Whenever we are happy and enjoying working together to serve those in need, God will be there, since his Spirit is the uplifting fellowship and companionship which underlies such happiness.

In other words, when we live as God's people we shall experience his character and it will show in the way we behave at all times and in all our relationships, even the trying ones.

John 3:16-18

The most profound way in which God's nature is shown to us is in Jesus of Nazareth, the carpenter turned itinerant preacher, who slept, ate, got tired, knew fear and understood failure. This fully human being was, in some way that is impossible to explain in human terms, also God. In him mankind could see the nature of God expressed through voice, tears, healing hands, and dusty, travel-worn feet. Never before had God's qualities of tenderness and compassion, patience, kindness and faithfulness been so clearly seen.

Having seen Jesus we can understand more of God, and by believing, or putting our trust in him instead of ourselves or man-made commodities, we can be saved and liberated. We can also turn a blind eye to God's offer, and reject it and all the hope it contains. The choice is ours.

Bidding Prayers

Celebrant Gathered together in the love and fellowship of God, let us speak to the Father of our needs and cares.

Reader We pray for the work of the Church in suburbs, cities, slums and villages, especially where there is violent opposition, complacency or apathy; that all who work with Christ may be blessed and encouraged, so that many find peace in God's love.

Pause

Father, hear us: **keep us in your love.**
For the world, with its mistakes and misunderstandings; for all areas in which there is a breakdown of communication between individuals, groups or nations; that the unifying love of God may draw people together, helping them to find common, shared ground to build on, rather than dwelling on hurtful divisions.

Pause

Father, hear us: **keep us in your love.**

For those who are without homes or live in crowded, inadequate accommodation; those living alone and isolated; for the hungry and malnourished; that God's love, working through us, his body, may reach those in desperate need and give them new hope.

Pause

Father, hear us: **keep us in your love.**

For a greater love and fellowship amongst ourselves in this parish and in our families; that God's life living in us may make us more ready to respond and forgive, to put ourselves out and to listen.

Pause

Father, hear us: **keep us in your love.**

Celebrant Father Almighty, in the Spirit we pray, and ask you to hear our prayers through Jesus Christ our Lord. **Amen.**

Ideas for Adults

Try a Japanese-style flower arrangement using three flowers and three twigs or branches. Include some clover or shamrock if it is available. Aim to express the idea of three-ness in one-ness. This kind of arrangement is really a visible meditation, and can be very helpful and stimulating.

Ideas for Children

Begin by playing a game. The teacher says, 'I'm thinking of someone who . . .' giving three ways of knowing the mystery person, such as wearing her hair in plaits, playing the violin, enjoying playing with Richard etc. The others have to guess who it is. Do this several times.

Then say, 'I'm thinking of someone who made the world, who healed people because he loved them, and who can live in each one of us now. Who is it?' Explain that God shows himself to us in different ways, and we can get to know him by seeing the beauty of nature, reading about Jesus in the gospel, and by asking for his Spirit (or life) to live in our own lives now.

Give the children three sheets of greaseproof paper each. On sheet 1 there is a 'G' and they draw the created world. On sheet 2 there is an 'O' and they draw Jesus healing, or on the cross. On sheet 3 there is a 'D' and they draw people singing, praising or helping each other. When all three sheets are stapled together at the top and held up to the light, we can see that, by expressing the Father, Son and Holy Spirit we have been shown GOD, who is all three persons in one. These could be stuck on a window to show them effectively.

Music
Recorded Music

Britten – N*oye's Fludde*: the handbells as the rainbow appears

'Live' Music

Of the Father's love begotten *(ONE, 388)*
One, one, eternal one *(ONE, 417)*
Russian Sanctus *(SONL, 38)*
We believe in God almighty *(ONE, 588)*

ORDINARY TIME

2nd Sunday in Ordinary Time

Theme
Jesus is revealed as the Chosen One of God

John bears witness to Christ, as the Holy Spirit leads him to see Jesus as the Saviour of the world. Like a light, that witness spreads outwards from the chosen people to reach every nation; through living in the Spirit, we too are witnesses.

Penitential Rite

For our inadequate witness to your love,
Lord, have mercy. **Lord, have mercy.**

For our concern with trivialities,
Christ, have mercy. **Christ, have mercy.**

For the opportunities we have wasted,
Lord, have mercy. **Lord, have mercy.**

Notes on the Readings

Isaiah 49:3, 5-6

God is a personal God – he works through individuals. When a whole nation is chosen to witness to him, it is possible for their light to spread far and wide. Beginning with internal commitment, repentance and reconciliation among the chosen people, God goes on to a far bigger plan, much more far-reaching than the prophet had envisaged; in time every nation will be able to participate in God's work of salvation.

God's power is enormous, and he will use us, if we co-operate, to take on even the deadliest evils of our time and defeat them. When we fail to co-operate, we are limiting his power in our lives and our world; we do so at our peril.

1 Corinthians 1:1-3

This passage emphasises our bond with all other Christians; not just in other countries but in other generations as well. Unlike others, Christians do not see death as a cut-off point, so its threat does not underpin our earthly activities. We do not need the frenetic exertions to fend off aging, or distractions to keep our minds from the fear of our existence coming to an end.

Knowing that we all, both this and the other side of death, are bonded into one community, united in worshipping our Lord of time and eternity, we can be stronger, more light-hearted, more bold in our witness, more generous with our time and our money. The life we share in Christ is not going to be affected by where we live, the age at which we die, or any other consideration. When we really grasp this we start to experience the heady freedom that alters our whole life.

John 1:29-34

John knew that his job was to prepare the people for the coming of the Messiah, God's Chosen One, even though he did not know who it was going to be. No doubt John knew Jesus, his cousin, and perhaps about him; but he had to trust God and get on with his own job first, until God chose to reveal his next task: witnessing that Jesus was the Chosen One. Accordingly, he was given the necessary insight and understanding to enable him to witness with conviction.

We will often find ourselves being led by the Spirit in a similar way. We may be given some task to do and wish we knew where it is leading or how it can be of any use. If we simply trust God and get on with it, he will lead us step by step, allowing us to see just enough at a time to make our work possible. It may not be good for us to know too much at first; humans are impatient creatures, and may destroy God's plans by trying to complete them too hastily. We need to trust God more: he knows what is best.

Bidding Prayers

Celebrant As fellow members of the body of Christ,
let us join in praying to our Father
for the Church and for the world.

Reader Let us pray for a strengthening of our
Christian witness regardless of our
personal safety or comfort; that we may
all re-dedicate ourselves to proclaiming
God's saving love in every situation
in which we find ourselves.
Pause
Almighty Father: **you are our only strength.**

Let us pray for those who cry in distress
but are not heard; those who suffer
injustice but have no power to object;
for the weak, the hungry,
the desperately poor; that we, and all
God's witnesses, may strive to bring
the Light of Christ into their
shadowed lives.
Pause
Almighty Father: **you are our only strength.**

Let us pray for the people with whom
we worship, and for their families and
neighbours; that we may be more alert
to God's calling and more ready
to tackle his work.
Pause
Almighty Father: **you are our only strength.**

Celebrant God our Father, you know us better than
we know ourselves; we ask you to hear
our prayers through Jesus Christ,
your Son. **Amen.**

Ideas for Adults

Beg or borrow a globe – the larger the better, and place it in a prominent position today, with a light burning in front of it or lights in a circle around it. These could be lit at the Bidding Prayers.

Ideas for Children

Begin by singing a song which acknowledges Jesus, our friend, as the Son of God. Some examples are: *I have a friend*; *All of the people (MWTP)*.Have some children playing instruments, if possible, and everyone can dance. Help them experience the happiness of knowing Jesus. Then sit down quietly with the children in a circle, with everybody holding hands, and thank God for joining us all in his love.

Discuss ways we can let other people know about the happiness of living with Jesus. It may help to have pictures of mouths, hands and feet (old mail-order catalogues are a good source) to get everyone thinking. Try to explain that we can help people to know Jesus by what we do, as much as by what we say. Some children may have already met opposition or scorn; discuss the possibility frankly and remind them that Jesus will always stand by them, even if they are laughed at for believing in him or going to church.

On a large sheet of paper, make lots of hand and footprints. The least messy way to do this is to have a shallow seed tray of paint next to a large bowl of soapy water and a towel. Lip prints can be made using lipstick. On the paper write 'We'll use our hands, feet and mouths to SHOW GOD'S LOVE.'.

If you have time, sing, stamp and clap: 'Wanted – good hands' (MWTP).

Music

Recorded Music

Elgar: Symphony No. 1

'Live' Music

Be still, and know I am with you (ONE, 57)
Christ is my light (ONE, 83)
I am the Light (SONL, 20)
Tell out my soul (ONE, 514)
Trust is in the eyes (ONE, 576)

3rd Sunday in Ordinary Time

Theme
Christ has come to enlighten his people

As the prophecies foretold, Christ has come among us to be our light, our healer and our Saviour. Turning towards him means turning away from all divisive arguments, selfishness or rivalry, for if we are to follow him it must be on his terms of uncompromising love.

Penitential Rite

For our quarrels and arguments,
    Lord, have mercy. **Lord, have mercy.**

For our criticising and unkindness,
    Christ, have mercy. **Christ, have mercy.**

For our complacence,
    Lord, have mercy. **Lord, have mercy.**

Notes on the Readings

Isaiah 8:23-9:3

No earthly leader is capable of establishing a perfect society; when we put our trust in human leaders and systems we are bound to become disillusioned and disenchanted, for we are unable to create a Utopia. The real, limitless power lies with the Creator: God himself. When we redirect our adoration to him alone, our hopes and longings have an unassailable foundation on which remarkable lives can be built.

It is this salvation which the prophet foretells – a salvation which is complete, full of goodness and truth, and utterly secure. It will result in the joy and gladness of harvest time, when relief and accomplishment are mingled with the happy hope of enough food to last the winter; the joy and gladness of a hard-worked slave having his heavy yoke snapped, so he is suddenly light and free. This is the hope Christ brings, which can set all men free.

1 Corinthians 1:10-13, 17

Any community is prey to the divisions, arguments, gossip and cliquishness which result from lack of love. Particularly when there is no common enemy such divisions can thrive, and in some church communities they are dismally prolific. This internal bickering is so common that it is what many comedy programmes pick out as the hallmark of churchgoers. What a witness to the world! What can we do to improve matters?

First, it is vital that Christians never lose touch with their Light; otherwise their grotesque shadows may turn outsiders away from the hope of Christ. A constant, lively and regular prayer life must include as many parishioners as possible, all through the week.

Second, it is essential to repent when we turn to Christ. This means renouncing sin and making a determined decision not to carry on in the critical, spiteful, or blinkered way into which we have perhaps lapsed. For repentance is not an immediate gateway to perfection, but a lifetime struggle of getting up every time we fall down.

The great gift of salvation is worth so much more than petty injustices or minor changes of liturgy. In the unending glory of God such irritations melt into insignificance.

Matthew 4:12-23

In Jesus the prophecies were at last fulfilled. Here was a man who showed the Light of God in his teaching, curing and compassion. And the message he had was the need to repent; he called people to follow him instead of selfishness, and they in turn would call others.

Jesus has called us, and he wants us to follow him. He wants us to bring others to him until at last all men are reconciled to their creator.

Bidding Prayers

Celebrant My brothers and sisters in Christ, let us bring the luggage of our cares and concerns to the generous love of our heavenly Father.

Reader We bring to his love the varied parish communities worshipping today, in remote villages, crowded cities, impoverished and affluent areas, in cathedrals, chapels and in the open air; that every Christian worshipper may be uplifted and strengthened to work for Christ in the world.
Pause
Light of the world: **shine on us now.**

We bring to his love all who teach in schools, colleges and universities; all writers and artists; film, video and television producers; all whose work may influence the way people think; that their influence may be positive and constructive.
Pause
Light of the world: **shine on us now.**

We bring to his love the disabled and chronically ill; those suffering long-term effects of war, injury and

disaster; that some good may come out
of their suffering and that they may be
comforted by the presence of Christ.
Pause
Light of the world: **shine on us now.**

We bring to his love our own dear ones,
both living and those who have died;
any friends or relatives who live
far away from us, and whom we miss;
any family problems or sadness
known to us; that the God of love
may heal, protect and comfort.
Pause
Light of the world: **shine on us now.**

Celebrant Father, rejoicing in the richness of
your love, we ask you to accept these
prayers for the sake of Jesus Christ. **Amen.**

Ideas for Adults

At the offering of the gifts, involve people from different
races or cultures.

Ideas for Children

So as to get across the idea of fulfilled prophecy, make a
'scroll' by rolling a sheet of paper stuck on to sticks at
either end, with a ribbon on it for fastening. If possible,
copy a little Hebrew writing on to it.

Show it to the children, ask them to guess what it is, and
explain how, many years before Jesus was born, some
people (prophets) were used by God as messengers.
Through them, God told his people that one day he would
send someone very important who would save them and
show them the right way to live. Read from the scroll today's
prophecy, then roll and tie it up.

Tell the children how people waited a very long time for
that hope to come true, and each generation passed the
hope on to its children. Until one day they met a man
called Jesus. They began to wonder if he was the Chosen
One of God. Read the prophecy again, bit by bit, matching
it with what they know of Jesus. You could have pictures
or an illustrated Bible available to refer to.

So the hope had come true – in Jesus. Sing 'All of the
people' (MWTP) and let the children make their own scrolls
with the prophecy written on it.

Music
Recorded Music

Walton – *Symphony No. 1: slow movement*

'Live' Music

God forgave my sin *(ONE, 175)*
God's Spirit is in my heart *(ONE, 183)*
If we only seek peace *(SONL, 76)*
I sing a song to you, Lord *(ONE, 257)*
Our hearts were made for you, Lord *(SONL, 36)*

How the Kingdom grows

Questions for Discussion Groups
1. Where is mission needed today, and what form should it take
(and not take!)?
2. How do we cope when God's work causes difficulties in our
relationships/organisation of time?

4th Sunday in Ordinary Time

Theme
Happy are the poor in Spirit

Like a pulse beating steadily through the Old and New
Testaments is the need for humanity – the poverty of Spirit
which does not cling on to anything except God, and regards
everything material and financial as something to be used
for God's glory, rather than possessed. God's values may
appear foolish in worldly reckoning, but they bring
indestructible joy.

Penitential Rite

For our possessiveness of people and goods,
Lord, have mercy. **Lord, have mercy.**

For our lack of mercy,
Christ, have mercy. **Christ, have mercy.**

For our mean-hearted response to your love,
Lord, have mercy. **Lord, have mercy.**

Notes on the Readings

Zephaniah 2:3, 3:12-13

The prophet sees all around him the blatant disregard for
God's laws, and a general renunciation of all that is good,
wholesome and pure. God's retribution in terrible anger
seems inevitable. Only for the small remnant of those still
seeking integrity and humility is there hope: through this
tiny but loyal group the covenant between God and his
people will survive. The rest have sealed their own fate.

1 Corinthians 1:26-31

God has made some strange choices through the years.
Jacob cheated Esau out of his father's blessing; the geneal-
ogy of Jesus includes several figures of dubious reputation;
Jesus chose a motley assortment of characters to be his
special friends, and was often in the company of tax-collec-
tors for an occupying power, prostitutes and others despised by the upright community as a whole. He even
chose you and me!

If God is wise, then there must be some reason for this.
Paul explains that when the foolish nobodies are taken
over by Christ, amazing things happen. We can see evidence of this in other Christians and in our own lives, where
we know perfectly well that we could not have been patient
or forgiving, or wise in a particular situation if we had been
relying on ourselves. It was Christ, working in us, that enabled us to do his will. The more this happens, the more
people will start thinking there must be something worth
having in this Christianity business; and perhaps good
looks, brains and money are not so important after all.

Of course, it puts us, who call ourselves Christians, in a
highly responsible position. For if outsiders do not see any
evidence of God's power in us, they will draw the conclusion
that he has no power, and that good looks, brains and
money are a better bet.

Matthew 5:1-12

When we grasp the meaning of the first beatitude, we find that the others follow on from it in sequence. If we put God first and regard ourselves not as possessors but stewards of worldly goods, we shall be poor (or unpossessive) in spirit. That will make us less aggressive, defensive and ambitious materially, so we shall become more gentle in our dealings with others, having no need to fight to protect ourselves any more.

Those who are gentle are more sympathetic, and that makes us vulnerable, easily affected by the pain we see around us, so we shall find ourselves mourning, due to more loving involvement.

Seeing the causes of suffering will make us long to put right the areas of injustice and cruelty which harm and damage, so that we shall hunger and thirst after righteousness.

Yet, loving oppressors as well as the oppressed, we shall want to act with God's mercy, rather than fighting for good with the weapons of evil. Such involvement will make us increasingly aware of the contrast between God's purity and the chaotic corruption of misdirected humanity, which is bound, in turn, to inspire us to work towards peace, reconciliation and love.

Once we are set on that route, as history bloodily endorses, we are bound for the cross; and it is highly likely that, having stuck our necks out, we shall become targets for persecution.

Yet the journey has been one towards greater and greater closeness to the Spirit of God; towards the peace of knowing we are doing his will; towards finding our true selves and serving him. And that is certain happiness.

Bidding Prayers

Celebrant United in Christ, let us join in prayer, my brothers and sisters, trusting not in our own strength but in God's mercy.

Reader Let us pray for all who witness to Christ, in both ordained and lay ministries; that we may become so aware of our richness in Christ that we may be poor in spirit, till our happiness draws others to God, the source of all happiness.

Pause

Merciful Father: **your grace is sufficient for us.**

Let us pray for our world, particularly wherever people are ambitious for power and prestige both locally and internationally; that God's spirit of truth may lead us all to get our priorities right, so that we seek integrity and humility instead.

Pause

Merciful Father: **your grace is sufficient for us.**

Let us pray for those whose lives have been damaged by slander or perjury; for any who are in prison for crimes they have not committed; for all who are imprisoned and tortured for their faith; that they be upheld and strengthened, and know the reality of God's presence.

Pause

Merciful Father: **your grace is sufficient for us.**

Let us pray for our homes and those with whom we live or have lived in the past; for our relationships at work and at school; that we may enjoy the challenge of spreading God's love in every room we walk into, and with every person we meet.

Pause

Merciful Father: **your grace is sufficient for us.**

Celebrant Father, we lay before you these prayers, and ask you to accept them for the sake of Jesus, your Son. **Amen.**

Ideas for Adults

During the week a group may like to collect slogans and captions from advertisements which encourage greed, self-indulgence and covetousness. (There are plenty to choose from!) These are then displayed against a coloured background as if they are blocks of wood or stone crashing down on some little pin men figures.

Over this have a rainbow superimposed, with the words: How happy are the poor in spirit; theirs is the kingdom of heaven. Here is an idea of what it may look like:

They can bring it up to the altar at the offering of the gifts.

Ideas for Children

Bring along an assortment of advertisements mounted on a board so the children can see them as they come in. You could have some on tape as well from television and radio.

Why do firms advertise? So as to get us to buy their product. Every day we are encouraged to WANT and to GET. The more we GET, the more we WANT. Stick a thin strip of paper over the advertisements which says: GET, GET, GET. WANT, WANT, WANT. GET, GET, GET all across it.

But if *things* are most important in our life, they make life harder, not happier. Have some heavy chains, stone-filled bags with straps etc. with labels on such as:

– I wish I could have . . .
– If only I could . . .
– I want . . .
– Leave that alone – it's MINE.

One by one, hang them around yourself or a child who volunteers, until he is really loaded down.

Jesus says to us: 'Trust in me, instead of in THINGS. You'll find you're much happier.' Then unload your volunteer and pin on him an 'I'm for Jesus' badge. Now he is less cluttered, able to move and run about (let him demonstrate).

When we trust in Jesus we can enjoy what we are given, but also enjoy giving away. We can enjoy owning, but also enjoy sharing. We can be happy when we have lots of toys, but also be happy when we haven't got many.

Let the children make an 'I'm for Jesus' badge to wear, and ask them to try giving instead of getting at least once each day this week.

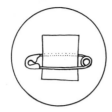

Music
Recorded Music

Mozart – *Concerto for flute and harp*

'Live' Music

A new commandment *(SONL, 34)*
Blest are the pure in heart *(ONE, 66)*
Lord of life *(SONL, 63)*
Love is his word *(ONE, 338)*
Oh the love of my Lord *(ONE, 430)*

5th Sunday in Ordinary Time

Theme
Your light must shine to lead others to Christ

When we live kind, caring lives, we shall be showing the brightness of God's love, and that will commend people to trust him far more than philosophical argument. Following Christ is not merely knowing about him, but knowing him personally so that he seeps through our lives.

Penitential Rite

We have excused ourselves from giving till it hurts, Lord, have mercy. **Lord, have mercy.**

We have excused ourselves from loving when rejected, Christ, have mercy. **Christ, have mercy.**

We have excused ourselves from risking full involvement, Lord, have mercy. **Lord, have mercy.**

Notes on the Readings

Isaiah 58:7-10

Here we see love in action. Love is a gradual turning away from self-centredness and it is in no way dependent on emotional attraction or warm feelings. Often it involves putting ourselves out, either financially or physically, or both. Sometimes it may mean challenging the accepted attitudes around us, and risking ridicule or even rejection by 'friends' who feel their own consciences pricked, but have no desire to change. Living in love means that we shall not be able to pass the buck any further; it is we who must do the inviting, sharing, visiting and giving.

But though it is a duty, it is also our delight. Spreading God's love is by far the happiest way to live: we are rather like servants of a good king, sent out to deliver all kinds of gifts and parcels to the people he loves, together with invitations to everyone to come and celebrate at his table. That is a crude analogy, but it is important to see ourselves as privileged members of a great and good plan – the work really should make us full of joy.

1 Corinthians 2:1-5

The Greeks were used to philosophical arguments. They prided themselves on their civilised discussions and persuasion by logic and, up to a point, the existence of God can be argued in this way.

But when the uncompromising love of God floods into our life in the person of Jesus, culminating in the crucifixion and resurrection, there comes a point at which even philosophy is swept away in the wash.

Accordingly Paul shows the Corinthians how he is quite contented with being a nervous and unremarkable preacher because it has highlighted the evidence of God himself – the outpouring of his Spirit of love. Thus there is less chance of his hearers giving Paul glory; they are far more likely to direct their praise and glory to God, the source of all power and love.

Matthew 5:13-16

We, who have been entrusted with the building up of God's kingdom on earth, must, without fail, recognise the source of our power and pass the glory on to God. Otherwise we are not working for him, but for ourselves, and that is both dangerous and destructive.

Salt was not just a seasoning but a food preserver, so that it was actually important for life. Worldly, material values have a powerful grip on many people's minds. The greed and selfishness they engender can cause decay and rot in family life, society, and in individuals. We, the Church, are the salt which can preserve, purify and decontaminate: that is how vital our work as Christ's body is. It is desperately important for our world that we are effective grains of salt.

Similarly with light: we may all be burning brightly with God's love due to our worship and communion with our heavenly Father, but if we share his love only with other Christians we shall be hiding our light under a tub. We Christians are supposed to be the world's light: is its darkness due to our wasted, under-used or dim light? If we do not shine, how will anyone see?

Bidding Prayers

Celebrant Companions in Christ, let us pray to our heavenly Father, trusting in his generous mercy.

Reader For the Church as it witnesses to Christ in the world; that its members may be always aware that they are called to be servants, ready and happy to minister to the spiritual, emotional and physical needs of all people.
Pause
Lord of light: **kindle us so that we shine.**

For the leaders of every community and nation; that their government may reflect the values of responsible caring, compassion and integrity, so that no individual or minority group is abused or left in need.
Pause
Lord of light: **kindle us so that we shine.**

For all who are rejected or shunned, neglected or despised; for babies and young children who are abused physically or emotionally; all whose minds are disturbed and all who live fearfully; that God's will may be accomplished so that they are healed,

restored and comforted.
Pause
Lord of light: **kindle us so that we shine.**

For a breaking down of our complacency
and blindness until we are able to see
the needs around us, and can work in
God's strength, giving our whole lives
away in loving those whom he loves.
Pause
Lord of light: **kindle us so that we shine.**

Celebrant Father, God of love, increase our love
for one another, and hear our prayers,
for the sake of Jesus Christ. **Amen.**

Ideas for Adults

The gifts today could include salt and light, as a sign that
we are intending to be used by God for the good of our
world. Salt and light can also be the theme in flower arrangements this week. If you live near the coast, some seashore
plants and pebbles may be included.

Ideas for Children

Bring along the following:
  – some sea salt;
  – something preserved in brine (e.g. frankfurters);
  – some small cubes of cheese (enough for one each);
  – a candle;
  – a large metal saucepan.

First sprinkle some grains of salt on a plate and talk about
what it is (they can taste it if they like). Explain how it was
used to keep food before anyone had freezers and fridges.
Sometimes it is still used like that (give examples) and in
hotter countries it is still used to preserve meat and fish.
See if they can taste the saltiness in cheese – the salt
keeps it fresh.

Now read what Jesus said about us being salt. Discuss
with them what this means for us: how can we be salt in
the world? It may be helpful to have this question written
on a board or sheet of paper, and jot down their ideas to
keep track of them.

Then light the candle, and talk about useful lights such
as torches, street lamps, car lights etc. Cover the light with
the saucepan, and help them see how silly this is, if we
want to light the room.

Now read the second part of today's Gospel and jot
down ideas under a second question: how can we be the
light of the world?

Sing I'*m gonna let my little light shine* and help the children to
make these Chinese lanterns from stiff paper. They can carry
these into church.

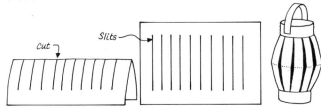

Cut   Slits

Music
Recorded Music

Rachmaninov – *Symphony No. 1: slow movement*

'Live' Music

Forth in the peace of Christ (*ONE, 147*)
In bread we bring you, Lord (*ONE, 243*)
I no longer live (*SONL, 6*)
Thine be the glory (*ONE, 554*)
You touch my soul (*SONL, 62*)

6th Sunday in Ordinary Time

Theme
God gives us his Law to guide us in his wisdom

The Spirit of the Commandments is much deeper and
broader than a set of rules. The Commandments are clues
and signposts to the unimaginable depth of God's wisdom,
and when we mould our lives round the loving essence of
this law we shall be drawn more closely to the pulse of
God. But we are perfectly free to choose whether or not
we want to avail ourselves of the opportunity.

Penitential Rite

We have gone our own way, instead of yours,
    Lord, have mercy. **Lord, have mercy.**

We have failed to keep God's law,
    Christ, have mercy. **Christ, have mercy.**

We have not centred our lives on your love,
    Lord, have mercy. **Lord, have mercy.**

Notes on the Readings

Ecclesiasticus 15:15-20

The Commandments provide useful guide-lines for a way
of life which is faithful and leads to life in its fullness. So
to keep the letter of the law but not the spirit of it, or to
find handy loopholes to excuse our sinfulness, is to exercise
our free will in favour of death, rather than life; to renounce
God rather than follow in his footsteps.

For none of us can shirk the responsibility that God has
provided in giving us free will, however much we may like
to. There are plenty of occasions when it would certainly
be less difficult if we were forced to decide in a particular
way. After all, we could blame the consequences on someone else, then! Having free wills means that whatever decision we make regarding good and evil, we must accept
the consequences and not try to put the blame on other
people or God.

God will never force us to be good; nor will he give us
permission to sin, whatever the exceptional circumstances.
If we sin it is because we choose to: it will be no one's
fault but our own.

1 *Corinthians 2:6-10*

The Law is rather like a compass, in that it points us in the
right direction for travelling to a deeper understanding of
God's love. It is not the path itself, and it is not a detailed,
precise guide, but a valuable aid. For the wisdom of God
is simply too enormous and profound to be spelt out; it
is so much bigger than minds and hearts, that trying to
grasp it is like trying to catch the wind in a paper bag. We
end up with a mere token of what we hoped to master.

Yet, living in Christ, we have free access to the Spirit of
God, through which we are given insight into the heart of
God's being which would be utterly impossible in human
terms.

Matthew 5:17-37

Jesus was not punctilious about observing the exact letter
of the Law. On a number of occasions he healed on the
Sabbath instead of resting from all work, and this raised
doubts and righteous anger in others.

So Jesus takes pains to explain the purpose of God's
Law. He shows the people not only its limitations but also

its demands. Instead of conserving narrow, pedantic behaviour, the Law is now thrown open so that in one sense
we are freed from exclusive and rigid rules and in others
we are given the grown-up responsibility of observing God's
loving will in all its awesome ideals.

Our whole selves are to be brought under his Law in this
way – what we think as well as how we act; what is hidden
as well as what is seen by others.

Since rules define limits, the temptation is to go no
further than they explicitly demand. That gives us a sense
of having 'done our duty' and 'arrived'. When Jesus speaks
of the Law as complete loving, the limits are swept away,
and we can see that there is no point at which we will have
completed our duty, for the duty of love in God's terms
has no boundary.

Bidding Prayers

Celebrant Fellow pilgrims, as we travel the Way of
Christ, let us pray to our heavenly
Father who guides us.

Reader For all who teach the Christian faith
by word and example, especially those
responsible for the Christian education
of children; that God will work through
them to touch the hearts of many and
bring them to the joy of knowing
his abundant love.
Pause
Father of mercy: **write your law in our hearts.**

For all who strive to uphold civil
peace and individual human rights;
for the police, magistrates,
solicitors and those serving on juries;
that the wisdom of God may guide them
in the ways of honesty, justice and mercy.
Pause
Father of mercy: **write your law in our hearts.**

For the lonely and the bereaved;
for any who are finding life
particularly difficult at the moment,
for those whose problems seem impossible
to solve; that as we hold them here
in God's love they may begin to know
peace and the certainty of
his comforting presence.
Pause
Father of mercy: **write your law in our hearts.**

For ourselves and those with whom
we worship; that we may increase in love
which goes far beyond understanding
and brings us face to face with Christ
Pause
Father of mercy: **write your law in our hearts.**

Celebrant Father, we ask you to hear our prayers,
for the love of Jesus, your Son. **Amen.**

Ideas for Children

It is important that children become familiar with the Ten
Commandments as well as Jesus' interpretation of them;
otherwise they will not see how he fulfilled the Law.

Have a chart with the Ten Commandments clearly written
in simple language, and read them or have them written
separately on placards which are fixed on to ten children,
and each is looked at in turn. Explain that there were lots

of other little rules which were also part of the Law which
were a bit like brushing your teeth after eating sweets,
washing your hands before a meal and so on.

Talk about how some of the rules are easier and some
harder to keep, and throw in some of the problems Jesus
tackled, e.g.

- The Sabbath is a day of rest; but what if you are a
  doctor and someone is very ill, should you still
  work to make them better?
- You must not murder; but what if you really hate
  someone? Even if you don't actually kill them, are
  you still keeping the Law?

These questions may seem far too difficult, but even young
children have a highly developed sense of rules and justice,
and will have a surprising amount of wisdom to share.

Help the children make a belt to wear, on which is written
the whole Law in the way Jesus explained it: 'Love God,
love each other'.

Music
Recorded Music

Palestrina – *Missa Papae Marcelli* – *Kyrie*

'Live' Music

Faith of our fathers *(ONE, 130)*
O Lord, all the world belongs to you *(ONE, 403)*
Our hearts were made for you, Lord *(SONL, 36)*
Thy hand, O God, has guided *(ONE, 572)*

7th Sunday in Ordinary Time

Theme
Love your neighbours; love your enemies

We are called to nothing less than holiness, since God,
whom we serve, is holy. This entails approaching other
people with God's loving acceptance. We can understand
such loving with those we like, but to be Christ-like we must
extend the boundaries of our love to include even those we
dislike; even those who work for our destruction. Though
foolishness in worldly terms, this leads to the wisdom of
God.

Penitential Rite

A *New Commandment* (SONL, 34),
or *Alleluia for forgiveness* (SONL, 18).

Notes on the Readings

Leviticus 19:1-2, 17-18

The message which Moses is given for the children of Israel
concerns God's call for them to be holy. Holiness will be
expressed by love, and love will be expressed by forgiveness.

Such a message is reassuring, for although the ideal of
holiness is distressingly impossible, the path towards it
does not presuppose perfect beings who never irritate
each other or offend. Since we know we all spend considerable time (and even effort!) in irritating and offending

each other, it is good news to find there is hope for us yet.

For the holy loving to which we are called is about how we react to our own sin and that of other people. It is about forgiving, in the sense of really wiping the offence away; if we dredge it up years later in a spiteful argument we have not really forgiven at all. Nor must we tot up the injustices we have suffered and store them ready for some mammoth explosion of rage and 'righteous' indignation. Far better to talk about what has upset us, being ready to hear the other point of view, recognising that, unlikely as it may seem, we may actually be mistaken or be over-reacting. Then, with full forgiveness, our loving will have developed, and we shall have progressed along the road to holiness.

1 Corinthians 3:16-23

Being full of Christ's love, we are like holy temples, filled with the presence of God. When we remember this it can comfort us during danger and strengthen us when we are tempted to abuse our bodies.

For we do not belong to ourselves any more, but to Christ, and when that still point is fixed, all other loyalties and commitments will fall into place. No personality or theory is as important as our relationship with Christ.

Matthew 5:38-48

Many societies have used the maxim of 'an eye for an eye, a tooth for a tooth' and, up to a point, it works quite well. Certainly there is a strong element of deterrence in it. Certainly it is absolutely fair and just. But there is no route to lasting peace; just a ricochet of revenge which cultivates hatred, rejection and prejudice.

Christ's way of love comes as a breath of fresh air in the maze of violent retaliation of our world. It sounds crazy, yet is more sane than any complex army tactics; and the root of it is that we start giving ourselves away. Of course this would be foolish, and even suicidal, if our lives ended at death, if we were ultimately living in our own strength and if survival meant only protecting a group of cells which make up the physical body.

The difference comes with the point at which we stop living for ourselves and live for Christ instead; when his living Spirit comes to us and empowers us with the stunning love of a creating God.

Suddenly many threats lose their sting. Much violence is a disguised cry for help; a longing to 'matter' and be of worth. Seeing with God's loving eyes, we shall see the real need, and our response to that, instead of to the violent threat, will begin the healing and, in many cases, prevent the attack by taking away the cause.

It is not enough for Christians to be pleasant and friendly within the world's narrow boundaries. We must make it quite clear in our conversations, our choice of friends, our reaction to violence, and in our capacity to laugh at ourselves sometimes, that we do not live for ourselves, but belong to Christ whom we can trust absolutely, and in whom there are no unlovables.

Bidding Prayers

Celebrant Brothers and sisters in Christ, in the knowledge of God's great love for us let us pray for the needs of our Church and our world.

Reader For all clergy serving in deprived or violent areas; all who are in personal danger for teaching the faith of Christ; that they may be reassured, upheld and inspired by the life of Christ and that their work may be blessed.
Pause
Abba, Father: **we belong to you.**

For all universities, colleges and other centres of learning; for all discussions, debates, congresses and summit meetings; that as people use the God-given power of reasoning, they may be led towards truth and not wander away from God's wisdom.
Pause
Abba, Father: **we belong to you.**

For all who hate; all whose hearts are distorted by bitterness or resentment; all who delight in revenge and have forgotten how to forgive; that the Spirit of God may touch them to promote healing, to melt and soften, enlighten and renew.
Pause
Abba, Father: **we belong to you.**

For our own lives, especially our relationships with those we find difficult, and with those who pose a threat to us and our families; for increased love one for another, more willingness to forgive, and a breaking down of our prejudices.
Pause
Abba, Father: **we belong to you.**

Celebrant In silence we re-dedicate ourselves to your love, and ask you, Father, to hear our prayers, through Jesus Christ. **Amen.**

Ideas for Adults

Dance of Reconciliation

To the slow, regular beating of a drum, two men walk up the centre miming an argument which gradually gets more angry and heated until one is thrown to the ground.

Two relatives rush to mourn over the fallen man, one of whom approaches his killer full of determined revenge. They face each other, and then the killer falls. Two of his relatives rush to mourn and one of those rises and faces his brother's murderer.

They begin to fight but as they do so, a group of voices starts to chant, with a flute or recorder playing in the background, or you can use the fourth movement of Mahler's *Symphony* No. 4.

The words chanted are from today's Old Testament reading: 'You must not exact vengeance, nor must you bear a grudge against the children of your people. You must love your neighbour as yourself. I am the Lord.' This is repeated while the two men stand still, look out at the group, back to their dead, then back to each other. Slowly they extend hands to each other and embrace. Together they get the mourning relatives to join hands so they are all in a circle. Finally, they lift their joined hands high and join in with the last two sentences: 'You must love your neighbour as yourself. I am the Lord!'

Ideas for Children

Have on display a selection of things we are given by God which make life possible and enjoyable:

- a glass of water
- lump of coal
- salt
- pictures of a sunrise or sunset
- picture of rain
- plants and flowers

Talk about how much God must love us to give us all these, and many more they can add. Then sing a 'thank you' song.

Now present them with a problem. If they lent a friend one of their toys, and the friend did not use it properly, and broke it, how would they feel? Angry? Upset? What might they do? Take it back? Not lend them anything again? Hit them? (You could write the main points of this discussion up on a board or sheet)

Then show them some pictures of people spoiling God's world and each other; children quarrelling, being unkind and destructive, people starving while others feast, the aftermath of a bomb explosion etc.

Explain that God sees us all spoiling what he has given us. He feels just as angry and upset, and he could, if he wanted, take the gifts away. As you say this, take away the water, sunlight etc. until the table is bleak and bare.

Why do they think he doesn't do that? Because he loves us so much, even when we are horrid. He hates what we do, sometimes, but he never hates us.

Let the children help put back all the lovely things. If God loves us that much, we must love each other that much.

Music
Recorded Music

Indian sitar music such as a morning Raga

'Live' Music

Alleluia for forgiveness (SONL, 18)
God forgave my sin in Jesus' name (ONE, 175)
Make me a channel of your peace (ONE, 342)
Whatsoever you do to the least of my brothers (ONE, 606)

8th Sunday in Ordinary Time

Theme
Don't worry

God loves us and will always look after us; he sees our needs and he will never, ever forget us. So we are safe and secure in his hands, and need not fret our lives away worrying. He alone is our strength, our provider and our judge.

Penitential Rite

1. Teach me, Lord, to trust you. Train me, Lord, to see

ev- en where the path is dark- est you are guid- ing me.

2. Teach me, Lord, to trust you.
   Train me to be still,
   resting on your love with patience,
   open to your will.

3. Teach me, Lord, to trust you,
   so that I may grow
   deeply rooted by the stream
   where living waters flow.

Notes on the Readings

Isaiah 49:14-15

The bond between mother and child is normally a particularly powerful and often instinctive one. Mother animals of all species are renowned for their defence of their young and it is this image of steadfast loyalty and protection that the prophet uses to describe God's constant love and care for his people.

Not that we are always aware of it: there are times when God seems to be hiding his face, or when we suspect that he may only be a figment of our imagination, since there seems a great lack of activity on his part and evil appears to have the upper hand everywhere. The desolation and loss at such bleak times is painful and distressing. We may well feel that God, if he exists at all, has abandoned us.

Foolish though it seems at the time, it is important to trust that God is still with us even if we cannot see him; our dogged perseverance will be a great act of faith, even if it feels like empty, meaningless words and actions at the time. But God does not remain hidden longer than we can bear, and if we have done our best to clear away any sinfulness that may be blocking us from him, he will, in the best time for us, make his presence clearly felt. And our love and faith will be deeper for the experience.

1 Corinthians 4:1-5

Not only do we need to trust God; we also need to be people he can trust. He has called each of us to work with him for the good of the world, and all our time, gifts, abilities and money have been lent to us by him to be used. If we dedicate them to his service, God will make brilliant use of them. But we cannot expect everyone to agree with what God reckons most useful.

Saint Francis, for instance, could have become a highly successful businessman; God decided his gifts would best be used in uncomfortable poverty, and many reckoned Francis mad. We shall not find the world patting us on the back when we take on Christ's work; we may be criticised, written off as cranks, or, perhaps worse, merely passed over, ignored, unappreciated and unvalued. Many areas which Christ considers important are not rated highly by society; they are unfashionable, embarrassing or may not make any money and therefore elicit little interest.

- But the world's judgement simply does not matter if we are serving Christ. His opinion of us all is what counts, and any prejudging, either of or by us, is unnecessary and a waste of time. For he sees the whole of us – intention as well as action – and at the end of time everything will be made clear. For the time being we can stick closely to what God wants us to do and be, and not be put off by what other people think about it.

Mother Teresa has said 'God has not called me to be a success, but to be faithful.'

Matthew 6:24-34

In fact, we are easily put off by outside influences. So many trivial things seem important, and we are not helped by the vast amount of advertising, which aims to create a need and then fill it. An offshoot of this is that many cravings and expectancies are roused which give rise to guilt and anxiety when they cannot be fulfilled.

Many of us waste time and energy worrying about what shape we are; which clothes we should wear; whether our children are intelligent, brave, relaxed, fat, thin, noisy or quiet enough; whatever would happen if . . . and so on.

Life is not only more pleasant, but a good deal healthier if we take this teaching of Jesus to heart. It only demands a change of attitude, not necessarily life-style. If we begin every day by consciously submitting our energy and resources to working with God, and putting our worries into his capable hands, the pressure is immediately eased. Praying people have been found to acquire the therapeutic alpha brain waves, so praying is good for you in many ways!

Worrying is also connected with pride and selfishness. We may feel very self-righteous about worrying for those we love, thinking that it proves our love. But isn't it sometimes an inflated sense of our own importance which makes us worry, assuming that we have the key to other people's happiness and survival? If we acknowledge that the key really belongs to God, then we can start seeing that the world will not crumble if we forget the peas, or our children do not make the grades we hoped for, or the new neighbours are a different colour.

With God at the helm, problems can become exciting opportunities, and we shall be able to face whatever life throws in our way with confidence and enthusiasm.

Bidding Prayers

Celebrant My brothers and sisters, we serve God and trust him to look after us; let us pray to him, then, bringing our cares and concerns to his love.

Reader We bring to his love all who are called upon to witness to Christ in the political arena, where there is large media coverage; that, drawing all strength from God, they may witness faithfully to his truth and love.
Pause

Lord, our rock: **help us stand firm.**

We bring to his love all who have power and influence over people's lives; all national leaders and monarchs, all involved in advertising and communication media; that they may use their influence for good, and reject the temptation of corruption.
Pause

Lord, our rock: **help us stand firm.**

We bring to his love all who are anxious and fearful; all who find life a constant worry and cannot cope with their problems; all who are unable to relax; all who feel unable to escape the pressures of work; that through each may flow the healing peace of God, to allow them to unwind and rest in his love.
Pause

Lord, our rock: **help us to stand firm.**

We bring to his love ourselves and those we love; any particular problems that are worrying us or them
(pause)
that we may really trust God's love for us, and put ourselves consciously into his care, knowing that he will not let us come to any harm.
Pause

Lord, our rock: **help us to stand firm.**

Celebrant Father, in confidence we pray, and ask you to accept these prayers through Jesus Christ. **Amen.**

Ideas for Children

Make up a story about Mr Worry-a-lot, illustrating it with flannelgraph pictures. He might worry about what he's going to wear, what he's going to eat, who he's going to invite, where he should go on holiday etc.

Then he meets Mr Trust, who finds him in a bad state of nerves. One by one he sorts out Mr Worry-a-lot's problems with him, showing him that he is worrying unnecessarily because God is sure to look after him. When the next worry arises, they remember to stop and ask God to help them and are then much happier, knowing that God will not let them down. You could make the characters look something like this:

Mr Worry-a-lot   Mr Trust

and give the children cut-outs of each character to colour in and take home.

Music
Recorded Music

Dvorak – Cello concerto

'Live' Music

Do not worry over what to eat *(ONE, 123)*
Lord, for tomorrow and its needs *(ONE, 322)*
Lord, let me know *(SONL, 2)*
You shall cross the barren desert *(ONE, 627)*
Lord, when I turn my back on you *(SONL, 40)*

9th Sunday in Ordinary Time

Theme
Listen to God's will and act upon it

The Law set out a code of behaviour based on mutual love and respect, springing from love and respect for the Creator. Remembering it would help keep his people aware of their special relationship with God. Jesus showed God's will clearly and is able to save us from our sinfulness if we listen to him and act on his words. If we are foolish enough to ignore him we shall speed our own destruction.

Penitential Rite

Help us to hear and listen,
  Lord, have mercy. **Lord, have mercy.**

Help us to see and understand,
  Christ, have mercy. **Christ, have mercy.**

Help us to do your will,
  Lord, have mercy. **Lord, have mercy.**

Notes on the Readings

Deuteronomy 11:18, 26-28

Moses well understands the way human memories are short and easily side-tracked. He knew from experience the initial bursts of enthusiasm gradually sinking into slackness. Few of us can keep going with sustained vigour for long; mostly we get distracted, and progress by lurching fitfully from resolution to resolution.

That is why Moses suggests fastening the Law, quite literally, to our bodies, and the Law itself is a memory aid, useful for keeping us pointing in the right direction and turning us back if we have turned away.

So we must never listen to the whisper of temptation which tells us we have done our choosing and our turning to God, and can sit back and relax. We may suddenly find that we have been worshipping all kinds of idols for quite some time.

We may find that some of our worst problems are actually the result of worshipping (or 'considering of great worth') the wrong things, and if we turn ourselves back to God, the problems may be solved or healed.

It is best to acknowledge our capacity for getting side-tracked, and set regular, thorough times for examining ourselves in the light of God's law of love. Then we can start to be reconciled with God before we have blundered too far in the opposite direction.

Romans 3:21-25, 28

Paul, too, was very aware of human frailty. But living in the light of Jesus, God made man, he could see that however firmly we attach the Law to our bodies, whatever steps we take in treading the 'rules' path, we shall never be able to be reconciled with God by our personal efforts alone. That is the bad news. The good news is that we do not have to.

Jesus undertook to take on our weakness without falling, and he managed it.'Our faith is like a life line which secures us to him, so that we can be hauled to a right relationship with God. The Law can guide, but Jesus saves.

Matthew 7:21-27

Since the man who built on sand is called 'foolish', we can assume that he had the choice of rock for his site, but for some reason decided against it. Perhaps the sand involved less work, and would provide quicker results. Both as individuals and in society and the Church we are often guilty of similar short-sightedness, and pay for it later.

Spiritually, we are particularly loath to dig deep foundations into hard rock, since it is painful and humiliating. And the house will look just as impressive from the surface whatever it is built on. Through history 'Christians' have been notorious for this: singing hymns while slaves died below decks; using their faith as an excuse to wage war and plunder; using their status as respectable people to lead self-indulgent or cruel lives. The whole body of the Church is weakened by the shame and sadness of such hypocrisy.

Tragically, many fine, sensitive people, and many longing for faith, have rejected Christ because of our pathetic building on sand. Jesus offers us strong rock on which to build lasting houses; lives built on Christ work – for the good of the whole world.

Bidding Prayers

Celebrant Fellow members of Christ's body, we come, united in his love; let us pray together for the needs of the Church and the world.

Reader For every newly baptised Christian; for all who have recently been confirmed; that they may all be strengthened and encouraged to witness faithfully and bravely, listening to God's will and acting on it.
Pause
Hear us, Father: **and let your will be done.**

For our world, so richly blessed and so full of potential; that wherever people have turned from God's love and wherever resources are squandered or destroyed, there may be a turning back, a reconciliation, new hope and deeper trust.

Pause
Hear us, Father: **and let your will be done.**

For all whose bodies or minds are weak
and diseased, especially those suffering
from long-term, chronic illness, and for
those who nurse and care for them;
that they may be brought to wholeness,
and some good may come from their
suffering.
Pause
Hear us, Father: **and let your will be done.**

For all of us here, and all who worship
God in this town/city; for all whose
lives we shall touch this week; that we
may never forget Christ's presence,
but introduce his love into every
situation in which we find ourselves.
Pause
Hear us, Father: **and let your will be done.**

Celebrant Loving Father, we ask you to accept these
prayers for the sake of Jesus, your Son. **Amen.**

Ideas for Children

Bring along two sets of building bricks (not interlocking
ones). Divide the children into two groups and let each
build a house. One is based on a firm block of wood, the
other on thick layer of sand in a tray.

When both are finished, tell the children Jesus' story of
the two houses. At the point of the stormy rain, pour water
round the bases of each in turn. The sand will cave in and
the 'rock' will not.

Make sure you explain what Jesus told the story for, or
they will not understand. Point out how silly it was not to
have a good strong foundation, (they may have seen houses
being built with foundations deep in the ground) and that
we can choose to build our lives on strong rock or slipping
sand. Sing 'I'm gonna build my life'.

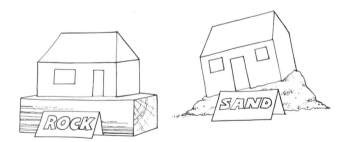

Build on God – put him *first*.

Music
Recorded Music

Mozart – *Piano concerto No. 23*

'Live' Music

Guide me, O thou great redeemer *(ONE, 190)*
Lord Jesus, think on me *(ONE, 327)*
On days when much we do goes wrong *(SONL, 68)*
The King of love my shepherd *(ONE, 528)*

10th Sunday in Ordinary Time

Theme
What God wants is mercy, not sacrifice

External, ritual sacrifice can look impressive, but be only
an empty shell which does not demand much real offering
at all. Faith and love, on the other hand, are actually costly
sacrifices, for they require total, personal giving, forgiving
and acceptance. With these we can reach out to those who
are sick or in need, and allow God's healing to take place.

Penitential Rite

Heal us of prejudice and bigotry,
  Lord, have mercy. **Lord, have mercy.**

Heal us of complacency and pride,
  Christ, have mercy. **Christ, have mercy.**

Heal us of intolerance and carping criticism,
  Lord, have mercy. **Lord, have mercy.**

Notes on the Readings

Hosea 6:3-6

On his side, God is utterly dependable. If he promises us
something he will never go back on his word and he never
reaches a point beyond which he loses interest in us or
feels we are no longer worth bothering with.

In contrast, our love for him is often spasmodic and wavering, as ephemeral as clouds or morning dew. Since we
are made in the likeness of God, we are actually capable
of much deeper, stronger love, and do often give it to
parents, marriage partners or close friends.

This is the kind of love God wants us to have for him,
and for those he has made, rather than a casual habit of
going through the motions of sacrifice (or, in our terms,
church-going and prayer reciting).

Romans 4:18-25

Abraham is a shining example of faith, since he believed
God's promise in spite of all its seeming impossibility. The
practical details were left trustingly in God's capable hands
because Abraham had no doubt about either God's power
or his unswerving loyalty. It was this great faith which saved,
or justified him, as it is our faith which speaks for us.

We may have to begin by wanting to believe, and asking
for faith. We may be helped to it by being encouraged to
step out, without support being visible, like a beginner on
to an ice rink. Gradually we will be encouraged to take
greater 'risks' trusting in God instead of the more obvious
support of our own strength, energy, intelligence or influence. That is not easy, especially if we prize our independence and resourcefulness. But it is essential if we are to
learn to trust God. The fruit of that trust will be increased
love for one another.

Matthew 9:9-13

The Pharisees set themselves high and exacting standards
of behaviour. They observed the Law with strict adherence
and were very committed, religious people. A personal rule
of life is very necessary, and in particular, regular religious
observance is useful in reinforcing our allegiance to God
and giving opportunity for worshipping him.

But the temptation is to start condemning anyone who
does less; and as soon as we do this we are right outside
the essence of the Law ourselves, for we are not looking
with God's eyes of love at his created beings.

Bidding Prayers

Celebrant   My dear companions of the Way, in thankfulness for our heavenly Father's constant love and loyalty, let us pray to him for all our needs and concerns.

Reader   For those involved in the planning of the liturgy and all who prepare music and readings for worship; for all regular worshippers; that all our worship may be an outward expression of deep, personal commitment and never become careless or empty repetition.

Pause

Father, hear us: **we know we can trust you.**

For those involved in welfare services, prison management, those working in industry and commerce, all whose work helps maintain peace and order; that justice may always be administered with mercy, and policies followed which are grounded in loving care.

Pause

Father, hear us: **we know we can trust you.**

For all who have become prisoners of habits – whether smoking, drugs, alcohol, ritual divorced from meaning, self-indulgence or constant criticism; that God may give us the power and confidence to break those habits which prevent us from loving fully, and that there may be mutual support and encouragement as we recognise our mutual needs and weaknesses.

Pause

Father, hear us: **we know we can trust you.**

For our families and friends and neighbours; that we may serve God in serving one another cheerfully and ungrudgingly, so that his kingdom of love and joy may be established throughout the world.

Pause

Father, hear us: **we know we can trust you.**

Celebrant   Father of mercy, we rejoice at your welcoming forgiveness, and ask you to accept our prayers through Jesus Christ. **Amen.**

Ideas for Adults

The Old Testament passage can be read chorally, using groups of men, women and children.

All:	Let us set ourselves to know the Lord;
Men:	that he will come is as certain as the dawn,
Women:	his judgement will rise like the light, he will come to us as showers come,
Children:	like spring rains watering the earth.
Men:	What am I to do with you, Ephraim?
Women:	What am I to do with you, Judah?
All:	This love of yours is like a morning cloud,
Children:	like the dew that quickly disappears.
Men:	This is why I have torn them to pieces by the prophets, why I slaughtered them with the words from my mouth,
Women:	since what I want is love, not sacrifice;
All:	knowledge of God, not holocausts.

Ideas for Children

Tell the children the story of today's Gospel as a narrator of a play. Arrange the chairs as an audience and set up one end of the room to be the 'stage'. If there is a screen, or space for a background picture of hills, so much the better. Give the children their parts in advance, but they can sit as audience until needed.

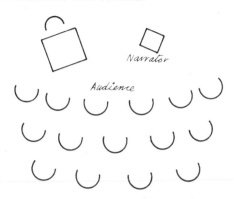

As the characters are mentioned, another helper discreetly tells them to move to the stage, and they act out what the narrator is saying. You may find they join in and speak their own words. If not, they can either use the narrator's words or mime. Speak slowly and clearly, and give enough time for the children to act their parts at each stage of the story. Here is a possible 'script':

On stage: Matthew, sitting at money table, a beggar, two women buying cloth from a man, one man paying his taxes, and Jesus.

One day Jesus was walking slowly through a town, chatting to the people. He saw a man called Matthew sitting collecting money from the Romans. Jonah was poor and told Matthew he couldn't afford to pay today.

(*Jonah*: I can't afford to pay you today.)

Matthew shook his fist at Jonah angrily. He told him he *had* to pay or he would put him in prison.

(*Matthew*: You'll *have* to pay. If you don't, I'll put you in prison.)

The man went away sadly. Just then Jesus came up to Matthew and shook hands with him. The other people were surprised to see a good man like Jesus talking to a bad man like Matthew. They told their friends about it.

(*One of the women to audience*: You know that good man, Jesus? Well, he's being friendly with that tax-collector, Matthew! It doesn't seem right to me.)

Then Jesus told Matthew he wanted him as one of his followers, one of his special friends.

(*Jesus*: Come and follow me, Matthew.)

Matthew was very happy that Jesus had chosen him. He was quite surprised, too. He jumped up straight away and told Jesus he would love to follow him.

(*Matthew*: Yes, Jesus, I'll come. I'd love to follow you!)

He even invited Jesus to dinner that day.

(*Matthew*: Will you come to dinner with me today?)

Jesus thanked him and said that he would love to come.

(*Jesus*: Thank you, Matthew. I'd love to come .)

So together they went off to Matthew's house. On their way home, Matthew kept inviting his friends to join in the dinner party.

(*General conversation*: Would you like to come to dinner? – Yes please; thank you, etc.)

Till by the time they reached Matthew's house there was quite a crowd. Matthew showed them all where to sit down, and gave Jesus the seat at the head of the table. Then they all had a lovely feast with lots to eat and drink. There were quite a lot of bad people among the guests, but Jesus was quite happy to be with them. A church leader came and looked at Jesus eating with all the sinners. He asked Jesus why he was with people like that. Didn't he know what kind of people they were?

(*Pharisee*: Why are you mixing with these sinners, Jesus? Don't you know what they're like?)

Jesus came over to him. He explained that God loves people whatever they're like, so we must be forgiving as well.

(*Jesus*: God loves people whatever they are like, you see. So if God is ready to forgive, we must forgive too.)

He said it was like a doctor – he does not visit the healthy ones, he visits those who are ill.

(*Jesus*: I'll try and explain. A doctor doesn't come to see the healthy people, does he? He comes to help those who are ill. And God comes to put us right when we go wrong.)

And Jesus went back to eat dinner with all the sinners who needed his love to heal them.

Music
Recorded Music

Haydn – *Symphony No. 49 (La Passione)*

'Live' Music

All my hope on God is founded *(ONE, 25)*
Look around you, can you see? *(ONE, 316)*
Lord, make me an instrument of thy peace *(ONE, 328)*
Lord of life *(SONL, 63)*
O King of might and splendour *(ONE, 398)*

11th Sunday in Ordinary Time

Theme
We are God's people whom he saves and sends

God has shown massive evidence of his faithfulness both in rescuing his people from slavery and through Christ, in dying for us in spite of our sinfulness. As we trust him, he will lead us into great hope and joy, and he sends us out to proclaim this good news to the world, so that many others can know the freedom of living in his peace.

Penitential Rite

Use the 'Jesus prayer', repeated 9 times, either said, or chanted to this music in a round:

Je - sus,   Son   of   God,   have   mer - cy on me   a   sin - ner.

Je - sus, Je - sus,   Son   of   God   have   mer - cy on me   a   sin - ner.

Notes on the Readings

Exodus 19:2-6

God has given the people of Israel good proof of his power and his faithfulness. They can always remember how they were rescued from slavery in Egypt and that will remind them that God really can be trusted to keep his word and look after them.

If they are prepared to keep their side of the bargain, they will be a people set apart, or consecrated, with a special assignment: to be the means through which the whole world will be saved.

We, too, are called by God, adopted as his own sons and daughters with a particular task to do. But with God it is a serious undertaking of mutual trust; he will not be able to make much use of us if we only honour him when we feel like it, go to Mass only when it suits us, or pray only when all the other jobs are done. God puts us first. We must put him first if our covenant is to be realistic.

Romans 5:6-11

Jesus did not wait until we were worth saving before he died for us. (There might have been a long wait if he had!) Sometimes we become so accustomed so hearing about Jesus dying for us that we are tempted to take it for granted.

It is a sobering thought to remember that God need not have gone out of his way to save us. We may see a wasp struggling in a spider's web and think about setting it free. But we do not have to do anything to help it, and the realisation that it might well sting us if we do, may make us decide not to bother after all.

In a sense, we are like trapped wasps, and God, if he chooses to free us, is making himself vulnerable to our sting: since he loves us, he can be deeply hurt by our cruelty and selfishness. Suppose, then, he had walked away? What hopelessness and anguish there would be as humanity saw its creator turn his back and abandon it.

That is why a shout of joy echoes down centuries of Christian thankfulness; God did not abandon us but decided to save us, stings and all. No wonder we can trust him absolutely with our lives, hopes, problems and celebrations.

Matthew 9:36, 10:8

Jesus shows us God's character. When he sees the people so anxious and harassed, expending so much energy on things of so little importance, their priorities all wrong and their lives so encumbered and restless, he does not get irritated or angry; instead he feels sorry for them, longing to give them peace of mind, joy, a sense of direction – longing to shepherd them.

Being practical he starts straight away, by delegating. One man cannot do enough; eventually freed from the limits of a body, his Spirit would be able to spread far and wide, and in a way this sending of the apostles is a foretaste of the power of Pentecost, starting, as is usual with God, in a small way. Just twelve men are delegated to be Jesus-people, working in his power to heal, console and teach.

We are only here now because God has called and commissioned us. And there are others working with us in every country, also called and commissioned.

The honour can easily go to our heads, but it is no good flitting off in a gust of emotion to do it all our way. We must have Jesus' authority, and he will certainly make our work clear to us, so long as we listen in attentive silence and stop giving him advice!

Bidding Prayers

Celebrant   My brothers and sisters, we know that our heavenly Father cares for us; trustingly, then, let us pray.

Reader   For all those involved in missionary work all over the world; that their work may be blessed and fruitful, and that they may be constantly strengthened and encouraged by the caring presence of Christ.
Pause

Lead us, good shepherd:
and work through our lives.

For the leaders and advisers of all nations, for diplomats, envoys and negotiators in all areas of difficulty, where tact and delicacy are needed; that people may learn to respect and honour one another, to work together for the common good.
Pause

Lead us, good shepherd:
and work through our lives.

For all who are harassed and dejected, overworked, stressed or bewildered; that they may come to know the calm of God's peace fixed faithfully beneath all the activity and clamour, secure and liberating.
Pause

Lead us, good shepherd:
and work through our lives.

For an increased trust and faithfulness in our own lives; for clearer knowledge of God's will in how our time and ability is used; for a greater readiness to listen to God's voice and respond to his calling.
Pause

Lead us, good shepherd:
and work through our lives.

Celebrant   Father, we ask you to hear these prayers through Jesus Christ, our Saviour and our brother. **Amen.**

Ideas for Children

Talk with the children about times in their week which are muddly and rushed – such as before school in the mornings, or packing to go on holiday or moving house. Everyone gets grumpy with everyone else, and it is lovely when things get sorted out and there is time to be friendly again, to listen to each other, and feel peaceful. You could show a selection of pictures of people rushing about, or in a panic, to aid discussion.

Now explain how Jesus felt sorry for all the people when he saw them like this. He wanted to tell them they need not worry, because God loved them and would look after them. He felt they were like sheep without a good shepherd. (The children may have seen the way sheep scatter in any direction and don't seem to see further than immediate danger.)

As you tell them Jesus' plan, of sending out twelve of his special friends to help him help the people, fasten name stickers to twelve children and let them all read the names a couple of times. Then help them make a line of twelve apostles each, and write their names on them. On the back write: 'I belong to Jesus. He needs me to help in his work.' Put one word on each apostle.

Music
Recorded Music

Brass Band playing: *'When the saints'*

'Live' Music

God forgave my sin *(ONE, 175)*
God is love, his the care *(ONE, 178)*
God's spirit is in my heart *(ONE, 183)*
Go, the Mass is ended *(ONE, 188)*

12th Sunday in Ordinary Time

Theme
Don't be afraid – you are safe in God's hands

Whatever the danger, whatever the pain, we shall never be left to cope unaided. God loves us, supports and sustains us, and keeps us ultimately safe. Only he has power over eternal life; nothing on earth can destroy more than the body. So we need never be frightened of witnessing to Christ, for the God who is all-powerful also loves us. In him we are secure.

Penitential Rite

Fix our eyes on your brightness,
   Lord, have mercy. **Lord, have mercy.**

Fix our hearts on your compassion,
   Christ, have mercy. **Christ, have mercy.**

Fix our wavering faith on your steadfast love,
   Lord, have mercy. **Lord, have mercy.**

Notes on the Readings

Jeremiah 20:10-13

Jeremiah's cries are searing, and may touch chords in our own experience when we have felt threatened, misunderstood and alone. Bitterly he finds out which are his real friends and which have turned away when he needs them.

The real friend is God, whom he finds has not abandoned him when the going gets rough; in spite of his misery he feels the assurance of God's promise and knows that, since God is in control, all will ultimately be well.

The low, difficult times may feel like struggling through a deep valley of misery, but it is possible to use them and learn from them. Every suffering is a chance to learn patience; a chance to increase our sympathy and capacity to help others afterwards; a chance to have some share in the passion of Christ.

Although this does not ease the distress or the discomfort, it enables us to see the pain as something positive – like the pain of childbirth, or running a marathon.

Romans 5:12-15

Some days the newspapers are full of so many stories of destruction, corruption and cruelty that evil in our world appears to be more powerful than good. Even the natural world is capable of great cruelty.

We know there is much evil; we are often very conscious of its power in ourselves. Mankind, personified by Adam, is diseased with sin, which breeds death. Its results are always negative and destructive, both in individuals and, alarmingly, in the context of society.

Perhaps it seems a hopeless pipe-dream that one man, however good or holy, might be able to cancel out such widespread and deeply rooted sinfulness. Many point to all the evil continuing since Jesus' crucifixion as proof that his followers' claims are fatuous and naive. Yet we have all seen considerable evidence, through the centuries, of lives amazingly transformed by encountering Christ, and social atrocities curbed and healed by the influence of good people, faithful to Christ.

For a while evil may appear to be in charge, but always it is usurped by a gradual upsurge of good, sometimes accelerated by the evil itself. Even natural disasters, illness and pain can become, remarkably, springboards to kindness, trust, compassion and love. War is renowned for bringing out qualities of good neighbourliness and self-sacrifice.

The path forward cannot be expected to be a well-laid, weatherproof road. Because of the existence of sin there will be much contortion and disruption of progress, and the road must be built painstakingly, stone by stone. But it is progress; God's kingdom is being established and evil will never be able to win now that God has intervened.

Matthew 10:26-33

So we need not be afraid, as we are sent out to bring the kingdom of God nearer. We are working on the side of one who is able to answer for us in eternity, as well as in time, and if we have witnessed for him during our lives here, he will know us and speak for us the rest of our lives on the other side of death.

It is immensely liberating to know this. It means that we are free to go ahead with whatever unusual or seemingly hopeless jobs he gives us to do, without worrying what will become of us, where the money will come from, what people will think or whether it will be appreciated by them. God promises that he will look after us. And he can be trusted.

Bidding Prayers

Celebrant   Fellow members of Christ, let us approach our heavenly Father, acknowledging the wonder of his involvement with us, and asking him to help us.

Reader   We pray for all who labour to spread the Good News, especially those who face threatening behaviour, imprisonment or persecution; for those who are tempted to remain silent in order to avoid danger to themselves or their families; that they may be calmed and given courage by the promise of Christ's determination to keep them eternally safe.
Pause
Lord, in our weakness: **we ask for your help.**

We pray for all the injustice, cruelty and oppression of our world; for its confusion of priorities, its lost opportunities and misdirected zeal;

that we may be guided unceasingly by
the level-headed, compassionate
leadership of God's Spirit.
Pause
Lord, in our weakness: **we ask for your help.**

We pray for all who are wounded and
injured – those undergoing surgery
and all in pain; that they may find
Christ alongside them in their
suffering; we pray for those who
inflict pain on others, for terrorists,
murderers and all who are fired
with hatred; that their lives may be
transformed by encountering Christ,
who loves them.
Pause
Lord, in our weakness: **we ask for your help.**

We pray for our families, friends
and neighbours; for the very young
and the very old in our care; for the
wisdom to see opportunities of
showing Christ's love and for enough
energy and time to do
what God needs us to.
Pause
Lord, in our weakness: **we ask for your help.**

Celebrant Merciful Father, protect us during
this week and through all our lives,
and hear these prayers for
the sake of Jesus Christ. **Amen.**

Church Decoration

Give the text 'Do not be afraid' to several groups during the
preceding week for meditation, and let each group express
the words in different ways, such as:
  - in a titled arrangement of flowers
  - among a collection of pictures and photographs
  - in a fabric collage
  - in a small prayer card which can be duplicated and
    distributed

Ideas for Children

Remind the children of how Jesus sent out his friends to
help him look after the world and heal and comfort it. Before
they left, he gave them some useful advice, and he gives it
to us, as well, because he needs us to help him too.
    Give each child a duplicated paper, personalised with his
or her own name.

Don't be afraid, . . .
even if you get hurt when
you work for me.
People may hurt your body
but they cannot hurt your soul,
because I will look after you
and keep you safe.
You stick up for me
and I will stick up for you.
Together we'll make the world
a happier place.

**Talk about how people do sometimes get hurt (even killed)
for doing God's work. Then split into small groups to play
this Snakes and Ladders game.**

Ladders
  1. Offering to dry up.
  2. Put a surprise bunch of flowers on
     the table.
  3. Turning down an invitation because
     it is during Mass time.
  4. Trying to stop your friends teasing
     somebody.
  5. Admitting you are a Christian even
     if they laugh at you.

Snakes
  1. Pretend to have full marks when you
     copied an answer.
  2. Make fun of a new person at school.
  3. Go to church, but don't join in at all.
  4. Make a mistake, but pretend you
     haven't.
  5. Let your friend down because you
     don't feel like keeping your promise.

SNAKES AND LADDERS

Music
Recorded Music

Simon and Garfunkel –
    Bridge over troubled water
Handel – *Water music*

'Live' Music

Deep calls to deep *(ONE, 119)*
On days when much we do goes
    wrong *(SONL, 68)*
The Church's one foundation
    (ONE, 518)
Though the mountains may fall
    (ONE, 569)
With you, O God *(SONL, 50)*

13th Sunday in Ordinary Time

Theme

Live for Christ, serving him in one another

As Christ was willing to die, we must be prepared to die to all that is evil in us. That will enable us to live the resurrection life with him. To do this we must put Christ before everything, and every time we serve others in need we shall be ministering to Christ himself.

Penitential Rite

Help us to break our bonds of selfishness,
Lord, have mercy. **Lord, have mercy.**

Help us to hold nothing back from your love,
Christ, have mercy. **Christ, have mercy.**

Help us to live entirely for you,
Lord, have mercy. **Lord, have mercy.**

Notes on the Readings

2 Kings 4:8-11, 14-16

The wealthy noblewoman is very kind and hospitable, and her generosity is rewarded in a way which money could not buy but which fulfilled her dream of having a child.

She was hospitable because of the obvious need of Elisha, not because she was likely to receive anything in return. We never know who it is we minister to, except that whoever it is, and however dirty, poor, spoilt, rich or disease-ridden they may be, they are God's loved ones. Surely that is reason enough to help, whatever our emotions and prejudices may tell us.

Romans 6:3-4, 8-11

The symbolism of baptism is easier to understand in total immersion, as early Christians would have known it. Wading into water and then being ducked right under it is a powerful reminder of drowning. Anyone who has seen the possibility of immediate death, whether by accident or illness, receding, will know the fresh clarity and thankfulness with which life is suddenly seen. Bird songs seem more lovely than ever, colours brighter, nature full of miracles and the privilege of being alive so great that one feels one will never grumble again.

Dying to sin and being alive to Christ is just like this; it creates a state of fresh joy and wonder at all that is hopeful, unobtrusively persevering, beautiful or touchingly honest. For it is the relief and heightened awareness that comes from being released from the condemned cell and told that we can go free. That is what resurrection means, and that is why it can be brought with powerful effect into every situation: having found ourselves set free we shall have a different outlook, and that will bring new hope to all areas, no matter how wearying and despairing they may seem.

Matthew 10:37-42

Being alive to Christ is bound to alter our attitude to everything and everyone else. It does not mean that we are being told to abandon our families and loved ones – rather the opposite, because it is through serving others that we shall be serving Christ.

The passage really deals with getting things in proportion, and having our priorities right. When we love God first, our love for others increases by leaps and bounds: we may even find ourselves loving those we couldn't stand before. Our love for God may lead us to see areas of our character which need to be changed, subdued, curbed or developed in order that we can be more loving; and because we love God we shall be willing to have a go at what he suggests, even if it is a bit humiliating and demands stepping down from a position proudly defended before. It may be only the equivalent of a cup of cold water that we give, but it will serve to increase our love both for God and for the recipient.

On the other hand, if our loving gets trapped in one area – either for a person or a thing – it will not be able to spread and grow in the same way since it is not rooted into the source of all love. It is likely, instead, to become possessive, narrow and exclusive. It must be defended against anyone threatening it, and if it lets us down (as may well happen) our world will seem devastated, for our ground of being will have been devastated.

That is why Jesus urges his followers to give their full allegiance to Love itself: all the rest, and more, will follow us all the days of our life, both here and in eternity.

Bidding Prayers

Celebrant My brothers and sisters in Christ, mindful of God's steadfast love for us, and with our hearts full of thanks and praise, let us pray to our heavenly Father for the Church and for our world.

Reader For faithfulness among all Christians, particularly when conflicts arise between Christian values and social expectations; for a drawing together towards unity of the different denominations and an increase of the kind of caring that makes Christ's followers stand out.
Pause
Father, live in us: **fill us with love.**

For all factories, mines, quarries, all processing and refining plants, and all those who work in them and live nearby; that they may be safely and responsibly managed, and that industrial relations in them may be based on mutual respect, courtesy and goodwill.
Pause
Father, live in us: **fill us with love.**

For the malnourished and the starving, the grief-stricken and the bereaved; for the homeless and those surviving in inadequate or dangerous accommodation; that our eyes may be opened to see Christ among all who suffer, so that we are inspired to spend our lives in helping those in great need.
Pause
Father, live in us: **fill us with love.**

For everyone who has helped us during this week at home, at work, or at school; for anyone in need who is known to us and whom we could help; that we may be more prepared to take the initiative in caring for others, and take ourselves less seriously.
Pause
Father, live in us: **fill us with love.**

Celebrant Almighty God, accept the prayers we bring you here, for the sake of Jesus Christ. **Amen.**

Ideas for Adults

The Old Testament reading is effective when dramatised, with characters speaking their parts as well as acting. You will need:

> a narrator
> Elisha
> the woman of rank
> her husband
> Gehazi

Ideas for Children

First give the children a maze to do, individually with a pencil. Here is one you could use:

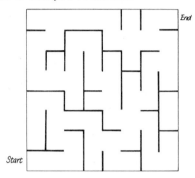

Talk about what happens when they go down a dead end;

- – they are out of the main route
- – they can't make any progress
- – the only way out is to retrace their steps
- – if they just stay there they may be imprisoned with no freedom.

Now show them a large picture of the maze either on a blackboard or sheet of card. The beginning of our maze, as Christians, is when we are baptised. (Stick a picture of baptism, or a font at the start of the maze.)

All the time we go on the right route we are putting Jesus first. In his love we can enjoy loving Mum and Dad, playing with brothers and sisters, enjoy football, painting, going on holiday, helping Nana, having friends to tea etc. (Write these, and their ideas, in coloured pencil along the route, with a cross, as Jesus' sign, in between each one.) Because Jesus is Love, he helps us love and appreciate other people.

But suppose one thing starts to be more important than our love for Jesus? (Write one item, such as 'football' or 'having friends to tea' at a dead end.) It will cut us off from the supply of Love, and our lives will be stuck at a dead end. So what can we do if that happens? We have to go back the way we came, meet up with Jesus, and then we can live in his love again.

Now read them the first part of the Gospel, which continues Jesus' advice to the friends he was sending out. Then tell them the story of the woman of rank who, because she loved God, was kind and loving to Elisha, and was rewarded. Being loving does give us a reward – it makes us happy!

Music
Recorded Music

Holst – *Planet Suite: Jupiter*

'Live' Music

All creatures of our God and King (ONE, 10)
Alleluia, sing to Jesus (ONE, 15)
Lord, enthroned in heav'nly splendour (ONE, 321)
Lord of my life, the ground of my being (SONL, 21)

> ### The mystery of God's Kingdom
> *Questions for Discussion Groups*
> 1. Why did (and does) Jesus so often speak indirectly, and in parables – would it not be better for everyone if he spoke out and left no room for doubt?
> 2. Can you think of modern equivalents to some of the parables which bring out their significance more sharply?

14th Sunday in Ordinary Time

Theme
Find rest in God, who is gentle and humble of heart

Jesus offers us rest from our troubled and overburdened lives which weigh us down with anxiety, for he is full of compassion and tenderness. Although he is so powerful, important and strong he does not throw his weight about, but humbles himself to meet us at our own level, share our sorrows and difficulties, and welcome all, regardless of physical or mental attributes.

Penitential Rite

In our love of personal esteem,
    Lord, have mercy. **Lord, have mercy.**

In our untrusting anxiety,
    Christ, have mercy. **Christ, have mercy.**

In our misplaced values,
    Lord, have mercy. **Lord, have mercy.**

Notes on the Readings

Zechariah 9:9-10

A donkey was a symbol of peace and humility, since it was associated with the ordinary, day-to-day carrying of burdens, rather than the horse which would be used in war, and was a far grander animal.

With remarkable insight the prophet sees no incongruity in victory and triumph being associated by God with humility and peace. His prophecy speaks of a time beyond the need to settle disputes by war, because God's peaceful kingdom will have spread far and wide, to encompass the heathens as well as the Hebrew people.

When, on Palm Sunday, the passage was literally fulfilled, the people fell joyfully into their role of cheering and shouting with gladness. Yet even then, in spite of the donkey, many expected a horse-riding style of Messiah, and could not believe he would go through with the humility idea when it came to the crunch. Even as Christ hung on the cross, many waited for the time when, at the last moment, he would break loose from the power of encroaching death and become the challenging war lord they hoped for, in order to sort out their immediate problem of Roman occupation.

Perhaps, we, too, find it hard to accept, deep down, a donkey-riding Saviour. Why does he let such diseases and catastrophes happen? we demand indignantly. Why doesn't he do something to stop the suffering if he is so powerful? How can he be a loving God if he allows wars to carry on?

Surely it all depends on what kind of victory is being gained. If God had fulfilled Judas' dreams and overcome the Romans, he could never have overcome sin and death. To do that, he had to submit, go through it, and emerge resurrected. And ever since, countless beautiful deaths, joy-filled sufferings and radiant losers have testified to the triumphant victory of a donkey-riding God.

Romans 8:9, 11-13

Through God's grace we can acquire his character, or Spirit, in our own selves. This means that the mortal part of us – the body shell – is no longer of such urgent importance, because it is not that bit of us which houses life. And although the shell will eventually weaken and decay, our life which God has given us will be unaffected, and carry on living whether it has a body or not.

Not that our bodies are unimportant: rather, they put into practice the life of the Spirit; the way we use and treat our bodies stems from our spiritual life.

Matthew 11:25-30

I may be wrong, but it always seems to me that it came as a delightful surprise to Jesus that God had chosen straightforward, unlearned men in revealing his wisdom.

When he was twelve years old, it was to the company of the learned scribes that he went to do his Father's business, and throughout his life he worked within the context of the Law, so perhaps he had expected his teaching to be taken up and spread by the clever, learned professionals.

In an exclamation of praise Jesus sees God's character of beautiful humility extending to those he chooses to understand him. The result of this fresh insight of his relationship with his Father floods out as welcoming love for all who need him in their weakness and vulnerability. As we may long to help a young child who is heavy-eyed, lost and frightened, so he longs to help us, who wander, often heavy-eyed, lost and frightened, through life. He calls to us because he can help and comfort us. If we run to him he will enfold us gently in everlasting love and we shall know real rest at last.

Bidding Prayers

Celebrant Dear friends in Christ, let us gather together the concerns and needs of our world and bring them before our heavenly Father, who welcomes us with love.

Reader Let us bring him the needs and difficulties encountered in parishes all over the world; the individual disappointments and the corporate weaknesses; that all difficulties may lead to growth, based on Jesus' generous love.
Pause
Lord, you have called us: **Lord, we come.**

Let us bring before him our world, particularly its areas of war and unrest, deeply held grievances, disillusion, careless violence and corruption; that wherever the world is sick God's great love may work towards healing and wholeness.
Pause
Lord, you have called us: **Lord, we come.**

Let us bring before him the blind and partially sighted, all with impaired hearing or deafness, all whose bodies or minds are handicapped in any way; for new parents of handicapped babies, and all those coping with the daily problems of having an ill or handicapped member of the family; that they may be given patience, understanding, strength and joy.
Pause

Lord, you have called us: **Lord, we come.**

Let us bring before him our families and loved ones; those living with us, those separated by distance or death, those we need to love more; that as our love for God deepens, so we may be enabled to be more generous, outgoing and caring in our daily life.
Pause
Lord, you have called us: **Lord, we come.**

Celebrant Heavenly Father, we rejoice in your abundant love for us, and ask you to hear our prayers, for the sake of Jesus Christ. **Amen.**

Ideas for Children

Clear the room so that there is sufficient space for everyone to move about without bumping into each other. Tell them that as it's a lovely day we're going for a walk. First we all put on some boots in case it's muddy, then we set off enjoying the blue sky, the birds, stopping to look at a squirrel or a flower, jumping in the puddles, etc. and we get into a wood. We decide to explore, so we leave the path, and push away the brambles, untangle ourselves from nettles, and climb over fallen trees and cross a stream.

Suddenly we find there is no path anywhere near us. We move faster, a bit worried. (More brambles etc.) The wood is very thick and we realise we are completely lost. Very worried now, we push on and recognise a fallen tree – we have walked round and round, and don't know how to get out. We sit down, tired and miserable, and eat a fluffy sweet we find in a pocket. Look at the sky – it's starting to get dark, and there are shadows all round.

Suddenly we hear the voice of someone calling our name – our dad's voice! He has come to find us. Forgetting how tired we are, we break through the branches and nettles and run into his arms. (At this point open your arms wide and gather all the children for a big hug.) How lovely it feels to be safe!

Still in a big huddle, sing a song of how Jesus keeps us safe, and calms us when we are frightened, such as 'I have a friend who is deeper than the ocean' (MWTP).

Music
Recorded Music

Beethoven – *Quintet*

'Live' Music

Dear Lord and Father of mankind *(ONE, 116)*
Farmer, farmer *(SONL, 37)*
Firmly I believe and truly *(ONE, 143)*
Take my hands *(ONE, 509)*

15th Sunday in Ordinary Time

Theme
God tends his creation so that it can bear fruit

With care and painstaking love, God provides all that is necessary for his creation to be fruitful. Sometimes, what is needed is unpleasant, but ultimately will be for the best. The process of growing always involves pain, and the whole created order is still 'growing'. The speed of growth in us can be altered according to the extent of our receptivity.

Penitential Rite

Use the song *Farmer, farmer* (SONL, 37).

Notes on the Readings

Isaiah 55:10-11

The natural cycle of water, with its rhythm of falling rain and evaporation, through which plants are nourished, provides a clear image of God's constant tending of his creation. Lovingly he plans for and cherishes the natural world and humanity, the crown of his creation. And just as the visible, steadfast pattern of rain and cloud brings growth, so God's word will bear fruit in some way, even if it appears to go unheeded. In his good time it will be fulfilled.

Romans 8:18-23

All growth is bound to involve some discomfort or pain. From the unwillingness to be led from what we know to what we don't know, to the flexing of untried muscles, the readjustment to a new role, and the breaking down of lifestyles we have grown out of: in all this there is likely to be emotional, spiritual, even physical pain. But it is positive and full of hope, because we live in the knowledge that everything is working gradually towards a completion and accomplishment, when the Creator's plan is brought to perfection and the work will be finished.

Fleetingly, sometimes, we glimpse the glory of that time, or grasp something of the almighty power which guides. Sometimes we sense, beyond words or reasoning, the whole, symphonic majesty of this movement towards accomplishment and total freedom set in total alignment of wills with the will of God.

Compared with such endless, timeless joy and fulfilment, any suffering during this life is brief and fleeting.

Matthew 13:1-23

Even when God actually walked the earth as a man, the Word was not soaked up by everyone. Their eyes and ears were fully functional, yet they did not notice the obvious, because their inner eyes and ears were shut fast by expectation, complacency and lack of desire to change in any way.

None of this alters the quality of the seed itself, which, if it falls on good, rich soil, can produce an excellent crop. But the parable of the sower does emphasise the other factors involved in fruit production – our own responses, perseverance, capacity to learn to trust and our willingness to be committed whole-heartedly.

It is a good idea to use this parable sometimes during self-examination, as, of course, there is always the possibility of even good soil becoming stony or choked with weeds!

Bidding Prayers

Celebrant My brothers and sisters, united in the bond of Christ's love, let us join in praying together for our common needs and difficulties.

Reader For the Church, and all who teach the faith by word and example in homes, schools and parishes all over the world; for those areas where there are no priests, or too few; that more people may be alert to God's calling so that there are more labourers for the harvest.
Pause
Father, hear us: **we pray to you in trust.**

For the world with its great potential, its hopes and its capacity for destruction; for those who perpetuate its divisions and for those who have responsibility for areas of its welfare; that all mankind may work for the common good, shared interests and mutual support.
Pause
Father, hear us: **we pray to you in trust.**

For all who listen, yet do not hear; all who look yet do not see; for those whose lives are choked with worries, materialism or the desire for immediate gratification; that they may be spiritually brought to life and enabled to be fruitful.
Pause
Father, hear us: **we pray to you in trust.**

For ourselves, our neighbours here in church, and those who live near us; for our families and friends; that our lives may be deeply rooted in Christ, so we are nourished by his unselfish love and not put off by the shifting changes of worldly things.
Pause
Father, hear us: **we pray to you in trust.**

Celebrant Merciful Father, we thank you for providing for us and for blessing us so richly, and ask you to accept our prayers, through Jesus Christ. **Amen.**

Ideas for Adults

1. Bowls of grain, stalks or corn and loaves of bread can be introduced into flower arrangements today.
2. Have posters of farmers in many countries displayed on pillars or walls (CAFOD, Christian Aid and Traidcraft have large calendars with some beautiful pictures.)

Ideas for Children

Have some grain (pearl barley will do, if no wheat is available) and a baking tray arranged with the varied surfaces on it like this:

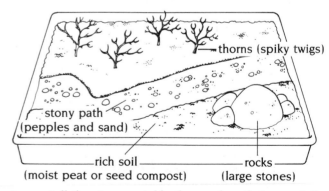

As you tell the story, sprinkle the seed so that some falls on each section. Talk about which will not grow and which will do best. You could have some fresh plants to press into the good soil to emphasise the point.

Now explain how Jesus used this story to tell us about how people react to God's good news. See if they can work out what some of the images mean. Then help the children to write captions for each section, stick them on lolly sticks and push them into the model. Others can decorate the background and title. The whole model will then look something like this:

A sower once went out to sow...

Bring the model into church and display it where the rest of the congregation can see it as they come to receive Communion.

Music
Recorded Music

Tchaikovsky – *Symphony No. 6 ('Pathetique')*

'Live' Music

Come to me, all you who labour *(ONE, 109)*
Comfort, comfort, my people *(SONL, 88)*
For you will be my people *(ONE, 153)*
Thou wilt keep him *(ONE, 570)*

16th Sunday in Ordinary Time

Theme
God is lenient with us

Through our human weakness we often sin, and sin is always destructive. Yet although we deserve God's punishment, he treats us mercifully when we are sorry, and gives us plenty of opportunities to become sorry if we are not repentant. His Spirit is needed to lead us to the point where we are repentant, and he gives us his promise that he will forgive everyone who turns to him.

Penitential Rite

Help us to see where we have turned away,
    Lord, have mercy. **Lord, have mercy.**

Help us to be truly sorry,
    Christ, have mercy. **Christ, have mercy.**

Help us to turn back to you,
    Lord, have mercy. **Lord, have mercy.**

Notes on the Readings

Wisdom 12:13, 16-19

So often do human leaders become corrupted by the power they wield, that it is difficult to imagine great power hand in hand with great goodness. Magnified to God's complete, almighty power, it becomes mind-boggling. If God is able to do anything, and if we let him down and spoil the good

he has created, why on earth does he not act forcefully and impressively?

Does mercy sometimes seem close to foolishness to us who are used to expecting heavy-handed power? Paul talked about becoming fools for Christ's sake; in a sense, God himself is prepared to become a fool out of love for us. His is the gentleness of a parent, who, though not condoning bad behaviour, is sometimes prepared to bend the rules or understand and accept it, simply because feelings of love towards the misbehaving child outweigh cold justice. Seeing the child's vulnerability and misery drives one to hug, rather than reject.

Romans 8:26-27

When the prodigal son returned home, his father went out to meet him; in the same way, God's Spirit comes to us as we turn towards him – he does not sit, distant and unconcerned, as we struggle ineptly towards him.

As soon as our hearts turn, with great longing, to face in the right direction, God's Spirit is there to help us forward and speak for us.

No amount of poetic and beautifully phrased prayers will draw us closer if we have not first set foot on the Way; it is far more important to get ourselves right within our hearts: if that first step is right, the Spirit will see to it that our prayers are heard, and we are led, step by step, to the full peace and joy of his love.

Matthew 13:24-43

While in this life we may well find that weeds and thorns seem to be flourishing better than the wheat. Incredible sums of money change hands for things which are of little lasting value; dubious entertainers and money jugglers are highly paid and esteemed by many, while many less glamorous yet infinitely valuable and caring work is poorly paid and unacclaimed.

If we are tempted to be hurt by the injustice of how, often, evil appears to receive all the rewards, we can re-read this parable which acknowledges that good and evil must grow alongside each other until the end of time, when only what is good will survive.

Bidding Prayers

Celebrant Fellow travellers, we are united in the
    love of Christ. In that love let us
    unburden our needs and cares to
    our heavenly Father.

Reader We bring him all lapsed Christians; all
    who have known him but rejected him;
    all who doubt his love or are hesitant
    to trust him with their lives;
    that they may all be led back
    to his welcoming arms.
    Pause
    Just as we are: **we come to you for help.**

    We bring him our world with its
    blundering mistakes, its weaknesses for
    self-indulgence and greed, its misplaced
    affections and well-meant interference;
    that lives may be ordered and calmed
    by the breath of his Spirit.
    Pause
    Just as we are: **we come to you for help.**

    We bring him all missing persons and
    their families; all who have lost
    their way emotionally or professionally;
    all who are senile and whose minds

are blurred or confused; that all who
are lost may be found, and know the
security of being loved and
protected by their creator.

Pause

Just as we are: **we come to you for help.**

We bring him our own lives; that they
may be re-ordered, calmed and refreshed
by his Spirit; that they may be healed
of all that shuts them off from his love.

Pause

Just as we are: **we come to you for help.**

Celebrant Father, in thankful love we ask you to
hear our prayers, for the sake of
Jesus Christ. **Amen.**

Ideas for Children

The Palm Tree Bible Stories series has a very readable version of this story, which could be told to the children first. It is called 'Evil *Beezel's Wicked Trick*'.

Talk about what things they think are like the weeds, and which the wheat, and how sensible God is not to risk damaging the crop by pulling up the weeds before the wheat is strong enough. Then divide them so that some draw and cut out wheat and some thorny weeds. Stick them all on to a poster, on which is written: 'Let them both grow till the harvest.'

Music
Recorded Music

Wagner – *Siegfried Idyll*

'Live' Music

Breathe on me breath of God *(ONE, 70)*
If we only seek peace *(SONL, 76)*
In the earth the small seed is hidden *(ONE, 250)*
This day God gives me *(ONE, 555)*

17th Sunday in Ordinary Time

Theme
Lasting treasure

God plans for us to become images of his Son, and he works unceasingly for our good to that end. As we know him better we shall gain the wisdom of discernment, allowing us to see with God's insight. When we realise what kind of being God is, and the extent of his love for us, it is like finding treasure of priceless value in comparison with which many other possessions seem expendable.

Penitential Rite

Realign our vision, so we see as you see,
  Lord, have mercy. **Lord, have mercy.**

Realign our minds, so we think as you think,
  Christ, have mercy. **Christ, have mercy.**

Realign our hearts, so we love as you love,
  Lord, have mercy. **Lord, have mercy.**

Notes on the Readings

1 Kings 3:5, 7-12

Solomon's legendary choice of gift, and God's pleasure at it, has been echoed in stories of similar nobility in many other cultures. It does, after all, show man at his possible best, rather than in his more usual human petty-mindedness. We may hope we would choose a similarly noble gift, but have a sneaking suspicion that, on the spur of the moment, we might well have plumped for a repaired car (to make us more useful, of course) or a bigger house (so as to be more hospitable).

Solomon was feeling rather vulnerable. He was conscious of his raw youth, aware of his inexperience and probably very nervous about the daunting prospect of ruling the people of Israel. In some ways all that put him at a disadvantage; yet in another, important way, his misgiving gave him an advantage, because whenever we are at our most vulnerable, and most aware of our weakness, we are also at our most receptive. There is no play-acting about trusting in prayer, when people are confronted with the possibility of immediate death in an accident or disaster. Desperate people are driven to pray, and there are many stories of fervent prayer during shipwrecks, or while waiting for rescue.

In Solomon's vulnerability he asks for what he needs, instead of what he wants. It is something we need to cultivate in our prayers, so that, instead of thinking of short term answers we would like to suggest God tries, we acknowledge the actual difficulties of our own weaknesses, and leave it in his hands. Things are far more likely to fall into place if we do.

Romans 8:28-30

God is on our side. He loves us and works with us, and when we stick with him our unpromising lives will gradually be coaxed into articles of beauty which actually change the world for good. As the number of committed followers of Christ grows, so the influence for good must increase. We can be proud of being Christians, not embarrassed by it. We are caught up in the greatest event that can ever happen, and we are on the winning side, because evil will never win. Christ has seen to that. From the resurrection on, everything is drawing together into the glorious completion at the end of time.

Matthew 13:44-52

One of the most striking aspects of this parable is the excitement following discovery. It is a feeling we have all experienced at one time or another – the sheer delight welling up and bubbling over which takes you back to childhood magic. (I can clearly remember the thrill of finding that raindrops made colourful diamonds in lupin leaves.)

Sometimes among church-going people, where one would expect to see much of this excitement at having found some treasure, there is instead the dullness of habit and no sparkle.

What does Jesus mean, then, by saying that the kingdom of heaven is like finding treasure? Can it really be a perpetual thrill of discovering something precious? In which case, why doesn't it show?

It may be that we can easily forget about the treasure when we are distracted by the frantic business of living; or we can put it carefully in a special box and spend more trouble polishing and fussing with the box than with its contents. For there certainly are Christians who 'bubble'; who seem to have a happiness and excitement about life which is based on their faith and gives them great inner peace. It can attract some, and make others envious, as there are always people who seem quite happy to do unpleasant as well as pleasant work, who are outgoing, friendly and slow to take offence. It must be quite some treasure to have an effect like that on an ordinary person's life.

And so it is! But we cannot just go and collect it, for it is not available until we start searching for it – and then we shall find it when we are least expecting to: but the discovery will make us want to rethink and re-order our whole life.

Bidding Prayers

Celebrant My dear companions in Christ, knowing that our heavenly Father loves to provide for us, let us approach him with the needs and weaknesses of the Church and the world.

Reader We pray for all who have recently been given new responsibilities in the Church; those who are working in unfamiliar areas; for the parishioners, who serve on Church councils; that in all posts of responsibility we may see our relation-ship with God of primary importance so that we may be instruments of his peace.

Pause

Lord, hear us: **help us discern your will.**

We pray for all newly emerged nations and all nations and states with uneasy peace or open hostility among their peoples; that they may be led in ways of acceptance, integrity and fair judgement, so as to provide a peace-ful and just society where human rights are honoured and respected.

Pause

Lord, hear us: **help us discern your will.**

We pray for those who have recently retired or face a change or readjustment in home or business circumstances; for those who are weary from the burden of constant care for an elderly, sick or handicapped relative; for all who are taking important and difficult decisions; that in all life's changes we may know the unchangeable, steadfast love of Christ.

Pause

Lord hear us: **help us discern your will.**

We pray for the people either side of us here, for our families and our friends, and all who live in this parish, that we may increase in love for one another, notice needs and be prepared to help.

Pause

Lord, hear us: **help us discern your will.**

Celebrant Father, we rejoice in the treasure of your love, and ask you to hear our prayers, for the sake of Christ, our Lord. **Amen.**

Ideas for Children

Begin by staging a treasure hunt, either round the room or in small groups using a treasure map on a grid, like a 'battleships' game. Also look through a magnifying glass to 'see' things not noticed before.

Talk about how they would never have discovered the treasure unless they had decided to start looking. Point out that they may or may not have discovered yet that life with Jesus is the best thing that ever happened to them. The search can take some time, but it is certainly worth it.

Now tell them the story of how Solomon acquired his great gift of wisdom, and help them to work out how they might start 'digging the field' to discover Jesus, not just as a name but as real treasure. The list might include:

- reading the Bible every day
- talking to Jesus every morning and night
- singing a praising song
- doing a good turn and trying not to be found out
- offering to help in the home/car/garden
- finding out during the week about such saints as Francis, Paul, Mary, Margaret (of Scotland) or Joan of Arc
- writing to an elderly or lonely person

They can take home a reminder of what they have decided to do, and come next week ready to talk about how they got on.

Music
Recorded Music

Bach – Mass in B minor

'Live' Music

Glory be to Jesus *(ONE, 165)*
In you, my God *(ONE, 254)*
Lord, however can I repay you *(ONE, 324)*
Take me, Lord *(SONL, 92)*

God's Kingdom on earth

Questions for Discussion Groups
1. Why did Jesus found a Church?
2. Is the Church doing its job?

18th Sunday in Ordinary Time

Theme
The Lord provides us with all we need

God's love for us spills out in his constant provision of food and resources and all the rich gifts we receive through life. There is generosity in all his giving, but especially in the gift of his Son, Jesus. Many were fed at his hands by the five loaves and two fishes; countless millions are nurtured and sustained spiritually by Christ's life, and nothing can ever cut us off from that source of love.

Penitential Rite

You are the Giver of all good gifts,
   Lord, have mercy. **Lord, have mercy.**

You are our Provider and Sustainer,
   Christ, have mercy. **Christ, have mercy.**

You are Constant, unflinching Love,
   Lord, have mercy. **Lord, have mercy.**

Notes on the Readings

Isaiah 55:1-3

Free gifts in cereal packets and washing powder cartons often turn out to have strings attached when the small print is examined; in the world of commerce there has naturally to be a good reason for giving something away. Perhaps that is what makes us slightly cynical at the thought of anyone deliberately giving something away for nothing; we are on the alert for the catch!

God's giving is free whether we thank him for it or not; whether we acknowledge him as giver or not; whether we use what we are given wisely or not. Rain, sun, wind, air, plant life and animal life are available to everyone, both good and wicked, both those filled with love and those eaten up with hatred.

The loving creator calls to every generation and to human communities throughout the entire world, including us. If we take him up on his offer we shall be bound to start leading happier, more meaningful and fulfilling lives.

Romans 8:35, 37-39

When we are down on our luck, feeling at our worst and least pleasant or attractive, or needing the kind of help which involves using people's time and energy – these are the times we find out who our real friends are. Mysteriously, some 'friends' are nowhere around, while others (often those who surprise us) turn out to have accepted us, warts and all, and are prepared to put themselves out to help us.

God's love is of that steadfast, persevering and loyal kind, which means that we do not need to put on any mask in his company. He knows our bad tempers, irritating habits, personal indulgences and particular nastinesses, which we prefer not to be seen too often. He knows us at our very worst, and yet still loves us and tenderly cares for us, boots us sharply if we need it, gives us opportunity for rest when we are getting frayed at the edges, plunges us into hard work when we can cope and buoys us up on a calm sea of peace when everything around us is in turmoil.

That is the kind of love which binds us to Christ, and the bond is surer and firmer than any glue. Nothing can worm its way between us and not even the most terrible catastrophes affect it: not even death itself. He holds out his hand to us; if we take it, we shall never be lost or alone again.

Matthew 14:13-21

We get a glimpse of the extent to which Christ is prepared to expend himself, in the way he reacts to the crowd. He was desperately in need of quietness and time to think and pray. The last thing he wanted was another large, demanding crowd. Surely he would have been quite justified in telling them to leave him alone for a while and go home. Or he could have left them standing there and sailed somewhere else.

But, of course, he did not. He loved them too much to do that. They must have looked somehow pathetic, having gone to the trouble of getting there with their sick in the hope of seeing this miracle worker, who spoke in a way that excited deep hope and touched their jaded hearts to the quick. Jesus' heart went out to them and he set to work, tired as he was, healing, listening and teaching. How immense is the task of healing the world.

Yet that is the responsibility Jesus takes on, and shares with all his disciples. We are not to send people away – we are to feed them. Jesus shows how, through prayer, it can be done, until all are satisfied and there is even some food left over. All the world can be fed, both physically and spiritually. All the world can be made whole, listened to, and taught about God's love. And we are the ones chosen to do it in Christ.

Bidding Prayers

Celebrant   My brothers and sisters, let us gather together our thoughts, needs and concerns and pray to our heavenly Father who is always ready to listen and eager to help us.

Reader   We pray for the Church, especially in its work of counselling and welcoming those who approach in great need or difficulty; that the Christian witness may vividly reflect the generous love of Christ.
Pause
Hear us, Father: **and let your will be done.**

We pray for the world's leaders and all who hold positions of authority and responsibility; that the world's resources may be shared and fairly distributed, so that all its inhabitants have enough to eat.
Pause
Hear us, Father: **and let your will be done.**

We pray for the starving and malnourished, and all who are weakened by lack of sufficient food; for refugees and those whose mental incapacity prevents them from being adequately fed, clothed or housed.
Pause
Hear us, Father: **and let your will be done.**

We pray for our own lives, and those we meet each day; that we may be more prepared to give our time, energy, talents and money in serving those in need, and working hand in hand with Christ.
Pause
Hear us, Father: **and let your will be done.**

Celebrant   Father of mercy, you are always more ready to give, than we are to receive; in thankfulness we welcome your Spirit into our lives, and ask you to accept these our prayers through Jesus Christ, your Son. **Amen.**

Ideas for Adults

1. 'Oh, come to the water' (SONL, 67) can be sung (or the tape played) in place of the Old Testament reading today.
2. Homemade bread as five small loaves can be offered today to be consecrated and shared.

Church Decoration

Have a display made by a group of people during the week, with pictures of those who need to be fed – the malnourished and the very poor. The title of it should be 'Give them something to eat yourselves.' Perhaps a special collection for Famine Relief could be made today.

Ideas for Children

Have displayed a selection of pictures of crops, preferably from different parts of the world, so that they can see the variety and abundance of plants God provides.

Now tell the story of the feeding of the five thousand. You may like to use a children's version, such as the Palm

Tree Bible Story called *Five Loaves and Two Fish*. Or you could tell it in your own words, keeping in the first part of the gospel where Jesus is tired and hoping for some peace and quiet. As you tell it have some bread (five bread rolls, for instance) and a few fish fingers or sardines which you break into a basket. There should be enough for everyone to have a taster. Then, when you tell them how many people were fed with that amount they will have a better idea of it. They will also have experienced the communal sharing of God's gifts.

Look again at the world's harvests, and talk about how we, like the disciples, are called to feed the world. You could play the '*Feed the World*' song at this point, and pray together about the problem. If some practical suggestion comes out of this prayer time (a sponsored activity or a weekly giving programme, for instance) follow it up.

Music
Recorded Music

Pachelbel – an extract from one of the Concertos

'Live' Music

As bread my Lord comes to me *(ONE, 43)*
Come and be filled *(SONL, 59)*
Fear not, rejoice and be glad *(ONE, 137)*
If you are thirsting *(SONL, 83)*
We plough the fields and scatter *(ONE, 597)*

19th Sunday in Ordinary Time

Theme
God's voice was a gentle breeze

If we listen we shall know when God is making himself known to us, even though it may not be in the way we would have expected. Wherever he is present he brings peace, and this was true even in terms of the wind and waves when Jesus calmed them. There is great tragedy in the way so many fail to recognise the authentic voice of God. We must be alert, so that we do not miss him when he comes.

Penitential Rite

We have failed to recognise you,
  Lord, have mercy. **Lord, have mercy.**

We have led blinkered lives,
  Christ, have mercy. **Christ, have mercy.**

We have tried to avoid deeper commitment,
  Lord, have mercy. **Lord, have mercy.**

Notes on the Readings

1 Kings 19:9, 11-13

Elijah was dejected and fearful, doubting his vocation and threatened by his enemies. God shows him these 'storms' projected on to elemental forces of nature in the wild turmoil of the fierce wind, destructive earthquake and explosive fire. But he does not project his own presence in these things; that is not the truth about himself that he wants Elijah to know. It is his profound peace which he wants Elijah, his loved child, to understand.

He shows him, by the gentle breeze with its connotations of relaxed peacefulness, that whatever turmoil and aggression Elijah may be living through, there is a fundamental core of peace which is unshakeable, since it is God himself.

For us it is tremendously valuable to have regular periods of silence and stillness, waiting on God. We may protest that there is no time for such luxuries, but in many ways it is a necessity, not a luxury at all. For some the complete quiet of the church for a while is the best place, possibly with several others as a regular meeting time. For others it may be a time in the train to work, during the washing up, or even in the bathroom. There is often a pocket of time we may not yet have explored which could be used. And it is our silence and stillness, more than external silence, which is necessary.

Concentrating on the 'now', and deep, regular breathing can help put us into stillness. As we get used to it, we shall find we are able to sense God's peace at many different times, and it is a great source of refreshment and strength.

Romans 9:1-5

Paul is deeply saddened by the way so many of his fellow Jews do not accept Jesus as the promised Messiah. Having discovered the pearl of great price himself he longs for his own people to find it, too, especially as they are, after all, the people chosen by God to bring about the world's Saviour – he is their own flesh and blood, and they have been led step by step through the Law and the prophets to the glorious moment of fulfilment in Jesus. The voice was there, but it was not recognised.

Those parents whose children reject the faith so precious to them will know how Paul feels. So will those whose partner is not a believer; there is bound to be deep anguish and longing that those we love and to whom we belong should share in the breathtaking good news of Christ which, we have found, brings a whole new dimension to life.

We must never lose hope, or stop praying, for the power of prayer can prepare the ground for personal response; it can also prepare us to speak and act the way God needs us to whenever any opportunities for witness arise. Often it is the continuing, steadfast prayer of relatives which brings people to Christ.

Matthew 14:22-33

Like Elijah, the disciples are feeling buffeted and in danger; they are struggling against the head wind and in the middle of all the wild weather they see Jesus walking towards them. Because he is doing something unexpected they do not recognise him, but slot the experience into the only compartment of their minds where it will fit: they assume it is a ghost, and panic.

Jesus is always behaving unexpectedly, since our minds tend to run on narrow tracks of our own limited human experience. But we may not recognise him if we will only accept what falls in with our expectations of his behaviour.

Peter, for all his faults, has the great quality of being prepared to try anything, and he is prepared to believe that this figure on the water is his Lord. His faith is rewarded by Christ's confidence in him and spiritual encouragement as he calls him to share in the humanly impossible.

So far, so good. We can accept the call to seemingly impossible tasks in our lives and we shall be enabled to do them. But the force of the wind will not die down while we do it, and there may be times when we, like Peter, panic, and wonder what on earth we are doing sticking our necks out – we seem to have bitten off more than we can chew.

If and when that happens, we may feel as if we are sinking, but Christ will never let us sink. He will take hold of us and lead us back to calm and safety if we are desperate. Time and again there will be someone or something to encourage us, minister to our wounds or provide a small breakthrough in what has been a long struggle – somehow God will provide for us, even though our sinking has been a lapse of trust. After all, we have proved our will to trust him by setting out in the first place, and that act of faith will be honoured by the God who loves us.

Bidding Prayers

Celebrant   Fellow travellers of the Way of Christ,
let us bring to the feet of our heavenly
Father all that concerns or worries us,
trusting in his infinite gentleness
and love.

Reader   We bring to him the need for the Church
to communicate effectively with those
who are searching but uncommitted;
we pray for those with special
responsibility for preparing young people
for their first communion
and confirmation;
that more of God's children will hear
his voice, and experience the joy
of living in his love.
Pause
Father, teach us to listen:
so that we hear your voice.

We bring to him the need for the nations
of the world to be more trusting and
more ready to work together towards
peaceful settlements; the need for
prejudice to be broken down and
dissolved in love; and the need for
corruption to be dispelled
by courageous honesty and integrity.
Pause
Father, teach us to listen:
so that we hear your voice.

We bring to him those who are suffering
in mental or physical pain, those who
sometimes despair of getting better and
those who are approaching death;
that even in the darkest, bleakest
times they may have sure knowledge of
God's deep love for them as individuals.
Pause
Father, teach us to listen:
so that we hear your voice.

We bring to him our loved ones and
their particular needs; we bring all
our relationships and opportunities for
serving others; we bring our need for a
closer, more wholehearted commitment
to our Creator and Saviour.
Pause
Father, teach us to listen:
so that we hear your voice.

Celebrant   Merciful Father, hear us as we pray,
for the sake of Jesus, our Saviour. **Amen.**

Ideas for Adults

This week perhaps a quiet half hour could be arranged as a time for the whole parish to 'listen' to God. It may not be suitable to gather for this; individuals can keep their quietness pledge wherever they happen to be, knowing that many others are as well.

Ideas for Children

Today's Gospel is splendid for acting and can be first told to the children in a suitable translation, such as the *Good News Bible* or the second part of *Jesus on the Sea* (Palm Tree Bible Stories).

After the children have heard the events, talk briefly with them about why the disciples thought it must be a ghost, how Peter showed his trust in Jesus, and why Jesus rescued him.

Have a large white sheet pegged on a line and a bright lamp shining behind it, so that the story can be acted out in a shadow play. Show the children how shadows can be made and then help them make the necessary props.

They will need a length of material to be the sea, a cardboard boat, a figure of Peter and of Jesus. The card shapes are fixed on to sticks. Other children can make sound effects, such as dried peas in a plastic bottle, a few jam jars filled with different amounts of water to play with a metal fork, and sand in a tin to make swishing sounds.

When actors and orchestra are ready, narrate the story, slowly and clearly while the figures move and the wind and surging sea get wilder, and then calm as Jesus and Peter go back to the boat.

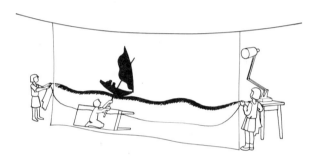

Music
Recorded Music

Dvorak – *Symphony No. 9* ('*From the New World*')

'Live' Music

Be still and know *(ONE, 58)*
It came upon the midnight clear *(ONE, 258)*
Listen, let your heart keep seeking *(SONL, 26)*
Oh the love of my Lord *(ONE, 430)*

20th Sunday in Ordinary Time

Theme
God's mercy embraces all the earth

Although the Jews were chosen by God as the means of bringing about his plan of salvation, the salvation extends to include all nations. Not all Jews recognised Jesus as Messiah when he came, and Jesus was impressed by the obvious faith of some pagans. God shows us, therefore, that his mercy is deep and abundant, and freely available to all people – none is excluded.

Penitential Rite

You who have created every individual,
  Lord, have mercy. **Lord, have mercy.**

You who love all of us, whatever our race, class or colour,
  Christ, have mercy. **Christ, have mercy.**

You who long for us to be healed,
  Lord, have mercy. **Lord, have mercy.**

Notes on the Readings

Isaiah 56:1, 6-7

The prophet was convinced of the very special role played by the people of Israel in God's plan to save the world he had created. But salvation was not to end there: God loves each part of his creation and would never contemplate the possibility of saving a few while others are excluded. Working with human material it was essential to start small, using particular individuals and then a particular race, so that the message would gradually spread from strong roots to the whole world.

Whenever justice and integrity, loving care and acceptance are practised conscientiously, there God is acting, whatever the creed or culture may be. Some of those practising God's covenant would deny his existence; many would probably doubt it. But that does not alter the fact that they are living in close association with him. Often what they do not believe in is a false image with which they have been presented, possibly through Christians who should know better.

For our presentation of Christ is the only Christ many will meet; it is vital that we present him as well as possible, then, so that we cause none to stumble.

Romans 11:13-15, 29-32

Paul, being a fervent Jew himself, longs for his own people to come to the point where they can accept that they have drifted away from their special covenant relationship with God, and will be reconciled to him when they acknowledge Christ as the promised Messiah, who has fulfilled the prophecies they hold so dear.

The covenant between him and his people stands for ever: God will not make a promise and then think better of it in view of new circumstances or unforeseen hitches. His side of the pact is unchangeable, and in his mercy he rejects no one.

Matthew 15:21-28

We may find this accepted inequality difficult to reconcile with the God who loves and sustains all people regardless of creed or race. But Christ was fully man; man of the age in which he lived, and nurtured in the culture and expectations of his time.

Canaanites recognised the pact between God and the people of Israel as something rather exclusive and nationalistic, and would not therefore have expected their prophets and miracle workers to perform any of their wonders on them. Neither would Jesus have gone out of his way, at this stage, to teach and heal those outside the people of Israel, as they were to be the first fruits from which the rest of the world could be saved.

But something about the character and charisma of Jesus prompts this woman to waive conventions and speak out boldly, knowing she has every likelihood of being rebuffed. Again, it is desperation which drives her to approach him, for her daughter is very disturbed and probably making life extremely difficult and agonising.

Jesus is amazed by the trust she shows in his power; she is quite convinced that he can heal her daughter, and almost convinced that he will be prepared to help her even if she is a Canaanite. Having enquired more deeply into her argument for receiving help, Jesus lovingly and gladly restores her daughter to peace and wholeness, marvelling that the faith he had expected to find among the children of Israel is bubbling up here, in a foreigner.

Humans are generally clannish beings; the bonds between those sharing the same family name, the same sectarian view of religion, the same country of origin or the same values, are immensely strong and have often been the cause of fierce fighting.

That is not what a loving God wants of his creation; he was, after all, prepared to intervene personally in order to show the broader, more open-minded nature of his character and the extent of his love which has no narrow boundaries, is always flexible, and never exclusive. That is what we must show if we are his followers. Any strait-jacketing of God's love into pedantic rules or defensive sectarianism will only block God's plan to save the world.

Bidding Prayers

Celebrant Led by the spirit we have come here today. Trusting in our loving and merciful Father, let us pray together for the Church and the world.

Reader Let us pray for unity among Christians; that in mutual love we may learn from each other, grow together and worship together.
Pause
Merciful Father: **hear our prayer.**

Let us pray for all peace initiatives, all negotiations between nations, all attempts at integration; that, knowing God's love for every individual, we may all respect and honour one another.
Pause
Merciful Father: **hear our prayer.**

Let us pray for those who are far from home, and those who are exiled or who fear for their lives; that they may be kept safe, and know the strength of God's presence no matter what dangers they face.
Pause
Merciful Father: **hear our prayer.**

Let us pray for our own loved ones – our families and our friends; for greater understanding of those from whom we feel distant; that we may show Christ's love in the way we order our lives and relationships.
Pause
Merciful Father: **hear our prayer.**

Celebrant Father, we trust in your unswerving love, and bring you these prayers through Jesus, our Saviour. **Amen.**

Ideas for Children

Begin by talking about pets the children may have, and how they sometimes eat the scraps of food that get left over or fall off the table. (Babies' high-chairs are usually a good place to wait if you are a hungry dog.)

Now tell them today's Gospel, explaining that the woman would not have expected Jesus to minister to her people as she did not belong to their religion, but that Jesus helped her anyway, because he loved her.

Then discuss with them how some helpful, kind things are nice to do (such as baking cakes or shovelling snow), while others are less attractive (such as washing up or clearing your bedroom) – but that to show real love we need to do both sorts cheerfully. And some people are nice to help (because they thank you and perhaps give you a treat), while others are less so (they may grumble, not thank you, or criticize the way you have done something) – but all people need our loving care, whether they are pleasant to help or not.

Now show some pictures of people doing something beautiful for God, even though it may be uncomfortable, smelly or tiring work. e.g.

- Mother Teresa of Calcutta,
- the Sisters at Helen House,
- those helping the homeless at St. Martin's in-the-field.

Is there a job they could do sometimes which would really show God's love? Ask them to talk about it at home and come with their suggestions next week. Give each child a card to fill in when they have decided what to do.

Music

Recorded Music

African music

'Live' Music

All the nations of the earth *(ONE, 30)*
Build, build your church *(SONL, 41)*
He's got the whole world in his hand *(ONE, 209)*
I am the Light *(SONL, 20)*

21st Sunday in Ordinary Time

Theme
You are the Christ, Son of the living God

Through faith Peter had recognised the glory, majesty and wisdom of God in this man of Galilee, and he was prepared to stand up and voice his belief. Because of his faith Jesus chose Peter as the foundation rock on which his Church would be built. What Peter had glimpsed was something of the great power combined with compassion which is beyond understanding but can change our lives. For if Jesus of Nazareth is none other than God himself, then we have such hope as was never possible before.

Penitential Rite

Help us in our unbelief,
  Lord, have mercy. **Lord, have mercy.**

Increase our faith and trust,
  Christ, have mercy. **Christ, have mercy.**

Help us to know your wisdom and your love,
  Lord, have mercy. **Lord, have mercy.**

Notes on the Readings

Isaiah 22:19-23

Anyone in a position of power possesses potentially dangerous authority; any abuse of power will have far-reaching effects on those who are led. Corruption among those with authority can damage a whole nation. It is vital, therefore, that anyone working in God's service should reflect his integrity, wisdom and goodness.

When the prophet finds that the authority entrusted to Shebna has been abused, he sets about healing any possible damage by removing him from his position and appointing Eliakin instead.

Paul, too, was always aware of the danger of complacency, and worried that, having led others to Christ, he should himself be found unworthy. He was right to be concerned: it is healthy for all those in any authority to use regular self-examination, with the selfless, unflinching love of God as their only yardstick, in order to check that they are not becoming slack or abusing privilege – and most of us are in some kind of authority, so it will not do to pass the buck. We must start with ourselves.

Romans 11:33-36

The God we believe in is not a whimsical idea which we use to prop ourselves up when we feel low, nor is he a man-sized being whom we pacify by giving a regular weekly hour or so of our attention.

Sometimes we can lose sight of the enormity of the concept of God, and when, perhaps in real need, we pray with real earnestness, the immense power we glimpse can come as a shock. Being caught up in a group of praying people is even a little frightening at first, as we realise that we are not as much in control of everything as we may like to believe. In, through, round and above the whole created order is the presence of the creator and sustainer, who is uncompromising in his love.

God can never be controlled, or packaged, or battened down into forms, or even creeds, which suit us. He is always revealing his presence unexpectedly and using people we would not have chosen. He asks outrageous things of his followers and then provides, coaxes and supports till they are achieved. Time and again, the impossible gets done. For God is infinitely vaster and closer than we ever realise; confessing belief in him is the most profound, far-reaching step we shall ever take.

Matthew 16:13-20

Peter was prepared to take that step. As a Jew he knew that God would, at some stage, send the Messiah to save his people, but to acclaim a living, local man as being one with the creator God, was to risk terrible blasphemy. It was the great risk involved which proved Peter's great faith and insight.

Here was a man who must already possess God-given wisdom which, with his straight forthright character, made him so suitable for the foundation on which to build the body of Christ – the caring body, to minister to a wounded world and bring it sure and joyous hope.

Bidding Prayers

Celebrant My brothers and sisters in Christ, trusting in our heavenly Father's unchanging love, let us bring him our cares and concerns for the Church and for the world.

Reader We bring before him the daily demands, difficulties and problems of those

involved in all ministries, both lay
people and the clergy; that they may be
supported and encouraged by God's
presence, and trust in his steadfast love.
Pause

Unchanging Lord: **to whom else could we go?**

We bring to his love the areas of our
world where changes have caused suffering;
all those responsible for reorganisation
in government and in industry; that every
decision may be the result of careful
thought and be carried out with integrity
and respect for all those involved.
Pause

Unchanging Lord: **to whom else could we go?**

We bring to his love those who have
recently been made redundant, those
who are unemployed and their families;
those whose work separates them from
home, and all who are without homes
or adequate accommodation.
Pause

Unchanging Lord: **to whom else could we go?**

We bring to his love our own families
and friends, especially those with whom
we find it difficult to live; all
families with newly born babies or where
changed circumstances are making
readjustments necessary.
Pause

Unchanging Lord: **to whom else could we go?**

Celebrant   Heavenly Father, we want to fix our lives
on your enduring love, and we ask you to
accept these prayers for the sake of
Jesus Christ. **Amen.**

Ideas for Adults

The reading from Romans can be dramatised using four
voices – two men and two women.

All:	How rich are the depths of God
1st Woman:	how deep his wisdom and knowledge
1st Man:	and how impossible to penetrate his motives
2nd Man:	or understand his methods!
Women:	Who could ever know the mind of the Lord?
Men:	Who could ever be his counsellor?
2nd Woman:	Who could ever give him anything
1st Woman:	or lend him anything?
Women:	All that exists comes from him;
Men:	all is by him and for him.
All:	To him be glory for ever! **Amen.**

Ideas for Children

Have a display of things which are drawn from an unusual
angle, so that they are not easy to recognise. Here are a few
suggestions, but you may find others in photographs.

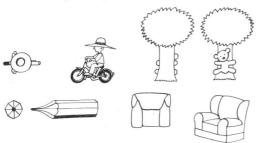

Talk with the children about how they might recognise
someone in disguise – the way they move, talk etc. In other
words, their *behaviour* tells us who they are.

In a way, Jesus was God in disguise, but how did his *behaviour* show that he was God as well as man?

– healing people
– teaching them well
– being loving and kind, etc.

(Of course, those who knew and understood God most,
would be the first to recognise, through his behaviour, that
Jesus was acting just as God would act.)

Now tell the children how Peter answered Jesus' question
about who he was, and how that showed Jesus what a strong
'rock' Peter would be on which to build the Church. If we get
to know Jesus well, we shall see him around all over the
place. You could all use St Richard's Prayer at this point:

Most merciful redeemer, friend and brother –
may I know you more clearly,
love you more dearly,
and follow you more nearly
day by day.   Amen.

All the children can add to a poster headed: 'We have seen
Jesus at work today . . .' by sticking on either drawings or a
short description of something good, kind, loving or forgiving going on. This poster may be displayed in church where
everyone can see it.

Ask the children to look out for Jesus during the coming
week – he may be in disguise, but loving behaviour will
show where he is.

Music
Recorded Music

Vivaldi – *Violin concerto*

'Live' Music

Glorify the Lord *(SONL, 17)*
He brings us in to his banqueting table *(ONE, 204)*
Open your ears, O Christian people *(ONE, 422)*
O praise ye the Lord *(ONE, 425)*
Without seeing you we love you *(SONL, 13)*

22nd Sunday in Ordinary Time

Theme
Think God's way

Worshipping and serving God needs to involve a surrender
of all our pre-conceived ideas and a readiness to think and
act in God's way, which may be very different from behaviour in our contemporary society. The worldly tenets of
survival, gain and material comfort give rise to quite different codes of behaviour from God's canvas of total giving, unending life and sacrifice. His way may well include suffering,
but it also includes rich life, joy and peace.

Penitential Rite

Use the music for *'Take up your Cross'* (SONL, 42).

Notes on the Readings

Jeremiah 20:7-9

Things were not going too well for Jeremiah. He was
ridiculed, belittled and abused; the message of gloom and
doom did not go down well, however true it was, and he was
very tempted to give up the whole business, keep quiet

and let people get on with their destruction unchecked.

The trouble was, he knew that God needed him to speak out, and since he loved God, that placed him in a tricky and painful dilemma. His love for God won and he was then prepared to put up with any insults and ill-treatment for the sake of following the God he worshipped.

If we find ourselves in the minority, with values that are despised and scorned by many around us, and pressures on our children to conform to different standards of behaviour, we may well feel like Jeremiah. It will test our reasons for standing out; if we have been working towards gaining adulation and respect, then these difficulties will probably dissuade us and cause us to falter. If, on the other hand, we are giving our lives for our love of God, then we shall find that the difficulties deepen our resolve and give us clearer understanding of how important the work is.

Romans 12:1-2

All action begins with the mind; if we are thinking in God's way we shall start to act his way, too. So often we assume we know how God expects us to act and career off enthusiastically without consulting him at all. All kinds of schemes and projects have failed for this reason. The danger is especially great among well-established Christians who feel they know all the procedures by now and are remarkably confident in their assessment of God's requirements.

Yet in fact, our God is a God of surprises. Fully in control of the shifting, changing needs and gifts of his people, he can see clearly what needs doing, by whom and how. Holding past, present and future intricately balanced in his being, he knows the right timing, so that different factors can be brought into sharp focus simultaneously and thereby work brilliantly.

So we cannot make any decision without consulting God, if we want to be involved in the perfect thing to do. And the perfect thing may not be what we had in mind; it may involve a lot more action, or even a lot less action and more patience; it may involve drastic change, or an acceptance of a situation as it is. The important thing is to offer our lives to be used by God, and then listen intently by spending time with him, so that he can make perfect use of us.

Matthew 16:21-27

It is quite encouraging, in a way, to find that Peter, who was so obviously close to God and had such faith, also had times of blindness, when his thinking was not aligned with God's mind. Saints are not born perfect, but are very ordinary people like us.

Why was Jesus so quick to stamp on what Peter said? He was, after all, showing love and concern for Jesus, and it seems a natural reaction if a loved friend talks of walking openly into certain death. So why was Peter wrong? He was thinking with the mind of man; the concern for his loved friend and master was not wrong in itself but it did not go nearly far enough. It became trapped at the immediate instead of going further to see sacrifice as necessary for the much wider context of all humanity. And it therefore pulled the human Christ towards immediate, smaller gains and away from the very costly, divine plan for mankind's salvation.

There is, in other words, an element of grit and rigour in thinking God's way which may lead to a harder, longer and more expensive course of action than seems necessary to those around us. But if we find God asking such costly action of us, it is only because the long-term effects, perhaps on us or perhaps on society, will be immeasurably greater.

Bidding Prayers

Celebrant   Fellow travellers of the Way of Christ,
we know that God our Father loves us; let

us therefore pray to him now about all that concerns us in the Church and in our world.

Reader   Especially we pray for the groups of Christians worshipping alongside us, but in other communities and other countries; for all who risk persecution for their faith; that we may support and encourage one another and serve the world as Christ's body, whatever the personal cost.
Pause
Take us, Father: **and use our lives.**

We pray for the leaders of the nations, all members of government and the financial and social advisers; that they may be led in the Spirit of Christ to work in harmony with God's will, so that his values are reflected in all policy making.
Pause
Take us, Father: **and use our lives.**

We pray for all in intensive care at the moment; all those undergoing emergency surgery; all women in labour, and their babies; all who are approaching death; that God's great healing love may pervade them and wash through their bodies and minds in a surge of peace.
Pause
Take us, Father: **and use our lives.**

We pray for ourselves; for a lessening of our selfishness and a broadening of our characters, until we are prepared to welcome, love and care for whoever is in need, and work hand in hand with God, wherever we are sent, and on his terms.
Pause
Take us, Father: **and use our lives.**

Celebrant   Father we thank you for your constant, loving provision for us, and want to become better able to do your will; please hear our prayers through the pleading of Jesus, your chosen one. **Amen.**

Ideas for Children

Bring along a bucket, spade and sandcastle flag, some school uniform and a wooden cross (not crucifix). First produce the seaside things, and talk with the children about what they make them think of; if we were all grandmas and grandpas, would we think differently? Or what if we were coastguards? Or crabs? The idea is to help them see that the same object produces different reactions according to who you are, and how you think.

Now show the uniform, and talk about how that makes different people react –

children?
teachers?
caretakers?
younger brothers and sisters?

Finally, show the cross. Tell them how Peter reacted when Jesus told him he would be put to death. Jesus saw it differently. Although it would be very painful and a terrible experience, he saw it as a good chance – an opportunity to show the people in the world (including us) how much he loved us.

> Did he have to go through with it?
> How could he have got out of it?

But that would mean choosing not to be human after all. If he didn't escape, even when he could, we would understand that he really did want to be with us in all the worst, horrible times, as well as the happy times.

Sing 'Think Big' or another song which combines God's great power and his love for us. Then give the children a cardboard cross each with this prayer:

Lord
if things seem hard
help me
see them
as
chances
to show
love

Music
Recorded Music

Chopin – *Piano concerto No. 2: slow movement*

'Live' Music

Breathe on me, breath of God (ONE, 70)
God be in my head (ONE, 171)
I am the Light (SONL, 20)
Take me, Lord (SONL, 92)
Without seeing you we love you (SONL, 13)

23rd Sunday in Ordinary Time

Theme
Lovingly correct one another

Loving our neighbour is the essence of the Law, and loving may sometimes mean caring enough to correct wrong behaviour. This can be done gently and discreetly, only being brought to public attention in the last resort. Often a quiet word in friendship is all that will be needed.

Penitential Rite

We recall the ways we have hurt and upset each other.
> (Silence)
> Lord, have mercy. **Lord, have mercy.**

We recall all our selfishness and mean-mindedness.
> (Silence)
> Christ, have mercy. **Christ, have mercy.**

We recall our lack of self-control.
> (Silence)
> Lord, have mercy. **Lord, have mercy.**

Notes on the Readings

Ezekiel 33:7-9

The sentry on duty must be alert and watchful, and has a great responsibility in that he can prevent enemies from gaining access. A false sentry therefore jeopardises many lives.

Ezekiel uses the image to express the seriousness of his task as God's spokesman or prophet. If he falls down on his job of warning and pointing out God's will for his people, he will be, in effect, opening wide the city gates to all that is evil. Having entrusted him with the spiritual well-being of

his people, God will hold him responsible for their death if he has made no effort to save them.

All too often we deceive ourselves by thinking that, so long as we have not done anyone any harm, we have been good Christians. But what God wants to know, is whether or not we have actually done anyone any good? If we have had opportunities to bring anyone to Christ, or change any evils in society, or right any injustices in our world, and have not taken those chances, then we are responsible for any destruction or catastrophe which results.

Does that sound too severe? Well, God has enormous love for his world – he created it to be good, and deeply desires for all those in it to be saved, not destroyed and lost. So he means business and enlists our help as responsible loving people who have pledged their lives to working with him. If we offer ourselves he will most certainly use us, because there is so much at stake. We cannot offer our lives and then plead deafness when volunteers are called for.

Romans 13:8-10

If we get into debt it usually means we have been overspending; and that is just what Paul suggests we do with love: overspend. We can be quite reckless and unreserved in this kind of spending, without quantifying areas of good investment with high returns, and without keeping reserves just in case.

For love, unlike money, increases with spending and makes us richer the more liberally we give it away. This is why it is the centre of all the Commandments, as loving our neighbours will prevent us from hurting their feelings, taking advantage of them or envying them.

Matthew 18:15-20

Sometimes when our feelings are hurt, or when someone has wronged us, our instinct is to talk about it with other people; partly to gain their support in justifying our grievance and partly to gather a bit of sympathy. (Perhaps too, if we are really honest, to get some of our own back on the one who has wronged us!)

Jesus does not advise this escalation of involvement. We know from personal and international experience that the more people who are involved in a dispute the more complex and unwieldy it becomes as feelings run high and other issues become grafted on to the original complaint.

So it is very practical, providing we do genuinely want a peaceful reconciliation, to keep the matter private and provide an escape route or an opportunity to step down without losing too much dignity. Obviously, if we are waiting, ready to point the finger and smugly crow over our offenders, they are not going to stand down or alter their behaviour gladly. It is vital that we practise the art of correcting in a non-judgemental way, and that art is a natural offshoot of Christlike love.

It may be that using humour is the way to defuse an explosive situation; or cheerfully acknowledging our own fault; or giving praise whenever it is due so that criticism is not the only time there is contact. Whatever our character, God's love will polish it till it reflects his own nature and works his will in all our relationships.

Bidding Prayers

Celebrant Our heavenly Father assures us that wherever two or three meet in his name he will be with them; in confidence, then, let us bring him our needs and cares.

Reader We pray that God's love will spill out through his Church to the world, filling all teaching, all advice and counsel, all correction and guidance.

Pause
Father, hear us: **renew us in love.**

We pray that God's Spirit of forgiveness and acceptance will permeate the social and political fabric of our world, till we are able to criticise gently and accept criticism honestly; discuss differences calmly and be prepared to negotiate rationally.
Pause
Father, hear us: **renew us in love.**

We pray that God's comfort and consolation will soothe those who are afraid or in great pain, refresh those who are mentally or physically exhausted and be a life line to those who are broken hearted or in despair.
Pause
Father, hear us: **renew us in love.**

We pray that the light of Christ may shine in our hearts to show us our faults and enable us to admit them; to shine through our lives in the way we treat each other, especially when we disagree or feel hurt.
Pause
Father, hear us: **renew us in love.**

Celebrant Father, we ask you to gather up these prayers of your people, through the merits of Jesus, our Saviour. **Amen.**

Ideas for Children

Use a tape recorder today, with three short conversations, illustrated by three cartoon pictures on large sheets of paper, all showing different ways of being corrected.

1.
Girl: Auntie, can you help me with my knitting?
Auntie: Certainly, Katie. What are you making?
Girl: A scarf for Teddy, but it seems a bit wiggly.
Auntie: Just let me find my glasses ... now, let's see. Oh, good gracious, you have been busy. It's got a bit tangled up, hasn't it! But I bet it will keep Teddy warm. Now, I'll just get this row right (sound of knitting needles) and set you off again.
Girl: Thanks, Auntie. Now I can do it. In...round ...through...off. I've done another stitch!
Auntie: Well done, Katie. You'll be knitting me some gloves before long!

2. Sound of two girls skipping.
Amanda and Rachel: Apple tart, apple tart. What is the name of your sweetheart? A...B...C...D

Sound of boy being a rocket.
Matthew: Whooooooosh shsh
Amanda: Hey, Matthew, you clumsy idiot. You stopped our skipping rope!
Matthew: Well it was in my orbit...bleep...bleep... bleep (into distance)
Rachel: Let's tell the others. He's always spoiling our game.
Amanda: Yes, let's. (sound of running) Hallo Catherine, hallo Claire. Matthew's just been messing up our skipping again.

Girls: Oh no, not again; he's always doing that etc.
Catherine: Let's tell the teacher about it.
Rachel: But then he'd get detention. Let's tell him off ourselves.
Girls: Yes! (sound of running) Matthew – we've got something to tell you.
Matthew: Eeeoow – screech. Oh yes, what?
Amanda: If you don't stop spoiling our games we'll spoil yours
Rachel: and tell of you.
Matthew: O.K., O.K., I only got into the wrong orbit. I've adjusted the instruments now. It won't happen again. 5 4 3 2 1 Blast off!!

3. **Teacher's voice:** Number one...3 sweets at 2p. each. Number two...if 8 biscuits are shared between 2 children, how many does each child eat? Number three...
Tony: (whispers) Hey, stop it Tracy – you're looking at my answers.
Tracy: (whispers) No I'm not.
Tony: You are, I saw you.
Teacher: ...5 balloons at 5p. each.
Tony: You *are* looking – isn't she, Paul?
Paul: Yes, you cheated, Tracy, we saw you.
Tracy: No I did *not.*
Tony: Excuse me please, Miss Carter.
Teacher: Number four...yes, Tony, what's the matter?
Tony: Please, Miss Carter, Tracy's cheating.
Others: Yes, she is, Miss Carter, we saw her.
Paul: She's a rotten cheat!
Teacher: Now then, Paul. There's no need for that! Tracy, bring your book out here. (footsteps) and you, Tony. Mm, well, it's certainly odd that you made the same mistakes Tony made, isn't it, Tracy? What's the point in copying – you make mistakes quite well on your own!
Tracy: I'm sorry, Miss Carter.
Teacher: Very well. Now sit here in the front where you can't see anyone's work. Number four... if three cars each have four wheels... (fade out)

Discuss each conversation, bringing out how we can correct people and still stay friends if we do it in a kind way. Jesus suggests:
1. Talk to them yourself.
2. Talk to them with a few others.
3. Tell someone in charge.

Have Jesus' plan drawn up clearly and let them take home their own copy of it for future use.

Music
Recorded Music

Elgar – *Cello concerto*

'Live' Music

Alleluia for forgiveness (SONL, 18)
But I say unto you (ONE, 75)
God forgave my sin (ONE, 175)
Make me a channel of your peace (ONE, 342)
Man of Galilee (ONE, 343)

24th Sunday in Ordinary Time

Theme
Unless we forgive, we shall not be forgiven

It is no good expecting God to be merciful and forgive us unless we are willing to behave in a similar way to those around us. We have a wonderful example of this costly forgiveness in Jesus, whose obedience, even to death, shows his immense love and brings us unending life.

Penitential Rite

Let us first have a time of silence for remembering and confessing our lack of love for God and for our neighbours.

1. Je - sus Christ, I love you; all that I am, all I can ev - er be I give you, Je - sus Christ, I love you; you have brough peace to me.

2. Jesus Christ, I need you.
   Time and again, you have forgiven me
   and healed me.
   Jesus Christ, I need you.
   Your life has set mine free.

Notes on the Readings

Ecclesiasticus 27:30-28:7

We are given sound, practical advice here, obviously based on a wide knowledge of human behaviour and yet not losing sight of idealism. Difficult though it may be, sometimes, to bring ourselves to forgive when the wounds are very deep and the pain very sharp, we still sense, albeit grudgingly, that our own wounds will fester unless we forgive those who made them.

As soon as we begin to bless, instead of curse, we find, like Coleridge's Ancient Mariner, that the heavy albatross drops away from our neck, and there is once more a breeze to sail by.

But if we are entrenched in resentment, or have been very badly hurt, how can we start forgiving? It is certainly no good pretending we have – that only drives the damage deeper into us, and may cause longterm harm.

The first step is to meet the problem face to face; we need to admit to ourselves that we really have been angered, upset, unjustly treated or whatever, and that we really do consider a particular person, group or government to blame for our distress.

Now it is out in the light of our consciousness we can either clutch it back to ourselves or offer it to God. It is not a bad idea to do this physically; we can kneel with our hands, palms down, as we face up to our grievances, and then slowly turn our hands over and imagine releasing them to God. We can visualise those who have wronged us kneeling beside us, and say the Jesus Prayer (*Jesus, Son of God, have mercy on me, a sinner*) over and over until we are able to feel we are praying not for, but with them; then the healing will begin. We shall notice a difference, a deepening of understanding and, eventually, a real love. They will have done us a favour, by giving us a chance to learn more of God's love, and offer him real sacrifice.

Romans 14:7-9

We are children of eternity; the life we live in Christ is never going to end. That is bound to affect the way we react to every situation, from everyday routines to momentous decisions. Some things will seem less important and some busyness unnecessary. Our lives may well become less complicated and less cluttered.

On the other hand, some things, like quickly forgiving, spending time cultivating our relationship with Christ, or making ourselves available during this first stage of our unending life – these will become more important to us.

For the realisation that we belong to a Lord who does not stop when our bodies wear out, gives us new freedom; it is as if, instead of being part of a photograph, we are in the actual location; we are like actors in a play whose lives are not finished at the final curtain, because their real lives continue outside the theatre.

Matthew 18:21-35

When we hear this story, we probably share the indignation of the fellow servants at such injustice. The issue is clear and easily seen.

Unfortunately, in real life things are rarely so glaringly black and white, and it is quite possible for us to find we have been behaving like the unforgiving servant without even realising it. Often, it happens when we are under pressure: if we have a deadline to meet, we shall probably take out our anxiety on those who hold us up; if money is scarce, we are more likely to flare up at anyone causing expensive damage.

Yet, when you think about it, such pressure is really caused by us keeping a tight grip on our lives instead of giving them away to Christ. If, when we feel the tension, we take a deep breath and remember that, as children of eternity, our lives are now spaces for God to work in, then the irritations and setbacks become opportunities to grow in patience, to spread God's kind of peace which the world lacks, and to put into practice his loving forgiveness.

Bidding Prayers

Celebrant My brothers and sisters in Christ, in
thankfulness for all God's blessings to us,
let us share with him our loving concern
for the Church and for the world
in which we live.

Reader We lay at his feet the painstaking,
persevering and often unnoticed work of all
who minister to the world in Christ's name;
that every effort towards goodness may be
blessed and made fruitful; and that
during times of weariness and despondency
Christ's servants may be upheld and
invigorated by his real, living presence.
Pause
Father, in our weakness:
we call on you for strength.

We lay at his feet every attempt at
peacemaking, every stand against injustice,
all who try to improve unsatisfactory
living conditions, all who work to relieve
suffering; that God's healing power
may spread throughout the world.
Pause
Father, in our weakness:
we call on you for strength.

We lay at his feet all who are in
prisons, borstals or detention centres;
all those who have been victims of
violence and aggression, and any who
have been bereaved; that where deep
wounds have been inflicted, whether
emotionally or physically, God may
bring his healing Spirit of forgiveness.
Pause
Father, in our weakness:
we call on you for strength.

We lay at his feet our own lives, our
energies, gifts, sorrows and joys;
that he may transform us into the
kind of people he wants us to be,
even if the transforming hurts.
Pause
Father, in our weakness:
we call on you for strength.

Celebrant Heavenly Father, we know that in you
we shall be safe; give us courage
to do your will gladly, and hear our
prayers in mercy, through Christ,
our Lord. **Amen.**

Ideas for Adults

Today's Gospel is excellent for acting out. You will need:
  a narrator
  the king
  2 or 3 servants
  the man who owes 10,000 talents
  the man who owes 100 denarii
  torturers

You can include a few props, such as a crown, some money, a rope and a whip, for instance.

When the narrator begins, have the king and his servants counting piles of money and looking at long bills. You can alter some of the narrative passages to be direct speech (such as when the king cancels the debt). Try it out first as it stands and wherever direct speech comes naturally, put it in.

At the end, all the actors would walk to the centre and say the last sentence together: 'And that is how your heavenly Father will deal with you unless you each forgive your brother from your heart.' This could either be performed at the Gospel, or just after a straight reading of the Gospel, in place of a homily.

Ideas for Children

Begin by asking them the question Peter asked Jesus – how often do they think they should forgive their brothers and sisters if they keep irritating/breaking toys/teasing etc. It will probably become clear that there is quite a gap between ideals and reality, so help them to be honest!

Then tell them how Peter asked Jesus the same question and how he explained his answer with a story. Tell the story, using different headgear for the various characters, some bills and play money and a pair of handcuffs, or something similar. You can grab hold of a volunteer when the second servant is nearly throttled. If the children have enjoyed an entertaining telling of the story, and been involved in it, they will remember it more.

So having told it and talked about what it says about the way we should behave, let all the children join in an acted version.

Music
Recorded Music

Ravel – *Pavane pour une infante defunte*

'Live' Music

A new commandment *(SONL, 34)*
God is love, his the care *(ONE, 178)*
My God, how wonderful thou art *(ONE, 357)*
When I survey the wondrous cross *(ONE, 610)*

Authority and Invitation
Questions for Discussion Groups
1. How did Jesus disappoint the expectations of many religious people?
2. How can we strike the right balance between being 'at home' with Jesus and dishonouring him by casual behaviour?

25th Sunday in Ordinary Time

Theme
God's values are different

Ordinary human standards, often based on survival, lead to ways which are quite different from the ways of God. All his justice is shot through with generosity, which the world often misunderstands. We have been called to live in him and he in us; that closeness of wills helps us to see things God's way, and reach out in love to others, as he does.

Penitential Rite

We have not looked with eyes of love,
Lord, have mercy. **Lord, have mercy.**

We have not spoken words of love,
Christ, have mercy. **Christ, have mercy.**

We have not lived out caring lives,
Lord, have mercy. **Lord, have mercy.**

Notes on the Readings

Isaiah 55:6-9

The people of Israel had slid slowly away from keeping the covenant, and for many a far lower standard of behaviour was accepted practice. Everyone else was doing the same, so it must be all right. The prophet breaks that illusion and shows them that to turn back to God now will mean completely abandoning their present way of life since it is wholly unacceptable to the character of a generous, unselfish God.

Adolescence is renowned for healthy rebellion against taught values. Such rebellion is vital if we are to make mature commitments thrashed out from our own experience and questing.

Far more dangerous, perhaps, is the slide towards habit and complacency which can set in very easily unless we are careful, especially if we are not often challenged in what we believe or why we do things. That is why frequent small changes are good for us; to be working for God we need to be flexible, and long periods of no change are bound to make us pretty stiff. Then, when we are eventually challenged, it will be quite painful to move!

Society's influences can be insidious, and we need to refer regularly to the Maker and his values if we are to avoid losing touch with what is of real importance in life.

Philippians 1:20-24, 27

This reading is a bit like choosing between two chocolates – it is difficult to select one because both have much to commend them. For there to be such a dilemma in Paul's mind, one thing is clear: his amazingly strong faith in Christ. He is really enjoying the prospect of living with Christ through eternity, once death has allowed him to, so that dying holds just as much promise and delight for him as living.

Do we get as excited about the prospect of death? Often, although we state our belief in a continuing life in Christ, we frantically make sure that the ageing process is not too obvious; and often a complex lying procedure is brought into play when a close relative is approaching death, with few people feeling able to talk about it honestly, let alone enjoy the excitement of preparing for it, rather as we prepare to go on holiday.

Perhaps it is time we tried to approach death with real faith in Christ's promise. It will surely be a wonderful and thrilling event, with the prospect of all the time in the world to do what makes our whole being filled with joy and deep-seated peace – praising the God who made us and who, through our lives, we have been getting to know; the God whose company makes us relaxed and happy. Death is not nearly so bad, after all – it is something to look forward to.

Matthew 20:1-6

Humans are often blinkered when it comes to justice. Generosity in justice rouses suspicions that we may be losing out, and that would never do. Being competitive, we usually feel rather grudging when we meet people who are good at everything and even look attractive as well;

we also spend time squashing these feelings in favour of good sportsmanship, but their existence cannot be denied.

In God's kind of justice there is joy for everyone who turns to him, especially those who looked as if they were heading for destruction but finally received God into their hearts, or those who have had such little help and guidance and yet turn to Christ.

If we are really living in Christ ourselves, we shall start to share his generous-hearted way of looking at things, rejoicing in people's gifts and the good use they are making of them, and delighting in newcomers to the Church bringing freshness and different outlooks to enrich and enliven the worship.

Bidding Prayers

Celebrant Fellow members of the body of Christ, let us bring before our loving Father all the needs and concerns of the Church and of our world.

Reader Let us pray that all Christians may daily renew their commitment to Christ, daily deepen their love for him and joyfully spread the good news of hope and unconditional inner peace.
Pause
Lord, hear us: **we offer you our lives.**

Let us pray that all over the world, voices speaking words of good sense, compassion and goodwill may be heard among the clamour of greed and self-interest, and influence all the nations in their decisions and policies.
Pause
Lord, hear us: **we offer you our lives.**

Let us pray that in hospitals, nursing homes and clinics, all healing may be blessed, and those who are ill in body or mind may experience the tender love God has for each of his children, all of whom are special to him.
Pause
Lord, hear us: **we offer you our lives.**

Let us pray that in every home and in every street God may be invited to live, so that family life is enriched, relationships strengthened, and rifts healed.
Pause
Lord, hear us: **we offer you our lives.**

Celebrant Merciful Father, you alone give meaning to our lives; help us live in closer communion with you, and accept these prayers, through Christ Jesus. **Amen.**

Ideas for Adults

Try a flower arrangement on the vineyard theme, with possibly a travel poster of vines growing in a warm climate, bunches of grapes and vine leaves. Ivy, or Russian vine would trail nicely if no one has grown grapes. A carafe of wine can be added, too, together with a few coins.

Ideas for Children

First discuss with the children what work there is in a vineyard, such as grape picking, treading the grapes, weeding, pruning etc. Everyone can act out each job.

Without telling the story first, begin acting it out, with one child taking the part of the landowner. Narrate it simply, and split the other children into five groups (or fewer if numbers are small) to be the workers hanging around the market place. Make sure that the first group is quite clear about how much money they will earn – let them shake hands on the deal. And make much of those who work hard during the hot blistering day.

When it comes to the giving out of wages, see how the children react to the amount the last workers are given, but don't give away the surprise. When the first workers receive their wages it will be interesting to see how they take it, and it should give rise to some lively discussion on what is fair and what is generous.

Bring out two points:

1. Jesus never gives up looking for us in the market place to see if we'd like to work for him.
2. If we do decide to give him our time and energy, then even if we were a long while getting there, Jesus will welcome us and we shall not lose the good reward at the end.

Help the children make a model of the vineyard and workers out of plasticine, and assorted boxes, paper, string, pipe cleaners etc.

Music
Recorded Music

Handel – Jeptha: 'Waft her, angels, to the skies'

'Live' Music

I want to build my life (SONL, 95)
Lord, thy word abideth (ONE, 333)
There is a world (ONE, 542)
This is what Yahweh asks of you (ONE, 563)

26th Sunday in Ordinary Time

Theme
Whenever we turn from our sin, God will forgive us

We are constantly falling, so we constantly need to turn back to God to put right our relationship with him. He is always ready to welcome us into his life again, but he cannot forgive us unless we recognise our need of his healing.

Penitential Rite

Use the song Lord, when I turn my back (SONL, 40).

Notes on the Readings

Ezekiel 18:25-28

There is always the danger that, after a heart-searching time leading to commitment, we may get lulled into the belief that everything will now be all right between us and God, since he has saved us from our sin.

This rather sobering reading reminds us that there is always the possibility of throwing away our treasure by rejecting integrity and living in sinfulness again.

As Christians we are never allowed the luxury of living off past goodness while we spend the rest of our lives indulging ourselves. Salvation is a living thing, concerned with the present and our behaviour at this particular moment. God only gives us one moment at a time, thankfully, and we can spend each one as it appears either working in conjunction with the God of love, or against him. We need to keep on our toes, then, and put matters right quickly if and when they go wrong.

Philippians 2:1-11

Paul urges us to aim for the sky – to model our behaviour on Christ Jesus. And what shines out in his life is that incredible humility which made him willing to obey and to expend everything at colossal cost in order to help and save those he loved.

So, too, we are encouraged, by the strength of Christ's love in us, to be outgoing, caring, generous and willing to put up with hardship and suffering in order to help and save others.

Internal bickering among Christian groups usually results from looking too much at each other and too little at Christ. If friction raises its ugly head, it is usually better if we break off everything we are doing for a while, and all look together at Christ. Then, having been touched again by his humility, open-mindedness, love and obedience, we shall be enabled to put our bickering right and heal our rifts, even if we still do not agree about a particular issue.

Matthew 21:28-32

It must have caused Jesus great sadness to find that the bastions of faith, the teachers and leaders of God's Law, were unable to see how far they were from God's will, even when it was pointed out to them in prophets like John the Baptist. They had catalogued their own interpretation of God so neatly and thoroughly that they could not recognise him in any other way.

How can we prevent ourselves from falling into the same trap? Partly by living as much as possible in the world by serving those who are in need, rather than only socialising with church groups and similarly-minded people. If we feel we are rather cut off, and the daily news seems to be talking about a world we do not live in, then that is the time to get more involved – as Christians we should be 'praying our newspapers', writing to our members of Parliament, offering our services in all the many ways, sometimes unpleasant but always rich in experience, which bring us into contact with real problems.

Also, we need to pray without always using set prayers, but honestly and simply approaching God and asking him to show us our faults. Beware, though! He will do this by providing us with all the situations in which we are at our worst, and, if we have forgotten our request, this can be unnerving, to put it mildly. At the same time it can be of tremendous value, however humiliating. And since God loves us, he will 'polish' us, even using our weaknesses until they, too, can be things of value in our renovated characters.

Bidding Prayers

Celebrant My brothers and sisters in Christ, bound in love, let us pray together for the needs we see around us.

    Reader For constant renewal, re-dedication and regeneration among all Christ's followers, so that God's love is clearly seen in their lives and can draw many to the joy of his peace.
Pause
Father, in mercy: **hear us and help us.**

For enlightenment and honesty in all
business transactions, decision making
and discussion, so that people really
listen to each other and work towards
agreement rather than personal gain.
Pause

Father, in mercy: **hear us and help us.**

For healing, reassurance and support
among all who are ill, injured,
confused or heavily burdened by sorrow,
so that they may be made whole, and
so that out of their pain there
may come some good.
Pause

Father, in mercy: **hear us and help us.**

For a greater desire to know and
love God, a deeper sense of his
presence, and more willingness to
make ourselves available for him to use.
Pause

Father, in mercy: **hear us and help us.**

Celebrant   Father, in you we hope and place
our trust; please accept these
prayers, and help us to do your
will, through Christ Jesus. **Amen.**

Ideas for Children

First of all give each child this hood to wear, which effectively produces narrow blinkered vision.

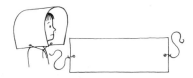

Wearing these hoods, they can try walking slowly about
the room, which has chairs dotted about. They will probably
bump into chairs or people from time to time. Discuss this
once they are de-hooded, and how we sometimes have
'hoods' of selfishness on without realising, and may hurt
others or not use ways we could help because we just do
not notice them. In prayer, ask God to help us walk through
this week without hoods, and see how much more useful
to each other we can be.

Now show them some traffic signs from the Highway
Code which show choice in the road ahead: i.e.

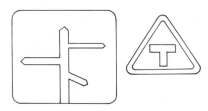

Explain how we can always make choices in our life road,
and show various objects which we can use either well or
badly, such as:

- a 10p piece (all on ourselves/share)
- an exercise book (doing our best/working
  carelessly)
- a clock (using our time/wasting other people's time
  to help)
- knife and fork (being greedy/offering salt and
  pepper or laying the table)

Give the children a card traffic sign to draw in, and on the
back write:

*Lord
when I
choose, help
me choose the
good way*

Music
Recorded Music

Mendelssohn – *Midsummer Night's Dream*

'Live' Music

I'll turn my steps to the altar of God *(SONL, 16)*
Lead, kindly light *(ONE, 297)*
Lord Jesus, think on me *(ONE, 327)*
Lord, when I turn my back on you *(SONL, 40)*
Oh the love of my Lord *(ONE, 430)*

27th Sunday in Ordinary Time

Theme
God the master of the vineyard

God puts great faith in us and provides us with everything
we need to produce good fruit. But if we abuse his gifts,
reject him and betray his trust, then the opportunities will
be given elsewhere. If, on the other hand, we trust and
lovingly commit ourselves to God, we shall experience his
lasting peace.

Penitential Rite

Through your love we can be renewed,
   Lord, have mercy. **Lord, have mercy.**

Through your life we can grow,
   Christ, have mercy. **Christ, have mercy.**

Through your tending we can bear fruit,
   Lord, have mercy. **Lord, have mercy.**

Notes on the Readings

Isaiah 5:1-7

In this lovely poetic passage is all the tenderness and
perseverance of a truly loving God, and all the sadness
and disappointment of being badly let down by his people
who have thwarted his plans for goodness by their sin.

At this stage, God's just retribution is threatened, for the
prophet is profoundly disturbed by the moral decline
among his people and acutely aware of how far they have
moved from keeping the covenant. As yet, there is little
evidence of God's mercy, only his perfect right to abandon
a people who have rejected their side of a binding promise.

But this acknowledgement of deserving nothing after behaving badly is a very necessary prelude to penitence,
from which confession springs, which in turn gives access
to forgiveness. We must not rush on to the assumed forgiveness of God too quickly; while there is no need to wallow,
there is certainly a need for real sorrowing penitence if we
are to be forgiven.

Philippians 4:6-9

Just as in Isaiah we saw a vision of things going wrong, so
here we see a vision of how good life can be when things

go right, and we work our lives in accordance with God. The result is peace of mind; delight at all that is beautiful; abundant creativity and constructive thinking; hope and order without nagging worries and anxieties. It is altogether an attractive and fulfilling life style. What is more, it is freely available to everyone.

Matthew 21:33-43

Both Jesus and his audience would have known the Isaiah story of the vineyard, and Jesus uses their knowledge with dramatic effect. Just as the chief priests and elders are settling comfortably into what they think is a story they know well, and in which they are the heroes who have remained within the Law, suddenly Jesus branches off and starts talking about tenants and ill-treatment of the owner's servants. They listen intently, indignation rising at every stage, and are unequivocal about the punishment for those wretches.

Then quietly, Jesus shows them that they themselves have behaved like the tenants. That is the moment when they are bound to be cut to the quick, resulting either in full and joyful repentance or in defensive hatred.

There was nothing wrong in their moral reasoning throughout the story – they just could not see their own behaviour in that light.

Bidding Prayers

Celebrant We belong to our heavenly Father, who loves us. Let us pray to him now for all the concerns of our world.

Reader Let us pray for all areas where the presence of the Church challenges social evils and corruption, and lives are endangered by speaking out.

Pause

Lord, hear us: **keep us living in you.**

Let us pray for areas of tension, unrest and violence in our world; for all in positions of power and influence in international affairs.

Pause

Lord, hear us: **keep us living in you.**

Let us pray for those who are tortured, neglected or badly treated; for those mentally or physically handicapped and for their families; for the babies being born, especially where there are complications.

Pause

Lord, hear us: **keep us living in you.**

Let us pray for our homes, and all the homes in this parish, particularly where there is friction, distress, loneliness or poverty; for our own relatives and friends, neighbours and those with whom we work or travel.

Pause

Lord, hear us: **keep us living in you.**

Celebrant Father, we thank you for your steadfast love, and ask you to accept our prayers, through Christ our Lord. **Amen.**

Church Decoration

Following the vineyard theme, an arrangement of flowers can include grapes and vine leaves and a bottle of wine.

Offering of Gifts

In the procession of gifts, corn and grapes can be brought up at the same time as the bread and wine, and placed near the altar. Afterwards they can be given to someone in the parish who is unwell. This reinforces the importance of us, as tenants, giving the produce of our 'vineyard' to the master.

Ideas for Children

Tell today's Gospel story using the model that was made two weeks ago (see 25th Sunday in Ordinary Time) and either use more plasticine people or toy people from a construction set.

When you have told the story, ask them Jesus' question about what the master would do to the servants. Then read to them from a Bible (or let them find it themselves) what the reaction of the chief priests and elders was. In discussion, draw out the similarities between the master and God, his servants and the prophets, and his son and Jesus. Give them these certificates of tenure, which they can fill in and colour.

Music
Recorded Music

J.S. Bach – Trio sonata No. 2: *Largo*

'Live' Music

Christ is made the sure foundation *(ONE, 82)*
Forth in thy name, O Lord, I go *(ONE, 148)*
I am the vine *(ONE, 227)*
Oh, come to the water *(SONL, 67)*

28th Sunday in Ordinary Time

Theme
We are invited to God's banquet

The climax of God's creative act in making, sustaining and redeeming the world, is that all the created order will join in a celebration to end all celebrating; a joyful feast or banquet where there is no more sorrow or distress, but a common praising and thanksgiving. Of course, we are free to turn down the invitation, and if we choose to accept, we must do things God's way – otherwise we shall not be included.

Penitential Rite

Lord, you have called us to share in the banquet,
    Lord, have mercy. **Lord, have mercy.**

Lord, make us worthy of our calling,
    Christ, have mercy. **Christ, have mercy.**

Lord, your grace is sufficient for us,
    Lord, have mercy. **Lord, have mercy.**

Notes on the Readings

Isaiah 25:6-10

Having berated the people for their sin and disrespect to a loving God, the prophet has brought them to the point of repentance; and now God's loving nature reveals itself in his willingness to forgive, take back and prepare the homecoming celebration, very much as the father of the prodigal son was happy to do.

Penitence and forgiveness are wonderfully joyful, involving relief, lightness of heart, refreshment and liberation. We sense great well-being, a lack of worry, and a security which, unlike the effect of alcohol or drugs, will not wear off. God's forgiveness celebration has no adverse side effects, either.

Philippians 4:12-14, 19-20

Since Paul's well-being is not dependent on material comforts or possessions, he can enjoy both richness and poverty, and be just as happy whether he has little or plenty.

Our society is highly materialistic, which makes it difficult to latch on to Paul's outlook; we are pressurised constantly by the media, advertising and social expectations, to be concerned about achieving better material comforts for ourselves and others, and to see health and wealth as necessary for happiness.

To train ourselves to delight in whatever God provides, it sometimes helps to make ourselves say, 'thank you, Lord' every time we miss a bus, spill our best whisky, cannot afford a new coat or use our holiday savings on repairing the car. Thankfulness is a habit, and when we remember to rejoice in the not-having as much as the having, we shall be much richer and, incidentally, happier.

Matthew 22:1-14

There is no question of people not being invited to God's celebrations – no one is left out or ignored. But invitations demand a response, and many of those invited have chosen not to come. The hollow, terrible words: 'but they were not interested' are immensely sad. From the children of Israel onwards, people have not been interested in coming to share the celebration that would make them happier and more fulfilled than anything else, they prefer to concentrate, with heads down, on immediate gratification, the temporary accumulation of comforts and self-centred ambitions, and throw away the chance of a life-time.

Others agree to come, but do not take seriously enough the honour of being invited by the Author of all life and creation. If we are casual and half-hearted, disrespectful and arrogant in God's presence, we cannot expect him to welcome us to his celebrations: it is, after all, a tremendous privilege to have been invited.

Bidding Prayers

Celebrant My brothers and sisters in Christ, our heavenly Father invites us to make our requests known to him; let us therefore pray to him now.

Reader We pray for all those involved with home visiting, preparation for baptism and marriage, for all chaplains working in schools, prisons, hospitals or factories; that they may be given the right words to say, and be channels for God's peace to flow through, out into the world.
Pause
Heavenly Father: **hear your children call.**

We pray for all who have been chosen to act on behalf of others – for all members of parliament and local councillors, for international delegates and representatives; that they may be true to those who elected them, and responsible and honest in their work.
Pause
Heavenly Father: **hear your children call.**

We pray for the very poor, the malnourished and starving, the badly housed and the homeless; for all who suffer and find life a burden; that they may be refreshed and provided for, both through immediate aid and long term planning.
Pause
Heavenly Father: **hear your children call.**

We pray that our own lives may be more ordered and peaceful, more firmly rooted in Christ's love, and better able to express his tenderness and care.
Pause
Heavenly Father: **hear your children call.**

Celebrant Lord, in thankfulness for all your rich blessings to us every day, we offer you our prayers, through Christ our Saviour. **Amen.**

Church Decoration

One of the flower arrangements can echo the theme of a banquet in the Isaiah reading and the Gospel with candles, wine, napkins and fruit included in it, and perhaps a crisp table cloth under it. It could be spot-lit during the readings. On a gilt-edged invitation card should be elegantly written: 'You have prepared a banquet for me.'

Ideas for Children

Today's Gospel is good to use for making a 'television' programme. The television is a cereal packet with two wooden spoons for winding the 'film' on, and the story is displayed in a series of pictures on a long strip of paper, marked into numbered frames. Either the words can be written underneath each picture, or they can be read on to tape with a clicker between each frame so that the winder knows when to do his bit.

Tell the children the story first and have each part written on a separate card. These are then given out in order to the children, who work on a particular frame, either drawing or colouring in the appropriate picture. It may be easiest to work on the floor, or to stick separate sheets on to a strip when they are finished.

The finished story can be presented to others, perhaps during visits to the elderly, or those in hospital. It can be kept as useful resource material.

Music
Recorded Music

Tchaikovsky – *Swan Lake*

'Live' Music

At the Lamb's high feast we sing *(ONE, 49)*
Come and be filled *(SONL, 59)*
My God and is thy table spread *(ONE, 356)*
The Lord's my shepherd *(ONE, 533)*

29th Sunday in Ordinary Time

Theme
God alone is supremely worthy of our praise

God, the instigator and upholder of all things, is all-powerful; even those who do not know him are used by him and eventually all creation will honour his name. All other powers and dominations are subordinate to God, and we must be careful to order our priorities so that God comes first. Our dedicated allegiance to the God of love will bring joy and hope into our lives.

Penitential Rite

God alone can forgive sins,
  Lord, have mercy. **Lord, have mercy.**

You, alone, have the words of eternal life,
  Christ, have mercy. **Christ, have mercy.**

Lord, to whom else could we go?
  Lord, have mercy. **Lord, have mercy.**

Notes on the Readings

Isaiah 45:1, 4-6

The powerful Cyrus was about to break Babylon's rule; perhaps this would be the way in which the people of Israel could be freed from Babylonian captivity. It seemed to the prophet that Cyrus would actually be used for God's will to be accomplished.

It is certainly true that God works through many and varied means, using a far wider spectrum than those who know him. They may not believe in him, but he believes in them; and if many of us pray fervently for all those who lead and influence in national and international affairs, God's plans will be put into practice in the most unexpected ways and through surprising people.

For God is more powerful than any individual or group, no matter how important or aggressive it may temporarily seem. Even in the worst horrors of war and disease, some shaft of hope and goodness lights up among the terrible shadows; even evils can be used by the one creative and caring God to bring about the birth of hope and understanding. This is because our God reigns – over all time, in all places and throughout all existence, whether excellent or appalling.

Thessalonians 1:1-5

The Thessalonian Christians do not just know *about* God – they know God, and that is what makes all the difference in their lives. They are showing the extent of their faith in everything they do and in their attitude and outlook, even when things look bleak, because they are happy to persevere in hope.

No amount of Bible study or recitation of prayers and scripture can, on its own, give us such close relationship with God. It will remain just words, just knowledge, unless the power of God's life (or Spirit) breathes into us to lift us, and the words we use, into living fellowship with him.

The only thing we need for this to happen is an open-heartedness which is prepared to accept Christ's love and the changes his presence will bring. Then our lives, as well as our lips, will sing his praise, even if we are not aware of it.

Matthew 22:15-21

The Pharisees have been faced directly with the need to turn their expectations and thinking upside down if they are to be saved. But they have, like Dives, the wealthy man, too much to lose, and so begin scheming for the downfall of this man who threatens their comfortable lives.

Cleverly, they lay the trap for Jesus to fall into: Roman taxes are a volcanic issue and if he denounces them the authorities will be enraged; but if he does not, his integrity as a Jewish teacher will be in question. The scheming is particularly ironic, since it hinges on the forfeiting of esteem – the very thing the Pharisees themselves could not cope with.

So Jesus not only confounds them, but also uses the situation to teach, if they will only listen. The real question is one of priorities, and whereas what Caesar both represents and requires is money, or materialism, what we owe God is on a different plane altogether – more costly, more demanding, more far-reaching, but also more fulfilling and rewarding.

Bidding Prayers

Celebrant My dear companions of the Way of Christ,
as we journey through life let us lift
our eyes to the Father who loves us, and
share with him our needs and cares.

Reader We commend to his love all who spend
their lives working to spread the Good
News of Christ; that their words and
behaviour may sow seeds which develop
and yield good fruit, so that many
who are lost or weary find joy and
peace of mind in following Jesus.
Pause
Heavenly Father: **we put our trust in you.**

We commend to his love the leaders and
figureheads of every nation, all
opposition leaders and all who have
political and social influence; that
God's will may be done through them,
and our world liberated from
all that is evil.
Pause
Heavenly Father: **we put our trust in you.**

We commend to his love all who are
in exile, all refugees and those
imprisoned unjustly; those who are
in bad health and those in constant,
wearying pain; that their suffering
may be in some way a channel for
Christ's love, and that all who suffer
may be comforted and made whole.
Pause
Heavenly Father: **we put our trust in you.**

We commend to his love all those near
and dear to us, and especially those
from whom we are separated by distance
or death; that in all our relationships

the sparkle of God's loving may shine,
and our limits of loving care may
stretch to embrace more and more
of God's family.
Pause
Heavenly Father: **we put our trust in you.**

Celebrant In joy, we offer you our prayers and
our praise, Father, through Christ
Jesus our Saviour and our brother. **Amen.**

Ideas for Children

Jesus' lifetime can sometimes appear like a fairy tale to children, and today's Gospel provides a good opportunity to fasten it firmly in history, with the Romans.

Have a book on the Romans (the local library will have some available) and show the children how they lived, and which countries they ruled. Point out that the people of those countries (Britain as well as Israel) disliked paying taxes to foreign rulers. Also show the children some pictures of Roman coins, and some of our own coins to see whose head is on those.

Now tell the story of the Pharisees' clever question, pointing out how difficult it was for Jesus to answer without getting into deep trouble, either with his people or the Romans. Tell them how Jesus answered, and have this answer written out clearly ready to display: 'Give back to Caesar what belongs to Caesar – give back to God what belongs to God.' They can all say this together, or even learn it for next week.

What does belong to God, that we can give him back?
- our time
- our life
- our thanks
- our praise. . . *ourselves!*

Sing '*Father, you have given us a bright new day*' or '*The clock tells the story of time God gives us*' (MWTP).

Music
Recorded Music

Scottish or Irish melodies played by James Galway

'Live' Music

All people that on earth do dwell *(ONE, 27)*
Immortal, invisible *(ONE, 242)*
Praise, glory, to you, O Lord *(SONL, 71)*
Praise to the Lord, the almighty *(ONE, 456)*

30th Sunday in Ordinary Time

Theme
Love God and love your neighbour

The greatest and most important command is that we love God with our whole being, and this will lead us on to love our neighbours, and all those in need, with as deep a concern as we have for ourselves. All other laws and rules of behaviour, including good manners, really reflect an attitude of caring concern. Love for God and love for one another go hand in hand, since loving God will make us into more loving people.

Penitential Rite

We come to your love for healing,
Lord, have mercy. **Lord, have mercy.**

We lean on your love for strength,
Christ, have mercy. **Christ, have mercy.**

We long for your love to transform us,
Lord, have mercy. **Lord, have mercy.**

Notes on the Readings

Exodus 22:20-26

For most people, it helps to have an ideology worked out in practical terms, with everyday examples given. That is really what many of these rules are doing – explaining the meaning of loving one's neighbour in a practical way.

The advice is a recipe for a compassionate and caring society, appealing to the 'how would *you* like it if. . .' syndrome. One of the advantages of any suffering is that it can increase the capacity for understanding and compassion; often, sadly, it hardens the desire for revenge instead.

But God's nature is full of pity – sympathetic and concerned. That is how we must be, too, consciously using any painful experiences we may have to deepen our love and understanding of others.

1 Thessalonians 1:5-10

When people start abandoning their lives to God, word spreads fast, because onlookers can really see the difference! The way we act proclaims the way we think, and where our treasure is; so if money, or promotion, or clothes or sport have been filling our conversations and time recently, it might be an idea to spend some while in stillness with God re-appraising our values and re-ordering our commitments financially and socially.

With Christ at the centre of our lives the pressure is off and we can be happier, more actively involved, less self-conscious and more able to laugh at ourselves, able to enjoy life and delight in the fun of God's creation yet at the same time being more affected by its injustices and sorrows. In a world where personal success and financial security rate highly, such behaviour is likely to be noticed and stir the dissatisfied with the possibility of hope – that, perhaps, there is meaning after all.

Matthew 22:34-40

It all stems, then, from a right relationship with God. We owe everything about us to him, and as we acknowledge our debt in thankfulness we are accomplishing his will and allowing his ideas to be fulfilled.

No number of rules for good conduct can hope to include every eventuality, so, rather than thinking in terms of rules, it is better to start with loving God and go on to loving others in his way. That will drop us in at the deep end because it has no limited policies or marked boundaries, but it is much more useful because it will always put the help where it is needed, and in a way which is not deprecating or insulting to those who are helped.

Bidding Prayers

Celebrant My brothers and sisters, humbled by the wonder of God's love for us all, let us lay before him all our concerns.

Reader We lay before him all Christians who are troubled by doubt, all who have lapsed from worshipping or whose prayer life is threatened by over-busy lives; that they may know the nearness of Christ, and be touched by his calm and stillness.
Pause
Father of all: **we love you very much.**

We lay before him the heated arguments,
industrial action, blinkered vision
and stubbornness of our world; that
the power of God's love may soften,
ease and coax us all to be more
understanding, wise and forgiving.
Pause
Father of all: **we love you very much.**

We lay before him widows and
widowers and orphans, all broken
families and all the socially rejected;
those who are disfigured or
incapacitated, and those who persevere
in the daily tending of a physically
or mentally sick relative; that the
warmth of God's love may radiate all
aspects of life, even the most painful,
to heal, comfort and transform.
Pause
Father of all: **we love you very much.**

We lay before him the areas of our
own lives which are in shadow and
darkness; that in the light of God's
love we may see our faults and
weaknesses more clearly, and notice
the needs around us more readily,
so that in Christ's strength we can
show love in practical ways.
Pause
Father of all: **we love you very much.**

Celebrant Father, we ask you to work your love
in our lives, and accept these needs
we have brought you, through Christ,
our Lord. **Amen.**

Ideas for Adults

If there is no Good Neighbour scheme operating in the area, today is a good time to launch it. Have a chart with the names of roads written on it, and during the week ask people to sign up against the road for which they will take responsibility. Any needs which become apparent can be met more effectively, matching needs with those prepared to offer help in different ways. The list of helpers should be duplicated and made available for each street representative, and help can range from shopping and cleaning to reading, ironing or baby sitting.

This is a fairly simple means of enabling Christians to carry out practical care. The lists can be brought up and the work blessed at the offering of the gifts.

Ideas for Children

Have written out a list of the Ten Commandments; we cannot build on these unless children are familiar with them and how Moses received them from God.

But before you draw their attention to these, talk about good manners, and rules they have been told at home and at school. These can be added to a poster entitled 'Remember your manners' and might include:

Keep to the left in the corridor.
Don't speak with your mouth full.
Please and thank you.
Say 'hallo' and 'goodbye'.
Don't interrupt.
Offer food.
Turn T.V. down or off if visitor comes.
Open classroom door to teacher.

Stand at side for people to pass.
Wait your turn in a queue.
Point out that these are ways of caring for others and respecting them. If you love someone, you do this anyway. The rules remind you to act lovingly however you feel about the other person.

Now show them God's Commandments, and Jesus' way of simplifying them: (1) Love God and (2) Love your neighbour as yourself, drawing lines from the first four and the last six to make it clear.

Give the children card circles on which to write the two Commandments, one one each side. These can be coloured and decorated and taken home to remember.

Music
Recorded Music

Grieg – *Lyric Suite*

'Live' Music

A new commandment *(ONE, 39)*
I give my hands *(ONE, 253)*
I now no longer live *(SONL, 6)*
Peace, perfect peace *(ONE, 445)*

31st Sunday in Ordinary Time

Theme
Living our faith without hypocrisy

Preaching the Good News is all very well, but our message will be far more effective if our words are borne out in loving action. In fact, we can seriously lead people astray if we, who speak of belonging to Christ, behave in an uncaring way. As Christians we gladly divest ourselves of all rank and are happy to become servants in order to spread God's saving love among all people. The living power of God is then able to work in every area our lives touch.

Penitential Rite

You are ready to welcome us back with joy,
Lord, have mercy. **Lord, have mercy.**

You touch our lives and we are charged with life,
Christ, have mercy. **Christ, have mercy.**

You offer us the joy of being forgiven,
Lord, have mercy. **Lord, have mercy.**

Notes on the Readings

Malachi 1:14-2, 8-10

It was a measure of how far the people had strayed, that even the priests were slack and corrupt. Their fault was that they had stopped bothering to give God of their best; their careless, casual slackness showed how little they honoured and respected God, and when they, the teachers, behaved like this, the whole people would be led astray. There is a world of difference between the informality which results from love and trust, and the carelessness which results from a lack of any respect or reverence.

Both in private prayer and public worship it is surely of utmost importance that God in his greatness is highly revered; we must never give him less than our best, however that is expressed.

1 Thessalonians 2:7-9, 13

Here, in contrast, we see an example of teaching and example coinciding: real, deep belief in what we preach means rolling our sleeves up and getting to work, spending time and energy because it is fervently believed to be worthwhile. That kind of preaching gets people interested because they can see it is genuine – and, quite rightly, everyone is sceptical of hypocrisy.

An actor knows that, if his audience is to believe in the character he is playing, he must first really believe in the part himself. The same enthusiasm fires people wherever a charismatic leader emerges.

Christ's followers, if they have the 'charisma' or life of Christ living in them, will be able to teach and draw others to peace and joy by their love in action.

Matthew 23:1-12

The hypocrisy of the Pharisees really sticks in Jesus' gullet, because their damage is so great. God loves his people tenderly, longs to guide them and encourages every move in the right direction. Yet here are his own spokesmen proclaiming, by their cruel, vain and pompous attitudes, that God gives hard rules without help, and impossible demands without compassion. No wonder it galls Christ to see his beloved sheep led astray and left shepherdless by those who are assumed to be ambassadors for God!

All of us, who are privileged to be members of Christ's body, must be constantly alert, rigorous in self-examination, flexible and open-minded, so that at the first hint of hypocrisy, either individually or communally, we can be checked, and start again. This step is obviously going to be humiliating, but if we put it off it will get harder, not easier, with more damage done to the very people God loves and longs to help – which includes us.

Bidding Prayers

Celebrant We are all brothers and sisters in Christ; as children of God, our heavenly Father, let us draw near and tell him of our needs and cares, asking for his help and blessing.

Reader Let us ask God to bless and guide all those who serve him; to inspire their teaching, nudge their memories, instruct them through their failures and mature them through their experiences, so that in all their undertakings, God's will may be done.
Pause
Merciful Father:
work on us till we shine with love.

Let us ask God to direct and guide the people of the world towards harmony and peace, mutual respect and appreciation of one another's cultures and traditions; so that we are prepared to learn from each other.
Pause
Merciful Father:
work on us till we shine with love.

Let us ask God to ease the burdens of those who are bowed down with grief, depression, pain or guilt; to encourage the timid and frightened; refresh all who are overworked or have not been able to sleep; and break down all barricades of hatred and revenge.
Pause
Merciful Father:
work on us till we shine with love.

Let us ask God into our homes and places of work, so that all our friendships and business transactions, shopping and leisure times may be opportunities for rejoicing in his love and spreading his peace.
Pause
Merciful Father:
work on us till we shine with love.

Celebrant Father, in your love accept our prayers, through Christ our Saviour. **Amen.**

Ideas for Children

Using two old white socks, make two sheep puppets to use today. Tuck the heel in between your thumb and fingers for the mouths.

One of the sheep is wearing a hat, and is very pompous, telling the other one where he can't eat grass, which flowers are bad for him, how scruffy he looks, but how he isn't allowed to use the river except on Thursdays etc. – any rules which make life difficult and which do not affect the sheep giving the orders because as 'head sheep' he is 'important'. (He might insist on being called 'master'.)

The children should be able to see an image of someone who is smug and hypocritical, with the ordinary sheep ending up without really knowing where he is.

Now tell the children how Jesus is very sad to see people behaving like the 'Master Sheep' because he loves all his sheep and wants to help them in ways of kindness and goodness. Smug sheep don't help, especially when they claim to be chosen by the shepherd. If we are bossy, smug or unkind, others may think Jesus, our shepherd, is like that!

Help the children to make a sock puppet which wears a badge saying 'I love Jesus'. But they must only wear the puppet to do something loving and kind, such as carrying, putting away, laying the table etc. That way, their sheep will always put into practice what he says.

Music
Recorded Music

Mozart – *Clarinet quintet in A major*

'Live' Music

Blest are the pure in heart *(ONE, 66)*
If we only seek peace *(SONL, 76)*
Let us break bread together on our knees *(ONE, 307)*
My God, accept my heart this day *(ONE, 355)*
This day God gives me *(ONE, 555)*

32nd Sunday in Ordinary Time

Theme
Be prepared for Christ's second coming

The highest form of wisdom is to acknowledge God as the supreme power in our universe and in our lives, and even the yearning to do so is the beginning of an understanding which will eventually be made clear when Christ comes again in glory. No one else's goodness or perseverance will help us be ready: we must each take personal responsibility for being prepared. At that last day both the living and those who have already died will rise from the dead with Christ – we must keep ourselves ready.

Penitential Rite

Father, you have power both through life and death,
  Lord, have mercy. **Lord, have mercy.**

Jesus, by your death you have won the victory over sin,
  Christ, have mercy. **Christ, have mercy.**

Spirit, you lead us in wisdom and truth,
  Lord, have mercy. **Lord, have mercy.**

Notes on the Readings

Wisdom 6:12-16

In this lovely passage, wisdom means far more than know-ledge or shrewdness. It is the essence of God's love and understanding, which goes beyond reasoning and leads us to an extraordinary inner peace and tranquility: it is the kind of insight which is possessed by quiet-centred, prayer-ful people. They may not be particularly well-read or know-ledgeable, but they seem able to touch people's real needs and questions, however much they have been uncon-sciously camouflaged. One thinks of Mother Julian, Francis or Anthony, to whom many were drawn for counsel and advice: what they possessed was God's wisdom.

The manuals and handbooks available for helping us discover wisdom are partly the lives and thoughts of such great saints, but our most useful handbook is simply time spent in the presence of God. It is not time-wasting to do nothing but wait on God for a regular space of half-an-hour or so. It is the most valuable activity we can engage in, and will allow us access to the deep pools of wisdom at the heart of all being.

1 Thessalonians 4:13-18

Since, in the early Church, everyone expected the second coming to be imminent, some people became worried that those who died before it happened would miss out. Paul reassures them that both the living and the dead will see Christ coming in glory. Death is not the end of living but the beginning of a new dimension. We need not worry about our loved ones, or feel they are no longer in existence, because they are safe in the loving protection of Jesus, and at the last day, we and they will see the accomplishment of all things – the coming of God's everlasting kingdom.

Matthew 25:1-13

As we have seen, the early Christians expected Jesus to come in a matter of weeks or months. He did not, and here we are, nearly 2,000 years later, still waiting.

So this story of long waiting, yet still being prepared, is very useful. There is no doubt in the bridesmaids' minds about whether the bridegroom would come or not, and they had all brought their burning lamps with them. The only difference is that the five sensible ones had an extra oil supply with them so that their lamps would not go out after the initial burst of enthusiastic preparations.

We do need to refuel regularly if we are to stay 'alight', alert and ready to welcome Jesus. But we must do it our-selves – it is no good resting on other people's prayer lives, good works or depth of commitment to worship and care. Just because we are all members of the Church does not mean that we can jog casually along, not getting too involved while others dedicate their lives to serving Christ. If we do this, we shall find that our lamps are out when we need them most, and no borrowing of beautiful lives is possible.

In other words, how we live every second and every day determines how bright our lamps will be. Seconds may not seem very important, but life in Christ is built painstakingly, piece by piece, and a few grand gestures followed by months or years of complacency will not enable us to be made new in Christ. If we treasure each moment as an

opportunity to refuel, offering whatever we are doing quite consciously to be used for God's praise and glory, then, when we meet him face to face, he will recognise us as loyal friends, and welcome us with joy.

Bidding Prayers

Celebrant My brothers and sisters, let us pray together in the Spirit of Christ, for the needs of the Church and of the world.

Reader Let us pray that the Church and all its members may never become stagnant but flow forward in the direction God wants it to go, true to Christ's teaching, unswerving in loyalty to him and undistracted by worldly values.
Pause
Lord, give us wisdom:
  to know and love you more.

Let us pray that we may tend and care for the world God has given us, that its food and riches may be shared and wisely used, and its resources safely and thoughtfully deployed without waste or destruction.
Pause
Lord, give us wisdom:
  to know and love you more.

Let us pray that all those who are ill, injured or distressed may be touched by the healing hand of Jesus and be made whole, comforted by his presence.
Pause
Lord, give us wisdom:
  to know and love you more.

Let us pray that we may be more watchful, preparing ourselves more thoroughly day by day to meet our Lord, face to face.
Pause
Lord, give us wisdom:
  to know and love you more.

Celebrant Father, whose character is full of mercy and compassion, accept these prayers for the sake of Jesus, our Saviour. **Amen.**

Ideas for Adults

Have a wedding theme to a flower arrangement, with lengths of ribbon, some confetti and a little posy of flowers among the main display.

Ideas for Children

Tell the children today's Gospel, making clear that it is a story Jesus told, not a real event. To help in the telling, have two strips of card, each with five bridesmaids on it.

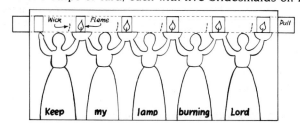

Five have extra oil in a flask, five do not. At the point where the lamps go out, pull the strip along, so that the wicks show instead of the flames.

When they have heard the story and what it tells us about keeping ourselves ready for Jesus, the children can make their own strip of bridesmaids with flames that go out. Write on each: 'Keep my lamp burning Lord' with one word on each bridesmaid.

Dance of the Bridesmaids

Ten bridesmaids, with long dresses and flowers in their hair, carry their lamps during this dance. The lamps are small bowls with nightlights inside.

As the music begins they dance up the centre in two lines of five, doing basically a quick waltz step but free within this to turn and sway or join hands sometimes in pairs. They adjust their hair, smooth each other's dresses, check their lamps in an atmosphere of excited preparation.

Gradually they start to fidget and yawn, resting in different positions – some leaning, some sitting, some lying down. The lamps go out.

From the back comes the trumpet call to announce that the bridegroom will soon be here. The bridesmaids nudge each other awake, flutter about getting neat again, and then the five with extra oil mime their refuelling. The other five kneel and beg them to lend some oil, which the first five refuse to do, pointing out where the oil can be bought.

The five foolish bridesmaids scamper (in contrast to their waltzing) off to buy oil, as the bridegroom, bride and guests come in grand procession up the centre.

The wise bridesmaids dance down to greet him, curtsey and light the way to the centre front. As the bridegroom goes to 'close' the door, the foolish bridesmaids run up with their lamps alight again, but are turned away and walk to the back, dejected, and looking wistfully behind them at the others enjoying themselves.

Handel's *Water Music* has three sections which reflect the three moods of this parable.

Music
Recorded Music

Holst – *Planet Suite: Neptune*

'Live' Music

Father you are living in us now *(SONL, 65)*
Jesus, gentlest Saviour *(ONE, 276)*
Jesus, my Lord, my God, my all *(ONE, 283)*
Let all that is within me *(ONE, 301)*
Save us, O Lord *(SONL, 53)*

33rd Sunday in Ordinary Time

Theme
Use your talents

Our life, energy, strength and gifts are given to us by our Creator to use for good. If we are wise stewards we will further God's glory and hasten the coming of his kingdom. Like the valuable wife in Proverbs, we shall be valuable members of the family of Christ. However little we feel we have to offer, we need to use and develop it, not hide it away.

Penitential Rite

Use the song *Take me, Lord* (SONL, 92).

Notes on the Readings

Proverbs 31:10-13, 19-20, 30-31
In spite of the fact that few wives work assiduously at their distaffs these days, there is something in this account of the perfect wife which has a lot to say to all modern members of God's family.

It is the thoughtful care for others, shown in work; or, as Kahlil Gibran puts it, 'work is love made visible'. A carefully prepared meal, a well-ironed shirt or a newly decorated room – whoever does these things and whoever they are done for, tell a great deal about love.

There is little value in love being expressed in words if no demonstration of practical caring is ever forthcoming. Christianity is a 'body' religion; after all, our God wore a body in order to show his love for us. And, using our bodies to work, carefully and lovingly, we are making our lives a prayer of praise.

1 Thessalonians 5:1-6
Since God comes unexpectedly, it is a good idea to get into the routine of being ready, living each day as if it is the Day of the Lord when Christ comes in glory to judge the world and to draw together all the threads of love in unimaginable joy.

It is not a question of dashing out to take on extra 'religious' activities, but rather of doing ordinary things simply and faithfully, offering them to Jesus.

Actually, it usually works the other way round; if, as we start the pile of greasy washing up, we repeat in the silence of our hearts: 'I want to do this for you, Jesus', then we find ourselves doing the job in a kind of 'reverent' way, and we can end up refreshed instead of weary.

The principle of work being prayer has been cultivated in the monastic life for centuries, but there is no reason why it should not be extended to those of us living in the world's bustle.

Matthew 25:14-30
Some people keep their best china permanently behind glass doors; some have precious jewellery in bank vaults instead of round their necks; some keep a large 'nest-egg' of money and rarely dip into it, even if the carpet is threadbare.

All these precautions are taken because greatly valued things are precious, and we want to preserve them from damage. But the need to preserve can get out of hand, until, since we are not using something, we come to value its value, rather than itself. And then, in a way, its possible use is being wasted.

Gifts and talents are often under-used and hidden away as well. Sometimes this is because of an inverted vanity, rather than real modesty: perhaps other people will not appreciate our gift sufficiently – they may even laugh at our efforts.

Sometimes we hold back because our sophisticated society brings a slick professionalism into every home through the media, and home-grown talent is thought of as second best.

What Jesus wants us to know is that we are all valuable and have all been given talents which can be used to good effect in our world. We really ought to use them, or the world will suffer – yes, even if one, seemingly meagre talent is wasted, the world will be poorer.

If we are willing to have a go, try anything once, or make fools of ourselves in a good cause, we might well unearth talents we did not even know we had!

Bidding Prayers

Celebrant Gathered here by Christ's calling, let us now pray in his Spirit to our heavenly Father who loves and cares for us.

Reader   We commend to his care all who work to
spread the Good News of God's far-
reaching love; those abroad and in this
country; that they may work in God's
strength, and be upheld and encouraged
by his nearness.

Pause

Lord, help us: **work through our lives, we pray.**

We commend to his care all who are
responsible for the spending of public
money, all town and city planners,
those in charge of aid programmes in
disaster areas; that they may be
guided to see practical and sensitive
use of money, land and resources,
directed at real needs.

Pause

Lord, help us: **work through our lives, we pray.**

We commend to his love our own
particular needs, problems or anxieties;
(pause)
that we may learn to trust God more,
placing our whole lives and those
of our families and friends,
in his wise, safe keeping.

Pause

Lord, help us: **work through our lives, we pray.**

Celebrant   Heavenly Father, grant these prayers
which we bring before you in the name
of Jesus Christ. **Amen.**

Ideas for Adults

At the offering of the gifts today arrange for everyone to
bring up in the procession a small token of what they do
in life. For instance, a builder could bring a brick, a cook
a wooden spoon, a gardening enthusiast a trowel. Ask
everyone a week beforehand to think about what to bring
and explain that we shall be offering our lives for God to use.

As all the people approach the altar with these tokens,
it is a moving experience to see the ordinary things of life,
and the wide variety of lives presented, being offered. It
makes everyone aware of their membership of Christ's
body, too.

All tokens are placed near the altar, and taken out into
the world again. It is a powerful symbol of our stewardship
of God's gifts.

Ideas for Children

Have three boxes with slits in the lids, and some play
money. Label the boxes as follows:

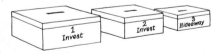

Secretly place five pounds inside box 1, two pounds inside
box 2 and nothing in box 3.

Tell the children the story of today's Gospel, using more
play money. Post five pounds into the first box, two pounds
into the second box and one pound into the third.

When you tell the children about the master's return,
open each lid. There will now be ten pounds in the first
(give him a round of applause), four pounds in the second
(another round of applause), and still only one in the last.

Explain how Jesus needs us to use the gifts he gives us,
otherwise they will be wasted. Talk with them about their
own gifts and things they are good at or advantages they
have been given. These may include, for instance, being
friendly, strong, a fast runner, musical, clever, artistic, sympathetic, good with animals, a clear reader, funny, or a good
listener. They may also include having enough money to
share, outgrown toys which could be given away, or time
which might be used in helping.

Music
Recorded Music

Haydn – *Symphony No. 84*

'Live' Music

God's spirit is in my heart *(ONE, 183)*
Go in peace to be Christ's body *(SONL, 45)*
O King of might and splendour *(ONE, 398)*
Take my life *(ONE, 510)*

Last Sunday in Ordinary Time
Our Lord Jesus Christ,
Universal King

Theme
Christ is our King

As our good shepherd, Christ watches over us and sorts us
out if we get into difficulties; he is in complete charge and
has overall authority in our universe. At the end of time
we shall be judged by our actions during life, and if we
have lived for Christ we shall enter with him into the glory
of his unending kingdom.

Penitential Rite

Good Shepherd, who finds us when we stray,
  Lord, have mercy. **Lord, have mercy.**

You, who are present among the poor and needy,
  Christ, have mercy. **Christ, have mercy.**

You, our King of all time and place,
  Lord, have mercy. **Lord, have mercy.**

Notes on the Readings
Ezekiel 34:11-12, 15-17

As we read this passage we experience a childlike sense of
security that settles and calms; everything is under control
and we are safe in the care of a wise shepherd who loves us.

The feeling is not a sentimental indulgence, though, for it
is how God wants us to feel; he made us for himself and we
only find lasting peace in his presence. For many of us this
is difficult to swallow. We want to be shepherd, not sheep,
and it feels like a blow to our pride and independence to
accept the obedience that is required in serving Christ.

Ironically, that route of careering off to please ourselves,
leads not to the expected freedom but to a kind of prison,
and a hardening in us which we do not really want but
accept as part of being experienced in life; while accepting
God as our shepherd actually makes us liberated, with our
sensitivity to others still intact.

1 Corinthians 15:20-26, 28

It is impossible to explain eternal matters in terms of time,
or to explain the relationship between Christ and the Father
in human terms, since these things are more vast and extraordinary than we can ever understand. But Paul does his
best, and through his earth-bound words we can glimpse

something of the cosmic glory of God's plan surging into a splendid accomplishment, ordered and perfect, bearing along with it, as a huge glacier collects varied rocks and minerals, all sorts of different lives.

Death is the great barrier between time and timelessness and Christ has already broken through it. When all who belong to him in every age have been raised to life, death will itself have died, and the great work of an almighty, loving God will be complete in a perpetual state of joy, peace and love.

Matthew 25:31-46

Following our own way and living for ourselves has the effect of thickening our skins and dulling our sensitivity to others. It is an insidious process, and may be quite advanced before it becomes noticeable to others, though we usually see it in ourselves before that.

Gradually we find we can shrug off the suffering of the malnourished as a problem for their own governments to solve: it is no concern of ours. Prisoners deserve to be severely punished – what is the point in showing them kindness? Yes, it is bad when volcanoes cause such damage, but what a stupid place to live! The homeless have usually brought about their own problems by squandering money and making trouble, and in any case, I need my money to look after my own family. So it goes on, a daily hardening and toughening which is justified conveniently every time.

Yet Christ pierces the excuses, and in his light, selfishness will be revealed for what it is – a rejection not just of the needy but of God himself, who suffers alongside them. Our attitudes and behaviour during life, then, will be interpreted as our attitudes and behaviour towards God. But he does not wave a flag or sound an alarm to let us know his presence, and warn us to behave generously on a particular occasion, so unless we are alert, we may find that our ordinary, everyday behaviour counts against us. God requires a thorough 'conversion' or turning round of our outlooks, not few magnanimous gestures or an occasional smug good turn. But if we want to change, he will rush to transform us.

Bidding Prayers

Celebrant As sons and daughters of our heavenly Father, let us join together in praying for the needs of the Church and our world.

Reader Let us pray for the Christian communities worshipping all over the world; in small groups and large gatherings; simply or elaborately; that as our planet spins, God may be glorified unceasingly in a constant wave of praise.
Pause
Gracious Lord: **help us to serve you well.**

Let us pray for all earthly kingdoms, states and nations, particularly for those in positions of great power; that, acknowledging their limitations of authority they may remain humble and seek to act justly and with wisdom.
Pause
Gracious Lord: **help us to serve you well.**

Let us pray for those undergoing emergency treatment today, especially those in intensive care at the moment; for those who have no one to nurse them adequately; for all who will die today alone and frightened; that the Lord of all healing may comfort, reassure and bring to wholeness all who need help.

Pause
Gracious Lord: **help us to serve you well.**

Let us pray for our families and neighbours, and all those with whom we socialise, travel and work; that, looking with the compassionate eyes of Christ, we may be led to see needs around us, and actively involve ourselves in relieving them.
Pause
Gracious Lord: **help us to serve you well.**

Celebrant Trusting in your great love, dear Father, we lay our prayers before you, and ask you to hear our requests through Christ Jesus. **Amen.**

Ideas for Adults

The Ezekiel passage can be read chorally. Divide the readers into three groups: high, medium and low voices.

Low: The Lord says this:
All: I am going to look after my flock myself
Medium: and keep all of it in view.
High: As a shepherd keeps all his flock in view when he stands up in the middle of his scattered sheep,
All: so shall I keep my sheep in view.
Low: I shall rescue them from wherever they have been scattered during the mist and darkness.
Medium: I myself will pasture my sheep
High: I myself will show them where to rest –
All: it is the Lord who speaks.
High: I shall look for the lost one,
Medium: bring back the stray
Low: bandage the wounded
All: and make the weak strong.
Low: I shall watch over the fat and healthy,
All: I shall be a true shepherd to them.
Medium: As for you, my sheep, the Lord says this:
All: I will judge between sheep and sheep, between rams and he-goats.

Ideas for Children

Give the children a paper with a mixture of goats and sheep on it, and see if they can help the shepherd divide them into two groups by drawing a line round all the sheep and all the goats. If possible, show the children some slides or pictures of goats and sheep in Israel, where they are all looked after together most of the time.

Then tell them how Jesus said that we are like sheep and goats which the shepherd will divide at the end of time. But we will be divided not into sheep and goats but into loving and unloving people (put like this, the children will not confuse goats with badness!)

Now scatter around some circles of card on which are drawn loving or unloving actions. Discuss whether each action is loving or unloving and sort them into two separate piles. Finally, read them today's Gospel, which should now be more readily understood.

Music
Recorded Music

Beethoven – *Symphony No. 9*

'Live' Music

Christ is our king *(ONE, 84)*
Loving shepherd of thy sheep *(ONE, 340)*
The king of love my shepherd is *(ONE, 528)*
This world you have made *(SONL, 73)*

Year of Mark : B

ADVENT

1st Sunday of Advent

Theme
Stay awake

It is difficult to keep alert and watchful when no definite date or time of coming is known. There is always the temptation to slacken off or turn away. In Advent we are reminded of the need to be constant and vigilant. The Holy Spirit strengthens us in our task, and we know that, however difficult it may be, we are loved and sustained by the God who made us.

Penitential Rite

When our attention wanders, and priorities are confused,
  Lord, have mercy. **Lord, have mercy.**

When we listen to selfishness instead of love,
  Christ, have mercy. **Christ, have mercy.**

When temporary pleasures assume more importance than
    lasting joy,
  Lord, have mercy. **Lord, have mercy.**

Notes on the Readings

Isaiah 63:16-17; 64:1, 3-8

There is such pathos in this yearning for God from the rags of human frailty. We are so vulnerable, so easily led, and so quickly rebellious that without God's grace it is quite impossible to remain loyal for long. Like withered leaves we are left to drift in the wind and, the further away we are blown, the more difficult it becomes to 'catch hold' of God.

Depressingly accurate as this picture is, it is not the whole picture. The passage ends with the prophet's reminder that we shall not be left to shrivel and scatter because, although only clay, we belong to a potter who is forming us painstakingly into his own vessels.

1 Corinthians 1:3-9

Fortunately, God our Father is all too well aware of our habit of drifting away from the right path. He knows how good we are at giving in to temptation and forgetting to be watchful. That is partly why he built the Church, which is (or should be) a huge supportive network of teaching and caring in which individual Christians are comforted, strengthened, disciplined and guided. Through its fellowship and shared worship the people of Christ are richly blessed; it is far too useful and beneficial to ignore, or only use half-heartedly. Within the Church we shall find ourselves enriched in a direct and powerful way through the living Jesus.

Mark 13:33-37

We need this help in keeping ourselves prepared as good stewards, since there is no way of knowing when our master will return. Even Jesus did not know exact dates – only that at the right time God would bring everything to completion. And he warns us all to stay awake, as if the end is imminent. That way we shall not be caught unawares at the most important moment.

Sometimes a deepening of fervour is followed by the temptation to relax and be spiritually lazy; Jesus is concerned that we do not get lulled into a sense of false security, for we are often weak and cannot afford to allow our relationship with Christ to lapse. Since he loves us though, he will help us unceasingly.

Bidding Prayers

Celebrant   My brothers and sisters in Christ,
      as we watch together for his coming,
      let us pray together for his world.

Reader   For all those who strive to keep the light
      of the Gospel burning in our hearts,
      even when they are in danger;
      for all who are weary and
      tempted to reject their calling.
      Pause
      Father, help us: **strengthen our faith.**

      For all who are able to influence large groups
      or nations; that their influence may be for
      lasting good, so that God's kingdom may be
      established on earth.
      Pause
      Father, help us: **strengthen our faith.**

      For the disillusioned and disappointed;
      for those who have been brought up in
      an atmosphere of hatred and aggression;
      for those who feel lost and afraid.
      Pause
      Father, help us: **strengthen our faith.**

      For our own circle of friends,
      and the other members of our family;
      for an increase of Christian love in
      our dealings with one another.
      Pause
      Father, help us: **strengthen our faith.**

Celebrant   Lord, our creator, we thank you for
      the wonder of our being, and ask you to
      hear our prayers through Jesus Christ. **Amen.**

Ideas for Adults

Arrange for people to bring a collection of pottery today. Try to include a wide variety of shapes and sizes, glazes and uses; some pieces should be works of beauty and others very practical. Set them on a low table which is draped with a length of suitable material, and ask someone to copy out the last part of the Isaiah reading to 'label' the display:

  And yet, Lord, you are our Father:
  we the clay, you the potter,
  we are all the work of your hand.

Ideas for Children

Bring along a large suitcase with labels to a distant country, a passport, some foreign coins and a map. Also a pile of newspapers and letters, toy pet and an indoor watering can. Dress up and pretend you are going off on your travels. You will be coming back but you don't know when.

Now bring out a large notebook and write in it the jobs you must do before you leave, at the children's suggestions:

* ★ cancel the milk and newspapers
* ★ arrange for a neighbour to feed the cat
* ★ ask a friend to water the plants
* ★ ask a neighbour to push letters through your letterbox and keep an eye on your house

Select various children to do the tasks, then lock up, wave goodbye and walk out of the circle. From the outside, direct the neighbours and friends to do their jobs on Saturday, then Sunday, then Monday . . . till perhaps they start to give up/lose interest/find they're too busy etc. Do they feel they ought to do it anyway? Suppose the owner is going to be away for a long time? Try to help them see that we are all tempted to give up; as you call out the next few days, some of the jobs don't get done.

Suddenly burst back into the circle, telling everyone you are home! Which friends and neighbours will you be pleased with and which will you feel have let you down?

Now read today's Gospel, and give each child a picture postcard. The message on the back is:

and they can fill in their own name and address and colour in the front.

Music
Recorded Music

Haydn – *Surprise Symphony*

'Live' Music

Guide me, O thou great Redeemer *(ONE, 190)*
Rain down justice *(ONE, 459)*
Wake up, O people! *(SONL, 44)*

2nd Sunday of Advent

Theme
Planning and preparation

Before anything can be built in a desert wilderness there has to be straightening out and reordering. Advent is a good time to prepare our lives for Christ to build on, by rigorously cutting out and reshaping the areas which are barren. Then, as he builds, we shall be taking part in the establishing of God's kingdom, which culminates in the new heaven and new earth, where God reigns for ever with unending love, peace and joy.

Penitential Rite

We dear-ly want to love you, Lord. We real-ly long to serve you, Lord. So

take us, melt us, then re-make us: use us to your glo-ry.

Notes on the Readings

Isaiah 40:1-5, 9-11

Although the terrain is far from promising, and much has to be done before the highway can be constructed, the overriding message here is of great joy. The people are given comfort and consolation. This is because turning towards God and away from sin has put them in a right relationship with their creator, and all the hard work will now be positive: they will be working with God instead of against him. We have only to look at the way people throw themselves into the preparations for a street party, carnival or Christmas decorating to see how eagerly we work for something special and exciting. This is the spirit in which we are urged to prepare ourselves for the Lord. Having faced up to sinfulness, having apologised to God for it and resolved to make amends, we can enjoy the hard work, enjoy getting our hands dirty by physical involvement in his service, and be happy that we are tired by the end of the day. We can get excited about the highway we are building and delight in the fellowship we share with all the other road workers. For when it is finished the dazzling glory of our God will be revealed so that everyone can see it. That is well worth a few blisters and bruises.

2 Peter 3:8-14

If you are expecting visitors or waiting for a train, the time passes much more slowly after the scheduled time of arrival has passed. And, for many of the Christians to whom Peter is writing, Christ seemed slow in coming and they were getting very tired of waiting. Was he ever going to fulfil his promise and return to the earth in glory?

Peter reassures them by explaining the timelessness of an eternal God, which we creatures of time find so hard to grasp. God's good time takes into consideration all factors, all circumstances; in his loving mercy he will patiently give us the time and opportunities we need. Sometimes wild claims are made about actual dates for the second coming of Christ, but in fact no one has such inside information. We can spend too much time and energy worrying about the finer details of exactly how and when it will happen. All we really need to do is to trust Jesus to keep his promise, and get on with leading the kinds of lives that will hasten the coming of his Kingdom.

Mark 1:1-8

Mark begins his Gospel with the prophecy in Isaiah being fulfilled. John the Baptist's call to repentance is exactly the kind of highway building that was necessary to prepare people for the ministry of Jesus. The excitement quickens, the sense of urgency and immediacy grows, and crowds flock to set about straightening their lives out and starting afresh. How easy it would have been for John to hang on to the glory himself instead of making it quite clear that he was only a forerunner; his humility taught as powerfully as his words. Repentance puts us right with God, but the Spirit of Jesus living in us daily is what enables us to grow and yield fruit.

Bidding Prayers

Celebrant   Let us bring to God our loving Father
all the cares that weigh on our hearts,
knowing that he understands us better
than we understand ourselves.

Reader   We bring the daily work of those who
labour to spread the good news of Christ amid
apathy, ridicule or prejudice;
that they may be encouraged and strengthened.
Pause
Father, hear us: **and make us ready to serve you.**

We bring our daily work with all the
pressures, monotony, enjoyment and mistakes;
that we may know God's presence
and trust in his love.
Pause
Father, hear us: **and make us ready to serve you.**

We bring the lives of all those who
are trapped by physical or mental illness,
all whose lives seem bleak and without meaning;
that God may release them, unburden them
and bring them his joy.
Pause
Father, hear us: **and make us ready to serve you.**

We bring all our loved ones with
their hopes and their disappointments,
their struggles and their successes;
that they may be built
and nurtured by Christ's love.
Pause
Father, hear us: **and make us ready to serve you.**

Celebrant   In great thankfulness for your
compassionate love, dear Father,
we ask you to accept our prayers,
through Jesus Christ our Lord. **Amen.**

Ideas for Adults

Either for the Old Testament reading or as people are coming into Church, play a recording of 'Prepare ye' from *Godspell*, or the setting of this prophecy from *Messiah*.

Ideas for Children

From now until Christmas the children can take part in building 'the highway of the Lord'. First talk with them about how their town or country prepares its streets for important visitors such as royalty, a winning football team or a film star. There may be flags hung up, streamers waving, a red carpet rolled out on the pavement and flowers planted round all the lamp posts, for instance. If you have any photographs of such events, or of a local carnival, show them around.

Now read them Isaiah 40:3-5 and unroll a length of white material, about a yard wide and four yards in length. (A double sheet split down the middle and joined end to end makes the right size: it is important that it looks big.)

The children are going to turn this strip of boring material into a highway for Jesus. At Christmas it can be laid down in church so that when the Christ child is brought to the manger he is carried along the children's highway.

Have ready plenty of colourful oddments of material, a really efficient fabric glue, scissors, pens and templates. Discuss ways in which we can prepare ourselves for Jesus, and write these at intervals along the highway with coloured pens. Here are some suggestions:

- I'm sorry, Jesus.
- I want to get to know you better.
- I apologise for being unkind.
- Please help me to be more loving.

- I know I'm selfish – please help.
- Please, Jesus, teach me to share.

Then between and around the words, all work together to make a really beautiful roadway ready for Jesus.

Music
Recorded Music

Handel – Messiah
Stephen Schwartz – Godspell

'Live' Music

Comfort, comfort, my people (SONL, 88)
In you, my God (ONE, 254)
Maranatha! (ONE, 311)

3rd Sunday of Advent

Theme
Being happy and thankful

Christian people have a deep-seated joyfulness and an attitude of constant thankfulness, since their hope and security is based on unflinching love. We know we are ultimately safe in the arms of our God; that the beautiful world he has made is part of a great plan in which Goodness has the victory. So we should try to make sure that minor irritations do not cloud the profound joy that is our heritage.

Penitential Rite

Your joy can shower our lives with light,
   Lord, have mercy. **Lord, have mercy.**

Your joy dispels all sadness,
   Christ, have mercy. **Christ, have mercy.**

In joy we will sing of your love,
   Lord, have mercy. **Lord, have mercy.**

Notes on the Readings

Isaiah 61:1-2, 10-11

Full of hope and expectation, this prophecy is rooted in God's forgiveness of his wayward people. It is his will that they shall be set free from all that imprisons them, that their emotional wounds be healed and soothed, and an atmosphere of festival replace the dejection.

Jesus staggered his listeners at his home town by announcing that the prophecy was now being fulfilled. Since they had all known Jesus as one of the local children, they could not believe that the ancient, revered text could start coming true in their own small town, through one of their own residents – and a family with questionable morals at that.

Sometimes we, too, doubt that God really means what he says, because it seems too simple – too good to be true. Yet, if we can forget our adult, sophisticated scepticism for a moment, we shall find Jesus right there, perfectly natural and friendly but also inspiring and gracious. It is rather like learning to dive: C.S. Lewis used to say that although swimming involves learning to 'do' certain things, diving requires 'non-doing' – allowing your body to let go and fall. It often takes practice to learn physical relaxation, and trust is a kind of spiritual relaxation. It is worth working for, because it will make us so happy that we shall start jumping for joy!

1 Thessalonians 5:16-24

We are given good sound advice here. Lasting happiness which is independent of circumstances is everyone's dream. All sorts of ways have been tried to achieve it, and many accept cheap or dangerous substitutes and end up either resigned or desperate. God, who formed us in the first place, can offer the only permanent joy, and his offer does not cause air pollution, hangovers, aggression or decay. It simply involves keeping in close touch with him and putting him first in our lives. All the rest he undertakes, for to him each one of us is infinitely precious and important.

John 1:6-8, 19-28

In this account of John the Baptist's witness we see the heralding of the long awaited Messiah, in images the people – with their sound knowledge of the prophets – would be likely to understand. John was fulfilling a role that was essential in preparing the way for Israel's Saviour. It would alert many to look for signs of God visiting his people, and guide them to see his presence where they may not have been expecting to find it.

If we join the crowds around John and whole-heartedly repent of all that is evil, ugly and damaging in our characters, we too shall be alerted to recognise Christ and see him more clearly.

Bidding Prayers

Celebrant   Confident in the love our Father has for us,
         let us approach him with our needs and concerns.

Reader   That there may be an increasing joy and
         enthusiasm among all who follow Christ;
         that any who have lost their sparkle spiritually
         may be revitalised.
         Pause
         Hear us, Father: **you alone give life and joy.**

         That the apparently insoluble problems of
         our world may be healed and soothed;
         that opportunities for reconciliation
         may be well used both nationally
         and internationally.
         Pause
         Hear us, Father: **you alone give life and joy.**

         That wherever despair or disillusion
         has distorted the truth about love or freedom,
         we may allow Christ greater access,
         so that he can enlighten and guide.
         Pause
         Hear us, Father: **you alone give life and joy.**

         That Christ may show us any areas in
         our lives which hinder our relationship
         with him; and that his love may spill over

into our relationships with one another.
Pause
Hear us, Father: **you alone give life and joy.**

Celebrant As part of your generous creation, Father,
we give you thanks and praise,
and ask you to accept these prayers
through Christ Jesus. **Amen.**

Ideas for Adults

The Isaiah reading is well worth preparing chorally, using a group of men and women. Arrange for the speakers to stand, kneel and sit instead of all standing in a line; visual harmony is important and often improves the quality of presentation.

Begin with all speakers taking a deep breath and exhaling audibly through open mouths over a silent count of four.

All: (*softly but very clearly*) The spirit of the Lord has been given to me,
(*slightly louder*) for the Lord has anointed me.
Men: He has sent me to bring good news to the poor,
Women: to bind up hearts that are broken;
1 Man: (*others look towards soloists as they speak*) to proclaim liberty to captives,
1 Woman: freedom to those in prison;
1 Man: to proclaim a year of favour from the Lord.
All: (*loudly*) I exalt for joy in the Lord, my soul rejoices in my God,
Women: for he has clothed me in the garments of salvation,
All: he has wrapped me in the cloak of integrity,
Men: like a bridegroom wearing his wreath,
Women: like a bride adorned in her jewels.
Men: (*softly*) For as the earth makes fresh things grow,
Women: (*louder*) as a garden makes seeds spring up,
All: so will the Lord make both integrity and praise (*loudly*) SPRING UP in the sight of the nations.

Ideas for Children

Remind the children of the highway they are preparing for Jesus, and spread the cloth out to see how they started – with saying sorry and asking God to forgive them.

Now read them a clear translation of today's second reading. Have it written out on thick paper, then folded and sealed like an important letter, and explain that this letter was written to the Christians in Thessalonica to help them prepare *their* highway. Show them on a modern map whereabouts Thessalonica is in Greece. It is very important that children realise early on that we are teaching them about real events in actual places.

Help the children to thank their loving Father for one or two things in this world that they appreciate very much, and write these with coloured pens on flower-shaped pieces of material to add to the highway.

Thank you for my goldfish

Thank you for giving us water to swim in

Music
Recorded Music

From Taizé – *Confitemini Domino*

'Live' Music

Morning has broken *(ONE, 350)*
My God, how wonderful thou art *(ONE, 357)*
This world you have made *(SONL, 73)*

4th Sunday of Advent

Theme
Through Mary the secret of ages will be revealed

God promised that from the house of David would come a king who would rule for ever in peace and righteousness; and now, at last, Gabriel approaches Mary with amazing news. She is betrothed to Joseph of the House of David, and in her child the world will meet the one eternal King. Mary's ready response teaches us how to react to God's calling in our own lives.

Penitential Rite

Make us receptive to your voice,
Lord, have mercy. **Lord, have mercy.**

Help us to recognise your will,
Christ, have mercy. **Christ, have mercy.**

Teach us to obey your word,
Lord, have mercy. **Lord, have mercy.**

Notes on the Readings

2 Samuel 7:1-5, 8-11, 16

The ark of the covenant was a symbol of God's constant presence among his people. He had heard their cries of anguish in Egypt and led them across the Red Sea to freedom; he had supported and guided them throughout their wandering years in the wilderness, and kept faith with them through their grumbles and idolatry. Now, for a while, King David had established peace, and had the leisure to start plans for a permanent building to house the ark.

At first sight it seems to be a very good idea: noble, generous and necessary. But Nathan, being a man of God, mulls it over during the night and begins to see things in God's way. Perhaps a permanent house for the ark would destroy some very powerful symbolism: God is not anchored to one spot, but travels with us in times of danger, failure and victory; God is there among his people where they need him, and he will never abandon them.

In God's eyes the time is not yet right for such an enterprise, but he reaffirms his promise which spans a far broader plan even than building a magnificent temple: from the family of David will come one who displays God's eternal glory to the whole world.

We, too, need to be wary of planning ambitious works for God. They may not always be what he has in mind, or the timing may be wrong. We would be better advised to ask him first!

Romans 16:25-27

Paul, as a devout and learned Jew, believed passionately that those ancient prophecies and promises would be fulfilled for the chosen people of Israel. He had, before his conversion, been utterly convinced that those who claimed Jesus of Nazareth as Messiah were guilty of nothing short of blasphemy.

Yet here we find him full of excitement, bursting to let everyone share the good news that those prophecies really have been fulfilled in none other than Jesus. The great barriers of his preconceived ideas and narrow expectations have been sent flying, and we can sense his exhilaration as he feels the breeze of God's Spirit and the light of understanding. As so often happens with God, the truth far exceeds our wildest dreams.

Luke 1:26-38

Many factories have machines in which several products, labels and packaging materials converge in order to emerge as a unit, ready for transportation. For the system to operate efficiently, exact, precise timing is needed.

We are made in God's likeness, so our ability to plan in this way gives us a faint reflection of how God orders and plans in his universe. Although we recognise such order in the laws of physics and the structure of matter, we are sometimes blind to it in less tangible forms.

In this gentle and tender moment of the Annunciation, we are witnessing the convergence of many events, many lives and many spiritual journeys. They all merge at this particular point in time to enable the next great stage of God's salvation to be accomplished. And it all depends on Mary's response.

Bidding Prayers

Celebrant   Fellow travellers of Christ's Way,
as we walk together through life,
let us pray together in his spirit.

Reader   For all who profess to be Christians
in every community,
whether remote and isolated
or crowded and sophisticated;
that they may always hold firmly
to their unchanging Lord,
and rejoice in his abundant love.
Pause
Loving Father: **let your will be done.**

For all those who are uncertain
about their future, those who are unemployed
or unhappy in their place of work;
that they may be attentive to God's will,
and trust him to use their lives
in the best way.
Pause
Loving Father: **let your will be done.**

For all who are anxious and nervous,
all who suffer from phobias or mental stress;
for those who worry about everything
and have no sense of peace;
that they may find receptive stillness
in the peace of Christ.
Pause
Loving Father: **let your will be done.**

For the people with whom we live
and those we meet each day;
that we may learn to see Christ in one another
and grow more caring and responsive.
Pause
Loving Father: **let your will be done.**

Celebrant   Heavenly Father, accept our prayers,
and make us channels of your peace,
through the power of Jesus Christ. **Amen.**

Ideas for Adults

Today's Gospel reading lends itself particularly well to dramatising. Use Nativity play costumes or albs, with a blue cloak for Mary. Spotlight the angel when he comes in. Those acting should spend some time meditating on the words they are going to say, as familiarity can sometimes cloud our perception.

Ideas for Children

Beforehand, prepare a picture of some houses in a street drawn on thin card, and cut round the doors so that they open and close. Also make a simple wooden-spoon or mop puppet.

First talk with the children about any good news they would like to share, and choose someone to knock on the door of each house to tell their news.

At the first house let the puppet say: 'Go away – I'm busy!'; at the second house: 'Pardon? . . . pardon? . . . I can't hear a WORD!'; at the third house: 'You don't expect me to believe THAT, do you?'; and at the fourth house: 'Hallo! Nice to see you! . . . oh really? How lovely!'. Discuss with them the different ways of receiving news, and how we need to welcome Jesus when he speaks to us, instead of being deaf, or too busy, or not believing what he says.

Now show the children a picture of God's messenger bringing some very important news to Mary. Who was the messenger? What was his news? Think back to the ways people sometimes react – did Mary say she was too busy, or couldn't hear, or didn't believe the angel? Read together the way Mary listened carefully and said she would certainly let God's will be done in her.

Unfold the children's 'highway' now, and complete it by adding Mary's words. Use them as a prayer to make them part of our preparation for the coming of Jesus into our lives.

Music
Recorded Music

Mahler – Symphony No.4: slow movement

'Live' Music

Mother of God's Living Word (ONE, 353)
Stretch out your hand (SONL, 2)
The love of God (SONL, 46)

CHRISTMASTIDE

Christmastide

Questions for Discussion Groups
1. Why do you think God chose to enter your world as a baby?
2. Using a concordance, discover some of the other times that Bethlehem is mentioned in the Bible. Are there any links between these events and Christ's birth?

The Nativity of Our Lord (Midnight Mass)

Theme
Christ our Saviour is born

At a particular time in history, eternal God breaks into human existence to transform and redeem it. In the darkness of night, God's majestic glory becomes a vulnerable, new-born baby; Creator of all is entirely dependent on those he has created. Such is the measure of his infinite love.

Penitential Rite

God our Father, creator of the world,
  have mercy on us: **have mercy on us.**

God the Son, redeemer of the world,
  have mercy on us: **have mercy on us.**

God the Holy Spirit, who gives life to the people of God,
  have mercy on us: **have mercy on us.**

Notes on the Readings

Isaiah 9:2-7

The prophet perceives that a merely temporary king, however benevolent and strong, could not be compatible with God's plan to save his people, and his vision broadens to encompass a kingdom of absolute peace and harmony and justice.

We sense the weariness, dirt and rags of protracted battles and oppression which, bringing a wonderful feeling of relief, are finally coming to a close. In the new age there will be security, rest and integrity for ever.

Now, as God, unannounced except by angels, slips into the middle of human life, we can join in the exultant joy of all heaven – for that eternal, saving king has just been born.

Titus 2:11-14

No one is left out of this message of salvation; Christ loves every individual in the entire human race, and longs for each one of us to be reconciled to our Father in heaven and to each other as brothers and sisters in one close-knit family.

Christmas, with all its hope and happiness, is a wonderful opportunity to deepen bonds of love, offer reconciliation where there has been coldness or hostility, and push back the frontiers of our caring a little more, to include a wider circle of 'brothers and sisters'.

Luke 2:1-14

The first reaction of the shepherds to seeing their familiar hillside filled with glory, is absolute terror. Faced with such awesome and obvious naked power, they recognise their own weakness and vulnerability. Once the angels have re-assured them, their amazement at God's power turns into ecstatic joy at the love such a powerful God must have if he is prepared to put aside that glory in order to save the creatures he has made.

Sometimes a glimpse of God's majesty stuns us and may scare us. We may feel tempted to argue it away, so that we can stay in our familiar territory. Many back away from the real God of glory because he is so unpredictable and disturbing. They prefer their own, controllable, watered-down version.

But the one, omnipotent God is not only powerful; he is also a God of tenderness and compassion, and if we listen, we will always hear him reassure us whenever he challenges.

Bidding Prayers

Celebrant Brothers and sisters in Christ,
  together with God's people
  throughout the world, let us pray.

Reader That many hearts may be touched
  by the wonder of what we celebrate tonight;
  that we may be changed
  by the unswerving love of our God.
  Pause
  Most merciful Father: **we bring you our lives.**

  That there may be peace –
  true and lasting peace –
  between individuals, between families,
  between tribes and between nations.
  Pause
  Most merciful Father: **we bring you our lives.**

  That this time may mark the beginning
  of hope for any who are lonely, homesick,
  rejected or oppressed;
  that in Christians they may meet
  the friendship and compassion of Christ.
  Pause
  Most merciful Father: **we bring you our lives.**

  That we may all be filled with God's gift of joy
  as we begin to grasp the amazing depth
  of his love for us.
  Pause
  Most merciful Father: **we bring you our lives.**

Celebrant Father, with the shepherds we adore you;
  please accept our prayers through Jesus,
  our Redeemer. **Amen.**

Ideas for Adults

Focus on Advent and Christmas has many suggestions for making the celebration of Christmas rich and meaningful for the whole parish.

Ideas for Children

Have the children's highway installed in church, taped down if necessary.

Music

Recorded Music

Handel – *Christmas Oratorio*

'Live' Music

Let all mortal flesh *(ONE, 300)*
Peace is the gift *(ONE, 443)*
– and plenty of carols

The Nativity of Our Lord
(Christmas Day)

Theme
The Word was made flesh

No longer hidden, no longer veiled, God has revealed himself to us directly in the person of Jesus. The Word, the expression of God, is now among us in the form of a human baby, worshipped by the very angels. And in every age new generations mingle their praise with that of Mary, Joseph and the shepherds.

Penitential Rite

This is particularly suitable for a family service where children are involved.

Notes on the Readings

Isaiah 52:7-10

The loveliness of this passage excites every generation with its conviction of hope and joy. The prophet has a vision of the age of peace, when the Lord will be seen face to face, and all the world will perceive his glory coupled with his compassion – for he is bent on rescuing and saving mankind.

His presence will heal, console and restore; the deep, lasting comfort that every wandering soul craves will become a reality, as God touches his people and walks among them.

Hebrews 1:1-6

Even before the swirling gases of our solar system were formed, God was fully present and active. It is well worth star-gazing, sometimes, to remind ourselves of the vastness of the universe and the immensity of God who had no beginning and will have no end. For that is the power which broke into a particular point in history by being born of a human woman at Bethlehem.

All through the world's development and birth pangs; all through the developing spiritual consciousness of humanity; and all through the visions and prophecies of perceptive, prayerful people, God was revealed. But never so clearly as when he lay in Mary's arms as the first-born baby in a human family.

John 1:1-18

For here the full expression of God shines out, as the Word becomes flesh. The Incarnation is an impossibility come true; we wonder at the enormity of it, delight in the beauty of it and perhaps balk at the courage of it. Can it really be possible that the creative force behind every galaxy, every bacterium and life itself, is actually here, with the name of Jesus, walking about healing, teaching and listening to us? Yes, says John, incredible though is seems, it is true; because we saw his glory and it was the glory of God himself. If

(Accompany with triangles or handbells.)

Ma-ker of all stars and light: Lord,   have   mer-cy;   Je-sus born that ho-ly night:

Christ,   have   mer-cy;   Spi-rit keep us shin-ing bright: Lord,   have   mer   -   cy.

we, also, are convinced by our experience of Jesus that he really is God, we are bound to accept his teaching and open our hearts to his love. And he will not only make us his disciples, but also his brothers and his sisters, all sharing God as our loving Father.

Bidding Prayers

Celebrant Let us pray to God our Father,
because he loves us dearly.

Reader That the light of the world
may shine so brightly in our lives
that other people notice it
and are attracted to Jesus
by the way we live and love.
Pause
Lord of the universe: **be born in us today.**

That the world may stop its noise, chatter
and arguing long enough to hear
the angels singing of hope and peace.
Pause
Lord of the universe: **be born in us today.**

That God will bless and support
all expectant mothers and those in labour;
and that all newborn babies
and young children may be loved, cherished
and protected from harm.
Pause
Lord of the universe: **be born in us today.**

That there may be more understanding
and more mercy in our family relationships,
with Christ always among us –
not an occasional visitor.
Pause
Lord of the universe: **be born in us today.**

Celebrant Father, we can never thank you enough
for coming to rescue us;
please hear our prayers which we offer
through Jesus, your Son. **Amen.**

Ideas for Children and Adults

The children's highway should still be in evidence in church.

During the offering of the gifts, why not let the children offer a carefully wrapped gift for a group of children in a poorer parish or a local community home. Remind parents and children beforehand and suggest a nearly-new (but in very good condition) toy, or book. It is sensible to have the sex and age group for whom it is suitable, written on the label.

Get a large greeting card which can be passed round and signed by everyone in church. This can accompany the presents.

Music
Recorded Music

A carol from another country.

'Live' Music

Focus on Advent and Christmas includes some new Christmas hymns. Also try varying the treatment of traditional carols; accompany the singing with violin and recorders, for instance, or have one sung in parts unaccompanied.

The Holy Family of Jesus, Mary and Joseph

Theme
Christ's family

The basic unit of human society is the family, and God reaffirmed its importance when he sent his Son into the world by being born as a baby in a family. In that holy family we can see a pattern for our own homes – Christ born into them. In a broader sense, too, we are all brothers and sisters with Christ in the family of God, and all children of the same heavenly Father.

Penitential Rite

Our homes need you to be places of light,
Lord, have mercy. **Lord, have mercy.**

Our homes need you to be centres of love,
Christ, have mercy. **Christ, have mercy.**

Our homes need you to be havens of joy,
Lord, have mercy. **Lord, have mercy.**

Notes on the Readings

Ecclesiasticus 3:2-6, 12-14

In this passage we find the practical kind of caring love which Jesus taught and showed. It is so much easier to talk about love as a general ideal, than to tend patiently to an irritating child, or repeat the same pieces of news time after time to an elderly relative whose memory is failing. Somehow, these mundane, everyday opportunities for loving seem to be especially difficult and demanding.

Yet it is from these threads that the strong fabric of real love is woven. Perhaps if we think of them as opportunities, instead of as frustrating time-wasters, we may find them easier to cope with, and even start enjoying the challenge!

Part of the honour spoken of here is a respect which acknowledges wisdom. Some societies are very bad at learning from the elderly, and it is often assumed that wisdom is a by-product of health, strength and fitness instead of experience. We are all losers in such an atmosphere. It is not enough just to provide nursing homes and good meals, vital though all this obviously is; we need also to ask their advice and draw on their experiences in solving present problems, invite their prayerful involvement in parish life and share their silence. Then we will be caring in a way which values their worth as full members of our society.

Colossians 3:12-21

'Wearing' kindness, compassion and humility is quite different from carrying them around. Once on, clothes go everywhere we go, and unless they are definitely unsuitable for our activity we tend to forget about them and concentrate on what we are doing. Having chosen overalls to wear, we can paint the window frames without worrying about accidental spills; having chosen a raincoat and wellies we can take the children to school without moaning about getting wet. In other words, if we choose to wear suitable clothes, our attitudes and outlooks alter.

These qualities of compassionate caring are suitable clothes to wear for living a Christian life. If we mentally put them on when we dress each morning, we shall find them helping us through the day. It will not be an introverted obsession with how our 'clothes' look, but a practical confidence which enables us to fling ourselves whole-heartedly into the business of Christian caring without worrying about any possible damage to us. For these fruits are the loving Spirit of Christ living in us, and they equip us for the task of establishing and forging loving relationships, and making reconciliation a priority.

Luke 2:22-40

Both Simeon and Anna must have been in constant touch with God, dressed for action spiritually and therefore ready to recognise, among the daily routines of the Temple, the coming of the promised Saviour, even though he was only a baby.

Their insight perceived the ancient prophecies in fulfilment through this small child – the pain as well as the victory. Joseph and Mary had the incredible task of nurturing God's Son. God chose a home which was not over-privileged, materially; the family was not famous, wealthy or well connected. The best upbringing for God's Son was a home where he was loved and cherished, teased and laughed with, had local children as friends, and trained in his father's craft. So we need not worry about how our children are losing out if we cannot afford all the latest toys or clothes. If we concentrate on the values God chose for his own Son we shall be giving our children the best possible start in life.

Bidding Prayers

Celebrant   My brothers and sisters in Christ,
as members of one family,
let us talk to our heavenly Father
about our needs, cares and concerns.

Reader   Let us pray for the life, teaching
and fellowship of the Church,
our Christian family;
that we may support and care for one another
as true family members,
regardless of physical, cultural
or intellectual differences.
Pause
God our Father: **hear your children's prayer.**

Let us pray for friendship and goodwill
between all the different nations
in our world;
that we may enjoy the variety as richness,
rather than fearing it as a threat.
Pause
God our Father: **hear your children's prayer.**

Let us pray for all who have been damaged
by a disturbed or violent upbringing;
for children who are growing up
amid hatred and cruelty;
that they may be healed by love.
Pause
God our Father: **hear your children's prayer.**

Let us pray for God's blessing and guidance
in all the homes of this parish;
that in each problem and difficulty,
God's loving wisdom may steer us
in the right direction.
Pause
God our Father: **hear your children's prayer.**

Celebrant   Heavenly Father, dwell in our hearts
and homes, and accept these prayers
through Jesus Christ,
our brother and Redeemer. **Amen.**

Ideas for Adults

It is easy to take the blessings of family life for granted; why not arrange a display board full of family snapshots which capture the fun and laughter, comfort and support which is often much in evidence. Make sure each picture is named on the back, so as to ensure its safe return. The parish family can also be included, but avoid set portraits; catch people in action – caring, rejoicing, praying, working and dancing.

Such an exhibition can develop parish affection and a sense of shared experience of God's blessings.

Ideas for Children

Talk with the children about some of the things that have to be done when a baby is born, such as registering the child (show a birth certificate, and suggest they ask to see their own at home) and having a check-up with the doctor (put on a toy stethoscope) and preparing for the baby's Baptism (show a Christening robe or a picture of a baby being baptised).

Now tell them how, in the Law of Moses, whenever the first son was born, he was brought to the Temple to be offered to God, together with a present of two doves or pigeons. (Show two paper ones.)

Now, using a doll and four children to be Mary, Joseph, Simeon and Anna, tell today's Gospel reading with the children miming the actions. The other children should mime the parts of people in the Temple so no one is left out.

Finally, help the children to make a pair of turtledoves each:

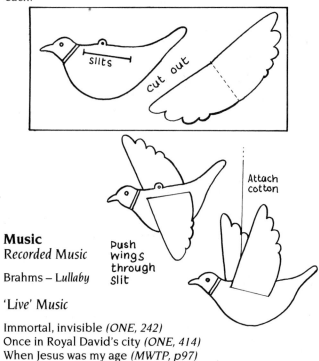

Music
Recorded Music

Brahms – *Lullaby*

'Live' Music

Immortal, invisible *(ONE, 242)*
Once in Royal David's city *(ONE, 414)*
When Jesus was my age *(MWTP, p97)*

Solemnity of Mary, Mother of God

Theme
Through Mary, God's Son was born

God chose Mary to be the instrument of his Incarnation. All the blessings handed down through the generations of the people of Israel now bore fruit to feed the world, as Mary gave birth to Jesus and nurtured him through childhood. Her example fills us with love and gratitude.

Penitential Rite

Train our hearts to desire your will,
  Lord, have mercy. **Lord, have mercy.**

Train our hearts to accept your will,
  Christ, have mercy. **Christ, have mercy.**

Train our hearts to do your will,
  Lord, have mercy. **Lord, have mercy.**

Notes on the Readings

Numbers 6:22-27

The image of warm sunlight which this lovely blessing invokes, tells us much about the warmth and tender affection God has for us. There will be times in our lives when clouds seem to cut us off from the radiance, and we *know*, rather than *feel* that God loves us. But even the cloudy times draw us closer, and Mary experienced acute pain as well as intense joy.

Then, when the clouds clear, and we are bathed in the light of God's tenderness, the sense of his presence uplifts, soothes, sustains and inspires us.

Galatians 4:4-7

Jesus was born in direct line to the Law and the promises of salvation. He explained the essence of the Law and fulfilled the promises by saving us from our deadliest enemy of sin. In doing so he enabled us to be drawn into a radically new relationship with God: fully human through being born of Mary, Jesus is our brother, and we, as his adopted brothers and sisters, can now call God our Father.

Luke 2:16-21

Luke gives us a very special glimpse of these early days in Christ's life: what an amazing time it must have been for Mary and Joseph, with so many confirmations of God's promise from all sorts of unexpected areas, so much excitement and astonishment, and yet so much peace and assurance in the tiny being they cuddled, washed and fed!

Obediently they bring him up according to the Law's requirements, and that obedience is the hallmark of their integrity, and their undivided loyalty to God. Obviously Mary questioned and wondered about what it all meant and how it would all be achieved, but her questioning was fixed on the solid rock of her faith, and her obedience was willingly and joyfully given.

Bidding Prayers

Celebrant In the presence of Mary and all the saints
  let us pray to our heavenly Father.

Reader For the will to serve God
  more whole-heartedly, rejoicing in
  every opportunity to learn patience,
  humility and obedience.
  Pause
  Let it be to us: **according to your will.**

For a willingness to share
  the resources of our universe,
  conserve its riches
  and use our knowledge for good.
  Pause
  Let it be to us: **according to your will.**

For wisdom to know
  how best to help those in need;

for healing and wholeness
  in pain and distress.
  Pause
  Let it be to us: **according to your will.**

For the tuning of our lives
  so that they express the beauty of God's love.
  Pause
  Let it be to us: **according to your will.**

Celebrant Father, hear our prayers
  and bless our lives with your presence,
  through Jesus Christ. **Amen.**

Ideas for Adults

If you have a particularly lovely picture, window or statue of the Christ child with his mother, highlight it with spotlighting and flowers. Slides of Michaelangelo's *Pieta* and other works of art depicting the tenderness between Mary and Jesus may be projected on to a bare wall to catch the imagination and lead to a deeper understanding.

Ideas for Children

Moulds are available from craft shops for making plaster models of Mary and Jesus. Modelling plaster is easy to mix and does not take long to set. Perhaps the children could make these and/or paint them. They can be blessed at Mass.

Music
Recorded Music

Bach – *Cello Suite*

'Live' Music

Baruch Attah Adonai Elohenu *(SONL, 27)*
Sing of a girl *(ONE, 485)*
Sleep, holy babe *(ONE, 496)*

2nd Sunday after Christmas

Theme
From the very beginning, we were chosen

Right from the expression of God in the creation, we have been marked out and chosen to be his adopted sons and daughters through the restoring and saving power of Jesus. To know and perceive the nature of God, both through his created world and through his Son, is perfect wisdom; such purity of heart and integrity allows us to see his will for us more clearly.

Penitential Rite

Have a large globe carried in silence to a space in front of the altar and set down. Then have representatives of all age groups to set down night-lights around the globe, again in silence. Sing this simple round very softly; it could be taught in a few minutes before Mass.

a. Lord,
b. Christ, } have mer - cy;
c. Lord,

Lord,
Christ, } have mer - cy;
Lord,

Lord,
Christ, } have mer - cy   on   us.
Lord,

Notes on the Readings

Sirach 24:1-4, 12-16

Wisdom means far more than shrewd common sense in this passage. It is linked with the concept of an absolute ideal of purity and integrity, which is only accessible in the character of God himself. As humanity searches for such infinite goodness, the mist is sometimes penetrated, and true wisdom glimpsed or gazed upon.

But, in a very special way, God's wisdom has taken root like a young plant in the chosen people of Israel. There it is nurtured, and grows until it flowers in the person of Jesus.

Ephesians 1:3-6, 15-18

Jesus, by shattering the barriers that split us off from God, has enabled us to come close to him in a way that was not previously possible. With Paul, we feel quite bowled over by the privilege, once the enormity of it hits us.

To be adopted into his family means that we are full members, not just employees or wistful onlookers: this close fellowship and sharing is what God had in mind for us all along, and now it has happened. Nor does it stop with us; as we become more and more responsive to God's love and power, we shall be able to participate in drawing the whole cosmic entirety into a perfect relationship with its maker and redeemer.

John 1:1-18

Instead of analysing the separate words and phrases intellectually, it is sometimes worthwhile approaching the passage differently. In an atmosphere of silence and stillness, allow God's peace to take charge. Then let the words and images wash over and through your consciousness. Gradually the blending of timelessness and perfect timing can be 'caught', as if you are looking through eyes of eternity instead of time. Planning, creation, development and fulfilment are held in a harmony which is quite incompatible with measured time, but, in the mind of God, fundamental.

Having no hands but ours to work through, God needs us to have deeper knowledge of him, so that he can act with and through us; a regular habit of such stillness and silence allows him access.

Bidding Prayers

Celebrant   God has chosen us
          as his adopted sons and daughters;
          in the Spirit of Jesus Christ,
          let us pray to him now.

Reader   For all who are working to spread the news
          of hope and joy for humanity;
          that their teaching may be inspired
          so as to draw many, through Christ,
          to their loving creator.
          Pause
          Father of Wisdom: **open our eyes to your truth.**

For all who sit on committees;
all decision makers and policy planners;
that they may be guided to work
in accordance with God's will,
so that the world is governed
and ordered wisely.
Pause
Father of Wisdom: **open our eyes to your truth.**

For those who are chronically ill,
or suffering from a long-term disability;
that even through intense pain
there may be positive, spiritual growth,
and a deeper awareness of God's presence.
Pause
Father of Wisdom: **open our eyes to your truth.**

For all children separated
from their families by circumstances
they do not understand;
for those who long to be fostered
or adopted into an ordinary loving home;
for an increase in receptive families
to welcome them.
Pause
Father of Wisdom: **open our eyes to your truth.**

Celebrant   Almighty Father, hear our prayers
          and make us alert to your response,
          through Christ our Lord. **Amen.**

Ideas for Adults

Sometimes the discipline of silence is easier to cultivate in a small group who meet at a regular time week by week in church for half an hour. Busy people often come to value that pool of silence in their week, and, in praying together like this, experience great fellowship, even though no words are spoken.

Dance

This dance expresses how a growing awareness of God flows out into our relationships with one another.

Accompany the dance with *The Light of Christ* (ONE, 529). Begin with six dancers placed in a central area absolutely still and staring fixedly straight ahead. Have two sitting, two kneeling on one knee, and two standing; the group should look something like this:

Chorus: During the first chorus they remain completely still, while the whole area is very gradually lit up. A dimmer is ideal for this, but not essential.

Verse 1: Two dancers notice the light and slowly move their heads to gaze in a wide arc to the sides and above; then they raise one arm forward and trace an arc, palm outwards, in the air, as if they can see shape and form around them.

Chorus: Two more dancers notice the light, and the last two start at the second 'light of Christ', each couple repeating the slow smooth actions. The first couple begins to find they can move shoulders, arms and bodies, which they do with a sense of wonder as if the experience is quite new.

Verse 2: The dancers move their hands, studying them as a baby does, fascinated with the fingers, and looking at the hands from different angles. At 'so that all men who believed in him' all faces turn upwards to the light, back to the hands and then up again, bringing the hands upwards as well, in worship.

Chorus: Those who are kneeling stand and turn around as if trying their feet out; at the second 'light of Christ' the seated ones join in; and at the third 'light of Christ' the standing ones join in.

Verse 3: The dancers begin to notice each other and move, hesitantly at first, towards each other into groups of two, then three, exchanging a greeting of peace – embracing, linking hands and kissing. Each should make contact with all the rest.

Chorus: The dancers draw into a circle and all kneel, bowing their heads. Slowly they raise their arms and their heads in a gesture of praise, then stand and walk out among the congregation spreading the sign of peace throughout the whole worshipping community.

Ideas for Children

Discuss with the children what it means to be adopted. Someone may have personal experience of being 'chosen' into a family in this way. They may have come across 'Cabbage Patch' dolls which come with an adoption certificate; there are often advertisements in local newspapers about children in care who are hoping to find a family willing to adopt them.

It is important that even young children have the opportunity to talk about such matters in a caring, sensitive atmosphere, and they are often touchingly aware of the importance of belonging to a family unit.

Now give all the children lumps of plasticine, clay or play dough, and ask them to make some kind of person-creature that they would like as a friend if it were alive. When the creatures are finished, display them and enjoy them.

Wouldn't it be wonderful if we really could bring them to life! Explain how God created beings whom he loved and actually brought to life, and see if they can guess the names of some of them. And not only did he give us life, he adopted us; so that makes us very, very special – we must be children in God's family. He is our parent who loves us enough to want us to eat, sleep, play, work, sing, laugh and cry in his company.

Write this notice to put with the models and bring the whole thing into church.

God made us, gave us life, and chose us as his children

Music
Recorded Music

Prokofiev – *Peter and the Wolf* – Peter's theme

'Live' Music

Hark the herald angels sing *(ONE, 202)*
Let all mortal flesh keep silence *(ONE, 300)*
Listen, let your heart keep seeking *(SONL, 26)*
Of the glorious body *(ONE, 389)*

The Epiphany of the Lord

Theme
Christ's Light is shown to the world

As foretold by the prophets, the light of hope, personified in Jesus, is not for the chosen people only; it is for all humanity in every nation. The wise men, from distant countries and different cultures, pay homage to this child whose power and greatness they acknowledge.

Penitential Rite

King above all kings,
    Lord, have mercy. **Lord, have mercy.**

Power surpassing all temporal power,
    Christ, have mercy. **Christ, have mercy.**

Light of the universe,
    Lord, have mercy. **Lord, have mercy.**

Notes on the Readings

Isaiah 60:1-6

Israel is to be the focus of the most astounding event of history. Through all her wanderings, escapes, defeats and exile, she has waited. God had kept by her, encouraged, chided and forgiven her, but still the long-term promise has yet to be fulfilled.

Now the prophet sings with the thrill of conviction and hope, of the time when Israel's greatest hour will come. On her is conferred the privilege of being the centre of God's revelation; like a pulsing light glowing in the surrounding darkness, God's glory will attract all peoples, and the light will eventually flood the whole world.

It is a remarkable privilege, which excites national pride and awe-filled humility. Israel cannot fail to experience a deep-seated hope and expectation.

Ephesians 3:2-3a, 5-6

Paul was acting as an ambassador. Himself a Jew, he was fulfilling Jewish prophecy by reaching out into the world's darkness with the light of God's saving love. The full, rich extent of God's promise had taken quite a time to dawn on Paul, and the dawning had been traumatic. But once enlightened, he worked fervently to spread the news.

Perhaps it has taken us years to realise that Jesus really is the son of God, and that if we can bring ourselves to 'fall back on him' he does not let us drop. Perhaps a relative or friend has drifted away and seems to be taking anxious years to return.

It is important to remember that it is never too late to bother; however old we are, we can work whole-heartedly, and youth is not a prerequisite for being a full-blooded Christian. Also, some wanderings may be necessary for growth in some people's spiritual development and, if constant prayer is offered for their return to faith, they may well come back stronger and more receptive. What we must never do is give up on them, even secretly. God never does that and neither must we.

Matthew 2:1-12

This event has always fascinated astronomers, and there are various possible explanations for the great bright light that led these enigmatic strangers to a small child living at Bethlehem. Whoever they were and wherever they travelled from, they knew they had arrived when they saw Christ. Here the searching stopped and the worshipping began; the focus of their lives was readjusted and they responded by giving.

Jesus, when he grew up, promised that everyone who searches will find. Sometimes people fool themselves into thinking that they are searching when really they have their hands over their eyes! But thorough searching involves setting out on a risky journey, asking directions from the scriptures and from those who have studied them, and being prepared for the star being occasionally hidden from view. Do we provide enough help to those who are struggling through their search? Do we offer accommodation and hospitality on the way? Are we too ignorant of scripture to be able to answer their questions? Perhaps we could do more, as individuals and as a parish, to guide them towards their destination.

Bidding Prayers

Celebrant   Fellow travellers of Christ's Way,
let us pray together for the Church
and for the world.

Reader   That our Christian witness
in a confused and nervous world may shine
with a piercing integrity and warmth
that awakens people's hearts
to the love of their creator.
Pause
Light of the nations: **shine in our lives.**

That all travellers and pilgrims
may be blessed and protected;

that we may learn to cherish the beauty
of our world and share its riches.
Pause
Light of the nations: **shine in our lives.**

That we may be directed to see
the best practical ways of providing shelter
for the homeless, safe accommodation
for those who live in fear of violence,
and food for the hungry.
Pause
Light of the nations: **shine in our lives.**

That we may learn to see Christ
in the eyes of all those we meet,
and delight in giving God glory
by serving others without expecting rewards.
Pause
Light of the nations: **shine in our lives.**

Celebrant   In thankfulness, Father, we offer you
our lives and our prayers,
through Jesus Christ. **Amen.**

Church Decoration

Incorporate gold, frankincense and myrrh into flower arrangements today.

Ideas for Adults

Arrange a visit to a planetarium; or perhaps there is a keen astronomer in your parish group who would be willing to lead an evening's star watch. In either case, begin or end with a short time of worship, involving a reading from Matthew 2 and Psalm 8. The experience will enhance the Sunday parish worship, as well as being an unusual and fascinating evening out!

Ideas for Children

Prepare a cereal box 'television' and a strip of paper showing the night sky, the wise men on their journey, their visit to Herod, their adoration of Jesus and their departure by another route. Use these drawings as a guideline, or cut out pictures from Christmas cards and stick them on.

Tell the children the story of the wise men, rolling the pictures along as you do so; or ask two children to do the spoon-twisting.

Talk about how we can all be like the star by shining brightly to lead people to Jesus. With their help, make a list of practical ways we can do this:

- stay close to Jesus
- get to know the Bible
- be kind and loving
- stand up for what is right
- let others know you're a Christian
- enjoy and care for God's world

Have six strips of card about 1 metre long and 5 cms wide, lay them down on the floor to make a star shape like this:

Write one of the six guidelines for being a star on each strip of card and let the children decorate them with tinsel and glue. Staple the strips together and carry the star into church, placing it near the altar, if possible.

Music

Recorded Music

Sound track from *2001 Space Odyssey*

'Live' Music

Lead us heavenly Father *(ONE, 298)*
Lord of my life *(SONL, 21)*
The day thou gavest *(ONE, 521)*

The Baptism of the Lord

Theme
'This is my Son, the beloved. Listen to him.'

Associating himself with all those flocking to put their relationship right with God, Jesus, though sinless, came to be baptised by John. As the Spirit, like a dove, descends on him, God audibly confirms both his status and his mission. Through Jesus the Spirit confirms us, too, and lives within us to carry out the work of establishing God's kingdom on earth.

Penitential Rite

It is a good idea to sprinkle the people, as baptismal vows are renewed. During the sprinkling sing *Alleluia for forgiveness* (SONL, 18).

Notes on the Readings

Isaiah 42:1-4, 6-7

The servant is the chosen one, personally appointed by God for a specific mission; he is to establish justice (in the sense of the right and honourable way of behaving) in line with the will of God.

In contrast with worldly empire builders, he is not going to throw his weight about and impose his ideas on people. However good the ideas, forced acceptance of them is diametrically opposed to God's character; and, what is more, it never results in real acceptance anyway.

The gentler, considerate and genuinely caring way points us directly to the way Jesus lived. That is the way we are to walk as well. All too often in history, Christians have conveniently played down the image of the Servant, that Jesus made his own, and time and again it has resulted in attempts to bludgeon people into faith.

Such treatment produces not faith but fear; not freedom but oppression. However well meant, it is misguided and not the way God has chosen. Loving people into faith may seem to take longer, and in the process we may sometimes be trodden on or bruised, but in the end it is the only way that can bring others into the secure happiness of trusting a loving God.

Acts 10:34-38

Peter was still being surprised by God. Just when he thought he had everything sewn up, God would challenge him again. Straight after he had acknowledged Jesus as the Christ, he had been rebuked for tempting Jesus to think in terms of physical safety. Now he has been joyfully confining the good news of Christ to God's chosen people, only to discover that the celebration is to be shared by anybody who fears God and does what is right.

The mark of the Spirit dwelling in Peter is that he is willing to learn and accept the surprises as enlightenment, rather than rejecting them for the way they threaten the status quo. For it is the living Spirit of Jesus who makes his home in us, and nothing living ossifies – much as we may want it to. We should frequently find ourselves being surprised by God – by his choices, his methods and his will for us; if we have not been surprised lately, perhaps we need to spend some time listening instead of talking to him. It may be that the communication channels have got a bit blocked up.

Mark 1:7-11

John's mission was foundation building. He was to clear the ground, dig deep, and prepare God's people for a completely new stage in their relationship with him. By the means of word and sacrament he touched their hearts and consciences till they were receptive enough to know their Saviour when he stood among them in everyday clothes, looking like any other village carpenter.

For however clearly God thunders and makes his will known, those who have closed their minds will be unable to see or understand. By convincing ourselves that God is inactive, we effectively blind ourselves to his acts. And although he yearns for our acceptance of his love, he will find it almost impossible to attract our attention. So it is of utmost importance that we keep God's access routes clear of the debris of sin and daily clutter; then we shall be given the valuable gift of discernment.

Bidding Prayers

Celebrant   Bound together in love
by the power of the Holy Spirit,
let us pray to our heavenly Father.

Reader   For all newly baptised Christians,
all preparing for baptism,
and everyone involved in teaching the faith;
that the Word of God may take root,
grow, and produce good fruit.
Pause
Father of Jesus: **use us for your glory.**

For the world's political leaders
and all who influence them;
that there may be mutual respect
and courtesy, and a shared desire
for peace and understanding.
Pause
Father of Jesus: **use us for your glory.**

For those who carry heavy burdens
of guilt or anxiety; for the very ill
and the dying, and for their loved ones
who share their suffering;
that the Spirit of Christ will comfort,
soothe and strengthen them.
Pause
Father of Jesus: **use us for your glory.**

For ourselves and our spiritual development;
for all whom we irritate and annoy;
for any we have unwittingly hurt or damaged;
that in fixing our gaze on Jesus,
we may see our true selves more clearly.
Pause
Father of Jesus: **use us for your glory.**

Celebrant   Father, we rejoice
in your uncompromising love for us,
and ask you to hear our prayers,
through Jesus Christ. **Amen.**

Ideas for Children

Set up a treasure hunt with clues which direct the children
from one place to another, like this:

The 'treasure' is a bicycle lamp. Switch it on and talk with the
children about how useful it is in helping us find our way in
the dark, without tripping over things or causing accidents.

Now read today's Gospel and tell the children that you
are all going to discover Jesus. Give out these clues to
different children:

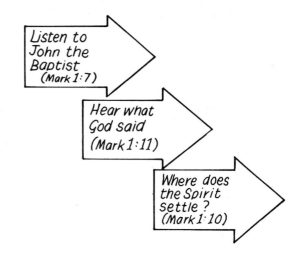

and using Mark's Gospel in their own copies of the Bible,
find out what John says to direct us (Mark 1:7); what God
says to direct us (Mark 1:11); and where the Holy Spirit, in
the form of a dove, settles (Mark 1:10). Explain that there are
lots of other clues every day which lead us to Jesus, such as
the beautiful and amazing things in nature; kind or unselfish
behaviour; Bible stories and stories of the saints; help when
we need it; songs and poems, etc.

Give the children this paper with a picture of Jesus in the
centre which they can colour in. Then fill in one circle each
day of the week, either with words or a drawing, with something that has directed them towards Jesus. Ask them to
bring these back next week.

Music
Recorded Music

Debussy – La Mer
Tchaikovsky – The Nutcracker: 'The kingdom of ice and snow'

'Live' Music

As gentle as silence (ONE, 430)
Dear Lord and Father of mankind (ONE, 116)
We shall be one (SONL, 10)

LENT

Lent

Questions for Discussion Groups
1. Study each of the temptations and Jesus' replies. What do they teach us about how to resist temptation in our own lives?
2. Time and again we hear of the importance of sacrifice. How can you translate this idea into sound, practical forms in the parish and as individuals?

Ash Wednesday

Theme
Reject sin and be reconciled to God

Thorough and ruthlessly honest self-examination is essential before we can be reconciled to the God of light. The experience is necessarily humbling and embarrassing, but is worth far more than any outward show aimed at impressing people. God sees the secret sorrowing and welcomes us back in joyful reconciliation. Now it will be God, working through us, who is really impressive.

Penitential Rite

The marking of ashes on each forehead provides the expressive penitential rite for today. If no choir is available, consider using a recording of the *Miserere*.

Notes on the Readings

Joel 2:12-18

After the appalling devastation caused by an onslaught of locusts, the people are shown how their behaviour has brought about such suffering. They are urged to own up to their sinfulness and make a full and sincere apology to God.

Outward hysterical drama of tearing their clothes is not necessary; other people may be impressed by it but God is never fooled. He sees clearly the hidden, secret thoughts in our hearts; and the complete altering of our values, so that God is central, is what prompts his complete forgiveness.

2 Corinthians 5:20-6:2

Panic following a threat to our survival (like Joel's story of ruined harvests) usually shocks us into action, and we begin to put things right in our relationships, realising that although bodies die, eternity goes on for ever! Often such zeal wears off once the threat subsides.

Paul is anxious to make it clear to the Christians at Corinth that reconciliation to God is not a one-off event we can then forget about. Jesus, by taking on human nature, and steering it through temptation and death without soiling it with sin, has enabled us to have a new and special relationship with God. So we must be sure not to waste or neglect that treasured gift of his grace. If we do, we shall be unable to work with him for the good of the world, and may well cause others to stumble.

Paul urges us not to wait, and not to waste a second more of our lives: there is only one time to do something about our spiritual debts, and that is now ... now ... now.

Matthew 6:1-6, 16-18

Jesus saw around him, among the religious community, some who did the right things for the wrong reasons. To him, looking with the discernment of God, it was quite obvious which ones were acting and what they were really after in their almsgiving, praying and fasting. They were being just subtle enough to take in those whose admiration they craved, and, as a result, were highly respected.

Sometimes we use even more subtle ways of pocketing the glory which belongs to God. Perhaps we casually let slip our good deeds in conversation, or recount our news with a heavy editorial slant in favour of Number One. It is quite a useful exercise to attempt to do three good deeds in a day without anyone ever finding out!

Of course, it all stems from the heart; if we are primarily concerned with serving God and pleasing him, we need not become neurotic about what others see or do not see. Their reactions will cease to be so important, and if they do notice us shining, we can gladly and willingly direct the praise to God in whose strength we live.

Bidding Prayers

Celebrant Let us come before God,
our creator and sustainer,
with the needs of the Church and of the world.

Reader We bring to his love all who have
committed their lives to his service;
that they all may be one,
bound together by God's Holy Spirit.
Pause
Father of mercy: **hear us with compassion.**

We bring to his love
all the areas of the world
in which there is hostility and unrest;
that new routes to negotiation
and reconciliation may emerge.
Pause
Father of mercy: **hear us with compassion.**

We bring to his love
all who have become hard and aggressive
through years of festering hate or jealousy;
that their unresolved conflicts
may be brought to God's light and healed.
Pause
Father of mercy: **hear us with compassion.**

We bring to his love
the members of our human families,
especially any we find it difficult
to get on with or understand;
that our love for one another
may enter a new dimension
of warm and positive caring,
seasoned with laughter.
Pause
Father of mercy: **hear us with compassion.**

Celebrant Lord and Father, hear our prayers,
and help us grow in the power of your Spirit,
through Christ Jesus. **Amen.**

Ideas for Adults

Have a vigil throughout the day and/or preceding night, with some times of silence and some of singing suitable hymns, chants or choruses. Taking time to prepare as a parish for Lent in this way will set the right attitude for really strong spiritual growth.

Ideas for Children

If possible, arrange for the children to be present when the palm crosses are burnt to ashes. If they witness the breaking down of matter into dust, they will better understand the symbolism of leaving our past in ashes and of remembering that God formed us from dust, and life in him does not end with physical death.

Music
Recorded Music

Mozart – Clarinet Concerto: slow movement

'Live' Music

King of glory, King of peace (ONE, 292)
Life pervading (SONL, 46)
Lord, let me know (SONL, 2)
Though the mountains may fall (ONE, 569)

1st Sunday of Lent

Theme
Water that signifies new life

Jesus' baptism was followed immediately by severe temptation, which he withstood and overcame by the power of the Holy Spirit. Noah put faith in God's promises and survived with his family in spite of the devastating flood. When we, in baptism, put our faith in the life-giving Christ, we shall also receive the strength and grace to resist temptation and overcome sin.

Penitential Rite

In time of temptation your power is our strength,
  Lord, have mercy. **Lord, have mercy.**

In time of temptation your word is our shield,
  Christ, have mercy. **Christ, have mercy.**

In time of temptation your love keeps us safe,
  Lord, have mercy. **Lord, have mercy.**

Notes on the Readings

Genesis 9:8-15

Every child (every grown-up child, too!) loves a rainbow. It is often used as a symbol of joy and hope, and the sight of one against dark storm clouds is often enough to make a day special. The wonder of their scientific explanation is just as exciting as their beauty.

Why not use all future rainbows as calls to re-dedicate ourselves to our side of God's covenant – to accept him as the Lord of our lives? For rainbows are, in a sense, a holy sign, blessed in ancient times as a sign to Noah and his family of God's faithfulness. They had been cradled in the ark as the waters of destruction swirled and churned; and now, as the flood recedes, they are 'born' into a muddy but fertile world of new life and hope.

1 Peter 3:18-22

Our baptismal pledge or promise is also a watery experience, for water is such a powerful symbol both of washing and drowning. Peter – who had at first refused to have his feet washed by Jesus and then demanded a full scale bath, when he realised what Jesus was trying to teach – speaks with great feeling about how baptismal water cleanses us from all that separates us from God. In pledging our lives to him we are effectively drowning our sinful nature, and surfacing, refreshed and bathed, to a new kind of living, grafted onto Christ.

Mark 1:12-15

Satan lost no time in attacking the greatest prize of all. If the Son of God, through the human weakness he had chosen, could be persuaded to work in Satan's way, then every chance for us humans being saved from sin's destruction would be utterly lost for ever. It is a bleak and terrifying prospect.

Mark's Gospel emphasises the force and desolation of that harsh time in the barren wastes near the Jordan river, where Satan hoped to destroy Jesus' ministry even before it had fully begun.

But Jesus, lifting our humanity into the divinity of God, remained steadfast and strong, until Satan slunk away unsuccessful and angels looked after Jesus in his exhausted weariness.

Sometimes we excuse ourselves from giving in to sin on account of the temptation being too strong, and with a sigh of relief we enjoy not having to try any more. If only we could hang on a bit longer in God's strength instead of our own, we should find that, although genuinely exhausting, the resistance would remain just within our capability, and the temptation would recede before we succumbed to it. Resisting Satan's attacks is a serious business and will stretch our wills almost to breaking point at times; but Jesus will never allow us to be tempted beyond what we can, in his strength, survive. And afterwards he ministers to us with immense tenderness.

Bidding Prayers

Celebrant In Christ we were baptised
        and became one with him;
        so in his Spirit let us pray to the Father.

Reader For all Christians whose faith
      is being tested by hardship,
      spiritual dryness or any outside pressures;
      that they may hold fast to Christ
      and emerge stronger in the knowledge
      of his loyal, sustaining love.
      Pause
      Lord, you are the rock: **on whom our security rests.**

      For those involved in advertising,
      broadcasting and journalism
      throughout the world,
      and for all in the entertainment business;
      that they may not encourage
      selfishness or violence,
      but discretion and insight.
      Pause
      Lord, you are the rock: **on whom our security rests.**

      For all who are blinded by prejudice
      or self-centred thinking;
      for all who are being dragged down
      by a drug or alcohol habit they feel
      powerless to stop;
      that they may be led tenderly to freedom.

Pause
Lord, you are the rock: **on whom our security rests.**

For the people either side of us now;
for the families represented here,
and all who live in the same street as we do;
that we may live out the pattern
of Christ's loving in a practical way.
Pause
Lord, you are the rock: **on whom our security rests.**

Celebrant Father, we thank you
for showing us the way to abundant life,
and ask you to hear our prayers
through Jesus Christ. **Amen.**

Ideas for Adults

Get the artists and technicians together this week to construct a huge rainbow, either to be placed behind the altar, or outside the building so that everyone walks under it to get into church.

Many ingenious ideas may emerge from your parish, but here is one suggested method: use lengths of garden wire bent into an arc, with coloured crêpe paper woven in and out of the wires to make the bands of colour.

Ideas for Children

With coloured chalks on a blackboard or marker pens on a large sheet of paper, start drawing a rainbow, colour by colour. Let the children guess what you are drawing. Talk together about when we see rainbows, what the weather is usually like, and which colours come where.

Now read a good children's version of Noah and his ark, such as *Noah's Big Boat* from the Palm Tree Bible stories series. Make sure that they understand the meaning of the rainbow sign at the end of the story: God loves us and will never destroy us. We promise to love him and obey him.

Give the children thin card rainbow shapes which they colour in. On each colour they write one word of the covenant between themselves and God, like this:

Music
Recorded Music

Britten – *Noyes Fludde*

'Live' Music

Comfort, joy, strength and meaning *(SONL, 68)*
Love divine, all loves excelling *(ONE, 337)*
Oh come to the water *(SONL, 67)*
Oh the word of my Lord *(ONE, 431)*

2nd Sunday of Lent

Theme
God was willing to sacrifice his own Son for us

For Abraham, everything, including even his cherished son, was in God's hands; and for such trusting obedience he is greatly blessed. So shall we be when we trust him with our lives, because Christ not only sacrificed his life for us; he has also come right through death to the throne of heaven where he takes our part and pleads for us to the Father.

Penitential Rite

Abraham's God and our God,
Lord, have mercy. **Lord, have mercy.**

Saviour who paid our debt of sin,
Christ, have mercy. **Christ, have mercy.**

Faithful and forgiving God,
Lord, have mercy. **Lord, have mercy.**

Notes on the Readings

Genesis 22:1-2, 9-13, 15-18

It must have seemed utterly incomprehensible to Abraham that God should ask him to sacrifice the very son through whom the promise of a chosen nation was to be fulfilled. If Isaac were killed, how could God's word possibly come true?

Perhaps Abraham was on the edge of trusting more in the means of achieving results than in the source of the power. Such a drastic threat to the 'means' threw Abraham's faith squarely onto the author of the promise. Since he was prepared to sacrifice even his beloved son, Abraham proved that even his most cherished hopes were second to his desire to serve God faithfully.

It was not any blood-sacrifice that God required; he needed the sacrifice of faith in other things, however closely those things may be tied up with his will. And it is all too easy to start trusting in the means instead of the source. If anything seems to be steering our attention away from God, we may find we are asked to abandon it, even though it is intrinsically good. Perhaps, once we have refocused our priorities, it will be given back abundantly; but by that time we will have sacrificed our faith in it, so our trust in God will have grown.

Romans 8:31-34

God loves us so much that as the Father, he is prepared to sacrifice his beloved Son; and as the Son, he is prepared to be obedient, even to the point of submitting to torture and death. All this because it was the only way that we could be set free from our self-centred sin. This time there was no alternative ram provided for the offering; the lamb was Christ himself.

Such extravagant generosity proves, beyond all doubt, that God will never let us be overwhelmed by evil. He is on our side and no matter what terrors or dangers we face, no matter how much we may be abused or criticised, ultimately we are perfectly safe, protected eternally by the God who loves us enough to undergo death for us. He holds us, with all our hopes, struggles and dreams, tenderly in the palm of his hand.

Mark 9:2-10

The practicalities of crucifixion are not in any way ennobling. It is a sordid and sickening business, designed to strip the victim of every scrap of human dignity. Those exhausting hours of torture, interrogation and slow, excruciating dying, would give an overriding impression of abject failure and shame.

It was important, then, that the three who would be most vulnerable to despair should receive some encouraging sign of Christ's divinity before the trauma of Good Friday. They had to see their Lord in his glory, so that they could hang on to this when all dignity was shrouded in pain and jeering. Even in the middle of their grief and horror there would be a memory insisting that Christ was greater even than death.

We, too, can use the memory of the transfiguration when grief or pain or bewilderment threatens to overwhelm us. In the back of our minds the image of the risen Christ instils calm and the confidence of victory: all is well, for he has overcome death.

Bidding Prayers

Celebrant As children and heirs through adoption,
let us confide in our heavenly Father
who knows us so well.

Reader Into his enlightenment and perception
we bring all whose faith is limited
by fear or prejudice;
all whose living faith has been replaced
by the empty shell of habit.
Pause
Lord, we believe: **please help our faith to grow.**

Into the depths of his wisdom
and understanding we bring those
with responsibilities, and all who have
difficult decisions to make;
all those in charge of hospitals, schools,
factories and all community services.
Pause
Lord, we believe: **please help our faith to grow.**

Into the gentleness of his healing love
we bring all who are in pain;
all those recovering from surgery;
those involved in crippling accidents
or suffering from wasting diseases.
Pause
Lord, we believe: **please help our faith to grow.**

Into his tireless faithfulness we bring
any who rely on us for help,
support or guidance;
any whom we are being asked to serve
or introduce to God's love.
Pause
Lord, we believe: **please help our faith to grow.**

Celebrant Father, whose character is always
full of mercy, hear our prayers
through the pleading of your Son,
Jesus Christ. **Amen.**

Ideas for Adults

Dramatise the Genesis reading by using a narrator and actors. Nativity play costumes can be worn by Abraham and Isaac and God's voice should come strongly from behind the congregation so that they are caught in the middle of the action.

As the great promise is confirmed, have an instrumentalist (on organ, keyboard or guitar) to play quietly, continuing for a phrase or two after the words have finished.

Ideas for Children

This is a particularly difficult theme for children to tackle, but if presented in a sensitive way it provides rich ground for teaching.

Beforehand prepare a duplicated sheet of A4 paper so that when folded it shows Abraham's offering on one side and God's on the other. Give them out and help the children fold them into zigzag books. Then read them through, looking at the pictures and adding details as you go. Help them to see why Abraham had already made his offering without actually doing anything to hurt Isaac. Are they ever asked to give anything up? Sharing toys willingly is offering God a sacrifice. So is giving up viewing time to help at home; offering someone your favourite sweet; sticking up for someone even if you get laughed at; being friendly when you feel like being thoroughly grumpy.

In the light of this discussion, read through the other side of the 'book'. Help them to see how the offering here was both in God offering his Son, and in Jesus being willing to go through with it. Many popular stories today explore this idea of an ultimate power of good conquering an ultimate power of evil. Use this shared experience and build onto it.

Music
Recorded Music

Handel – I know that my Redeemer liveth
Beethoven – Symphony No. 9: 'Ode to Joy'

'Live' Music

He is Lord (ONE, 206)
Jerusalem the golden (ONE, 273)
Take my hands (ONE, 509)

3rd Sunday of Lent

Theme
God alone has the message of eternal life

The full significance of the Law and the prophets culminates in the figure of the crucified Christ who is Lord even over death. The truth of this is so extraordinary that we can only perceive it with eyes of faith; otherwise it appears either as blasphemy or madness. Yet to those who believe, God's anointed Son being killed and rising again is the solution to the meaning of life.

Penitential Rite

Nowhere else do we find such love,
    Lord, have mercy. **Lord, have mercy.**

Nowhere else do we find such peace,
    Christ, have mercy. **Christ, have mercy.**

Nowhere else do we find such hope,
    Lord, have mercy. **Lord, have mercy.**

Notes on the Readings

Exodus 20:1-17

If we are to get the full impact of Jesus' teaching, we need to be familiar with God's Law as revealed to Moses. Although not the whole story, the commandments are still worth learning off by heart, however old-fashioned rote learning may be! Jesus certainly used them as the framework of his code of living.

The commandments are a God-given structure of right attitudes and behaviour, based firstly on placing God at the centre of life, and secondly on love and consideration for others. They may look negative with all those 'You shall not's' around, but if we look at them in the light of Jesus' summary of them, we can see that breaking any of the commandments involves a lack of caring love towards God and our fellow humans.

1 Corinthians 1:22-25

Paul has heard rumours that the Corinthians are beginning to form splinter groups, claiming to be a 'Paulist Christian', or a 'Peterist Christian' or an 'Appolloist Christian' or even a 'No-one But Christ Christian'. There is a sadly familiar ring here for us today.

So Paul's advice is very pertinent to all of us who yearn for Christian unity. What he does is to draw attention away from the individual differences of style and emphasis. Obviously people from different backgrounds come with different spiritual 'luggage', and are bound to express themselves in different ways. That is expressive of the rich diversity of God's creation and we should rejoice in it.

But the message that all Christians proclaim slices right across the spectrum of religious, cultural and intellectual differences. It is not something that makes any sense to any group nor is it attractive or comfortably assimilated. And yet the very fact that a crucified Christ is so shocking, uncomfortable and crazy, unites those who believe with a powerful bond given only by God and irrespective of individual styles and personalities. Deliberately God has chosen a sign which can only be understood through faith; and when understood it provides a complete answer to each individual search.

The more we train ourselves to think and act in the light of the crucified Christ, the stronger our bonds of unity will become.

John 2:13-25

Insidiously the Temple trading had grown, based first on genuine practices of devotion and sacrifice, but gradually debased by greed and corruption, which needed rigorous cleansing. Here, too, people had missed the real point of the message and were looking in the wrong direction. Jesus dramatically swung them round to look Godwards and many hated him for it. The sign they demanded was right there in front of them, but they had trained their minds to think in terms of matter and cost-effectiveness, so they could no longer perceive spiritual truth.

Bidding Prayers

Celebrant My brothers and sisters,
trusting in the power of God to save us,
let us pray to the Lord.

Reader For all those in lay and ordained ministry;
for every group of Christians
worshipping together,
in simple or elaborate settings,
throughout the entire world.
Pause
Heavenly Father, hear us:
    we commend them to your love.

For light, guidance and reconciliation
in areas of conflict and tension in our world;
for receptiveness to the commandments of God
and a genuine desire for wisdom and insight.
Pause
Heavenly Father, hear us:
    we commend them to your love.

For all whose lives have been
shattered by disaster;
all who have insufficient food or clothing;
all who suffer as a result
of violence and revenge.
Pause
Heavenly Father, hear us:
    we commend them to your love.

For our parents, brothers,
sisters and children,
and for all who serve us in the community;
for those whose company we miss.

Pause
Heavenly Father, hear us:
we commend them to your love.

Celebrant　Father, we thank you for giving us
this opportunity to pray,
and ask you to hear us
through Jesus Christ. **Amen.**

Ideas for Adults

For the Exodus reading, have ten people each with an unlit candle standing in a semi-circle round the Paschal candle. Each person proclaims one commandment (preferably from memory) and lights a candle, so that when all ten have spoken there is a circle of light all drawn from the resurrection light, complete with its reminder of crucifixion wounds. The candles are then taken and placed in various parts of the church where they witness to God's Law throughout the Mass.

Ideas for Children

Remind the children that when the people of Israel had escaped from Egypt and were going through the desert, God gave Moses ten commandments or rules for them to live by. Have the commandments written up clearly for everyone to see, and read them all out loud. Point out that the first four are all to do with loving God and the others are to do with loving each other.

Now tell or read today's Gospel, asking the children to see if they can pick out which commandment was being broken. (They had let their greed push God out of first place in their lives.) Explain how the different parts of our lives will stay healthy if we fix God right at the centre. As you say this, spread out the five sections of a jigsaw puzzle and ask two of the children to make the puzzle up.

Give out pieces of thin card, paper with the puzzle drawn on, scissors, crayons and glue, and help them make their own jigsaws to take home.

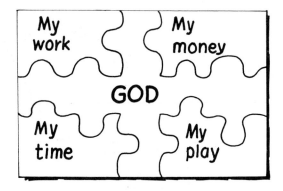

Music
Recorded Music

Bach – *St. Matthew Passion: Truly this was the Son of God*
Beethoven – *Symphony No. 6: The storm and thanksgiving after it*

'Live' Music

Alleluia, sing to Jesus *(ONE, 15)*
I want to build my life *(SONL, 95)*
Lord of all hopefulness *(ONE, 329)*

4th Sunday of Lent

Theme
Jesus brings hope to the lost and exiled

The selfishness of sin always brings about misery, destruction and death. For the people of Israel it produced the heartache of exile in a foreign country, and for all of us it brings a hopeless and desolate wandering, fraught and defensive, aimless and frightening. Yet, through God's immense love and mercy, we are saved from this 'death' existence; Jesus has broken into our prisons and set us free.

Penitential Rite

God of love and tenderness,
　Lord, have mercy. **Lord, have mercy.**

Always ready to forgive,
　Christ, have mercy. **Christ, have mercy.**

Offering the gift of life,
　Lord, have mercy. **Lord, have mercy.**

Notes on the Readings

2 Chronicles 36:14-16, 19-23

God had not ignored his people when they started to go wrong; time after time he had sent them prophets to remind them of their covenant and encourage them to reject evil and be reconciled with him. They took no notice, and laughed scornfully at the messengers' words. Moral dissipation and self-indulgence, with their immediate gratification, had become far more attractive than the ideals David had inspired.

The resulting destruction and exile were humiliating, lengthy and heartbreaking. Now, they realised what they had carelessly thrown away; here they wept as they were asked by their captors to sing songs of their homeland – songs celebrating God's faithfulness to his people.

The God of mercy, true to his nature, forgives and provides the opportunity to return to Jerusalem and rebuild the ruins; he will always do the same for us, too, from whatever distant exile our sin has landed us in. When we turn longingly in his direction again, he will provide the means to return and the opportunity to rebuild.

Ephesians 2:4-10

In all this God is the 'enabler', for we cannot get back from our exile and be reconciled with him by doing good works, however rigorously we apply ourselves or however busy we are.

Often we badly want to do things for God as a kind of 'bargain'; 'if he will only help me pass this exam, I will offer my services as a parish teacher', or whatever. But if we know that we have wasted our time and that is really why we are worried by the exam, then we shall remain in 'exile' from God until we admit that and ask his free forgiveness – even if we spend hours of our time teaching the parish children. In other words, we cannot, and do not need to buy God's forgiveness. It is freely given through the abundance of his love and mercy.

John 3:14-21

The ultimate in allowing people back from exile is to come in person and walk with them every step of the way. This is exactly what God has done, sending his Son into the world among all its evil, misguided foolishness and weakness, in order to walk with us each step of the road to reconciliation with our loving creator. Of course, we are quite at liberty to reject his offer and carry on struggling in our own independent darkness; even if we can't see where we are going, we tell ourselves, at least we will have been true to ourselves and made our own mistakes. On the surface that may sound a valid and mature attitude, but on closer inspection we can see that it is centred on self and therefore exclusive and potentially destructive. Any sin we commit has a damaging effect on those around us: we cannot sin in isolation. Rather, we spread the darkness flooding out from our selfish centres and block the light from ourselves and others.

The alternative is to accept Christ's offer. It will mean relinquishing our assertive independence, which is hard; it will also mean opening our shutters so God's light can stream in. The results will be startling, exciting and overwhelmingly joyful.

Bidding Prayers

Celebrant Followers of the Way of Christ,
let us lay at the feet of our heavenly Father,
all our burdens and concerns.

Reader We offer our concern for those
whose Christian witness has brought danger,
imprisonment and torture;
asking that they may be sustained
and their witness be fruitful.
Pause
Father, hear us: **for you are our hope.**

We offer our concern for all
whose human rights are denied
by defensive or corrupt government;
asking that all in authority may learn wisdom,
compassion and sensitivity.
Pause
Father, hear us: **for you are our hope.**

We offer our concern for the very poor,
the malnourished and the homeless;
asking that individuals and nations
may apply themselves whole-heartedly
to alleviating such suffering.
Pause
Father, hear us: **for you are our hope.**

We offer our concern for all those
who are dear and precious to us,
especially any living through a period
of distress or difficulty;
asking that they may be blessed
and guided by the light of the world.
Pause
Father, hear us: **for you are our hope.**

Celebrant Merciful Father, you know our
deepest needs;
let your will be done in our lives
and in the lives of those for whom we pray,
through Christ Jesus. **Amen.**

Ideas for Adults

To convey the atmosphere of exile as a symbol of our separation through sin and the joy of reconciliation, display pictures of refugees who, because of war or famine, have been forced to live in a strange country with few possessions. World aid programmes are willing to provide some very emotive pictures which help us to understand and increase our willingness to help. Today would be a good opportunity to act as a collection centre for blankets, shoes, food or other necessary materials for such areas of need.

Ideas for Children

Tell today's Chronicles reading with the aid of a model which the children can help to make. Cover a large area of the floor with a green sheet or tablecloth and let them build a fine city from non-interlocking bricks down at one end. At the other end set up model trees and cut a meandering foil river to flow between the trees. Give each child a small card person to move about.

Explain how the people in the city of Jerusalem (label the city) stopped following God and became lazy, greedy, selfish and mean. (The card people act this out.) God sent a messenger to warn them that their behaviour would lead to trouble, but the people only laughed at him (they do this). God tried again and again but they took no notice. One day the army from Babylon arrived. (Give each child a card soldier to hold in the other hand.) The people were not disciplined or prepared and the Babylonians defeated them, smashed their city and took them off to Babylon as prisoners. (They can act all this out with enthusiasm!) Now they were sad and lonely. They missed their lovely city and realised how they had let God down by allowing it to be destroyed. The Babylonians said, 'Sing us one of your songs – one of the psalms!' (the card people say this.)

That made the people even more sad and homesick and they started to cry. Play them a recording of Psalm 137 either from the parish choir or on record. After many years God worked through King Cyrus to allow the people back to Jerusalem. Very happily, and a lot wiser, they went back to their city thanking God and ready to work hard to rebuild. (They help their people to start building.)

Talk about how we are 'exiled' whenever we sin, and if we are sorry, God will give us the chance to come home to him and put things right. Pray about this together and write on the back of each card person: *Lord, when I turn away from you help me to turn back.*

Music
Recorded Music

A Spiritual, such as *Nobody knows the trouble I'm in*
By the Waters of Babylon

'Live' Music

Amazing grace *(ONE, 36)*
God forgave my sin *(ONE, 175)*
Lord, when I turn my back on you *(SONL, 40)*
Walk in the light *(ONE, 547)*

5th Sunday of Lent

Theme
Jesus is willing to suffer and die for us

Knowing the agony that is in store for him if he goes through with the plan to save us, Jesus does not flinch or avoid it. Obediently he accepts the necessary death which will bring life to the world. Thus, through him, Jeremiah's prophecy of a new, deep-seated bond between God and his people will become a reality. God's law will be written on the hearts of all when Christ's kingdom spreads through the whole world.

Penitential Rite

If you have an area of floor space in the church, set down in the centre of it a large wooden cross. Give the people votive candles and invite them to bring the lit candles up and place them on the floor around the cross. Everybody kneels on the floor with their attention centred on the cross surrounded by light, and the following words are sung:

Beginners on skiing slopes experience this feeling as the white expanse dips steeply away from them. If their fear leads them to lean back to the safety of the hill behind them, they actually slip faster and lose control. It is only when they lean forward into the frightening space that they find control and can tackle the slope confidently.

In other words, trusting our lives to God requires courage, but is rewarded with a far greater sense of security and confidence than if we rely on ourselves. In Christ we shall have access to the strength and help we need. We have it 'in Christ' because he, with all human fear and vulnerability, flung himself absolutely and obediently on to the will of his Father.

John 12:20-33

It was this need for complete obedience that Jesus stressed when the Greek Jews showed an interest in meeting him. Philosophical discussion and interest are all very well and can serve as introductions to Jesus, but eventually we are challenged with the requirement to obey, with all the courage and trust that this involves. No longer can we follow Jesus when the mood takes us, or when we approve of the liturgy/music/homily. No longer can we excuse our need for regular times set aside each day for prayer and reading the Bible.

If we really want to follow Christ we have no choice but to become obedient, and lay our ambitions, plans and loyalties down at his feet. We may find that we are enabled to do this in one fell swoop, as Paul did, or we may find it is a ques-

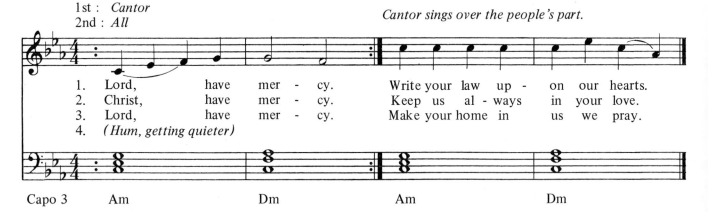

1st : *Cantor*
2nd : *All*

Cantor sings over the people's part.

1. Lord,   have   mer - cy.   Write your law up - on our hearts.
2. Christ,   have   mer - cy.   Keep us al - ways in your love.
3. Lord,   have   mer - cy.   Make your home in us we pray.
4. *(Hum, getting quieter)*

Capo 3   Am   Dm   Am   Dm

Notes on the Readings

Jeremiah 31:31-34

Our Bibles are divided into the Old and New Testaments, and there is a very good reason for this. When, at the Last Supper, Jesus offered the wine as the blood of the new covenant, or testament, he was saying that the prophesied new covenant between God and his people was now being made, through himself.

From now on the law would be written on people's hearts, rooted in love and cauterized with the ultimate sacrifice of giving up one's whole life freely and gladly. When we share in Christ's dying we give our lives away; we hand over the use of our time, our money and our gifts and energies and allow God to take over and be in charge of our lives. All the richness of communal worship and all the structuring of Christian care emanate from this kind of total, personal commitment to God.

Hebrews 5:7-9

Such complete obedience may appear distasteful and threatening; we want to grip our lives tighter in case relinquishing our hold sends us into situations we cannot cope with or control.

tion of peeling off skin after skin until we really understand just how much giving is required. But however it happens, it will be done in a supportive and encouraging atmosphere, because God our Father is not a domineering slave-driver but a tender and caring parent who enjoys our company and wills for our salvation.

Bidding Prayers

Celebrant Brothers and sisters in Christ,
trusting in the deep love
our heavenly Father has for us,
let us pray.

Reader For the grace and strength to be obedient
in whatever God asks us to do,
without thought for our personal gain or safety.
Pause
Wise and loving Father: **may your will be done.**

For greater trust and friendship between
the different nations on our planet;
for a universal desire for peace.
Pause
Wise and loving Father: **may your will be done.**

For Christ's calming reassurance
to bring peace of mind and spirit
to those worried about the future,
those dreading some difficult event,
and those who are frightened of dying.
Pause
Wise and loving Father: **may your will be done.**

For the capacity to be positive
and encouraging in all our relationships;
for the right words to say in order to be
peace makers and witnesses to God's love.
Pause
Wise and loving Father: **may your will be done.**

Celebrant With thankful hearts we offer these concerns
for the Church and for the world,
through Jesus, our Saviour. **Amen.**

Ideas for Children

Show the children a packet of seeds with a picture of the delicious food they will grow into. Sprinkle them into a tray so they can feel them without spilling them. If we put them back into the packet (do so) will they grow? What if we waited for a month or two – would we get a crop then? No, they would just stay as seeds. What needs to happen to them before they will grow?

Bring out a seed tray and a bag of seed compost, a trowel and a watering can, and let the children prepare the seed bed and plant the seeds. Help them to realise that the original seed has to die in order for all the life to come which brings about the harvest. (Keep this tray of seeds watered and cared for week by week, transplanting when necessary, so the children can watch the growing and eventually share the crop.)

Now read or tell the Gospel for today, relating the seeds both to Jesus and to ourselves. Sing *Love is something if you give it away* and give them all some seeds to plant at home. Put the seeds in an envelope on which is written:

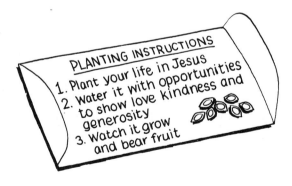

PLANTING INSTRUCTIONS
1. Plant your life in Jesus
2. Water it with opportunities to show love kindness and generosity
3. Watch it grow and bear fruit

Music
Recorded Music

Paul Winter – *Earth Mass: The Kyrie* (based on the sounds of howling wolves)

'Live' Music

Covenant *(ONE, 153)*
Farmer, farmer *(SONL, 37)*
Love is his word *(ONE, 338)*
My God, accept my heart this day *(ONE, 355)*
Our hearts were made for you *(SONL, 36)*

![HOLY WEEK]

Holy Week

Questions for Discussion Groups
1. Re-read the events surrounding the Passover in Exodus. What parallels and significance can you see which give you insight into the events of Holy Week?
2. Make a list of the people Jesus encountered during his trial and crucifixion. What influence do you think he had on each one?

Passion Sunday (Palm Sunday)

Theme
See, your king is coming!

Amid great rejoicing Jesus enters the holy city of Jerusalem, riding on a donkey. Ahead of him is betrayal, torture and death; but we still join our cheers with the crowds waving their palms, because we know that the route to the cross is the route to our redemption. Jesus is indeed our King.

Penitential Rite

King with power to forgive,
Lord, have mercy. **Lord, have mercy.**

King of love who heals us all,
Christ, have mercy. **Christ, have mercy.**

King of inner peace and joy,
Lord, have mercy. **Lord, have mercy.**

Notes on the Readings

Isaiah 50:4-7
Philippians 2:6-11
Mark 14:1-15, 47

Through his own personal suffering and humiliation, the obedient servant in the Isaiah prophecy is able to teach others about the uncompromising love of God. In Jesus this song takes on a new and astounding reality, for here is the Son of God, with whom God is 'well pleased', undergoing insults, slander, torture, death, and, perhaps most hurtful of all, desertion by every one of his followers and even a sense of isolation from his Father.

However can such a bleak and distressing drama be cherished generation after generation? Why did God not answer Jesus' desperate prayer that the horror might be averted?

When Jesus returned to find the disciples sleeping, perhaps his words applied also to himself: 'The spirit is willing but the flesh is weak.' For here is the essence of what it meant to save us from the prison of sin; God had to empty himself of all rights, privilege and status and become utterly weak and vulnerable; he had to submit to the very worst that evil could throw at him and still continue to love, forgive and trust. Had his flesh not been weak he would not have been able to make this complete sacrifice; had his spirit not been willing, he would not have been able to achieve this ultimate in loving obedience.

Yet even at his most helpless, most cruelly treated and

most terribly alone, Christ still loved the world which rejected him, and it is the incredible wonder of such love that draws us stumbling to his feet.

Bidding Prayers

Celebrant   In the spirit of Jesus let us pray
to our heavenly Father who knows us so well.

Reader   For wisdom and guidance
in all areas of Christian teaching;
for discernment and perseverance
in all who spread the news of God's love.
Pause
King of love: **reign in our hearts.**

For honesty and integrity among
all national leaders and ambassadors,
all employers and employees,
all local councillors and administrators.
Pause
King of love: **reign in our hearts.**

For an awareness of God's undergirding love
in all those who are suffering physically,
emotionally, mentally or spiritually.
Pause
King of love: **reign in our hearts.**

For increased generosity and mercy
in our dealings with one another
in our daily routines and everyday problems.
Pause
King of love: **reign in our hearts.**

Celebrant   Father, we rejoice in your companionship
and loyalty, and ask you to hear our prayers
for the sake of Jesus our Saviour. **Amen.**

Ideas for Everyone

The procession of palms is a chance to witness to the local community; it is a chance to 'dance with all our might before the Lord' as David did when the ark of the covenant was carried into Jerusalem. Ask everyone to wear bright clothes and bring along percussion instruments (home-made if possible) and branches from tree-pruning that are large enough to wave like flags. Have a practice session during the week to teach the music and dancing and plan a slightly longer route as the procession will be moving faster than usual! No books will be needed as the words are easily learnt. Such a procession may be different, but it is in no way irreverent; just as the woman lavished expensive ointment on Jesus to show her 'worthship' of him, so we should have times when we move our whole bodies in worship of the king who rides into Jerusalem on his way to achieve our salvation.

The basic step for everyone is:

Step, together, step, hop;

encourage people to improvise on this, introducing turns, swaying and clapping and, of course, waving their branches. The words are a constant reminder of whom we are dancing for.

The music is given below.

Music
Recorded Music

Bach – St. John's Passion (one of the arias or chorales)

'Live' Music

Let all that is within me cry holy *(ONE, 301)*
My song is love unknown *(ONE, 363)*
Rejoice! The Lord is king *(ONE, 463)*

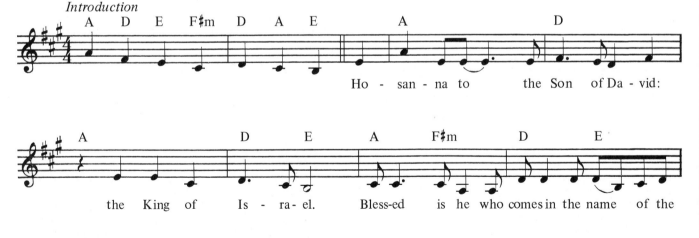

Holy Thursday

Theme
Christ gives the Passover new meaning

The Passover feast, celebrated year after year, was a celebration of God intervening to liberate his people from slavery. The blood of the lamb protected them, and the lamb was both a sacrifice and food for them as they began their journey. Now Christ offers himself in the bread and wine and in the washing of his disciples' feet. His sacrifice liberates us from the slavery of sin.

Penitential Rite

Lord and Master, so ready to serve,
Lord, have mercy. **Lord, have mercy.**

Knowing our weakness we come to you,
Christ, have mercy. **Christ, have mercy.**

You alone can make us pure,
Lord, have mercy. **Lord, have mercy.**

Notes on the Readings

Exodus 12:1-8, 11-14

The precise instructions for preparing and eating the Passover meal served to stress its importance; all ritual does the same thing, whether it is blowing out the cake candles and singing 'happy birthday' or dressing up for a wedding. Obviously it is no good merely going through the motions without any inner commitment, but neither is it helpful to dismiss ritual as empty actions we should have grown out of.

With obedience and reverence the people are to commemorate this great act of deliverance. So often God blends the spiritual with the highly practical, and here he insists that everyone has sandals on, belts fastened and walking staffs at the ready, so there is no mad rush and scramble after the feast in the Lord's honour. Instead, in ordered and expectant confidence, the people can go out to the world, having been physically and spiritually fed.

1 Corinthians 11:23-26

Now, having been brought up in the tradition of the Passover, Jesus takes its symbolism and broadens it to include an even greater deliverance. The lamb without blemish, offered to protect, sustain and deliver, is himself; for this feast marks the willingness of God to save the entire world from the enslavement to sin and selfishness. Through his sacrifice we will be enabled to walk freely and purposefully into the future.

John 13:1-15

Strangely (in worldly terms at least), our liberation from servitude to sin results in our acting as servants to one another; not very important servants either, if feet washing is anything to go by. So how can we account for this peculiar paradox?

The answer is in the word 'love'. There is all the difference in the world between grudgingly doing something because we are forced to, and lovingly doing something because we care in a personal way. Christ's death did not free us from unpleasant or difficult situations, nor from demanding relationships; what he does free us from is the inward-looking

self-centredness that makes us see our personal survival, comfort and success as being of primary importance. As soon as love for God and each other usurps that self at the hub of our lives, attitudes change, resentment melts, bitterness softens to understanding, needs become opportunities to show our affection in practical ways and duties turn into joy-filled privileges.

That is the freedom that Christ died for; and it enables us to realise our potential as co-workers with our loving creator.

Bidding Prayers

Celebrant Followers of Jesus, as we gather to share
in this celebration, let us cast our burdens
on the loving mercy of our heavenly Father.

Reader We commend to his care and protection
all who are abused, imprisoned
or insulted because of their faith.
Pause
Lord, by your example: **teach us all to love.**

We commend to his light and truth
all governments and committees,
every head of state, and all leaders.
Pause
Lord, by your example: **teach us all to love.**

We commend to his healing and wholeness
all who are ill or injured;
those undergoing emergency surgery
and those who are nearing death.
Pause
Lord, by your example: **teach us all to love.**

We commend to his long-suffering
patience and compassion, ourselves,
with our frequent misuse of his blessings
and failure to serve.
Pause
Lord, by your example: **teach us all to love.**

Celebrant Merciful Father, fulfil our needs
in the way which is best for us
in the context of eternity;
we ask this through Jesus Christ. **Amen.**

Ideas for Adults

Many helpful and practical ideas are given in *Focus on Holy Week* which are well worth trying.

Encourage people to bring bells to ring during the *Gloria* and invite a broad cross-section of the parish to take part in the feet washing, giving them a special preparation session during the week. Use the notes on the readings and study the passages chosen for Holy Thursday so that the group is fully aware of what it is doing.

Ideas for Children

Some children will be able to accompany their parents and join in the celebration and drama of this day. But if they are too young, suggest that families have a special shared meal during the day, before which the Exodus and Gospel passages are read, and a family blessing is said. Holy Thursday, the feast of the Passover, is an important time for families (or groups of families) to pray and eat together.

Music
Recorded Music

Bach – St. John's Passion

'Live' Music

A new commandment (ONE, 39)
Take this and eat it (SONL, 77)
The freedom song (ONE, 154)
The king of love my shepherd is (ONE, 528)

Good Friday

Theme
Through his wounds we are healed

Jesus yearns so much for us to be saved that he is prepared to lay down his life for us, allowing the burden of the whole world's evil to rest on his shoulders. Not once does he stop loving and forgiving. His death is no failure, then, but an accomplishment of cosmic proportions. Christ, by taking the just reward for our sin, has brought us life and freedom.

Penitential Rite

This is provided today by the Veneration of the Cross.

Notes on the Readings

Isaiah 52:13-53:12

It is certainly amazing, and proof of God speaking through the prophets, that this passage strikes to the very core of how the world was to be saved. The idea of God's obedient servant being prepared to suffer and die in order to bring others to peace and understanding, is taken up and richly fulfilled by Jesus on the cross. The unthinkable insult – of the creator being destroyed by his created – has actually happened: God is being put to death while 'praying all the time for sinners'.

Hebrews 4:14-16; 5:7-9

This act, more than any other, points to the end of our hopeless yearnings and desolate loneliness. God is not a distant and unapproachable ideal but a person – warm-blooded and tactile, with pulse and breath. His loving is not a condescending 'playing' but a close relationship with deep affection and empathy. So much so, that he identifies completely with us in all our best moments and our most appalling ones. At the times we come, exhausted, to the end of our strength, and have nothing left to draw on, we find Jesus – not in the distance with his back to us, but right next to us, lifting us up to carry us to safer ground. His willingness to die the crucifixion death is our guarantee that he will never, ever desert us, and no suffering we face is beyond his reach; always he suffers alongside us and leads us through it to new life.

John 18:1-19, 42

Friday was the day for sacrificing the Passover lambs in the temple. At the Last Supper Jesus had prepared his disciples for the new Passover when he gave them the bread and wine and spoke of sacrificing his own body and blood for the forgiveness of the sin of the whole world.

Now, with the Passover preparations complete, the Lamb of God is slaughtered at the same time as the Passover lambs. While their death marks and celebrates physical liberation, Christ's death marks and celebrates the freedom of eternal and universal salvation.

Bidding Prayers

The General Intercessions are used today. It may aid concentration if a duplicated sheet is produced with appropriate pictures alongside each intention.

Ideas for Adults

Instead of having a reader for the Isaiah passage, make sure that everyone has the words and read it aloud, slowly and carefully, together.

Ideas for Children

While older children can actively participate in the drama and liturgy of Good Friday and gain much from its richness, younger children may find it all too overwhelming and distressing. It is probably better for them to have a separate liturgy to walk the Way of the Cross, and some suggestions are given in *Focus the Word* (Luke).

If there is space outside your church, a very moving and valuable experience can be offered the children by organising an outdoor Stations of the Cross. Use planks of rough wood, rope, masonry nails, cloth, piles of stone, thorns and pictures to set up each Station with the children's help. Utilise any natural symbols that are already there, such as thorn bushes, piles of rubble or narrow places; the area does not need to be beautiful.

Let several of the children carry a really large wooden cross on the journey, and teach the children two choruses to be sung as rounds between Stations. If the weather is bad, wear suitable clothing and carry on. Such a physical Way of the Cross speaks directly to children and can help them a lot. Finish in church with the cross laid on the floor, a hand-made crown of thorns laid on it, and everyone gathered kneeling around it in a short time of silence.

Keep each stop simple and straightforward and quite short.

Music
Recorded Music

Lloyd Webber – Requiem: Pie Jesu

'Live' Music

Fear not, for I have redeemed you (ONE, 136)
I am the bread of life (ONE, 226)
Life-pervading, all-containing (SONL, 46)
Our God reigns (ONE, 223)

EASTER

Holy Saturday
The Easter Vigil

Theme
New life through the resurrection

Having been obedient even to death, Jesus has accomplished our redemption, and now breaks through death's barrier into new life which will never end. We too can share that everlasting life as we die to sin in baptism and are raised to a new, rich and fulfilling life engendered by our Saviour.

Liturgy

This night is the most significant and important in the whole liturgical year; the central point of Christianity and the focus of all the Church's belief and teaching. The worship therefore deserves particular thought and planning, worthy of such a great and special occasion.

The liturgy provides an abundance of powerful symbolism which can heighten our understanding of the paschal mystery we are celebrating. It is worth using these symbols to the full, so that they are caught and experienced by the whole community.

There is a fund of ideas in *Focus on Holy Week* which will ensure that the Vigil is as meaningful as possible.

Notes on the Readings

Genesis 1:1-2:2
Genesis 22:1-18
Exodus 14:15-15:1
Isaiah 54:5-14
Isaiah 55:1-11
Baruch 3:9-15, 32-4:4
Ezekiel 36:16-28

Just as a family, on some special occasions, likes to go through the photograph albums, reminiscing over the shared events which have forged their common roots, so we, as the Christian family, spend some time tonight looking back over the past events which have led up to the joy of the resurrection.

God our Father and Creator is in control. We see again how his love forms, leads, forgives and sustains humanity, and how the promises and prophecies look forward to the events we are now privileged to have seen.

Romans 6:3-11

Not only have we seen the world being redeemed, or 'brought back' from sin, but we are also part of the redemption ourselves. Whenever, in the strength of Jesus, we renounce sin and reject evil, we share both in the crucifixion and in the resurrection. Fresh growth springs up where there was desert; ice-bound rivers of love begin to flow again; and hope blossoms straight out of the deadwood of despair. The resurrection is both a unique event and a constant state of renewal which sets our lives dancing.

Mark 16:1-8

As Creator, God had rested on the seventh day after accomplishing his work. Now, as Saviour, God keeps the Sabbath after the accomplishment of his redeeming work. With the beginning of a new week comes the most amazing new life which is forever free of the threat of death. Now Jesus emerges triumphant over humanity's fall from grace; the blockade is down, just as the stone has been rolled away, so that the way is now clear for us to be children of our heavenly Father, loving and beloved in a close relationship which death cannot destroy.

It was raw power of universe-building proportions that the women witnessed that Sunday morning; no wonder they were scared out of their wits! No wonder, either, that once they had grasped the consequences of such an incredible event, their joy was inexhaustible. For the resurrection means that there is always hope and opportunity in every conceivable situation. Evil can never be the end of the story; pain and failure are not barren deserts but dark places where strong growth begins. Jesus has claimed us back and in his arms we are safe.

Ideas for Adults

Vary the presentations of the Old Testament readings, using music, slides, drama, dance and choral reading. Those who have been practising during Lent can now offer their work for the strengthening of others. More specific ideas are given in *Focus the Word* (Luke).

Ideas for Children

Older children can be involved with the adults in some of the presentations. Since it is a very special occasion, and there is plenty going on, many families may decide to bring younger children as well, complete with a blanket to cuddle up in if and when they fall asleep!

It may also be worth considering whether the renewal of baptismal vows, with the lighting of each person's candle and the sprinkling of water, could not be incorporated into the Easter Day Mass for the benefit of those children who are not able to come to the Vigil.

Another possibility is to time the Vigil so that instead of being very late it is very early – perhaps 3.00 am. – so people sleep beforehand and the Vigil is followed by a parish breakfast.

Music
Recorded Music

Tchaikovsky – *1812 Overture*

'Live' Music

At the name of Jesus *(ONE, 50)*
Praise to the holiest *(ONE, 455)*
Tell out, my soul *(ONE, 514)*

Easter Sunday
(Mass of the Day)

Theme
H*e is risen*!

The tomb of death is empty and Jesus, thoroughly dead on Good Friday, is thoroughly alive today and for ever. The victory over evil has been won, and his glorious risen life empowers us to bring hope, joy and healing to the world's darkness and decay. God has brought new life to our world.

Penitential Rite

Help us to turn from all that is evil,
  Lord, have mercy. **Lord, have mercy.**

Help us to turn to the light of your love,
  Christ, have mercy. **Christ, have mercy.**

Help us to live resurrection lives,
  Lord, have mercy. **Lord, have mercy.**

Notes on the Readings

Acts 10:34, 37-43

You cannot get a more reliable witness of the resurrection than Peter, who has eaten and drunk with the risen Christ. When Jesus had raised Jairus' daughter to life he had told her parents to give her something to eat; this was the confirmation that she was truly alive and well.

The disciples had discovered Jesus among them at the breaking of bread, and he continues to be found in the breaking of bread day by day in the Eucharist. We too, then, can be confident witnesses to the fact – not opinion – that Christ rose from the dead, is still alive now and will be alive for ever.

Colossians 3:1-4

Not only has Christ conquered death and sin; he has also brought us back to life lived in the way God planned when he created us. Like bulbs in winter, our growing in Christ gets started in secret and will in due course burst into flower. But flowers don't just happen; the hidden growth is essential. So we are encouraged to keep ourselves fixed on Christ, looking with his eyes at the world, until we see everything lit by eternity.

Alternative Reading

1 Corinthians 5:6-8

Life in the risen Christ is a continual growing, and we must never fall into the trap of thinking we have arrived. That is the moment pride takes hold and blocks all further growth until it is eradicated. We need to knock all the hot air out of ourselves, so to speak, taking as our yardstick the values of sincerity and truth. This is the best and only way to celebrate Christ's sacrifice and resurrection.

John 20:1-9

The breathless excitement and wonder of this morning of mornings is caught, like rainbows in a diamond, in this account of the resurrection. The darkness, the running feet, the fear and nervousness, the curiosity and the amazement; all showing ordinary people swept against the unimaginable, eternal power of God. Like a great shock wave, the impact of that unprecedented Sunday morning has rocked people's established ideas about life and death in successive generations. After this, nothing will ever be quite the same again; God has visited and redeemed his people and Christ has claimed the world for goodness, love, peace and everlasting joy.

Bidding Prayers

Celebrant   Filled with the hope and joy of Easter,
    let us pray confidently to our loving Father.

Reader   For the newly baptised and their families;
    for those who are sensing God's call
    and need reassurance in it;
    for all God's people
    in every part of the world.
    Pause
    Life-giving Lord: **reign in our hearts.**

For the areas in which there is fighting,
    unrest and unresolved conflict;
    for the unprincipled, the corrupt
    and those who thirst for revenge.
    Pause
    Life-giving Lord: **reign in our hearts.**

For those who are finding life very trying
    and difficult at the moment;
    for those who are coping with personal tragedy
    or mourning; for all who are ill or frail.
    Pause
    Life-giving Lord: **reign in our hearts.**

For our neighbours here; in our street;
    and at school and at work;
    for any who may be wishing they knew someone
    willing to share their burden.
    Pause
    Life-giving Lord: **reign in our hearts.**

Celebrant   Father, in the name of the risen Jesus,
    we ask you to bring the hope, healing
    and joy of the resurrection
    to all these people for whom we pray. **Amen.**

Ideas for Adults

Why not try constructing a festal archway outside the church using two step ladders with a third ladder lashed across the top? Weave plenty of greenery in and out until the main structure is hidden and then decorate with flowers and ribbons.

Another possibility is to have a festival of flowers in the church this week. Get together a team of about a dozen people to decide on themes and who is going to be responsible for each, ask someone to write labels, and pool ideas and resources. The main theme should be the resurrection; within this, you could either trace God's promises through from the creation, the fall, Noah, Abraham, Moses and the prophets; or you could select the main events of Jesus' life. Either way the festival will provide good teaching material both for those involved and for all the visitors.

Ideas for Children

Bring along a large metal tray, a tub of fine earth, moss, stones, twigs and flowers, and help the children to construct a garden with a tomb cave in it. To keep flowers fresh, sink small paste jars into the soil and use as tiny vases.

With everyone sitting round the garden, read or tell the Easter events, making your fingers walk or using simple models of the people involved.

Carry the garden carefully into church, with an acolyte leading the way.

Music
Recorded Music

Greig – *Peer Gynt Suite: Morning*

'Live' Music

All the nations *(ONE, 30)*
Praise the Lord! Ye heavens adore him *(ONE, 452)*
Sing to the mountains *(ONE, 495)*

2nd Sunday of Easter

Theme
Believing without seeing

It takes a leap of trust to believe, without visual or tangible proof, that Jesus is risen from the dead. But having made that leap of faith, we are empowered to win over all that is evil and destructive within ourselves and in our world. For when we believe, the spirit of Jesus makes his home in us so that our love, mercy and integrity can develop and spread through the world.

Penitential Rite

In our areas of doubt,
    Lord, have mercy. **Lord, have mercy.**

In our hesitating faith,
    Christ, have mercy. **Christ, have mercy.**

In our excuses and denials,
    Lord, have mercy. **Lord, have mercy.**

Notes on the Readings

Acts 2:32-35

The early Christians did nothing by halves! Many had been first-hand witnesses of the living, risen Jesus, as well as having seen him hanging dead on the cross. Since Pentecost they knew that even though they could not see him, he was living there among them now.

And this is the clue to their incredible lifestyle, full of love for one another, full of generous sharing and joy. Just supposing Jesus of Nazareth walked physically into our own parish, shared meals with us, worked and prayed alongside us, came with us on parish visiting, sat in on church meetings and helped plan our activities so as to be of most service to the community – what would happen? The result would

surely be the same joy and unity of purpose and loving affection that we see in Luke's description of the early Church.

Well, they did not see Jesus physically at this stage any more than we do. And he is just as much alive and present among us now as he was among them then. So if we spend some time letting the events of the resurrection sink in until we really *know* Jesus is alive, we will find him really present in all our parish worship, work, plans and problems; and his life will transform any areas which have become jaded, critical, narrow, outworn or dead.

John 5:1-6

Through this faith we become children of God, and that loving relationship lets loose incredible power over evil. We do not, like Hercules, have to perform all kinds of spectacular deeds; we have only to do something very natural: love the heavenly Father who spiritually begot us. If we think of our love and praise directed towards God as a beam of light aimed towards one of those globe mirrors you find at dance halls, we can see how our God-directed love is used to shine outwards in many directions on all kinds of people. Loving God first enables us to love the rest of his children. And love is unsurpassed as a dissolver of evil.

John 20:19-31

Jesus was still wearing his human body, and still retained the wounds which had caused his death. The disciples had lived and worked with him for many months; they recognised him now and were overjoyed to see him again.

We can all sympathise with Thomas. It is all very well to be told something incredible has happened but we need the proof of first-hand evidence before we commit ourselves to anything we may regret. We sometimes forget that the other disciples had been just as sceptical at the beginning, calling the women's claims 'idle talk' and running to the tomb themselves to see what had happened.

But if we are doubtful and want to be convinced, we have to put ourselves where we are likely to find proof; it is no good closing our minds and our Bibles or staying away from Mass because we are full of doubts. If we do that we shall miss Jesus when he makes his presence known, and give ourselves no opportunity to thrust our hands into his side. At first Thomas reacted by keeping away, and his doubts grew. Then, drawn by Christ's love, he put himself in the place to which Jesus had come before. This was his initial act of faith, and Jesus honoured it, coaxing Thomas' trust to grow and blossom.

Bidding Prayers

Celebrant Dear friends in Christ, as we gather here
in the presence of the living God,
let us ask for his help and guidance
in the Church and in the world.

Reader Let us join our prayers
with all other worshipping Christians,
for an increasing love and affection
between individuals and groups
in every parish; for open-heartedness,
outreach and generosity of spirit.
Pause
Unchanging Lord:
    we pledge ourselves to your service.

For the breaking down of suspicion,
double standards and hypocrisy in our world;
that the nations may work together
to conquer the problems of food

and water distribution,
so that our planet's resources
are shared and not wasted.
Pause
Unchanging Lord:
we pledge ourselves to your service.

For those involved in medical research,
and all who suffer from diseases
which are as yet incurable;
for any who are too weak or exhausted to pray;
for any who are desperate or suicidal.
Pause
Unchanging Lord:
we pledge ourselves to your service.

For the homes and families,
represented here, with all their particular joys
and sorrows, needs and resources;
that our lives may be practical witnesses
to our faith.
Pause
Unchanging Lord:
we pledge ourselves to your service.

Celebrant   Trusting in your immense compassion, Father,
we offer you our prayers
and ask you to hear us,
through Jesus Christ. **Amen.**

Ideas for Adults

The second reading is more clearly understood if it is dramatised chorally. Use a group of six – three men and three
women. If they all wear similar clothing, such as cassocks,
that will help people to concentrate on words and actions.
The group walks in this formation:

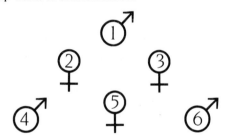

starting from the back. When they reach the area of best vis-
ibility they all stop. (1) turns to face the congregation.

WORDS	ACTION
(1): Whoever believes that Jesus is the Christ	
(2), (3): has been begotten by God	*They turn to face congregation.*
(1), (2), (3): and whoever loves the Father that begot him loves the child whom he begets	*They raise right arm slowly, looking upwards.* *They extend arm and rest on shoulders of (4), (5) and (6) turn to face congregation.*
(4), (5), (6): We can be sure that we love God's children	
all: if we love God himself	*All form a circle, holding hands and looking up.*
all: and do what he has commanded us	*All turn outwards, arms in 'offering', palms up*
(2): this is what loving God is –	*(2) stays standing; others kneel on one knee facing her.*
(2): keeping his commandments	

all: and his commandments are not difficult	*Stay kneeling, but swing head round over shoulder to look at congregation.*
(1), (2), (3): because anyone who has been begotten by God	*Walk into centre of circle, others look towards them.*
all: has already overcome the world;	*All stand up and raise arms.*
(4): this is the victory over the world –	*He takes 4 steps down the church.*
all: (Loudly) our faith.	*All turn and face altar.*
(4): Who can overcome the world?	*All lower arms.*
(1), (2), (3): Only the man who believes that Jesus is the Son of God;	*All turn to face congregation in this formation*
(5): Jesus Christ who came by water	*All turn to look at (5).*
(6): and blood,	*All turn to look at (6).*
(4): not with water only	*Walks up to others.*
all: (slowly) but with water and blood;	
(3): with the Spirit as another witness –	*All turn to look at (3).*
all: since the Spirit is truth. (Pause) This is the Word of the Lord.	*All group into original form holding hands with others in same row.*

Formation diagram:

```
          1
      2       3
   5             6
          4
```

They walk in formation to the back of the church.

Ideas for Children

Believing without seeing is something young children usually find easy; their natural trustfulness was used by Jesus as
a model for us all. Begin by performing a very careful mime
of some everyday action such as sewing, or sealing and ad-
dressing a letter. Let the children guess what you are doing,
and give them a turn if there is time. Would they have known
the answers if they had never seen someone do these
things? The more familiar something is, the better we shall
'see' it if it is invisible.

Now ask them to close their eyes and point to you. Help
them see that it is hard to do if they don't know where you
are, but easy if they know where to find you before their
sight of you goes.

Now pass round two strong magnets and let them feel the
power of attraction and repulsion. It is very strong and real
but invisible.

Explain how this is like the risen Jesus who lives among us
but is not usually seen. The better we get to know him, the
more we can recognise him; and his power is just as real as
the magnetic power. We can know his presence by the way
people act when he is living in them. What would we notice?

– love – readiness to forgive – thankfulness etc.

In a shallow tray show how iron filings behave if shaken on
to a sheet of paper over an invisible magnet. Immediately
there is order and beauty; the magnet's power directs them.
We are not like iron filings because we can choose whether
to be affected by the life of Jesus or not. But if we ask him
into our lives, we will certainly feel his power.

Sing *Wander in the sun* (MWTP) and give each child a small
magnet to try out. Write on the field of magnetism: Lord, we
cannot see you, but we *know* you are here.

Music
Recorded Music

Beethoven – *Piano Concerto No. 4*

'Live' Music

I see your hand and your side *(ONE, 256)*
Peace is the gift *(ONE, 443)*
Without seeing you we love you *(SONL, 13)*

3rd Sunday of Easter

Theme
Through Christ's sacrifice our sins can be wiped out

God's revelation was a slow and very gradual unfolding, which we can trace in the Law of Moses, the Prophets and the Psalms; and all this points to the necessary suffering of the Christ in order to save the world from sin. Now Christ has fulfilled his mission, and as Easter people we witness to the new life he has made possible.

Penitential Rite

Wise, creating Father,
  Lord, have mercy. **Lord, have mercy.**

Saviour, suffering for our sin,
  Christ, have mercy. **Christ, have mercy.**

Spirit of healing love and grace,
  Lord, have mercy. **Lord, have mercy.**

Notes on the Readings

Acts 3:13-15, 17-19

Speaking to the Israelites, Peter guides them through their religious history to the point where the appalling truth dawns on them: they have insisted on killing the God they worship.

This is the moment of decision for them. Either the truth will seem so terrible that they prefer to reject Peter's claims, or else their sense of guilt will drive them to try and put things right as quickly as possible.

Peter hastens to soften the impact with God's mercy – Jesus' prayer as he hung dying had been 'Father, forgive them; they do not know what they are doing.' And he also offers them the route out of the terrible burden of guilt. Christ's suffering and death have actually made it possible for their sin to be wiped out. The suffering was necessary in order that we could be saved from the consequences of sin.

1 John 2:1-5

Imagine standing accused of a crime for which death is the penalty. There is no doubt that you are guilty, but that does not make the punishment any more attractive. You are very sorry for what you have done and, if only you could find someone to speak on your behalf and plead eloquently for you, you would love to spend the rest of your life making amends.

As you stand miserably and hopelessly in the dock, the best advocate in the country walks in. He is very famous and you may have thought he would only bother to use his expertise for those who can pay well. But he has come specially to plead for you, even though he knows you cannot

pay any fees. Because he is so highly respected and speaks so wisely and compassionately, the judge accepts his surety and pronounces that you can go free.

That lifting of burdens, that joy rushing to the head, that fervent desire to spend our redeemed lives in lavish praise and thanksgiving – all that is freely available whenever we turn back to Jesus from our sin.

Luke 24:35-48

Even though Peter and some of the others had realised that Jesus was the anointed Christ, about whom the prophets had written, they were still hard put to grasp that God has power even greater than death. Perhaps they thought his spiritual life was to help them, rather as Elijah's power fell on Elisha. Perhaps they felt they ought to be strong enough to carry on as they had after being sent out by Jesus two by two. Then, they had come back thrilled and confident; now they felt weak and frightened, and probably very guilty and embarrassed by their pathetic cowardice and disloyalty on Thursday and Friday.

Could it be that their own guilt and embarrassment was what prevented them from looking truth in the face? Was their wounded self-image causing them to hide from God's face just as Adam and Eve had done? At any rate, they are in great need of reassurance, so Christ reassures them by being with them once again, just like the old times; and they do not believe their eyes.

Triumphant over death and sin, and knowing how delighted his friends will be once the penny drops, Jesus' sense of humour shows through as he voices their fears: 'Touch me and see for yourselves; a ghost has no flesh and bones as you can see I have.' At last they look at him with both physical and spiritual eyes wide open, so that they are once more receptive as Jesus patiently explains again about his fulfilment of the scriptures.

Bidding Prayers

Celebrant Sharers in Christ's risen life, in trust
  and thankfulness let us pray to the Lord.

Reader For the work of the Church in
  every country, especially where
  Christian witness brings danger;
  that the Spirit of Christ may nurture life
  and hope in the world's darkest areas.
  Pause
  Risen Lord: **instil in us your peace.**

  For all who encourage others to squander
  their time, money or talents;
  all who lead others into drug addiction;
  that they may come to know Christ
  as the only treasure worth worshipping.
  Pause
  Risen Lord: **instil in us your peace.**

  For all whose characters
  have become hardened and twisted
  through jealousy, resentment or hatred;
  that they may at last recognise
  their need for repentance,
  and come to Christ to be restored
  to the joy of new life in him.
  Pause
  Risen Lord: **instil in us your peace.**

  For those who helped to bring us
  to know Christ, and those who turn us
  back to him when we wander away;
  that in humility we may always be

glad to learn and ready to accept criticism,
in order to grow as Christians.
Pause
Risen Lord: **instil in us your peace.**

Celebrant   Heavenly Father, slow to anger
and quick to forgive,
immerse us in your Spirit
and let your will be done in our lives,
through Jesus Christ. **Amen.**

Ideas for Adults

Make a display for today composed of a selection of quotations from the Law of Moses, the Prophets and the Psalms which are fulfilled in Christ. Write out each quotation clearly on paper of different colours, and using matching cord or ribbon, direct attention from each to a central cross.

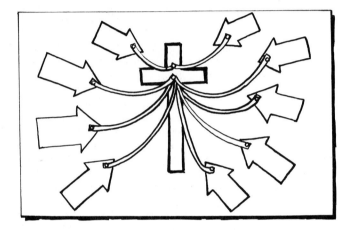

Useful references:
Genesis 12:2-3; Psalm 108/109:4; II Samuel 7:16; Job 19:25; Psalm 21/22:7,8,16,18; Psalm 70/71:11; Psalm 117/118:22; Isaiah 7:13,14; 9:6,7; 11:1,2; 35:5,6; 40:11; 53; Daniel 2:44a; Micah 5:2-5; Zephaniah 9:9; 11:12,13; Malachi 3:1.

Ideas for Children

Talk about what happens when you get a nasty graze. What happens before the comfortable plaster is put on? The wound has to be thoroughly cleaned up – otherwise it does not heal. Often the cleaning up hurts, and we have to be brave; but putting up with the sting makes sure our wound will get better. (You could have a small first aid kit to help discussion.)

Now show them some pictures of other times when suffering is necessary for something good to happen. Here are some ideas:

  ★ setting a broken leg
  ★ taking medicine
  ★ cleaning out your rabbit's hutch
  ★ God letting himself be killed by
    our evil, but still loving us
  ★ forgiving your brother when he
    breaks your aeroplane

Leave the crucifixion until last, and then help them to see that his suffering was necessary for the healing of the world from evil. You could sing *Do you believe?* (MWTP) at this point.

Music
Recorded Music

Beethoven – *Piano Concerto No. 5 (Emperor)*

'Live' Music

Glimpses of glory *(SONL, 51)*
Love divine, all loves excelling *(ONE, 337)*
Now the green blade riseth *(ONE, 376)*

4th Sunday of Easter

Theme
The good shepherd lays down his life for us

We actually belong to Christ, so his care of us is responsible and whole-hearted, like a good shepherd who owns his sheep and is prepared to defend them with his life. Through the strength of Christ's life in us, we can bring healing and wholeness to the world; through him, one day, we shall be enabled to see the full glory of God.

Penitential Rite

We come to you in need of healing,
   Lord, have mercy. **Lord, have mercy.**

We come to you to be renewed,
   Christ, have mercy. **Christ, have mercy.**

We come to you to be forgiven,
   Lord, have mercy. **Lord, have mercy.**

Notes on the Readings

Acts 4:8-12

Peter and John are being embarrassing. They keep talking about Jesus of Nazareth as if he were still alive, even though everyone knows he has been put to death. The priests and elders just wish they would keep their fanciful, threatening ideas to themselves and let life go on in the comfortable, established way it always has done.

Unfortunately there is this tiresome cripple standing up in front of the people, large as life and twice as healthy; in fact, perfectly healed. Obviously some power *must* have been at work.

Why were they unable to accept the joyful truth of the resurrection on the evidence of such 'fruit'? Surely because they knew that acceptance would utterly change their lives (as it did in Paul's case, of course); and having put a lot into establishing their life-style, they reckoned they had too much to lose. Whereas the cripple, whose life had been held physically tight and rigid by his handicap, was wildly delighted at the flexibility and capacity for movement that God had now given him.

Two things, then, about the resurrection life: it shows, and it liberates; but not everyone wants to be liberated. Perhaps some area in our own life-style is causing us to hobble, spiritually. If so, the risen Jesus has the power and the desire to set us leaping!

1 John 3:1-2

Wonderful though our new life in Christ is, even this is not the whole treasure. Living as constant companions and disciples of Jesus we shall become gradually more and more like him. We shall see changes in our attitude to people, in the way we organise our time and money, in our perception of others' needs and in the way our gifts are used. But still there is more. Eventually we shall be given the greatest treasure of all: to see the God we worship as he really is, in all his glory, and be brought to perfection in him.

John 10:11-18

The image of the good shepherd is so full of thorough caring and security that it has been a source of comfort for centuries. In the beautiful 22nd/23rd Psalm David took the standpoint of the sheep being led by his Lord, the shepherd. His own experience of tending his father's sheep gave him particular insight and sympathy.

It is quite possible that as a child Jesus also tended the village sheep, and he would certainly have known David's Psalm. So it is particularly apt that he should take the same beautiful image and refer to himself as the good shepherd.

There is all the difference in the world between being a hired man and being the shepherd to whom the sheep belong. Working as usual from the practical situations that his hearers would understand, Jesus explains the kind of love he has for us: it is costly love – responsible and completely dedicated. His death proved his words could be trusted; and as we live in his risen life that same unlimited love will blossom and fruit in us.

Bidding Prayers

Celebrant Rejoicing in the amazing love
of God our Father, let us pour out to him
our needs, cares and concerns.

Reader As we see, with sorrow,
the divisions between Christian groups,
let us ask our Good Shepherd to enable us
to become one flock.
Pause
Father, hear us: **and help us to hear you.**

As we see the glaring injustices of wealth
and food distribution in our world,
let us ask God to give us courage
to work in his strength towards building
a safer and more caring society.
Pause
Father, hear us: **and help us to hear you.**

As we see and read in the news of all those
afflicted by natural disasters,
by terrible accidents and by war,
let us ask God, the Lord of Life,
to bring good out of every evil
and growth out of every suffering.
Pause
Father, hear us: **and help us to hear you.**

As we watch our children growing up
and feel anxious for their future,
let us ask God for the assurance
of his steadfast love,
as we entrust their lives to his perfect care.
Pause
Father, hear us: **and help us to hear you.**

Celebrant Loving Lord, we thank you
for this opportunity to pray,
and ask you to answer our prayers
in the way that is best for us.
In the name of Jesus we pray. **Amen.**

Ideas for Adults

Incorporate into a flower arrangement a shepherd's crook and a lamb model or ornament, stones and a label:

'I am the good shepherd, says the Lord;
I know my own sheep and my own know me.'

I am the good shepherd, says the Lord; I know my own sheep and my own know me

Ideas for Children

Beg or borrow some photographs or slides of the Holy Land to show the children today. The local library or Christian resource centre should be able to lend some. Point out the wildness of the land, where wolves prowl, and the importance of having a shepherd who knows what he is doing, really cares for his sheep and is prepared to protect them.

Now read today's Gospel and act out with them the difference between the hired shepherd who runs away when danger comes, and the good shepherd who loves his sheep so much that he will even face death to protect them. Choose someone to be the wolf, and the rest can be sheep with a teacher as shepherd.

If there is time, they can make two models using plasticine: one with the sheep being abandoned to the wolf, and the other with them being protected by the good shepherd.

The good shepherd lays down his life for his sheep

The hired man runs away if there is danger

Music
Recorded Music

Elgar – *Cello Concerto*

'Live' Music

At the name of Jesus *(ONE, 50)*
Spirit of love *(ONE, 499)*
Walk in the light *(ONE, 547)*

5th Sunday of Easter

Theme

Whoever remains in me bears fruit in plenty

Jesus is the true vine, and if we, the branches, grow out of him, then his love will show through in the way we act, think and speak. The more we allow ourselves to be transfused with his life-giving Spirit, the richer will be our harvest and the more good we shall be empowered to do in the world.

Penitential Rite

2. Come, Spirit, come, take charge of my mind.
   Show me the darkness that you find.
   Help me to trust you, even with my shame,
   till I freely acknowledge where I am to blame.

3. Come, Spirit, come, bring life to my soul.
   Your forgiveness makes me whole.
   Then from the pain and stress of sin set free
   I am dazed by the awesome love you have for me.

Notes on the Readings

Acts 9:26-31

Paul is a striking example of how a person's life can be turned upside-down on becoming grafted to Jesus. He was the very last person the disciples expected to be a Christian; they reckoned he must be pretending so as to infiltrate and destroy. That would be far more in keeping with his record to date.

Fortunately for Paul and for us, Barnabas had a hunch that Paul was genuine. He took the trouble to get to know him, and then introduced him to the others. So, once again, the precious good news was on the move.

Before we dismiss anyone's claim to be a follower (or an enemy) of Christ, it is a good idea to look carefully at their 'fruit'. Whatever their background or past record, their present behaviour will help us to see if they are really working for or against God's will. God has always had a tendency to choose surprising people for his work, so we sometimes need to curb our suspicious natures in case we inadvertently close our doors to someone God has sent to help us.

1 John 3:18-24

Sometimes the Christian life seems like trying to walk a tightrope. There is always the danger of losing our balance. We have to make sure that we do not become glib about having been saved from our sin, and start behaving in a smug, complacent way. But, on the other hand, there is the temptation to dwell so much on our sin and unworthiness that we become restricted by our guilt and lose our sense of joy and forgiveness.

John reminds us here to keep our balance by keeping our priorities right. Our love must show in practical, active caring, based on our belief in Christ. Having resolved on that direction in our lives, we shall be walking with our Saviour, and need not be frightened in his presence as we trustingly tell him our hopes and anxieties, our disappointments and our failures, our celebrations and our successes.

Of course we shall sin, but living in Christ will urge us to repent quickly and learn from our mistakes; such occasions can often lead to deeper love for our forgiving Lord. So we can walk with heads high, enjoying the good life he has given us.

John 15:1-8

Jesus is quite clear and definite: if we do not live in him as closely as a branch lives on a vine, we shall bear no fruit at all. Not even the occasional grape! If you visit a vineyard, look closely at any succulent cluster of fruit and trace its stem. It may be trained some distance from the main branch, but eventually it joins the true vine with its strong root system (never a weak sucker shoot).

That is how we, too, will bear fruit – fruit in great clusters, like the grapes. But before we can flourish we shall need to be pruned, as any gardener knows. Any side shoots of distractions or weakening habits and sins need to be cut out, so that all our growth and energy are concentrated along the main fruiting branch. We may well dislike this pruning, and not recognise that it proves God's love for us. It can be useful, sometimes, to look again at some disappointment or failure we resent, and see if we can discern in it something that perhaps we needed to learn the hard way; or perhaps it may be the very thing to spur us into action from which great good will come.

Bidding Prayers

Celebrant Fellow members of the Body of Christ,
full of thankfulness for his abiding love,
let us pray to our heavenly Father
who knows us so well.

Reader Let us ask God to deepen
the personal commitment of every Christian,
so that the life-giving sap of the true vine
can flood through the Church
and out into the world.
Pause
Live in us, Father: **that we may bear fruit.**

Let us ask God to direct and further
all international discussions
so that they lead to peace, goodwill
and greater understanding.
Pause
Live in us, Father: **that we may bear fruit.**

Let us ask God to bring healing
to those who are ill, peace to the anxious,
courage to the fearful and rest to the weary.
Pause
Live in us, Father: **that we may bear fruit.**

Let us ask God to make his home in us,
in our marriages and our homes,
our places of work and in our local community,
so that our characters can be forged
by his Spirit in us.
Pause
Live in us, Father: **that we may bear fruit.**

Celebrant Merciful Father, fulfil our needs
according to your loving wisdom,
through Jesus Christ. **Amen.**

Ideas for Adults

Decorate the church with cut-outs of vines and grapes on walls and pillars; and instead of a flower arrangement have a fruit arrangement.

Ideas for Children

Bring along a gardening book with clear illustrations to explain pruning, a pair of secateurs and gardening gloves, and a bunch of grapes.

First put on the gloves and hold the secateurs, and discuss what kind of job you are ready for. If your church has a garden take the children out into it and show them how the roses have been pruned so they produce better flowers. Also find any flower and trace it back to the main stem and roots, from which it gets all its life. Cut off one twig. Will this be able to produce flowers?

Back inside, show the children how gardeners have to learn to prune all their fruit trees and bushes, so as to produce more fruit. Then read today's Gospel, and help the children understand that we need to be (1) joined on to Jesus and (2) pruned, if we are to produce fruit.

On a large sheet of paper draw a central vine with many branches and some leaves. Let the children stick on lots of clusters of grapes which they have coloured and labelled like this:

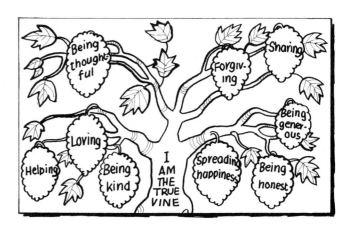

Then share out the grapes to enjoy together.

Music
Recorded Music

Dvorak – *Symphony No. 8*

'Live' Music

A new commandment *(ONE, 39)*
If we only seek peace *(SONL, 76)*
Make me a channel of your peace *(ONE, 342)*
Walk in the light *(ONE, 305)*

6th Sunday of Easter

Theme
Love one another as I have loved you

God is the source of all love and is therefore present wherever unselfish loving is being put into practice, regardless of creed or culture. We can delight in this, for it shows us the richness of God's unlimited giving; and it is this kind of generosity that we need to cultivate in all our relationships.

Penitential Rite

Impoverished, we seek your spiritual treasure,
    Lord, have mercy. **Lord, have mercy.**

Blind, we come to you for insight,
    Christ, have mercy. **Christ, have mercy.**

Blinkered, we come to you for vision,
    Lord, have mercy. **Lord, have mercy.**

Notes on the Readings

Acts 10:25-26, 34-35, 44, 48

Peter, showing the down-to-earth humility which makes him

so lovable, brushes aside Cornelius' rather effusive respect. For Peter has come freshly from yet another humbling learning experience and is well aware of his limitations. But he does not wallow in them. As soon as he realises God's will he sets off to put things right, plunging straight into a new course of action. That shows real love for his Saviour; above his pride and his reasoned arguments for keeping Christianity Jewish, is set whatever Jesus wants to be done. If Jesus wants to include pagans just as they are, then that is fine by Peter – he wants it too; even if it means changing his mind.

Whenever there is disagreement or heated discussion about any issue, we need to take a leaf out of Peter's book. First, setting ourselves to find out God's will by seriously asking him with prayer and fasting; and then, when we are receptive, recognising his will and acting on it, whether we agree with it or not. Obedience to God's will is what proves the extent of our love for him.

1 John 4:7-10

The consequences of loving God are very far-reaching, for it unavoidably affects every relationship we have, both casual acquaintances and life partners. Loving God and loving each other are so inextricably related that if we look around our own lives and find any area at all where there is prejudice, meanness or lack of loving consideration, then our professed love for God is to some extent a lie. Perhaps that sounds rather strong. What about God's mercy? What about all the extenuating circumstances in this or that particular case? How does God expect me, in my weakness, to put up with all I have to go through and still stay loving all the time?

Well, thankfully, he does not. The important truth that John makes clear is that it doesn't all start with us but with him. He first loved us. What we have to do is to stay receptive and accessible, so that his love can take root and grow in us; and that is what will enable us to love each other in that unlimited, responsive way. And since our loving will then be rooted in the source of all love, we will not find ourselves running out of supplies at the crucial moment.

John 15:9-17

We have the perfect example of such loving in Jesus himself. He was able to show us the sort of committed, responsible caring that God has for us, worked out in practical, human ways. He was filled with compassion and sympathy for the bereaved, the crippled and the diseased, and used his power to heal, comfort, visit, encourage and feed. He was sensitive to people's needs – even their unspoken needs – and listened to what they said. He had no invisible boundaries, so no-one was ignored or considered unimportant. He deliberately cut across social and religious strata, making friends over a very broad spectrum. He spent many hours on his own in prayer, was obedient to the Law, worshipped with the community and was prepared even to lay down his life for us humans, whom he loves.

We are offered not only the example but the power as well. If we commit ourselves whole-heartedly to Christ, his love in us will turn us into exceptionally beautiful people – people whom the world desperately needs.

Bidding Prayers

Celebrant   My Christian brothers and sisters,
as we rejoice at being called
and chosen by our heavenly Father,
let us speak with him
of our needs and concerns.

Reader   We commend to his love all leaders
and teachers in the Church;
that in all they do

they may stay close to God,
alert to his will and constantly prepared
to move where he guides.
Pause
Father, hear us: **increase our capacity to love.**

We commend to his love all talks
and negotiations in industry
and in matters of international importance;
that they may be marked by the generosity
of spirit, and desire for reconciliation
that comes only from God.
Pause
Father, hear us: **increase our capacity to love.**

We commend to his love all outsiders
and outcasts, all who have been rejected
by their family or their country;
that rifts may be healed,
relationships repaired
and new bonds of love forged through Christ.
Pause
Father, hear us: **increase our capacity to love.**

We commend to his love
all who are especially precious to us,
and all with whom we find it difficult to relate;
that we may always treat each other
with Christlike love.
Pause
Father, hear us: **increase our capacity to love.**

Celebrant   Heavenly Father,
so unrestrictive in your mercy,
accept our prayers
and fulfil our needs
through Jesus Christ. **Amen.**

Ideas for Adults

When there is an area of special concern, either within the parish or the wider world, arrange a day of prayer, perhaps linked with fasting, and joining with other Christian or non-Christian religious groups. The aim should be a serious seeking after God's will, and a willingness to be changed in our views if necessary. A 'still' listening is important, and faith that God will make the way forward clear. Finish with a simple shared meal; the deepened sense of fellowship and healing will be powerfully evident.

Ideas for Children

Using a roll of wallpaper, make separate letters of the word LOVE at least one metre tall. Let a couple of the children arrange them on the floor to spell LOVE. Then talk about what kind of decoration would best show what it means. Use bold marker pens to put their ideas into practice. Then explore what it is that makes LOVE such a bright, happy, joyful word. How do they know when it is there? Have a display of pictures of people showing loving and unloving behaviour, and discuss which ones are about love. Pictures can be from family photo albums, magazines, newspapers and comics, and can include friends laughing together; the exchanging of presents; tending a sick person; a grandparent reading a story; world leaders shaking hands in agreement; survivors in a disaster being helped to safety; as well as some showing mean, destructive or threatening behaviour.

Now read the Gospel passage and help them to see that Jesus is present wherever such loving goes on. Let them make a big notice for the display with decorated letters:

Music

Recorded Music

Mozart – *Piano Concerto No. 23*

'Live' Music

God is love: his the care *(ONE, 178)*
Listen, let your heart keep seeking *(SONL, 26)*
Love is his Word *(ONE, 338)*
O love of loves *(ONE, 405)*

7th Sunday of Easter

Theme
United and bound together in love

If we live in Christ we shall be able to witness to God's truth by the way we love one another. Matthias was chosen to replace Judas because he had been with Jesus right through his ministry and was a first-hand witness. We shall only be effective witnesses if we dwell in God and he in us. That involves caring till it hurts.

Penitential Rite

Unending source of caring love,
  Lord, have mercy. **Lord, have mercy.**

Still centre of all energy,
  Christ, have mercy. **Christ, have mercy.**

Our constant comforter and friend,
  Lord, have mercy. **Lord, have mercy.**

Notes on the Readings

Acts 1:15-17, 20-26

Peter's decision to elect a replacement for Judas is not just a sudden whim, or change for change's sake. It has emerged from prayerful thought and crystallized in the words of a verse from Psalm 108/109; so God has led Peter to take this important and symbolic step, making twelve apostles again to match the twelve tribes of Israel under the old Covenant.

The whole operation is carried out in an orderly way. Peter explains the scriptural basis, and the initial screening is thorough: only those who have been constant companions of Jesus are eligible, and eventually two names are put forward. And before the votes are cast, everyone prays. They do not pray to ask for help in choosing well; instead they recognise that God has already made his choice and what

they need is to be shown what that choice is. The atmosphere is full of faith and love.

Perhaps we would make fewer wrong decisions if we tackled each situation in this way. There would certainly be fewer frayed tempers and discussion deadlocks. Our task as Christians involves spreading the good news of living by the power of love. One way we can do this is by bringing the power of love into discussions; coaxing towards reconciliation, encouraging order, praying for each speaker and for God's will to be made clear: the way we reach decisions can be just as eloquent as what we decide.

1 John 4:11-16

We are so used to seeing the power of hatred in action. Terrorism, violent crimes, child abuse, revenge killings – the news is packed with details of destructive behaviour by individuals and nations based on hatred and fear.

At first sight it does look powerful. Innocent people lie dying as the murderer escapes with both life and money; aggressive threats extract secrets; brutal selfishness can pile up easy money quickly.

Yet through the history of the chosen people of Israel, and in the person of Jesus, God unfolds a much stronger power, which not only makes living more joyful and secure, but actually works better as well. Loving our enemies annihilates them more effectively than any gun can, because the door is then opened towards friendship. Rebels can be won over by kindness and a genuine concern for their cause, while repression and strong-arm tactics are more likely to turn them into underground revolutionaries. Love has inspired people to great acts of loyalty and courage and prolonged self-sacrifice; love has succeeded in uniting families and countries when war has weakened both and failed to bring lasting peace.

God's way of living by love, through every situation without exception, is both profound wisdom and sound good sense.

John 17:11-19

It is a great privilege to be given this insight into Jesus at prayer. We can learn so much from the way he pours out his heart to his Father, voicing his fears and talking things through in perfect trust. His love and affection for the little group he has trained is protective and deeply caring but not in any way possessive. Of far more importance than their personal bodily safety is that they are kept true to God, consecrated and set apart to that end. For love is stronger than death; when we live in God (who is Love) we live a life that can never be destroyed.

Bidding Prayers

Celebrant Companions in Christ,
      as we travel together,
      let us pray for one another
      to our loving and merciful Father.

Reader We pray for all who have been sent out
      by Christ to witness to the liberating truth
      of God's great love and mercy;
      that they may be blessed in their work
      and protected from evil.
      Pause
      Holy Father: **consecrate us in your truth.**

      We pray for the confidence
      and courage to speak out against evil,
      so that, working in the strength of Christ,
      we may contribute to the building
      of his kingdom on earth.

Pause

Holy Father: **consecrate us in your truth.**

We pray for the underprivileged
and deprived; any who are being physically
or emotionally abused;
and all whose warped, distorted lives
spread misery and destruction.

Pause

Holy Father: **consecrate us in your truth.**

We pray that from today,
the rest of our lives
may be set more firmly on Christ,
so that we seek his company and his will
before anything or anyone else.

Pause

Holy Father: **consecrate us in your truth.**

Celebrant   Trusting in your love for us,
and full of hope in your promise to hear us,
we offer you these prayers in the name
of Jesus Christ, your Son. **Amen.**

Ideas for Children

Show the children last week's display with its title, to re-mind them that God is Love. Encourage them to share any times during the week when they have seen love in action, or any cases where it is needed; make these into a prayer time of joys and concerns.

Now tell them Jesus' prayer for us, in a simplified form, which brings out his love and concern for us.

Help the children make this Jack-in-the-box which they can try out on their friends and family:

Who fills us with love

Who can we always trust

Music
Recorded Music

Bizet – *Symphony No. 1: Adagio*

'Live' Music

Bind us together *(ONE, 62)*
May all be one *(SONL, 10)*
Spirit of love, Spirit of truth *(ONE, 499)*

The Ascension of the Lord

Theme
Jesus is taken up into heaven

Having appeared to his disciples many times after his resur-rection, Jesus is now taken beyond our physical sight until he returns in glory. His ascension proclaims our hope: that we shall one day join him in heaven and spend eternity in joyful praise and adoration.

Penitential Rite

Father you are living in us now (SONL, 68)

Notes on the Readings

Acts 1:1-11

For forty days Moses had communed with God on the mountains, concerning the Law on which his chosen people would be built. Now, after the resurrection, Jesus spends forty days instructing and explaining the building of the new Israel (the kingdom of heaven) on earth, so that this small group of believers will be able to spread the good news to the whole world, beginning at the holy city of Jerusalem.

Having done this, it is necessary for Jesus to stop being *with* his disciples and be *in* them instead. He is taken with his physical risen body into the presence of his Father in heaven, and his disciples prepare themselves to receive his power.

Ephesians 1:17-23

The power they await is unmatched by any other power in any generation. Its potency brought stars and planets into being, generates life, and charges the universe with pur-pose; in Christ it broke through death and destruction to unsurpassed glory. All time and space is poised in the har-mony of that power; and as limbs and organs of Christ's Body, the Church, we have it pulsing through us, vital and glowing. Through us Jesus reaches your neighbours and my family; through us he reaches everyone we talk to, everyone whose lives our lives touch. Through us he restores confi-dence, soothes and comforts, strengthens and supports, heals and reconciles. Whenever we decide not to co-operate, the whole Body's effectiveness is weakened.

Mark 16:15-20

As evidence of God's Spirit, all kinds of gifts will show. We must not all expect all of the signs; the body is composed of many different organs, each with a particular function, and the Body of Christ is just the same. Also, the gifts may alter through our lives according to the work God has prepared for us to do. He will always equip us for a particular task; so if we feel called to undertake some work, but know we lack the resources and skills necessary for it, we should not promptly put in our resignation. Rather, we need to ask for what we need. As we pray: 'Lord, you must be joking – I couldn't ever do *that*!', his reassurance is there: 'I didn't say *you* would do it; I said *I* would!'

Bidding Prayers

Celebrant In the Spirit of Jesus
let us pray to our heavenly Father.

Reader We bring to his love all those who are
being trained for ministries in the Church;
that their studies may teach them
not only knowledge but also perception,
not only skills but also sensitivity.
Pause
Guide us, heavenly Father:
to walk your paths each day.

We bring to his love
all whose positions of responsibility
create pressure and stress;
that in their weakness and weariness
they may come to Christ for refreshment,
and rely on him for their strength.
Pause
Guide us, heavenly Father:
to walk your paths each day.

We bring to his love all who are dying;
that their trust in Jesus may deepen,
until their fears are calmed
and they can look forward with real hope
to meeting their Saviour face to face.
Pause
Guide us, heavenly Father:
to walk your paths each day.

We bring to his love
our own friends and loved ones;
all who live with us and near us;
all who rely on us,
and all who are influenced by our behaviour.
Pause
Guide us, heavenly Father:
to walk your paths each day.

Celebrant God of all mercy, our hope and our joy,
we ask you to hear our prayers
through Christ Jesus. **Amen.**

Ideas for Adults

Dance of the Ascension

This dance conveys the spread of Christ's power of love as it reaches more and more people, bringing them new life and hope. For the music, use Psalm 97 as set to music in *Focus on Parish Music*.

Begin with the dancers arranged like this, each one

```
            2
       1        3

   4,5              8,9
           6,7

   10              12
           11
```

crouched down close to the ground and completely still. Together they all say: "Jesus said to them, 'Go out to the whole world, proclaim the Good News to all creation.'" They kneel, sitting back on their heels during a silent count of three, then repeat the words. They kneel up, with arms raised during a silent count of three, then repeat the words loudly and clearly for the third time. The choir and/or congregation now sing the psalm, beginning with the verse, not the response.

WORDS	ACTION
Let us sing a new song to the Lord	*All dancers sit back on heels again, except 1, 2 and 3. They stand facing inwards holding hands, heads bowed.*
for the wonderful things he has done;	*They step forward, swinging joined hands up to the centre; step back, swinging arms back; step forward, swinging arms up; release hands and each turn.*
with his holy and powerful arm	*They join right hands in centre, weight on bent right leg, as left arm is brought up, over shoulder and extended to cover right hand.*
his salvation is brought to us all.	*They hop on right foot, step back transferring weight to left foot as left arm is extended like this:*

then pivot on left foot as right arm is brought up to 'match', before both arms are brought forward in a gesture of offering.

WORDS	ACTION
All the ends of the earth have now seen	*They bend knees and lower arms, turn palms upwards and gradually 'unfold' until they are poised on tip-toe (only for a split second!) with both arms raised, palms still flat up and eyes up.*
the salvation brought to us by God.	*They each run to the nearest group and kneel facing them, arms extended from the elbow.*

During the next verse the new groups go through the same action. At the end of the next response they run and re-group like this:

```
      1                    3
    10   4              8    12
                  2
                6   11

            5   7
              9
```

The actions are now repeated with even more people participating. At the end of the response this time each group of three holds hands.

WORDS	ACTION
O sing psalms to the Lord with the harp	*They skip 4 steps to the right.*
and with music sing praise to the Lord;	*They skip 4 steps to the left.*
with the trumpet and blasts of the horn	*Holding hands in a line, each group skips across to the centre, where they form one circle.*

we acknowledge the Lord who is King.

They stand with feet apart, transferring weight from foot to foot 4 times, arms extended up like this:

All the ends of the earth have now seen

They bend knees as before and gradually unfold, facing outwards.

the salvation brought to us by God.

They take 2 steps and on 'salVAtion' they all make a great leap of joy with one arm up, as in victory; then slowly kneel down on one knee, raising head and right arm on 'God'

Ideas for Children

Start by showing the children a bright cut-out sun, then cover it from sight with a cut-out cloud. Is the sun still there? Show that it is. We do not always see it because it is sometimes hidden from view, but we know it is always there. How?

Talk about life and growth and light and warmth. If we shut ourselves in where the sun cannot reach us we couldn't survive. Can we see Jesus? No. Then what do we mean when we say he is alive? Where is he?

Read them an account of the Ascension as told in Acts. His friends had seen him a lot after he had come back to life on the first Easter Day, and now, like the sun behind a cloud, he is hidden from sight for a time. (Show a bright card with JESUS written on it, and put the cloud in front.) But he is just as much alive as before. As our King he reigns over everything – people, animals, the sun, the stars, the universe!

Ask some children to draw and colour flowers and trees, some animals and people, some stars and planets, mountains, seas and weather. Then mount all their work on a big collage banner, with OUR GOD REIGNS written over the top. This can be carried into the church in procession.

Music
Recorded Music

Sibelius – *Symphony No. 6*

'Live' Music

Lord, enthroned in heavenly splendour *(ONE, 321)*
My love for you will never leave you *(ONE, 362)*
Our God reigns *(ONE, 223)*

Pentecost

Questions for Discussion Groups
1. What evidence have you actually seen of Christ's living Spirit active in people today?
2. Re-read the conditions under which the Spirit came at Pentecost. Are there any ways in which our preparation, both individually and corporately, needs to be different?

Pentecost Sunday

Theme
The Church receives the Holy Spirit

Like tongues of fire and a rushing wind, the Holy Spirit of God anoints the apostles with amazing power. Its immediate effect is to send them out, proclaiming the marvels of God; and as a sign of the unity and universality of the kingdom of heaven they are lucid in many languages. As Christ's Body, we are called to proclaim the wonderful truth that the Spirit has revealed to us.

Penitential Rite

All that we need we find in you,
Lord, have mercy. **Lord, have mercy.**

All that we lack you can provide,
Christ, have mercy. **Christ, have mercy.**

All our sins you can forgive,
Lord, have mercy. **Lord, have mercy.**

Notes on the Readings

Acts 2:1-11

Pentecost marks the beginning of a new era, a fresh stage in God's plan. The rest of time is to be spent relaying the message of salvation through Jesus, the Son of God, until it has reached the people in every part of the world. When that is accomplished God will come in full glory and heaven and earth, as we know it, will end.

Through the outpouring of the Spirit Jesus is spread among all who believe in him, beginning with these men of Galilee who have witnessed God's Son daily, and have been taught by him directly.

Deeply prepared, vigilant and receptive, they are filled to overflowing with the Spirit, and cannot help pouring out a stream of marvelling joy at all that God is and all he does. The devout people living in Jerusalem hear their words without any language barrier: for they, too, are prepared and receptive.

When we ask for God's Spirit we also need to work at being fully receptive; we are talking about nothing less than the power of life, and so we should be ready for drastic changes and constant growth when our bodies become temples of the Holy Spirit.

1 Corinthians 12:3-7, 12-13

The Spirit unites us as nothing else can, regardless of race, culture, education, age, wealth or position; for in the Spirit we are all equally special and important as children of God.

And it is given to us through God's generosity – it is not something we can earn by good behaviour or even by coming to church regularly. It does not depend on how long we have been members of a particular community (in fact, introspective cliquishness can sometimes be a barrier to our receptivity). It is not automatic or static, and the more open to God we become the more effects of his Spirit we shall see. It is not pride to acknowledge the good God has worked in our characters; after all, it is his work – not ours, and we can enjoy praising and thanking him for it.

John 20:19-23

The whole purpose of receiving the Spirit, then, is to use it. We are sent out in the Spirit's power to tell others that God loves them in a way they have always longed to be loved: loyally, honestly, uncompromisingly and tenderly. We are to invite others to come and meet Jesus for themselves; to introduce them to him both through our attitudes to people and events, and also by suggesting passages in the Bible that they read, praying with them and telling them what Christ means to us and how he has changed our lives.

It is all too easy to assume everyone knows where to come and what to read if they are interested; but we cannot make any such assumptions. There is widespread ignorance today about the good news that means so much to us, and we are commissioned to make sure the news is spread. We never need worry about what words to use; if we live in the Spirit he will give us the best ones.

Bidding Prayers

Celebrant   As the Body of Christ
we are bound together in love.
Let us pray, then, for our fellow members
in the Church and for our world.

Reader   That all who profess to be Christians
may allow the Spirit to penetrate their lives,
prune them where necessary,
realign, train and support them
so that they produce good fruit.
Pause
Lord, hear us: **we give our lives to you.**

That the common bond of humanity
may draw people closer,
develop international understanding
and friendship, break down prejudice
and generate peace.
Pause
Lord, hear us: **we give our lives to you.**

That all who are damaged
and scarred physically,
mentally, emotionally or spiritually
may be given wholeness and healing;
and that all who are floundering and confused
may find assurance in Christ,
the source of meaning.
Pause
Lord, hear us: **we give our lives to you.**

That we may use the gifts
of the Spirit within us to the full,
walking cheerfully and thankfully
in the way God has prepared for us,
and delighting in every opportunity to serve.
Pause
Lord, hear us: **we give our lives to you.**

Celebrant   Loving Father, rejoicing in your strength and
fellowship we lay these prayers before you,
through Jesus Christ. **Amen.**

Ideas for Adults

Fire is a powerful symbol. Consider the possibility of having a preparation time of prayer gathered round a fire near the church, on a beach or in a garden.

Ideas for Children

Read the children the account of Pentecost from Acts and have an atlas to show them some of the places all the people came from. Talk about the different languages people speak (they may have heard some in friends' homes, on the television or on holiday), and about how hard it can be to make yourself understood.

Now make a wall of building blocks, and explain how language can be like a barrier between people. So can other things, such as money, anger and bad temper, sulking, fear etc.

What the Holy Spirit does is to break down barriers (let them break down the wall) and in its place build bridges (let them build some). Label the bridges:

- God's Spirit works for peace
- God's Spirit cares about people
- God's Spirit tells people about Jesus
- God's Spirit forgives

Ask them to look out for barriers during the week. If they find one, remind them to use God's Spirit to break it down and build a bridge in its place.

Music
Recorded Music

Pachelbel – *Canon*

'Live' Music

Freely, freely *(ONE, 175)*
God's Spirit is in my heart *(ONE, 183)*
The Spirit of the Lord is with us *(ONE, 549)*

The Most Holy Trinity

Theme
God is eternally present as Father, Son and Spirit

All authority in time and space belongs to the almighty God who made himself known in his creativity, loyalty, power and leadership, making his will clear through Moses and the prophets. The risen Christ establishes the new, full covenant with us as God's sons and daughters who, in sharing his suffering, inherit his glory.

Penitential Rite

Almighty God, who was in the beginning,
Lord, have mercy. **Lord, have mercy.**

Almighty God, who is now,
Christ, have mercy. **Christ, have mercy.**

Almighty God, who will be for ever,
Lord, have mercy. **Lord, have mercy.**

Notes on the Readings

Deuteronomy 4:32-34, 39-40

Moses proclaims to the people the uniqueness of their God and their relationship with him. They are to be surrounded by many exotic, colourful and tempting religions based on greed, and self-indulgence, just as we are today. To strengthen and encourage them, God speaks through Moses, reminding them of the unprecedented reality of the one true God. Nowhere, in any other religion, has a god identified so closely with his people, giving constant, practical leadership and help, guiding them and making his presence known. Everything points to him being the one, true deity by whom they are privileged to be called

Romans 8:14-17

Now, through Christ, we have received the Spirit which makes us God's children. 'Abba' is much nearer to the meaning of 'Daddy' than 'Father', so it throws us into the relationship of a young, trusting child with a loving parent. It speaks of dependence, comfort, discipline, belonging and binding love. No longer struggling on our own to uphold moral standards, we are freed from so much pressure and stress. We do not have to go it alone and carry the day's and the world's problems on our own shoulders. Those fears are something from the past: in the present we belong to God. His patience, his forgiving nature, and his willingness to show mercy are all there at our disposal to use liberally in all our relationships.

Matthew 28:16-20

In Matthew the events after the resurrection are concentrated, so that we have a kind of condensed version. The forceful significance, however, is sharp and clear. Beyond doubt, the Lord is God indeed, of heaven, earth, time and eternity, life and death; there is nothing and no one to out-class him, for he is supreme and almighty.

Just as Moses commissioned the people to keep their covenant as the chosen race, so Christ commissions us, bound in the new covenant, to witness, teach and baptise in every country and neighbourhood. There is no way we can side-step this commission; nor is it a job for someone else to do because they have more time/ know their Bibles better/ are older/ are younger or any other justifications we are adept at making to excuse ourselves. We need to stop making excuses and get cracking. God has important work for us to do and he is waiting for us to report for duty!

Bidding Prayers

Celebrant   As sons and daughters of the living God, let us trustfully pray to our heavenly Father.

Reader   We pray that we may all recognise our calling to be missionaries, and use every chance, every day, to proclaim God's love by our words, actions and example.
Pause
Abba, Father: **hear your children.**

We pray that the whole world may come to acknowledge God as supreme Lord of all; so that as one people, under God, we are enabled to live in love, harmony and integrity.
Pause
Abba, Father: **hear your children.**

We pray that all who doubt may be helped towards faith; all who are burdened by repressed guilt may be given the courage to confess, and experience the liberation of forgiveness.
Pause
Abba, Father: **hear your children.**

We pray that we may be shown any areas in our lives which hinder others from turning to Christ; and having been shown, receive the grace to renounce them and re-tune our lives to God's will.
Pause
Abba, Father: **hear your children.**

Celebrant   Heavenly Father, eternal and always present, we offer you these prayers in the name of Jesus. **Amen.**

Ideas for Adults

For the Lord's Prayer, teach the people the *Abba, I belong to you* chant which becomes a pulse over which the familiar words are sung. (SONL, 69)

Ideas for Children

Talk with the children about being given jobs to do. Share some of the things they are appointed to do at home or at school. Sometimes we try to get out of doing jobs; but if we don't feed the cat she will go hungry; if we don't help keep our home clean, germs thrive etc.

Tell the children how Jesus gave us a job to do, before he went back to heaven, and how he needs us to do it. Read them Jesus' commission to go and tell everyone about God and the way he loves us. Discuss with them the kind of things they would like others to know about their special friend, Jesus – who he was, how he helps them and what he is like.

Write down their words on coloured paper which they can illustrate, and then staple the whole lot together to make a book. If possible have it duplicated and used as an aid in mission; children's straightforward and trusting faith is a great witness.

Music
Recorded Music

Elgar – *Serenade for strings*

'Live' Music

God's Spirit is in my heart (ONE, 183)
Go in peace (SONL, 45)

ORDINARY TIME

Ordinary Time 1 – 5

Questions for Discussion Groups
Who is this man? Calling
1. What do we learn about Jesus' character from the way he calls his disciples?
2. What is our vocation – individually and corporately – and how can we best respond?

2nd Sunday in Ordinary Time

Theme
Responding to God's call

Just as Samuel and the apostles were personally called by God, so also are we. When we respond to his calling we become members of Christ's spiritual Body; different parts of one organism, filled with Christ's life. In doing so we give away ownership of our selves, for we have allowed Christ to buy us out of slavery to sin; from now on we use our bodies for the glory of God.

Penitential Rite

You call us, but we do not always listen,
  Lord, have mercy. **Lord, have mercy.**

You choose us, but we often let you down,
  Christ, have mercy. **Christ, have mercy.**

You invite us home, but we make excuses,
  Lord, have mercy. **Lord, have mercy.**

Notes on the Readings

1 Samuel 3:3-10, 19

Even before he was born, Samuel had been consecrated to the Lord; and now, while he is still a child, God calls him to prophesy. It would seem that few other people were receptive enough to hear the word of God, for it was 'rare' at that time. The priesthood had degenerated in greed and self-indulgence, with Eli's own two sons the worst offenders, and Eli had already been warned of God's retribution. He had spoken to his spoilt sons but done nothing to put things right.

Samuel does not recognise God's voice straight away, and Eli, well-meaning but weak, recognises that God is speaking to this child and teaches him how to respond. So begins a lifetime of close communion with God; Samuel treasured the word of his Lord and always acted on it, however unpleasant or unexpected it proved to be.

Communal worship is essential and of great value, but it is also vital to keep times of silence to commune with God, listen to his presence and respond to his calling.

1 Corinthians 6:13-15, 17-20

We tend to think of our bodies as being our own private property; when we over-indulge them, paint or disfigure them, wear them out or poison them, it is doing nobody else any harm so why should it matter? We can surely do what we like with our own bodies!

But supposing they are not our property? If we give our lives to Christ we offer arms, legs, head and torso as well as minds and hearts. When Christ dwells in us he lives in our physical body. This may make us feel somewhat uncomfortable at first, when the completeness of it dawns on us. It will mean having nowhere to go to 'escape' from God while we surreptitiously indulge ourselves every so often. That may mean big changes in our lifestyle; it may mean the end of some relationships or avoiding certain company. It may mean being ridiculed for saying 'no', or refusing to watch certain videos.

Well, the Corinthians had very similar pressures of widespread indulgence and immorality to contend with as we have today, and the truth applies to us all: when we accept Christ into our lives our bodies are his temple, with all the reverence that this implies; and we need to use them for his glory, not for our selfish pleasure. Often, of course, we will find such service becomes freedom, as our bodies are used in a pleasurable way to show sympathy and affection, to express joy and peace, and to work in a healthy, positive way in the community.

John 1:35-42

Some time before being called to commit their whole lives to following Jesus, the disciples are directed to him by John the Baptist, who points him out as being the promised Lamb of God. They trail along behind him, rather than approaching him directly, until eventually he turns and asks them what they want. And isn't that so human? When we have the chance to meet someone we have longed to talk to and learn from, we become quite tongue-tied when we actually see them!

But Jesus is compassionate, welcoming, understanding and straightforward. Whenever he finds us hovering nearby, he will invite us to spend time with him and get to know him better. Then we can go and tell our family and friends news that will transform their lives, too.

Bidding Prayers

Celebrant Bound together in the life of Christ,
    let us pour out our needs and concerns
    before our Lord and Father who knows
    and loves us so well.

Reader We commend to his love
    all who have recently been ordained;
    that the people to whom they minister
    may accept and love them
    and help them to grow in Christ.
    Pause
    Lord, here I am: **I come to do your will.**

We commend to his wisdom
    all who wield power;
    that they may encourage reconciliation
    rather than revenge, friendship
    rather than aggression, and flexibility
    rather than stubborn intransigence.
    Pause
    Lord, here I am: **I come to do your will.**

We commend to his healing
    all who are ill or in pain;
    all who are recovering from surgery;
    all who depend on others for life and movement;
    any who long for a friend
    who would visit them during their illness.
    Pause
    Lord, here I am: **I come to do your will.**

We commend to his peace and joy
our homes and all the homes in this parish,
especially any where there is conflict
or distress; that, being dwelt in by Christ,
our homes may speak
to every visitor of his love.
Pause
Lord, here I am: **I come to do your will.**

Celebrant   Loving Father, we thank you for calling us,
and ask you to hear these prayers
we offer through Christ, our Saviour. **Amen.**

Ideas for Adults

The reading from Samuel can be effectively dramatised using a narrator, Eli and Samuel. Insist that everyone speaks clearly and audibly; it is so frustrating for the congregation to miss what has been carefully prepared. Check that they can be heard all over the church.

Ideas for Children

Tell the children the story of God calling to Samuel, involving two of them in the story to mime the events.

Now divide them into two groups to play a game. One line of children are given a different short message which they have to shout across to their partner on the far side of the room. The trouble is that everyone will shout their message at the same time! See how long it takes before everyone has received the right message. Then gather everyone round in a circle and hold up a pin. Try to hear the pin drop. Once this stillness has been achieved, talk quietly with them about the need to be quiet and still in our prayer if we are to know what God wants us to do.

Finish with a time of prayer based on the sounds we can hear when we close our eyes and really listen. Pray for travellers and drivers when you hear traffic; for those with colds and others who are ill; for babies and those being born; thank God for the wind or the rain, and so on. Encourage the children to add to their prayers; there is no better way to learn to pray than by praying.

Music
Recorded Music

Beethoven – *Piano Sonata* (Moonlight)

'Live' Music

Here I am *(ONE, 360)*
Listen *(SONL, 26)*
Take me, Lord *(SONL, 92)*
We're the people of God *(ONE, 351)*

3rd Sunday in Ordinary Time

Theme
Turn away from sin and believe the Good News of Christ

We are at present in the last age, and the world as we know it will only last until Christ comes in glory. It is important, therefore, to get our priorities right straight away; to repent, turn to Christ, and not to let worldly possessions, materialism or even good relationships take over God's central position in our lives.

Penitential Rite

Source of all power and majesty,
    Lord, have mercy. **Lord, have mercy.**

Love that shames our niggardly hearts,
    Christ, have mercy. **Christ, have mercy.**

Hope of all who turn to you,
    Lord, have mercy. **Lord, have mercy.**

Notes on the Readings

Jonah 3:1-5, 10

Jonah had been so anxious to avoid giving God's word to the citizens of Nineveh that he had at first set off in the opposite direction and hopped on a boat bound for Spain! It took a perilously close look at death to convince him that he was in the wrong place at the wrong time! God, firmly insistent and full of patience, gives him a second chance, and this time Jonah obeys straight away.

The outcome of his obedience is that a whole enormous city is saved. Contrary to Jonah's expectations, the threat of destruction brings the people to their senses, and they repent of the way they have been behaving.

Every day we come across instances of grossly unjust, greedy, destructive and abusive behaviour in our world, and no doubt they cause us great concern. Could it be that such behaviour continues and thrives because there is no one prepared to speak out against it and warn of the effects of such a way of life? Like Jonah, we are tempted to busy ourselves elsewhere, fearing the consequences of speaking out boldly. But we are Christ's Body on earth; our whole purpose here is to bring others to repentance so that they, too, can accept the joy and freedom of his forgiveness.

1 Corinthians 7:29-31

The early Christians were expecting the second coming of Christ to happen very soon; probably within a lifetime. So Paul advises the Corinthians to become less and less possessive, with relationships and worldly sorrows and delights always secondary to standing in readiness before God and spending their lives in doing his will.

We are nearly two thousand years closer to the second coming now, and should not assume that it will not happen for countless generations. Rather, we would be better advised to follow the spirit of Paul's letter, and take care not to become engrossed in worldly matters or dominated by materialism. Thankfulness and generosity can help prevent the clogging deposits of material dependency.

Mark 1:14-20

Jesus' call, too, concerns repentance. This is always the necessary first step; nothing can happen, not one sin can be forgiven, no growth can start at all, until we confess that we are to blame and our sinful way of going on is our own fault. The buck stops here.

If you recoil from the unpleasantness of full repentance you are not alone; neither are you misguided: taking the blame and renouncing excuses is a humiliating and painful experience. It hurts. But, as any dentist will confirm, no filling will be effective, not even a gold one, if the cavity is not first drilled clear of all decay.

After the bad news comes the Good News! A new life, new confidence independent of circumstances, a fresh delight and enthusiasm, an outlook of hope and challenge. The fishermen left their old life and followed Jesus' call. Dare we do the same?

Bidding Prayers

Celebrant My brothers and sisters in Christ,
let us draw near to our heavenly Father
and pray in the Spirit of Jesus.

Reader For all who labour in the painstaking work
of building up God's kingdom;
that they may be encouraged in seeming failure,
guided in uncertainty
and trained through perseverence.

Pause

Father of great mercy: **hear us as we pray.**

For newspaper editors,
television and film directors,
show business personalities
and all who influence our attitudes and values;
for every consumer, viewer and reader;
that the world may be led to search
for real and lasting values,
and so find peace and joy.

Pause

Father of great mercy: **hear us as we pray.**

For all who have lost their way in life
and need to be rescued
and loved back to wholeness;
for those who are as yet blind to the damage
they are doing themselves and society;
that they may recognise their sin
and turn from it.

Pause

Father of great mercy: **hear us as we pray.**

For guidance in the way we use our time,
money and abilities this week,
and courage to follow Christ in a more
committed, demanding, sacrificing way.

Pause

Father of great mercy: **hear us as we pray.**

Celebrant Rejoicing that we have been called
to serve you, Father,
we offer you these prayers,
along with our lives for you to use;
through Christ we pray. **Amen.**

Ideas for Adults

Repentance and believing the Good News involve rededication and renewed commitment. Before the Creed today have a time of silence for people to reflect on all that Jesus means to them in their lives. Then use the renewal of Baptismal Promises as the profession of faith.

Ideas for Children

Bring along a household repair manual which has clear diagrams in it, a piece of sandpaper for each child and an assortment of wood offcuts or driftwood, and plenty of varnish.

First show the children how important it is to prepare a wall before you paint it – otherwise the paint will not last. Show them how cracks need to be cleaned out before they can be filled and wood sanded down before it is varnished. Explain how repentance is the necessary cleaning out and preparation before any growing can start in our Christian lives. This is made clearer if you have a chart with diagrams similar to the repair manual like this:

Give the children a chart to use in prayer during the week, which helps them review areas in their lives which need to be sanded down or cleaned up for Christ to make beautiful and useful.

Now let the children select a piece of wood and sand it down smoothly before varnishing it. It may be used as an ornament, or a paper weight.

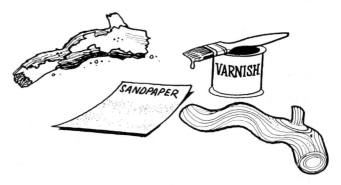

Music
Recorded Music

Mozart – *Clarinet Concerto: slow movement*

'Live' Music

I want to build my life *(ONE, 260)*
Lord, when I turn my back on you *(SONL, 40)*
My song is love unknown *(ONE, 363)*
Oh, the love of my Lord is the essence *(ONE, 430)*

4th Sunday in Ordinary Time

Theme
Jesus teaches with authority

Directly in the tradition of Moses and the prophets, Jesus speaks the word of God to his listeners at Capernaum. Instead of quoting accepted explanations of the Scriptures, he teaches with an astonishing insight and understanding and shows authority over both the Scriptures and the forces of evil. We acknowledge him Lord of all, giving him the central place in our lives so that he can use us to reach out and rescue.

Penitential Rite

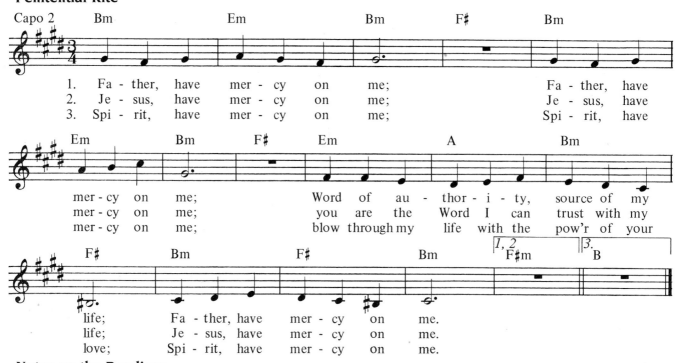

Notes on the Readings

Deuteronomy 18:15-20

Although Moses' prophecy was fulfilled in one sense throughout the Old Testament, as the line of prophets spoke God's word to bring the wayward people repeatedly back to their covenant, the prophecy was to be fulfilled completely only with the coming of Jesus.

The people had found direct contact with their God so powerful that they could not 'bear' it: none could see God face to face and still live. Only Moses, wholly at one with his creator could commune with God in this way, and even then his face glowed with the reflected light of God's glory, making it necessary for him to wear a veil afterwards.

We need to remember, in our private prayer and public worship, the immensity and galactic power of the God we worship; certainly he is full of tenderness and compassion, but he is also brighter, greater and more dynamic than we can begin to imagine. We should always stand in awe of him, for he is full of majesty and great glory.

1 Corinthians 7:32-35

All of us who are married and have children to look after know from experience that by the time everyone is fed, cleaned, clothed, taken or collected, played with, read to, listened to, rescued, comforted and finally put to bed, there is not a great deal of spare time left! Perhaps, we may feel ruefully after a particularly trying day, Paul was right.

But of course the important message in this passage is that we recognise Jesus as the Master of our life. From his words and actions we know him to be the Son of God, and our whole existence should proclaim that conviction. Some are called to celibacy, some to marriage; but whatever our estate we can devote it entirely to God's glory – even the constant clearing up, commuting or repetitive routines which take up so much of our time. Done with and for Christ they become prayers through which our homes and places of work can be abundantly blessed.

Mark 1:21-28

What was it about Jesus' teaching that so impressed his listeners at Capernaum? He used no new material or eccentric behaviour; just the same old Scriptures which had been taught week after week for generations. Yet somehow this was different – inspiring, uplifting and enlightening.

For Jesus brought the Scriptures to a living reality. Instead of quoting the borrowed opinions of accepted interpretation, he was speaking warmly, with inside information, communicating God's Word directly to his people. The same authority is exhibited even over the powers of darkness, as Jesus was seen to be capable of controlling and healing physical, mental and spiritual disease.

Jesus promised that the Spirit would continue his work of leading us into truth and wisdom. And whenever we read the Scriptures in an attentively prayerful way, we experience first hand the same enlightening, personally applicable teaching as did that gathering in Capernaum.

Bidding Prayers

Celebrant Summoned by Christ to live his risen life,
let us pray in the assurance of faith
to our heavenly Father.

Reader That many may be receptive to God's calling
and, acknowledging his authority,
be prepared to relinquish personal
ambitions and plans in submitting
their lives to his service.
Pause

Lord of all creation: **may your will be done.**

That the leaders of the nations
may be sensitive to the needs of their people,
just and merciful, caring and constructive.
Pause

Lord of all creation: **may your will be done.**

That all who work to heal,
restore movement, hearing, sight or speech,
may be blessed as they work
in harmony with God;
that those they tend may be given courage,
patience and wholeness.
Pause

Lord of all creation: **may your will be done.**

That in every person we meet this week
we may look for the good
and be alert to needs;
that we may be ready to serve cheerfully,
without grudging, but happy
to be serving Christ.
Pause

Lord of all creation: **may your will be done.**

Celebrant Most merciful Father,
we ask you to accept these prayers
through Jesus Christ. **Amen.**

Ideas for Adults

In a central flower arrangement today, incorporate an open Bible and/or some scrolls, and a candle. Have a carefully written label giving the response of Psalm 94: O *that today you would listen to his voice! Harden not your hearts.*

Ideas for Children

Today is a good opportunity to introduce children to the Bible as being the book of God's love. Have enough Bibles available for each child to handle one; if possible use an edition with pictures and clear print, or have an assortment of editions, from paperbacks to family heirlooms.

First show the children pictures or slides of the kind of church Jesus went to – a synagogue – and the kind of Bible he read from. The local Christian resource centre may be able to help here.

Now give out the Bibles and help them find the Scriptures that were available in Jesus' time. It is important that they realise these are still here in our Bibles today. Point out how the 'Bible' is not a book, but a library; and take them on a whistle-stop tour of some of the books on the library shelves. Pick out the stories they have heard about, such as the Creation, Noah and the flood, Abraham, Joseph, Moses, David and Goliath etc. Don't spend hours on each, though; the aim is to help them to see the overall 'shape' of God's plan and promise which leads up to Jesus and the New Testament, Covenant or Promise.

So long as well illustrated Bibles are used, it is possible for even quite young children to explore the Bible like this occasionally. Encourage them to ask questions about it, and tell them about where some of the original scrolls were found. Show them archaeological sites where interesting finds have been made, too. Suggest that they ask their parents to show them where a favourite story is in their own Bible during the week.

Music
Recorded Music

Purcell – *The Moor's Revenge: Suite*

'Live' Music

Firmly I believe and truly *(ONE, 143)*
Lord of my life *(SONL, 21)*
My Lord, my master *(ONE, 361)*
The Freedom Song *(ONE, 154)*

5th Sunday in Ordinary Time

Theme
Jesus fills our life with meaning

God created us for himself, so we can only find lasting peace and fulfilment in him. It is both our duty and our joy, as followers of Christ who have seen his transforming power in action, to bring others to share his life. Once people see the real God working in our lives they will come searching for him with their own needs and questions.

Penitential Rite

We know that you alone can save us,
Lord, have mercy. **Lord, have mercy.**

We know forgiveness brings us peace,
Christ, have mercy. **Christ, have mercy.**

We ask you to remake our lives,
Lord, have mercy. **Lord, have mercy.**

Notes on the Readings

Job 7:1-4, 6-7

Anyone who has experienced deep depression like Job's, will recognise the sense of utter futility and bleakest isolation. The edges of reality are blurred in a landscape of seething misery, in which you have no worth and no substance. It is of no importance whether you live or die.

Christians are not immune; Job was a righteous man who

loved God. Sometimes it is caused by wounding circumstances, sometimes by suppressed rage or unrepented sin; sometimes it is part of a necessary mourning and sometimes its roots are genetic and chemical.

Job poured out his anguish to God, never pretending or hiding his hurt, anger, sense of injustice or resentment. The pus in a boil has to come out before healing is possible. We too need to pour out our hearts to the Lord, and explain how we feel – for this is part of the healing.

Then Job contends with the 'comforters', whose advice does not help a great deal; it is the closeness of God himself who brings Job to the point where he can recognise God's charge over all things, even things like suffering which we cannot understand. We may at first become aware that Christ is suffering alongside us; if we let him, he will sustain us as we struggle, and lead us step by step to wholeness.

1 Corinthians 9:16-19, 22-23

People today are highly aware of what they consider to be their 'rights'. Righteous indignation inflates every issue where our rights are threatened or violated, and sometimes we are so concerned with protecting our rights that we fail to remember our privileges.

Paul is not in the least concerned with his rights; he is more than willing to sacrifice them all if it means gaining more souls for Christ. We may not live under the Mosaic Law any more, but we do live under God's law of love; and that can often cut clean across the worldly view of rights. Our unselfish caring, our willingness to forgive completely, our self discipline (all of which should be hallmarks of our life in Christ) may often be regarded as weakness and foolishness by a world which is obsessed by what it can gain rather than what it can give. And we are required, as part of our allegiance to Christ, to work for the spread of his kingdom using his methods. They are, in the end, the only methods which work.

Mark 1:29-39

God is the ultimate creative, positive being, and it is his nature to bring healing and wholeness in every scrap of his creation. Whenever Jesus was put in touch with illness, injury, or torment, he brought divine healing which sprang from his compassion.

So many who reject the negative, narrow Christ they have been shown by negative and narrow Christians, would never reject the true Christ who loves with such personal affection, looks us straight in the eye, accepts, forgives and heals.

Bidding Prayers

Celebrant Companions in Christ,
as we remember with gratitude
all that God has done for us,
let us bring to his love the needs and concerns
of the Church and of the world.

Reader We bring to his love the daily work
of each member of Christ's Body;
that in constant prayer we may learn
God's will and his way of doing things,
till we work exclusively for his glory.
Pause
In you we trust: **we look to you for help.**

We bring to his love the mistakes,
short-sightedness and arrogance of our world;
that in Christ we may learn
to respect one another
and the treasures of the planet we inhabit.
Pause

In you we trust: **we look to you for help.**

We bring to his love the wounded
and the afraid, the despairing
and the rejected;
that they may find Christ
suffering alongside them
and allow him to restore them to full life.
Pause
In you we trust: **we look to you for help.**

We bring to his love our busy concern
with unimportant things;
that in spending more time
in Christ's company we may learn to act
and react with the character of Jesus.
Pause
In you we trust: **we look to you for help.**

Celebrant Almighty Father, hear the prayers we offer,
and use our bodies, minds and spirits
in establishing your kingdom.
In the name of Jesus we pray. **Amen.**

Ideas for Adults

Dance of the healing Christ

This dance expresses the suffering of a person in physical, emotional or spiritual torment. She looks in vain for God and rages at his hard-heartedness, only to find that he is there beside her. He has been suffering with her all the time. The knowledge of his presence sustains her, and he leads her to joy and new life.

The music is the second movement of Sibelius' Symphony No. 5 in E flat. You will need a group of eight dancers to express the torment, and two others: the Sufferer and the Presence of Christ. Play the music through several times, following the dance instructions so that you get the 'shape' of it, as I have left plenty of room for improvisation.

As the music begins the Sufferer enters, running fitfully while the tormenters chase and threaten, blocking her way wherever she tries to go. The group works sometimes in twos and threes, sometimes as a unit. Everywhere the Sufferer goes, the Presence of Christ goes with her and is similarly persecuted, but the Sufferer acts as if she is entirely alone.

As the horns begin their theme the chase should reach the main performance area, and the Sufferer pleads, wringing her hands, trying to push the tormenters away (hands palm to palm). Sometimes they are pushed back a few steps but then they advance and send her off balance, then insolently watch as she staggers to her feet before they claw and jostle again.

They form a large circle and push her from one to the other round it, and then use her and the Presence (back to back) like a rope in a tug of war.

One ties blindfolds on them and they spin them round, teasing, frightening and causing them to stumble. As the music goes quiet, they run to escape, and the tormenters hide; they seem to have gone, but as the Sufferer walks timidly about, they pop out and grab her, or stealthily follow. The horn's theme comes again, and again she pleads for God to hear her. She is bewildered and dazed and seems to have lost her way. The tormenters now slide and slither towards her from different directions until she is cut off. They begin to reach up, as if dragging her down, however hard she resists. At the crescendo she shakes her fist towards the sky, holds her head in agony and collapses from weakness.

With the horn's theme she slowly realises that she is not alone; the Presence of Christ is lying, weak and wounded, beside her. He stands and painfully the Sufferer rises to her feet. As if she cannot quite believe he is real, the Sufferer traces the face and arms of the Presence who puts his arm round her for support and helps her limp towards the altar. In a frenzy the tormenters try to stop them. The Presence of Christ lifts the Sufferer on his shoulder where they cannot reach her. When they reach the altar the Sufferer is lifted down, and finds that she can stand upright. In joy she embraces her rescuer and bends and stretches to the music, delighting in being free.

The music ends with six chords. During the first four of these, the Presence of Christ, holding hands with the Sufferer he has saved, points with authority, all fingers outstretched, at the tormenters who are writhing, grouped in twos. Each time, the couple pointed at cower and freeze, until by the fourth chord, all the tormenters are still. On chord five, the Sufferer and the Presence of Christ stand facing the altar with arms raised like this:

On the final chord they kneel on one knee, like this:

Ideas for Children

So as to reinforce last week's lesson, give the children a Bible each and help them find first the New Testament, then the Gospel of Mark, and then Chapter 1:29-39. Read it with them, clearly and slowly. Then re-tell it with their help, using questions and answers, and pictures if possible.

Now that they know the events, dress them up in lengths of material, towels, tie-belts etc, and act out the story. Lead them by narrating while they mime, but encouraging them to speak as well. A few props such as a tray and bowls, and the odd bandage help participation.

Point out how Jesus needed to spend time on his own with God just as we do. Above all, help them understand that Jesus loved the people and was always glad to make them well.

Music
Recorded Music

Sibelius – *Symphony No. 5*

'Live' Music

Be not afraid *(ONE, 627)*
Our hearts were made for you *(SONL, 36)*
Walk with me O my Lord *(ONE, 582)*

Ordinary Time 6 – 13

Questions for Discussion Groups
Who is this man? Healing
1. What part does faith play in the healing works of Jesus? Was faith shown by others as well as the patient?
2. What different methods did Jesus use to heal? Why were these appropriate for particular problems?

6th Sunday in Ordinary Time

Theme
'Of course I want to!' said Jesus. 'Be cured!'

The leper came to Jesus hoping he would rid him of the disease which cut him off from society. Willingly and lovingly, Jesus restored the man to full health. We, too, approach him, knowing his power to heal and liberate us; and his response is warm and rich. Our lives are transformed by his grace and reflect his love to the world.

Penitential Rite

You have the power to forgive our sin,
    Lord, have mercy. **Lord, have mercy.**

Stretch out your hand and heal us now,
    Christ, have mercy. **Christ, have mercy.**

Restore us to full life in you,
    Lord, have mercy. **Lord, have mercy.**

Notes on the Readings

Leviticus 13:1-2, 45-46

To us, this ruling for lepers and other diseased people appears crude and harsh. What has such a practice to do with a God of Love, we may ask.

We need to bear in mind the conditions under which these rules were made. The people realised how important it was for them to keep themselves as a pure nation, with physical, moral and spiritual health proclaiming the holiness and purity of the God to whom they belonged. In this way, other nations would see the greatness of the one true God.

Isolating disease was a practical and effective way of curbing the spread of infection. The priests, who had been shown the first signs of the illness, were therefore in charge of examining those who claimed to be healed; and once they proclaimed the patient well, he was allowed back in society again.

But, however effective, the system must have made any disease-ridden person feel rejected, lonely and despised.

1 Corinthians 10:31 — 11:1

When we are filled with the Spirit of Christ we can afford to be outgoing and open-hearted; we no longer need to be defensive or narrow. This is because our survival no longer depends on avoiding death. Since we have been promised life which will not end with decay of our physical shell, we can use our bodies in God's service without worry. Instead, every action, every muscle we stretch, every word we speak, becomes an act of praise as our whole being works in harmony with its creator.

Mark 1:40-45

We can sense the ingrained feeling of rejection in the way the leper approaches Jesus. He is quite sure that this man has power to heal him; what he is not so confident about is whether he would want to! His low self-image is the result of being constantly unwanted and devalued. There is wonderful hope for anyone who shares the leper's sense of worthlessness and inadequacy. For Jesus reacts with a spontaneous rush of affection and acceptance: 'Of course I want to!' he says, and promptly cures him.

Bidding Prayers

Celebrant   Fellow members of the Body of Christ,
in his Spirit let us pray
to our almighty and merciful Father.

Reader   For the work of the Church
in all deprived areas of the world;
that in the name of Jesus we may reach out
to the poor and hungry,
the outcast and the despised,
and spread God's healing love.
Pause
Father of life: **hear us and help us, we pray.**

For law makers and politicians,
leaders and advisers;
that God's law of love for one another
may permeate our planet
and lead to international harmony.
Pause
Father of life: **hear us and help us, we pray.**

For all lepers and those suffering
from any debilitating or disfiguring disease;
for those who work in medical research;
that God may bring about abundant healing.
Pause
Father of life: **hear us and help us, we pray.**

For any relatives, friends or neighbours
we have rejected, hurt or despised;
that God's love may flood into the relationship
to promote forgiveness and joy.
Pause
Father of life: **hear us and help us, we pray.**

Celebrant   Father, your amazing compassion
fills us with wonder;
in joy and thankfulness we offer you
our praise and intercession
through the person of Jesus. **Amen.**

Ideas for Adults

Today is a good time to alert people's attention to the fact that although leprosy can be cured, it is still widespread in some areas due to lack of money and resources. Posters and information can be obtained free from: British Leprosy Relief Association, Fairfax House, Causton Road, Colchester, Essex CO1 1PU (Telephone 0206 562286).

Organise an exhibition and collection towards this work of widespread healing, and ask people to commit themselves to pray for the elimination of this and other debilitating diseases, such as malaria and bilharzia.

Ideas for Children

Read or tell the children the story of how Jesus cured the leper. Talk with them about what leprosy is and why lepers used to be sent off to live on their own. (They may have been kept away from school when unwell for the same reason.)

When we are in need of curing, either from illness or from sin, we can come to Jesus and ask him to help us. Pray together for any of their friends or relatives who are not well.

Show them a large poster on which is written Jesus' conversation with the leper. Using 'tiles' of small pieces of different coloured paper, the children can make a mosaic, sticking on the pieces with glue. The finished mosaic can be placed in church alongside the leprosy exhibition.

Music
Recorded Music

Tchaikovsky – *Symphony No. 6*

'Live' Music

Lay your hands *(ONE, 295)*
Living Lord *(ONE, 326)*
Lord, however can I repay you? *(ONE, 324)*
Tell out my soul *(ONE, 514)*

7th Sunday in Ordinary Time

Theme
God has authority to forgive our sins

God alone can blot out our sins and is always willing to do so as soon as we confess them with sorrow. That spiritual healing is a most precious gift, which transforms our whole future by completely dissolving the guilt and hurts of the past.

Penitential Rite

Forgiver of sins, we come in need,
    Lord, have mercy. **Lord, have mercy.**

Healer of souls, we come in hope,
    Christ, have mercy. **Christ, have mercy.**

Giver of new life, we come in trust,
    Lord, have mercy. **Lord, have mercy.**

Notes on the Readings

Isaiah 43:18-19, 21-22, 24-25

God speaks here as a parent to a wayward child. The people of Israel are chosen and cherished; God loves them tenderly and has wonderful plans for them to be a light to guide all nations to worship their creator. Yet time and again they have let him down, turned away, abandoned him and broken the Covenant.

Instead of abandoning and rejecting them, God assures them, through his prophet, that although they have sinned, all is not lost. Though there is no way they can redeem themselves, he, as their Redeemer, can and will do it for them. He will forgive their sins so that they are completely eradicated and can be forgotten. The way is then open for an entirely new beginning.

This is the kind of forgiveness we need to strive for in our relationships. If we think of other people's sins against us as financial debts written in our creditor's book, forgiving them has to be as thorough as scribbling through that entry so much that the entry cannot be read; it will be as if that debt never ever existed. Have we sincerely forgiven all those who throughout our lives have hurt or offended us, in such a whole-hearted way?

2 Corinthians 1:18-22

God is in no sense a ditherer. He is not the kind of person who promises something one day and retracts it the next. Nor does he ever promise anything he does not intend carrying out. Nor are his promises only guaranteed as valid for a limited time; however far we have wandered and however great the sin that separates us from him, we shall never find that the warranty has expired.

Without fail and without question his promise to forgive and transform us holds good for ever. Whenever we turn back to him from any sin, however appalling, deep-seated, destructive, embarrassing or despicable, we shall meet his steady gaze and loving acceptance. We will begin to realise that his interest and caring has not once wavered while we have been carelessly hacking our way selfishly through life; yet he looks at us now with no trace of resentment or bitterness, but only joy that we have returned. Not one instance of our nastiness has been hidden from him, yet in full knowledge of what we are like at our worst he loves us whole-heartedly and cancels out all the past sin; we are offered the chance to start completely afresh.

Mark 2:1-12

Jesus always heals in the way that will bring most lasting good. As in a symphony, many parts are often brought together in superb harmony. So often God's way of answering prayer touches far more lives with blessing than the solution we had envisaged.

Here the remarkable faith of the paralytic's friends provides the opportunity for Jesus to touch the raw nerves of suspicion in the scribes, and gives them the opportunity to believe in him as God's chosen one for whom they have been waiting.

The friends do not murmur when Jesus forgives the man instead of enabling him to walk straight away, because they trust him, and their trust makes them patient and accepting. For the scribes, this met their suspicions head on. They knew that only God has power to forgive sins. What a wonderful opportunity Christ gave them, here, in immediately following his absolution with healing. What joy there might have been if this direct, startling proof had been sufficient for them! We need to pray that our eyes will be able to discern the power of God in action. Closed minds face the bleak prospect of failing to recognise the only one who can save them.

Bidding Prayers

Celebrant My brothers and sisters in Christ, knowing the deep love that surrounds us and reaches out to us in every distress, let us unload our burdens of care to the healing power of our heavenly Father.

Reader We bring before him the Church's work among the homeless, the disillusioned and the apathetic, in parish communities all over the world.
Pause
Life-giving Lord: **hear us and help us we pray.**

We bring before him all areas of the world where lack of communication breeds suspicion and fear; where lack of understanding breeds insecurity and a spirit of revenge.
Pause
Life-giving Lord: **hear us and help us we pray.**

We bring before him all whose lives are crippled by unrepented sin or the refusal to forgive; all whose lives are constantly restless and devoid of peace.
Pause
Life-giving Lord: **hear us and help us we pray.**

We bring before him each member of this community, each individual anxiety and sorrow, each hope and dream, each weakness and special need.
Pause
Life-giving Lord: **hear us and help us we pray.**

Celebrant Heavenly Father, so full of power and yet so personally involved with us, accept these prayers and let your will be done in our lives; through Jesus Christ we pray. **Amen.**

Ideas for Adults

The Isaiah reading can be dramatised chorally today. Use a group of nine voices; three each of light, medium and dark.

Dark:	Thus says the Lord:	(pause)
Medium:	No need to recall the past,	
Light:	no need to think about what was done before.	
All:	See, I am doing a new deed,	(louder)
Light:	even now it comes to light;	
Medium:	can you not see it?	(soft)
All:	Yes, I am making a road in the wilderness, paths in the wilds.	(pause)
Dark:	The people I have formed for myself will sing my praises.	
Light:	Jacob, you have not invoked me,	
Medium:	you have not troubled yourself, Israel, on my behalf,	
Dark:	instead you have burdened me with your sins, troubled me with your iniquities.	
Medium:	I it is,	
All:	I it is, who must blot out everything and not remember your sins.	<

Ideas for Children

Tell today's story of the paralytic who was let down through the roof, using a simple model which the children make first. One group makes a house from a white shoe box. At this stage do not mention the way the man's friends got him to Jesus; just talk about the typical design of such a house, with outside steps to a flat roof in which there was often an opening.

Other children make a stretcher-bed with a paralysed man on it, and others make a large crowd of people. Arrange the model on sand-coloured paper and put a few model donkeys and chickens around, and a palm tree or two.

Place Jesus and his friends in the house first, and add other visitors as you explain how word got around that Jesus could heal the sick. When the men arrive with their paralysed friend the children will see that they can't get to Jesus. Ask what they might do now. Give up? Seeing the problem will help them appreciate the men's faith and their determination and persistence. They may even suggest using the hole in the roof!

All through the story help them to identify with the different characters so that they can, in some sense, become 'eye witnesses' to the events.

Music
Recorded Music

Elgar – *The Dream of Gerontius*

'Live' Music

Alleluia for forgiveness *(SONL, 18)*
Amazing grace *(ONE, 36)*
Fear not, for I have redeemed you *(ONE, 136)*

8th Sunday in Ordinary Time

Theme
Christ, our bridegroom, loves us faithfully and tenderly

In spite of his people's waywardness and lack of fidelity, God loves them with constant, unswerving affection, and whenever they stray he labours to bring them back. His love, transforming our lives, makes us influential witnesses, rather like written testimonials which can introduce others to the joy of living in his presence.

Penitential Rite

Though we have strayed, please take us back,
  Lord, have mercy. **Lord, have mercy.**

Increase our faithfulness and trust,
  Christ, have mercy. **Christ, have mercy.**

So steadfast is your love for us!
  Lord, have mercy. **Lord, have mercy.**

Notes on the Readings

Hosea 2:16-17, 21-22

The Northern kingdom was fast approaching the threat of collapse after generations of unfaithfulness, self-indulgence and decadence. As the prophet Amos had pointed out, they deserved all they were going to get, for they had rejected God utterly, and God would be quite justified in abandoning them to their fate. But Hosea, personally wounded by his own beloved but unfaithful wife, was able to balance the justice of God's character with his tender mercy and forgiving love. He is the loving and faithful husband of his people, and though deeply hurt and grieved by them, he is always willing to start afresh with them and welcome them back.

2 Corinthians 3:1-6

Handwriting gives away aspects of our character; so do the clothes we feel comfortable in. But, more than anything, our character is shown in the way we behave – the way we act and react in the different circumstances of our daily lives. Perhaps we have sometimes seen a good Christian person we would like to emulate, and tried to graft their way of behaving, like a package deal, on to ourselves. It never works, of course! There is no short cut to being a shining, effective Christian.

But the more we allow his Spirit to write on our hearts, the more effective witnesses we shall be. It will be a testimonial which is unique, since God loves us personally, and the indwelling of his Spirit simply makes us more fully ourselves. A lively Christian community, then, will be a very colourful collection of people, with a whole range of variety.

Mark 2:18-22

John the Baptist had corresponded with what people generally expected of a man of God, but Jesus seemed to be behaving out of character for a prophet; he went to wedding feasts and parties, and enjoyed company. There is plenty of evidence that he had a good sense of humour. Some of the people are curious about this.

Jesus' reply harks back to the words of Hosea; in the person of Jesus, God is celebrating the everlasting betrothal with his own people, and that is surely an occasion for rejoicing. It also marks the beginning of a new age: some of the old expectations and traditions are going to recede in importance in the light of newly revealed truth. If they want to be part of the dynamic new covenant, the people need to be ready for this, and not try to hang on to their rigid, unyielding traditions.

Bidding Prayers

Celebrant Dear companions in Christ,
  let us trustfully pray to our heavenly Father
  who loves us so much.

Reader For the freedom of all who are imprisoned
  or persecuted for their faith;
  for the continued spread of the Gospel
  till every person is introduced
  to the saving love of Christ.
  Pause
  Father of mercy: **may your kingdom come.**

  For the growth of good international
  relationships and an urgent desire for real peace
  in all the troubled areas of the world.
  Pause
  Father of mercy: **may your kingdom come.**

For those whose lives feel
like a tangled mess at the moment;
for those who feel cheated or let down;
that they may allow Christ
to rescue them and lead them to peace.
Pause
Father of mercy: **may your kingdom come.**

For God's presence in the times of mourning
and celebration in our own families;
for increased mercy in all our relationships.
Pause
Father of mercy: **may your kingdom come.**

Celebrant   Father, we have so often experienced
your loving kindness in our lives;
accept now these prayers and answer them
in the way that is best for your creation,
through Jesus Christ we pray. **Amen.**

Ideas for Adults

Ask people to lend wedding photographs, and make a display of these outward signs of vowed faithfulness and love. One of the flower arrangements can also be given a festive, wedding atmosphere, incorporating ribbons, perhaps. Any whose wedding anniversary falls this month can come forward and renew their marriage vows.

Ideas for Children

Play a recording of the Wedding March and have two dolls or teddies dressed up as a bride and groom. Bring along any photos or keepsakes from weddings you have known, and discuss with the children any memories they may have of the good food, special clothes etc. at the wedding of a relative or family friend.

Explain what the man and woman promise each other in front of God, and ask what sign they give each other of the unending promise (the unending shape of a ring). They may like to ask grandparents how many years they have been married.

Now read the first section of today's Gospel and show them how Jesus liked to think of himself as the bridegroom of the Church. Like a bridegroom he promises to be faithful to us always and to love us in the good and bad times, the healthy and ill times, the rich and the poor times. What is the best way to show our thanks for his love? Love him and be faithful to him.

Using the fingers of a plastic glove, help the children make an unending ring on which they write: Jesus loves me. It can remind them that his promise is for always.

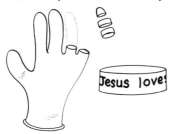

Music
Recorded Music

Mendelssohn – A *Midsummer Night's Dream: The Wedding March*

'Live' Music

Go in peace to be Christ's body *(SONL, 45)*
Our hearts were made for you, Lord *(SONL, 36)*
Sing to the mountains *(ONE, 495)*
Turning the world upside down *(ONE, 403)*

9th Sunday in Ordinary Time

Theme
The Son of Man is master even of the Sabbath

Since it had been instituted by God himself in the organising of creation, the Sabbath was extremely precious and holy. The law surrounding it arose out of proper awe and respect for God. Yet Jesus showed that allegiance to the God of Love is even more important; and when he dwells in us, our lives are radiant.

Penitential Rite

Focus our minds, so easily distracted,
  Lord, have mercy. **Lord, have mercy.**

Soften our hearts, so easily hardened,
  Christ, have mercy. **Christ, have mercy.**

Broaden our vision, so easily tunnelled,
  Lord, have mercy. **Lord, have mercy.**

Notes on the Readings

Deuteronomy 5:12-15

Keeping anniversaries is important. Birthday parties, wedding anniversary gifts, and remembering loved ones who have died – all help to remind us of special or significant events. And remembering helps us recall God's abundant blessings to us so that we are thankful and rededicated to the author and sustainer of life.

The liberation from slavery in Egypt was such an event, and prompted not yearly but weekly remembrance. After such an unprecedented and dramatic intervention by God in their distress, the people had ample proof that theirs was the only, true and all-powerful God, who really loved them. The pulsing rhythmic order of six days' work followed by one day's rest, set a divine order in their lives. Its weekly insistence marked their living as people in harmony with the God who had made them and set them free.

2 Corinthians 4:6-11

There are extraordinary paradoxes in the Christian life. So many Christians have recorded the odd and remarkable experience of finding wonderful assurance and peace at the lowest, weakest and most terrifying points in their lives; of sensing the great company of the faithful while in solitary confinement, or inexplicable peace before execution. The right words pour out (often to our own astonishment!) when we are called to witness to Christ in a difficult situation; and when we know full well we would normally be exploding, we are buoyed up with patience that can have only one source.

These are the daily miracles that happen to all people of prayer. They strengthen our faith as we see that praying really works, and they witness powerfully to others – especially those who know our weaknesses and limitations all too well. For it all points to Christ's power working in us; and when other people see how our faith allows us to accept disaster calmly (not with a stiff upper lip, necessarily), to remain forgiving in the face of attack, or to stay outgoing during long-term illness, they will be drawn to seek this power for themselves.

Mark 2:23-3:6

The Pharisees were right to honour the Sabbath and keep it holy: it was God-given and valuable. But they had begun to lose sight of the wood from looking so intently at the trees.

The whole point of the Sabbath was to help people remember their close relationship with God; when it started to actually hinder people from acts of God-like loving-kindness, something had to be wrong.

Similarly, we may have good, valuable rules for church attendance which occasionally need to be waived so that we are able to tend a sick child or run a neighbour to hospital in an emergency. We would hardly be serving God if we refused to help because we had to be at Mass!

Sometimes, too, acts of kindness, like providing the tea and biscuits after church, or singing in the choir, can get out of hand and assume more importance than the main event of worship which they serve. It is as well to check, quite frequently, that we are still committed to Christ, and not some related activity.

Bidding Prayers

Celebrant   Companions in Christ, in confidence
let us pray to our loving Father.

Reader   That all baptised Christians may pray
without ceasing and work enthusiastically
to spread the good news of the Gospel
with love and sensitivity.
Pause
Almighty Father: **radiate in our minds.**

That all disputes and misunderstandings
may be brought to a settled peace,
based on mutual respect, honour and
concern for each other's grievances.
Pause
Almighty Father: **radiate in our minds.**

That any who are in great pain
may be granted relief and comfort;
that all who live in constant fear or distress
may be given a real assurance of
Christ's undergirding and full protection.
Pause
Almighty Father: **radiate in our minds.**

That every home in this parish
may be enfolded in God's love,
brightened by his joy and calmed
by his unbroken peace.
Pause
Almighty Father: **radiate in our minds.**

Celebrant   In praise and gratitude
we offer you these prayers, Father,
through Jesus Christ. **Amen.**

Ideas for Adults

Ask everyone to bring along an ordinary earthenware pot. It may be a clay flower pot, or a plain mug or small jug. As people come into church they place a votive candle in their pot, and at the offering of the gifts the candles are all lit. (Tapers passed down the rows are a practical way of organising this.) They are kept burning for the rest of the Mass, and afterwards placed in front of the altar as a reminder of how Christ is to shine in our weakness throughout the week.

Ideas for Children

Prepare three large posters each with four sheets of paper stapled at the top, like this:

Look together at the one about going to church. The answer to the first two questions is going to be YES; the third circumstance is more difficult. In the end the answer should still be YES, as long as they plan to rearrange other activities that day to make sure the necessary jobs get done as well. The fourth circumstance helps the children explore the kind of situation when a good rule has to be broken in order to do God's will. Obeying God's law of love must always take precedence.

Next, deal with the question of Bible reading in the same way, and finally the question of prayer. This one will be different, because there is no time at all when keeping in touch with God is wrong; in fact, the more difficult the situation, the closer we cling!

After this discussion, show the children a picture of Jesus healing the man with the withered arm. Was it a good thing he was doing? Tell or read how the Pharisees reacted and how Jesus showed that even the best rules are not as important as living life in God's loving way.

Music
Recorded Music

Tchaikovsky – *Serenade in C for strings*

'Live' Music

If I am lacking love *(ONE, 232)*
I give my hands *(ONE, 235)*
Open your ears *(ONE, 422)*

10th Sunday in Ordinary Time

Theme
God's eternal power for good is stronger than all evil

Since the beginning of humankind, people have been tempted by the evil power of Satan. It was not possible for humans to overcome that evil on their own: that is why God intervened by becoming man and redeeming us. Each one who believes and does God's will becomes part of Christ's life, with all the security and lasting joy that contains.

Penitential Rite

You can wash our sins away,
Lord, have mercy. **Lord, have mercy.**

You see us as we really are,
Christ, have mercy. **Christ, have mercy.**

Your forgiveness sets us free,
Lord, have mercy. **Lord, have mercy.**

Notes on the Readings

Genesis 3:9-15

The serpent had said that Adam and Eve would be like gods once they had eaten of the fruit forbidden by God. In fact it only drives home to them just how naked and vulnerable they are compared with the great power of their creator; that is why they suddenly become frightened of God, and hide from him. It is like the drug pusher who promises a good experience with enhanced vision, yet the new addict discovers only narrow misery and the threat of death.

We may wonder why on earth God put that tree there at all. Wouldn't it have been better to censor the garden so that humanity had no opportunity to be led into sin?

If we think of that precious moment when a baby gives you her first spontaneous hug, we can begin to understand the necessity for freedom of choice in fostering real love. God risked rejection but still considered it a worthwhile price for the joy of responsive love freely given.

2 Corinthians 4:13-5:1

Freely given obedience is most clearly seen in Jesus. Even while on the receiving end of man's rejection, he submitted willingly to God's law of outreaching and forgiving love. In him the rejected God, and the man choosing to love, are fused together, producing such a highly potent force that evil can no longer win.

This would only be useful to us if we could in some way join forces with Jesus, this man/God; if only there were some way of soaking up his life-force, we could actually share the triumph over evil in our own lives!

Happily for us, that is exactly what God makes possible. The only credential needed is to believe in Jesus, and then we are given a free pass for the very qualities which seem so unattainable. We are promised new, rich, full lives, not just in this world but in the world to come; in the light of which, the alluring glitter and neon, tempting us to sin, are shown up clearly for the sham and deceitful trash they are.

Mark 3:20-35

Jesus was proving to be an extremely attractive person. His authoritative teaching, coupled with a warm, responsive approach, brought the crowds flocking to his door. Not all those in the groups of inquisitive people were friendly, however; the scribes were finding this man increasingly dangerous to their status, and set about one of the most efficiently destructive forms of attack: the malicious rumour.

All this no doubt worried Jesus' family. Perhaps, knowing his purity and selflessness, they were concerned that he should not be abused, either by the adoring with their endless needs, or by the offended with their deceit, or both. Jesus' reaction to their anxious inquiries is reminiscent of his reply when he was found as a twelve-year-old in the temple, and would help to reassure them, as well as teaching the listeners.

All was well, for he was doing God's work here in healing, teaching and bringing wholeness to people's lives; his way of love was not to reject the family but to broaden the boundaries of human family love to include all those who wanted to be part of God's family. The close relationship Jesus had with his mother was to be extended to all who, like her, did the will of his heavenly Father.

Bidding Prayers

Celebrant As trustful children, let us confide
in our loving Father,
and pour out to him our cares and concerns.

Reader For all lapsed Christians
and all whose faith is being tested;
all whose spiritual growth is being stunted
by material cares or possessions;
and all who are hesitantly approaching Jesus
for the first time
or after long separation from him.
Pause
Almighty Father: **your power is sufficient for us.**

For the areas in which corruption
has splintered the integrity of government;
for the instances of double-dealing
and hypocrisy which blunt honour,
and breed suspicion and revenge.
Pause
Almighty Father: **your power is sufficient for us.**

For all who are trapped and frustrated
by physical or mental disabilities,
illness or weakness; for the lonely
and those for whom no-one prays.
Pause
Almighty Father: **your power is sufficient for us.**

For enlightenment as to our own areas
of spiritual weakness: for the courage
to desire real, fundamental changes there,
and for the will to persevere in growing.
Pause
Almighty Father: **your power is sufficient for us.**

Celebrant Most merciful Father who knows us so well,
accept our prayers through Christ Jesus. **Amen.**

Ideas for Adults

The reading from Genesis is very effective if acted out in the style of the early Mystery Plays. Have God dressed in white, Adam and Eve in brief, simple tunics, and the serpent in leotard and tights of one colour.

Begin with a recording of bird song to create the atmosphere of the lovely garden, which mankind's sin has spoilt. Adam and Eve run up together from the back, looking furtively behind them every so often. At the front they stand pressed against a pew or lectern, as if concealing themselves. (Use a sheet of cardboard to make the sound of distant thunder to suggest inevitable threat.)

God walks slowly up the centre aisle as the narrator starts to read. God's 'Where are you?' is repeated as he nears the front. God stops before he gets really close to Adam, so that they have to call to each other. When God asks why he knows he is naked, Adam and Eve look at each other in silent panic, for they have been found out. They hold hands and agree not to answer.

When God opens the way for Adam to own up, he and Eve release hands and Adam moves slightly away from Eve, so as to disassociate himself from blame. The woman covers her face with her hands. At this point the serpent is seen crawling between Adam and Eve and God. When God asks the woman: 'What is this you have done?' she sees the chance of blaming something else and comes forward pointing accusingly at the serpent as she speaks.

As God addresses the serpent, who writhes in resentment and frustration, Adam and Eve listen in fear, clinging to each other. The thunder crashes as God retraces his steps to the back and Adam and Eve move, weakened and frightened by the silent garden, in another direction. The serpent slinks off a different way.

Ideas for Children

Talk together about how difficult it is to be good. Even quite young children will have discovered the tiresome truth that Paul also found: the things we don't intend to do, we end up doing; and some of the good things we mean to do, don't get done! Such a discussion does not damage a child's self image; rather, it helps him see that doing wrong sometimes is part of being human, and the important thing is to say sorry and put things right quickly.

Now tell them the story of Adam and Eve being disobedient. This is a sin they will readily understand; they may also pick up the way Adam blames Eve and she blames the serpent. They had chosen not to do what God wanted, and that spoilt things. Help them see how we, too, are always free to choose whether to be loving or unloving. Who can help us make the right decision? Jesus can. Why? Show them a picture of Jesus healing, then teaching, so they can see that, though a man like Adam, Jesus was God's Son, and always, without fail, chose to be loving.

Even when people were horrid and cruel to him he went on loving. (Show them a crucifix.) Even when they killed him, he loved and forgave. So if we trust him as our most special friend, he will help us to grow more and more loving.

Using two spent matches and a wire bag-fastener, the children can make a small cross to carry about in a pocket, to remind them to ask Jesus to help when they are tempted to be unkind, mean or selfish.

Music

Recorded Music

Telemann – *Suite in A minor for flute and orchestra*

'Live' Music

Mother of God's living Word *(ONE, 353)*
Oh! How good is the Lord *(ONE, 396)*
Praise to the holiest in the height *(ONE, 455)*

11th Sunday in Ordinary Time

Theme
The seed of God's kingdom grows in our hearts

Like the tiny mustard seed, which grows into a shady bush, God's Word, when planted in our hearts, flourishes until we are able to work with our creator to bring news of comfort and joy to a restless world. The more God's love transfuses us, the more we shall yearn to do his will; oneness with Christ will become more important than whether we live or die physically.

Penitential Rite

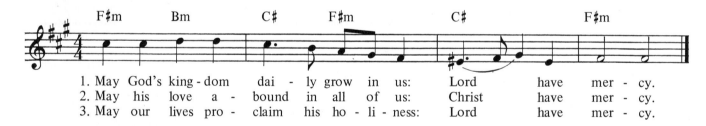

1. May God's king-dom dai-ly grow in us: Lord have mer-cy.
2. May his love a-bound in all of us: Christ have mer-cy.
3. May our lives pro-claim his ho-li-ness: Lord have mer-cy.

Notes on the Readings

Ezekiel 17:22-24

Recurrent in so many Old Testament prophecies is the theme of a small remnant from the bulk of corruption being saved and becoming the basis of hope. In many cases the hope is centred on just one person, under whose leadership the people would be restored to good and lasting harmony with their creator.

Here, Ezekiel foretells the coming of the Messiah who will spring as one small shoot from the royal family tree of King David, and flourish to provide safety and shelter for many.

2 Corinthians 5:6-10

Paul speaks here as one who has made his home in the shade and shelter of his Lord. He has no fear of death, as that will not bring separation from the one he loves; and his joy at pleasing Christ will not change, whether he remains in his body or out of it.

As professing Christians, our attitude to death is fundamental in our witness to others. It must differ radically from that of anyone who reckons death to be the end of personal existence. If in the face of approaching death (our own or that of a loved one) we find our faith challenged, or weaker than we thought it was, it may help to retrace our steps to faith, rather like running our hands over a favourite, familiar piece of furniture or musical instrument.

Work slowly and imaginatively through the Creed, remembering how the whole universe was made by God. Think of what you could see through a telescope and a microscope as well as with the naked eye. Having recalled the power and wonder of God, think about the life of Jesus until you are able to say with Peter, 'You are the Christ, the Son of the living God.' Then let him reassure you of his promise which, coming from the all-powerful God, you can believe: his promise is to raise you up, as he was raised up on the first Easter Day.

Mark 4:26-34

The kingdom of heaven is busy growing quietly, now, in many, many people throughout the whole world. It's an exciting thought. Sometimes in our impatience, we make a renewed commitment one day and expect to find a full-grown, fruiting tree by the next morning; but like so many things in our existence, the material is a reflection of the spiritual, and growth never works like that except in Jack and the bean-stalk.

It is the steady, persevering, habitual leaning towards God that makes for strong spiritual growth; the kind of loyalty to our Lord that goes on praying when we miss the train, when we feel anger boiling up inside us, when we win the pools or lose our pension book. And the taller we grow, the more welcome shade and shelter we can provide, both individually and as part of a strong and vigorous Church, nourished with the life of Christ.

Bidding Prayers

Celebrant Rooted in Christ, let us call to mind now
all those in need, and pray for them
to our heavenly Father.

Reader That all who teach the Christian faith
may be given appropriate language
to get through to those who hear,
so the Word of God takes root in many hearts.
Pause
Lord of life: **help us to grow.**

That all diplomats and negotiators may promote
peace and friendship between the nations,
fostering mutual respect and understanding.
Pause
Lord of life: **help us to grow.**

That those whose lifestyle has been threatened
or shattered by crippling illness or injury,
may find new doors opening, new hope appearing
and new meaning transforming their outlook.
Pause
Lord of life: **help us to grow.**

That we and our families, neighbours
and friends may become daily more Christlike
and less self-centred;
more responsive to the needs
of those around us and less bothered
by what we get out of life.
Pause
Lord of life: **help us to grow.**

Celebrant Father, we lay our needs and cares before you,
and ask you to hear us through Christ. **Amen.**

Ideas for Adults

Make a central display of packets of seeds, a watering can, some seedlings and flowers in full bloom; the gardeners of the parish can have a field day!

Ideas for Children

Talk with the children about the country they live in and who is in charge of it, who makes the rules etc. Bring pictures of leaders of other countries. What about the kingdom of heaven? We are citizens in that country, too. Do they know who the king is? And where is it on the map?

Explain that Jesus' kingdom is all over the world because it is growing in people wherever they accept him as their Saviour and personal friend. As we grow in love, kindness and obedience, the kingdom of heaven grows. Drop some coloured ink on to blotting paper and watch it spread. That is what happens when we love Jesus – his love spreads out through us to the world. So if we let the kingdom of heaven grow in us we will be really helping our world and all the sadness and pain in it.

Read today's parable of the mustard seed, and then help them make a growth measuring chart for themselves, so that as their bodies get taller they remember the importance of growing in Jesus too.

Have the sheets of paper already measured in centimetres with the Bible references, to look up when they reach certain heights, written on separate strips of sticky peel-off paper. Fix the measuring charts all round the wall, let the children measure each other, and stick the first reference on their present height. The others are on each of the next five centimetres up. As they grow, their brothers and sisters or parents can help them read the words of Jesus.

The Bible references are these:
1. Mark 4:30-32
2. Luke 12:22-24
3. Matthew 22:37-40
4. John 8:12
5. Matthew 19:13-15
6. John 10:27-28

Music
Recorded Music

Music from Taizé – *Jesus, remember me*

'Live' Music

Crown him with many crowns *(ONE, 112)*
Dear Lord and Father of mankind *(ONE, 116)*
Let all the world in every corner sing *(ONE, 302)*

12th Sunday in Ordinary Time

Theme
We need not fear: God is fully in charge

Nothing exists that was not made by God, and even the fiercest tempest in our lives is not beyond the control of the Lord of Peace. The fear and panic that so often haunts us can be converted by his presence into quiet assurance, based on everlasting values. Such an assurance is felt, rather than argued, and has the effect of making us new, from the inside.

Penitential Rite

Bring our lives to rest in you,
Lord, have mercy. **Lord, have mercy.**

Realign our wills to yours,
Christ, have mercy. **Christ, have mercy.**

Flood our hearts with caring love,
Lord, have mercy. **Lord, have mercy.**

Notes on the Readings

Job 38:1, 8-11

From the depth of his suffering Job had hammered at God, and the turmoil of his feelings is reflected in the heart of the tempest from which God makes himself known; for he is there in the very centre of Job's distress. By way of answering his hurt and bewildered child, God directs Job's attention to the cosmic power that created and controlled in the unfolding of a universe. God himself was that awesome power; and as Job begins to grasp the inexhaustible grandeur and greatness of his Lord, he starts to understand his own frailty and weakness. His awareness drives him to repentance, and then inner peace, as God encourages him and restores his blessings.

2 Corinthians 5:14-17

Whenever we catch glimpses of God's astounding glory, we too are overwhelmed by the sense of our own unworthiness for the patient and loving way he deals with us. For, as Paul points out, if we were to get what we deserve for our sins, we should all be dead! But because the great, creating God was willing to die in our place, it is our sin and selfishness which dies with him, enabling us to live on in a new creation, provided we bind ourselves to Christ.

It is a constant 'dying', whenever sin sidles or charges into our relationships and behaviour; but it is also a constant 'resurrection' as we are tenderly shaped and moulded into new creatures filled with the life of our risen Lord.

Mark 4:35-41

Job had experienced God's peace at the heart of a raging storm; Elijah had heard him as a still, small voice after violent weather; and now that God is present among people as Jesus, the disciples find, in a very practical way, that God's peace is always there in any tempest. However terrifying the circumstance we find him there, 'just as he is', and his presence may be enough to calm us. Often it is not enough, and we panic, and scream at him to *do* something! Our panic is really an indication of our paltry faith, but God does not turn over and go back to sleep, ignoring our cries. He is never callous or thick-skinned, and if we ask, he will calm the storm until we are able to cope better by trusting him more.

Later in our lives, we may find we have managed to remain calm through far worse storms than we ever thought we could cope with. That is because by dwelling in Christ we are gradually being made into his likeness, and that includes becoming the still, secure point in a storm. Living in Christ will permit us to spread his peace.

Bidding Prayers

Celebrant Together we walk the way of Christ;
let us now pray together in his name,
to our Lord and heavenly Father.

Reader That the spiritual life of each parish
may be nurtured and grow,
so that Christians reach out increasingly
to the particular needs of their neighbourhood.
Pause
Lord of Peace: **be present among us.**

That God's will may prevail in the way we use
our world's resources, our intelligence,
our knowledge and our power.
Pause
Lord of Peace: **be present among us.**

That all those who are living through
some tempest, whether physical, emotional,
mental, or spiritual, may know the peace
and comfort of God's absorbent love
which soaks up all hurt
and promotes healing and wholeness.
Pause
Lord of Peace: **be present among us.**

That our homes may be havens of caring
and understanding, where all who enter
may find the tangible and attractive
peace of the God we serve.
Pause
Lord of Peace: **be present among us.**

Celebrant Father, rejoicing that you are
in overall charge of all creation
we offer these prayers
through Christ Jesus. **Amen.**

Ideas for Adults

The first reading is even more striking and beautiful if read chorally.

Before the reading, play some music which suggests a violent storm, such as the 'storm' passage from Beethoven's *Pastoral Symphony*. As the music plays, the whole group of speakers shouts above it:

All: Then from the heart of the tempest
the Lord gave Job his answer   *ff*
(*Fade the music gradually*)
Women: He said: Who pent up the sea behind closed doors
when it leapt tumultuous out of the womb,
Men: when I wrapped it in a robe of mist
Women: and made black clouds its swaddling bands;
Men: when I marked the bounds it was not to cross
and made it fast with a bolted gate?
All: Come thus far, I said, and no further;
here your proud waves shall break.

Ideas for Children

Read the story of Jesus calming the stormy sea, from the Palm Tree Bible stories: *Jesus on the Sea*. Talk with them about other kinds of storms we might have in our lives; times when everything seems to be going wrong, or we feel unsettled and sad. (Perhaps a new baby in the house might seem like a noisy and interfering storm, or a change of schools or classes or moving house.)

Help them to see, through the story, how Jesus will always be there in the boat with us, and if we ask him he will calm our fears. Use the discussion as a lead into a time of prayer, and encourage the children to pray aloud in the group for people they know or know about, who are specially needing our prayers.

Then help them to make this moving model of a rough sea with Jesus and his friends in the boat. Use thin card or thick paper. The sea and sky can be coloured or decorated. (Drawing overleaf.)

Music
Recorded Music

Mendelssohn – *Fingal's Cave*

'Live' Music

Lead us, heavenly Father, lead us *(ONE, 298)*
Listen *(SONL, 26)*
Lord of my life *(SONL, 21)*

13th Sunday in Ordinary Time

Theme
Christ brings us full, abundant life

Death is the result of sin; and God, who created a good world, loved it enough to send his Son to buy it back from sin with his life. Showing God's nature, Jesus worked zealously to heal and restore, comfort and encourage. In his spirit we too can cause waves of compassion and healing to wash round our aching and stressful world.

Penitential Rite

Acknowledging our frailty, we come,
  Lord, have mercy. **Lord, have mercy.**

Yearning for your wholeness, we come,
  Christ, have mercy. **Christ, have mercy.**

Just as we are, we come,
  Lord, have mercy. **Lord, have mercy.**

Notes on the Readings

Wisdom 1:13-15, 2:23-24

The world we live in is an incredibly beautiful place. One of the rewards of television is that we can all look in on the wonders of landscape, wildlife and the variety of life on our planet, and Christians cannot help but be led on from such richness to praise the master of creation. There is no doubt that it is, indeed, very good.

And that must always be our starting point. We must never accept evil or destruction with a hopeless shrug, as if things are bound to be that way because the world is basically bad and unfair, and we cannot, or even should not, expect anything better.

The world is *not* bad: it was created good by the God who is ultimately in control. All the evil in the world is not endemic, but an infection of sin, which can and will be overcome.

2 Corinthians 8:7, 9, 13-15

Flattery will get you everywhere! Paul is not actually buttering up the Christians at Corinth in order to increase their giving; but he is encouraging them by delighting in the good God is working through them. We do need to make our thanks and praise of others known, sometimes, and not take it all for granted. Too much back-patting is obviously unhealthy, but often a little encouragement is precious and stimulating, especially to those who are not highly considered by worldly standards.

Those to whom much is given will have much expected of them, so we can never judge our own generosity by comparing what we give with what someone else gives. Paul's advice is very sound: strike a good balance, remembering God's generosity in discarding the richness of splendour and majesty in order to make us rich. If we keep to this yardstick we shall be good stewards, sharing the abundance of a good world.

Mark 5:21-43

If we were to read the creation poem in Genesis, and then imagine how the God revealed there might react to a young girl desperately sick and dying, we would surely come up with the way Jesus feels deep sorrow, confronts the evil, overrules it with his authority of intense goodness, and creates an atmosphere of joy and wholeness.

Even though he is delayed by another act of healing (which remade the timid woman who had suffered for years), Jesus' power to make whole is not diminished. For Jesus it is never too late to bother; never too late to transform, heal and make whole. The wholeness may be different from what we were expecting, but God knows and loves us in terms of eternity, and will make us, and our loved ones for whom we pray, healed in the way which is eternally best for us. We need to touch him with faith, invite him into the home or hospital, and listen to his instructions. He will never refuse to come.

Bidding Prayers

Celebrant My brothers and sisters in Christ,
        let us lay at the feet of our heavenly Father
        all our cares and concerns for the Church
        and for the world.

Reader That those Christians whom God is calling
        to a particular ministry
        may recognise his voice
        and respond to it in trust.
        Pause
        Lord of Life: **we offer ourselves to your service.**

That the way we govern our country
may reflect the way we are governed
by the God of justice, mercy and compassion.
Pause
Lord of Life: **we offer ourselves to your service.**

That those who have become locked
in their guilt, resentment, revenge or hatred,
may be released through thorough repentance
and the joy of forgiveness.
Pause
Lord of Life: **we offer ourselves to your service.**

That we, and all others worshipping
in this city/town, may allow God access
to more of our life and personality this week,
so he can work through us to spread
healing and wholeness.
Pause
Lord of Life: **we offer ourselves to your service.**

Celebrant   Father, we thank you for drawing us here
to pray, and ask you to hear us,
through Jesus Christ. **Amen.**

Ideas for Adults

Today's Gospel lends itself to a different form of dramatisation in which the entire congregation is involved. It gives great immediacy and reality to the living, healing Jesus.

The characters of Jairus and his family, the woman suffering from a haemorrhage, Peter, James and John, are all trained beforehand, and need to know their words off by heart. The narrator stands separate from the action, and the priest takes the part of Jesus.

Warn the congregation in advance that they will be participating; and as Jesus moves out of the sanctuary, ushers invite them all to come out of the pews and crowd round him. Jairus pushes his way through them from the back, and everyone listens to him. As they all begin to follow Jesus and Jairus, the sick woman (no-one should know who it is) touches Jesus' clothes, and the crowd will find themselves reacting naturally: curious and then surprised, happy for her – even hugging her – just as they feel instinctively.

Jairus' house is located at the back of the church, with lots of weeping from the distraught family. This, too, will affect the crowd. Let the family ad lib when the girl has been brought back to life. They may bring her outside, and the crowd can cheer and clap before returning to their seats.

Ideas for Children

The children will get a lot from joining in the acting of the Gospel with the adults today. Before they come into church, have an assortment of wildlife pictures, sun, snow, fire, plants, animals, birds and people, for them to stick on to a poster entitled: *God made the World, and it was very good.* Have a time of prayer to praise and thank God for all his presents to us and pray for those who are ill, blind or deaf, or handicapped in any way.

They can bring their poster into church with them, and act out this wonderful example of Jesus restoring the created world to wholeness, person by person.

Music
Recorded Music

Dvorak – *Symphony No. 9 (From the New World)*

'Live' Music

Freely, freely *(ONE, 175)*
Jesu, the very thought of thee *(ONE, 287)*
Living Lord *(ONE, 326)*

Ordinary Time 14 – 20

Questions for Discussion Groups
Who is this man? Feeding
1. How did the feeding of the five thousand provide an important clue to Jesus' mission?
2. When, and in what way, have you experienced him as Living Bread in your own life?

14th Sunday in Ordinary Time

Theme
Whether they listen or not

We are called to tell others about God and the quality of life in his kingdom, whether they are responsive or apathetic. As Jesus himself found, there's none so deaf as those who know all the answers already! In reality, our very weakness and doubts can become strengths, since they teach us to rely trustingly on God to show us where to go, what to say and how to act.

Penitential Rite

For the chances to witness we have avoided,
   Lord, have mercy. **Lord, have mercy.**

For our lack of zealous commitment,
   Christ, have mercy. **Christ, have mercy.**

For our embarrassment at proclaiming your truth,
   Lord, have mercy. **Lord, have mercy.**

Notes on the Readings

Ezekiel 2:2-5

Half-empty churches should bother us. Not because actual numbers are important, but because the empty seats are 'full' of troubled, aimless, vulnerable people who need to know the love of Jesus in their lives, and do not. We may protest that they have had lots of opportunities to meet Jesus if they really wanted to, and many have chosen to live materialistic, self-sufficient lives instead.

Much of Israel had chosen to ignore God. What had begun in one generation was passed on in attitudes to the children, so that the whole structure of God-centred living gradually fell into ruins. God's answer then is also our call today. Ezekiel is commissioned to go to the people and tell them about God, explaining his will through his Word; and whether they listen or not, they will know there is a prophet among them. We, too, are to arrange for people in our area to hear and study God's Word; to have the opportunity to talk with convinced Christians about their faith; and to experience firsthand the outpouring of Christ's love through the practical help and care given by his friends. If we don't do this, we shall effectively be barring people from meeting Christ.

2 Corinthians 12:7-10

Having decided that it is time to start spreading our faith more, we may find ourselves meeting obstacles almost before we have started! When you think about it, that is not really surprising, as the last thing Satan wants is for us to bring more people to Christ's saving love. Paul's list of insults and sufferings gives us some idea of what to expect, and is not exactly inviting.

However, because it is the God of goodness, power and love that we are volunteering to serve, the strangest paradox becomes evident as soon as we set ourselves to do his will. The more difficult life is, the easier it seems to be to witness to others in an effective way that really draws them to our Lord. Hanging on to his hand for dear life, we experience such overwhelming support and such miracles of perfect timing, answered prayers and peace of mind, that we can witness to actual knowledge of a God who is alive and well, interested in us enough to want to help and remake us. There is only one conclusion we can draw: he must really love us! After that, the difficulties matter less; if they keep us relying on the Lord we love and who loves us, then we are happy to have things that way.

Mark 6:1-6

When Jesus returned to his home town he continued to do his Father's business, and taught in the synagogue with all the insight and understanding that only he could have. At first the congregation listens, spellbound; they are amazed and profoundly struck by what they hear. So far, so good. The atmosphere seems ripe for the delight at finding God's chosen one to be a next-door neighbour.

But something makes their admiration turn sour, leading them to reject Jesus instead, until he is left marvelling at their amazing lack of faith. What was it that blocked their belief? Perhaps, having been brought up alongside him, they considered themselves Jesus' equals. And now, here he is, preaching like a fine scholar and obviously grasping truths about the Scriptures that they have never even considered. What they thought they knew about Jesus is suddenly challenged, and in their jealousy they resent him.

As Christians, we ought never to think we have finished our education; constantly learning more about Jesus will make us less liable to reject out of hand some new insight which challenges our accepted image of him.

Bidding Prayers

Celebrant My dear companions in Christ,
let us pray together to our heavenly Father,
who loves us and knows us so well.

Reader For all who are working to build up
the Church in their local area;
that they may be guided to see the real needs,
and present the good news
in ways the people understand.
Pause
Lord of All: **give us power to witness.**

For all who work for good and just
legislation; for all who act to change
the politics in our world which are contrary
to God's law of caring love.
Pause
Lord of All: **give us power to witness.**

For the weak and the vulnerable,
the sorrowing and the disheartened;
for the very young and the very old;
for all who will wander aimlessly through life
unless someone brings them to Christ.
Pause
Lord of All: **give us power to witness.**

For ourselves and those next to us here;
that we may be encouraged to share
our experience of God's love
with some of the people
we shall meet this week.
Pause
Lord of All: **give us power to witness.**

Celebrant Father, we ask you to fulfil our prayers
to your glory; in Jesus' name we pray. **Amen.**

Ideas for Adults

It may be useful, in the light of this week's readings, to review the parish programme for teaching and outreach. Perhaps there are some areas in which a fresh approach is needed, or new needs provided for. Share a time of prayer (half an hour, perhaps) before going on to discuss possible outreach programmes.

Ideas for Children

Collect some pictures of missionary work, both at home and abroad, and discuss with the children what the needs are and how they are being met. Point out that the missionaries are telling people about the God of love not only by what they say but also how they behave and what they do.

Tell or read the passage from Ezekiel and then make a tape recording together. Start it with a song of praise, and then have different children explaining what they love about Jesus, how being a Christian helps them in their lives, what they would like everyone to know about God etc. A friendly and sensitive interviewer helps a lot, and after initial shyness, most children really enjoy speaking into a microphone.

The finished tape can be copied and played to others in the parish. Or it could be made available for visitors or to introduce a discussion and prayer group.

Music
Recorded Music

Ravel – *Piano concerto: slow movement*

'Live' Music

Go in peace *(SONL, 45)*
Go tell everyone *(ONE, 183)*
He who would valiant be *(ONE, 210)*
I give my hands *(ONE, 235)*

15th Sunday in Ordinary Time

Theme
We have been chosen to work for his glory

Even before the world was made, God's mind encompassed you and me, and our individual parts in his great redemptive plan. We were created solely for him, and all material worries fade as we lean on the God who loves, guides and supports us, sending us, if we will only listen, to the right place at the right time.

Penitential Rite

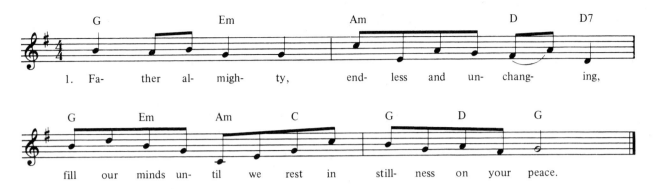

1. Fa- ther al- migh- ty, end- less and un- chang- ing,

fill our minds un- til we rest in still- ness on your peace.

2. Jesus our Saviour,
   radiant with compassion,
   break our hearts of stone
   and make us burn with selfless love.

3. Life-giving Spirit,
   streaming from the Godhead,
   steep us in your purity
   and drench us in your joy.

Notes on the Readings

Amos 7:12-15

Amos was by no means a welcome visitor to the northern tribes of Israel. Their centre of power and worship at Bethel had originally been set up to stop the people wandering off back to Judah to worship at the holy city of Jerusalem; so it had bad foundations, and pinpointed the beginnings of idolatry which had drawn people away from allegiance to the one true God.

Twice, Amos pleaded with God on behalf of Israel, but no repentance was forthcoming, so judgement seemed to be inevitable. That was the last straw as far as Amaziah was concerned! Why should they have to put up with hearing gloomy and uncomfortable messages from a prophet who did not understand their lifestyle? No doubt at that moment Amos' sycamores and flocks of sheep had never seemed more inviting, but he stands firm in what he knows God has called him to do. God recognised in Amos the right man for a difficult job, so he called him to do it, even though Amos had not been trained in the usual way.

Neither need we be hesitant about taking part in some ministry to which we sense God is calling us. If he wants us to do it he will certainly provide the necessary training and resources. Our task is to be available, and agree to do it.

Ephesians 1:3-14

When you walk up a hill or a mountain, you often head for 'false' summits on the way. They look like the top, but when you reach them you find the real summit is higher than you thought.

Imagining God's power, influence and control is a bit like that: however much understanding and awareness we grasp, there is always more than we can comprehend. But within it is the firm and dependable promise of Christ: that we have been chosen right from the beginning, and stamped with the seal of the Holy Spirit, to be freed sons and daughters of the God whose majesty is beyond us.

Mark 6:7-13

This sending out of the Twelve in pairs to preach repentance, and to heal, would have been in some sense a practice run for their commission after Pentecost. It would also have spread the news of the imminence of God's kingdom being established on earth. Jesus' instructions to them, as to us, are clear, practical and uncomplicated.

The point is not that we should all leave our families and set off in sandals without any spare clothes; rather, we need to spend time in the quietness of Christ's presence to listen to the instructions he has for us!

Bidding Prayers

Celebrant We are God's children, and he loves us;
let us pray to him now.

Reader We bring to his love those
whose Christian ministry is in prisons,
hospitals, schools or industry;
those who work among the homeless
and the very poor.
Pause
Father, you have called us: **we are ready to follow.**

We bring to his love the areas of
political tension and unrest in our world;
the unresolved conflicts and
the deep-seated grudges that hinder peace.
Pause
Father, you have called us: **we are ready to follow.**

We bring to his love the hurt and wounded,
the abused and the frightened;
women in labour and newly-born babies;
those who are approaching death.
Pause
Father, you have called us: **we are ready to follow.**

We bring to his love the special needs
and concerns known to us individually;
and any who have particularly asked
for our prayers.
Pause
(*The people may drop into the silence particular
names or needs.*)
Father, you have called us: **we are ready to follow.**

Celebrant With great joy, in the knowledge
that we can trust you unconditionally,
we offer you our prayers
through Jesus Christ. **Amen.**

Ideas for Adults

For the first reading, have two men dressed in costume to take the parts of Amos and Amaziah, learning the words by heart. A reader narrates only the first phrase. Encourage Amaziah to sound irritated and angry, and Amos to express the feeling that he would not have chosen to come and prophesy either, but that he is doing it because God has told him to.

Ideas for Children

Bring along twelve sticks and some pictures of Israel. Tell the children the story of how Jesus sent the twelve off in pairs; and as you get to each point, collect twelve children, let them take off their socks so they are wearing only sandals or shoes, give them a staff to take with them, just one set of clothing, and no money. All other children are the sick and their families, some of whom offer the disciples food and shelter, while others refuse to listen to them.

Show the pictures of Israel so the children can see that Jesus' instructions were practical for travelling light in that climate and terrain.

Gather round in prayer to ask Jesus to show us where he wants us to work for him today and through the week, and give them this prayer to colour and hang up in the bathroom at home and use every morning.

Music

Recorded Music

Bach – *Toccata and fugue in D*

'Live' Music

Build your church *(ONE, 74)*
Go, the Mass is ended *(ONE, 188)*
If we only seek peace *(SONL, 76)*
Make me a channel of your peace *(ONE, 342)*

16th Sunday in Ordinary Time

Theme
Christ shepherds his people

Seeing us through eyes of love, Christ is always ready to feed us words of life, steer us through crises, protect and sort us out. His personality draws in all hurt and hardness and softens it to healing, so that the barriers that divide us are broken down and we can all become one in love.

Penitential Rite

As your sheep and lambs, we need you,
  Lord, have mercy. **Lord, have mercy.**

We cannot find our way without you,
  Christ, have mercy. **Christ, have mercy.**

We want to travel close beside you,
  Lord, have mercy. **Lord, have mercy.**

Notes on the Readings

Jeremiah 23:1-6

When we hear news of corrupt police, a teacher molesting children or a nurse convicted of assault, it strikes us with an ominous dread; for these are the kind of people we look to for security and guidance, and if they betray our trust, the whole fabric of society cracks. This is what had happened to Israel: the very priests who were responsible for leading God's people had let them go wandering so they were scattered and lost. To abuse the privilege and responsibility of leadership is, in God's eyes, a terrible wrong against him and the people he loves.

But, as always with the God of hope, there is to be repair and healing. With the coming of the Messiah, the remnant of the flock will be gathered personally from wherever they have been scattered; they will be led and comforted, nurtured with peace and integrity and cared for by shepherds who can be trusted.

Ephesians 2:13-18

That remnant has another meaning, apart from the faithful of Israel and Judah. Early on in its history the Church was led by the Spirit of Truth to make a dramatic and courageous decision: Gentiles could become Christians without first becoming Jews. It was certainly a heated issue, with good people on each side aiming to do what they saw as God's will, and both sides could be strongly argued.

Quite possibly this could have led to a cavernous split, or to Christianity developing as a small Jewish sect. And those on whom this life-threatening decision rested were just ordinary people, like Church leaders today who are faced with similarly difficult problems.

But of course they were not making the decision without the presence of Christ; and his presence, eagerly sought, is what actually breaks down existing barriers. In this case, his peace dissolved the issues that were keeping Jews and Gentiles separate, and fused them into one unbroken, out-reaching community which could lead people to the Father.

What worked then will be just as effective today. Christ's presence is just as real and vibrant; he is just as successful in achieving the impossible, sealing rifts, bonding factions and inspiring right decisions. All we have to do is ask him and trust him.

Mark 6:30-34

It is vital for us all to have times of retreat in our heavy schedules. Jesus wisely shepherds his apostles to a lonely place where they can relax, rest and have 'space'. We need to do the same, setting aside some time each week, if possible; it is not laziness, but a valuable recharging of batteries.

Not that the plans always work out. Jesus arrived with his apostles at an isolated spot 'wound down' and ready for a time of quietness, only to find crowds of people eager to see him. They had struggled round with all their sick and crippled, hoping for more cures and help.

As a human, Jesus' heart must have sunk at the sight of so much need when he was tired; but as God, he lays the tiredness aside in a rush of sympathy, understanding and compassion. They need their good shepherd, and he responds to their need.

Bidding Prayers

Celebrant   Little flock, we have been called here
            by our good shepherd; let us pray trustingly
            to the loving God who made us.

Reader   For a strong witness of peace-making
        Christians in every community;
        for actively prayerful Christians who plead
        with urgency and compassion for those in need;
        for spiritual dynamism to refresh
        Christians whose faith is limp or frayed.
        Pause
        Father almighty: **with you all things are possible.**

        For clear light and guidance as our world
        faces the problems and crises of another week;
        for the willingness of leaders
        to be wisely advised.
        Pause
        Father almighty: **with you all things are possible.**

        For those who are addicted to drugs,
        alcohol, solvent abuse, violence,
        or any other habit which enslaves;
        for those whose bodies and minds
        have been damaged by abuse;
        for the desperate and the suicidal.
        Pause
        Father almighty: **with you all things are possible.**

        For a greater willingness in us
        to lay our burdens and worries at the feet
        of our Saviour; for a deepening of trust
        and a widening of our circle of loved ones.
        Pause
        Father almighty: **with you all things are possible.**

Celebrant   Father, in the sure knowledge of your promise
            to answer the prayers of all who are faithful,
            we offer you our cares and concerns
            through Jesus. **Amen.**

Ideas for Adults

During the week, collect pictures of news items which show people in need of the good shepherd's help, healing and guidance. World leaders in conference; political or industrial unrest; bad weather or natural disasters; local and international problems – use a wide variety and display them either on an exhibition stand or on different sides of covered cartons. Among the pictures have Mark 6:34 written out, and also Psalm 22/23:1. This can be used as a focus for intercession.

Ideas for Children

Children are very good at intercession and their gift should be developed and used.

Begin by telling them the story of how Jesus went away for a well-earned rest, but found all the people had guessed where he was going and had come to find him, with all their needs. Jesus did not send them home, but lovingly looked after them. Explain that there are many people who need Jesus today, and we can bring them to him by praying for them. That is called 'Intercession', and they are going to make an 'Intercession' book to help them bring some people to meet Jesus and be helped by him.

Give out several sheets of coloured paper to each child. These are folded and stapled to make a scrap book. On the cover, the children stick a duplicated title page, like this:

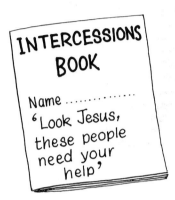

Inside they can stick pictures of people and situations to carry along to their good friend, Jesus, to ask for his help. Have a selection of pictures from magazines, newspapers, leaflets etc. showing both general groups of people (like nurses, priests, scientists and teachers), and also specific problems (like accidents, earthquakes or important meetings).

The idea is that more pictures can be added as the children hear about the needs, and others in the parish can be put in touch with particular children to be 'prayer partners' during an illness or some other need. If they can supply a photo for the child who is praying, so much the better. Failing that, their name can be stuck in the book.

Music
Recorded Music

Fauré – *Pavane*

'Live' Music

Feed my sheep *(SONL, 12)*
If you are thirsting *(SONL, 83)*
The king of love my shepherd is *(ONE, 528)*
Where would we be without Christ our Lord *(ONE, 617)*

17th Sunday in Ordinary Time

Theme
Christ, the generous provider

Taking the offering of one small boy's lunch, Christ provides food in abundance for thousands of people. Any gift we offer him will be blest, broken and multiplied for the good of the world; and we are all fed and sustained richly through his Word and the sacraments. We are called to pass on this liberal generosity in loving, caring lives, knit together in the unity of the Spirit.

Ephesians 4:1-6

Corporate faith results in God's Spirit binding us together in a firm bond of love. It is the same kind of bond as we find between brothers and sisters, parents and children – a family closeness; for we are all brothers and sisters in Christ, all with the same heavenly Father. In God's family we are not alone, or without relatives who care, or without the children we lost or could never have. It is good and comforting, sometimes, to look round the Christian family and remind ourselves that each one there is as closely related to us as blood relations! It also helps us to get along better with those we may find difficult, as the bonding overrides likes and dislikes, and makes us more accepting of each other's funny ways.

Penitential Rite

1. Out of the dark-ness and void God cre - a - ted, and so the slow bear-ing of life was be - gun, till it burst in its full - ness, in the per - son of Je - sus, show-ing all of the glo - ry of God's on - ly Son.

2. Tak-ing the splin-ters of life that we of - fer he pa - tient-ly builds us a tree with his pow'r; in the earth of our suff'-ring, plants a seed of his glo - ry which he care - ful-ly tends till he brings it to flow'r.

3. Come to us, Fa - ther, re - new us, your chil-dren and make us what we by our-selves can-not be: liv - ing mem - bers of Je - sus, grow-ing gra - dual-ly strong - er as we find that your ser - vice is set - ting us free.

Notes on the Readings

2 Kings 4:42-44

There was a famine in Gilgal, where Elisha was with the prophets, and God used the generous gift of barley loaves and grain to feed them. There was even a surplus, so there was no doubt that everyone had eaten enough. Elisha, living so closely in communion with God, was able to be a channel for God's generous and practical care.

We do not even have to be prophets: God has promised that when we call to him he will hear, and supply our needs. And just as through Elisha's faith many benefited from much-needed nourishment, so through our individual and corporate faith, many others will benefit.

John 6:1-15

Perhaps Philip needed to learn to rely less on buying answers to problems and more on God's freely given grace. A rapid calculation makes it obvious that in this case, anyway, money is not going to work.

The small boy's quick and willing response, with a prompt offer of his own lunch, shows just the lovely quality of children that Jesus warmed to and longed to find in adults. 'Use mine!' is so often the reaction even from very young children, and as a parent it is touching to find a favourite teddy shoved eagerly in alongside Dad when he has 'flu; or their special comforter shared with Grandma after an operation.

Andrew is obviously touched by the boy's gift, but has

natural adult misgivings about the actual use of it! But for Jesus, the willing offering, the spontaneous desire to sacrifice, is what enables him to feed the vast company of people with God's liberality. As soon as we show we are ready to put ourselves out, God can use us, often with far, far more effect than our meagre offering on its own could have achieved.

Bidding Prayers

Celebrant Let us approach our heavenly Father
with all that worries and concerns us
in the Church and in our world.

Reader We bring before him all whose stand
for Christian values and principles
brings with it the constant threat of danger,
betrayal, persecution or biting scorn.
Pause
Father of mercy: **we trust you to help us.**

We bring before him the spiritual deserts
of our world where many wander in lives
without hope, direction or meaning.
Pause
Father of mercy: **we trust you to help us.**

We bring before him those
who are in constant pain; the starving and
malnourished, the neglected and unloved.
Pause
Father of mercy: **we trust you to help us.**

We bring before him our own friends,
families and loved ones, with all
their particular worries, sorrows,
dreams and longings, needs and weaknesses.
Pause
Father of mercy: **we trust you to help us.**

Celebrant Father, your generosity draws us
to love more deeply; hear us as we pray,
and use us in fulfilling our prayers.
We pray through Jesus Christ. **Amen.**

Ideas for Adults

To emphasise the way a small gift was turned into such a wide-reaching service, cover a flower-stand with draped white material and surround the base with a profusion of flowers. But on the stand itself, place only a child's scruffy lunch box.

Ideas for Children

Cut out from card five small rolls and two fish, colour them and put them in a lunch box, and use this as you tell the children today's Gospel. It will help them imagine it all better if you enlist their help in being the crowd walking round the lake, listening to Jesus' words, one boy being Philip and another the one who had a lunch box which he offered and so on.

Then help them make five barley loaves and two fish each, using the card ones as templates. On the back of each item write a word which can be shuffled into a prayer, like this:

Music
Recorded Music

Feed the World (Bob Geldof et al!)

'Live' Music

As bread my Lord comes to me *(ONE, 43)*
Blest are you, Lord, God of all creation *(SONL, 47)*
In bread we bring you, Lord *(ONE, 243)*
This day God gives me *(ONE, 555)*
You are the bread *(SONL, 57)*

18th Sunday in Ordinary Time

Theme
The bread that gives life to the world

Every day God provides food to sustain us; in the wilderness he supplied manna, in Galilee sufficient bread and fish. Yet more importantly, Christ is himself the bread for our spiritual, unending lives. He nourishes and satisfies our craving for harmony, peace and wholeness. As we feed on him we become more and more Christlike in outlook, will and action.

Penitential Rite

In spite of our sin, you welcome us home,
Lord, have mercy. **Lord, have mercy.**

In you we touch the source of true peace,
Christ, have mercy. **Christ, have mercy.**

Only in you do we find our rest,
Lord, have mercy. **Lord, have mercy.**

Notes on the Readings

Exodus 16:2-4, 12-15

The enthusiasm and excitement of the great escape from Egypt has started to wear off; and the people begin to feel their vulnerability and precarious survival out here in the wilderness, far from their familiar routine. Their panic leads them to grumble at Moses who stirred them up to go in the first place. So what God provides is not just food, which is the immediate problem, but also reassurance, which feeds a much more fundamental need of his children who are frightened and feel threatened.

If we find ourselves doing more than our fair share of nagging and grumbling, it may be worth laying aside all those stupid and terrible things people are doing to irritate and make life difficult for us, and instead ask for God to give us reassurance of his love. When he does so, we shall probably find that the urge to nag has disappeared!

And if in our parish there seems a lot of carping and petty mindedness, it is often because the critics feel vulnerable and threatened in some way. Ministering to their fundamental need for reassurance of being loved, cherished and valued will promote deeper healing than head-on collisions over spiteful criticisms.

Ephesians 4:17, 20-24

Half-hearted, sauntering Christians are not a recent phenomenon; it did not take long in the early Church for the rot to set in. For a Christian's spiritual journey is very like the journey of the people of Israel: after the initial excitement and fervour of being liberated from the slavery of sin, we stride out eagerly into the desert, until the rigours and discipline of the wilderness make us hanker after the more easy-going habits of the old life again. Our feet may still be wandering through the desert, but our hearts have scuttled back to Egypt.

Well, today is the first day of the rest of our lives; what better time to choose to throw off any complacence, slackness or materialism we have accumulated, and have a spiritual revolution!

John 6:24-35

Does Jesus sound cynical here? Certainly he was under no illusion about human nature, and he shrewdly recognises that even the most eloquent and uplifting signs will only be interpreted by many in the light of what they can get out of it. The use in advertising of special offers and coupons appeals directly to this human trait.

Jesus uses what seems like a weakness to be a starting point for teaching. He draws the 'special offer' mentality further on, to get it wanting the only real, everlasting special offer there is. And then he provides it: it is himself.

Bidding Prayers

Celebrant Companions in Christ, bread-sharers with him,
let us pray, united in his Spirit,
to our heavenly Father.

Reader That all Christian people may proclaim
the full truth about Jesus Christ,
without watering it down or distorting it,
even if the truth may sometimes be unpalatable.
Pause
Bountiful Father: **feed us always.**

That we may be wise and careful stewards
of the resources of our world,
so as to live out our thankfulness.
Pause
Bountiful Father: **feed us always.**

That those who are physically hungry
may be fed; and those who hunger and thirst
for real meaning in life may be led
to find lasting nourishment in Jesus.
Pause
Bountiful Father: **feed us always.**

That having received Christ into our hearts,
we may joyfully, in words and actions,
spread the marvellous news of his saving love.
Pause
Bountiful Father: **feed us always.**

Celebrant Father, we can never thank you enough
for what you have done for us,
and for the way you are transforming our lives;
with grateful hearts we offer you
these prayers, through Jesus Christ. **Amen.**

Ideas for Adults

Make sure everyone has a copy of the Gospel, and have them all joining in the words of the crowd. Sometimes,

asking the questions aloud like this makes us listen more closely to the answers.

Ideas for Children

Remind the children of how the people were fed by Jesus, and say together the prayer written on the loaves and fishes. Tell them how the people all got into boats and followed Jesus to Capernaum (a map is useful). What do they think the people were hoping Jesus might do? Feed them with a meal again? They may have an uncle or family friend who often gives them a treat, so they hope for one whenever they meet.

Jesus tells them he has come to give them food that will not leave them hungry a few hours later (we may eat breakfast, but we still need more food by lunch time), and he calls this the 'bread of life'. Now read the last section of the Gospel, from '"Sir," they said.'

Whenever we eat bread we can remember that we need Jesus, our bread of life, as well. Help them make this bread basket to use at home, and pop a roll into each to eat with their lunch.

Music
Recorded Music

Thomas Tallis – any one of the *Motets*

'Live' Music

Come to Jesus *(SONL, 83)*
Fill your hearts with joy and gladness *(ONE, 142)*
I am the bread of life *(ONE, 226)*
Lord Jesus Christ *(ONE, 326)*
Take this and eat *(SONL, 77)*

19th Sunday in Ordinary Time

Theme
Christ is the living bread from heaven

God fed Elijah when he was weak, to strengthen him for his journey. In the same way he feeds all those who are drawn to him with the spiritual food of his beloved Son. From him we gather dynamic and fulfilling life which does not end with the heart muscle. Its effect should be obvious in the friendly and positive way we act towards each other.

Penitential Rite

Father, we hunger for your goodness,
    Lord, have mercy. **Lord, have mercy.**

Living bread, we need your sustenance,
    Christ, have mercy. **Christ, have mercy.**

Fill our lives to spread your love,
    Lord, have mercy. **Lord, have mercy.**

Notes on the Readings

1 Kings 19:4-8

Elijah had just made a superb witness to God in the astonishing and victorious challenge to the worshippers of Baal, when in answer to his prayer God sent fire to consume the sacrifice, and showed thousands of people that he was indeed the one true God worthy to be worshipped. We may expect Elijah to be on cloud nine after such a glorious occasion, yet instead we find him in the depths of depression.

Actually there is often a sense of 'sagging' after elation, especially when much energy and concentration have been used; and Satan is ready to use such times of exhaustion to undermine our faith and cause us to collapse in a soggy mass of self pity, doubt or self-indulgence. We need to pray for our priests *after* an uplifting homily or retreat, as well as before; and be spiritually prepared for such feelings ourselves so we are not thrown by them if they occur.

But how tenderly God ministers to his loyal servant, Elijah! There are no words of rebuke telling him to pull himself together; just the unobtrusive provision for practical needs, lovingly served, appetising and nourishing. God, the parent, feeds his child.

We are God's arms and legs; we may be needed to carry out his feeding, whether that entails baking, listening, consoling or encouraging. Unless we are tuned in to God, we shall not know when or where we are needed.

Ephesians 4:30-5:2

Those who love are bound to get hurt sometimes. Those who love deeply may get badly hurt. And all our loving is only a faint reflection of God's love for us, so every time we turn our backs on what is right, indulge our spitefulness, cause friction or sulk, we reject the one who loves us completely. Anyone who has ever been rejected or slighted will know how much that hurts.

So our sin, our selfishness, causes the Holy Spirit of God to grieve; it fills him with great sorrow and hurts him deeply, in a personal way. And similarly he is personally delighted when we reflect his nature by being responsive, warm and loving people.

John 6:41-51

Christianity must never, in any circumstances, become an élitist or exclusive religion; and if we catch even a hint of it, red lights of warning should start flashing in our heads. For when we read the words of Jesus it is quite clear that the good news of hope is freely available to *all* who believe, and no race or class is excluded.

Our spiritual feeding is provided to sustain us on our spiritual journey and we need it just as much as we need food for our bodies. It is also a source of great joy, because through it we experience the individual, personal love our heavenly Father has for each of us.

Bidding Prayers

Celebrant   United in the Spirit of Christ,
        let us pray in faith to the God
        who made us and sustains us.

Reader   We pray for all who are finding
        their Christian ministry hard and tiring;
        that they may be physically
        and spiritually refreshed.
        Pause
        Source of life: **live in us.**

        We pray for the seemingly insoluble problems
        of our world; that God will guide us,
        step by step, to peace, justice and mutual care.
        Pause
        Source of life: **live in us.**

        We pray for all who suffer from
        debilitating illness, senility, instability
        or progressive weakness; that they may experience
        the love of Jesus which is beyond understanding.
        Pause
        Source of life: **live in us.**

        We pray for ourselves, for those who love us
        and those who depend on us;
        that we may build our lives firmly
        on the foundation of Christ.
        Pause
        Source of life: **live in us.**

Celebrant   Father, we acknowledge our total dependence
        on you, and ask you to hear us as we pray,
        through Jesus Christ. **Amen.**

Ideas for Adults

Use home-made bread today for the Eucharist, baked by one or two people in the parish.

Ideas for Children

Remind the children of their bread baskets, and how Jesus said he was the Living Bread. Can they think of a special way we are fed with Jesus, the living bread? Show them some pictures of the Mass being celebrated in all kinds of different places: in different countries, beautiful cathedrals, hospitals, in the open air etc. Church newspapers, missionary magazines and leaflets are good resources. Help them to see that all over the world people come regularly to be fed and to worship God. Suggest that everyone writes a letter or draws a picture about themselves and their church. These can be sent or taken to another parish as greetings from one group of Christians to another. It may even be possible to send them to a parish in another country.

Music
Recorded Music

Mozart – *Flute concerto*

'Live' Music

Farmer, farmer *(SONL, 37)*
Sweet sacrament divine *(ONE, 507)*
The bakerwoman *(ONE, 517)*
The Lord's my shepherd *(ONE, 533)*

20th Sunday in Ordinary Time

Theme

Christ's blood is the wine of real and lasting life

Wine is festive, blood is the life-source; when Christ offers us his blood as real drink, he invites us to a life celebrated with joy, while fully aware of reality. Our lives are bonded closely to his, and our thanks and praise will spill out to kindle the world till it catches the fire of love.

Penitential Rite

Sometimes a shared silence is a valuable form of penitential rite. Suggest that everyone holds hands, and sits or kneels. During the silence each person is going to bring before Christ his or her own need for forgiveness and longing for God's mercy.

Notes on the Readings

Proverbs 9:1-6

Wisdom is pictured here as a noble and gracious woman who invites all who are hungry to a magnificent feast. Everything has been superbly prepared, but the invitations go out to those who need feeding, not just to a few exalted guests of appropriate status.

So it is with the Wisdom of God. We are drawn from the point of ignorance concerning God's character to an increasing understanding of him as we are 'fed' by Word and sacrament. If such joy-filled Wisdom were to be put on the market it would sell at such a high price that we would not be able to afford it! Fortunately for us, it is never offered for sale – only given away free.

Ephesians 5:15-20

In many ways the world Paul lived in was morally similar to ours. There was widespread drug abuse (mainly alcohol), sexual promiscuity and a general acceptance of violence and self-indulgence. Such a society makes it very hard for us, and especially for our young people, to remain uncontaminated by the lax moral standards which prevail. It is tempting, too, to excuse our sin, and blame our drift from God on the age we live in.

Paul reminds us of the obligation we have as Christians: our task is nothing less than to redeem our wicked age by our lives – not hide our families away in a church group where the children won't meet bad influences; not keep ourselves to ourselves and pretend AIDS victims and drug abusers only exist on another planet. We need to draw constant life and refreshment from Christ and his Church, and then go out into the world to spend our lives liberally and conscientiously to heal, enlighten, improve conditions, speak out against evil. Through it all, we should give thanks to our loving God on every train, in every queue, at every shop and round every corner.

John 6:51-58

To people of our time the language of this passage can be off-putting. There were some in Jesus' time who found the words unacceptable, and walked no more with Jesus after this. But the Jews had celebrated Passover throughout their development as a nation, and deep in their culture was the understanding of sacrifice. The pure lamb would have laid on it the sins of the people, so that when the lamb was killed, its blood became an offering to cleanse the people of sin; and then the animal was burnt, with the cleansed worshippers eating the meat with unleavened bread, in an act of praise and thanksgiving. At Passover the blood, sprinkled on the doors of the houses, had protected them from the angel of death and therefore brought them life, hope and freedom.

Now Jesus points them towards the culmination of all that important preparation in himself as the sacrifice which brings unending life, and freedom from the slavery of sin.

Bidding Prayers

Celebrant   My brothers and sisters in Christ,
with confidence and faith let us pray
to the true and living God.

Reader   For the newly baptised
and the recently ordained;
for those who have rejected their former faith,
and those who are besieged by doubt.
Pause
Father, we commend them:
into your safe keeping.

For those under pressure who are tempted
to compromise God's values of truth and love;
for all who make far-reaching decisions.
Pause
Father, we commend them:
into your safe keeping.

For all the victims of power struggles,
suffering, poverty, neglect, disease
and malnutrition; for all whose health
has been wrecked by drugs or AIDS.
Pause
Father, we commend them:
into your safe keeping.

For ourselves, our neighbours and
our friends; for any we have hurt or offended;
for any who have hurt or offended us.
Pause
Father, we commend them:
into your safe keeping.

Celebrant   Most loving and merciful Father,
we ask you to take over our lives
and live through them, and accept
these our prayers in the name of Jesus. **Amen.**

Ideas for Adults

Have a flower arrangement based on the theme of wine. It might include a carafe of red wine, grapes and vine leaves, as well as red and gold flowers.

Ideas for Children

Display some posters of vineyards – travel agents should be able to supply some pictures – and have a cluster of grapes on the table (seedless are best for young children). Share the grapes out, and talk about how the juice is squeezed out and mellowed carefully in vats before being bottled and drunk, perhaps on special happy occasions like weddings, or, in some countries, with everyday meals. When have they seen wine used in church?

Explain how on the night before he gave his life for us, Jesus left us a special instruction. We are to take bread and wine, give praise and thanks and offer them to God. Then, as we eat the bread and drink the wine we will be feeding on Christ and taking his everlasting life into ourselves. The children's Mass book, *Share My Love*, would be useful here.

Help the children make a card like this:

Music

Recorded Music

Saint Saens – *Concerto No. 3 for organ*

'Live' Music

Glory be to Jesus *(ONE, 165)*
Of the glorious body telling *(ONE, 389)*

Ordinary Time 21 – 25

Questions for Discussion Groups
Who is this man? Son of God
1. What evidence is there in Mark's Gospel that Jesus was indeed the Son of God?
2. What characteristics of God, revealed in the Old Testament, do we see in the character of Jesus of Nazareth?

21st Sunday in Ordinary Time

Theme
Lord, you have the message of eternal life

Christ loves his Church as a loving husband cherishes his wife, and his fond concern prompts our response of fealty, love and obedience. There is simply no other being, in or out of time, who speaks with words of full and everlasting life. Christ will always leave us free to go, with no emotional blackmail forcing us to stay against our will; but experience of his personality shows us that he is the inimitable Saviour.

Penitential Rite

In our need of guidance we come to you,
    Lord, have mercy. **Lord, have mercy.**

In our need of reconciliation we come to you,
    Christ, have mercy. **Christ, have mercy.**

In our need of fundamental peace we come to you,
    Lord, have mercy. **Lord, have mercy.**

Notes on the Readings

Joshua 24:1-2, 15-18

Joshua is old and nearing death, and he wants to leave the tribes of Israel fully aware of their covenant with God. The problem is that they are surrounded by the Canaanite religion which is highly seductive and utterly contrary to the principles God had revealed. Joshua is anxious to make sure the people know the position. It will be hard for them to remain dedicated to God in the face of such temptation unless they keep in the forefront of their memories all the wonderful acts of God they have witnessed.

He finishes with the voice of a true leader: he is going to serve God, even if they don't! It has the desired effect, and the people are moved to a show of great determination to serve God and be loyal to him alone.

Ephesians 5:21-32

Paul uses marriage as a beautiful illustration of the kind of relationship Christ has with his Church. At first sight it may look as if Paul's concept of marriage is irrelevant in our age of sexual equality, and is one of those bits of the Bible we can skip lightly over, looking the other way.

Look again. Obedience sometimes gets stuck in the groove of grudging duty, and love in the groove of emotion and instinctive desire; but what happens when Love becomes Law, as it has in Christ? Now, duty and obedience become full of delight and joy, freely chosen and always appreciated. This can only occur when both husband and wife live in obedience to the Law of Love, with all the patience, acceptance, kindness and humility that it entails. entails.

And that is the sort of marriage Christ has with his Church: bound by love, the Church becomes one with the body of Christ; our obedience to him springs out of our love for him and his rich love for us.

John 6:60-69

How easy and untroubling it would have been for Jesus to have allowed himself to become king in the way people had expected; there could have been lots of cheering and glorious battles, and food could be provided miraculously each day, so there would be no longer any need to work! When Jesus starts talking about the real, spiritual saving he has come for, many are disappointed, angry and disgusted. This is not what they had envisaged at all.

It must have been one of the hardest moments for Jesus, to watch so many turn physically away and reject him, in spite of all his painstaking planning, careful teaching and programming, deep prayer and unremitting effort. In his humanity, the enormous risk of redemption must have glared, ominous and threatening.

As he turns to his closest friends, we sense a foretaste of that terrible loneliness as death approaches at the crucifixion – he is in the world, the world was made by him, but the world does not know him. Peter and the other apostles were allowed the privilege of ministering to their Lord. Their firm acceptance of Jesus as the Holy One of God provided comfort and reassurance at the human level, and a spiritual preview of all Christians in every age and country, acknowledging Christ as Lord in thunderous praise.

Bidding Prayers

Celebrant Followers of Christ, let us pray together
in his presence to our merciful Father,
who feels with us in our needs.

Reader We bring to his love
all religious communities, who offer
a constant wave of prayer as the earth spins;
for those who sense that God
may be calling them to a life of prayer,
that his will may be made clear to them.
Pause
Lord of our lives: **hear us, we pray.**

We bring to his love all who wield power
in each community in our world;
those who persist in challenging injustice and
prejudice; those who bring to public attention
areas of need and unnoticed hardship.
Pause
Lord of our lives: **hear us, we pray.**

We bring to his love all those in hospital,
in wards and on operating tables throughout
the world; for those worn down
by constant pain; those who are struggling
to rebuild broken lives.
Pause
Lord of our lives: **hear us, we pray.**

We bring to his love our own
particular concerns, hopes, doubts and fears;
our difficulties at work and at home;
our responsibilities.
Pause
Lord of our lives: **hear us, we pray.**

Celebrant In great thankfulness for all your blessings
to us, heavenly Father, we offer you
these prayers through Jesus Christ. **Amen.**

Ideas for Adults

The reading from Joshua can be dramatised, using a group of about a dozen people. Have two or three important-looking people with scrolls; Joshua, helped to his seat reverently; and the rest of the group entering in ones and twos from different directions.

The narrator reads his words from a scroll, and Joshua says his words. The people's speech is split into separate sections, to be said by different people:

1: We have no intention of deserting the Lord and serving other gods! (*Murmurs of agreement*)
2: Was it not the Lord our God who brought us ...
3: ...and our ancestors ...
2: ...out of the land of Egypt, the house of slavery?
4: Was it not he who worked those great wonders before our eyes?
5: And preserved us all along the way we travelled?
6: And among all the peoples through whom we journeyed?
All: We too will serve the Lord, for he is our God.

Ideas for Children

Remind the children of how Jesus had fed the great crowd of people with five loaves and two fishes and how they had wanted to make him their king, there and then. Talk about how different Jesus' kingdom was from what they expected.

As you guide the children through this recap of material from previous weeks, it is helpful to show examples of their craft work as memory aids.

Tell them how some of the crowd reacted when Jesus talked about himself as bread and wine that feeds our spirits. Make up a scene of people standing looking at Jesus and turn some of the people round to face away from him. You can use flannelgraph for this. Show how the apostles reacted, and pray together that we will not turn away as soon as it gets hard being a Christian.

Then help the children make this movable picture of Jesus asking us personally if we are going to turn away from him as well.

Music
Recorded Music

Tchaikovsky – *Symphony* No. 6 (*Pathétique*)

'Live' Music

Abide with me *(ONE, 4)*
Alleluia, sing to Jesus *(ONE, 15)*
God is love: his the care *(ONE, 178)*
Without seeing you *(SONL, 13)*

22nd Sunday in Ordinary Time

Theme
God's commandments require full obedience

The Law of God is far more wide-reaching than a collection of rules. What is required is not lip service to the outward signs of obedience alone, but a deep-seated commitment of the heart and will to following God's will for his people. Without such commitment it is all too easy for the outward actions to become mechanical and meaningless.

Penitential Rite

You offer the only way worth living,
    Lord, have mercy. **Lord, have mercy.**

Your Word is a lamp to guide our feet,
    Christ, have mercy. **Christ, have mercy.**

You know the secrets of our hearts,
    Lord, have mercy. **Lord, have mercy.**

Notes on the Readings

Deuteronomy 4:1-2, 6-8

The pride and privilege of being God's people glows through these words. It really is something special to have a living God who takes a personal, parental interest; and the Law, as his mouthpiece, is naturally sacred and highly reverenced. Absolute obedience to it is the outward sign of the heart's dedication to the supreme God, and will serve as a great witness to other nations of God's wisdom and understanding, as seen in the Law and behaviour of his people. As we go through this week's activities, perhaps we should ask ourselves whether our obedience to God's law of love ever makes anyone around us exclaim at the God-given wisdom, insight, practical care or understanding and sympathy we show.

James 1:17-18, 21-22, 27

The practical James knows that the Word must always be a spring-board to action, and not a substitute for it. It is quite posssible to be swept up on to an emotional 'high' during some inspiring worship, and feel so good about it that we fail to notice glaring needs and opportunities for serving when we get out of the church. Or we can get so used to talking 'God-language' that we deceive ourselves into thinking we are practising the words we spout, when we have actually got stuck in a complacent rut.

Another temptation is to busy about all the *doing*, without any hearing first. (Or during, or afterwards!) God's word is our treasure, our strength and our foundation, and if we really steep ourselves in it, by attentive reading and receptive contemplation, we shall find ourselves urged to take positive action in ways which may surprise us. So long as we do not let Self plug up the channels, God's Word will flow through us for the good of the world.

Mark 7:1-8, 14-15, 21-23

When we remember that Jesus was himself the Word of God, we can understand how hurt and angry he felt about people who distorted God's truth, making a mockery of it by their vanity and hypocrisy. If they had really obeyed the letter of the Law, as they claimed to, they would have kept not only the pedantic yet practical health and hygiene rules, but also the necessity for a pure heart before God. Somehow, the things other people cannot see are always the first to slip whenever we get slack!

Bidding Prayers

Celebrant My companions in Christ, we have been
drawn here today by the power of God's love;
into that love let us now gather
all those for whom we pray.

Reader We commend to his love
all who are working for Christian unity,
that their work may be guided and blessed
with integrity, wisdom and purity.
Pause
Father, almighty: **let your will be done.**

We commend to his love
all judges and those serving on juries;
those who make laws in our own country
and throughout the world; that our human laws
may reflect the unchanging law and will
of the good and merciful God.
Pause
Father, almighty: **let your will be done.**

We commend to his love those whose minds
have been poisoned by exposure to violence;
children who have been abandoned or maltreated;
all who crave affection but are frightened
to become emotionally involved
in case they get hurt.
Pause
Father, almighty: **let your will be done.**

We commend to his love our own

areas of weakness, that we may be remade
by God's grace into the sort of people
he intends us to be.
Pause
Father, almighty: **let your will be done.**

Celebrant Heavenly Father, in your love
and mercy hear our prayers,
through the mediation of Jesus Christ. **Amen.**

Ideas for Adults

Have the summary of the Law (the two great commandments that Jesus gave: *Love God*, and *Love your neighbour as yourself*) displayed on banners using collage in either paper or fabric.

Ideas for Children

Beforehand make two simple hand puppets and join them to a piece of stiff card with lengths of string. On the card, stick a sheet of paper with a clearly written script on it. Use different colours for the two characters. Stick the second script on the other side of the card.

Script 1.

Boots: Loopy, you must help me.
I need to do a hard sum.
If you stop talking
I can do it.

Loopy: O.K. Boots. You do your sum.
I will not talk.

Boots: Thank you, Loopy.
Now, let me see . . .

Loopy: (sings) La la la la pom pom pom!

Boots: Loopy, stop it!
You said you would not talk
so I could do my sum.

Loopy: Yes I know I did.
And I have kept my promise.
I was not talking,
I was singing!

Boots: Oh, Loopy!!

Script 2.

Boots: What are you doing, Loopy?

Loopy: I'm sweeping these leaves
for Mr. Tod.

Boots: That is kind of you.
Loopy: I'm just doing it
to make him think I'm kind.
Then he will give me some sweets.
Boots: Wow! That's clever.
I'll sweep too.
He'll never know
we are not really
being kind.

Ask two children to wear the puppets and read the first script so everyone can hear. Was Loopy doing what she was told? Help them to see that in one way she was, yet in another way she wasn't – like when we rush our prayers but have not really talked to God at all.

Ask another two children to read the second script. Mr. Tod told all his friends about how kind Loopy and Boots were. Did they deserve his praise and his sweets? Help them to see that although they had done the sweeping, they had not been honest with Mr. Tod.

Now tell the children about some of the scribes and Pharisees who behaved rather like Loopy and Boots. They did all the right things, down to the very last detail (you could demonstrate all the washing and ritual they went through) but they were not really obeying God's main rule at all.

On a poster, write up God's main Laws, or rules, and see if they can learn them off by heart. Chanting them to a simple melody makes the learning easier, and the Law can be sung to their families in church. *London's burning* works well:

You shall love the Lord your God with
all your mind and all your heart and
all your strength! All your strength!
And love your neighbour, love your neighbour!

Music
Recorded Music

Prokofiev – *Romeo and Juliet*

'Live' Music

Be thou my vision *(ONE, 61)*
If we only seek peace *(SONL, 76)*
Love is his word *(ONE, 338)*

23rd Sunday in Ordinary Time

Theme
Christ opens ears to hear and tongues to speak

The great time of saving and comfort would be heralded with the deaf hearing and the dumb speaking, and Jesus fulfils the prophecy with compassion and power. If we tune our ears to his words we shall hear truth that leads us to live Gospel lives; lives with God-centred values and priorities, uncluttered by materialism, wealth or status.

Penitential Rite

Unstop our ears to hear your voice,
Lord, have mercy. **Lord, have mercy.**

Open our eyes to perceive your truth,
Christ, have mercy. **Christ, have mercy.**

Purify our lives with the fire of your love,
Lord, have mercy. **Lord, have mercy.**

Notes on the Readings

Isaiah 35:4-7

The beautiful compassion of a caring God spreads the light of hope in this uplifting and lovely prophecy. God comes to do justice but also kindness; he comes to restore and heal as well as revealing our sinfulness. And these were the signs that Jesus gave to reassure John the Baptist: as Christ, he was indeed opening the eyes of the blind and unstopping the ears of the deaf. To the Samaritan woman he described himself as Living Water which would, like streams gushing in a desert, bring life, growth and hope.

Wherever Jesus is, the sense of hope and restoration pours in too. He calms fear and panic, ignores the word 'impossible' and activates healing, understanding, reconciliation and peace.

James 2:1-5

Such generous, freely given love should also be the hallmark of all who have received the Spirit of Jesus. It is really a contradiction in terms for a Christian to be narrowly exclusive, snobbish or judgemental. Whatever the unwritten rules of our society regarding who mixes with whom and who the V.I.P.'s are, we as Christians should be living examples of the truth that in God's eyes everyone is a V.I.P. Just imagine what a witness it would be if we all reverenced every person we saw this week as much as we might instinctively reverence the famous or the glamorous.

Mark 7:31-37

Spittle was commonly used in the medicine of Jesus' time, so it is interesting that his healing incorporated this. When we pray for healing, our prayer may well be answered via a visit to the doctor or the hospital, for God delights in using us and our gifts in the work of healing. Every time researchers discover new ways to combat pain and disease, that is a victory for the God of Wholeness who enlightens and heals.

If we really want to see Jesus in action, we have only to visit a patient who has been 'prayed through' a major operation; there is an incredible radiance about such people that joyfully proclaims the peace which can only come from God. It shows plainly that wholeness is more than clinical health; that Jesus personally transforms the spiritual, emotional and physical structure of the people he is asked to heal.

Bidding Prayers

Celebrant My brothers and sisters in Christ,
bound together in his Spirit,
let us pray to our heavenly Father.

Reader That Christians may use their gifts
to minister to the world and to draw others
towards the joy of knowing Christ.
Pause
Our God and our King:
we want to do things your way.

That political and industrial disputes may be
handled with sensitivity, and understanding
of deeply felt needs and hurts.
Pause
Our God and our King:
we want to do things your way.

That the deaf, dumb, blind and crippled
may be accepted with warmth
and practical assistance by society;

that those involved in medical research
may be guided to knowledge
that can bring new hope to many.
Pause
Our God and our King:
we want to do things your way.

That our homes and places of work
may be filled with the light and joy
of God's presence; that we may see
in everyone we meet the mark of his love.
Pause
Our God and our King:
we want to do things your way.

Celebrant   Father, your character is so rich in mercy;
please hear our prayers which we offer
in the name of Jesus. **Amen.**

Ideas for Adults

In the light of today's readings, discuss the healing ministry in your parish. Some groups have a strong prayer chain which is called on whenever the need arises and is often composed of unemployed, bed-ridden or elderly Christians who have the gift of time to spend in this valuable and fruitful work.

Other parishes have a regular prayer group which meets specifically to pray for those who are physically, mentally or emotionally troubled, and the prayer life extends into hospital and home visiting, transport for out-patient care or child care when parents undergo treatment. If this seems a good idea for the needs in your parish, be thorough in planning the caring, with one person organising and centralising. Otherwise a lack of communication can cause problems instead of solving them. But the local church is a wonderful place to act as a centre for people who care enough about those living in the neighbourhood to provide prayer support and practical help in times of crisis and illness.

Ideas for Children

Help the children to find the Isaiah passage in the Old Testament and read it together. Point out that this was written many years before Christ, but that the words are like a forecast of what God would be like when he came to the world in person.

Now turn to today's Gospel passage in Mark and read it together. Point out how Isaiah's words had come true in Jesus. Ask the children to put their hands over their ears so that they can't hear. What would they miss if they were deaf? Help them understand a little of how cut off and lonely a deaf person's world can be. Jesus understood, and made contact with touch before healing the man.

Give the children balloons so they can feel the vibrations as they speak against the balloon skin; different sounds make different vibrations. Write on the balloons:

Jesus makes the deaf hear
and the dumb speak.

Music
Recorded Music

Vaughan Williams – *Fantasia on a theme of Greensleeves*

'Live' Music

In bread we bring you, Lord *(ONE, 243)*
Lay your hands *(ONE, 295)*
The eyes of the blind *(ONE, 522)*
You touch my soul *(SONL, 62)*

24th Sunday in Ordinary Time

Theme
Jesus is none other than the Son of God

When we recognise that Jesus is the Christ – God's chosen one – our whole life is challenged. Following him will not always be comfortable or easy, and may involve danger. But there is no other way, because our faith is bound to result in unselfish caring, time-consuming love and costly generosity. Surprisingly, such an uninviting recipe produces outstanding joy!

Penitential Rite

With our doubts and fears we turn to you,
Lord, have mercy. **Lord, have mercy.**

With our failures and mistakes we turn to you,
Christ, have mercy. **Christ have mercy.**

With our particular weaknesses we turn to you,
Lord, have mercy. **Lord have mercy.**

Notes on the Readings

Isaiah 50:5-9

The physical and psychological cruelty endured without retaliation here, foresees the mocked and crucified Christ, in heart-rending clarity. We sense the terrible rejection, the jeering and lack of understanding; but there is also the help and strength from God which empowers the suffering servant to submit to his agony in the knowledge that it is necessary for a greater good.

Suffering in our own lives can provide really fertile conditions for growth, much as we may laugh at the stupidity of such an idea in our initial anger, distress and hopelessness. The value of suffering is partly in the way it can nudge us into trusting God instead of our own strength which is in short supply. It helps us learn what it means to be dependent on God and draw help from him. It heightens our awareness of the suffering of others and will in the future enable us to be more sympathetic and useful. It gives us a glimpse of the suffering that Christ was willing to undergo, in order to buy us back from sin; and it can concentrate our attention on what is of lasting value, rather than living from one distraction to the next.

Suffering is bound to be acutely painful; but with Christ it can become a positive pain.

James 2:14-18

Faith is a bit like putting two and two together and making five; for although there is evidence, which points us in the right direction, actually believing that Jesus is the Son of God involves an extra leap without holding on. The leap is a commitment to a changed life, based on the love and teaching of the Saviour in whom we have put our faith; so if it is real we shall most certainly notice some changed behaviour.

Good works on their own are not a substitute for faith, they may result from holding on to the reins of our life instead of handing over control to God. But a claim of faith which is unsupported by good works does not say much for the faith!

Mark 8:27-35

Peter could see that all the prophecies in the Scriptures concerning the Messiah were coming true and being fulfilled in the carpenter from Nazareth who had called him from his fishing at Galilee. Reading the signs, he was prepared to accept that this man was indeed the one the Scriptures referred to; he must therefore be the actual Christ, walking about on the earth, eating and drinking, relating to people and responding to their needs.

But the Scriptures also prophesied that suffering and death would be a necessary part of salvation; and, being human, Peter did not want to perceive any revelation that spoke of danger to and destruction of the Lord he loved. We also have a desire to shrink back from witness which causes pain, not just in ourselves but also in others. We do not want our fellow Christians to stick their necks out too far by working in too dangerous an area, getting mixed up in court proceedings for upholding some principle in a corrupt society, or risking death in undertaking delicate negotiations in violent and unsettled countries.

Yet what else can we do if we claim to take up our cross and follow Christ? Our 'cross' does not mean the expected problems faced by everyone in the course of life: it is the suffering which comes as a direct result from living life Christ's way. And that is never a life of ease and comfort, for if we really love, we cannot remain detached.

Bidding Prayers

Celebrant   My companions in Christ, let us pour out
to our loving Father the areas of need
and concern in the Church and in our world.

Reader   We commend to our loving Father
all who persist in working to spread the news
of Christ's saving love in spite of
poor conditions, hostility or danger.
Pause
Lord, our strength:
with you all things are possible.

We commend to our loving Father
all who have been elected to govern,
both locally and internationally;
that being guided by the light of truth
and goodness they may be good stewards
of the resources in their care.
Pause
Lord, our strength:
with you all things are possible.

We commend to our loving Father
the chronically and critically ill,
and those who tend them;
the babies being born today,
and the people who will die today.
Pause
Lord, our strength:
with you all things are possible.

We commend to our loving Father
those we love who do not yet know Christ,
or have turned away from him;
that through circumstances and relationships
they may be drawn to seek him.
Pause
Lord, our strength:
with you all things are possible.

Celebrant   Father of mercy, hear our prayers
which we offer through Jesus, the Christ. **Amen.**

Ideas for Adults

The Isaiah reading is powerfully projected if it is read by a group of three men, giving full weight to the punctuated stops, and accompanied by a very slow and regular drum beat. The drum can be improvised, but aim at a low, resonant boom, as it should sound insistent, inevitable and threatening.

Ideas for Children

Tell the children how Peter recognised that Jesus was not just a good man but actually the Son of God. Draw a large cross as the sign of Jesus, in the centre of a sheet of paper. The prophets in the Old Testament spoke about what Jesus would be like and what he would do. Now draw in (or stick on) some people on the left side of the cross, looking towards it. Write in some speech balloons with quotations referring to the Christ:

> Daniel 7:13-14
> *I saw . . . there came one like a son of man . . . and to him was given dominion and glory and kingdom.*
>
> Micah 5:2
> *From you, Bethlehem, shall come a ruler . . . who shall feed his flock in the strength of the Lord.*
>
> Isaiah 60:3
> *Kings shall come to the brightness of your rising.*
>
> Isaiah 53:5
> *He was wounded for our wrongdoing.*

and discuss with the children how these fit in with Jesus' life. They will see that his suffering for us is mentioned; the cross is part of the loving.

Jesus told his friends that if they wanted to follow him they would have to be prepared to suffer as well. Ask the children to colour and cut out pictures of themselves to stick on the right side of the cross, looking towards it. Speech balloons above them can say things like:

> 'Don't worry – I'll help you.'
> 'I'll share my chocolate with you.'
> 'There's no need to be nasty to her; let's ask her to join in our game.'
> 'Please don't say those horrid things about Jesus – he happens to be a friend of mine.'

When we follow Jesus we have to learn to give up our time, money, plans or wishes whenever we are needed by our friend Jesus to help someone, or stand up for what is right.

The completed poster can be brought into church so that everyone can see it.

Music
Recorded Music

Beethoven – *Symphony No. 7: slow movement*

'Live' Music

A man fully living *(ONE, 246)*
Come to Jesus *(SONL, 83)*
Lord Jesus Christ *(ONE, 325)*
Man of Galilee *(ONE, 343)*

25th Sunday in Ordinary Time

Theme
Christ foretells his death

The disciples did not understand the weakness and vulnerability in the face of brutality that Jesus seemed to be suggesting. Their idea of greatness was still a worldly view, with status and privilege important. Jesus hugs a small child to help them see how different are the values of his kingdom of loving service, whether rewarded or not; where the best is the willing servant of all.

Penitential Rite

Teach us to strive for your values,
   Lord, have mercy. **Lord, have mercy.**

Teach us to serve one another in love,
   Christ, have mercy. **Christ, have mercy.**

Teach us to walk humbly before you,
   Lord, have mercy. **Lord, have mercy.**

Notes on the Readings

Wisdom 2:12, 17-20

Both in Hebrew prophecy and in Greek philosophy the idea emerges of a perfectly good man conflicting with the evil in people to the extent that they prefer to torture and kill him, rather than be changed or challenged by him.

We notice the dirt when the sun shines in; and can either draw the curtains and pretend the dirt is not there, or use the light to make a good job of the cleaning. Whenever we reject Christ's light, we join the crowd who screamed for his crucifixion.

James 3:16-4:3

Bickering in families, in churches, in politics or in industry is so often a cause of bad feeling, which can erupt into ugly and really destructive behaviour. Constantly taunting one another, finding fault, hinting confidentially about each other's inadequacies – all this weakens and damages; instead we could be constructive peace-makers, working at creating harmony and holiness.

James shrewdly pinpoints the reason for our antisocial behaviour: it is a symptom of what is going on inside us. So if we sort out our relationship with God first, and begin to align our wills with his, we shall find it far less necessary to prove we are better than everyone else, or force our opinions down everyone's throats so we can get our way.

Mark 9:30-37

Even those who were constantly in the company of Jesus fell prey to the tempting attractions of power and status. Aware that Jesus is approaching the climax of his ministry, when the new kingdom will be ushered in, the disciples start squabbling about which of them ought to have most power.

So Jesus explains in actions, with a visual aid, in this very beautiful scene. The child is obviously comfortable and happy in Jesus' hug, without any desire to be honoured for being there. And that is how we need to be – just unaffectedly happy in his presence. For, as Jesus explains, all are equally precious to God, so whether we welcome a famous celebrity or a small toddler we shall be welcoming God himself.

Bidding Prayers

Celebrant   As children of our heavenly Father,
   let us approach him with our needs and cares.

Reader   We bring the problems of communication
   in this parish and in all church groups;
   the difficulties of finding enough
   youth leaders/church cleaners/teachers/visitors
   to work effectively for God in our area.
   Pause
   Father, guide us: **according to your law of love.**

We bring the pressures on those in business
   to think only in terms of what is profitable;
   the problems of wealth distribution which
   cause unnecessary suffering in our world.
   Pause
   Father, guide us: **according to your law of love.**

We bring the shortage of money and staff
   in hospitals; the distress of those
   who have no hospital to go to;
   the suffering of those
   who are in physical pain,
   mental anguish or spiritual darkness.
   Pause
   Father, guide us: **according to your law of love.**

We bring the things that irritate, anger
   and frustrate us; the jobs that we find
   difficult to do cheerfully; the relationships
   we find demanding and tiring.
   Pause
   Father, guide us: **according to your law of love.**

Celebrant   Father, you always give us far more
   than we can ever deserve;
   please fulfil our prayers
   in the way that is best for us.
   We ask in the name of Jesus Christ. **Amen.**

Ideas for Adults

To emphasise the bond of Christ's peace which holds us together in love, invite everyone to move about the church freely so that everyone present can exchange the Sign of Peace with everyone else. And ask everyone to hold hands during one of the hymns.

Ideas for Children

Take along a selection of advertisements showing the product and the price. Some may include special offers. Try to pick some which seem reasonable and some which are far more expensive.

Show the advertisements to the children, and discuss whether or not they think each one is worth the price. Of course this will depend on how much they want the product; one may feel a pair of skates is worth spending money on, while another would be more willing to pay out for a doll. Aim to get across the point that the more we want something, the more we are prepared to pay for it.

Now show them a picture of an ordinary crowd of people. Jesus wanted all the people in God's world to be set free from evil, so they could live in peace and love. He wanted that badly, but the cost was very high. See if they can guess how much that would cost. Jesus knew it would cost more than money: it would cost his life. If he were to save these people, he would have to die for it!

What do they think Jesus decided? That it wasn't worth it?

Show them a picture of Jesus on the cross. He decided that we *were* worth it!

Give the children a 'bill of sins' with their name at the top. Then in red they can write across it: PAID IN FULL – BY JESUS.

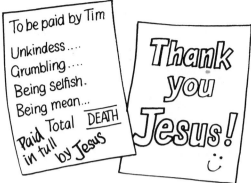

Music
Recorded Music

Handel – *Messiah*: *He was despised*

'Live' Music

Give me peace, O Lord, I pray *(ONE, 160)*
The love of God *(SONL, 46)*
There is a green hill far away *(ONE, 540)*
The Spirit of the Lord is with us *(ONE, 549)*

Ordinary Time 26 – 33

Questions for Discussion Groups
Who is this man? Teaching

1. What does Jesus teach us about the attitudes we should have towards marriage, money and status?
2. Which passages from the Old Testament might Jesus have referred to when he taught his disciples that the Son of Man would have to suffer and be put to death in order to save us?

26th Sunday in Ordinary Time

Theme
Anyone who is not against us is for us

We do not need to protect God by excluding or dismissing those who do good but may not be Christians. All good comes from God and he works through many different outlets. Nor can we expect God to deal mercifully with us if we claim to have faith but have accumulated wealth and a comfortable life through cheating or meanness. God's good fruit shows and lasts.

Penitential Rite

Come, Spirit, come, prise open my heart.
(The music is given on page 140.)

Notes on the Readings

Numbers 11:25-29

Like the young man in this passage, we sometimes become indignant when we see evidence of God's Spirit in the ministry of someone we would not have thought 'eligible'. It seems like a kind of insult to those we love and respect. With Joshua we may feel like saying, 'My Lord, Moses, stop them!' But Moses was such a close friend of God that he had begun to think like him; his generous-hearted response shows a complete lack of personal vanity, jealousy or petty-mindedness.

History has countless examples of characters spoilt and corrupted following success and great blessing, but we rarely learn. So people like Moses are a wonderful inspiration. He is not in the least bothered that Medad and Eldad are prophesying: his view is 'the more the merrier', for he is caught up in God's yearning to draw all people to him; for everyone to know the joy and peace that comes from serving him.

James 5:1-6

This is rather like a time-lapse film sequence where, with time effectively telescoped, we watch all our treasured possessions and favourite clothes degenerate from brand new, price tag attached, to rotting, mildewed rags and dust. Doesn't that sound like a nightmare – surely nothing to do with our newly fitted kitchen or our latest compact disc.

In one sense that is true; there is nothing intrinsically wrong with kitchens or discs or anything else we enrich our lives with. But if our high standard of living is causing others to go short of essentials like food or fresh water; or if we demand products which encourage child slave labour in other countries; or if we cheat on tax forms, business expenses and social security; then the cries of those we have failed to help will surely reach God's ears, and the nightmare will be a prophecy of future reality.

Mark 9:38-43, 45, 47-48

The disciples are concerned about an outsider working miracles in the name of Jesus; but Jesus is far more concerned about those who become obstacles to faith, or lead his flock astray. In fact he is so concerned about this that he uses strong and graphic language to shock his listeners into realising how vigorously they need to rid themselves of anything that causes them to sin.

So if we find that we are drinking too much, it is wise to avoid situations where we are tempted to go over the limit; if certain companions always indulge in gossip, we need to be quite firm and change either our approach or the company we keep. From time to time it is worth taking stock of our bad habits, to see if there is any way to avoid them; it may need quite a simple change in lifestyle to conquer a habitual weakness. We can set the alarm earlier to avoid screaming at the children in the usual morning rush. We can stop watching the kind of videos that encourage us to indulge in lust or violence. We can avoid anything that keeps us from spending time with God. In the process we shall find more fulfilment and enrichment than were ever provided by the distractions.

Bidding Prayers

Celebrant Christ has brought us here to worship;
in his Spirit let us pray to our heavenly Father.

Reader That the life-giving truth about Christ
may be proclaimed clearly in every generation
and in all parts of our world;
uncompromised, undiluted and pure.
Pause
Father, hear us: **keep us rooted in you.**

That the Christian values of caring love,
honesty and goodness may permeate society

and show in wise decisions,
constructive planning and just settlements.
Pause
Father, hear us: **keep us rooted in you.**

That those who are struggling to conquer
their addictions may be supported
and strengthened; that those who are ill
may be healed to wholeness.
Pause
Father, hear us: **keep us rooted in you.**

That we may be strengthened against temptation,
daily committing ourselves more whole-heartedly
to serve Christ in all we think, say or do.
Pause
Father, hear us: **keep us rooted in you.**

Celebrant With thankfulness and praise for
all your blessings to us, Father, we offer you
these prayers through Jesus Christ. **Amen.**

Ideas for Adults

Make a display of pictures showing God's work being done, though not necessarily through Christians. Magazines and newspapers are useful resources for this. There may be pictures of good neighbourly behaviour, medical research, surgery, deaf children being taught to speak, rubbish being cleared up, or a grandparent reading to a young child. Call the display: GOD AT WORK, and have all three of today's readings among the pictures.

Ideas for Children

Read today's Gospel from a Good News Bible, or another translation suitable for children. Children are mostly less squeamish than adults, and will understand what Jesus is getting at. Talk with them about the sort of thing they find starts them off behaving in an unloving way, and together work out some ways to 'cut off the offending hand'. (Perhaps going out to kick a ball when they feel like kicking a sister; setting a cooking timer to share a toy equally, giving each a set time – until the pinger rings – in which to play; writing a list of daily jobs that need to be done before bed, so things don't get forgotten; asking to sit next to someone in class with whom they are less likely to waste time!)

These practical ways of turning our lives to Christ are very valuable and it is never too young to start. They will not repress the children, as is sometimes feared, but rather increase their maturity.

Give the children paper cups and a pencil. They draw their own face on the side of the cup and punch holes in the bottom. Then, over the grass or a large bowl, pour water from an enormous jug through each child's cup. We are to be channels for God's living Spirit to flow through to the world; we have to work at increasing the flow!

Music
Recorded Music

Palestrina – *Pope Marcellus Mass: Kyrie*

'Live' Music

Make me a channel of your peace *(ONE,342)*
Many times I have turned *(ONE, 344)*
O thou who at thy Eucharist didst pray *(ONE, 432)*
You touch my soul *(SONL, 62)*

27th Sunday in Ordinary Time

Theme
What God has united, man must not divide

From the beginning, the unifying of man and woman in marriage was part of God's plan; the complete human state involves a harmony of the masculine and the feminine. A marriage to which Christ is invited and in which he lives, will be a strong and beautiful reflection of God's tender and affectionate love for his 'little children' of all ages.

Penitential Rite

Your light exposes our faults and weakness,
Lord, have mercy. **Lord, have mercy.**

Your forgiveness sets us free,
Christ, have mercy. **Christ, have mercy.**

Your strength is sufficient for us,
Lord, have mercy. **Lord, have mercy.**

Notes on the Readings

Genesis 2:18-24

In this second view of the creation, man and woman are not made at the same time. Man is created first and God decides that it is not good for him to be alone. What Adam felt is not recorded! Many of us have lived solo at some stage and know how easily we can become self-centred when there is no-one else to consider. There is none of the constant balancing of choices, moods, needs and expectations that living with someone involves. Man and woman together provide not only helpmates but also a built-in mechanism to encourage outreach and guard against selfishness.

The sexual drive is an urge to be physically united with another; in the marriage relationship this becomes both an expression and a symbol of a unity which is not just physical but emotional, mental and spiritual as well.

Hebrews 2:9-11

The Incarnation shows the extent of God's desire to be united with his creation. In Jesus he confines himself to become human and live alongside us, sharing our sensations, temptations and vulnerabilities. It is as if, instead of supervising the building of new lives from the distance, Jesus rolls his sleeves up and mucks in with the mud, cement and dust.

Becoming human allowed the most spectacular reconciliation of all time to take place. Christ could be both the priest and the victim; both the sanctifier and the sanctified. No other, easier, less dangerous or painful way was possible; and Christ was willing to go through with it because of his incredible love for us.

Mark 10:2-16

It is clear from Jesus' teaching here that God's will concerning marriage is that it should be between one woman and one man and that it should be a life-long partnership. Just as Jesus had developed the Mosaic law, about loving your neighbour, to include loving your enemy, so he develops the Mosaic rule concerning divorce. Under the new covenant, based on unlimited, selfless love, we are called to be so responsive to God and each other that our marriages work for life.

Unfortunately, it is very obvious that 'hardness of heart' still tears marriages apart, resulting in misery and heartbreak for parents and children alike. The break-up of strong family units is damaging the whole structure of our society; and there are many pressures to accept marriage as only a temporary state, valid until it becomes tiresome or inconvenient.

As with all Jesus' teaching about real loving, we are being asked the impossible. It only becomes possible when our whole life is founded not on our partner, our emotions, our instincts or society's expectations, but on the rock of Christ. He can reinforce crumbling marriages, heal deep hurts, refresh our love, promote forgiveness and soften hardened attitudes, so he is an excellent guest to invite to the wedding!

But we also need to remember that our God is loving and compassionate, understanding our weakness and willing to forgive. So if we have a wrecked or failed marriage in our past, we are not unredeemable; when we confess our failure and determine to build our future on Christ, he will not only forgive us but also give back the years that the locusts have eaten.

Ideas for Adults

Organise today as a family day, with an outing, shared meal, teaching film strip or video about family life, discussion groups and a party. Include non-churchgoing partners in the invitation and stress that as members of Christ's family, single people and married ones are all part of the family.

Ideas for Children

Bring along a selection of toy farmyard and zoo animals and people and let the children group them into families of mother, father and baby. Or you could use a Happy Families set of cards to sort into families.

Now read the children the story of creation; *Palm Tree Bible Stories* has a version called *God makes the world*. They will see how God started the family idea right at the beginning of humanity's creation. Show them some wedding pictures and point out that it is God who joins the couple in marriage.

Using card tubes, scraps of net and other material, colour pens and glue, help them make a bride and bridegroom holding hands.

Music
Recorded Music

Tchaikovsky – *Swan Lake: the love duet*

'Live' Music

Comfort, joy, strength and meaning *(SONL, 68)*
Covenant *(ONE, 153)*
Lead us, heavenly Father, lead us *(ONE, 298)*
We come to you, Lord *(ONE, 590)*

Bidding Prayers

Celebrant As members of the Church of Christ,
let us lay our needs and cares
at the feet of our heavenly Father.

Reader We ask that his love, peace and joy may fill
the Church in every corner of the earth;
that God's name may be held holy
in unending waves of praise.
Pause
Unchanging Lord: **fix our hearts on your goodness.**

We ask that all negotiators
and administrators may be guided to work
with sensitivity, care and integrity.
Pause
Unchanging Lord: **fix our hearts on your goodness.**

We ask that all strained marriages
may be healed and strengthened; that those
whose lives have been damaged or warped
may be emotionally repaired and rebuilt.
Pause
Unchanging Lord: **fix our hearts on your goodness.**

We ask that our homes may be built
on the solid rock of Christ,
so that when storms come they may stand firm.
Pause
Unchanging Lord: **fix our hearts on your goodness.**

Celebrant Father of compassion and mercy,
accept our prayers through the person
of Jesus Christ. **Amen.**

28th Sunday in Ordinary Time

Theme
The kingdom of heaven is far more valuable than riches

Possessions can be a severe obstacle to entering God's kingdom because they encourage getting rather than giving, defending rather than trusting. With all his wealth the young man still lacked something: the capacity to give his wealth away; his possessions were more precious to him than the lasting treasure Jesus has promised to any who give anything up for his sake.

Penitential Rite

Help us to be less preoccupied with possessions,
    Lord, have mercy. **Lord, have mercy.**

Make us more willing to give till it hurts,
    Christ, have mercy. **Christ, have mercy.**

Set our hearts on your treasure alone,
    Lord, have mercy. **Lord, have mercy.**

Notes on the Readings

Wisdom 7:7-11

'Wisdom' here does not mean the accumulation of knowledge, or even the shrewd grasp of what makes people tick, which is based on experience. It is an understanding, given in answer to prayer, that turns the world's values upside down. We can think of it as the spiritual gift of seeing through God's eyes; a new kind of vision that brings different priorities into focus, and views behaviour (both our own and other people's) from a different perspective.

Hebrews 4:12-13

It is a perspective based on God's capacity to see everything – even what is so carefully hidden. Nothing at all is secret from God; when we think of this in relation to our own lives we realise just how much we need to be changed! We may be looking pretty good from the surface, but God sees the murky interior as well.

The powerfully effective instrument that can enlighten those dim areas and transform them, is the Word of God. All of Scripture is available for our use, and can lead us to see how our lives shape up to his character and will. And the Gospels show the expression of God crystallised in the Word made flesh: Jesus.

It is vital that all of us steep ourselves in the Word of God, day by day and week by week, just as Jesus himself did.

Mark 10:17-30

It sounds as if the young man had put off his question to Jesus until the last minute, and just as Jesus is setting out on a journey he throws his misgivings to the wind and invites a calling by expressing his desire to follow.

Yet when the calling comes it has strings attached. Following Jesus will mean abandoning his wealth, and that he finds too hard. Perhaps he had half expected Jesus to suggest this, and that was why he had delayed approaching him.

Don't we do this too? We offer our day for Christ to use, and then when he accepts our offer and gives us some unpleasant job instead of what we had planned, we moan about what a tiresome day it has been! Our 'wealth' may be our time, energy, plans, and comforts, our routine, favourite programme, relaxing company or even the biscuits we were saving. And God asks us to be prepared to give them all away joyfully in his service.

Bidding Prayers

Celebrant My brothers and sisters in Christ, let us lay our hopes, fears, burdens and concerns before our heavenly Father who loves and understands us.

Reader We lay before him our schools and seminaries, our teachers and theologians; our need for more priests and our need for guidance as the Church faces contemporary problems.
Pause
Lord of all: **you are our wealth and our treasure.**

We lay before him our desire for an end to war and conflict, so that children may not be brought up in an atmosphere of hatred and revenge; and we offer ourselves as channels of his peace.
Pause
Lord of all: **you are our wealth and our treasure.**

We lay before him all those in our local hospitals, hospices, homes for the elderly and nursing homes; that they may be indwelt by God – places of warmth and friendliness, hope and serenity.
Pause
Lord of all: **you are our wealth and our treasure.**

We lay before him our attachment to material comfort, financial success and pleasure-seeking; that we may be weaned from these to a closer and deeper attachment to the riches found in Christ.
Pause
Lord of all: **you are our wealth and our treasure.**

Celebrant Father, in your great mercy, hear these prayers we offer through Jesus Christ. **Amen.**

Ideas for Adults

Today's Gospel can be presented dramatically with the different parts being acted out. The narrator stands where he can be heard clearly, but is apart from the action. The actors mime what is narrated and speak their own parts from memory. The action begins in the sanctuary and Jesus sets out on his journey with his disciples to a central point in the main aisle.

Ideas for Children

Tell the children the story of the rich young man and talk together about some of the 'treasures' in our lives that stop us following Jesus. He wants us to be generous in giving and sharing, not just in money but in time and energy too.

Help the children make a treasure box each, by covering a small cardboard box with foil (it shouldn't need glue) and pressing in a few brass paper fasteners to decorate it.

Write the word TREASURE on the box in gold felt tip pen.

Inside will be the letters of Jesus' name, each letter in a different colour. Our treasure is Jesus.

Music

Recorded Music

Brahms – *Symphony No. 3: second movement*

'Live' Music

Leave your country and your people *(ONE, 229)*
Love is his word *(ONE, 338)*
Our hearts were made for you *(SONL, 36)*
Peace, perfect peace *(ONE, 445)*

29th Sunday in Ordinary Time

Theme
Christ's suffering and death is a ransom for many

Christ's great love for us is shown in the way he was prepared to pay the debt of our sin with his own life. Through his agony and death we are brought back and saved. However cruelly we are treated in life, however severely tempted, we know that Christ our brother has been in this place too; so that he understands, sympathises and has the power to bring resurrection into every deadly, impossible situation.

Penitential Rite

You stand by us in all our suffering,
    Lord, have mercy. **Lord, have mercy.**

Never do you let us down,
    Christ, have mercy. **Christ, have mercy.**

Knowing us completely, you love us still,
    Lord, have mercy. **Lord, have mercy.**

Notes on the Readings

Isaiah 53:10-11

The wonderful thing about the Christian message is that we do not have to walk around with our faces set in a tight, determined smile. We are not to feel guilty about heartbroken sobs, the ache of missing our loved ones who have died, or the sense of abject misery that may wash over us in a seemingly endless illness. For the central event of Christ's life, the event that saves us, is the slow and lingering death by crucifixion. And we need to remember that Jesus was not anaesthetised. He felt it all. His loving Father allowed it to happen. That is how we know that Jesus stands with us through every heartache and tragedy; and we know that the result of his suffering was astoundingly good.

It would be wrong to teach people that turning suffering into joy means taking away the pain. Sometimes this may happen, but at other times God allows the suffering to continue, just as he allowed the crucifixion to continue unchecked. But, just as that was the only way to resurrection and wholeness, so God will act through our suffering, if we let him, to enrich us, and bring about a transformation for great good.

Hebrews 4:14-16

Jesus, our supreme high priest, who offers the sacrifice, is also the offering. He is the victim, through living as man and undergoing the worst man can ever suffer; but he is also the freely-giving Saviour, withholding nothing. That means that the Lord we worship is not a distant ideal or a remote, though benign, onlooker: he is a personal friend.

Mark 10:35-45

In the current wave of hostage-taking we can really appreciate the relief and joy which accompany freedom after a ransom has been paid. Families have, through history, been willing to make sacrifices in order to buy the release of a loved one. That was the reason Jesus was prepared to give his life: he loved us so much that he was willing to make the greatest possible sacrifice to buy us our freedom from sin.

Bidding Prayers

Celebrant   Companions of the Way, let us pray together
              to our loving Father.

Reader   For all who, in following Christ,
           have encountered suffering, danger or persecution;
           that they may be supported and sustained
           by the presence of the risen Christ.
           Pause
           Heavenly Father: **your love sets us free.**

           For the innocent who suffer as a by-product
           of the world's mistakes, ineptitudes,
           misplaced priorities or greed;
           that love may breach the walls of prejudice
           and bring fresh life
           to the deserts of hopelessness.
           Pause
           Heavenly Father: **your love sets us free.**

           For the aimless and bewildered;
           for those who grieve and those who try
           to repress their grief; for all who are
           finding a burden desperately hard to bear.
           Pause
           Heavenly Father: **your love sets us free.**

           For our own friends and loved ones,
           and for ourselves; that we may trust Jesus
           to bring good out of every situation,
           however hopeless it seems.
           Pause
           Heavenly Father: **your love sets us free.**

Celebrant Father, in your unfailing mercy, we ask you
to accept these prayers through Jesus Christ. **Amen.**

Ideas for Adults

Have a guitar playing softly as a background to the Isaiah reading, starting in a minor key and changing to major at: 'His soul's anguish over'.

Ideas for Children

Show a few pictures of athletes training, mountaineers climbing, an orchestra practising, or any other activities where hard work or discomfort is necessary for the reward of winning, giving a good performance, or some other worthwhile end.

Discuss times in the children's own lives when they have had to put up with pain or discomfort which was worth doing; getting bruised in the process of learning to ride a bike or skate, for instance. Father Damien, the priest who worked among the lepers in Hawaii, was willing to put up with suffering from leprosy so that the people would be cared for.

When Jesus suffered and died on the cross, it really hurt a lot. But it was worth doing because it led to us being set free from all that is evil and bad.

Help them make this card to take home.

Music
Recorded Music

Rachmaninov – *Piano concerto No. 2: slow movement*

'Live' Music

Alleluia, sing to Jesus *(ONE, 15)*
Life pervading *(SONL, 46)*
My song is love unknown *(ONE, 363)*
Praise to the holiest in the height *(ONE, 455)*

30th Sunday in Ordinary Time

Theme
Jesus gives sight to the blind

Christ was able to restore both physical sight and spiritual vision, fulfilling Jeremiah's prophecy of the manifestation of God's parental love for his children. Through faith we can begin to see spiritual truths more clearly; we become sensitised to God working in and through his creation. As we share such a vision we are given the privilege of being co-workers with Christ in the healing of the world.

Penitential Rite

You can open our eyes to see,
Lord, have mercy. **Lord, have mercy.**

You can open our minds to perceive,
Christ, have mercy. **Christ, have mercy.**

You can open our hearts to love,
Lord, have mercy. **Lord, have mercy.**

Notes on the Readings

Jeremiah 31:7-9

In spite of all God's warnings through his prophets, the people of Israel have refused to return to his ways, until the destruction Jeremiah has predicted is inevitable. Yet the prospect is not to be utterly bleak for ever; Jeremiah can also glimpse in the distant future the light of restoration and hope, which we are privileged to see expounded in the ministry of Jesus.

We may find that although some sin has been confessed with sorrow, and although we know God has forgiven us, we are still in some kind of exile caused by the sin. There may be disease or injury which has stayed with us. We may have effectively shut doors which can no longer be opened, or lost something that can never be replaced. All this is part of accepting the consequences of our behaviour, but in many people it leads to bitterness and an impotent nostalgia, full of deep regret.

These words of Jeremiah are of great comfort, for they proclaim the immense mercy of God, who will not leave us in our personal exiles for ever, any more than he abandoned his stubborn and idolatrous people. Different doors will open; new opportunities to serve him will crop up; the very bitterness itself may be used to understand and help others out of their exile. At the end of the desert is hope, growth and healing.

Hebrews 5:1-6

Jesus was not a self-styled type of high priest; he was God's Chosen One – 'My beloved Son'. A high priest for the whole human race, he is permanently able to offer atonement for us through his unique relationship with us. As man he gave his life for us, and as God he is resurrected to unending life; what is more, he calls us his brothers and sisters, and invites us to share both in his sacrifice and in his risen life.

Mark 10:46-52

We do not know what had made Bartimaeus blind, but when we meet him he strikes us as loud-mouthed, bitter and aggressive. He certainly antagonises some of the crowd, who tell him to be quiet. His cry sounds hard, and full of unresolved resentment at his condition. He demands that everyone should feel sorry for him, for he feels so sorry for himself.

We might expect Jesus to go running over to him straight away and put things right by making him see. But Jesus understands that the blindness is only part of the problem; healing will only happen to Bartimaeus' personality when he starts to reach out from himself and humble his heart to admit his need and ask for help, instead of nursing his self pity. (In treatment for addiction, healing begins when the addiction is admitted and the need for help acknowledged.)

Jesus sends instructions for the man to make the first move and approach him, and at the invitation Bartimaeus jumps up – he even flings off his cloak in his excitement. When he gets to Jesus there is a significant silence before Jesus prompts him to express his need. It comes out in a new, reverent and respectful manner, straightforward, and simply put. This changed attitude is an important part of the healing; his raw, desperate longing is fulfilled as he receives both sight and self respect.

Bidding Prayers

Celebrant Bound together in the Spirit of Christ,
let us pray together to our heavenly Father.

Reader That wherever there is blindness, prejudice,
or lack of vision in the Church,
Christ may work his healing power
to refresh, enlighten and transform.
Pause
Not our will, Lord: **but yours, be done.**

That wherever personality conflicts,
errors of judgement, or insensitivity
threaten peace, God's Spirit may be allowed access,
to work towards harmony and goodwill.
Pause
Not our will, Lord: **but yours, be done.**

That all who are troubled and distressed
by pain, illness, poverty, hunger or any other
suffering, may experience the personal love
and loyalty of the healing Christ.
Pause
Not our will, Lord: **but yours, be done.**

That we may be more sensitive to the needs
of those with whom we live and work;
less critical, and better prepared
to encourage and forgive.
Pause
Not our will, Lord: **but yours, be done.**

Celebrant Father, you pour out your blessings
so richly on us; with thankful hearts
we praise you, and ask you to hear our prayers
through Jesus Christ. **Amen.**

Ideas for Adults

The reading from Jeremiah lends itself to choral speaking, which emphasises the wonderful message of hope. Have a group of 9 to 12 people, arranged in three sections: Light, Medium and Dark voices.

Dark:	The Lord says this:	
Light:	Shout with joy for Jacob!	
Medium:	Hail the chief of nations!	
One Light:	Proclaim!	<
Medium:	Praise!	

All:	Shout:	f
Dark:	The Lord has saved his people	
	the remnant of Israel!	*slowly*
Light:	See, I will bring them back	
	from the land of the North	
Medium and **Light:** }	and gather them from the far ends of earth; (pause) all of them:	p
Dark:	the blind and the lame,	
Medium:	women with child,	
Light:	women in labour:	
All:	a great company returning here.	f
Dark:	They had left in tears,	p
Light:	I will comfort them as I lead them back;	
Medium:	I will guide them to streams of water,	
Light and **Medium:** }	by a smooth path where they will not not stumble.	
Dark:	For I am a father to Israel, and Ephraim is my first-born son.	

Ideas for Children

Tell the children today's Gospel story from Bartimaeus' viewpoint. Wrap yourself up in an old cloak, have a begging bowl and a stick, and introduce yourself. You are going to share with them the most amazing thing that once happened to you. Really shout when you tell them how you were shouting, and throw off your cloak when you are summoned to Jesus.

Then work together to make a frieze telling the story of Bartimaeus. Some children colour a background, some draw and cut out crowds of people, one draws Bartimaeus begging, another draws him being helped to Jesus, and others the group with Jesus healing Bartimaeus. A road connects the different events of the story, so that it can be 'read'. The finished frieze can be brought into church and displayed.

Music
Recorded Music

Mozart – Horn concerto No. 5: *slow movement*

'Live' Music

Amazing grace *(ONE, 36)*
Christ is our king *(ONE, 84)*
Glorify the Lord *(SONL, 17)*
Turning the world upside down *(ONE, 403)*

31st Sunday in Ordinary Time

Theme
Love God with your whole self, and love your neighbour

First and foremost must come an entire and whole-hearted love for God. All our behaviour will be realigned once he is central. No amount of dutiful service or priestly sacrifice is as important as the humbling of the spirit which allows one to offer God loving adoration. Such love, pulsing through our relationships, is what the Christian faith is all about.

Penitential Rite

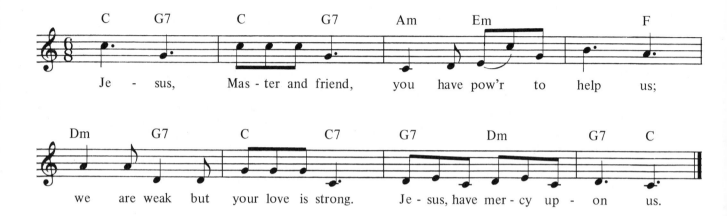

Je - sus, Mas - ter and friend, you have pow'r to help us; we are weak but your love is strong. Je - sus, have mer - cy up - on us.

Notes on the Readings

Deuteronomy 6:2-6

The Law, given through Moses, speaks of a love for God which is an expression of our whole being. There is real commitment in a love which involves our heart and our soul and our strength; it is a total bonding, with our entire self orientated towards God. And though it may seem demanding and excessive when we are used to pleasing ourselves and only fitting God in where we have space, it is in fact the most natural state for us, to be voluntarily at one with our creator. Everything else falls into place once this fundamental focus is right.

Hebrews 7:23-28

The Hebrew Christians, to whom this letter is sent, are finding it difficult to understand the full consequence of Christ, in connection with the Law as revealed through Moses. They are in some ways still stuck in the old Covenant, still offering burnt sacrifices and adhering strictly to all the Jewish rituals.

So it is explained that Christ is the only high priest we need, since he has offered and been offered in the one sacrifice that is sufficient for all time. He lives for ever, so he is perpetually able to atone for our sin; neither is he liable to corruption, having persevered through life and death in purity, resisting evil unswervingly. That makes him exactly the kind of high priest we desperately need, and we can be deeply thankful that Jesus Christ was sent to us to save us.

Mark 12:28-34

Regularly through Israel's history the prophets had declared God's loathing for lip worship without a committed heart, and hypocritical sacrifices that were empty of true repentance. Now, when the scribe approaches Jesus, he is genu-

inely concerned to find out where Jesus stands in relation to the Mosaic Law. Jesus focuses attention right back at the fundamental principles, from which all else springs, and the scribe warmly responds. He recognises that Christ is not a threat to the Law but is anxious to centralise what is really important, instead of looking so closely at the intricate rules and regulations that the basic rock is disregarded.

The Christian Church is not automatically immune from a similar near-sightedness. We need to be constantly rigorous in gazing steadfastly at our loving God, so as to avoid getting side-tracked in all the little extras that can distort our true vision.

Bidding Prayers

Celebrant   My companions in Christ,
we share a common faith and hope;
let us pray trustingly together
to the God who made us and sustains us.

Reader   Let us pray for all
who profess themselves Christians;
that in fastening our eyes on Christ
we may be led to unity.
Pause
Father almighty: **our life is in your hands.**

Let us pray for the political, industrial
and commercial administrations
throughout our planet; that our material
and economic organisation may reveal
good stewardship of the gifts God has provided.
Pause
Father almighty: **our life is in your hands.**

Let us pray for all convicted prisoners,
and for the victims of their crimes;
for all who are eaten up with hatred or jealousy;
for those who are finding it impossible
to forgive their enemies.
Pause

Father almighty: **our life is in your hands.**

Let us pray for the homes and families
represented here; for our loved ones
from whom we are separated by distance or death;
for a deepening of love towards each other,
in all our relationships.
Pause

Father almighty: **our life is in your hands.**

Celebrant With grateful thanks for the gift of life,
we offer you these prayers together with ourselves
for your service; in Jesus' name we pray. **Amen.**

Ideas for Adults

Have Christ's summary of the Law displayed on large posters in church, worked in appliqué or collage.

Ideas for Children

Have plenty of Bibles available and help the children to find the verses in which the first commandment is given. Remind them of how all the other commandments summarise loving our neighbour and then turn to the passage in Mark, chosen for today's Gospel.

Jesus would have learnt the commandments off by heart when he was a child. Say the summary of the Law several times together and suggest that they learn it off by heart during the week. You can offer a small reward for those who manage to do it. Sing it together, to refresh their memories. (See page 80.)

Have a lot of supermarket cartons, with the biggest labelled 'Love God with all your heart and soul and mind and strength'. Label the others: 'Friends', 'Money', 'Career', 'Home', 'Holidays' 'Car' etc. Then place the commandments box in the centre of the room and ask the children to help build their lives on it, to make a tall tower. What happens if we take away our base of loving God? Have a volunteer to pull out that main box and watch all the rest come tumbling down. You could sing I *want to build my life* (SONL, 95).

Music
Recorded Music

Mendelssohn – *Italian Symphony*

'Live' Music

For to those who love God *(ONE, 149)*
His name is higher *(ONE, 211)*
In you, my God *(ONE, 254)*
We behold the splendour *(ONE, 587)*
Worship, glory, praise and honour *(SONL, 22)*

32nd Sunday in Ordinary Time

Theme
Giving till it hurts

Both the widows mentioned today were willing to give at great personal cost. They gave lovingly, trusting that God would provide for them. God is well worth all the love we can ever lavish on him. Actual amounts of money pledged to God's work will vary according to circumstances; but the attitude behind really generous giving does not alter. We must steer clear of the hypocrisy which pretends to love God but is in reality festering with greed and vanity.

Penitential Rite

You are so generous with your gifts,
   Lord, have mercy. **Lord, have mercy.**

Your love enfolds us every day,
   Christ, have mercy. **Christ, have mercy.**

May our love be more like yours,
   Lord, have mercy. **Lord, have mercy.**

Notes on the Readings

1 Kings 17:10-16

God's timing is beautiful. Elijah meets the widow just as she is about to prepare her last meal before starvation, during a long, harsh drought. Consequently three people are fed throughout the drought, and generosity and faith blossom. Of course the widow could easily have refused to share her last scrap of food with Elijah. She did not even believe in Elijah's God, as she was not from Israel. But her willing gift opened up new possibilities of life for her and her son.

Hebrews 9:24-28

Continuing his comparison of Christ with the Jewish high priests, the writer of this letter looks at the necessity for regular, yearly sacrifice as a sin offering under the old Covenant. In contrast to this, Christ, taking upon himself all sin, only needed to offer one sacrifice. For this sacrifice was complete and full; nothing was left wanting.

The temple was designed with a series of courts, culminating in the holy of holies – the sanctuary where the stone tablets of the Law were housed – and this place was deeply reverenced. It was a kind of model of heaven itself. Now, in Christ, the real, original heaven has been entered by an everliving high priest who has completely atoned for the sin of the whole world; the temple and its sacrifices are therefore no longer the focus of our worship. With the destruction of the temple imminent, it was important that the Jerusalem Christians realised this, for their faith was about to be severely tested.

Mark 12:38-44

God is never fooled; he sees our motives, the bit we make on the side, the place our heart is, when we do the right things for the wrong reasons. However subtle we are, any hypocrisy will show up before his sight in all its glaring crudity.

Jesus hated to see hypocrisy anywhere, but he was particularly concerned at finding it among the religious leaders, for it is utterly contradictory to God's crystal purity. He loves to see the direct innocence of young children, and the straightforward integrity of adults.

Our world is so full of complexities, schemes and counter-schemes, wheeling and dealing, mixed motives and shady contracts; it is alarmingly easy to get caught up in it all. No-one will throw rosebuds at our feet for bringing these things to light, either. The only reward we will get for insisting on integrity is the knowledge that we are acting in accordance with God's will. But that is no mean reward!

The poor widow is held up as an example of generous giving even though she has only given a penny. God, in his purity, judges the heart.

Bidding Prayers

Celebrant   We have been given this opportunity
   to pray together; let us bring to our heavenly Father
   all our needs, cares and concerns.

Reader   We bring to his love the particular problems
   facing each parish in our city,
   our country and our world;
   that every Christian community may be guided
   and nurtured to reflect the love of Christ.
Pause
Giver of life: **we give our lives for your service.**

We bring to his love the run-down, neglected
and violent areas of our cities;
the unsettled, war-torn areas of our world.
Pause
Giver of life: **we give our lives for your service.**

We bring to his love the weak and vulnerable,
the hungry and the homeless,
the newly born and those who are nearing death;
that love may surround and undergird them.
Pause
Giver of life: **we give our lives for your service.**

We bring to his love the members
of our families, with their hopes and sorrows,
needs, joys and difficulties;
that we may learn to trust God
through both the good times and the bad.
Pause
Giver of life: **we give our lives for your service.**

Celebrant   Father, we thank you for bringing us here today,
   and ask you to accept our prayers
   through Jesus Christ. **Amen.**

Ideas for Adults

The reading from 1 Kings 17 is very suitable for acting out with a narrator, Elijah, the widow and her son. Simple costumes help bring the event to life, and the words of Elijah and the widow should be learnt off by heart.

Ideas for Children

Tell the children the story of Elijah and the widow, and then go through it again, acting it out. Bring along a few lengths of material, towels and ties to dress the actors in, and have ready some sticks, a small jar of flour, a jug of oil and a mixing bowl.

Give several children a chance to act, and each time renew the ingredients. When the flour and oil are mixed to a soft dough, give each child a lump to form into a little scone. They wrap their scone in foil and take it home to bake, with instructons on a slip of paper: Bake at Gas Mark 6, or 450° for 10 minutes. It is best eaten hot! Call them 'Elijah scones'.

Music
Recorded Music

Telemann – *Suite in A minor for flute and orchestra*

'Live' Music

Freely, freely *(ONE, 175)*
Go in peace *(SONL, 45)*
If we only seek peace *(SONL, 76)*
My God I love thee *(ONE, 358)*

33rd Sunday in Ordinary Time

Theme
Christ will come again in glory

Through his death Christ has offered the one complete sacrifice to free us from sin. No more is needed. In heaven, Christ, both divine and human, intercedes for us, and will return at the end of time to gather up his chosen ones from every part of the world. Though awesome and terrifying, it will be an occasion of rejoicing at the triumph of God's love over evil.

Penitential Rite

We can do nothing good without you,
   Lord, have mercy. **Lord, have mercy.**

Our only hope and strength is in you,
   Christ, have mercy. **Christ, have mercy.**

In penitence we turn towards you,
   Lord, have mercy. **Lord, have mercy,**

Notes on the Readings

Daniel 12:1-3

It can give us a mixed sensation of dread and excitement to realise that this vision of Daniel's depicts actual happenings that are still in the future; they may not necessarily be distant future either. They will affect us whether we are dead at the time or still alive, and we need to be prepared.

Since it has been so many centuries since Christ walked our earth, we can sometimes get lulled into a false sense of security. We assume that everything will carry on much as it has done for years; the inevitable crises and alarms, but nothing cataclysmic.

Daniel's vision nudges us to remember that God's plan is not yet complete, and he will most certainly bring all things to completion at the last day of all.

Hebrews 10:11-14, 18

Having made the one, full and complete sacrifice to take away all sin of the world, Christ has returned to heaven until the end of the world as we know it. He pleads on our behalf unceasingly, from the unique standpoint of being both human and divine.

The realisation of what an amazing freedom Christ has accomplished for us, urges us to a deep thankfulness that needs to be expressed in our lives as well as in words. For he has done this for us even while we are entrenched in our persistent sin and selfishness; he joins us in the garbage of our sin and loves us to freedom.

Mark 13:24-32

One of Jesus' roles was that of prophet, and here he foresees those last days on earth at the end of time. Again, as in Daniel's vision, there is terror and appalling distress involving all nations. Afterwards the whole world will see God in all his glory: the Son of Man will come back to the earth to gather every one of his chosen. Even Jesus himself does not know when this is going to happen; and there are obviously going to be terrible times to live through.

But no matter what devastation occurs, no matter how widespread evil will be, we need not be frightened. Holding fast to Christ, keeping his commandments and quickly repenting whenever our sin separates us from him, we shall be kept safe, and brought through it all to eternal life with the God we love and adore.

Bidding Prayers

Celebrant   My brothers and sisters in Christ,
   we have been chosen and called
   by our heavenly Father; let us pray to him now.

Reader   For the varied ministry of the Church
   over the whole earth;
   that in weakness we may be given strength,
   in danger courage, and in temptation
   the grace to stand firm in Christ.
   Pause
   Lord of the universe: **keep us in your love.**

For every peace initiative,
   all attempts to achieve just settlements,
   and each effort to put right
   whatever is corrupt, or insidiously evil.
   Pause
   Lord of the universe: **keep us in your love.**

For all who suffer from debilitating
   and progressive illness; for the physically,
   emotionally and mentally handicapped;
   and for those who nurse, encourage
   and support them.
   Pause
   Lord of the universe: **keep us in your love.**

For the areas in our own lives
   which need God's light and healing;
   that we may draw closer to understand his ways
   and walk in his will.
   Pause
   Lord of the universe: **keep us in your love.**

Celebrant   Trusting in your promise to hear us, Father,
   we offer you these prayers
   through Jesus Christ. **Amen.**

Ideas for Adults

Meaning can be emphasised by reading the passage from Daniel chorally. Have two groups of men and two of women and arrange the groups like this:

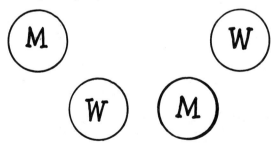

Men 1:	At that time Michael will stand up,
Men 1,2:	the great prince who mounts guard over your people.
Women 1:	There is going to be a time of great distress,
Women 2:	unparalleled since nations first came into existence
All:	When that time comes
Men 1, **Women 1:**	your own people will be spared,
Men 1:	all those whose names are found written in the Book.
Men 2:	Of those who lie sleeping in the dust of the earth
Men 2, **Women 2:**	many will awake
Women 2:	some to everlasting life,

All:	some to shame and everlasting disgrace.
Men 1,2:	The learned will shine as brightly as the vault of heaven,
Women 1,2:	and those who have instructed many in virtue,
All:	as bright stars for all eternity.

Ideas for Children

This can be a disturbing area for young children, and needs to be explored with sensitivity. At the same time, I feel it is important that we do teach our children about the reality of the Second Coming.

Together go over the events of Jesus' life, from his birth to when he returned to heaven at the Ascension. As each event is mentioned, mark it in on a 'life-path' drawn on a board or paper sheet. If you have small pictures of different events these can also be stuck on.

Now tell them how there is another event which has not yet happened; Jesus is going to return to our earth in glory. Read the passage from Mark 13 where Jesus tells his friends about that time. The next question is bound to be: 'When?'

Read them what Jesus said; he didn't even know himself when it would be. He just knew that it was certain. Help them to find the Creed, and look together at what it says about the Second Coming, when all people, both living and dead, will be judged.

Finish the chart of Jesus' life with pictures the children draw and colour of some of the signs Jesus mentions: the darkened sun, the dimmed moon, falling stars and the whole cosmos shaken, with Jesus 'coming in the clouds with great power and glory'.

Music
Recorded Music

Fauré – Requiem: Dies Irae

'Live' Music

All my hope on God is founded (ONE, 25)
I'll be with you to the end of the world (ONE, 238)
I need you, Lord (SONL, 40)
Rain down justice (ONE, 459)

Last Sunday in Ordinary Time
Our Lord Jesus Christ, Universal King

Theme
Christ is king of an everlasting kingdom

Christ's kingdom, based on the power of love instead of weapons, strong in weakness and vulnerability, and forgiving without revenge, presents a very different image from an earthly kingdom. Yet this is the kingdom that will never be overthrown, or decay from within. Love is the strongest power of all, and Christ is the king of love.

Penitential Rite

Teach us to love regardless of reward,
Lord, have mercy. **Lord, have mercy.**

Teach us to love without conditions,
Christ, have mercy. **Christ, have mercy.**

Teach us to love as you love us,
Lord, have mercy. **Lord, have mercy.**

Notes on the Readings

Daniel 17:13-14

This amazing vision looks through the darkness of time to the joy of heaven, as Jesus is led into God's presence, having accomplished the saving of humankind. Of course, no pictures can really grasp the meaning, but Daniel's language gives us a wonderful sensation of worth, dignity, grace, truth and rejoicing. Like a magnet, Christ draws many people from all nations into his kingdom which shall never end.

We have the privilege of living in this last age, when all the peoples of the earth are being brought to know and acknowledge him as Lord of All.

Apocalypse 1:5-8

When Christ rose again, in victory over death, he was the first but not the only one. When we put our trust in him, renouncing sin and embracing his promise of life, we too shall be raised to unending life. We feel right when we are serving and adoring God because that is what we were made for; only in him will our restless spirits find rest and complete peace of mind.

In the readings today we are bending our minds and imaginations round the unimaginable. We have to talk in the language of time about an existence outside time; about a God who had no beginning and will never end; about cosmic realisation of God's glory, involving millions and millions of individual journeys. It can seem just too much, too far beyond our understanding.

If that is how you feel, I would recommend giving the mind a break; choose somewhere quiet, and simply be still in God's presence, just gazing at the One who made you, loves you, and has all things under control.

John 18:33-37

Jesus turns his interrogation into a meeting of souls. It is an encounter that impresses Pilate deeply; encounters with Christ are bound to change us in some way. The kind of kingship that Jesus claims here throws a completely new light on all earthly kingdoms and empires, from Imperial Rome onwards. It topples the world's values and overturns the concepts of power and majesty. But it really works.

Christ's kingdom has not only survived, but grown and flourished through nearly 2,000 years so far. Whatever attempts have been made to stamp it out, pervert it, or dismiss it, it bursts out again in the blossoming of selfless lives, praise and unconditional love.

Bidding Prayers

Celebrant We belong to the family of God; as sons and daughters let us pray to our heavenly Father.

Reader For all who have devoted their lives to serving Christ and spreading the good news of his saving love; that they may be channels of God's peace and work always in his strength.
Pause
Our Lord and our King: **work your will in us.**

For all monarchs, presidents and national leaders; that their governments may be wise and just, careful and compassionate.
Pause
Our Lord and our King: **work your will in us.**

For the oppressed and despised, the lonely and those who have lost all hope; for those in constant pain or distress; that God will use their suffering for good, and ease their burdens.
Pause
Our Lord and our King: **work your will in us.**

For those with whom we live and work; for the people who serve us in this community; that God's kingdom of love may spread through the whole landscape of our lives.
Pause
Our Lord and our King: **work your will in us.**

Celebrant Most merciful and loving Father, we ask you to hear and answer our prayers which we offer in the name of Jesus. **Amen.**

Ideas for Adults

Decorate the church today with banners proclaiming Christ as our King, floodlight any windows or pictures expressing his kingship and, if you have a trumpeter among you, use him or her before the reading from Daniel.

Ideas for Children

Read the children what Daniel saw in his vision. Does it remind them of an event in Jesus' life? You can refer to last week's chart. Where is Jesus' kingdom? It can be found wherever the Spirit of Jesus is found – wherever there is caring, unselfish love.

Pray together for Jesus' kingdom to grow in us, and then help the children to make crowns, decorated with jewels, of love, peace, kindness and joy. They can wear their crowns into church.

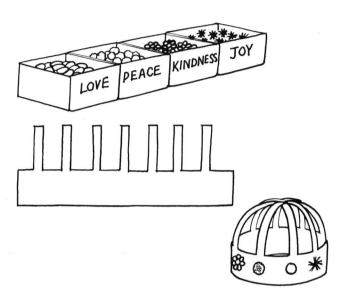

Music
Recorded Music

Rachmaninov – *Piano concerto* No. 2: *last movement*

'Live' Music

All the earth proclaim the Lord *(SONL, 79)*
Christ is our king *(ONE, 84)*
Let the mountains dance and sing *(SONL, 4)*
Rejoice! The Lord is King *(ONE, 463)*
The head that once was crowned with thorns *(ONE, 524)*

Year of Luke : C

ADVENT

Questions for Discussion Groups
1. By jotting down your weekly/daily timetable, compare the time you spend in God's company with the time you spend pleasing yourself. Is some reorganisation needed? Thrash out a possible Rule of Life with the members of the group.
2. How can we get the attention of the world God longs to save? What are the most effective means of spreading the Good News?

1st Sunday of Advent

Theme
Get ready straight away

We have no way of knowing exactly when Christ will come in glory. We can be ready only by living the kind of life he means us to live.

If Christ comes upon us while we are unprepared, we will see him, through our guilt, as terrible and threatening.

If we are already walking towards him, we shall be able to greet him with confidence and unbounded joy.

Penitential Rite

For our shallow commitment to you,
  Lord, have mercy. **Lord, have mercy.**

For our half-hearted attempts to follow you,
  Christ, have mercy. **Christ, have mercy.**

For our careless rejection of you,
  Lord, have mercy. **Lord, have mercy.**

Notes on the Readings

Jeremiah 33:14-16

The recurring promise of a branch emerging, full of virtue and integrity, takes on a new urgency and excitement as we prepare for the coming of the Saviour at Christmas. The wearying story of human disloyalty, rejection, disobedience and corruption does not end in despair but great hope: God loves his people and is willing to save them, whatever the cost.

We who have the privilege of living after Christ's coming can see how wonderfully Jeremiah's prophecy was fulfilled in the person of Jesus.

Thessalonians 3:12; 4:2

A child who has not yet acquired the taste for avocado pears will not appreciate them however beautifully they are prepared and served! In a sense we all have to work at acquiring a 'taste' for living life Christ's way. Loving in the full Christian way can be demanding, exacting, tedious and difficult at times, and is certainly not something that gushes out of us from babyhood onwards. It needs conscious, daily application, and real effort.

But, just as different dishes look appetising according to the tastes we acquire, so the selfless loving shown by Christ will become more and more attractive and desirable as we work on acquiring the taste for it.

Luke 21:25-28, 34-36

The worst trap is to think there is no hurry. In fact, the only thing we know for certain is that the Son of Man will come suddenly, at a time we may not be expecting him at all. Any of us who have tried to get physically fit in the last couple of days before a holiday or a hike, know all too well that it doesn't work: the muscles protest! Neither will it be much use trying to get spiritually 'fit' at the last minute. Rather, we need a strenuous training programme, a daily work-out, if our goodness and love are to develop. That's why we must start straight away.

How we react at the Second Coming will depend on how we act now. From time to time we need a thorough re-think of where we are, where we are heading and where we fall disastrously short. Advent is just the time for such a stock-check. Which times, for instance, would we be pleased for Christ to see us? And when would we prefer him to be looking the other way?

Bidding Prayers

Celebrant Let us pray together as we prepare ourselves
      for the great coming of Christ;
      let us bring to his healing and love
      the needs of the Church and the world.

Reader For all Christian people,
      for increased love and commitment,
      working within the world like yeast.
      Pause
      Lord, come to us: **live in us now.**

      For those in authority,
      that they may base their priorities and decisions
      on the foundation of God's power, justice
      and mercy.
      Pause
      Lord, come to us: **live in us now.**

      For those who suffer;
      for God's strength and support
      during pain, grief or distress,
      so that their very suffering
      may become a channel
      for God's redeeming love.
      Pause
      Lord, come to us: **live in us now.**

      For the local community,
      that God may be present
      in the varied, separate lives surrounding us;
      that, alerted to their needs,
      we may work in Christ to care and provide.
      Pause
      Lord, come to us: **live in us now.**

Celebrant Father, you came to show us
      the true way to life.
      Help us progress along that way
      in your strength.
      Through Jesus Christ, our Lord. **Amen.**

Ideas for Children

Advent frieze

The road to Bethlehem is drawn on a long sheet of paper. Week by week through Advent, the donkey, with Mary and Joseph, are moved along it towards the stable. Blu-Tac works well. Children stick on all the extras: star; trees;

animals; khans (shelters on the roadside); etc. Each week link this journey with our 'journey' through Advent in a particular way.

On this First Sunday focus on 'Getting ready for the journey': how we prepare. Talk about firemen, lifeboatmen, etc., who don't know when they may be needed, so they are always ready. How? By practising rescues, keeping machinery well-oiled and repaired.

> Loving Father,
> help us to get ourselves ready
> so that we can welcome your Son Jesus with joy.
> **Amen.**

Advent calendars are commercially often linked with getting rather than giving. Older children could make a calendar, with the emphasis on giving, instead.

Each day has a slit, down which a two pence piece is dropped. After Christmas, the money is collected at church to give to a charity. Or a visit to a hospice may be arranged and calendars could be emptied there and some carols sung.

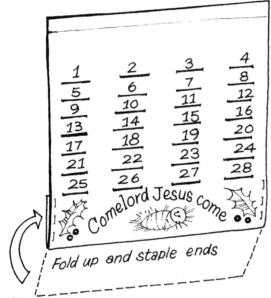

Music
'Live' Music

Come to the waters (SONL, 86)
Now watch for God's coming (ONE, 378)
Put on the armour of Jesus Christ (SONL, 11)
The Courtyard (SOS 3, 260)
There will be signs (ONE, 544)
Wake up, O people! (SONL, 44)
When is he coming? (MSOS, 119; BSOS, 6)

2nd Sunday of Advent

Theme
Work in Christ with hope and joy

God has promised that he will finish the work which he has started in us. We need have no doubts. As we work in him to become more loving and increasingly perceptive we can be confident that, in spite of our sin, God is using us to help establish his everlasting kingdom of joy, love and peace.

Penitential Rite

For the opportunities of loving that we have missed,
  Lord, have mercy. **Lord, have mercy.**

For our stubborn preference for twisted lives,
  Christ, have mercy. **Christ, have mercy.**

For our blindness and our pride,
  Lord, have mercy. **Lord, have mercy.**

Notes on the Readings

Baruch 5:1-9

God has plans for a new Jerusalem. No longer sin-stained, broken and devastated, she is to be dressed as a bride, her honour and integrity so glowing as to attract every nation to the beauty of God's kingdom. Such beauty, both in the city and in the structure of our lives, is always the result of full acknowledgement of our guilt, sorrow and repentance for our sin, and the joy of accepting God's complete forgiveness. We are not to try and pay God back for the gifts he hands out; we can't, anyway. It is his good pleasure to give us the kingdom, and we need to accept gracefully – with delight.

Philippians 1:3-6, 8-11

There is obviously a strong bond of affection between Paul and the Christians at Philippi. He draws a great deal of encouragement from the knowledge that they are working with him for the spread of the Gospel. Any work is less daunting and more fun when you know others are doing their bit as well. Surely that is partly why Christ founded the Church; working together for the kingdom, we can encourage one another along the way, sympathise, inspire and support. In the process we shall be changing increasingly into reflectors of Jesus.

Luke 3:1-6

Precisely, Luke establishes the date of John the Baptist's mission. The Good News he is reporting is historically valid, and God's plan for salvation is real.

John the Baptist was alerting people to the nearness of what they had long been awaiting, not just for years but for generations; it was this new urgency which made a thorough repentance seem vital. The urgency is still there in each individual lifetime, and the present is the best time to act. As Anne Frank wrote in her diary: 'How wonderful it is that nobody need wait a single moment before beginning to improve the world.'

The Christian Good News does not mean the easy, lazy, spoil-yourself, relax-and-have-a-good-time news of the advertisements. It is, as Paul Tillich says, 'healing in the ultimate sense; it is final, cosmic and individual healing.' How do we work towards its completion?

If we do it in our own strength, the nice-ness wears thin, patience wears out and exhaustion, indignation and resentment squeeze in through the cracks. It is what we are which speaks to those who are lost, doubtful, frightened or embittered. And what we are depends on what we let Christ make us into.

Bidding Prayers

Celebrant Let us pray to God our Father to make us
        spiritually supple, so that we can be
        of better use to him in
        spreading the Good News
        of his saving love.

Reader That the Church may be
      constantly renewed and deepened
      by the patient guidance of the Spirit.
      Pause
      Take us, Lord: **use us, we pray.**

That the world's leaders
will interpret all immediate issues
in the eternal light of God's fullness.
Pause

Take us, Lord: **use us, we pray.**

That the dying may be
comforted, their fears so calmed
that they are able to use
the rest of their lives in preparing
themselves in stillness and expectant joy.
Pause

Take us, Lord: **use us, we pray.**

For our families and friends,
that we may walk joyfully along the way
of Christ Jesus, expending our lives
in his service.
Pause

Take us, Lord: **use us, we pray.**

Celebrant   Father, as you prepared mankind
for your coming in Bethlehem,
prepare us to receive you in our hearts.
We ask this through Christ our Lord. **Amen.**

Ideas for Children

Continue the journey to Bethlehem. This week, talk about building a railway, with tunnels, embankments, cuttings etc. Use a model if possible.

Why do the engineers prepare the ground like this? To make it possible for trains to travel as easily and directly as possible.

Read the prophecy from Baruch.

We must make our own paths straight. We need to cut out and build up (pride, unkindness, forgiveness, helpfulness, etc.)

Continue to add to the frieze with fellow travellers, stars, trees, etc.

Dance

The idea of light and individual preparation can be 'caught' by a dance on this theme.

Use the music of Mozart's 23rd Piano Concerto, about three minutes of the end of the slow movement.

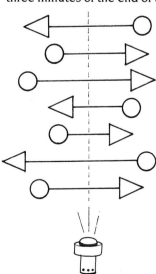

Dancers stand in centre aisle, relaxed, feet apart, hands at sides. As music plays dancers should move individually, sometimes walking and stretching arms towards the centre line, sometimes turning away and walking away, always along the arrowed direction. It should look like a constantly moving, disunited group. Then a low spot light shines straight up the centre aisle towards the altar. The dancers sense it at different times; some immediately line themselves up with it, kneeling, arms raised. Others take longer. Eventually all are in line, worshipping as the music ends.

This is simple enough for any group to tackle, but very effective if all movements are deliberate and controlled.

Music

Recorded Music

Mozart – *Piano Concerto No. 23: slow movement*

'Live' Music

Here I am, Lord *(SOS 3, 213)*
I give my hands *(MSOS, 123)*
O comfort my people *(ONE, 385)*
Take me, Lord *(SONL, 92)*

3rd Sunday of Advent

Theme
Rejoice, the Lord is very near

As Christmas draws closer we sense with growing excitement and joy the approaching of Christ himself. In love we prepare our hearts to meet him, both as child of Bethlehem and as Lord and Saviour for all time and in all places.

Penitential Rite

You come to heal sinners,
   Lord, have mercy. **Lord, have mercy.**

You come to make us whole,
   Christ, have mercy. **Christ, have mercy.**

You come in deepest love and great humility,
   Lord, have mercy. **Lord, have mercy.**

Alternatively sing: 'Lord, when I turn my back on you' *(Songs of New Life, 40)*

Notes on the Readings

Zephaniah 3:14-18

The mood of Advent certainly involves rigorous soul-searching and repentance, but it is equally a time of hope and joy. For as this lovely reading proclaims, when the Lord, our God, is right here in the midst of us, all things are well and there is no evil we need fear. Think of Paul and Silas, beaten with rods and imprisoned with their feet in the stocks; they spent the night praying and singing, and obviously entertaining the other prisoners! When we ask God to give us the assurance of his real presence among us he often responds by filling us with a quite unexpected joy.

Philippians 4:4-7

The Christian happiness does not come from a failure to look at reality. It is not a sign of blindness to the world's problems. On the contrary, Christian happiness invariably results in a lot of energy and positive action. But it is not God's will that the problems and injustices of the world should suffocate sensitive people with grief and despair; rather, we need to learn to shift the focus of our vision. First we are to love God; that will empower us to love the world and serve others selflessly without finding ourselves overcome by the heartbreaks we are bound to encounter.

Luke 3:10-18

With anything that fascinates us we work with terrific commitment while inspiration lasts, but if that fades we stop bothering to practise; it does not seem worth the effort any more. John's followers had been fired by the realisation of God's absolute power and the imminence of his wielding that power. Suddenly it mattered again that their lives had become shoddy. As John helped them to see God's blinding brightness they became conscious of their own tawdry existence.

As we begin to grasp something of how vast, how devastatingly powerful God is, and yet how he never bullies or throws his weight about, but waits, if necessary, welcomes and forgives; then we too are inspired to ask 'what must we do?' Practical details of our lives are challenged. Have our standards of loving and forgiving slipped to conform with what the world is prepared to accept? But it is not the world which calls us. Christ is our measuring stick and his living peace, though far beyond our understanding, is nevertheless astoundingly real.

Bidding Prayers

Celebrant   Let us pray that as we prepare
our homes for Christmas,
we may also prepare our lives.

Reader   That the Church may always be watchful,
rigorous in showing the brightness of
God's glory to the world.
Pause
Lord of all power: **save us, we pray.**

That both employers and employees
may think not only of their rights
but also of their responsibilities;
not only of justice but also of tolerance
and mutual understanding.
Pause
Lord of all power: **save us, we pray.**

That all who are suffering from anxiety,
depression, loneliness or grief
may be granted such a real knowledge
of God's presence that they are comforted.
Pause
Lord of all power: **save us, we pray.**

That we may order our daily lives
as true sons and daughters of God,
full of generosity and compassion.
Pause
Lord of all power: **save us, we pray.**

Celebrant   Father, we ask these things through Jesus
Christ our Lord. **Amen.**

Ideas for Adults

Zephaniah 3:14-18
First Reading. This could be effective with a group of 5 or 6 voices giving a dramatised reading. Here is a fully worked out example using three men and three women.

All: Shout for joy, daughter of Zion. Israel
shout aloud!
Women: Rejoice, exult with all your heart,
daughter of Jerusalem!
Men: The Lord has repealed your sentence;
(*pause*) he has driven your enemies away.

Man 1:   The Lord, the King of Israel, is in your midst.
Woman 1:   You have no more evil to fear.
All: (*low, measured*) When that day comes,
word will come to Jerusalem.
(*loud*) Zion have no fear. Do not let your hands
fall limp.
Men: The Lord your God is in your midst.
All: A victorious warrior.
Women: He will exult with joy for you. (*pause*)
He will renew you by his love.
All: He will dance with shouts of joy for you,
as on a day of festival.

Ideas for Children

1. Stained glass windows using tissue paper and black paper are very effective and several children can work together on one picture. The finished windows can become part of the church decorations at Christmas.

2. Tell the story of John the Baptist and then give each child a part in the story; the crowds are just as important.
Tell the story again with the children acting their parts.
A few costumes such as lengths of material, a sheep skin rug and a leather belt help create the right atmosphere.
3. The journey to Bethlehem continues.
4. Talk about how your life changes according to what you are getting ready for.
   - How do you get ready for a party? Have beads, necklace, make-up, etc.
   - A football player? Have clean kit, dubbin, boots, exercises.
   - A plumber? Overalls, old clothes.
   - We are preparing to meet Jesus. How should we do that? Dress up in hat labelled 'love', coat labelled 'kindness', boots labelled 'helping and forgiving', gloves labelled 'caring and sharing'.
   Give the children a card to take home and remind themselves each morning as they dress.

Music
Recorded Music

Elgar – *Serenade for strings*

'Live' Music

Love divine, all loves excelling *(ONE, 337)*
Seasons come, seasons go *(ONE, 470)*
Seek ye first the kingdom of God *(ONE, 473)*
Wake up, O people! *(SONL, 44)*
Zephaniah's Song *(SOS 3, 219)*

4th Sunday of Advent

Theme
God's promise of salvation needs our acceptance and co-operation

Sacrifices of the old Law could never atone for sin; that needed Christ himself, God made man, to accept death in perfect obedience and become the one true sacrifice. And Christ could only embark on this redeeming work if Mary were prepared, in perfect obedience, to become his mother. She was prepared; she did believe: God could become man and the way was opened for our salvation.

Penitential Rite

In order to save us, you became man,
Lord, have mercy. **Lord, have mercy.**

In perfect obedience, you accepted even death,
Christ, have mercy. **Christ, have mercy.**

Your coming recharges our lives with joy,
Lord, have mercy. **Lord, have mercy.**

Notes on the Readings

Micah 5:1-4

Faith seems easier to manage when there is rational, concrete evidence to support what we believe. Yet, in fact, real faith is only begun when that evidence is missing; like Peter, we often start sinking at the thought because it makes us feel desperately vulnerable. It was during the blackest times of exile that the prophets remained convinced of God's promise to come and save.

Micah, seeing beyond the fallibility of human rulers, however noble, looks forward to the time when the Prince of Peace will rule over the whole land in a reign of unparalleled integrity and majesty, founded on the majesty of God himself. Like the great king David, he will hail from the insignificant town of Bethlehem, and the fact of his coming is not in doubt, however hopeless the immediate situation appears.

Hebrews 10:5-10

Replacing the Law's regular sacrifices for sin, which needed to be repeated and could not redeem us back to holiness, Jesus becomes the one perfect sacrifice who can actually take away the sins of the whole world. This he does through his complete obedience to the Father's will, thus filling the concept of sacrifice with new meaning. It is our lives, expended in obedient service to our creator by working with him for the establishing of the kingdom of heaven on earth, which constitute the sacrifice most pleasing to God.

Luke 1:39-44

Elizabeth's husband, Zechariah, had found it impossible and too far-fetched to believe that his elderly wife could conceive. We may sympathise in our scientific age: the evidence was all against it. But Zechariah was reprimanded. Greater faith had been hoped for.

No wonder Elizabeth, after her own experience, had become wiser, and could see what an outstanding faith Mary had shown at the Annunciation.

We need to cultivate this kind of acceptance and trust, even if we have no idea how things can possibly work out. We need to be able to say, 'Lord, I trust you; use me.' And whenever we do, we share with Mary the privilege of allowing God's unbounded power of healing love to be set loose in all the world.

Bidding Prayers

Celebrant   Coming together in faith, let us pray
for a deeper trustfulness among all Christian people, so that they may become more and more open to your will.

Reader   That love may make his home in the hearts of men all over the world.
Pause
Lord our Redeemer: **deepen our love.**

That every family may become filled with the life of Christ and know his joy.
Pause
Lord, our Redeemer: **deepen our love.**

For all expectant mothers,
for the children growing within them,
and for the babies being born today.
Pause
Lord, our Redeemer: **deepen our love.**

Celebrant   In thankfulness we ask you, Father, to hear our prayers, through Christ our Lord. **Amen.**

Ideas for Children

Journey to Bethlehem. The arrival at the stable. Preparing for a new baby – cot, warm sheets, blankets, clothes, clean water.

We are like stables for Jesus to come to, and we can get ourselves ready for him.

Act of Contrition

Lord Jesus, we are sorry for the hard,
sharp corners in our stable
when we are spiteful.
Please make us kind and
gentle with others.
Come, Lord Jesus, live in us now.
We are sorry for the coldness of our stable
when we are mean and unfriendly.
Please make us warm and generous.
Come, Lord Jesus, live in us now.
We are sorry for the dust and rubbish
in our stable
when we are selfish
and want things our own way.
Please make us thoughtful and caring.
Come, Lord Jesus, live in us now.

Planting bulbs

Bulbs are a lovely image of God's promise. They also show us that to be fulfilled, we have to do our part, too. Some Iron Age wheat grains were found in a jar recently, and, when planted, they grew! God's promise lasts for ever, but he needs us to provide ourselves for his love to grow and bear fruit.

Daffodil and crocus bulbs planted now will begin to flower in Spring ready to be a symbol of the resurrection. Or, if you have garden space, try planting some grains of wheat.

Music
Recorded Music

Fauré – *Pavane*

'Live' Music

For all the saints *(ONE, 146)*
Oh Lord, my God *(ONE, 404)*
Tell out my soul *(MSOS, 161)*
Thy hand, O God, has guided *(ONE, 572)*
Without seeing you *(SONL, 13)*

CHRISTMASTIDE

Questions for Discussion Groups
1. What are some of the biggest risks you have taken? Did they all work out as you hoped? What risks was God taking when he became incarnate?
2. Are there any ways that we could keep the Christmas spirit of goodwill going for longer than Boxing Day? Make some practical plans!

The Nativity of Our Lord (Midnight Mass)

Theme
Jesus, our Saviour, is born

The God who made the world confines himself willingly and generously within the form of man whom he has created. The humility of such an act is a measure of God's love for us.

Penitential Rite

In great humility you have come to us,
    Lord, have mercy. **Lord, have mercy.**

Naked and defenceless you have come to us,
    Christ, have mercy. **Christ, have mercy.**

Love without limit you have shown to us,
    Lord, have mercy. **Lord, have mercy.**

Notes on the Readings

Isaiah 9:2-7

Darkness is like blindness: you cannot see. It means insecurity and the fear of falling; it means losing your way and your confidence. Light changes all that. In light, you can see where you are going and where you have been; you can see what is wrong and what needs putting right; you can see how to avoid accidents and disasters.

Men journeyed many miles in darkness, knowing that they needed light, but unable to generate it themselves. When Jesus was born in that stable in Bethlehem, light was born. In Jesus, men would be able to see. By his brightness they would be guided towards becoming their true selves.

Titus 2:11-14

Through Christ, not only the people of Israel but the whole human race received light. In him we can discern areas of growth and areas of decay, of hope and progress, and of danger and annihilation. But he came to live among us out of uncompromising compassion, so acceptance of his light is entirely voluntary: he will never force himself on us, any more than his parents forced themselves on the inn.

Luke 2:1-14

If we accept that, in the stable near some inn at Bethlehem, the source and creator of all has chosen to come and meet us in our human darkness, showing us by his light the purpose and direction of our existence; if we really accept that the

Christ child is God himself – then our lives cannot remain dark. We are bound to be made new creatures, brighter as we open more and more of ourselves to his light.

There are still many who walk in darkness. Perhaps our sluggish examples have shown them that the light is such a faint, confusing flicker that it is of no value. Perhaps they have never yet met anyone who reflects it at all. Yet Christmas shows us, if we peer behind the tinsel and glitter, God's stunning capacity for complete and unconditional giving. God risked everything that first Christmas, among fallible, foolish, bigotted humanity. If we risk everything, in completely giving ourselves to him this Christmas, we shall be placing ourselves in the everlasting arms; surrounding ourselves with the everlasting light; for we have his promise – to be with us for ever.

Bidding Prayers

Celebrant   My brothers and sisters, let us pray.

Reader   That the joy and wonder of Christmas
may infuse our lives, so that the Good News
may be spread throughout the world.
Pause
Loving Father: **we come to adore.**

That all in authority
may be filled with the wisdom
and compassion of God.
Pause
Loving Father: **we come to adore.**

That the lonely, the rejected
and the isolated may have knowledge
and confirmation of God's
abiding warmth and love.
Pause
Loving Father: **we come to adore.**

That all families may be blessed
with his lasting joy.
Pause
Loving Father: **we come to adore.**

Celebrant   Father, in wonder and adoration we offer our
lives to you with and through the holy child
of Bethlehem. **Amen.**

Music
Recorded Music

Handel – *Messiah: the Hallelujah chorus*

'Live' Music

Open your ears, O Christian people *(ONE, 422)*
Praise the Lord! Ye heavens adore him *(ONE, 452)*
The light of Christ *(ONE, 529)*

The Nativity of Our Lord (Christmas Day)

Theme
Christ our Saviour is born

At a particular time in history, eternal God breaks into human existence to transform and redeem it. In the darkness of night, God's majestic glory becomes a vulnerable, new-born baby; Creator of all is entirely dependent on those he has created. Such is the measure of his infinite love.

Penitential Rite

This setting is particularly suitable for a family service where children are involved. It can be accompanied with triangles or handbells.

Ma-ker of all stars and light: Lord,   have   mer - cy;   Je-sus born that ho - ly night:

Christ,   have   mer - cy;   Spi - rit keep us shin-ing bright: Lord,   have   mer -   cy.

Notes on the Readings

Isaiah 52:7-10

We are apt to take for granted the wonders which are familiar. Yet what an amazing thing it is that we can travel many thousands of miles to a huge variety of countries, and still find groups of Christians with whom to worship. One of the thrills of travelling is the opportunity it gives to experience the universal spread of Christianity at first hand. Today we can rejoice at the way the Good News is reaching to all the ends of the earth, just as the prophet foretold. Of course there is still more work to be done, but let us remember sometimes to acknowledge with deep gratitude the work that has already been successfully accomplished.

Hebrews 1:1-6

Never before has God's intervention been so remarkably direct. Jesus is not just another fine prophet proclaiming God's word to the people; he is not only a good man and miracle-worker preparing the people's hearts to turn back to God. He is none other than God himself, and that is what makes Christmas, the celebration of his arrival, such a wonderfully exciting time.

John 1:1-18

John gives the proof of an eye witness: trustworthy people actually met the grace and truth of God himself in the man, Jesus. Living closely in his company, they began to realise that he was the promised Messiah, the Word or expression of God, present from the beginning of time and now physically present in their lifetime.

Our task as Christians is to make sure that the people we meet each day are brought into contact with this same person, Jesus, who now lives in and among us. When they have spent time in our company, people should feel they have been in touch with an unselfish, natural and responsive love which is unusually marked with grace and truth, and which beckons them to find out more about the Jesus Christ we claim to follow.

Bidding Prayers

Celebrant Gathered with the shepherds in the presence of Christ, let us pray.

Reader That the Church may worship and adore faithfully and courageously in every age,
drawing more and more to know Christ.
Pause
Hear us, Father: **make our will yours.**

That the world may recognise and believe that Jesus is truly the Son of God.
Pause
Hear us, Father: **make our will yours.**

That all those in physical, mental, emotional or spiritual need may be comforted.
Pause
Hear us, Father: **make our will yours.**

That in our celebrations today we may be sensitive to one another's needs, kind, helpful and full of gratitude.
Pause
Hear us, Father: **make our will yours.**

Celebrant Heavenly Father, accept these prayers and give us the strength and the will to walk in love, through Jesus Christ. **Amen.**

Church Decoration

Pillars can be decorated with banners on various aspects of Christmas done by different groups in the parish. If they are made of material and the decorations tacked on, they can be used again another year or at Easter. Possible themes are:

- Light of the world
- Prince of peace
- Love came down at Christmas
- Hail Mary, full of grace
- The Word was made flesh
- Gloria in excelsis Deo

Outside

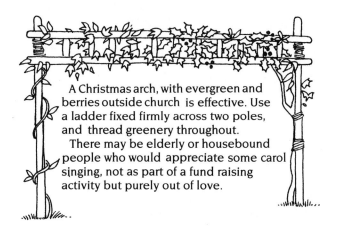

A Christmas arch, with evergreen and berries outside church is effective. Use a ladder fixed firmly across two poles, and thread greenery throughout.
There may be elderly or housebound people who would appreciate some carol singing, not as part of a fund raising activity but purely out of love.

Ideas for Children

Crib

One of the nicest things for children to do is construct their own crib which can either be displayed in the church or taken home. One simple but effective method is to start with a shoe box, stick straw on the roof and paint the inside walls wood or stone colour. The figures are made of plasticine or

self-hardening clay, in which case they can be painted. A star cut from gold card, attached to a lolly stick, is fixed above the stable.

The tray of a matchbox filled with straw makes the manger, and Jesus is wrapped in a thin strip of white material. Children are very good at devising little extras out of bits and pieces like toothpaste lids, silver foil, twigs, oddments of fur fabric and wool cloth etc.

If the cribs can be blessed the children can be encouraged to use them at home as a focal point for family prayers.

Church Crib

Think about who arranges the crib each year. It may be valuable for children to help, or for the figures to be placed during a carol on Christmas Eve. A free-standing altar could have the crib beneath it.

Music
Recorded Music

Britten – *Ceremony of Carols*

'Live' Music

Plenty of carols which the whole family can enjoy singing.

The Holy Family

Theme
At Christmas, Jesus became a member of a family

The holy family of Mary, Joseph and Jesus is an example and inspiration for all families. The qualities of mutual respect and understanding, affection and security which we see there are the qualities which provide the best conditions for children to grow and develop physically, emotionally and spiritually. The effects of a good, stable and accepting family life spread out into the whole of our society.

Penitential Rite

For our lack of love and respect for each other,
Lord, have mercy. **Lord, have mercy.**

For our trivial, unnecessary arguments,
Christ, have mercy. **Christ, have mercy.**

For the needs we have been blind to,
Lord, have mercy. **Lord, have mercy.**

Notes on the Readings

Ecclesiasticus 3:2-6, 12-14

When we are used to a welfare state, it is possible to forget the importance of the family code in Ecclesiasticus. But it actually goes far deeper than an insurance policy for old age. 'Familiarity breeding contempt' is always hovering just behind 'Relax, make yourself at home'. This passage reminds us of the courtesy and respect which oils the wheels of family relationships and suggests a certain amount of self control among family members, even though they know they will be accepted and loved no matter what they do.

Colossians 3:12-21

Paul's letter describes it as getting dressed in such 'habits' (clothes) as patience and kindness. The love, which holds everything together, is no sentimental sloppiness. This love is not shown by weakness or inconsistency. Rather, it is the love that Christ has shown to us: demanding, costly, firm and loyal; it is also rewarding, refreshing, full of fun and laughter, and able to sustain us through all the inevitable difficulties we face.

Luke 2:41-52

Jesus' own childhood was certainly not without problems. After all, he was born away from home and the family were refugees until he was a toddler. When they did get back to Nazareth, no doubt some of the villagers would have gossiped and drawn their own conclusions about his parents. And Luke's account of Jesus at twelve years old being left behind, his parents searching for him, desperately worried, gives us a glimpse of other special difficulties there may well have been in nurturing a child who was also God.

So it is not an absence of problems which marks out a Christian family from others. It is the way such problems are met; offered in love to God the ever lasting Father, accepted and used as an opportunity for growth in patience, unselfishness or compassion.

Bidding Prayers

Celebrant   My brothers and sisters in Christ, let us pray.

Reader   That we may open the door of our homes to welcome Jesus; that Christian families may be an example and a source of strength, a ministry of warmth and generosity.
Pause
God, our Father: **bless our homes.**

That our society may be based on mutual respect and understanding; on co-operation and care.
Pause
God, our Father: **bless our homes.**

For all our families who are suffering through poverty, sickness, separation or war; that God's presence may comfort and strengthen them.
Pause
God, our Father: **bless our homes.**

For our own families and loved ones, both living and departed.
Pause
God, our Father: **bless our homes.**

Celebrant   Father, we ask you to hear our prayers through Christ our Lord. **Amen.**

Ideas for Adults

Involve families:
- have the members of one family to lead the Bidding Prayers;
- have another family to process with the offertory gifts;
- perhaps there is one complete family which could play and sing a carol after the Communion.

Ideas for Children

Teachers and helpers show photographs of their families. Talk about each person in them being important.

Ask children to draw all the members of their own families (including pets if they wish). Write under the picture: 'God bless my family'.

Music
Recorded Music

Grieg – Peer Gynt Suite: Morning

'Live' Music

Once in Royal David's city (ONE, 414)
The bakerwoman (ONE, 517)
What child is this? (ONE, 605)

Solemnity of Mary, Mother of God

Theme
Through Mary, God was born as man

Mary is Christ's mother, and since we are, through grace, co-heirs with him, she is spiritually our mother too. Supported by her prayers and encouraged by her example we can be helped towards responding positively to God.

Penitential Rite

May we, like Mary, be receptive,
   Lord, have mercy. **Lord, have mercy.**

May we, like Mary, be obedient,
   Christ, have mercy. **Christ, have mercy.**

May we, like Mary, learn to trust you,
   Lord, have mercy. **Lord, have mercy.**

Notes on the Readings

Numbers 6:22-27

This blessing, suggested to Moses during one of his special times of communion with his Lord, reflects the close, affectionate relationship God has with his loved ones. Nothing is hidden and there is no pretence; with trustfulness and acceptance God, the parent, looks tenderly into the eyes, and the soul, of his child.

At one level such 'equality' seems ridiculous. How can we, with our ulterior motives, double standards and prejudices, ever be treated with such respect by the creator, who knows exactly what we are like at our worst as well as our best?

We may shake our heads in amazement, but the truth is that he really loves us – likes us, even! And he loves us into becoming people worthy of his love.

Galatians 4:4-7

That love is given very tangible form as the Christ develops from embryo to foetus, foetus to pucker-skinned baby in Mary's womb. Already we see hints of the obedience that would lead to the cross, for here the laws of nature are adhered to, and Jesus is born subject to the Law – truly one of us. All so that the reverse will be possible: we shall be enabled to become truly sons and daughters of God, our heavenly Father.

Luke 2:16-21

To Mary was given the responsibility of caring for the baby Christ. Hers was the privilege of feeding, cleaning, cuddling and soothing, which she undoubtedly sensed was a form of worship. The natural closeness between Jesus and his mother makes her close and special to us as well.

We can learn so much from her willing undertaking of God's will, her inner stillness and the total commitment of her love.

Bidding Prayers

Celebrant   As sons and daughters of our heavenly Father, let us pray for the Church and for the world.

Reader   That we may all be receptive to God's ideas and plans for us, and ready to carry them out.
Pause
Father, in your mercy: **hear our prayer.**

That people may look for the good in one another and know when to speak and when to stay silent.
Pause
Father, in your mercy: **hear our prayer.**

That all babies may be cared for with love and protected from danger.
Pause
Father, in your mercy: **hear our prayer.**

That in our homes there may be increased understanding of one another, and greater willingness to serve one another cheerfully.
Pause
Father, in your mercy: **hear our prayer.**

Celebrant   Heavenly Father, accept these prayers through the person of Jesus, our Saviour. **Amen.**

Ideas for Adults

Suggest that everyone uses the blessing from Numbers in daily prayers this week, in the knowledge that everyone else in the parish is praying it too.

Ideas for Children

Talk with the children about the excitement of having a new baby in the family, and all the jobs it involves. You could demonstate some of these with a doll, or, if a parish mother is willing, invite her in to bath her baby so the children can watch.

As they watch, help them to think of Mary looking after Jesus, and afterwards pray together to thank God for the care our parents give us, and for Mary's willingness to look after and bring up Jesus for us.

Music
Recorded Music

Brahms – *Lullaby*

'Live' Music

Holy Virgin, by God's decree *(ONE, 218)*
Mother of God's living Word *(ONE, 353)*
When Mary listened to God's Word *(ONE, 611)*

2nd Sunday after Christmas

Theme
The Word becomes flesh

In Christ's birth the eternal Word, present from before all time and all created things, breaks into the immediate human world. Through him, we are called to share in the vast plan of God's glory.

Penitential Rite

For all anguish and sorrow caused by sin,
    Lord, have mercy. **Lord, have mercy.**

For all physical wounds and suffering caused by sin,
    Christ, have mercy. **Christ, have mercy.**

For all abuse of our world's resources,
    Lord, have mercy. **Lord, have mercy.**

Notes on the Readings

Ecclesiasticus 24:1-2, 8-12

The whole purpose of God from the very beginning has been to make it possible for every person to become a member of the great, loving family of God; a child of the heavenly Father. The germ of this dynamic plan was sown in the creation of matter from formless void; it took root, like a seedling, in the chosen race of the people of Israel.

It is expressed here as the Wisdom of God, and the word embraces the idea of personality, and charismatic presence. Through the Old Testament we are able to track the developing process, as God's people are shown the mercy, loyalty, tenderness and purity of their God.

Ephesians 1:3-6, 15-18

Christ Jesus, by becoming man, living, dying and rising again, has broken down all the barriers that separated man from his creator, and enabled the next stage of God's plan to be accomplished. Through him we can all become children of God; not through any merit of our own, but through his sacrifice. He can lead us to a perception based on love that does not flinch. He can change our outlook until we see setbacks and problems as opportunities for growth; arguments as opportunities for reconciliations; social problems as chances to serve and befriend; life as a precious gift.

John 1:1-18

Jesus, the Word, is the expression of God's infinite and yet personal love. We, who have seen and known his love and its power in our lives, share the great privilege of spreading it throughout the whole world until the Word has come round in a full circle and the earth is filled with the glory of God as the waters cover the sea. As T.S. Eliot says in *Four Quartets*, 'In my end is my beginning'.

Bidding Prayers

Celebrant Full of thanks and praise, we come
        to worship God our Father
        for the earth is rich with his blessing;
        let us pray to him now.

Reader That the will of God may be accomplished
        in every life and every situation.
        Pause
        Father of the living word: **speak in our hearts.**

    That the world may be drawn into a
    deep, abiding love.
    Pause
    Father of the living word: **speak in our hearts.**

    For all those who are physically
    or mentally handicapped in any way,
    and for those who minister to them.
    Pause
    Father of the living word: **speak in our hearts.**

    That all of us here present may become
    more aware of the privileges and
    responsibilities of being
    the children of God.
    Pause
    Father of the living word: **speak in our hearts.**

Celebrant We ask this through Christ our Lord. **Amen.**

Ideas for Children

The children could present a simple nativity play or tableau, using a carol to accompany themselves.

Music
Recorded Music

Haydn – *Creation*
Sibelius – *Finlandia*

'Live' Music

Sing to our Father *(MSOS, 192)*
Something that we have seen *(SOS 3, 211)*
Song of Simeon *(SONL, 53)*

The Epiphany of the Lord

Theme
Jesus the Light is shown to the world

In fulfilment of old prophecies the promised Messiah is now revealed to all nations, symbolised by the three Wise Men. The offering of their gifts foreshadows the time when all nations will be drawn to acknowledge the omnipotence of God.

Penitential Rite

King of all kings, rule our hearts,
    Lord, have mercy. **Lord, have mercy.**

Mary's Son, yet God most high,
    Christ, have mercy. **Christ, have mercy.**

Light to scatter all our darkness,
    Lord, have mercy. **Lord, have mercy.**

Notes on the Readings

Isaiah 60:1-6

Dramatically the prophet describes the dawning of God's coming to his people, like the sunrise of a remarkably beautiful day. It will be the time of Israel's great mission to the world, for through her all nations will be brought to acknowledge and worship God.

Ephesians 3:2-3a, 5-6

It was some while before the literal meaning of such prophecies was understood. It was hard for many Jews to accept that through the dawning of Christ in the world pagans as well as themselves would be allowed to share in their special heritage. Now Paul, who had also had deep-seated misgivings originally, spends his life proclaiming the Good News to the Gentiles, for he realises that in Christ they are part of the same Body.

Matthew 2:1-12

The astrologers were inquisitive. The unusually bright star suggested a deeply significant cosmic event and they were prepared to go to great lengths and considerable hardship in order to unravel the mystery and be there when it all happened.

What the star actually led them to was quite unexpected. We might imagine that they would assume their calculations were wrong, and it was all a mistake. Instead, they were so convinced of the greatness of this young child in Bethlehem that they bowed down and worshipped him, offering their treasures as gifts to signify that, after this, their lives would never be the same again.

There are many different routes to Christ, and God is full of surprises. What we think we are looking for is often revealed in totally unexpected ways and in totally unexpected places. When this happens, it is not a time for doubt and rejection but a time for rejoicing and gratitude.

We have to be led forward a step at a time because we are not strong enough to cope with God's glory in larger quantities at first. We would not understand. Who knows – perhaps if the Wise Men had known what outwardly lay at the end of their journey, they may never have started at all. But in the journeying they were gradually prepared, so that by the time they reached the little house where Joseph and Mary and Jesus were living, their eyes could see more than the outward form: they recognised the presence of the Divine, and it fundamentally altered the priorities in their own lives.

Bidding Prayers

Celebrant   Let us pray to our heavenly Father who guides us.

Reader   That we may be ready to follow Christ wherever he leads us.
Pause
Lord of lords: **hear us, we pray.**

That all nations may rejoice in the light of goodness and reject the darkness of evil.
Pause
Lord of lords: **hear us, we pray.**

That in the brightness of love, Christ may be revealed, turning the doubtful to faith, the despairing to hope, and the revengeful to forgiveness.
Pause
Lord of lords: **hear us, we pray.**

That no opportunity may be lost in sharing the joy and peace of Christ with those we meet in our daily lives.
Pause
Lord of lords: **hear us, we pray.**

Celebrant   Father, we commend our lives to your loving care, through Christ our Lord. **Amen.**

Ideas for Adults

The Gospel can be acted out using a narrator, Herod, the scribes and the three Wise Men. An acolyte is the star who can lead the Wise Men in procession either to a group of the Holy Family, or to the church Crib. Costumes do not have to be elaborate. Cloaks, crowns, home-made scrolls to suggest characters are effective, but if Nativity costumes are readily available, why not make use of them here?

At the offertory, children dressed as the Magi with their servants can bring the gifts of bread, water and wine to the altar, led by an acolyte. If the Magi's caskets are large boxes, decorated by the children, they can be used during the collection, so that each person in church joins in the offering by the Wise Men.

Ideas for Children

The children may be taking part in the dramatised Gospel today in church. If not, the Gospel can be acted out in the children's teaching group. The figures of the Wise Men can be made to add to their Christmas Crib. Use plasticine, playdough or self-hardening clay. Alternatively, use cardboard tubes and scraps of material or wallpaper, wool and sequins etc. Here is the basic pattern:

Hand slit so present can slide in and out

Music
Recorded Music

Shostakovich – *Symphony No. 5: final movement*

'Live' Music

In you, my God *(ONE, 254)*
Lord of my life *(SONL, 21)*
Moses, I know you're the man *(ONE, 351)*
Our God reigns *(MSOS, 134, BSOS, 22)*
What child is this? *(ONE, 605)*

The Baptism of the Lord

Theme

Jesus is baptized by John, and the Holy Spirit confirms him as the chosen one

As Messiah, identifying with his people, Jesus receives the baptism of repentance, and as he does so, the Spirit of God descends upon him, showing him, beyond all doubt, that he is the promised Christ who is to save his people from their sins.

Penitential Rite

You alone can cleanse us from sin,
    Lord, have mercy. **Lord, have mercy.**

You alone can set us free,
    Christ, have mercy. **Christ, have mercy.**

You alone can make us new,
    Lord, have mercy. **Lord, have mercy.**

Notes on the Readings

Isaiah 40:1-5, 9-11

The comforting message of hope comes to a people weary with the results of sin in their lives, both individually and as a nation. With hindsight they can see how their breaking of the Covenant has caused the exile and misery in which they find themselves, and now in their distress they turn back to their God. He responds with the extraordinary mercy which is fundamental to his personality: his people are forgiven, comforted, and given fresh hope for the future.

Titus 2:11-14; 3:4-7

The way back from the exile of our sin is the way of Christ. Reborn in him at baptism we are empowered with his strength to resist temptation, strive for what is good, generous and loving, and live full of hope. Nothing is impossible for God, so no person or situation we encounter is beyond hope of redemption.

For it is not on account of any good deeds we do that we are saved; God saves us because of the great compassion he has for his 'creatures' – the beings he has created.

Luke 3:15-16, 21-22

For those with spiritual eyes open, the moment of Jesus' baptism reflects back through the landscape of ancient prophecies and the pulsing light of God's promise, from the misty distance of creation to this carpenter's son of Nazareth, standing on the river bed of Jordan. And the one most acutely spiritually aware was Jesus himself.

Having received confirmation in the Spirit so powerfully, Jesus withdraws to the silence of the hills where he meditates on what has happened and agonises over how his ministry is to be accomplished.

We are also given the Spirit of God which strengthens us for his service and enables us to do all things in Christ. But whenever we have the privilege of experiencing a particularly powerful awareness of God, we must not be surprised if it is followed by a particularly powerful temptation. We shall not be required to fight such battles single-handed; the Holy Spirit, the Comforter, is able to work in us and keep us faithful.

Bidding Prayers

Celebrant   My companions in Christ let us
            pray together.

Reader   That the Spirit of God
         will strengthen and uphold us
         as we try to live Christian lives.
         Pause
         Loving Father: **may your will be done.**

That all leaders and those in positions of power may understand the fundamental need for God's spirit of truth, peace and compassion.
Pause
Loving Father: **may your will be done.**

That any who are living under a burden of guilt may be led to complete repentance and find freedom and joy in God's forgiveness.
Pause
Loving Father: **may your will be done.**

That, being filled with the life of Christ, the quality and brightness of our lives may draw others into his love and peace.
Pause
Loving Father: **may your will be done.**

Celebrant   Father, confident in your love,
            we ask these things through
            Christ our Lord. **Amen.**

Ideas for Adults: Dance

To express the cleansing, life-giving properties of water.

You will need one group of six dancers and one group of three dancers.

1. A group of six dancers starts at the back of the church and moves up the aisle towards the altar. Each dancer holds a length of blue or green cloth or ribbon in each hand. They move in a line, one behind the other, in the following way:
   - one step forwards, raising arms forwards;
   - one step back, sweeping arms back;
   - turn on the spot to the right, arms outstretched;
   - repeat forwards;
   - repeat back;
   - turn on the spot to the left, arms outstretched.
   - When they arrive at the chancel they form a circle, continuing the forward-back-turn sequence until all dancers are in the circle.

2. Standing with feet apart, swing arms and body to the right, then to the left, four times, starting gently and gradually increasing the swing to give the effect of a rising wave.

3. In sequence, with leader beginning, go down on one knee as the arms swing in a circle up over the head and round to the floor. Then stand up. Repeated twice, this should make a continuous waving movement round the circle and it finishes with each dancer swirling on the spot, arms above the head.

4. The dancers form two lines of three, arms stretched in welcome, but constantly rising and falling like a sea.

5. Up the aisle come three dancers wrapped in dark cloaks with hoods (or lengths of dark material). They walk rhythmically and slowly, their heads and shoulders bowed, as if they are heavily burdened.

6. When they reach the water, they kneel down, covering their heads, in a triangle, and the water dancers stand round them in a circle.

7. They move arms backwards and then sweep them up and over forwards (rather like casting a line) so the ribbons should meet in the centre over the kneeling dancers. This is done slowly and deliberately three times.

8. The water dancers then kneel in their circle as the three others slowly stand up, their heads high and arms raised in joy. While they were kneeling, their cloaks were unfastened so that as they stand they are in white.

9. Turning together, they walk back down the aisle, upright and confident, leading the water dancers who are in two rows of three, moving in their forward-back-turn sequence.

Any waltz time music will work with this dance. Since its length will vary with the size of building used, a short melody which can be repeated as needed, may be best. If you use recorded music, try Mendelssohn – *Fingal's Cave*.

Ideas for Children

Have a collection of pictures of water, such as seas, streams, rain, baths and wash basins, vase of flowers, etc. Talk about how useful and important water is, and when we need it (even our bodies are mostly water).

Cut out the pictures and stick them on to a large poster which can be displayed in church, under the headings: 'Water makes things clean'. 'Water brings life'.

Show the picture of a baptism; some children may remember their own baptism or that of a relative. Ask if they can think why water is used. Let them refer to the water poster and see for themselves.

Tell the story of Jesus' baptism, using flannelgraph pictures.

Music
Recorded Music

Mendlessohn – *Fingal's Cave*

'Live' Music

If anyone is thirsty *(SOS 3, 252)*
Jesus, can I tell you? *(MSOS, 145; BSOS, 24)*
Oh, let all who thirst *(ONE, 400)*
Spirit of the Living God *(ONE, 501)*

LENT

Questions for Discussion Groups
1. Why do you think Jesus rejected the temptation to win followers through displays of supernatural power?
2. Are there any bad habits that we as individuals, as a parish and as a species need to get to grips with and eradicate?

Ash Wednesday

Theme
Be reconciled to God

We are to turn our backs on sin and reject it; we are to turn towards God and accept him. Lent is the time to take a long, hard look at our lives so that where necessary they can be re-shaped and re-directed. At baptism, turning towards God was begun, but our human sin and weakness means that we must constantly examine our consciences, repent and re-affirm our commitment to Christ.

Penitential Rite

This is expressed today by the distribution of ashes. During the distribution, as an alternative, or addition to the suggested psalms, Allegri's *Miserere* could be used.

Notes on the Readings

Joel 2:12-18

The two important marks of repentance expressed here are:
  – that it must be total and complete.
  – that the change of heart begins inside a person; outward forms are quite unable to replace this humbling of the spirit.

Nor is it entirely an individual matter: the prophet exhorts the whole people to join in a great communal act of penitence and at the same time assures them of God's profound tenderness and mercy.

2 Corinthians 5:20-6:2

Though without sin, Jesus identified completely with us and as a man, was even obedient to the point of death. So for his sake God freely pardons us if, in our lives, we identify with Jesus.

We do not need to wait any longer: the favourable time, the day of salvation, is now.

Matthew 6:1-6, 16-18

The Gospel scrapes away all the layers of traditional ritual which are in danger of superseding the vital business of a deep, inward contrition, generosity and humility.

It is this, rather than any outward show, which counts where God is concerned. That does not make giving or fasting easier; nor does it mean they are unnecessary or irrelevant. Rather, without the encouragement of admiration or image improvement, we are forced to ask ourselves why on earth we are bothering to do something which is not appreciated by anyone. How we answer will help us analyse our real position spiritually; it will only be worth bothering if we catch sight of the great gap between God's love and our mean response, and if we long for the gap to be narrowed.

Bidding Prayers

Celebrant   My brothers and sisters, let us use this season
of Lent for rich growth in the Spirit as we pray
for the Church and for the world.

Reader   That the Good News of God's salvation
may never be taken for granted
but accepted and shared
with thankfulness and joy.
Pause
Life-giving healer: **heal this world.**

That all countries
may have the courage to fight
against what is evil
and to nurture what is good
in an atmosphere of respect
and consideration for others.
Pause
Life-giving healer: **heal this world.**

For those whose lives have been
twisted and spoilt by sin;
that the lost and weary may turn to
the God of love for guidance and peace.
Pause
Life-giving healer: **heal this world.**

For all those living in this parish/city,
that we may use our gifts
in serving one another
and spreading the love of Jesus
throughout the world.
Pause
Life-giving healer: **heal this world.**

Celebrant   Father, we ask all these things
through Christ our Lord. **Amen.**

Ideas for Children

Prepare a LENT book, which will be added to week by week.

Explain that Lent comes from an old word meaning a lengthening of days. They will probably notice the gradual lengthening of daylight. Link this with all the new growth around them.

Look and see if any shoots are showing on their Advent bulbs. Or perhaps they have seen a snowdrop or crocus.

On the cover put a title:

Lord Jesus, may these
LONGER DAYS
become our
GROWING DAYS.

From green plastic (a carrier bag, for instance) cut full grown plants. Also cut coloured card pots. Staple pots on the cover, and tuck in plant, leaving just the top showing. Then the plants can be made to 'grow'.

Music
Recorded Music

Lloyd Webber – *Requiem: Pie Jesu*

'Live' Music

Alleluia for forgiveness *(SONL, 18)*
By the waters of Babylon *(ONE, 77)*
God forgave my sin *(ONE, 175)*

1st Sunday of Lent

Theme
Everyone who turns to Christ can be saved

However difficult, troubled or hopeless our lives may seem, God will listen to our distress and he alone has the will and the power to lead us to inward peace and richness. If we trust completely in the risen Christ, then in his strength we will have strength to overcome every temptation.

Penitential Rite

Come, Spirit, come on page 214.

Notes on the Readings

Deuteronomy 26:4-10

The people of Israel are reminded here that, during their hardship and suffering in Egypt, God heard them and acted powerfully to rescue them. It is only right that they should acknowledge this by an annual thanksgiving and harvest offering.

Romans 10:8-13

Paul reminds the Christians in Rome that a heartfelt conviction is bound to lead on to an acclamation of faith, and both are important. Nor is any person excluded from God's saving love: anyone of any colour and any race can approach God and will not be turned away.

Luke 4:1-13

It is important to remember that during the fast in the wilderness, Jesus was not only divine but also fully human, so the temptations were excruciatingly real and just as hard to resist as the temptations which face us all. As so often happens, they were couched in such a way that falling into the trap could be rationalised and even appear justifiable.

First, Jesus was experiencing the vulnerability and weakness of the physical body, which craved food. He knew he was entrusted with great power, and at the same time, he was in great need. Surely it would be sensible to use just a little of that power to alleviate physical suffering?

And then there was the desire to draw all men to God. Perhaps, after all, being a kind of Superman might be one way of attracting all those people who wouldn't be interested in things like humility, patience or repentance.

Then there was the urgency of his work; having only a lifetime, if that, to save God's people, perhaps a ministry of worldly power and influence might be quicker.

How, then, did he manage, as man, to resist such temptations? He was able to resist them because he was never, at any point, separated from the power of God.

Penitential Rite

1. Come, Spi- rit, come, prise op- en my heart. Where it is hurt, let heal- ing start. Cor- ners I keep well hid- den from your view. I now sur- ren- der, Lord, my God, to you.

2. Come, Spirit, come, take charge of my mind.
Show me the darkness that you find.
Help me to trust you, even with my shame,
till I freely acknowledge where I am to blame.

3. Come, Spirit, come, bring life to my soul.
Your forgiveness makes me whole.
Then from the pain and stress of sin set free
I am dazed by the awesome love you have for me.

The temptations were aimed at his humanity; strength and victory came from the Father. We are made co-heirs with Christ, which puts us in the same position. The weakness of our humanity will often be threatened and tempted. But our access to God's almighty power means that in Christ we shall have the necessary strength to cope with whatever happens to us. We have to fix ourselves in his life, and trust him.

Bidding Prayers

Celebrant My brothers and sisters, as we come together trusting in God's promises, let us pray.

Reader For all bishops,
priests and deacons,
and especially those persecuted
for their faith,
that nothing may prevent or
dissuade the Church
from upholding and proclaiming
the full truth of God's love.
Pause
Lord, our refuge: **you are our strength.**

For our local and national leaders,
that whenever feelings run high
God will guide them
to see where the way of justice
and integrity lies.
Pause
Lord, our refuge: **you are our strength.**

For those who are struggling
against temptation of any kind,
that they may be comforted by
the nearness of Jesus
and given the strength to resist

and overcome evil.
Pause
Lord, our refuge: **you are our strength.**

For those of this parish
who are preparing for the priesthood,
for lay ministry, for baptism,
that their hearts and minds may be filled
with the light and understanding
which comes from God.
Pause
Lord, our refuge: **you are our strength.**

Celebrant Father, we offer you our prayers in trust and love. Through Jesus Christ our Lord. **Amen.**

Ideas for Children

Try to show that the easy ways are not always the best or most effective ways of doing something.

a. Have two pictures of bread. One teacher tears one picture out ('I need to stick it on a poster and tearing is quicker'). The other cuts it carefully ('it took longer but it was much better').

b. Nana's birthday. Two brothers – one makes a card himself, the other asks Mum to buy him one. It may be very smart, and the homemade one may be a bit gluey, but which shows most love? Jesus was tempted three times:

'Use your power
to make bread'– *be selfish;*

'I'll give you the world so long
as you worship ME'– *take the easy way out;*

'Jump off the temple to
show them your power'– *show off.*

Instead, Jesus said 'No, I'll do it God's way – the hard, good way of love.'

Music
Recorded Music

Raga Bilashkhani Todi
or any sitar/sarod music with a similarly dignified grandeur, tinged with sorrow.

'Live' Music

Be with me, Lord *(SOS 3, 257)*
Forty days and forty nights *(ONE, 150)*
Loving you gently, Lord *(MSOS, 117; BSOS, 12)*
Oh, the Word of my Lord *(ONE, 431)*
When Israel *(ONE, 609)*

2nd Sunday of Lent

Theme
Faithfulness

Abram's faith in God's promise was rewarded and fulfilled. At the Transfiguration, the disciples saw the brightness of God's glory. If we have faith in him, our lives can be transfigured and infused with his brightness.

Penitential Rite

1. Teach me, Lord, to trust you. Train me, Lord, to see even where the path is dark-est you are guid-ing me.

2. Teach me, Lord, to trust you.
   Train me to be still,
   resting on your love with patience,
   open to your will.

3. Teach me, Lord, to trust you,
   so that I may grow
   deeply rooted by the stream
   where living waters flow.

Notes on the Readings

Genesis 15:5-12, 17-18

The act of sacrifice liberated the blood, and therefore the life, of the animal. So, in a legal sense, if two parties went between the two halves of a sacrificed animal, a profound, unbreakable bond had been made between them, uniting them by the consecrated life blood.

Here, it is only God who passes between the halves; man is in no way equal to him, and it is only God's freely given grace which enables man to participate in the covenant: even faith itself is not something we can achieve on our own but something that God gives and we receive. However, in accepting, we relinquish our desire to be independent, so we are giving God ourselves. This, then, is the only thing we can actually give God; it is also the only thing he wants from us.

Philippians 3:17; 4:1

So Paul urges his followers to remain faithful in this great hope of being made new in Christ, in such a way that priorities are changed, and nothing is anywhere near as important as our relationship with the powerful, almighty and faithful God.

Luke 9:28-36

This great transfiguring power of God was seen by the disciples as Jesus prayed on the mountain. It was beyond their understanding; but it must have remained, simmering in their minds, all through the humiliating crucifixion, till it burst out at the resurrection in an excited realisation that God had fulfilled his side of the promise, and any man who was prepared to accept that promise could now be assured of an eventual transfiguration such as they had once witnessed. God, in Jesus, had proved it would happen.

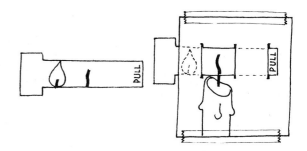

Bidding Prayers

Celebrant   In faith, knowing that where two or three are gathered in Jesus' name, God will grant their requests, let us pray.

Reader   For the Church,
that all priests may be given insight
and understanding to lead their people
into the light of God's truth.
Pause
Lord, we believe: **help our unbelief.**

For all councils, committees
and conferences, that a spirit of integrity
may underlie all discussion
and a desire for goodness inspire
all decisions.
Pause
Lord, we believe: **help our unbelief.**

For those in pain and distress,
physically, emotionally, or spiritually,
that they may hold to God
through all the bad times,
trusting in his love which never fails.
Pause
Lord, we believe: **help our unbelief.**

For all families,
especially those who have troubles,
that they may not be damaged
through their suffering,
but rather grow in compassion
and understanding.
Pause
Lord, we believe: **help our unbelief.**

Celebrant   Father, we ask this through Christ our Lord. **Amen.**

Ideas for Children

Tell the story of *the transfiguration*. This works well on tape with music in the background as Jesus is transfigured. Alternatively, have a guitar playing, or taped music while the story is told.

Have the children sitting in a circle round a table with a white candle on it. Have the candle lit as Jesus is transfigured, and blown out when the cloud passes over and only Jesus is left.

Give each child a candle (unlit). Show how one light can light all of these. In the same way, we can all be lit by Jesus.

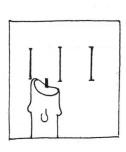

Give out squares of paper with candle drawn on and slits above.
Ask children to colour the candle and the flame and wick. Pull to make candle burn. Stick into books with a strip of sellotape top and bottom. Above it write: 'The bright love of Jesus can light my life.'

Music
Recorded Music

Vivaldi – *Gloria*

'Live' Music

O the love of my Lord *(ONE, 430)*
We behold the splendour of God *(ONE, 587)*
Without seeing you *(SONL, 13)*

3rd Sunday of Lent

Theme
Man's weakness; God's mercy

When we are truly sorry God always forgives us. If we try to excuse our weaknesses, he will give us every chance to change; but if we persist in evil, we cannot expect him to forgive us. We must neither presume on God's forgiveness by living carelessly, nor doubt it by living in despair.

Penitential Rite

For our constant excuses,
   Lord, have mercy. **Lord, have mercy.**

For our grudging forgiveness,
   Christ, have mercy. **Christ, have mercy.**

For our grumbling and complaining,
   Lord, have mercy. **Lord, have mercy.**

Notes on the Readings

Exodus 3:1-7, 13-15

When God calls Moses to act for him, Moses feels utterly inadequate and unsuitable: working in his own strength he would be inadequate and unsuitable. But God has other ideas. Moses will be the instrument of God's almighty power.

1 Corinthians 10:1-6, 10-12

God is always faithful and keeps his promise, so the Israelites were freed from bondage. But although they all witnessed the same wonderful and sustaining power, many of them were disobedient, easily upset, greedy and selfish. Often this led to death. It seems to remind us never to take God for granted.

Luke 13:1-9

Jesus is concerned to answer the perennial question 'Why should this happen to them? What have they done wrong?' He stresses that accidents and sufferings are not a direct punishment for evil people. Far from it – the casualties are no more guilty than those who escaped. Yet at the same time, in a sense all of us deserve accidents and suffering, for we are all guilty, and if we don't repent, there is just no reason why God shouldn't uproot us and throw us away.

Think of all the fruit we don't produce, all the help we excuse ourselves from offering; all the time we are too busy to give; all the love we are too 'committed' to share; all the mercy we are too strict to administer.

But Jesus does not give up on us. He digs us round, prunes us, puts manure round our roots – he does everything possible to bring us to our senses.

If it works, we acknowledge to him, and ourselves, all that is ugly, mean and selfish in us, and he will begin painstakingly to make us new creatures in his love. If it doesn't work, and we never bear fruit, then we have only ourselves to blame for whatever misery our lives produce.

Bidding Prayers

Celebrant Trusting not in our weakness
but in God's mercy, let us pray.

Reader For all God's people
that our self discipline during Lent
may make us spiritually stronger.
Pause
Lord of mercy: **hear us, we pray.**

For all builders, construction workers
and engineers
and all who work with machinery,
that all energy and power may be
used for good.
Pause
Lord of mercy: **hear us, we pray.**

For the mentally and physically
handicapped;
those injured or disabled in any way,
that they may be supported
and encouraged
through their pain and frustration.
Pause
Lord of mercy: **hear us, we pray.**

For those who are in any way persecuted
in mind, body or spirit,
that they may be given the grace
to persevere by the life and example
of our Lord Jesus Christ.
Pause
Lord of mercy: **hear us, we pray.**

Celebrant Merciful Father, accept these
prayers through Christ our Lord. **Amen.**

Ideas for Children

Read *Food in the Desert* (Palm Tree Bible Stories) to them, which shows how the people grumbled and had to learn to trust God.

Have a poster with slots in it. Each slot has a weed inside. Children each take out a weed and replace with a lovely flower picture. Heading of poster 'Lent is a time for Growing'.

Music
Recorded Music

Mendelssohn – *Song without words* Op. 30 No. 3
(available played on guitar by Segovia)

'Live' Music

From the depths of sin and sadness *(ONE, 155)*
God forgave my sin (Freely, freely) *(ONE, 175)*
If we only seek peace *(SONL, 76)*
Lord, when I turn my back on you *(SONL, 40)*
Make me a channel of your peace *(ONE, 342)*
On days when much we do goes wrong *(SONL, 68)*

4th Sunday of Lent

Theme
Reconciliation

God loves his people and leads them. He loves us so much that in order to reconcile us to himself, he is prepared to give everything, even to the point of becoming man and dying for us. Our job is to spread the joy of being reconciled to God through Christ; not begrudging, but delighting in others as they too find the peace and joy of salvation.

Penitential Rite

Use the song: *Many times I have turned from the way of the Lord.*
(ONE, 344)

Notes on the Readings

Joshua 5:9-12

The first thing the Israelites do on reaching the Promised Land at last, is to re-dedicate themselves to God by the act of celebrating the Passover. Theirs has been no ordinary escape, but a participation in an act of God, whose power and faithfulness they acknowledge.

2 Corinthians 5:17-21

God's liberating force did not end at Egypt. He has even chosen, out of love, to liberate us from evil, a seemingly impossible task, only made possible by the humility and obedience of Christ in becoming man. Since we are the ones who actually know that reconciliation to be true, we are entrusted with the work of spreading the life-shaking news to others.

How should we do this? Words? Actions? The way we react to suffering/cruelty/criticism? Do we act as Christ's ambassadors?

Luke 15:1-3, 11-32

If we feel sorry for the elder brother, we must remember the circumstances in which Jesus told his parable. The Pharisees and Scribes were not wicked men. They had remained faithful through the centuries of history and obeyed the Law minutely. Similarly the elder brother had remained as a good and trustworthy member of his father's house. The trouble is that in our human weakness, we tend to become jealous of our positions, and instead of being delighted when newcomers discover what we have known for years, we are tempted to stand on what we feel are our privileges and rights.

Living in Christ turns this upside down. For if what we delight in is a state in which all men are reconciled to God in one great Kingdom of love, then, when others accept Christ, we will be so thrilled that we'll be feasting and welcoming for all we're worth!

'Thy Kingdom come', we pray. Do we really want the Kingdom of God enough?

Bidding Prayers

Celebrant   While we are still far off from God our Father, he comes to welcome us and so we pray.

Reader   For all lapsed Christians;
for all who have lost their faith,
that they may return to God
and find him ready to welcome them home.
Pause
Father of love: **let your Kingdom come.**

For all who have been made redundant,
all unemployed,
all whose work is unhealthy or dangerous,
that we may strive to uphold each person's dignity and ease each person's burden.
Pause
Father of love: **let your Kingdom come.**

For the rejected and the homeless,
for those dependent on drugs and alcohol;
for those who have become bitter and
twisted or hard and mean,
that the generous warmth of God's love
will work within them
to thaw what is frozen, strengthen
what is weak, heal what is hurt
and repair what is damaged.
Pause
Father of love: **let your Kingdom come.**

For our homes,
that they may spread the Good News
of Christ's redeeming love by the way
they reflect his peace,
his understanding and his joy.
Pause
Father of love: **let your Kingdom come.**

Celebrant   Father, hear our prayers, through Christ our Lord. **Amen.**

Ideas for Children

The prodigal son is a lovely story to act out. Have a large assortment of dressing up clothes available (curtains, net, lengths of material, old ties and towels etc.)

Tell the children the story, showing pictures of the son:

(a) asking for money;
(b) waving goodbye;
(c) spending it all;
(d) as a pig keeper;
(e) returning home with Father's welcome.

The elder brother can be omitted with younger children, as there is plenty for them to grasp without it, and it may make the lesson too complicated.

(f) Angry brother with Father explaining.

Having given parts (plenty can be servants, girl friends and pigs) read the story bit by bit while the children act it out.

The value of this type of drama is in the involvement, rather than the standard of performance, so suggest what the characters might say as you go along.

Music
Recorded Music

Brahms – *Piano Concerto No. 2: third movement (Piu Adagio)*

'Live' Music

Glorify the Lord *(SONL, 17)* (use as responsorial psalm)
Let there be love *(SOS 3, 282)*
Many times have I turned *(ONE, 344)*
Oh Lord, all the world belongs to you *(ONE, 403)*

5th Sunday of Lent

Theme
God wipes out sin

Nothing in life stands still; everything either develops or decays. In Christ we can develop and go forwards because we are constantly being re-made by him. When he forgives us, our sin is completely cancelled and we are freed from its prison. Against this gift, all worldly riches pale into insignificance, and we can joyfully press on with the work of our Lord – establishing the Kingdom of Heaven on earth.

Penitential Rite

See music on page 219.

Penitential Rite

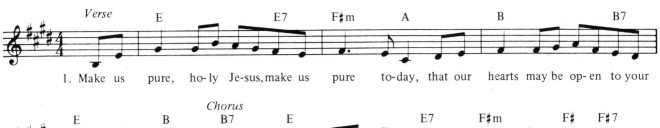

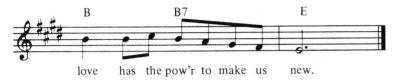

2. Make us good, holy Jesus, make us good, we pray,
   till the weight of our sinfulness is lifted away:

Notes on the Readings

Isaiah 43:16-21

Having failed to keep God's law, and having suffered in exile as a result, the people are given this consoling, refreshing prophecy. The punishment is to end for the sin has been forgiven. They have been freed from guilt and can now look forward with hope and joy.

Philippians 3:8-14

Paul has realised that his own efforts, however determined, will never be able to provide the lasting joy and peace which Christ offers, so nothing else is worth striving for.

Although living for Christ may well mean physical and spiritual hardship – even agony – it is worth every drop of suffering because the reward is so great. And the closer we get to being Christ-like, the more joy we shall find, and the more thankful we shall become.

John 8:1-11

We are now shown an illustration of God's forgiveness in the episode of the woman taken in adultery. She was dragged by the indignant crowd before this new teacher, and she stood in front of him as a convicted person, condemned already to death by stoning according to the law. Jesus does not excuse her, nor does he pretend she has done nothing wrong. He quietly and shrewdly points out to the crowd that all stand condemned by the law, for all have sinned. (Notice how it is the oldest member who is the first to realise this!)

When everyone has gone, Jesus 'redeems' the woman from her conviction and wipes out the sin of her past. Now she is free and told not to sin again in the future: before her is a completely new life.

To have her death sentence removed must have been wonderful enough; but to have her guilt and sin removed at the same time must have been utterly overwhelming.

Bidding Prayers

Celebrant Let us thank God for his priceless gift of forgiveness and lay before him our needs and cares as we pray.

Reader For all Christians worshipping God today in the country and in the towns and cities; simply or elaborately; in small groups or in vast crowds.
Pause
Lord bless them: **keep them in your love.**

For all world and national leaders, especially (use first names of Presidents, Monarchs, etc.)
Pause
Lord bless them: **keep them in your love.**

For the chronically ill, the disabled . . . the weak and the dying, especially (mention by name).
Pause
Lord bless them: **keep them in your love.**

For those either side of us here, our own families, our next door neighbours.
Pause
Lord bless them: **keep them in your love.**

Celebrant Father, help us to follow your example of forgiveness, and to love others as you love us. Through Christ our Lord. **Amen.**

Ideas for Children

Have a blackboard, coloured chalks, and an effective board rubber. Have an old dirty sack or bag labelled SINS in nasty looking letters. Inside have separate cards – jagged and irregular, on which are written:

- telling lies;
- stealing;
- pushing someone over;
- spoiling someone's toys;
  etc.

Ask one child to scatter them all around, and each picks one up. Each is written on the blackboard.

Explain how Jesus can wipe them right out, if we are really sorry. (Now rub them out.) How do we show we are sorry?

Stick cartoon in Lent book and colour in.

Music
Recorded Music

Mozart – *Flute and Harp Concerto in C major K.299: second movement*

'Live' Music

A new commandment *(ONE, 39)*
Love divine, all loves excelling *(ONE, 337)*
Our hearts were made for you *(SOS 3, 241)*
Seek ye first *(ONE, 473)*

HOLY WEEK

Passion Sunday (Palm Sunday)

Theme
Jesus of Nazareth is our Lord and King

As Prince of Peace, Jesus enters Jerusalem, and the people acclaim him as Lord. At the heart of our rejoicing is the pain of what he is bound to suffer in redeeming us through unflinching love.

Yet we still certainly rejoice, for we know him to have won the victory; he is our everlasting Lord and King.

Penitential Rite

We have failed to recognise you,
   Lord, have mercy. **Lord, have mercy.**

We have failed to honour you,
   Christ, have mercy. **Christ, have mercy.**

We have failed to follow you,
   Lord, have mercy. **Lord, have mercy.**

Notes on the Readings

Isaiah 50:4-7

Jesus, suffering and allowing himself to be abused, fulfils the role of the suffering servant, prophesied in Isaiah, who would become the means of salvation. Costly and full of agony, it is undergirded with the conviction that nothing is in vain.

Philippians 2:6-11

Paul reminds us of just how costly the sacrifice was. All-powerful God relinquished everything and accepted more humility than we could ever envisage, in order to save those for whom he had an undying love – us.

Luke 22:14 – 23:56

As the story of the human details unwinds, we witness not just an emotive drama, but the cosmic conjunction of God and man which radically and irrevocably alters all that ever was and all that ever will be.

Bidding Prayers

Celebrant   As we gather here, remembering the triumphal entry into Jerusalem, let us pray.

Reader   For Christians all over the world, especially those persecuted for their faith.
   Pause
   Lord, uphold them: **give them your strength.**

   For all rallies, mass meetings and congresses,
   that they may be guided and enlightened by the Spirit of Jesus.
   Pause
   Lord, uphold them: **give them your strength.**

For the crowded refugee camps,
and the shelters for the homeless,
that Christ's love may work within them
to heal, comfort and restore.
Pause
Lord, uphold them: **give them your strength.**

For this congregation
and all others in this town/city
that they may be so infused
with the life of Christ,
that others will be drawn
to his saving joy and peace.
Pause
Lord, uphold them: **give them your strength.**

Celebrant   Father, may we praise you not only with
our voices but in the lives we lead.
We ask this through Christ our Lord. **Amen.**

Church Decoration

A triumphal archway, made with ladders, could be erected outside the church and filled with branches and leaves. One floral arrangement in church could be based on dead wood or bark, from which Spring flowers are bursting, as a symbol of Christ's saving work through death.

Ideas for Children

If possible, all children should be able to take part in the *Procession of Palms*. In some churches a real donkey can be included. The excitement of participating and rejoicing is far better learnt from direct experience.

Try making a *Holy Week frieze* if time permits. The background is already drawn on, with mountains, Jerusalem, Golgotha and the tomb.

Tell the story today of the entry into Jerusalem. Ask each child to draw himself, colour and cut out. Stick all figures on around Jesus, together with tiny sprigs of leaves. This could be displayed in church.
Music for children – *Give me joy in my heart* (ONE, 159).

Music
Recorded Music

During the procession:
Pierre Attaignant – *Gaillarde*

'Live' Music

All Glory, laud and honour *(ONE, 19)*
How lovely on the mountains *(ONE, 233)*
Majesty, worship his majesty *(SOS 3, 232)*
Ride on! Ride on in majesty *(ONE, 465)*
We cry, 'Hosanna, Lord' *(ONE, 592)*

Holy Thursday

Theme
Christ fills the Passover with new meaning

God's lasting covenant with his people had always been celebrated as giving them freedom from slavery in Egypt. Now, in Jesus' institution of the eucharistic sacrament, there is a new covenant – God's promise to give us freedom from the slavery of sin.

The essence of the covenant is loving service, which Jesus shows by example when he, the master, washes his servants' feet. If we are to follow him, we too must freely and joyfully expend our lives in the service of the world.

Penitential Rite

We have not loved deeply enough,
Lord, have mercy. **Lord, have mercy.**

We have not been caring enough,
Christ, have mercy. **Christ, have mercy.**

We have not served generously enough,
Lord, have mercy. **Lord, have mercy.**

Notes on the Readings

Exodus 12:1-8, 11-14

The instructions given to the people of Israel emphasise the sense of urgency in looking forward to a new life in the promised land; it is to be a sacrificial meal, celebrated as a festival; and it will mark the promise God has made with his people to give them liberation.

1 Corinthians 11:23-26

Paul describes Jesus' acts at the Passover supper, showing how the bread and the wine are given new and mystical meaning. In this new Passover, Jesus himself offers and is the sacrifice; his death will bring us liberation from all sin – it will bring us life.

John 13:1-15

The washing of the disciples' feet shows how Christ's love turns upside down the worldly structures of rights and privileges. This love means relinquishing everything, even our self-images which we cherish, in the business of serving others solely for love. Impossible? Yes, utterly impossible unless, by dying with Christ, we also live with him. In the eucharist which he has supplied, knowing our weakness, we are able to become one with him and share his life of love.

Bidding Prayers

Celebrant   Filled with deep thankfulness and joy
for God's love to us, let us pray.

Reader   For all priests and ordinands
that each may be true to his calling,
open to God's will
and ready to serve Christ in his Church.
Pause
Father of mercy: **free us from sin.**

For the Jews, celebrating Passover,
that they may be drawn to see
their rich heritage fulfilled and
accomplished in Jesus.
Pause
Father of mercy: **free us from sin.**

For all who are imprisoned
physically or mentally;
for those who are desperately in need
of care and service.
Pause
Father of mercy: **free us from sin.**

For our own community here,
that we may be alive to the needs
and ready to help.
Pause
Father of mercy: **free us from sin.**

Celebrant   Lord, following the example of
your humility and love,
may we be freed from selfishness
and learn to give ourselves
in loving service,
through Christ our Lord. **Amen.**

Ideas for Children

You may wish to continue the frieze, showing through a window in Jerusalem the Last Supper. Otherwise let the children share this moving celebration of the Supper with the adults. Some of the children could be involved in the washing of feet ceremony.

Music
Recorded Music

William Byrd – *Ave, Verum Corpus*

'Live' Music

Come and be filled *(SONL, 59)*
Love is his word *(ONE, 338)*
Take this bread *(SONL, 57)*
This bread we break *(SONL, 80)*
This is my body *(SONL, 66)*
This is my body *(ONE, 556)*
This is the bread *(ONE, 559)*

Good Friday

Theme
Jesus lays down his life for us

Christ's great love does not even draw back from the act of death, a death in which the shame and guilt of the whole world was carried by one who was entirely innocent and sinless. Through that total sacrifice God redeems, or buys back, his lost people. If we are grafted on to him we too shall be able to give our lives away in service and receive through him the victory of abundant, everlasting life.

Notes on the Readings

Isaiah 52:13-53:12
Hebrews 4:14-16; 5:7-9
John 18:1-19:42

The 'suffering servant' in Isaiah suddenly takes on new and poignant significance, as Jesus, collecting to himself all the sin of humanity, undergoes such suffering and humiliation. Yet through that searing pain and wounding of body and spirit, Christ is obedient and thus triumphant, enabling all who place their trust in him to be saved from sin and death and brought through to eternal life.

Ideas for Children

Older children can participate in the events of Good Friday through today's liturgy, with all its solemn drama. But for younger children, this may be too disturbing or distressing. They can still follow the Way of the Cross, but at their own level, during a one or two hour session. You might like to call this 'Children at the Cross'. It needs careful planning, especially where large numbers are involved. Split the time into several sections, and have a drink and hot cross buns half way through. A possible programme might be:

10.00 a.m.   Introduction with brief talk (*What happened on Good Friday*), prayer and a song. Some Stations of the Cross may be used.

10.25 a.m.   Begin activities

10.45 a.m.   Break; drink and hot cross bun

11.00 a.m.   Resume and complete activities

11.20 a.m.   Gather for short litany, and a song and blessing

11.30 a.m.   End

Possible activities could be:

a. completing the Holy Week frieze with the crowd, the crosses and the tomb;

b. making a smaller banner for taking home. Have background material already stitched, and figure shapes out of felt. The children assemble it with glue, and thread two sticks through top and bottom, with a piece of wool to hang it up. These could perhaps be blessed at the end.

c. a standing cross could be made from wood. Have ready the base blocks and cross pieces. The children sand the wood down, glue and nail together and varnish. N.B. Very careful supervision necessary!

d. Blow eggs (pierce both ends with a needle, and blow contents into a bowl). Then decorate on them a cross made of flowers, coloured with felt tip pens. Use this as a symbol of Christ's death bringing new life. Make a holder for the egg from a small box covered and stuck with coloured paper, and filled with cotton wool.

The atmosphere should be calm and quiet, with the activities being looked on as part of their worship.

Music
Recorded Music

Mahler – *Symphony No. 5: Adagietto*

'Live' Music

Come to Jesus *(SONL, 83)*
I see your hands and your side *(SONL, 61)*
My people *(SONL, 85)*
Take up your cross *(SONL, 42)*

EASTER

Questions for Discussion Groups
1. Why is belief in the resurrection central in the Christian faith? What did the empty tomb signify?
2. Have you been surprised by the methods God is using to make you 'new'? Why does he never merely patch up?

Holy Saturday
The Easter Vigil

Theme
The night of Resurrection

According to his promise, and in accomplishment of his great, saving work, Christ passes through death into new and everlasting life. And we can share that life as, in baptism, we die to sin and rise to a new existence, powered and charged with his Spirit.

Liturgy

This night is the most significant and important in the whole liturgical year; the central point of Christianity and the focus of all the Church's belief and teaching. The worship therefore deserves particular thought and planning, worthy of such a great and special occasion.

The liturgy provides an abundance of powerful symbolism which can heighten our understanding of the paschal mystery we are celebrating. It is worth using these symbols to the full, so that they are caught and experienced by the whole community.

Take fire and candles, for instance. A good bonfire is too good a symbol to miss, and its significance will be highlighted if everyone also physically moves from darkness into the light and participates in spreading the light from one to another; the water, too, should not only be seen but also felt, in a really thorough sprinkling!

If a bonfire is impossible, one idea is to close off an inner porch, fill it full of incense, and then open the doors and light the paschal candle as the incense billows out.

Readings

The Liturgy of the Word gives a selection of readings, starting with creation, the law and the prophets and culminating in the risen Christ; all chosen to lead us to a deeper understanding of the resurrection. (Originally Christians spent the entire night in vigil, meditating on such texts.)

Since all pastoral needs vary, it is wise to choose readings which are most likely to 'speak' effectively to your particular parish community. The presentation of chosen readings can be varied and imaginative so as to reinforce their meaning.

A set of 'creation' slides, showing the wonders of God's world, may accompany the Creation reading, and taped music, used with sensitivity, can heighten perception here.

One or two readings may be dramatised, using voice groupings of men and women with some solos. Others may be heard as songs based on specific texts, such as 'As earth that is dry' (*Songs of New Life*) for Isaiah 55; and 'I will sing' (*Hymns Old and New*) flows on naturally from the Exodus 15 reading.

Since Lent has been a time for spiritual preparation, it could also be used beneficially for practical preparation; in learning a particular new song, mime or dance, for instance, to become part of the great Easter celebration.

The Easter Vigil is a tremendous opportunity for a reverent but joyful gathering of the whole parish, with all its gifts and energies being offered as worship.

Notes on the Readings

Genesis 1:1-2:2
Genesis 22:1-18
Exodus 14:15-15:1
Isaiah 54:5-14
Isaiah 55:1-11
Baruch 3:9-15, 32-4:4
Ezekiel 36:16-28

In this series of readings we trace the abiding love and faithfulness of God shown to his people since the very beginning. He has provided for them, saved them, comforted them and never forsaken them, in spite of all their waywardness and sin. Neither will he ever forsake us, for not only is he just, but he is also full of love, as we see for ourselves in Jesus Christ.

Romans 6:3-11

Death, the natural result of sin, has been overthrown by Jesus, because he has passed through its barrier into life, and will never die again. When we are baptized we actually die to our former selves. What does this mean?

It doesn't just happen that we are immediately perfect – we can still choose to live the old life: it means we are given the capacity for new life; to mature and develop we must fill ourselves with his life. How? Prayer, service, sacraments – in other words, fastening ourselves to the Spirit, we become more and more part of him.

Luke 24:1-12

In the resurrection, Jesus showed himself to be God. His rising again was so incredible that even the apostles thought it pure nonsense at first. Yet it did happen and cannot be explained away, so we are left with the mind-stretching challenge: Jesus, that good, wandering teacher from Nazareth, who was killed for expediency on Friday, must be one with the great, powerful God who made the whole universe! In that case, we now know, for certain, what God is like and the extent of his love for us. In the face of such wonder, we can only lay our whole lives before him and relinquish ourselves to his will.

A selection of ideas for the presentation of Readings

Genesis 1:1-2:2 The Creation

There may be a religious resource centre in your area from which you can borrow a set of 'creation' slides showing the whole range and development of life on earth. Otherwise, collect a set of slides showing the beauty of creation, such as sunsets, trees and animals, the sea and rivers, and people. It does not matter if they don't link precisely with the order of creation – they are there to help awaken people's wonder.

An organist may be able to play sustained chords which complement the reading and slides. Alternatively, try using the slow movement of one of Mahler's symphonies in the background.

Genesis 22:1-18 *The sacrifice of Abraham*

A dramatised reading.
The narrator reads the story while others act it out, speaking their own words. You will need:

> God's voice
> Abraham
> Two servants
> Isaac
> Angel's voice
> Length of rope and a knife
> A drum and cymbals
> Triangle
> Small handbell
> Row of mugs on hooks to play with a fork
> And, if possible, a spot light with punched card shade, to give the impression of stars.

Have God and his angel out of view and as far from the actors as possible. They should both have strong voices which carry well.

Abraham is sitting in the chancel. The drum starts a slow beating and the narrator begins. As God speaks, Abraham stands up and the spot light shines on his face. All the preparations for the journey are mimed, and the journey itself is from the chancel, round the church and back to a central area, where Abraham leaves the servants.

Abraham and Isaac walk on up to the chancel where a low table is Abraham's altar. As he starts to bind Isaac, the drum beats slowly again, and as Abraham raises the knife high the cymbals clash and Abraham freezes.

He helps his son off the table tenderly and the two begin to walk down to where the servants are waiting. But they are stopped by the cymbals and the angel's voice.

During the promise, triangles play, then mugs join in, then bells, and the spot light covers everywhere with stars.

Isaiah 54:5-14

A choral reading.
Have three groups placed at different levels in the chancel. They should be grouped according to voice tone: high, medium and low.

All:	For now your creator will be your husband, his name, the Lord of hosts;	*f*
Low:	your redeemer will be the Holy One of Israel,	
All:	he is called the God of the whole earth.	
High:	Yes, like a forsaken wife, distressed in spirit, the Lord calls you back.	*p*
Medium:	Does a man cast off the wife of his youth?	
All:	says your God.	
Low:	I did forsake you for a brief moment,	
Low &		
Medium:	but with great love will I take you back.	*f*
Low:	In excess of anger, (*pause*) for a moment (*pause*) I hid my face from you.	
All:	But with everlasting love I have taken pity on you, says the Lord, your redeemer.	
High:	I am now as I was in the days of Noah when I swore that Noah's waters	
All:	should never flood the world again. So now I swear concerning my anger with you and the threats I made against you;	*loud* *pp*
Low:	for the mountains may depart,	
Medium:	the hills be shaken,	
High:	but my love for you will never leave you	
All:	and my covenant of peace with you will never be shaken, says the Lord who takes pity on you.	
High:	Unhappy creature,	*slow*
Medium:	storm-tossed,	*slow*
Low:	disconsolate,	*slow*

High:	see (*pause*) I will set your stones on carbuncles and your foundations on sapphires.	*f*
Low:	I will make rubies your battlements,	
Medium:	your gates crystal,	
All:	and your entire wall precious stones.	*mf*
Low:	Your sons will all be taught by the Lord.	
Medium:	You will be founded on integrity;	
High:	remote from oppression, you will have nothing to fear;	
All:	remote from terror, it will not approach you.	*f*

Ideas for Children

It may be that many families will make a point of worshipping together at the Easter Vigil, especially if it includes a variety of imaginative presentation and involvement.

However, many young children are likely to miss the celebrations. It may be worth considering whether the renewal of baptismal vows, with the lighting of each person's candle and the sprinkling of water, could not be incorporated into the Easter Day Mass, so that even the youngest members of the family can participate.

Music
Recorded Music

Mahler – *Symphony No. 4*
Beethoven – *Symphony No. 9*
Stravinsky – *Rite of Spring*
any early lute or guitar music

Easter Sunday
(Mass of the Day)

Theme
He is risen!

Having passed through death to life, Christ has won the victory over everything evil and destructive. Full of glory and power, he enables us to bring the hope and joy of resurrection into the world's problems and tragedies. With God, nothing is impossible.

Penitential Rite

Love through our hearts, Father,
 Lord, have mercy. **Lord, have mercy.**

Think through our minds,
 Christ, have mercy. **Christ, have mercy.**

Act through our bodies,
 Lord, have mercy. **Lord, have mercy.**

Notes on the Readings

Acts 10:34, 37-43

In Peter's address to the centurion, Cornelius, and his gathering of family and friends, we hear a firm, eye-witness account of Jesus' life, death and resurrection. As Peter points out, it all began with a chosen few, but it is God's will that through them the news may spread far and wide because the promise to forgive sins and set people free is there for every person: past, present and future. It is for the whole of humanity.

Colossians 3:1-4 or 1 Corinthians 5:6-8

Having pledged ourselves to God, and renounced evil, it is vital that we really do continue to turn away from sin and towards goodness and love. If we don't, our half-hearted pledge will carry no conviction and no strength. If we do, our glory, though hidden at present, will grow, until at the end of time it will be seen as part of the great glory of God.

John 20:1-9

This very human, realistic account of Easter morning shows us the lovable, varied characters and their predictable reactions to an unimaginably amazing event. We see Mary of Magdala, distressed at finding the physical body of Jesus missing: the younger John racing ahead, but losing his nerve; the elderly Peter, puffing up behind and impetuously running straight in; we, too, all react differently.

The important thing is that they all suddenly understood what Jesus had meant about rising from the dead. It was not to be an other-worldly rising, from which they were excluded: suddenly they realised that he meant real life, fulfilled, accomplished, physical and spiritual – a total existence. Not only had Jesus become man: he had also brought humanity into the very essence of the Godhead.

Bidding Prayers

Celebrant Let us pray that our world may be
transformed by the light of resurrection.

Reader That the joy and conviction
of Christians may be so radiant
that all who are lost, weary and searching
may be directed towards the lasting,
inner peace of God.
Pause
Risen Lord: **live in us all.**

That from every world crisis
and tragedy some good may come;
every problem become an opportunity
for development and spiritual growth.
Pause
Risen Lord: **live in us all.**

That those in mental, physical
or spiritual distress
may recognise in their suffering
a privilege of sharing Christ's passion,
until in their acceptance, they also share
the joy of new life in him.
Pause
Risen Christ: **live in us all.**

For the newly born,
and for all families,
that the children may be nurtured,
and the elderly cherished,
in God's wide accepting love.
Pause
Risen Christ: **live in us all.**

Celebrant Father, in grateful thanks, we pray we may
be worthy of all your gifts and blessings.
Through Christ, our risen Lord. **Amen.**

Ideas for Children

Tell the story of Easter, either using a good, exciting children's version, or using felt or flannelgraph. Another method is to draw a picture strip on a scroll, and set it up on a cereal packet 'television', wound on by two wooden spoons.

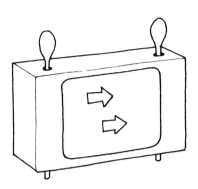

If the children make a resurrection banner, this could be carried through the church at the offertory, or hung on a pillar. Have a long sheet or piece of material, plenty of PVC glue, other scraps of material and scissors. Paper can be used instead. Possible ideas:

As they work, you could play a tape of some joyful songs, or they could sing some themselves. *Good Morning, Jesus* and *Many Ways to Praise* may be useful (both published by Palm Tree Press).

Music
Recorded Music

Handel – *Messiah: I know that my Redeemer liveth,
and Hallelujah Chorus*

'Live' Music

Earth in the dark *(SONL, 51)*
Easter Carol *(SOS 3, 289; BSOS, 144)*
Sing Alleluia! *(SONL, 31)*
The Lord is risen today *(SONL, 58)*
We are the Easter people *(MSOS, 108; BSOS, 7)*

2nd Sunday of Easter

Theme

He who was dead, is alive: he gives us his life

After his resurrection Jesus appears to his disciples, and the reality of his presence reassures them and strengthens their faith. In giving the gift of his Spirit he provides us all with the experience and knowledge of this presence, even though we cannot physically see him. Working in us, his Spirit leads us to share with others the best news since creation: we have been rescued from sin, and in Christ, we can be transfigured into the kind of people we were intended to be.

Penitential Rite

Use the song *Freely, freely* (ONE, 175)

Notes on the Readings

Acts 5:12-16

With the Spirit of Jesus living among his followers, the enthusiasm, joy and fervour of the early Christians is unmistakable and full of magnetism. Outsiders are so impressed by their sincerity and love, that many are drawn to join them.

Is this still true today? Wherever a group of Christians is set on fire with Christ, allowing him to take over their lives, outsiders are still drawn to join them. Christ has not become less alive with the years; he is just as real, and still gives us his Spirit. But we must hold nothing back, if we want him to have any real impact on our lives. It may be expensive, but what we receive in return is worth the cost.

Apocalypse 1:9-13, 17-19

The prophet John's vision gives his hearers the support, comfort and encouragement of knowing that whatever evils and sufferings afflict them, ultimately the ever-living God is in charge, and there is no need to fear.

John 20:19-31

What is the 'spirit' of a person? It is a person's life; his personality. Imagine how you would behave if you had the 'spirit' of your next door neighbour, say, or a colleague at work. You would act and react differently, view events from a different angle, etc.

What do we mean by 'receiving the Spirit of Jesus' then? In one sense the same — we will find ourselves noticing goodness and beauty; wanting people to be at peace with God and themselves; feeling thankful and joyful; wanting to help, to heal and to comfort. At the same time, because Jesus is not only human but God as well, he does not push our own personalities out of us when he gives us his Spirit: rather he grafts himself, as it were, on to us, so that in living with his Spirit, his life, we actually become more and more our true selves. It is a gift we cannot afford to reject.

'In whose service is perfect freedom'.

Bidding Prayers

Celebrant Brothers and sisters in Christ, let us pray
that his life will infuse and activate all
areas of creation.

Reader For the Church, especially
for missionaries both abroad
and in this country,
that with inner quietness
they may be ready to listen
to the voice of the Spirit.
Pause
Father of our risen Lord: **may your Spirit guide us.**

For world leaders and their advisers,
that nothing may tempt them from integrity,
and that they may boldly work
for what is good and honest and just.
Pause
Father of our risen Lord: **may your Spirit guide us.**

For those who doubt;
those who have lost their faith,
those whose faith is being tested;
that they may know the certainty
of God's presence and his love.
Pause
Father of our risen Lord: **may your Spirit guide us.**

For our own community,
that we may serve Christ
in caring for one another
and encourage one another,
in the faith of our loving Lord.
Pause
Father of our risen Lord: **may your Spirit guide us.**

Celebrant Father, we know that you are here present;
hear the prayers we make, confident of your
love. Through Christ our Lord. **Amen.**

Ideas for Children

The bulbs planted in Advent should have burst into flower now. Remind the children of the dead-looking bulbs, and how what results is not just a more cheerful-looking bulb but something beautiful and unexpected. So is resurrection like that. We are a bit like bulbs ourselves. God's life can make us more like daffodils/crocuses etc.

Or make Easter gardens in baking tins or shallow trays, using moss, rocks and pebbles and sunken 'vases' for flowers made from glass paste pots or cup shapes of aluminium foil sunk into the earth. They could be brought into church at the offertory.

Easter Dance — *Dance of New Life*

A very good symbol of resurrection is the butterfly which exists quite adequately as a caterpillar and has little idea of how amazingly it will be transformed.

Similarly our lives are transformed by Christ though we remain ourselves. While most of the children sing the 'Caterpillar song' from *Many Ways to Praise*, the others are dressed in a caterpillar type suit and squirm their way up the aisle until they reach the sanctuary.

The children can have made large plants out of crêpe paper which the caterpillars pretend to eat. When it is time for them to spin cocoons they fold themselves round in some cloth – a blanket or tablecloth will do nicely.

Then they curl up and rest until suddenly they burst out of their wrappings as butterflies. A leotard and wings cut out of an old net curtain and brightly painted makes an effective costume. The butterflies flutter about all over the church and finally settle in a position of praise in front of the altar.

Music

Recorded Music

Mahler – *Symphony No. 4: third movement*

'Live' Music

A man fully living *(MSOS, 193; BSOS, 5)*
Father you are living in us now *(SONL, 65)*
Ring out your joy *(SONL, 9)*
This joyful Eastertide *(ONE, 565)*

3rd Sunday of Easter

Theme
We, who know Jesus lives, must share the Good News

Jesus sends us out as witnesses of his resurrection, in order to establish his kingdom of peace, joy and love. All dangers and humiliations we may meet in the process, can be accepted gladly. For we know that, in doing God's will, we shall be sharing with the lamb of God who, through complete sacrifice, is completely worthy of all praise and honour.

Penitential Rite

In our lives we have denied you,
Lord, have mercy. **Lord, have mercy.**

In our priorities we have denied you,
Christ, have mercy. **Christ, have mercy.**

In our example we have denied you,
Lord, have mercy. **Lord, have mercy.**

Notes on the Readings

Acts 5:27-32, 40-41

Although they had already been punished for preaching that Jesus was the Son of God, the disciples were undeterred, and continued to publicise the Good News. From the distance of time we accept their determination as expected behaviour. But in our own lives, it is easy to back-pedal when we are threatened with ridicule or pitying looks; or we can excuse our lack of witness by saying we value people's freedom of thought and do not wish to persuade them differently.

But are we justified in not spreading such important news? If Jesus really makes a profound difference to the quality of our lives, are we not bound to introduce him to others?

Apocalypse 5:11-14

He, whom we worship, is not just of historical importance, but of cosmic eternal significance, worthy above and beyond all that ever was or shall be.

John 21:1-19

Even his close friends did not at first recognise Jesus. Perhaps their minds were still half-closed to the possibility of resurrection: they had even returned to the boats Jesus had called them from. But once they realise, there is no more doubt, even though the strangeness of it all frightens them.

As so often happens, a deeper knowledge of Jesus gives rise to a deeper responsibility. Peter, gently and deliberately forgiven for his denial, is commissioned as a shepherd, to look after the wayward and feed them. Jesus will never lead us forward so we can bask in the sun and enjoy our private insights. He will always lead us in order to use us, so we should not be surprised, but honoured, if we find ourselves in situations which may be difficult. We are probably there for a reason: God has work for us to do.

Bidding Prayers

Celebrant My brothers and sisters, as Christ
approaches us with welcoming arms,
let us approach him and pray in his Spirit
with humility and love.

Reader That Christ will use all Christians,
from the very young to the very old,
in witnessing to the reality of his presence
by the lives they lead.
Pause
Living Lord: **speak in our hearts.**

That, through the wonder
and beauty of God's created world,
many may be alerted to the sustaining
love of its creator.
Pause
Living Lord: **speak in our hearts.**

For the worried,
the confused and the anxious,
that in trusting Jesus
and laying their troubles before him,
they may experience the release
and freedom that his love provides.
Pause
Living Lord: **speak in our hearts.**

For ourselves,
our relatives and our friends;
that we may live more closely with Christ,
so that we see him more clearly
and become more like him.
Pause
Living Lord: **speak in our hearts.**

Celebrant Father, may we, who confess Christ as Lord,
live in his strength.
Through the same Christ our Lord. **Amen.**

Ideas for Children

Use the Gospel and tell the story of the disciples fishing and seeing Jesus on the beach.

Divide the group into two. One group prepares the acting out (give lots of help and participate to encourage the shy ones).

The other group cuts out lots of fish, all different colours, shapes and sizes. Have a net (old curtain) and an upturned table as a boat. Then the actors perform to the fish makers.

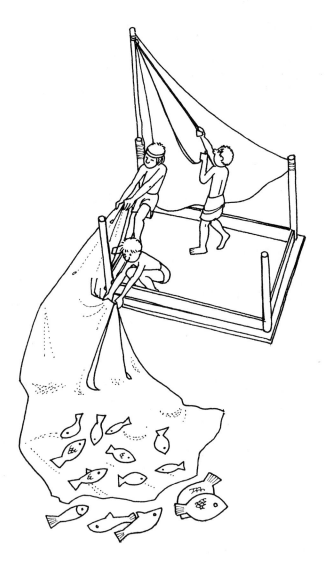

If this were prepared beforehand, the children could present their performance during the Gospel. Otherwise, let them take a fish home with them to remind them of what happened. Suggest they tell their families, or draw a picture of it to bring out next week.

Music
Recorded Music

Dvorak – *Cello Concerto: second movement*

'Live' Music

Colours of day *(ONE, 87)*
Give me joy in my heart *(ONE, 159)*
God's Spirit is in my heart *(ONE, 183)*
The rain and the snow *(SOS 3, 248)*

4th Sunday of Easter

Theme
Christ, the good shepherd, leads us into eternal life

Now, since the resurrection, the life of Jesus can spread far and wide, so that many, many people can be reached, touched with his love, and drawn into his saving presence, irrespective of colour and race. Jesus calls us all and he will lead us all.

Penitential Rite

Turn our weakness into strength,
   Lord, have mercy. **Lord, have mercy.**

Turn our anxiety into trust,
   Christ, have mercy. **Christ, have mercy.**

Turn our discontent to joy,
   Lord, have mercy. **Lord, have mercy.**

Notes on the Readings

Acts 13:14, 43-52

This reading shows humans acting at their meanest, in situations which must be familiar to all of us: we are all good at dredging up spiteful arguments which we justify by our righteous indignation. When we have cooled off a bit, and if we are honest, we often find that the real motive behind our spitefulness has been jealousy in some form, and we have leapt to defend what we considered as our own property.

No wonder the established Jewish community reacted as it did. Even the Christians, once established, have not been immune from this human weakness.

Apocalypse 7:9, 14-17; John 10:27-30

However, if the living Christ is invited into our lives, a startling change takes place. If we have given ourselves away, then we no longer have the same desperate urge to defend ourselves; we are therefore freed from seeing all new insights and different ideas as threats, and that enables us to be open-minded and receptive, without the pain and anxiety our imprisonment caused.

It is vital that we are open to God's word, because our faith is not a neat package, handed down unaltered through the ages; it is a living, growing organism, throbbing with vitality. Its full capacity for growth depends on our receptiveness: Jesus promises to lead us, but we must be prepared to follow.

Bidding Prayers

Celebrant As we follow our good shepherd,
      let us bring with us the needs
      of all our brothers and sisters.
      Together let us pray.

Reader For the Church,
      that in all its various ministries
      it may never lead any astray,
      but always follow faithfully
      the way of Jesus Christ the good shepherd.
      Pause
      Guide us, Father: **along the right path.**

For the world,
that in striving to do God's will,
we may not abuse or waste our talents
in thoughtless destruction,
but rather work with our Creator
to heal, conserve and fulfil.
Pause
Guide us, Father: **along the right path.**

For those who are ill,
and those who look after them,
that even in pain and discomfort
they may recognise Christ,
who also suffered, and who is full
of caring and compassion.
Pause
Guide us, Father: **along the right path.**

For all of us here,
and the families we represent;
that in trusting Jesus, the shepherd,
we may be liberated
to live selfless, generous lives.
Pause
Guide us, Father: **along the right path.**

Celebrant Father, in joy may we follow the way of Christ,
who alone has the words of eternal life.
Through the same Christ our Lord. **Amen.**

Ideas for Children

The good shepherd is a lovely image of Jesus which children readily understand. Have some pictures of sheep and shepherds and talk about the shepherd's job. Also show them how, in Jesus' time, the good shepherd would lie down across the pen's doorway, guarding the sheep with his life. You could act this out, using chairs to make the pen and the leader as the shepherd. The children make excellent sheep!

Let each child make a sheep, writing his own name on it. Stick on cotton wool to make it fluffy. Each sheep can be mounted on a large poster which already shows Jesus on a hillside.

Above the picture write: 'I am the good shepherd; I know my own sheep and they know me.' Display this in church if possible.

Music
Recorded Music

Gymel – *Jesu Cristes Milde Moder*
(for tenor recorder and medieval bells)

'Live' Music

Good Shepherd (SONL, 12)
Loving Shepherd of thy sheep (ONE, 340)
Open your ears (ONE, 422)
The King of love (ONE, 528)

5th Sunday of Easter

Theme
Love one another

In Jesus of Nazareth, we see the pattern of living by the rule of love, however costly or dangerous it may be. Others, seeing our love for each other, will be drawn to commit their lives to Christ. In love we are constantly being renewed and remade until all that is evil has passed away.

Penitential Rite

The light of your love exposes our selfishness,
Lord, have mercy. **Lord, have mercy.**

The warmth of your love exposes our indifference,
Christ, have mercy. **Christ, have mercy.**

The depth of your love exposes our meanness,
Lord, have mercy. **Lord, have mercy.**

Notes on the Readings

Acts 14:21-27

Above all in the early Church, we can sense the care and commitment that each had for the others. It was not a set smile grimly worn, but an expensive love which involved hardship and sacrifice as well as fellowship and joy. Individual weakness and despondency is not used as an excuse for general grousing and drifting away, but as an opportunity for encouragement and growth. How might Luke describe our own parish?

Apocalypse 21:1-5

In his vision, John glimpses this love made perfect in Christ. The crucial point in attaining such wholeness is the fact that God makes the whole of creation new. No amount of wallpaper, however splendid, will cure a damp or crumbling wall. No house, however pleasant, will last on poor foundations. We too, must allow ourselves to be made new; not just patched up in the parts that show.

John 13:31-35

The best encouragement of all is that Jesus has been glorified by the Father, and in him we can begin to understand how love transforms and fulfils humanity. But we do not have to gaze longingly from a distance and struggle ineptly on our own: the very love which suffuses Jesus makes him reach out personally to us and help us.

Bidding Prayers

Celebrant As members of the Body of Christ,
and united in his love, let us pray
to our heavenly Father.

Reader For the work of the Church
in spreading the good news
of Jesus who has brought
life and hope to the world.
Pause
Lord God of Love: **renew our lives.**

For all those with authority
and responsibility
in governing the nations of this world;
for peace, for compassion, forgiveness
and generosity.
Pause
Lord God of Love: **renew our lives.**

For those who shut love out;
those whom lack of love has hurt
or damaged; those whose love
has become distorted and twisted into hate.
Pause
Lord God of Love: **renew our lives.**

For those who live and worship here;
for particular areas in our own lives
where the love of God
is desperately needed
to transfigure, refresh and enrich.
Pause
Lord God of Love: **renew our lives.**

Celebrant Father, confident in your boundless love we
place these prayers before you.
Through Christ our Lord. **Amen.**

Ideas for Children

Aim to explore what loving means in terms of day to day life.
Have ready some sugar paper zigzag books. On the front is
written: LOVE IS . . .

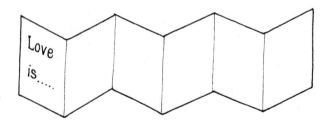

Inside, let the children stick a picture on each page which
represents a loving act. These could be duplicated sketches
or pictures photocopied from magazines. Some suggestions:
– parent reading book to child on lap;
– parent changing baby's napkin;
– child offering friend a sweet;
– child taking bunch of flowers to an old person;
– child making his bed or laying the table;
– child comforting someone who has fallen down,
even though other friends are running on.
Help children to see that love can be costly, but it often
makes *you* happy, as well as the person you have been loving
to.
Sing: *The clock tells the story* (MWTP).

Music
Recorded Music

Beethoven – *Symphony No. 6 (Pastoral): fifth movement –
Thanksgiving after the storm*

'Live' Music

Only a shadow *(MSOS, 131)*
Take me, O Lord *(SONL, 92)*
Thus! says the Lord *(SONL, 14)*
Walk, walk in love *(SONL, 44)*

6th Sunday of Easter

Theme
Peace

The peace which Christ gives is deeper and more far-
reaching than wordly peace. It is the ground which nurtures
rich spiritual growth. We cannot achieve it, then, by merely
following a code of rules; this peace is given to us only when
we allow God's living Spirit to permeate our whole being.

Penitential Rite

Our busy, hectic lives have left no time for peace,
Lord, have mercy. **Lord, have mercy.**

Our anxious, worrying minds have disregarded peace,
Christ, have mercy. **Christ, have mercy.**

Our carelessness and pride have undervalued peace,
Lord, have mercy. **Lord, have mercy.**

Notes on the Readings

Acts 15:1-2, 22-29

The way the Church dealt with this delicate and profoundly
significant problem says a great deal for the genuine love
and open-heartedness of those involved. No issues are
dodged; no one's opinion is 'steam-rollered'; hurt pride
does not atrophy into intransigence. Full of conviction that
Jesus Christ is Lord, they know without doubt that all things
are possible with God, and in that deep, trusting peace the
living Spirit of Jesus can speak and work.
    It is not a sign of weakness to allow our minds to be
changed, sometimes. Nor have we any right whatsoever to
gloat over others when they change theirs. Inter-church
discussions are watched by the world. Regardless of outcome they can be a powerful witness to Christian love.

Apocalypse 21:10-14, 22-23

Here is a vision of perfect radiance and fulfilment. It is the
vision of Jesus' promise accomplished: the kingdom of
heaven established for ever. Everything is so infused with
God's glory that even the splendour of sunlight is surpassed.
    When Jesus promises peace, joy and love, he means a
quality so extraordinary, so full of wonder, that it is really
indescribable, and passes beyond our understanding. Yet
the reality of it can be experienced to the very core of our
being.

John 14:23-29

We have been promised something even better than future glory. Jesus has given us his word that when we turn our lives to him, he and the Father will come and live in us; not at the end of time, but now.

When we are troubled or afraid, we can turn to one who is not only all-powerful but also loving. He will help us to get our priorities right; he will encourage and fortify us; he will replace the panic with tranquility and the terror with serenity. He does not promise an easy undisturbed life: what he does promise is his peace.

Bidding Prayers

Celebrant Let us quieten our hearts to listen
to the Lord of peace, and to pray to him.

Reader For all monks and nuns;
for the teaching, nursing
and contemplative orders;
for the growth and development of
a strong prayer life in every Christian.
Pause
Unchanging Father: **give us your peace.**

For the world of industry and commerce;
for those whose decisions affect many lives;
for those who determine the use of our
world's resources.
Pause
Unchanging Father: **give us your peace.**

For those who are suffering
from stress and depression;
for psychiatric nursing staff;
for those who cannot cope with
the burdens of their lives.
Pause
Unchanging Father: **give us your peace.**

For ourselves and our families;
for a greater simplicity in the ordering
of our lives; for deeper trust and acceptance.
Pause
Unchanging Father: **give us your peace.**

Celebrant Heavenly Father, accept our prayers,
through Christ our Lord. **Amen.**

Ideas for Children

Today's theme of peace will be best understood by children as Jesus being a very special friend whom they can trust, and who is always at their side. Talk about their own friends and why they like to be with these particular people. On a large sheet of paper make a collection of qualities that make a good friend:

- they like you;
- they don't boss you around;
- they are pleased when you do something well;
- they keep a secret;
- they share toys with you;
  etc.

Sing 'Jesus is my friend' from *Good Morning, Jesus* or 'I have a friend who is deeper than the ocean' from *Many Ways to Praise*.

Colour a picture of Jesus with the children, and write on it: 'Jesus is my friend'.

Music
Recorded Music

Langrave of Hesse – *Pavan (guitar solo)*

'Live' Music

Be not afraid *(MSOS, 196; BSOS, 72)*
Listen! *(SONL, 26)*
Lord of my life *(SONL, 21)*
Make me a channel of your peace *(ONE, 342)*
On eagle's wings *(SOS 3, 208)*
Peace, perfect peace *(ONE, 445)*

7th Sunday of Easter

Theme
Jesus lives in glory

Having accomplished his great, saving work through his life, death and resurrection, Jesus lives in glory which transcends all time and place. Dimly we sense the amazing truth and beauty which will one day be made abundantly clear.

Penitential Rite

We have often heard but failed to listen,
Lord, have mercy. **Lord, have mercy.**

We have often looked but failed to see,
Christ, have mercy. **Christ, have mercy.**

We have received but failed to share,
Lord, have mercy. **Lord, have mercy.**

Notes on the Readings

Acts 7:55-60

Stephen was so convinced of Jesus' eternal presence that death was a gateway to a life more rich and fulfilling than anything this world could offer. Sometimes we confess this belief with our words, but the way we behave denies it. Are we really convinced that God will keep his promises, even when a loved one is at the point of death, or when witnessing to Christ threatens our popularity or our lifestyle?

Being children of eternity does not preclude grief and heartache: in the person of Jesus we see that love is often compatible with tears. Yet it does mean that at bedrock level when we are confronted with the bleak, barren landscape of despair, Jesus alone, Lord of earth and heaven, time and eternity, reaches across death, across annihilation and keeps his word to be one with us for ever, in this world and the world to come.

Apocalypse 22:12-14, 16-17, 20

This is the life-giving truth shown to John in his revelation, which is food to the hungry and drink to the thirsty: Jesus will be with us to comfort and strengthen us in every situation. We have only to turn to him and ask for his help.

John 17:20-26

From this greatly moving prayer of Jesus we can catch something of the extent of God's love for us: his deep longing for us to share in the life which alone can give us the complete joy, peace and fulfilment that we crave. Our craving leads us down many false turnings and into many blind alleys from which we emerge frustrated, disillusioned and cynical.

Hence the prayer that we will be united in love; love alone can bind us to God and each other, and love breaks down all barriers that divide, however high they have become and however long they have been standing. God is with us, and with God nothing shall be impossible.

Bidding Prayers

Celebrant As one family in Christ, we come before
our heavenly Father, and pray to him now.

Reader For all those Christians
who are persecuted for their faith;
that they may be strengthened
by the certainty of Christ's presence
for all time and in all places.
Pause
Come to us, Father: **our hope and our joy.**

For all politicians
and government ministers;
that they may discern Christ's truth
and be given the courage
to walk faithfully in it.
Pause
Come to us, Father: **our hope and our joy.**

For the malnourished and the starving;
for those diseased from
contaminated water supplies;
that as fellow human beings
we may be led by love to share
the world's resources.
Pause
Come to us, Father: **our hope and our joy.**

For our own community;
for the many groups of Christians;
that Jesus' love and desire for our unity
may inspire us to break down barriers
and build bridges.
Pause
Come to us, Father: **our hope and our joy.**

Celebrant Father, trusting in your love we lay these prayers
before you through Christ, our Lord. **Amen.**

Ideas for Children

In an effort to steer clear of false impressions, we sometimes avoid teaching children about heaven. Today is a good opportunity to put that right. Start with a game. In a box have slips of paper which describe things in terms of other things:

- a bit like an orange but not so sweet,
  and coloured yellow;
- a kind of chair which has no back;
- a tall sort of cup;
- a wax stick that you can burn slowly; etc.

Point out that if you had not known before what a lemon was, you would have a better idea now, but not an exact idea until you actually saw a lemon yourself. Show them one. And similarly with the other items described.

It is the same with heaven. Pictures and words in the Bible give us clues but no more.

Show a large round poster with these words written all round the edge:

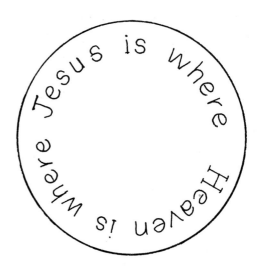

Then make a collection of words inside the circle which give us an idea of what heaven is like:

- happy
- beauty
- peace
- joy
- no worry
- Daddy finds you when you were lost
- like when you give Nana your best drawing
  and she's very pleased
- like when your friends ask you to join in
  their game, etc.

Stress that these are only clues, but try to show them some idea of what being with Jesus means in feelings they can understand, rather than looking at the idea of 'place'.

Let the children decorate the words with lovely bright colours and patterns and if possible display the poster in church.

Music
Recorded Music

Ravel – *Piano Concerto: slow movement*

'Live' Music

Glorify the Lord *(SONL, 17)*
Jerusalem the golden *(ONE, 273)*
You shall cross the barren desert *(ONE, 627)*

The Ascension of the Lord

Theme
Jesus Christ ascends into heaven

The ascension marks the end of Jesus' historical physical life, and the beginning of a far-reaching, all-pervasive presence unlimited by time or location. We who believe are given his promise that we will one day share his glory.

Penitential Rite

Story of love (SONL, 76) either sung by everyone or by a small group with the congregation joining in the chorus.

Notes on the Readings

Acts 1:1-11

With typically human narrow-mindedness, the disciples were still unable to grasp the breadth of God's plan, even after the resurrection, and in their need for security, wanted to pin him down to details of time and place that they could cope with.

Jesus explains the truth both in words and in actions. They are to wait patiently until they receive power which will enable them to be witnesses. They see that in removing himself from their presence physically, Jesus is allowing himself to be spread far and wide through all ages and all nations, so that all men can be drawn to know the peace and joy which comes from being at one with their Creator.

Ephesians 1:17-23

What do we mean by God's glory? All the richness and abundance of our own planet, the solar system and the vastness of the universe help to direct our minds to the enormity, splendour and vitality of God. We see his power in the raising of Christ to life and in the meeting of earth and heaven at the incarnation.

But whatever we see is only a shadow, a reflection, of what God's glory must really be; in fact no one would be able to see it and live, for it is larger than our capacity – like trying to fill a jug with the sea.

It should not worry us that we do not understand everything about God; we can rejoice in the glimpses of glory we do have, and also rejoice that the glory stretches on, far beyond our human limits and boundaries. God's love is large enough to take us in our entirety, absorb and support us, with plenty of room to spare. That is why God is the one person worth trusting.

Alternative Readings

Hebrews 9:24-28; 10:19-23

Christ had made the ultimate sacrifice which, unlike past priestly offerings, is complete and so never needs repeating. He has promised that when he comes again it will be to gather in the harvest. Trusting his promise brings us freedom from worry and tension about where the world is going, and we can throw ourselves enthusiastically into encouraging each other, so that the harvest will be good.

Luke 24:46-53

Jesus emphasises the fact that his death and suffering were all a necessary part of his work of salvation. Without his physical presence which they had always relied on, the disciples needed to understand the mystery of how death is a source of life, suffering a source of joy, and giving a means of receiving. They cannot understand these things without Jesus, so he promises them his ever present life – his Spirit; and the disciples, trusting him, return to Jerusalem full of joy.

Bidding Prayers

Celebrant   Christ has given us hope. In this hope let us pray.

Reader   For all those involved in spreading
the word of truth and joy;
that their lives may be instruments
of God's love.
Pause
King of Glory: **enable us to do your will.**

For the many different cultures
and races on this planet;
that we may all learn from one another,
until God's kingdom is established on earth.
Pause
King of Glory: **enable us to do your will.**

For the casualties of materialistic, unjust
or corrupt society;
that, in the light of Christ,
people may recognise needs and have
the courage to act.
Pause
King of Glory: **enable us to do your will.**

For each person here,
and the circle of lives linked to each one,
at home and at work;
that with these immediate contacts
we may open the way for God to act
by becoming channels of his peace.
Pause
King of Glory: **enable us to do your will.**

Celebrant   Father, fit us for heaven, to live with you
for ever. Through Christ our Lord. **Amen.**

Ideas for Children

Some churches have a Mass specially for children today, with the songs and homily geared to their understanding.

Readings at such a Mass might be taken from the *Good News Bible* or a suitable children's version.

There are several songs for Ascension in *Many Ways to Praise* including:

'When the Lord returns';
'There's a seed in flower';
'Shout aloud for Jesus';
'Think BIG . . .'

Music
Recorded Music

Elgar – *Dream of Gerontius*

'Live' Music

Holy, holy *(SOS 3, 218)*
Hymn of glory *(MSOS, 173; BSOS, 9)*
Lord, enthroned in heavenly splendour *(ONE, 321)*
Rejoice! The Lord is King *(ONE, 463)*
Whom do you seek? *(SONL, 30)*

Pentecost Sunday

Theme
The Church receives God's Holy Spirit

Coming first to the apostles as they waited in prayer, the Holy Spirit has continued to be poured out on Christ's followers ever since. If we open ourselves to receive it, the Body of Christ will be charged with his life.

Penitential Rite

Clear our lives of all that blocks your Spirit,
Lord, have mercy. **Lord, have mercy.**

Thaw our cold, unbending hearts,
Christ, have mercy. **Christ, have mercy.**

Break our chains of selfishness and pride,
Lord, have mercy. **Lord, have mercy.**

Notes on the Readings

Acts 2:1-11

The first effect of the Holy Spirit at Pentecost is the breaking down of barriers. All those present are able to understand the ecstatic message of God's saving power and love, unleashed as the Church is born. It is like the first fruits of a great harvest which still goes on today; it challenges the world with a radically new law of love; it is the victorious Christ, alive, strong and in charge. No wonder the disciples were full of such rapturous joy – if God was with them to this extent, then who could possibly be against them?

When we know this experience it is indeed breathtaking, invigorating and tremendously exciting. God has overcome the world. He comes with us in person.

1 Corinthians 12:3-7, 12-13

God is never narrow minded; we have only to look at the colossal variety of the created world to see this. We should not then expect such a God to provide or demand uniformity among his followers, whom he loves as individuals. It is human insecurity which clings to an ideal of sameness and can, at its worst, result in tight, exclusive cliques.

With God it is quite different; his living Spirit gives people the confidence to realise their own potential, and this will of course result in a riot of shades and shapes of character which can serve the world in many different ways. Before we ever criticise another person's faith or way of showing it, let us be sure that we are not criticising God's rich gift of variety, all the many different gifts of one Spirit.

John 20:19-23

Jesus was entrusted with the work of reconciling men to God; of saving them from themselves. Now he entrusts his followers with the work of continuing what he has begun, of joining him in establishing his everlasting kingdom of love and peace.

We have been chosen. How shall we respond?

Alternative Readings

Romans 8:8-17

When we commit ourselves to Christ, we begin to live in the power of his life, or Spirit. Obviously that is going to change our whole outlook, our attitudes and our values, since they are now charged with the unselfish goodness of God. Not that it happens overnight, of course; what we notice is much more of a journey towards than an arrival. But since the life of the Spirit is everlasting, the ageing, dying body is no longer so tragic, for our life will continue long after our physical, earth-bound bodies are worn out.

John 14:15-16, 23-26

The condition of receiving the living Spirit of God is uncompromising: if we love and obey God, he will make his home in us; and if we don't we shall not even recognise his existence when we see clear evidence. It is all too easy to get short-sighted about this. We all need regular check-ups to ensure that we are not missing out on the chance of a spiritual lifetime – *what if* the God of love were to knock at our door, and we failed to answer because we did not even notice him there?

Bidding Prayers

Celebrant In wonder let us pray to the almighty and everlasting God.

Reader For the Church;
that in constant prayerfulness Christians may be attentive and receptive to the Holy Spirit.
Pause
Father almighty: **may your Spirit fill us with life.**

For the world;
for its mistakes and tragedies, that God's active Spirit will bring order, serenity and hope.
Pause
Father almighty: **may your Spirit fill us with life.**

For those whose lives are darkened by guilt, resentment and despair; for those who live violent and cruel lives; for drug pushers and all who corrupt young minds; that God's generous Spirit of love will bring light to their hearts.
Pause
Father almighty: **may your Spirit fill us with life.**

For our loved ones and for anyone we find difficult to love; that God's Spirit living in us will increase our love for each other.
Pause
Father almighty: **may your Spirit fill us with life.**

Celebrant Father, accept these prayers through Christ our Lord. **Amen.**

Ideas for Children

After telling the children the Pentecost story, divide them into groups, each with a large sheet of paper, with one of the fruits of the Spirit on it. Have ready plenty of colourful magazine pictures, pens, coloured paper and glue and scissors.

Help the children to create a collage picture to express the quality they have been given. For example: *peace* may be expressed in restful colours, wide scenery; sleep, anything which makes for a feeling of peace; *joy* may be bright colours, flowers, balloons; etc.

Music

Recorded Music

Dvorak – *New World Symphony: Largo*

'Live' Music

Alleluia for forgiveness *(SONL, 18)*
Go tell everyone *(SOS 3, 229)*
If God is for us *(ONE, 231)*
Listen *(SONL, 26)*
Look at the sky *(MSOS, 179; BSOS, 73)*

The Most Holy Trinity

Theme

The Father, the Son and the Spirit are one God, whom we worship

Since before the beginning of creation, as Creator, Word and Spirit, God existed and will exist for ever. Through faith in him we can have abundant life, and grow to understand more and more of his goodness and love.

Penitential Rite

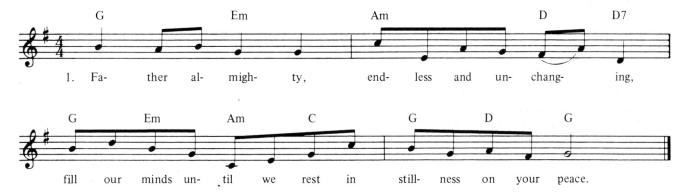

1. Fa-ther al-migh-ty, end-less and un-chang-ing, fill our minds un-til we rest in still-ness on your peace.

2. Jesus our Saviour,
   radiant with compassion,
   break our hearts of stone
   and make us burn with selfless love.

3. Life-giving Spirit,
   streaming from the Godhead,
   steep us in your purity
   and drench us in your joy.

Notes on the Readings

Proverbs 8:22-31

It is so difficult to imagine something that has no beginning, since we are ourselves creatures of time. This poetry gives us some idea of God's brooding Spirit, present before the most ancient landscapes were formed. Its effect is emphasised if it is read by a team of people chorally, grouped imaginatively and wearing simple costumes, such as similar coloured clothes within a group, or cassocks.

Divide the readers into three groups: men, women, children. Where they stand will depend on the type of building, but one suggestion is:

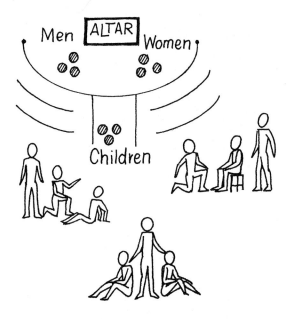

Arrange the reading as follows, accentuating the dynamics so that the effect is almost musical. If a flute or recorder player is not available you could use some taped flute music.

Music begins first and continues as a background to the reading.

Men:	The wisdom of God cries aloud.
Women:	The Lord created me when his purpose first unfolded, before the oldest of his works.
Men:	From everlasting I was firmly set, from the beginning.
Children:	The deep was not when I was born, (*pause*) there were no springs to gush with water.
All:	Before the mountains were settled, before the hills, I came to birth.
Woman 1:	before he made the earth
Woman 2:	the countryside
Woman 3:	or the first grains of the world's dust.
Men:	When he fixed the heavens firm I was there,
Man 1:	when he drew a ring on the surface of the deep,
Man 2:	when he thickened the clouds above,
Children:	when he fixed fast the springs of the deep,
All:	when he assigned the sea its boundaries – (*pause*) and the waters will not invade the shore –
Women:	when he laid down the foundations of the earth,
Man:	I was by his side, a master craftsman,
All:	delighting him day after day,
Children:	ever at play in his presence,
Women & Children:	at play everywhere in his world
All:	delighting to be with the sons of men.

Besides helping others to catch the meaning of this reading, a dramatised approach such as this is fun and rewarding to prepare and should not take long to rehearse.

Romans 5:1-5

Paul reminds us that we are not in a state of grace through our own efforts but through the person of Jesus, so we must always guide people's praise for any good we may do towards Christ, in whose strength we live and work. Even suffering provides opportunities to boast of God's love, for out of suffering can spring patience, perseverance and hope: the strong hope which comes from trusting in the all powerful, loving God.

John 16:12-15

Jesus teaches his disciples about the nature of the Spirit which they are going to receive. He explains that this power of wisdom, discernment and truth is inextricably part of himself, just as he is in the Father and the Father in him. So when we open ourselves to the Spirit we open ourselves to the full force of the Godhead.

Bidding Prayers

Celebrant My brothers and sisters, let us pray in the Spirit to God our Father through Jesus our mediator.

Reader For the Church, that it may be guided through suffering and persecution, temptation and difficulty by the powerful spirit of God's truth.
Pause
Everliving Lord: **hear us, we pray.**

For the world
and the leaders of every nation;
that it may be God's will
that is accomplished,
so that men care for one another
and live in peace together.
Pause
Everliving Lord: **hear us, we pray.**

For the lost and undecided;
for those who do not know
which way to turn
or what to do for the best;
that they may be reassured
of God's presence,
and, waiting in stillness on God's love,
receive the clear guidance of his Spirit.
Pause
Everliving Lord: **hear us, we pray.**

For our own community,
that all the trying circumstances
and troubles of our lives
may not weaken our faith
but rather strengthen us in hope.
Pause
Everliving Lord: **hear us, we pray.**

Celebrant God our Father, may we be led by the Spirit to a deeper knowledge of you.
Through Christ our Lord. **Amen.**

Ideas for Children

Begin by exploring relationships in the group, asking the children to stand in the 'daughter' ring, if they are daughters and the 'son' ring if they are sons (use lengths of wool, or hula hoops to make the rings). Now ask the sisters and brothers to go to other rings, such as cousin, grandchild, friend and nephew. Some children will have changed rings several times.

Sit the children in a circle and show them a picture of someone they all know about – it may be the Queen; or a photo of the teachers, perhaps. Work out together all the different things the person is, such as mother, daughter, woman, sister, grandmother, queen, horse rider. Write all these down beside the picture.

Now show them a poster with the word GOD in the middle.

Uncover the first picture of trees, mountains, animals and flowers.
What is God?
He is our Father, the Creator.
Uncover the second picture of Jesus, healing and teaching.
What else is God? He is Jesus Christ.
Uncover the third picture of wind and fire and the disciples full of joy, which they will remember from last week.
What else is God? He is the Holy Spirit.
Just as they are themselves, although they are also sisters, friends, and cousins, so God is God, although he is also Father, Son and Holy Spirit. Give each child a triangle of coloured card. They write GOD in the middle and Father, Jesus and Spirit at the three corners to take home with them.

Music
Recorded Music

Albinoni – *Adagio*

'Live' Music

Father, we adore you *(ONE, 134)*
Glorify your name *(SOS 3, 271)*
Glory to God *(ONE, 167)*
God is love *(ONE, 178)*
Holy is the Lord *(SONL, 78)*

ORDINARY TIME

2nd Sunday in Ordinary Time

Theme
We are chosen and cared for

God has chosen us and cares for us as a bridegroom loves and cares for his bride, to the extent that he has put away our sin and gives us the gift of his living Spirit which enables us to work powerfully for good in his strength. He can transform us into living members of his Body.

Penitential Rite

We have been obstinate and wayward,
  Lord, have mercy. **Lord, have mercy.**

Our sin has weakened the Body of Christ,
  Christ, have mercy. **Christ, have mercy.**

We have not trusted in your saving power,
  Lord, have mercy. **Lord, have mercy.**

Notes on the Readings

Isaiah 62:1-5

God's forgiveness is supremely generous; his loyalty is unswerving. He has promised to save his people and he will keep his word, so that they are uplifted and redeemed.
  Why will he do this? Simply because he loves his people.

1 Corinthians 12:4-11

His love is outpoured on his followers in a wealth of diversity, an abundance of gifts and talents, which are all valuable in building up Christ's Church.
  It is no good wasting our time and God's in hankering after a different gift. Nor can we decide in advance our first choices and recommend God to take our advice!
  God is so much greater than we often arrogantly imagine, and he sees, with complete knowledge and insight, what the needs are, and how and by whom they can be met. In some ways this makes life a good deal lighter and happier, for we have no need to worry any more about what we can or cannot do; instead we have only to love and trust Jesus, the Lord, and he will bring out in us all kinds of gifts which are often unexpected and sometimes a complete surprise and joy. Having been made rich, we can spend our gifts as liberally and freely as God wants; then, together, we will be helping to reap God's harvest.

John 2:1-11

In the first miracle of his ministry, Jesus shows himself as he who transforms and provides. He will transform the old Law into the wine of Love's salvation; he will transform our narrow, selfish lives into the wine of Christ-filled open-heartedness and joy; he transforms jars of water into sweet wine.
  To do this he needs the consent and obedience of the servants, just as Mary told them to do whatever Jesus said. If he is to transform us he needs our consent and obedience as well; sometimes we beg him to help us but when he tells us what to do we are not prepared to obey, especially if it seems rather foolish, unnecessary or unlikely to succeed.

But if we trust him and are prepared to fill our water pots up to the brim, he will honour his word and transform us into ourselves at our best, our most fulfilled.

Bidding Prayers

Celebrant As God's family let us pray to our heavenly Father.

Reader For the pilgrim Church,
with all the weak and strong members,
its mistakes and failures,
joys and achievements,
hopes and anxieties.
Pause
Father, help us: **to trust in your love.**

For the world of commerce,
industry and advertising;
the influence of the mass media,
the inequalities and injustices.
Pause
Father, help us: **to trust in your love.**

For the injured and the dying,
the threatened and abused,
the rejected and distressed.
Pause
Father, help us: **to trust in your love.**

For those with whom we live and work,
those whom we have met this week,
for our refuse collectors, paper boys and girls –
all who have served us during the week.
Pause
Father, help us: **to trust in your love.**

Celebrant God our Father, may the richness of your transforming Spirit refresh and renew our lives. Through Christ our Lord. **Amen.**

Ideas for Children

Have the room looking festive, with chairs and tables arranged as for a wedding party, cups on the tables, sweets, perhaps, and a pretty veil (net curtains) ready for the bride.
  When the children come in, tell them they are at a party as they are celebrating Ezra and Judith's wedding (choose two children to be the happy couple). Have some cheerful music and let everyone have a good time. Then announce in a loud whisper that the wine has run out.
  At this point tell the children that Jesus was once at a wedding party, when this happened, and this is what he did. Narrate the rest of the story, using children to act it out as you tell it. Large bowls can be the water pots.

Afterwards, let the children make water pots themselves out of thin coils of plasticine. If possible let them take these home to remind them of how God can use ordinary things to make special things.

Music
Recorded Music

Beethoven – *Piano Concerto No. 4: Largo*

'Live' Music

If God is for us *(ONE, 231)*
Send forth your Spirit, O Lord *(SOS 3, 237)*
Spirit of the living Christ *(ONE, 500)*
Spirit of the living God *(ONE, 501)*

3rd Sunday in Ordinary Time

Theme
God lives in his people

Just as the chosen Israelites felt the great privilege of God's special relationship with them through the Law, so we all share the great privilege of being members of Christ's Body, charged with his life, so that the ancient Law is fulfilled.

Penitential Rite

We have failed to keep God's law of love,
Lord, have mercy. **Lord, have mercy.**

We have compromised his challenge to our lives,
Christ, have mercy. **Christ, have mercy.**

Our separate sins have weakened the whole body of Christ,
Lord, have mercy. **Lord, have mercy.**

Notes on the Readings

Nehemiah 8:2-6, 8-10

Restored to the holy city after exile, the people commit themselves to God's Law as the foundation of their daily lives and the whole structure of their society. The occasion is very moving in its solemnity and in the sense of privilege they feel as the Law is read, and carefully explained. The realisation that they have been specially chosen enhances both their desire to work with their God, and also their shame and regret for past failures.

Ezra, Nehemiah, the priests and scribes urge the people to concentrate on the positive side; a day when God's people return to him must be a day of great rejoicing.

1 Corinthians 12:12-30

The Christian community extends this invigorating power wherever it reaches, for we are not individual saviours who have disastrous feet of clay: we are separate bits and pieces of one organism, and the organism functions better or worse depending on the effectiveness of each part of it, however small or insignificant or large it may be.

If we fool ourselves that we are able to be Christians without being part of the worshipping community, we not only weaken ourselves, but the whole body; for an eye cannot see unless it is linked to the brain, nor can a foot walk unless it is joined to the leg.

Such independence accepts God's privilege without taking responsibility; accepts the freedom of Love without its discipline. If we accept Jesus' call, we must accept it completely, even if some parts of it are less attractive than others.

Luke 1:1-4; 4:14-21

The drawback of a Law to live by, however noble, is that since a Law encourages conformity, it can also lead to narrow-mindedness and exclusive behaviour. When Jesus came to fulfil the Law through love, he was able to retain the value of discipline and guidance, while throwing open the closed gates of rigid pedantry. In this new Law of selfless love all kinds of gifts and qualities were free to blossom, and all kinds of healing, liberating acts were bound to occur, in an explosive burst of God's love for his world.

Bidding Prayers

Celebrant   As members of the Body of Christ,
let us pray together.

Reader   For all those who form the Church,
in its variety and richness
throughout the world;
that we may be encouraged
and strengthened,
and our weariness constantly refreshed
by the living Spirit of Jesus.
Pause
Take us as we are: **and use us, Lord.**

For all councils, committees
and governing bodies;
for those serving on juries;
for air, sea and mountain rescue teams;
that in working together they may strive
for what is good, just and honest.
Pause
Take us as we are: **and use us, Lord.**

For the poor and for the hungry;
for the blind, the downtrodden,
and for those imprisoned;
that God's Spirit, alive in his people,
will work its healing love.
Pause
Take us as we are: **and use us, Lord.**

For ourselves; that we may be given
deeper insight, more awareness
and greater love, so that we can
more effectively serve the world
as living members of the Body of Christ.
Pause
Take us as we are: **and use us, Lord.**

Celebrant   Father, we ask you to hear our prayers
through Christ our Lord. **Amen.**

Ideas for Children

Have ready a large selection of Lego, or other building bricks. Give a bag of it to each child on arrival. Let them sit in a circle. Together build a church on the table in the middle of a children's circle, each child contributing his bricks, one by one. As you build, point out that we need Anne's bricks here, we need John's over there, etc.

You could sing a song about building the Church at this point e.g. *Build, build your Church* (ONE, 74; SONL, 41).

Show the children a large poster with the outline of a church drawn on it.

Explain that the Church is made of living stones – the people who are baptized into it. Who are they? If the children name people outside the parish that's lovely. If not, suggest some well-known people yourself. They should realise that by 'the Church' we mean the whole Church, world-wide.

In groups let the children draw faces of themselves, their friends and families, and a family in another country. Cut them out and stick all the faces on to the poster so that it is a 'living' church.

Music
Recorded Music

Pachelbel – *Canon*

'Live' Music

A new commandment *(SONL, 34)*
Build, build your Church *(ONE, 74; SONL, 41)*
God's Spirit is in my heart *(ONE, 183)*
I give my hands *(MSOS, 123)*
The body of Christ *(MWTP)*

4th Sunday in Ordinary Time

Theme
Love is the greatest gift of all

Love is the generosity of spirit which transforms every action into an outpouring of God himself, full of compassion, patience and perseverance. It enables us to fulfil our task, as Christians, of going out to serve the world and bring it hope and joy.

Penitential Rite

Love is patient and kind, *(silence)*
    Lord, have mercy. **Lord, have mercy.**

Love is never jealous, boastful or conceited, *(silence)*
    Christ, have mercy. **Christ, have mercy.**

Love does not take offence and is not resentful, *(silence)*
    Lord, have mercy. **Lord, have mercy.**

Notes on the Readings

Jeremiah 1:4-5, 17-19

Jeremiah did not set out to be a prophet to the nations without a great many misgivings; but this vision convinced him that if he was to obey God, then this was the role he had to play, whether he liked it or not. God gave him the confidence and courage necessary for the work he needed Jeremiah to undertake. His words were not going to be popular, and he would be bound to suffer, but the stubborn and idolatrous behaviour of the people had to be shown up for what it was and condemned, if they were to repent and turn back to their God.

We may be surprised or annoyed at what God asks us to do. It may be far more difficult than we think we can cope with. But, of course, it will be God working in us, and not just us on our own, so we do not need to be frightened off, or make excuses for busying ourselves with something more 'useful'.

If we trust God and obey him, he will always, without fail, provide us with everything we need for the job he asks us to do. And we will never know that is true until we try it out!

1 Corinthians 12:31 – 13:13

This most beautiful passage on Christian love is worth reading every day this week. It is so different from the world's values, and reaches to the heart of all Christ's life and teaching.

If we try putting our own name instead of 'love', we shall very quickly see how mean and lacking in love our lives often are.

But there is plenty of hope; by God's grace there are times when we do reveal these qualities, and so often these are the times we feel, surprisingly, not burdened by their weight, but refreshed and full of joy. The way of love is not heavy and oppressive at all – it actually brings the very peace and freedom that selfishness tries desperately to buy. God gives it to us, hands it out for free: can we afford not to accept it?

Luke 4:21-30

Jesus began the day as a popular star, whom everyone admired and approved of. How tempting it must have been to hang on to this popularity, using it to influence some people, perhaps; rather like turning stones into bread and appealing to men's desire for an idol who will never require anything from them.

But Jesus knows that he must sometimes give unpalatable truths; if people are to be saved from their own selfishness they must learn to be open, and prepared for change. We may have to relinquish fond personal ambitions, or private indulgent resentments, smug critical attitudes or mean characteristics we rather enjoy keeping, like rudeness, or a strong temper. Jesus does not hesitate to speak out when it is necessary, even though what he says often winds people up and enrages them as they rush to their own defence.

If we find ourselves doing this, perhaps it is not because the accusation is false, but because it is nearer the truth than we wish to admit?

Bidding Prayers

Celebrant   Let us pray to our loving Father,
trusting not in ourselves,
but in his mercy.

Reader   For a constant renewal in the Church;
for a constant deepening of love
and thankfulness.
Pause
Loving Father: **teach us your ways.**

For the world in which we live;
for more tolerance and forgiveness
among its peoples;
for more understanding and less fear;
for more friendship and less bitterness.
Pause
Loving Father: **teach us your ways.**

For all who hate, for all who
seek revenge, for all who refuse to forgive;
that love may transform their hearts
and minds.
Pause
Loving Father: **teach us your ways.**

For the person next to us here;
that, being open to God's grace,
our community may be
more deeply filled
with his Spirit of outgoing love.
Pause
Loving Father: **teach us your ways.**

Celebrant   God our Father, give us all those qualities
of faith, hope and love which last for ever.
Through Christ our Lord. **Amen.**

Ideas for Children

Talk about any special jobs the children may have been put in charge of, such as being a door-opener at school, being responsible for laying the table on Thursdays at home, or giving out straws for milk. Have a chart with the children's names on it, and write down beside them particular jobs to do, such as:

- bringing flowers; arranging candles;
- lighting and blowing out candles;
- giving out scissors;
- collecting rubbish in the bin; etc.

Arrange it so that everyone has a job, however small. It will help the smooth running of your group and, more important, it will give the children a sense of responsible involvement.

Now tell them about a man who was given a special job – Jeremiah; and how God promised him it would not be easy, but that he would be given God's strength to cope with it. Show them that we all have this promise of God to help us cope with difficult times in jobs he gives us to do, so if we are finding it hard, we need not worry – just ask God to help us and he will.

At this stage, pray together for God's help in the job he gives us of being loving and caring, even to people we don't much like. Then let each child think of a God-job they find hard work and make it into a written prayer on a card which they can decorate and hang up in their bedroom.

Music
Recorded Music

Vaughan Williams – *Fantasia on Greensleeves*

'Live' Music

If I am lacking love *(ONE, 232)*
Life pervading *(SONL, 46)*
Love divine *(ONE, 337)*
Love is his word *(ONE, 338)*
Love is patient *(ONE, 339)*

Questions for Discussion Groups
Jesus' ministry and teaching

1. How can we make sure we shall be able to hear whenever God calls us?
2. On the surface, some of Jesus' teachings appear rather unfair; no paying back those who abuse us, no limits to our forgiveness etc. Yet we know God is good and just. What kind of justice is Jesus talking about?

5th Sunday in Ordinary Time

Theme
'Vocation' or calling

God calls people in many different ways and leaves them free to respond by accepting or rejecting their calling. Acceptance is not the end of the matter, but only the beginning; and all the necessary power, strength and words will be provided so long as we remain bound in Christ.

Penitential Rite

We have followed our ways instead of yours,
Lord, have mercy. **Lord, have mercy.**

We have obeyed our will instead of yours,
Christ, have mercy. **Christ, have mercy.**

We have looked for our glory instead of yours,
Lord, have mercy. **Lord, have mercy.**

Notes on the Readings

Isaiah 6:1-8

When the prophet sees a vision of God's glory, it brings home to him the shame of man's mean response to God and his corrupt hypocritical life, so empty and pompous.

God shows that he has power to forgive, so that the situation is not as hopeless as it seems. Having experienced the generosity of this forgiveness, the prophet is ready to offer himself as God's messenger.

1 Corinthians 15:1-11

Paul's calling was radical and spectacular and he never loses his amazement that God should choose one who had actually persecuted his followers. But having accepted the call, he gets on with the important business of spreading God's saving truth, devoting his entire life and energy to it, and finding that God's rich grace is always sufficient for all his needs.

Luke 5:1-11

Peter's calling begins with an apparently futile suggestion from Jesus which Peter is perfectly free to reject. He must have already been impressed by Jesus' teaching since he is prepared to pay out the nets again just because Jesus says so.

Having made this first step of hesitant faith, he interprets the huge catch as much more than a coincidence. The realisation of Jesus' power highlights his own sinfulness, so that he can hardly bear Jesus to be near him. Again, it has been an acknowledgement of his need and God's acceptance of him regardless of his faults, which results in Peter and his brother taking up the calling, and leaving everything else to follow him.

Bidding Prayers

Celebrant   Brothers and sisters in Christ, let us wait
on God our Father, to know his will
as we pray.

Reader   For Christian witnesses
all over the world
and those who are touched by
the good news of Jesus
that they show in their lives.
Pause
Whom shall I send? **Here I am, Lord; send me.**

For the lives where complacency
and material comforts
have dulled people's hearts to deeper needs
and deafened their ears to God's calling.
Pause
Whom shall I send? **Here I am, Lord; send me.**

For any who have rejected God's
calling through fear of the demands it may
make or doubt about its possibility.
Pause
Whom shall I send? **Here I am, Lord; send me.**

For this worshipping community;
for the removal of all blockages
to receiving God's word and acting upon it.
Pause
Whom shall I send? **Here I am, Lord; send me.**

Celebrant In silence let us pray for the strength and
dedication to offer ourselves to do his will.
Through Christ our Lord. **Amen.**

Ideas for Children

As the children come in, make a point of having various jobs that need doing. In each case say something like: 'Now, we need someone strong to move this table.'; 'We need two people to arrange these lovely flowers Matthew brought.'; etc.

When everyone is ready, remind the children of these needs which various people offered to do. When God has work to be done, we can offer to help as well. Lead the children in prayer –

Heavenly Father,
here I am –
please use me;
I do want to help you.

Tell the children that all of us here have been chosen and asked to help, just as the fishermen, Peter and Andrew, were chosen in Galilee. Sing the 'Follow Me' song before telling the story of the Gospel. Have a fishing net (or net curtain) and ask each child to make a fish with his own name on it clearly marked. (Teachers too.) Poke the fish into the net so the names show and hang the net up. Put a notice beside it saying: 'I will make you fishers of men'.

Music
Recorded Music

Palestrina – *Missa Papae Marcelli: Sanctus & Benedictus*

'Live' Music

Come, follow me *(SONL, 20)*
Follow Christ *(ONE, 144)*
Follow me *(ONE, 145)*
Here I am, Lord *(SOS 3, 213)*
He's a most unusual man *(ONE, 205)*

6th Sunday in Ordinary Time

Theme
Trust in God brings peace and joy

Those who trust in God are greatly blessed with a deeply rooted security which no amount of danger, suffering or persecution can alter. This is because they are deeply rooted in the God of love who nourishes and sustains; the God who, in Jesus, has even conquered death. If we trust in anyone or anything else, we are bound to be badly let down.

Penitential Rite

See Second Sunday of Lent, page 215.

Notes on the Readings

Jeremiah 17:5-8

We have all met people who have become bitter, hard and joyless; who bring a cloud of gloom with them and sour the atmosphere. Jeremiah sees this as a direct result of relying and trusting upon the weak frailty of human nature, as if it were God. The inevitable resulting disillusionment starts the rot.

Often sin is not a question of going too far, but of not going far enough; and in the area of trust, we are often very good at it, only we misdirect our faith instead of placing it in a foolproof and totally dependable person. It is rather like rejecting electricity because it doesn't make a faulty television work properly: but if you plugged it into a better set, you'd get a better picture.

When we root ourselves in God, that faith is honoured, and produces remarkable fruit.

1 Corinthians 15:12, 16-20

To believe in a great God of creation is, in some ways, easier than to believe that Jesus, in the familiar human form, is actually God.

Through the centuries people have found the resurrection an embarrassment and a stumbling block, for it disproves what we as humans feel we know about – that we die and stay dead. If Jesus did not break that barrier, then death must remain as final as ever.

But if he did break it, then he proves that he is both human and divine, and opens up the way for us, too, to pass through death to life. For Paul there is absolutely no doubt that the resurrection indeed took place, which means that for him, for us and our loved ones and all believers, an unnervingly exciting hope becomes an amazing reality.

Luke 6:17, 20-26

Jesus lists a strange set of qualities for bringing happiness, turning the world's values completely upside down. He acknowledges that living in such a way will bring criticism and persecution, but even this will not detract from the happiness. Why ever not?

Jesus, knowing and understanding our human nature, recognises that we are for ever restless and unfulfilled until we rest in the peace of accepting the God who made us. To achieve this, we must journey out of selfishness, relinquish our tight grip of dependence on temporal, worldly things, reject the illusion that we know the answers and become pilgrims, freed from self interest, flexible and receptive to

God who then becomes the ground of our being. This freedom which we find in binding ourselves to God, makes for a wholeness and depth of happiness which nothing can ever take away.

Bidding Prayers

Celebrant Gathered together in faith before our heavenly Father, let us bring him our burdens and cares.

Reader We bring to him
all who teach the Christian faith
by word and example;
that Christ will work,
even through their weakness,
to reach the world.
Pause
Abba, Father: **we belong to you.**

We bring to him
all who are striving
for peace and harmony,
in local government,
national and international negotiations:
that nothing may deter or divert them,
so that the Father's will
may be done on earth.
Pause
Abba, Father: **we belong to you.**

We bring to him all who trust
in wordly or man-made
solutions and systems;
for those whose ideals lead them
not to peace but violence;
that they may see the great rewards
which come from living and trusting
in a God of selfless love.
Pause
Abba, Father: **we belong to you.**

We bring to him our personal faith,
and our lack of faith;
our own efforts to reconcile,
and our sorrow for where we have failed;
we offer him ourselves and ask him
to increase our faith and trust.
Pause
Abba, Father: **we belong to you.**

Celebrant In silence, we commend all our cares to the God who loves us as his children. Through Christ our Lord. **Amen.**

Ideas for Adults

If anyone has slides of desert wilderness contrasted with fruiting trees by water these could be displayed during the first reading while music is played, or during the psalm.

Ideas for Children

Have ready two twigs and a margarine tub of earth or damp sand (or a block of polystyrene) for each child. Also some silver foil and green and pink tissue or crêpe paper, glue and scissors.

First show them some wilting and healthy houseplants, asking them how we could improve the drooping ones. Let the children help water them. Explain how we need food and water as well, to keep us healthy and give energy.

Now show them one of the pots and tell them this story:

'There was once a desert which had very little rain.
There was one stream which trickled through it
(add silver foil stream) and that was all.
There were two trees growing there (put in twigs)
one right beside the stream and the other further off.
For a while both trees did well,
as there was a good rainfall for two or three years
running. (Put on green leaves).
They had leaves, and blossom, and lots of fruit.
But then came a long, long time without rain.
The sun's heat burnt down fiercely
and the leaves of this tree started to drop (pull
off leaves).
The tree by the stream drew up the refreshing water
through its roots,
and went on flowering and fruiting all through the
dry, hot years.'

Tell the children that we need to be trees rooted in Jesus. Then we will go on fruiting, even if times are difficult and we have problems and sadness.

Pray together about this, then let each child make a model of the two trees like this:

Label the models: 'Keep me rooted in you, Lord.'

Music
Recorded Music

Shostakovitch – *Symphony No. 4*

'Live' Music

All my hope on God is founded *(ONE, 25)*
Be thou my vision *(ONE, 61)*
I want to build my life *(SONL, 95)*
Our hearts were made for you *(SONL, 36)*
Peace prayer *(SOS 3, 222)*

7th Sunday in Ordinary Time

Theme
Mercy

Cold justice demands retaliation and revenge, inciting hatred and death. By contrast, God shows that acting with mercy – acknowledging the fault in another, forgiving and remaining in fellowship – brings with it hope, reconciliation and peace. This is the way of Life.

Penitential Rite

Our world is bruised with unforgiven sin,
   Lord, have mercy. **Lord, have mercy.**

Hate and resentment stain the world with blood,
   Christ, have mercy. **Christ, have mercy.**

The world is weak from reprisals and revenge,
   Lord, have mercy. **Lord, have mercy.**

Notes on the Readings

1 Samuel 26:2, 7-9, 12-13, 22-23

This is a very graphic description of the noble young David refusing to take advantage of Saul in spite of everything he has suffered at Saul's hands. The fact that Saul was once anointed by God sets him apart, as far as David is concerned, and in not taking revenge, David is honouring God.

If we believe that all people are made in God's likeness then we, too, must honour God in each person, whether we like what they do or not.

1 Corinthians 15:45-49

Our human nature is material and mortal; life in Christ transforms it, allowing us to participate in what is eternal and spiritual. The closer we came to imitating Christ, the less hold our earthly natures have on us.

Luke 6:27-38

Some of Christ's basic teaching has been gathered here so that we can get a clear view of what 'loving', in God's vocabulary, really entails. What we hear is beyond all boundaries of reason and inclination, and involves becoming 'fools for Christ's sake'.

Since the words are so familiar, it is all too easy to assume that we know it, in the sense that we understand and have assimilated such an attitude in our own relationships.

But what about when we are unjustly accused?
   – unfairly treated?
   – upholding ideals against dangerous opposition?

Yet the way that Christ teaches has no list of exceptions or special cases where the loving can be waived for expediency: it is an all-inclusive response to honouring every sordid scrap of humanity as being God-made and valuable. It is relinquishing all the independence of self until our lack of defensiveness leaves us free to serve.

Bidding Prayers

Celebrant My brothers and sisters, let us pray together, committing our cares to the mercy of God our Father.

Reader For the Church;
   that it may always show the face of

compassion and understanding,
even in times of persecution.
Pause
Blessed be God: **from whom all mercy flows.**

For all multi-ethnic communities,
and for all areas where cultural differences
flare into violence;
that tolerance and mutual respect may
replace divisive bitterness
until seeds of trust and friendship can grow.
Pause
Blessed be God: **from whom all mercy flows.**

For the innocent sufferers caught up
in the tensions and conflicts of rival factions;
for the refugees, the wounded and
the oppressed.
Pause
Blessed be God: **from whom all mercy flows.**

For our own families,
neighbours and friends;
that we may strive daily to live out our faith,
not complaining but rejoicing in every
opportunity to forgive,
to show mercy, and to learn patience.
Pause
Blessed be God: **from whom all mercy flows.**

Celebrant   God our Father, may your love strengthen
and encourage us all.
Through Christ our Lord. **Amen.**

Ideas for Children

Children have a highly developed sense of fairness and enjoy keeping to self-imposed rules in playground games. Have two big boxes with slits in the top labelled FAIR and UNFAIR. Let children pick a card from a pile and discuss whether the situation on it should go in the FAIR or UNFAIR box e.g.

- Janet hadn't finished her painting, so she had to miss playtime to finish it.
- John's bus was late and he was told off for getting to work late.

Explain that sometimes we do deserve punishment. If someone decides to let us off with a warning, we feel very thankful.

Tell the story of David as an example of this. Make plasticine models to show the scene where Saul is surrounded. Display it on a barren hillside scene and write: 'Love your enemies' beside it.

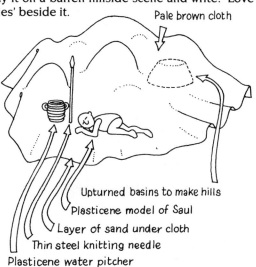

Pale brown cloth

Upturned basins to make hills
Plasticene model of Saul
Layer of sand under cloth
Thin steel knitting needle
Plasticene water pitcher

Music
Recorded Music

Holst – *Planet Suite: Neptune*

'Live' Music

Fear not, for I have redeemed you *(ONE, 136)*
Lead us, heavenly Father *(ONE, 298)*
O Lord all the world belongs to you *(ONE, 403)*
Shout aloud! *(MSOS, 141)*

8th Sunday in Ordinary Time

Theme
What we are shows in how we behave

Just as good fruit is evidence of a sound tree, so our words, attitudes and actions reflect the inward state of our heart and spirit. Knowing this we should aim to be more rigorous with ourselves and less critical of others. In Christ, that struggle is always worthwhile and we must never give up trying.

Penitential Rite

Our harsh and thoughtless words have caused distress
and pain,
Lord, have mercy. **Lord, have mercy.**

We have been critical of others yet blinded to our
own faults,
Christ, have mercy. **Christ, have mercy.**

We have condemned, and not encouraged,
Lord, have mercy. **Lord, have mercy.**

Notes on the Readings

Ecclesiasticus 27:4-7

The wise teacher who wrote these hints and guidelines for living a good life, shows a shrewd understanding of human nature, both in its personal behaviour and in its criteria for judging others; and people have not changed a great deal since he was writing.

Appearances can indeed be deceptive, and we are frequently surprised by how different someone actually is from what our first impressions led us to believe. Of course, it is not just the words people use which give their character away – the manner in which words are said also reflects a person's attitude to other people. And although we must not condemn, neither should we be so gullible that we are taken in by imposters – those who pose as caring friends, only to gossip about other people's business in a damaging way.

1 Corinthians 15:54-58

Underlying all our efforts and desire to become better, more loving people, is the inspiring fact that God has intervened to save us from our own destructive and mortal nature by becoming man himself and gathering all that experience, including death, into the realm of eternity. Knowing this, we need not be down-hearted, however badly things appear to be going, or however little we are appreciated. As Mother Julian of Norwich said: 'All shall be well, and all manner of things shall be well.'

Luke 6:39-45

These cartoon-like illustrations are marvellous for making the absurdity of our behaviour obvious to us. Even as we laugh at the incongruity of the blind men, and the chap with a great plank in his eye, we get nudged by a suspicion of these characters being sometimes dangerously like our own. If the plank is too big, we don't even notice the nudge!

However are we, then, to change and improve our behaviour? Jesus makes it quite clear that there is one foolproof way of bearing good fruit: it is to be a sound tree.

In other words, if we stop worrying about everything, and concentrate instead on spending more time with Jesus, getting to know him more and listening to his will, then the rest will follow automatically. As we become more Christ-like, we will not have to 'act' good lives any more because our inward goodness is bound to prompt us to speak and work in a loving way.

Sometimes our great efforts and busyness are really proof that we are trusting too much in ourselves, and not nearly enough in Christ, who, since he has all power and compassion, is actually a wiser bet!

Bidding Prayers

Celebrant Fellow pilgrims, let us pray to God our Father,
bringing before him
our needs and concerns.

Reader For the Church,
its leaders and all the faithful;
that in setting our hearts steadfastly
on the eternal truth of God's love,
we may be nourished and yield good fruit.
Pause
Lord, support us: **make us whole and strong.**

For those in news coverage
in the mass media;
for all whose words influence
our human society;
that integrity and honour may be valued
and responsibility never abused.
Pause
Lord, support us: **make us whole and strong.**

For those who delight in scandal
and gossip, and for those whose reputations
are damaged by others;
that God's love will heal and renew,
challenge and convert.
Pause
Lord, support us: **make us whole and strong.**

For this parish, its worship,
learning and social groups;
that our genuine love for one another,
and desire for one another's good,
may cleanse our hearts from all envy,
intolerance or spitefulness.
Pause
Lord, support us: **make us whole and strong.**

Celebrant God our Father, in our weakness may we
rely on your constant and almighty strength,
we ask this through Christ our Lord. **Amen.**

Ideas for Adults

Have a central flower arrangement which incorporates deadwood and dry twigs in one section and strong growth with real fruit in another.

Ideas for Children

If you have two leaders (or guests) who don't mind making fools of themselves, start today's session with a short entertainment, based on the Gospel reading.

The two leaders are blindfolded. One knocks at a pretend door.

'Ah, come in, come in!' says the other, walking in the opposite direction, and opening the window.

'I'm over here!' shouts the first. etc.

The idea is that they act out the absurdity of one trying to help the other to a chair, or to find a book or whatever. It should be as funny as possible, and, like a pantomime, encouraging the children to help: 'look – its *behind* you!!'

Finally, take off the blindfold and show how easy it is then.

Trying to pick figs from brambles; the plank and the splinter can also be acted out in clown fashion.

Next, sing a song, as this makes a useful bridge between one mood and another. Then tell the children today's Gospel, which they will now be able to imagine clearly. Finally let them draw a tree with lots of fruit on it (or colour in a duplicated picture). Write over it: 'Good fruit comes from a good tree.'

Music
Recorded Music

Brahms – *Symphony No. 3: end of last movement*

'Live' Music

If we only seek peace *(SONL, 76)*
There is a world *(ONE, 542)*
Walk in love *(SONL, 44)*

9th Sunday in Ordinary Time

Theme
God's Good News is for everyone

It is God's will and longing for every individual to be saved by the outpouring of his grace. He never limits or withholds his love. No wonder, then, that we can see and be inspired by Christ-like qualities in many who are not Christian, just as Jesus found greater faith in a Roman centurion than in many of the Jews.

Penitential Rite

We have not recognised your face in other faces,
   Lord, have mercy. **Lord, have mercy.**

We have undervalued treasures you have given,
   Christ, have mercy. **Christ, have mercy.**

We have not used our opportunities for growth,
   Lord, have mercy. **Lord, have mercy.**

Notes on the Readings

1 Kings 8:41-43

Displaying some of his remarkable wisdom and insight, Solomon grasps the universal nature of God's salvation. For God is not the exclusive property of the chosen people; he is Lord of all creation and he loves all mankind, even those whom we might prefer to leave out of the picture.

Galatians 1:1-2, 6-10

Just as God is universal, so there is only one Good News which is to be shared with the whole world.
   Naturally differences of expression will happen as a result of human diversity, but fundamentally it must not be impaired or falsely taught, for that would have the terrible consequence of leading people away from Christ. We, who have been privileged to hear the Good News already, are given the responsibility of spreading it to other people.

Luke 7:1-10

Recognising in Jesus a fellow figure of authority, the centurion is able to trust his authority in a way that puts many to shame.
   He was obviously a man sensitive to needs, as he commanded wisely and had made friends with the people, even contributing to their synagogue. In many ways he was already touched by the grace of Christ.
   Now, out of surprising concern for a servant, he sees Christ in action, even though he never actually meets him personally. It does not seem to occur to the centurion that Christ would need more than a command to make the servant well again.
   When we pray, do we really expect our prayer to be answered? Are we afraid to expect in case our God lets us down and proves impotent? Yet time and again Jesus says: 'Your faith has saved you.' He acts when we trust him to act.

Bidding Prayers

Celebrant As children of our heavenly Father,
            let us quieten ourselves and pray.

Reader For the Church;
         that having led others,
         Christians may not themselves

be found wanting;
that they may be open to what Christ
needs them to do.
Pause
Lord, I believe: **help my unbelief.**

For the busy, rushed and anxious world;
for those weighed down
with responsibilities,
and for the daily routine of millions
of individuals on this earth;
that God's abundant grace
may touch and light up each
separate person.
Pause
Lord, I believe: **help my unbelief.**

For those who profess to believe
but whose lives are dark and joyless;
that they may experience
the welcoming love of Christ
and be drawn more closely
to his life-giving presence.
Pause
Lord, I believe: **help my unbelief.**

For ourselves and our families,
that we may not waste any
of our life on earth
in pursuing futile goals,
but commit ourselves absolutely
to following Christ,
who has power to save us.
Pause
Lord, I believe: **help my unbelief.**

Celebrant Heavenly Father, we ask you
            to hear our prayers, through
            Christ our Lord. **Amen.**

Ideas for Children

Tell the story of the centurion, using flannelgraph or plasticine models to illustrate it.
   Begin with a game of 'Simon Says'. They only obey if Simon gives the order. Talk about who gives orders that are obeyed:

- policemen in traffic;
- teachers at school;
- doctors about medicine;
- Mums and Dads about looking after the home;
- soldiers in battle.

It is necessary for safety and peace to have someone *in charge*.
   Now tell the story of the Roman centurion (if possible, have a picture of one commanding his men) showing how he was used to being in charge, and recognised Jesus as being in charge as well. Use a flannelgraph or models to illustrate the story.
   Using coloured pencils or pens, let the children decorate these words on a card:

   'Lord, I am not worthy to receive you.
   But only say the word and I shall be healed.'

Do they recognise it from the Mass? And from the centurion story?
   Encourage them to read this from their card next time they are at Mass, and remember how the centurion trusted Jesus to be in charge.

Music
Recorded Music

Sitar music

'Live' Music

Firmly I believe and truly *(ONE, 143)*
Go in peace *(SONL, 45)*
Lord of all hopefulness *(ONE, 329)*
Sing the good news *(MSOS, 155; BSOS, 65)*

10th Sunday in Ordinary Time

Theme
Life restored

All life is brought into being by God; we depend on him for our whole existence. He also has power to restore life and wholeness and is not immune from the sadness and heart-break that death brings. By his grace we can be healed and enlivened in amazing ways; this is the message of hope we can bring to others.

Penitential Rite

Without Christ there would be no life,
  Lord, have mercy. **Lord, have mercy.**

Without Christ there would be no joy,
  Christ, have mercy. **Christ, have mercy.**

Without Christ there would be no peace,
  Lord, have mercy. **Lord, have mercy.**

Notes on the Readings

1 Kings 17:17-24

Having been fed and sustained by the widow, Elijah wrestles with what seems such cruel injustice. Surely God will not allow her son to die after she has shown such trust and kindness to the man of God.

Elijah pleads with God for the child's life, and his prayer is answered: the child lives, and the widow's faith is strengthened. Had Elijah not intervened, the child would surely have died.

Sometimes it takes a state of desperation and heart-breaking anguish to get us praying – really praying – with our whole being. God never rejects such prayer. But, seeing life as he does, in terms of eternity, restoration to life and vitality may sometimes involve vitalising spiritual deadness, rather than physical, and therefore temporary, health.

When we throw ourselves on his mercy in times of terrible need and despair, we can trust him absolutely to do what is best for us and the one we pray for.

Galatians 1:11-19

Paul wants to make it quite clear that God intervened personally in his own life to show him the good news of Christ's saving love. It was a direct challenge to his destructive and prejudiced behaviour; a direct invitation to an entirely 'new' life.

Luke 7:11-17

There are only three cases, recorded in the Gospels, of Jesus bringing a person back to life; this young man, the son of a widow, reflects the story of Elijah, with Jesus similarly deeply touched with sorrow and compassion. It also looks forward to the resurrection. The young man will physically have to die again, so his restoration to life is only transitory. The resurrection offers a much longer-lasting restoration to life: in the living Christ we can be made spiritually alive; and that life will never ever die.

Bidding Prayers

Celebrant Let us pray, my brothers and sisters, in the knowledge of our Father's infinite mercy.

Reader For all Christian people,
especially those whose belief
has been battered
through disaster and suffering;
that they may know the certainty
of God's abiding presence,
which transforms and rebuilds.
Pause
Touch our lives, Lord: **that we may live.**

For all administrative bodies
and political institutions;
that they may be always aware
of the real needs of those they serve,
and be effective in providing for them.
Pause
Touch our lives, Lord: **that we may live.**

For the dying and those
who love and tend them;
for the bereaved and desolate;
that they may draw strength
from the reality of Christ's life
and his victory over death.
Pause
Touch our lives, Lord: **that we may live.**

For our local community
with all its needs and cares;
that we may be ready to serve Christ
in our own area and spread his
life-giving joy.
Pause
Touch our lives, Lord: **that we may live.**

Celebrant God our Father, hear our prayer
and help us to do your will.
Through Christ our Lord. **Amen.**

Ideas for Adults

The first reading lends itself well to being mimed or acted.

Ideas for Children

Ask the children to remember some of Jesus' healing works when he was living as a man in Galilee. Explain how he aways felt sorry for people who were sad or ill, and wanted to make them well.

Now tell the story of today's Gospel, referring to a picture if possible.

If the children know of anyone who is ill the whole group can pray for them, imagining Jesus comforting them and asking him to make them well.

Then the children can make this pop-up card. They will need a piece of folded paper, and a semi-circle marked with fold lines; coloured pencils, scissors and glue. Decorate the inside as brightly as possible, and keep the outside plain so that the contrast will be greater when they open the card up.

Music
Recorded Music

Rachmaninov – *Prelude in G No. 5 Op. 32*

'Live' Music

I now no longer live *(SONL, 6)*
Living Lord *(ONE, 326)*
Morning has broken *(ONE, 350)*
The Lord is there at your side *(SOS 3, 287)*
Walk with me, O my Lord *(ONE, 582)*

11th Sunday in Ordinary Time

Theme
Forgiveness

However strictly we may observe the Law, it will never bring us forgiveness or save us from sin. To be forgiven we need to acknowledge that we have shown contempt for our generous, loving God, and then have faith in his power to cleanse and heal us. In this way we shall die to our sin and live, not in our own strength, but in the strength of God.

Penitential Rite

Use Come, Spirit, come, from page 214.

Notes on the Readings

2 Samuel 12:7-10, 13

Through Nathan, God touches David's heart by showing how his selfish action had insulted his maker and sustainer. It says a lot for David's character, that he did not lose his temper and banish Nathan, or try to excuse himself or shift the blame. Very simply, and in sorrow, he admits his guilt; immediately this opens God's forgiving heart.

No one is ever too far entrenched in sin to be forgiven, provided they turn to Christ in contrition and are committed to making amends wherever possible. Forgiveness will always involve living differently in the future: if we have no intention of changing our behaviour, then we have not really repented at all.

Galatians 2:16, 19-21

Paul had been a very committed and conscientious rabbi, following the Law astutely. He is therefore well qualified to speak on this question bothering the Galatians: the importance of the Law in being saved and liberated from one's sins. If anyone could find salvation by strict adherence to God's Mosaic Law, it would be Paul himself.

Yet he confidently asserts that the Law, though valuable as a guideline, creates its own type of prison; for although it suggests a good, noble and godly way of living, it does not provide the strength and power which weak humanity desperately needs in order to achieve such a life.

With the coming of Jesus Christ, all this changed. God, humbling himself in becoming man, accepts the duties and confines of the Law, but also breaks through them to suffuse them with his own life and power. So, when we accept Christ, we too are enabled to plug into that power which can at last take us just as we are, without pretence, and make us new creatures, able to do all things; for it is no longer us, but Christ alive and working in us and through us.

Luke 7:36 – 8:3

Simon the Pharisee is a respected and honourable man, dutiful and fully committed to leading a good life. We may wonder what prompted him to invite Jesus to a meal at his house. Perhaps this surprisingly wise teacher from Nazareth spoke words so profound that he wanted to know more of him; perhaps he was merely sounding out a man whom people were beginning to claim as a prophet. His lack of courtesy suggests that he did not rank Jesus as anyone very important. Whatever his reasons, he is certainly taken aback when Jesus seems quite unembarrassed by the attentions of a woman of bad reputation. The incident makes him suspect that Jesus may be an imposter. Jesus' response, however, proves him to be a prophet whose vision is wider and more fundamentally satisfying and practical than any before him. Simon is led to the point where he can see the link between love and forgiveness. The Law went hand in hand with condemnation; Jesus brings it to life with reconciliation.

Bidding Prayers

Celebrant   We believe that God has power to help us,
so let us pray for the Church and for the world.

Reader   For those who work for the
spreading of God's kingdom on earth;
that when disheartened
they may be encouraged,
and when weak or spent
they may be sustained
by the strength of the living Christ.
Pause
Lord, give us grace: **to live in the life of Christ.**

For the leaders of the nations,
their advisers and administrators;
that they may promote and maintain
peace and justice
based on care and respect.
Pause
Lord, give us grace: **to live in the life of Christ.**

For those in prisons,
detention centres or labour-camps;
and for all whose guilt weighs
heavily upon them;
that they may be led to Jesus
and know the joy and liberation
of his forgiveness.
Pause
Lord, give us grace: **to live in the life of Christ.**

For our homes; for the people
with whom we live and work;
that we may forgive others
as eagerly and fully as God forgives us.
Pause
Lord, give us grace: **to live in the life of Christ.**

Celebrant   Father, we ask this through your son,
Christ our Lord. **Amen.**

Ideas for Children

Tell the story Jesus told Simon, using the children to help you. First choose a postman, and give him a bag and badge (or hat) with two bills to deliver.

'One morning the postman delivered a letter to Sam Butcher. (Postman gives one bill to him). Sam opened it (let him open it and show everyone) and inside was a bill for £5.

How do you think Sam felt? A bit fed up/miserable? "At least it's not *too* big a bill," he thought. "I'll have to go without all my sweets this week."

Then the postman delivered a letter to Robert South. (He delivers it). Robert opened it and looked inside. It was a bill for £5000!

How do you think Robert felt? He was very worried and sad, because he didn't have much money at all. "Oh dear," he thought, "I'll *never* manage to pay this. Not unless I sell my house – and then where could I live?"

He felt worried and sad all day. He hardly slept that night, for thinking about the way he couldn't pay that huge bill. Perhaps he would be sent to prison, even.

Next morning the postman delivered another letter to Sam and another to Robert. They opened them, rather nervously. Inside was an important looking letter. It said (let the children read it our together)

Dear Sir,
I am going to let you off.
You need not pay me
the money after all.
Best wishes,
Tom Smith (Manager)

Well, how do you think they felt? Happy/delighted/relieved? They felt very relieved and happy. Sam was glad he could buy some sweets as usual.

But who do you think felt most thankful? It was Robert! He had been so worried and sad, and it was as if a great heavy weight was lifted off him. He ran out to Tom Smith's office to thank him straight away. He would never forget Tom's kindness.'

Explain that Jesus is rather like Tom Smith, and we are like Sam and Robert. When we do something wrong or unkind it is like being in debt. When we are forgiven, our debt is paid, and we feel happy and relieved again. Let the children make these cards to remind them.

Music
Recorded Music

Vivaldi – *The Four Seasons: Largo from Spring*

'Live' Music

Bless the Lord, O my soul *(MSOS, 180; BSOS, 37)*
Lord, however can I repay you *(ONE, 324)*
Oh, the love of my Lord *(ONE, 430)*
The King of love *(ONE, 528)*

12th Sunday in Ordinary Time

Theme

If we suffer with Christ we shall also live with him

Strange as it may seem, the free and lasting peace of full life is only experienced when we stop defending and bettering our own comforts, and instead start giving ourselves away. Like Christ, this is bound to result in suffering, but it is not a hard, resentful suffering. Clothed with Christ we find that it leads to an unexpected and remarkable joy.

Penitential Rite

We have chosen our ways, instead of yours,
  Lord, have mercy. **Lord, have mercy.**

Our lives have not shown your love,
  Christ, have mercy. **Christ, have mercy.**

We have failed to recognise your face,
  Lord, have mercy. **Lord, have mercy.**

Notes on the Readings

Zechariah 12:10-11; 13:1

This prophecy looks forward to the suffering of God's chosen one, which will release a new spirit of kindness and prayer among his people, even though they have been instrumental in his death. In their guilt and grief they suffer with him, and having made themselves receptive, can be remade as his own people.

Galatians 3:26-29

Paul is stressing here the new-found unity which is a direct result of belonging to Christ. Baptism is like a kind of dying, in that it is a complete break with the world's categorising, compartmentalised society, divisive by its very nature.

New life in Christ is not the old with a few 'extras' thrown in; it is a complete remaking – more like a caterpillar's transformation into a butterfly.

We are often happiest with things as they are; reluctant to alter what we know and understand, even if there are difficulties. Yet we must risk ourselves with Christ if he is to change us.

Luke 9:18-24

Not surprisingly, when the people were faced with the promised Christ in person, they were full of suggestions about his identity which would not demand too shattering a change to their lives and beliefs. When Peter acknowledged Christ as God's chosen one, he was taking a tremendous risk. After all, at this stage there had been no resurrection, and Jesus looked and functioned in a perfectly normal way. To acknowledge Jesus as 'the Christ of God' meant unavoidable and radical change in Peter. The years of waiting had a certain safety about them, but if the Messiah was actually there standing next to him, the waiting was over and man had entered a new phase in his relationship with God.

Straight away, Jesus speaks of the inevitable action of suffering and death. There is no possible way to save the world other than the Creator himself submitting to his creation in an entire self-offering of love.

Bidding Prayers

Celebrant Together let us quieten ourselves in God our Father's presence and pray to him.

Reader For all who teach the Christian faith;
  that they may lead others
  by word and example
  to know Jesus as Lord and Saviour.
  Pause
  Heavenly Father: **sustain us in your love.**

For all countries involved in war,
  and those whose peace is fragile;
  that the forgiving Spirit of Jesus
  may be present in all negotiations,
  so that a lasting peace may be established.
  Pause
  Heavenly Father: **sustain us in your love.**

For all who suffer for Christ;
  for those who are persecuted
  or despised for their faith;
  that their witness may bear fruit.
  Pause
  Heavenly Father: **sustain us in your love.**

For those who live
  in this parish,
  especially any whose needs
  are known to us.
  In silence we commend them by name
  to the comfort of God's everlasting
  tenderness.
  Pause
  Heavenly Father: **sustain us in your love.**

Celebrant Father, we ask for your mercy,
  encouragement and support.
  Through Christ our Lord. **Amen.**

Ideas for Children

The readings this week are very difficult for children to grasp, but the underlying principles can be explored.

There are several traditional stories which show how trying to keep a precious thing to oneself causes it to wither or die. Or you could invent your own:

'There was once a man who loved gardening. He had the most beautiful garden for miles around. But he found that the children and animals came to play in it, so he built a low wall around it. The children and animals jumped over the wall. "It's my garden," said the man angrily to himself. "I'll build the wall so high that no one can get in." So he did. But the sun and wind and rain couldn't get in either, and the garden plants started to fade and wither and die. When it was almost too late, the man sat miserably in his dark, shadowy, lonely 'prison' and suddenly realised what he must do. It was hard work, but he smashed and crashed at that high wall till the sun beamed in and the weak flowers lifted their heads towards it. On and on he worked, till the wall was a pile of rubble all round his garden. It wasn't long before all the plants sprouted and blossomed and fruited for all they were worth; it wasn't much longer before the children and animals came back to play. The man was very happy, and enjoyed his garden better than he ever had before. And what is more, the rubble became a most beautiful rockery to frame the garden.'

(If you like, accompany the story with pictures, homemade film strip or overhead projector)

Explain that we are sometimes like the gardener when we

want to keep our time, energy or gifts (abilities) to use just for ourselves.

Jesus shows us how we will be much richer, happier people if we are ready to break down the high walls we build by living selfishly.

Activity

Let the children make a moving picture. Use fairly thin white paper so the bottom picture can just about be traced. Have this already drawn. Following the outline, trace the front picture, but making the sun full and the plant happy with the wall gone.

To work it, curl the corner of the top picture tightly round a pencil. Then use the pencil to flatten the paper. As you slide the pencil back, the curled paper springs round it. Move the pencil backwards and forwards quickly and the picture 'moves'.

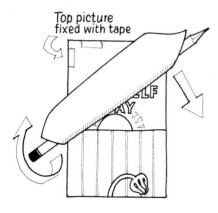

Top picture fixed with tape

Music
Recorded Music

Bach – *Violin Concerto in A minor: Adagio*

'Live' Music

Take up your cross *(SONL, 42)*
Though the mountains may fall *(ONE, 569)*
You may cross the barren desert *(ONE, 627)*
You touch my soul *(SONL, 62)*

Questions for Discussion Groups
What makes a good pilgrim?
1. Working from the parables Jesus told, what seem to be the qualities displayed by a committed follower of Christ?
2. How can we avoid advertising a cheap, easy (and false) Christianity, while still proclaiming God's wide accepting love?

13th Sunday in Ordinary Time

Theme
Total commitment

Those whom God calls or appoints for particular ministries are free either to accept or reject the callings; but there are no half measures – Christ demands our complete allegiance and gives in return the power for us to become complete, fulfilled people, no longer enslaved by sin.

Penitential Rite

Love is encouraging and kind,
    Lord, have mercy. **Lord, have mercy.**

Love is willing to serve and give,
    Christ, have mercy. **Christ, have mercy.**

Love is disciplined and strong,
    Lord, have mercy. **Lord, have mercy.**

Notes on the Readings

1 Kings 19:16, 19-21

Elisha is appointed Elijah's successor by the sign of receiving his cloak, while he is about his normal, everyday farming tasks. His acceptance of appointment involves the surrender of his past life: he slaughters the pair of oxen and gives them to his men to eat. Having thus broken completely with his former life, he commits himself entirely to being Elijah's servant.

Galatians 5:1, 13-18

Commitment to Christ needs constant renewal, because our weakness as humans makes us constantly vulnerable to temptation, and we are quite mistaken if we think that, having consciously turned to Christ, our future lives will automatically remain true to him. They won't. We will find that there are times when we are submitting ourselves again to the yoke of slavery and then the destructive behaviour is bound to follow. Paul shows us the only way to avoid this: we must allow ourselves to be led by the Spirit and he will both strengthen us to protect us from falling, and help us get up again when we do fall.

Luke 9:51-62

In this reading we see both Jesus' and man's commitment. Firstly, Jesus, fully aware of the distress and agony he is certain to encounter, nevertheless resolutely takes the road to Jerusalem, obedient to his calling, regardless of the risks and cost.

Secondly, we see several examples of men offering to follow or being called. 'I will follow you wherever you go,' says one. We sense in Jesus' reply that perhaps the man was not fully aware of the hardships and discomforts his decision would entail.

Others make excuses for not immediately obeying their call. Their reasons may seem humane and valid, but this is not really the point. They serve to point out how radical and absolute our approach to Christ must be: we are little use to him unless we are prepared to commit ourselves whole-heartedly.

Bidding Prayers

Celebrant Companions in Christ, let us pray,
opening our hearts to the love of our Lord
and Saviour.

Reader For all who are called
to follow Christ
in lay and ordained ministries;
that they may be strengthened
and blessed in their work.
Pause
Father: **make us instruments of your peace.**

For peace in the world;
for respect and co-operation between
nations and individuals;
for the humility which sees criticism
as an opportunity instead of a threat.
Pause
Father: **make us instruments of your peace.**

For all children and young people
at risk, either physically or emotionally;
for those who are abused and damaged;
that they may be protected, healed
and sustained.
Pause
Father: **make us instruments of your peace.**

That God's love will pervade
our own relationships,
to make them more positive,
constructive and supportive.
Pause
Father: **make us instruments of your peace.**

Celebrant Lord and heavenly Father, as we commit
our lives afresh to your service,
we ask you to hear our prayers.
Through Christ our Lord. **Amen.**

Ideas for Children

Have ready an envelope with a children's party invitation inside. Ask the children if they've ever had something like it, then read it out. Also read out the reply slip.

What do we have to do with this part?

Through their answers make it clear that when we are invited somewhere, we can either say 'yes' or 'no'. Then fill in the 'yes' section with them. Explain that Jesus invited people to come with him and help him in his work, and some said 'yes', some said 'no' and made excuses. (Perhaps they can name some of those Jesus called – Peter, Matthew, John, etc.)

Now give each child a party invitation written with his own name like this:

Dear John,
You are invited to spend your life
helping me to give love, joy
and peace to the world.
It will be hard work, but
it will make you very happy.
I do hope you can join me.
Love from Jesus.

Dear Jesus,
Thank you for inviting me.
I do/do not want to be your friend and help you.
Love from . . .

These can be filled in and cut off. Then, perhaps at the offertory, the slips can be taken up to the altar.

Dance based on the song 'Follow me' from *Good morning, Jesus*.

SONG	DANCE
Verse 1 Jesus went a-walking by the sea shore, walking by the sea shore, walking by the sea. Jesus went a-walking by the sea shore, said to the fishermen, 'Follow me.'	*Have one group of children miming hauling in their nets, rowing, winding ropes, etc. Jesus walks jauntily along, breathing in the sea air and then watches the fishermen.* *He beckons and they all leave their nets.*
Chorus 'Follow, follow, follow me; follow, follow, follow me; follow, follow, follow me; and I will make you Fishers of men.'	*They link hands in a long chain, dancing in a central area.* *Jesus stands still and raises his arms while fishermen separate, turn and face members of congregation.*
Verse 2 Jesus goes a-walking through the wide world, walking through the wide world, walking through the world, Jesus goes a-walking through the wide world, saying to everyone, 'Follow me.'	*Slowly Jesus and the fishermen walk down the aisles and stop at different places, offering hands.* *They 'collect' a number of people and join up into several chains.*
Chorus 'Follow, follow, follow me; follow, follow, follow me; follow, follow, follow me; and I will make you Fishers of men.'	*These chains of people dance all round the church, weaving in and out.* *All stop. Jesus stands in front of altar and raises his arms. Everyone turns to face him, kneels with arms raised*

Music

Recorded Music

Widor – *Symphony No. 5: Toccata*

'Live' Music

Come, follow me *(SOS 3, 269)*
Farmer, farmer *(SONL, 37)*
Lord of my life *(SONL, 21)*
This day God gives me *(ONE, 555)*
Walk with me *(ONE, 582)*

14th Sunday in Ordinary Time

Theme
Peace

Peace is part of the very nature of God, and flows from him like a river. It provides the warmth and wholeness which satisfies our deepest needs, and yet it is in no way dependent on comfort, for it often flourishes through suffering. Our commission is to be remade in Christ until we can spread this peace to our anxious, desperate world.

Penitential Rite

We are in need of your stillness in our lives,
    Lord, have mercy. **Lord, have mercy.**

We are in need of your light in our minds,
    Christ, have mercy. **Christ, have mercy.**

We are in need of your peace in our hearts,
    Lord, have mercy. **Lord, have mercy.**

Notes on the Readings

Isaiah 66:10-14

These words of hope and comfort are for any who feel exiled, whether physically, mentally, emotionally or spiritually. We shall not be left comfortless, but given peace, like a flowing river. The image is one of life, refreshment and movement, and strangely this experience of God-given peace often emerges before the danger of exile has gone. So Christians are not dependent on worldly success, popularity or financial security for peace of mind; trust in a loving, personal yet all-powerful God brings a flowing peace even in exile or uncertain, dangerous times.

Galatians 6:14-18

Paul stresses that nothing like race or customs are important: what really matters is man and God working together to make a new creature. This involves utter, abandoned surrender to God, which has the effect of releasing an outpouring of mercy and peace.

Luke 10:1-12, 17-20

When Jesus commissions the seventy-two to spread his peace, we see again the paradox of being a follower of Christ. Without comforts or security they and we are sent out into the world as vulnerable lambs among predatory wolves. Yet they are rich and generous with the qualities which really matter; they spread the peace of God which brings hope, joy and healing to those who receive it.

Working hand in hand with God is not only a great privilege, but also an infectious delight.

Bidding Prayers

Celebrant My brothers and sisters, in the peace of our Creator and sustainer, let us pray.

Reader For the Church throughout the world,
especially in areas of apathy,
and rejection of spiritual values;
that through Christian witness
many may come to find peace
and fulfilment in Jesus, the Saviour.
Pause
Heavenly Father: **give us your peace.**

For all places of conflict;
for countries at war,
for all areas of violence and bloodshed,
bitterness and hatred.
Pause
Heavenly Father: **give us your peace.**

For all who are distressed, bewildered,
lost or confused;
for those making painful decisions;
for those who have no one
to turn to for help;
that they may be given guidance,
comfort and serenity.
Pause
Heavenly Father: **give us your peace.**

For ourselves, the special needs
and concerns known to us;
for our own spiritual growth
that our ordered lives may proclaim
the beauty of God's peace.
Pause
Heavenly Father: **give us your peace.**

Celebrant Father, knowing that you alone have the words of eternal life, we lay our prayers before you. Through Christ our Lord. **Amen.**

Ideas for Adults

Show slides of peaceful ideas, such as a child asleep, sunrise and sunset, calm water, shady trees, etc., while music is played. (See music suggestion).

Or have a display board with pictures and quotations arranged to draw attention to the theme.

Ideas for Children

Tell the children the story of Jesus sending out seventy-two of his followers, and how they got on. It would be helpful to illustrate the story with drawings on a roll or an overhead projector. For instance:

In their groups talk about how Jesus sends us out to do his work:

- some to be Mums and Dads, teachers, nurses, drivers, miners, etc.;
- some to help Mums, Dads, teachers (that's us!);
- some to befriend a lonely or ill or old person (is that me?); and so on.

Help the children to see that Jesus needs them *now*; they don't have to wait until they are grown up.

Let the children decorate a postcard to put up in a place they will see it each morning.

Here I am,
Lord:
use me!

Music
Recorded Music

Mozart – *Clarinet Concerto: Adagio*

'Live' Music

Do not be troubled *(SOS 3, 255)*
Give me peace, O Lord, I pray *(ONE, 160)*
Go in peace *(SONL, 45)*
Peace is flowing *(ONE, 442)*

15th Sunday in Ordinary Time

Theme
The Law of Love

Through Moses the law of loving God and one's neighbour was given; God also gives strength within us to obey it, and see its relevance in our daily lives. Without this insight the law is a dead set of rules; yet with it, the wounded and abused world can be healed and set free.

Penitential Rite

We have not noticed other people's needs,
    Lord, have mercy. **Lord, have mercy.**

We have excused ourselves from getting involved in your work,
    Christ, have mercy. **Christ, have mercy.**

We have been deaf to your will,
    Lord, have mercy. **Lord, have mercy.**

Notes on the Readings

Deuteronomy 30:10-14

When Moses gives the people God's Law he makes it quite clear that they have not been given an impossible task, because the strength and will for obeying come from God himself who lives actually within a person. Having made us in the first place, he knows us even better than we know ourselves, and so he fully understands our weakness, lack of perseverance and capacity for rebellion.

Yet his knowledge of us is not all: he also loves us and longs for our well-being and peace of mind. Knowing that man can only find these things in loving God and his neighbour unselfishly, he provides not only the Law of Love, but the strength and power to achieve it.

It is when we separate ourselves from that strength and power that things begin to go badly wrong, both in ourselves and in our world.

Colossians 1:15-20

This reading explains how the ancient Law of Love becomes a personal reality in Jesus of Nazareth. He was the 'Word', or 'Command', through which all creation came into being, and his life and death 'fulfilled' the Law, or in other words, 'filled it full'. In the way Jesus lived and died, we can see clearly the Law in practice.

He gave no extra, complicated regulations, and he broke through much of the accumulated deadwood of empty ritual; he gave instead the perfect example of life lived in its proper perspective, with Love the central power house.

Luke 10:25-37

This Gospel shows us how, all too easily, our mouths can utter honourable vows of commitment which our lives belie. We can probably think of many vows we have made which we thought, at the time, we understood, but only later discovered what was really entailed. Perhaps we may regret ever having promised anything, at that point!

But if we have kept the vow even in the hard times, we can look back gratefully to the way the difficulties have enabled us to grow. The lawyer who approaches Jesus thinks that he understands the Law inside out and back to front. He is really hoping to make a fool of this new upstart.

Jesus shows him, in the story of the Good Samaritan, what the Law really entails when it has soaked into a man's whole being. It is no longer a case of doing certain things and not doing certain other things. It involves the much more open-ended and therefore far costlier commitment which sees with eyes of love, recognises needs with insight, and works for another's good without counting the cost.

Bidding Prayers

Celebrant Dear brothers and sisters, let us pray in Christ, bringing before our loving Father all our needs and concerns.

Reader For the Church, the Body of Christ;
that all its members,
being each important to the whole,
may be bound together
in the outreaching,
selflessness of God's love.

Pause

Lord, teach us your will: **and help us to carry it out.**

For this planet as it moves
in the vast universe;
that each individual may honour
and value both his neighbour,
and all creation.

Pause

Lord, teach us your will: **and help us to carry it out.**

For the victims of violence and disaster,
for refugees, the homeless and those
living in shanty towns;
that they may be relieved of pain
and restored to human dignity,
and that those of us more fortunate
may be moved to help them.

Pause

Lord, teach us your will: **and help us to carry it out.**

For ourselves;
that we may know more and more clearly
the work God needs us to do,
and be given his courage and obedience
gladly to do whatever he asks of us.

Pause

Lord, teach us your will: **and help us to carry it out.**

Celebrant Lord God of love, we offer you these prayers through Christ our Lord. **Amen.**

Ideas for Adults

A group of adults could act out the Good Samaritan story during the Gospel, with narrator and mime or speaking parts. Alternatively, it could be mimed to appropriate music: see the music section for suggestions.

Ideas for Children

The Good Samaritan is an excellent story for the children to act out, but it needs to be clearly explained first.

If the priest and the Levite touched a dead man they would be considered 'unclean' by the Law. The man looked dead, so they passed by, pretending they hadn't noticed.

The Samaritan came from another country so it was extra strange for him to bother with the man. But because he saw the man needed help he felt sorry for him, and helped him as best he could.

There are several book versions of the story which can be used. Give the children lots of help with what to do and say, setting out the room first with a road, an inn, Jerusalem and Jericho. Have strips of material for bandages and some pretend ointment in a small pot, some play money in a bag and some plastic cups for the people at the inn.

Music
Recorded Music

Lloyd Webber – Requiem: Pie Jesu
Palestrina – practically any Kyrie
Holst – Planet Suite: Saturn

'Live' Music

Colours of day (ONE, 87)
Make me a channel of your peace (ONE, 342)
Story of love (SONL, 76)
You touch my soul (SONL, 62)

16th Sunday in Ordinary Time

Theme
Welcoming Christ

The central message of Christianity is that Christ lives among us and is happy to make his home in every receptive heart. Abraham recognises God's presence in the visitation of the three travellers and welcomes them generously. Martha and Mary welcome Jesus to their home. Gently Jesus explains to Martha that welcoming may sometimes involve listening, rather than busily 'doing'.

Penitential Rite

We have shut our doors against your love,
  Lord, have mercy. **Lord, have mercy.**

We do not always open the door when you knock,
  Christ, have mercy. **Christ, have mercy.**

We have been too busy to hear your words of life,
  Lord, have mercy. **Lord, have mercy.**

Notes on the Readings

Genesis 18:1-10

Here we have a delightful picture of Abraham's practical yet reverent nature. He sees and values the significance of the three men's visit, and he hurries about making sure that every possible comfort is provided – the very image of a perfect host. Sarah prepares a delicious meal, and Abraham presents it to them, standing by, rather than joining in, as a mark of respect.

It is right, and often instinctive, to express our admiration, respect or love for a guest in giving of our best in a practical way.

Sometimes we are so concerned not to have 'empty' ritual that we become more casual with God than we would be with a respected friend. We must not forget our manners when we are in God's presence; he is a most precious guest, and we can enjoy welcoming him with the delight and courteous attention of Abraham.

Colossians 1:24-28

Paul proclaims the fact that Christ is actually among us now; he is our guest and we are privileged to see his glory in a more personal, open way than any of the Old Testament prophets could.

His presence brings great joy and strength, but it also challenges us to join Christ in his redeeming work. This will certainly create problems, hardships and suffering in our lives, but since Christ, in person, has commissioned us, we can take up the work gladly, knowing he will support and uphold us always.

Luke 10:38-42

While on earth Jesus became the guest of Martha and Mary. Like Abraham, Martha bustled about to prepare the very best for a guest she honoured and respected. Unlike Abraham, she became so anxious about the practical side that she began to lose sight of the really important part of welcoming a guest: that of giving him her loving and receptive attention.

Jesus does not need us to busy ourselves doing thousands of jobs we think he might find useful; he wants us to welcome him with a young child's enthusiasm, to be happy in his presence, enjoying his company and learning at his feet through a loving relationship.

Bidding Prayers

Celebrant In stillness let us pray
to our heavenly Father.

Reader We lay before him the weaknesses,
misunderstandings, mistakes
and foolishness in the members
of Christ's Body, the Church;
that in teaching us humility
and forgiveness they too may become
a source of strength and renewal.
Pause
Lord of all: **we welcome you into our lives.**

We lay before him all worldly distrust,
revenge, and corruption,
the deceit and injustice;
that God's living Spirit may inspire,
guide, repair and renew
even where it is darkest.
Pause
Lord of all: **we welcome you into our lives.**

We lay before him all those whose
busy lives leave little time for stillness;
for the overworked: those suffering
from stress and exhaustion;
that they may find God's inner peace
a constant strength and refreshment.
Pause
Lord of all: **we welcome you into our lives.**

We lay before him all the relationships
in our everyday lives;
the ordering of our own timetable;
that living closely with Christ

we may learn how to make room
for the important things
of eternal significance.
Pause
Lord of all: **we welcome you into our lives.**

Celebrant God our Father, we ask you to help us fix
our lives on you. Through Christ our Lord. **Amen.**

Ideas for Children

Talk about some of the special occasions in their families, like birthdays, Christmas, friends round to a meal, etc., and the preparations we make to show our love.

Sit them down round a table, and as you talk about preparing for a special guest, lay the table with a pretty cloth, candles, flowers nearby, plates and glasses. Make it as beautiful as possible.

When all is ready, ask the children if the table reminds them of something in church. Explain how the Mass is a special meal with a very important guest, then lead their prayers.

Dear Lord Jesus,
we welcome you!
We give you our hands,
our voices,
and our hearts
for you to use.
Please live in us,
now and always.
Amen.

Music
Recorded Music

Modern Jazz Quartet – *Exposure*
Beethoven – *Symphony No. 6 (Pastoral)*

'Live' Music

Praise the Lord (Psalm 150) *(SONL, 43)*
Take my life and let it be *(ONE, 510)*
Tantum ergo / Come adore *(ONE, 672)*
Walk with me, oh my Lord *(ONE, 582)*
We come to you, Lord *(MSOS, 165; BSOS, 1)*

17th Sunday in Ordinary Time

Theme
Praying to our Father

Through his death and resurrection Jesus has made it possible for us to become sons and daughters of God. As our loving Father, God will listen to our requests, and give us whatever is good and necessary for us, and for our spiritual growth and development.

Penitential Rite

You know the secrets of our inmost hearts,
    Lord, have mercy. **Lord, have mercy.**

You know our weaknesses and our strengths,
    Christ, have mercy. **Christ, have mercy.**

You know our hidden needs and fears,
    Lord, have mercy. **Lord, have mercy.**

Notes on the Readings

Genesis 18:20-32

We sometimes confuse God's mercy with an indulgent tolerance which is no part of his character. Jesus wept over the crowds at Jerusalem frantically racing after fatuous goals in the wrong direction, and he was angry at man's misuse of the house of prayer. This conversation between Abraham and God, concerning the destruction of Sodom and Gomorrah, shows Abraham pleading for mercy on account of the innocent. What better, more conscientious father could God have chosen for his people!

God shows his compassion in agreeing to save the cities, in spite of the way they have sinned against him, for the sake of merely ten just men.

God's standards are high and we must not underestimate them. They require self discipline, self control and rigour as well as forgiveness and understanding. We do not honour him by allowing evil to flourish around us or within us in the name of tolerance and freedom. We shall only be truly free if we live as God's people, on his terms of disciplined love.

Colossians 2:12-24

Seeing man's sinfulness and his inability to rise above it, God intervenes at his own expense to cancel the great debt of sin. To do this, he does not admit defeat, and lower his standards to accept man's dismal record of habitual sinning. After all, he knows man's potential and longs for him to know happiness and peace. So the only way he can cancel the debt is by paying it himself, in full. In the agony of the passion, we see this sacrifice in action, but this is only the historical focus of it: in terms of eternity, that debt is constantly being paid off; we see the suffering Christ in every starving, maltreated, exiled face.

Having paid the debt, Christ was raised and lives for ever; the first Easter Day was the historical focus, but in terms of eternity that resurrection victory continues too, in every barrier of hatred, broken by love; every act of loving service replacing resentment; every God-inspired rejection of evil and commitment to goodness.

Luke 11:1-13

The disciples could see that when Jesus prayed it was an altogether different experience from the praying they knew. What he taught was not so much a form of words as a new

relationship with God. Just as we would expect our children to be given good things from their earthly father, so we, as God's children, can trustingly ask and expect to receive good things from our heavenly Father.

It is sometimes helpful to think of the Lord's Prayer as headings, and spend much longer on each phrase than is usual, remembering throughout each phrase and silence, that God is our loving Father and we are conversing with him as his loving children.

Bidding Prayers

Celebrant   Invited by our heavenly Father, as his sons and daughters through Christ, we pray.

Reader   For the continuous worship of the Church in every different climate, culture and season;
that the waves of constant praise and thanksgiving may never be broken;
that Christians may pray attentively, joyfully and faithfully.
Pause
Our Father in heaven: **may your Kingdom come.**

 For all those in positions of authority, that they may neither abuse their power nor ignore their responsibilities but act with integrity, compassion and generosity of spirit.
Pause
Our Father in heaven: **may your Kingdom come.**

For all families split by political boundaries, war or natural disasters;
for all who have nowhere to call their home, and those for whom no one cares or prays.
Pause
Our Father in heaven: **may your Kingdom come.**

For our own fathers; for family life throughout the whole world;
that all homes may be blessed with love and security and reflect God's love for his children.
Pause
Our Father in heaven: **may your Kingdom come.**

Celebrant   God our Father, rejoicing in your tenderness and compassion, we bring these prayers before you. Through Christ our Lord. **Amen.**

Ideas for Children

Talk with the children about asking. Suppose they would like a friend round to play or some help with a tricky model they are building, what would they do? Ask Mummy and Daddy, and if they can help, they will. It's no good just thinking to ourselves, 'If only I could have my friend to play.' We have to ask, and then we've got a good chance of our hopes coming true. (At this stage show the first sign: 'Ask and you will receive.') Point out that it's the same with our heavenly Father; it's no good just thinking to ourselves, 'If only I didn't get bad-tempered so often!' or 'If only I wasn't so scared of owning up!' But is we ASK our heavenly Father, he will help us to change!

Have ready hidden an object in the room. Tell the children something is hidden. How can they find it? By looking! (Let them hunt till they find it. Then show the second sign: 'Seek and you will find.') Point out that in the same way we will never find out about Jesus, or ourselves or other people unless we get up and make an effort to find out, by reading the Bible, asking people, thinking and being aware.

Show a picture of a front door. How can you get someone to open it? By knocking or ringing the bell – no one will answer unless you do! (Show third sign: 'Knock and the door will be opened to you.') It is the same with God, our Father. He is there, alive, strong and he likes us – in fact, he loves us! But he will never push in to our lives; if we want his help, or if we want to know about his way of living, we must ASK, SEEK and KNOCK at the door.

Let three groups colour and decorate the three signs, to be put in church where everyone can see them. Then join in prayer together, encouraging the children to add their prayers too.

Music
Recorded Music

Bach – *Harpsichord Concerto No. 3 in D: Adagio*

'Live' Music

I ask your blessing, Lord *(ONE, 229)*
Jesus, gentlest Saviour *(ONE, 276)*
Listen *(SOS 3, 225)*
Our Father – Abba, I belong to you *(SONL, 69)*
Seek ye first *(ONE, 473)*
Take me, Lord *(SONL, 92)*

18th Sunday in Ordinary Time

Theme
True richness is not material wealth

A great deal of life is spent labouring for material possessions and material security, but in the last resort these things will never provide the permanency and peace we crave.

Much better for us to recognise God as the source of everlasting richness, and break our dependency on physical wealth. Then we shall be able to enjoy the created world without being enslaved to it.

Penitential Rite

Free us from all that keeps us from you,
    Lord, have mercy. **Lord, have mercy.**

Increase our faith, our hope and our love,
    Christ, have mercy. **Christ, have mercy.**

Centre our lives entirely on you,
    Lord, have mercy. **Lord, have mercy.**

Notes on the Readings

Ecclesiastes 1:2; 2:21-23

Often in our highly materialistic society, we are encouraged to see labouring for possessions as reason enough for our existence. In one sense it is almost refreshing to find the accompanying increase in depressive illnesses for it shows that at least human beings have not been brainwashed into automatons: whatever the media may say, people still know that fundamentally such a reason for existence is fatuous, vain and without meaning.

Perhaps we may need to recognise this the hard way, even experiencing the black depression along the route, before we can begin to appreciate what an amazing, extravagantly generous offer we are made by Christ.

Colossians 3:1-5, 9-11

For in Christ we can at last stop pretending; stop inventing distractions to keep us from uncomfortable questions about real values; stop lurching from one craze to the next for fear of drowning in the conviction that, though materialism is all, it is entirely unsatisfying.

Christ is not just a set of ideas, but the living God with a human face who can show us what life is really about, and confirm our suspicions that the material world is not the reason for our existence.

He can help us break our dependency on the created world, until we have reshuffled our priorities and begin to know the relief of centering our lives on something of real, cosmic, and ultimate value which puts our whole existence in a new perspective and brings with it an inner peace and order we could never have believed possible.

Luke 12:13-21

Although the man in the crowd seems to be asking for justice, Jesus sees behind his demand the seething resentment and ill-feeling created by putting so much value on ownership. Acquisitions obviously loom larger in his life than anything else.

Jesus' parable exaggerates the contrast between assumed and actual security to drive home the foolishness of relying on temporal things as if they were permanent.

Our lives as Christians should proclaim a far better, richer and more fulfilling alternative. But if we merely say these things and yet live as materialistically as everyone else, how can we ever expect people to believe us?

Bidding Prayers

Celebrant Recognising that we depend on God
          our Father for all things, let us pray.

Reader   For the needs and hopes of this
          pilgrim Church,
          working within our anxious, frantic world;
          that, being rooted and fixed on Christ,
          she may offer his lasting richness,
          abundant joy, refreshment and peace.
          Pause
          Father, in you we trust:
            you have power to make us new.

          For our troubled world
          with its conflicts, greed, fear and suspicion;
          that its peoples may come to know
          God's love, live in his light
          and experience the freedom of his service.
          Pause
          Father, in you we trust:
            you have power to make us new.

          For the rich, the ambitious, and the poor;
          those whose financial security blinds them
          to spiritual needs; all who have set their faith
          on a fleeting, material world;
          that they may realise, before it is too late,
          the everlasting security and wealth of Christ.
          Pause
          Father, in you we trust:
            you have power to make us new.

          For our families, neighbours and friends;
          that we may offer our possessions,
          skills, gifts and time;
          that all we are may be used and expended
          in the work of Christ.
          Pause
          Father, in you we trust:
            you have power to make us new.

Celebrant Lord our God, acknowledging your greatness,
          we ask you to accept these prayers,
          through Christ our Lord. **Amen.**

Ideas for Children

The parable from today's Gospel explains the day's theme very graphically, and can be made into a frieze for the wall.

As with all parables, make it quite clear that Jesus often enjoyed telling stories to explain what he meant; it is important they realise which are acts of Jesus and which are stories.

If possible, prepare a tape recording of the story using different people (men and women) to take part, and music as background. It is quite enjoyable making a recording, and should not take too long. Having completed it, you will have it as another resource.

Script for Tape

Music from Beethoven's *Pastoral Symphony* fades in.

Narrator:	There was once a rich man who had a very good harvest. *(Sound of running)*
Slave:	Master! Master!
Rich man:	*(snoring) (wakes up)* Oh! Yes – what is it slave?
Slave:	Master, we've filled all the barns with the crops but there's still lots more left to store.
Rich man:	*(laughs)* Well, Well! Such a good harvest that there's no room to store my crops, eh? Now what can I do about that, I wonder.
Slave:	Perhaps you could give some away?
Rich man:	What!! Good heavens, no! I know what I'll do. Slave – start pulling the barns down.
Slave:	Pulling them down, Master? B...b...but we've only just filled them up.
Rich man:	Then empty them, you fool! We're going to build ENORMOUS barns – enough to hold all my grain.
Slave:	Very well, Master; your wish is my command. *(runs off. In distance his voice is heard)* Come on, lads, get busy. All the grain is to be moved.
Other farm hands:	*(generally groan)* – Oh no! What on earth for? After all that work, etc. *(Sound of workers pouring grain fades out into music. Music fades into building sounds.)*
Slave driver:	Come on, there, stop wasting time. *(Whip)*
Rich man:	Ah, good, the new barns are splendid! Keep up the good work. *(Music fades in).* Now I've got so much grain I can enjoy myself for years to come. I think I'll start with a feast. No more worries for me! *(sounds of eating and drinking)* *(Cymbal or saucepan lids)*
God:	Fool! Fool! *(Cymbal)*
Rich man:	*(flustered)* Eh? Oh, my goodness, who said that? *(Cymbal)*
God:	I, God, tell you that you are a fool! This very night you are going to die. What use will your hoard of grain be to you then? *(Cymbal)* What use, then, fool? *(Music fades up to finish)*
Narrator:	So the man saw that getting rich did not make him safe and secure, after all.

Talk with the children about the things that do last for ever, like kindness, giving, loving, helpfulness, etc. Then ask them to illustrate the story:

– filling barns;
– knocking barns down;
– building bigger barns;
– barns full of grain;
– rich man eating and drinking;
– rich man frightened as God's voice says 'Fool'.

Display these in order, or play tape again and show each in turn.

Music
'Live' Music

If you are thirsting after righteousness *(SONL, 83)*
I want to build my life *(SONL, 95)*
Love is his word *(ONE, 338)*

19th Sunday in Ordinary Time

Theme
Trust God and be ready for him

We are called to have a faith which trusts God's promise even before there is any evidence of it being fulfilled. Living in the conviction that the Lord will certainly come, we will make sure we are not found unprepared; this will affect all our actions and relationships, as well as our willingness to repent and to forgive.

Penitential Rite

Help our unbelief,
  Lord, have mercy. **Lord, have mercy.**

Our selfish lives have betrayed you,
  Christ, have mercy. **Christ, have mercy.**

Prepare us for your coming,
  Lord, have mercy. **Lord, have mercy.**

Notes on the Readings

Wisdom 18:6-9

God has not just made some impressive promises and then kept a low profile for generations before fulfilling his word. Certainly there are times when he seems hidden, but there are many occasions when God acts, and if we have our spiritual eyes open we shall find these clear signs a source of strength and joyful courage. The writer of Wisdom retraces the steps of the chosen people to show them God in the act of saving his flock.

In the person of Jesus, we can see this action no longer veiled but clearly revealed. And since Jesus is still alive now, we should expect evidence of it around us today.

It is certainly there. Anyone who prays in faith – not merely uttering over-familiar words but really praying with concentration mentally, emotionally and physically – will find prayer answered in moving, remarkable, unexpected and sometimes amusing ways.

Hebrews 11:1-2, 8-19

Faith, or trust in God, is the firm ground on which we stand as we journey towards a deeper relationship with our Creator. It is unaffected by our moods, feelings, state of health or the weather. It is not altered by hardship, suffering, success or failure.

How can anything so constant exist in us who, being human, are generally inconstant? The reason is that it is nothing man-made or man-invented. It is a present which God will give us if we ask him for it. His close friends, from Abraham onwards, have known it and lived in its hope, and that is why it is so strong – it is based on a hope which is certain and goes deeper and further even than death.

Luke 12:32-48

Living in such a certain hope means living in a state of constant preparation so that we are always ready for Christ whenever he comes. Peter, listening to the parables illustrating the need to be prepared, did not see how Jesus could be talking to the chosen few: surely they were prepared already? Jesus' reply is a warning to all of us who are committed Christians. We must always be on our guard against complacency; against relaxing our own standards; against anything approaching smug attitudes or assumptions of privileges.

For we are to be judged by God's standards, and he expects a great deal from those to whom a great deal has been given. We must make sure that we do not throw our inheritance carelessly away.

Bidding Prayers

Celebrant Knowing that God the Father has promised
  to hear us, and is always true to his word,
  let us pray.

Reader For the world-wide Christian family;
  that in the strength of Jesus,
  it may offer hope to the despairing,
  peace to the distressed,
  fulfilment to those who seek,
  and refreshment to the weary.
  Pause
  Lord, you are our strength:
    we believe and trust in you.

For a shrinking world
  and those whose authority can affect it
  for good or ill;
  that we may all learn to trust one another
  and forgive each other more readily,
  and share our resources so that none
  may starve.
  Pause
  Lord, you are our strength:
    we believe and trust in you.

For those who are chronically ill
  and in constant pain;
  for those who are frightened by their illness
  and those who are approaching death;
  that they may receive the sustaining peace
  of Christ, who knows them personally,
  and whose love for them extends
  even through death itself.
  Pause
  Lord, you are our strength:
    we believe and trust in you.

For the members of our own families
  and their particular needs and difficulties;
  for our own lives and spiritual
  development and growth;
  that we may learn to trust more in God
  than in ourselves,
  and be alert to his guidance each day.
  Pause
  Lord, you are our strength:
    we believe and trust in you.

Celebrant God our Father, as we learn to trust more
  in your promise, may we grow to be more like
  Christ and reflect the radiance of his love.
  Through the same Christ, our Lord. **Amen.**

Ideas for Children

Today is a good opportunity to learn about Abraham. To avoid confusion begin by explaining that Abraham lived many, many years before Jesus was born.

Start with a prayer about trusting and being ready, and a song (e.g. *Forward in faith.*)

Then use a model and plasticine or card figures to tell the story of his calling. A green towel or cloth spread over various upturned bowls on a table makes a good landscape.

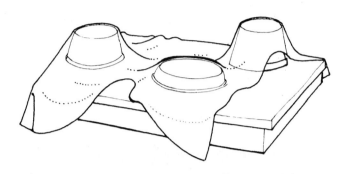

The children can help prepare it, and put on large stones, pebbles, boxes for buildings and the characters needed:

> Abraham
> Sarah
> his son, Isaac,
> sheep and cattle,
> a ram,
> etc. (farmyard models)

Spend the first half of the session making this model, and when all is ready, let the children sit round the model while you tell the story of Abraham, moving the figures as you tell it.

At each stage emphasise how Abraham and Sarah trusted God, even when it came to sacrificing their son; and how God rewarded their trust.

> Start at Haran, where God makes his promise;
> (*Genesis* 12)
> go on to the oaks of Mamre, where the three visitors tell him his elderly wife will have a son; (*Genesis* 18)
> and the birth of Isaac;
> then to Moriah (in the mountains)
> where God tests Abraham in asking him to sacrifice his son, but provides a ram. (*Genesis* 22)

Music
Recorded Music

Handel – *I know that my Redeemer liveth (Messiah)*

'Live' Music

Come, follow me *(SONL, 20)*
God is love: his the care *(ONE, 178)*
Immortal, invisible *(ONE, 242)*
Leave your country *(ONE, 299)*
Wake up, O people *(SONL, 54)*

20th Sunday in Ordinary Time

Theme
Following Christ brings hardship, but he will support us

God's special friends have often been persecuted, and we must not be alarmed or surprised if we encounter dangers, difficulties or hardships. We can persevere through all suffering, sustained by the love and strength of Christ, and encouraged by the saints.

Penitential Rite

In times of temptation,
    Lord, have mercy. **Lord, have mercy.**

In times of persecution,
    Christ, have mercy. **Christ, have mercy.**

In times of suffering,
    Lord, have mercy. **Lord, have mercy.**

Notes on the Readings

Jeremiah 38:4-6, 8-10

Jeremiah was the bringer of bad news and that made him a nuisance. Never mind if his prophecies were likely to be true; never mind if they grasped the truth of God's will with new insight; the blinkered people could only see the way forward in terms of military victory, and so they tried to get rid of Jeremiah, who was urging them to accept defeat in order to progress as God's people.

Conflict always gives rise to propaganda, and then truth is disguised or abandoned, prejudice reigns, and the hopes for peaceful settlements fade into the distance.

Like Jeremiah, we must never become party to such blindness, but fix ourselves on God's will, so that whatever the personal consequences, we are prepared to stand up for his truth, no matter how unpalatable it may be to those around us.

Hebrews 12:1-4

The author recognises that the race of this life is often a struggle and we shall not always find it easy going. But we have the examples of all the patriarchs, prophets and saints to cheer us on, and always with us is Jesus himself, our leader and our prize. Even he had to undergo suffering and death, but he was glad to do it so that we could be saved. One other thing to help us is travelling light: we often hang on to sins as habits which weigh us down unnecessarily. If we get rid of any sins quickly by confessing them and making amends, we shall be able to run much more easily.

Luke 12:49-53

Here we glimpse the inner agony of Jesus as he approaches his crucifixion. Perhaps we talk too glibly of Christ gladly or joyfully enduring the cross. Certainly he was fully prepared to accept it, and certainly he was deeply motivated by the good it would accomplish.

Yet at the same time, he was fully human: sensitive and acutely aware of the torture, rejection and isolation he was bound to face.

If ever we choose the good instead of the easier way, we travel along a road which Christ treads with us. Strangely, once we have made such a decision, we find his presence so comforting that the road is not nearly as impossible as we might have thought: there is an inner peace which brings real joy in the most unlikely circumstances.

Bidding Prayers

Celebrant My brothers and sisters, remembering our
dependence on God for all things, let us
pray to the Lord.

Reader For all those whose Christian witness
has brought embarrassment, rejection
or persecution;
that with their sight fixed on Jesus
they may be strengthened and encouraged,
and remain his faithful friends.

Pause

Hear us, Father: **you are our strength and joy.**

For all negotiators, diplomats, envoys
and advisers;
that they may seek peace rather than war,
unity rather than division,
and justice rather than personal success.

Pause

Hear us, Father: **you are our strength and joy.**

That the healing love of God
may work within those who have been
discouraged or hurt;
all who harbour resentment
and the desire for revenge;
the lonely, the timid,
the vulnerable and the abused.

Pause

Hear us, Father: **you are our strength and joy.**

For our local community
and all its homes, shops,
schools, surgeries and leisure facilities;
that we, as Christians, may bring
Christ's life and brightness to this place
so that it is infused with his love.

Pause

Hear us, Father: **you are our strength and joy.**

Celebrant Loving Father, hear our prayers,
through Christ our Lord. **Amen.**

Ideas for Adults

A dance, showing a Christian pilgrim encountering many
difficulties on his way, is an effective means of conveying
today's theme. The Christian should be carrying a heavy bag
or suitcase as he travels round the church towards the altar,
and a cross. On the way have groups of dancers providing
the difficulties: e.g.

- having a party and coaxing him to stay and join in; –
(he stays a while, dancing, then goes on);
- jumping out at him with masks on to frighten him
and turn him back; (he is scared, then holds his
cross firmly and passes them);
- making a dense forest that he has to work hard to
get through.

Have some saints to cheer him on (the congregation) and
a shout of triumph when he arrives and kneels, arms raised,
at the altar. (The case is abandoned just before the finish, so
he is free to dance up to the altar.)

Ideas for Children

If there is an outside area available, this could be used for
today's teaching, based on races. If not, have the indoors
area clear of chairs and tables for the first part of the session.

Tell the children you are going to have some races, and
choose two or three to race first. Have the others cheering at
the side lines.

For the next race, give the runners baggy clothes to wear,
which will slow them down.

For the third race, have obstacles to get round, over or
through. In each case encourage the runners by cheering.

Then gather the children round for prize giving. A nice
surprise – everyone who finished gets a prize (small sticker
or badge).

Now arrange the chairs in a circle, or several if numbers
are large.

Show a large sheet of paper with 'The Race of Life' on it.
Talk about what sort of obstacles life has (people nasty to
us; moving away from friends; illness etc); how cheering
crowds help us (the saints, other people, and we can cheer
on others); how the heavy clothes and baskets in life are our
sins (being greedy, unkind, selfish, wishing for what we cannot have, being lazy) so that they relate their races to life.
Now each child can make a plasticine model of him or herself
running, and put it somewhere along the track.

Music
Recorded Music

A march played by a brass band

'Live' Music

Farmer, farmer *(SONL, 37)*
Fight the good fight *(ONE, 140)*
If God is for us *(ONE, 231)*
Take up your cross *(SONL, 42)*
You shall cross the barren desert *(MSOS, 196; BSOS, 72)*

21st Sunday in Ordinary Time

Theme
People from all nations will be drawn into God's Kingdom

Having begun with the nucleus of a chosen race, the Kingdom of God is to spread throughout all countries so that everyone has the chance to be saved. But the dedication, self discipline and commitment necessary in living life God's way means that many will turn down that chance of salvation while others unexpectedly claim it.

Penitential Rite

For our lack of perseverance,
Lord, have mercy. **Lord, have mercy.**

For our lack of self discipline,
Christ, have mercy. **Christ, have mercy.**

For our lack of charitable love,
Lord, have mercy. **Lord, have mercy.**

Notes on the Readings

Isaiah 66:18-21

There is a lovely picture here of the great trail of people from all over the earth all arriving in their different ways to worship God in Jerusalem. It foretells the magnificent fulfilment of God's plan; the completion and realisation of all the training, suffering and preparation. Every nation will be included, for in God there are no second class citizens or unwanted minorities.

If we are working with Christ for the coming of his Kingdom, we must have nothing to do with racial discrimination, or any other discrimination, come to that. We are all brothers and sisters, children of our heavenly Father.

Hebrews 12:5-7, 11-13

As God's children we have the privilege of being trained by him. If we decide to learn a sport or tone up our bodies in an aerobics session, we happily pay money for lessons during which the trainer makes us use our bodies till they ache. We understand that the aches and pains are all part of getting fitter, so we don't abandon classes if we feel stiff; in fact we are encouraged, as it proves we are getting stronger.

It is just the same with spiritual fitness. We will never learn patience, for instance, unless we are given situations to practise it; nor will we ever learn perseverance unless we have long term difficulties sometimes. If instead of thinking, 'Why does God let this happen to me?' we think 'This is a good opportunity to learn – Lord, help me to use it,' then we will not only develop spiritually, but also be uplifted and encouraged during the learning, as we might be during the last few press-ups at rugby training.

God loves us enough to want to bother with us and remake us. This is not an insult, but a great honour.

Luke 13:22-30

Jesus takes up Isaiah's prophecy and confirms that his salvation is not pre-booked by a chosen minority, but extends to all men everywhere. It is not for us to judge who will enter the Kingdom of God, and we must certainly never assume that because we are Christians we will automatically be among the first.

We must make sure that we do our best to enter through the narrow gate. 'Doing our best' is not an excuse to abandon the idea of striving for perfection. It is not a rather lazy compromise, or a casual commitment which does not like religion to interfere too much with the serious business of life. If that is the extent of our 'best' then we will find ourselves last in the line.

Doing our best is devoting our entire life to knowing God better and working with him in his strength.

Bidding Prayers

Celebrant My friends in Christ, in the stillness of God's peace let us pray together.

Reader For all those involved with missionary work, both abroad and at home;
that they may be protected from danger and disease,
and led in the way of God's will,
so that their caring, forgiving lives witness to his love.
Pause
Take us; remake us: **and use us for your glory.**

For all the peoples of this earth who do not know God; for those who see him only as a threat or an excuse for violence;
that they may be brought into contact with the living Christ who longs to give them his peace.
Pause
Take us; remake us: **and use us for your glory.**

For those in physical or mental pain;
those weakened and exhausted by illness,
those in intensive care or undergoing emergency surgery;
that God's healing power will sustain them and make them whole.
Pause
Take us; remake us: **and use us for your glory.**

For all those with whom we live and work and worship;
that we may use every opportunity to care for each other and grow in patience and understanding.
Pause
Take us; remake us: **and use us for your glory.**

Celebrant God our Father, accept these prayers, through Christ our Lord. **Amen.**

Ideas for Children

Today is a good time to look at how the Good News of Jesus is spread to people all over the world; how it was brought to our own country and what missionaries are doing today.

Have on the wall a large map of the world, or if possible a large globe on a table. Begin by finding our own country and a few others.

Next show them where Jesus lived, worked and died, and ask if they know how the Good News spread.

Select a few particular people and areas (your own patron saint may be a possibility) to study:

- Mother Teresa
- Augustine
- Patrick
- Columba
- Queen Margaret
- David Livingstone
- Paul

Give each group of children a sheet of paper to arrange as a display of people spreading the Good News. Use photographs from Missionary Magazines etc.

Music
Recorded Music

Any 'Black Gospel' music – 'Missa Luba'

'Live' Music

African Our Father *(SONL, 90)*
All the nations of the earth *(ONE, 30)*
Be exalted, O God *(SOS 3, 262)*
In Christ there is no east or west *(ONE, 244)*

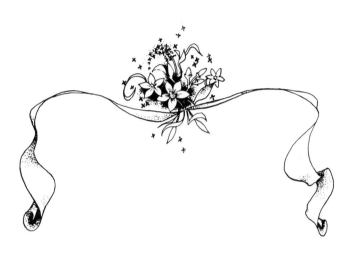

22nd Sunday in Ordinary Time

Theme
Humility

However much the world may be impressed by rank or position, in God's eyes the greatest are those who behave humbly, putting others before themselves and acknowledging that they still have much to learn. The humble will be blessed, and brought to the full joy of heaven.

Penitential Rite

You laid your glory aside to save us,
    Lord, have mercy. **Lord, have mercy.**

Obediently you went to the cross,
    Christ, have mercy. **Christ, have mercy.**

Without you we would be nothing,
    Lord, have mercy. **Lord, have mercy.**

Notes on the Readings

Ecclesiasticus 3:17-20, 28-29

The humility recommended by the writer of this passage has nothing in common with the cringing self-abasement which is only really a twisted kind of pride.

Here, humility is that characteristic which is always open to learn fresh insights or deeper understanding. The humble never assume that they know all the answers, however old, well-travelled or educated they may be. Such humility, the writer suggests, should actually increase with greatness. If we find ourselves rejecting changes or resenting new ideas because we have already done our thinking and reached our conclusions, then we should take these warnings to heart: perhaps in assuming we have arrived, we may actually be right at the beginning.

Hebrews 12:18-19, 22-24

We need never feel that our journeying is not worth the effort, for our destination is almost indescribable and unimaginable in its wonder. The end of our journey will be a completion and fulfilment of all that is lovely, good, valuable and true; it is nothing less than the city of the living God, inhabited by all the angels and saints in its perfect, overwhelming glory. And we shall be given the honour of being made perfect as citizens of heaven.

So we are not striving towards a vaguely pleasant finish, but a glorious destination where we will know complete fulfilment for ever.

Luke 14:1, 7-14

We can imagine the atmosphere of this Sabbath day meal at the home of one of the most important Pharisees and his influential friends. They, intrigued and curious, watch Jesus closely, and possibly hope to impress him by their rank, which he will be able to judge from their position at table. Jesus, unfettered by the world's values, watches their petty ambitions being played out so clearly, and teaches them about humility by means of a very thinly-veiled parable (using a Wedding Feast as the setting instead of an ordinary Sabbath meal).

They, who thought themselves religiously secure and confident, find that their values are not as worthy as they had imagined.

Before we start patting ourselves on the back for not behaving like the Pharisees, we had better examine our lives very thoroughly. Do we invite and help those friends who repay the compliment? Can we take valuable criticism without being offended? Do we perhaps get quite niggled if a stranger sits in 'our' place? How do we behave in queues, on public transport or with those whose appearance marks them as belonging to a different race, class or culture from our own?

Humility is acknowledging the real worth of all other people we meet, based on the knowledge that all we have depends not on our cleverness but God's generosity.

Bidding Prayers

Celebrant Acknowledging our dependence on God who
        creates and sustains all things, let us pray.

Reader For the Church, the Body of Christ;
        that regardless of rank or position,
        its members may be noticeable
        by their unselfish humility,
        so that through their good work
        God may be glorified.
        Pause
        Holy Father: **teach us your ways.**

    For the world's leaders
        and their governments,
        and for all in influential positions;
        that they may make good use
        of their power,
        and aim to serve the needs
        of their fellow men.
        Pause
        Holy Father: **teach us your ways.**

For the crippled, the mentally
and physically handicapped,
and those whose bodies or minds
have been damaged through
accidents or violence;
in silence we commit them to the calm
and peace of Christ.
Pause
Holy Father: **teach us your ways.**

For those we serve in our daily lives,
and all who serve us;
that we may care for each other
with kindness and friendship,
knowing that we are all brothers
and sisters before God.
Pause
Holy Father: **teach us your ways.**

Celebrant   Lord God, giver of all good gifts, we ask you
to hear these prayers.
Through Christ our Lord. **Amen.**

Ideas for Adults

Today's Gospel can be dramatised effectively.

Ideas for Children

Tell the story of today's Gospel, spending as much time on
the actual event (the meal made ready, of the important
guests arriving and choosing a particular seat, etc.) as on the
parable Jesus told the guests, and his advice to his host. To
accompany the story have a table and chairs, and ask two
children to be servants laying it.

Have ready an assortment of dolls and teddies and hats
or grand cloaks for them to wear. Make them all come in, be
greeted by the host and sit down, saying things like, 'Ah, this
must be my chair as I'm so important,' and 'I'll sit in this
place of honour – I shan't sit down with the ordinary people
at the end,' etc.

When you have finished the story, think together about
how we could put Jesus' words into practice. Is there someone at school who is often left out? Perhaps they could come
round to play one day. What about parties? Is there someone, an elderly neighbour, who might appreciate a
visit with a slice of cake?

Children like to help in a practical way – here is a chance
for them to do so. They may like to write down what they
decide to do, so that they don't forget.

Music
Recorded Music

Grieg – *Peer Gynt Suite: Solveig's Lament*

'Live' Music

Jerusalem the golden *(ONE, 273)*
Life pervading *(SONL, 46)*
Lord Jesus, think on me *(ONE, 327)*
Magnificat! *(SONL, 35)*
My God, how wonderful thou art *(ONE, 357)*

23rd Sunday in Ordinary Time

Theme
Freedom

In many ways we are not free. We are all encased in perish-
able bodies; some are restricted by social and political
boundaries; others entangled by possessiveness of things
and people. Jesus shows us the way to escape this slavery
and to be free, but his way is not cheap. It will be demanding
and costly, yet its benefits in terms of life-enhancement are
supreme.

Penitential Rite

Lord of all wisdom: have mercy on us,
   Lord, have mercy. **Lord, have mercy.**

Christ our liberator: have mercy on us,
   Christ, have mercy. **Christ, have mercy.**

Lord our sustainer: have mercy on us,
   Lord, have mercy. **Lord, have mercy.**

Notes on the Readings

Wisdom 9:13-18

The author of this passage from *Wisdom* has no illusions
about man's abilities. He is well aware of human frailty,
human error and human weakness. There is no point in pretending we can grasp the mind of God, for we have difficulty
in making sense of our local, material world and its problems.

Yet God has chosen to explain and enlighten, and when
man latches on to God's Wisdom, or Spirit, then some of the
mysteries will become clearer, and we can glimpse the
enormous terms of reference within which God operates.
Through God's Spirit we are enabled to fly beyond the insur-
mountable barriers of human restriction into the freedom of
life in Christ.

Philemon 9-10, 12-17

Paul touches here on three kinds of freedom, as he appeals
to a fellow Christian on behalf of Onesimus.

Firstly, we see in practice what Jesus promised to us all –
that we should no longer be considered slaves, but children:
brothers and sisters with Christ. Onesimus had been a slave,
and following some incident, either ran away or was banish-
ed by his owner. Paul has obviously found in him a dear
friend, and values him highly. Now he may well be granted
his freedom.

Secondly, we see Paul physically chained and bound, yet obviously free in spite of this. He accepts the fact that his imprisonment has resulted directly from spreading the Gospel, but does not hesitate to call it 'Good' news, all the same. He is not pretending imprisonment is good fun, but he accepts it cheerfully for Christ's sake. No chains can bind Christ's life in us.

Thirdly, we see how Paul allows his friend freedom to make decisions. Though he wished to keep Onesimus, he regarded it as more important that gifts should be freely given and not grudgingly handed over because they are expected, or out of a sense of duty. For if we do this, we are merely presenting a parcel of resentment and bitterness disguised as an act of love. The recipient may not notice, but God certainly will.

Luke 14:25-33

Jesus explains how we need to free ourselves from all earthly ties if we are to bind ourselves to him. He is not suggesting that we turn our backs on the world and its needs, nor that we cut ourselves off from all relationships and live as hermits.

He is concerned about our great desire to possess and control other people, and our determination to be always in control of our own lives. If this hold is to be relinquished, then we will have to alter our entire life-style, our relationships and our attitudes to family and friends, so we cannot undertake commitment to Jesus lightly. We should recognise its cost so that we can embark on discipleship with our eyes open.

Once we have given away our rights to all possessions and ownership, we may well find we are still deeply involved with people, goods and money. But now we are no longer owners; we are stewards who handle God's assets, and in all our relationships our human commitment will be overspread and underpinned by our allegiance and obedience to God's will.

Often we will find that this actually improves our relationships and increases our care and love. For we no longer need to be so defensive or aggressive. His service sets us free.

Bidding Prayers

Celebrant My brothers and sisters, let us pray for the Church and all the world.

Reader For all whom God is calling
to serve him in his Church;
especially those who are uncertain
of his will for them;
that, waiting patiently in stillness,
they may learn how God wishes
their lives to be led.
Pause
Lord, in your service: **set us free.**

For those who are in prison.
especially those in solitary confinement;
for all countries in which personal freedom
is restricted for political reasons;
that men may learn to trust and respect
each other, so that they may live in peace.
Pause
Lord, in your service: **set us free.**

For those weighed down
with grief, illness, pain and despair;
that they may find Christ present
in the heart of their suffering
and understand his love more deeply
through their distress.

Pause
Lord, in your service: **set us free.**

For those whose lives
are closely bound up with our own;
that we may respect each other's needs
and individuality.
Pause
Lord
Lord, in your service: **set us free.**

Celebrant Father, all that we are, and all we are
capable of becoming, we pledge to your service.
Through Christ our Lord. **Amen.**

Ideas for Children

The cost of discipleship

Have ready two money boxes or piggy banks and some pretend money (or real, if you wish). Tell the children you are thinking of building a big tower to live in and enjoy the view. Ask them to help you plan the things you will need, and what it will cost.

As you suggest the items (bricks, cement, scaffolding, a clock, window frames etc.) write each down on a large 'Tower Expenses' list and then take out money for each.

If you run out of money say something like 'Oh, dear! Perhaps I'd better not build a tower after all. I would look a fool if I build half way and couldn't afford a roof, wouldn't I? What a good thing we checked first, wasn't it?'

Explain how Jesus said that following him might be rather expensive, too, and we'd better decide first whether or not we're prepared to pay the cost before we join him.

What expenses are there in following Jesus? On another 'Christian Expenses' list, write down what we have to spend or give up to be Christians:

- watching television on Sunday mornings;
- telling lies;
- keeping all our sweets to ourselves;
- joining in the unkind teasing; etc.

What do we pay with? Out of the second money box take money shaped cards with:

- kindness;
- love;
- thoughtfulness;
- helpfulness;
- peace-making;
- self-control;
- patience;
- cheerfulness; etc.

It costs a lot, doesn't it? But we couldn't spend it on anything that would make us happier. And remind them that Jesus has spent everything for us – even his life!

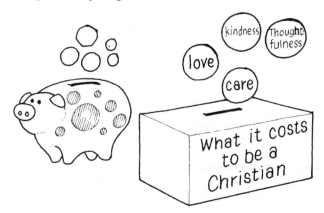

Give each child a box to decorate and cut out 'coins' to put inside.

Music

Recorded Music

Handel – *Water Music: Adagio*

'Live' Music

Jesus, can I tell you? *(MSOS,145; BSOS, 24)*
Let all that is within me holy cry *(ONE, 301)*
Living Lord *(ONE, 326)*
The Spirit lives to set us free *(ONE, 547)*

24th Sunday in Ordinary Time

Theme
Complete forgiveness

There is no limit to what God will forgive. Nothing we can ever do, individually or corporately, is beyond the possibility of forgiveness. All our sin causes God immense sadness and grief, and he longs to be reconciled to us. But for reconciliation and forgiveness to take place, one thing is essential: we must repent of our sin to the very quick.

Penitential Rite

Father, we have dishonoured your name,
   Lord, have mercy. **Lord, have mercy.**

Jesus, we have disgraced your love,
   Christ, have mercy. **Christ have mercy.**

Father, we are not worthy to be called your children,
   Lord, have mercy. **Lord have mercy.**

Notes on the Readings

Exodus 32:7-11, 13-14

With perfect loyalty God has kept faith with his people throughout their time of slavery and their great escape; he has transformed Moses from a timid, halting speaker into a great leader with whom he can converse. But the people, fed up with waiting, decide to create the god of their choice, who makes no demands and encourages indulgence. God's great anger springs out of his desire for his people to be fulfilled in working with him to accomplish the great work of salvation. Instead he finds them petty, mean and blind. (In a similar way Jesus wept over Jerusalem.)

Moses does not try to excuse their behaviour: he begs for forgiveness. God, who has been completely let down, deeply insulted, his ideals and values dismissed, shows his enormous capacity for love, even when rejected. All too often we feel very noble forgiving little things, which if we are honest, have not really hurt us a great deal. Yet we are tempted to count real hurts differently – 'Oh, that *really* destroyed me – I shall never be able to forgive *that*!' And we even feel justified; surely, we feel, there are some appalling sins against us which are beyond the boundary of our forgiveness. Let us remember the aching, despised, insulted God, who still responded with loving forgiveness.

1 Timothy 1:12-17

Paul never gets over his wonder at the way God chose such an ardent objector to Jesus Christ as his instrument. His love and enthusiasm for working with Christ are in direct proportion to the extent he knows himself forgiven. His conversion has the added advantage of witnessing more powerfully to those he previously worked with: having known him as he was, they are bound to be interested in the power which changed him.

Singing and talking about the joy of forgiveness will never have any meaning for us unless we are aware of our sin and its damage. Then, when we suddenly see how little right we have to expect anything but punishment from a just God, we will realise the meaning of being forgiven by him.

Luke 15:1-32

Those who followed the Law worked hard at keeping God's word. They could see others flagrantly flouting his authority and disobeying the sacred commandments. No wonder it surprised and upset them to see Jesus mingling with those whom the Law condemned. It may not all have been jealousy: some may well have been seriously concerned that it might damage the moral and spiritual values of the most high God.

In none of these parables does Jesus condemn the scribes and Pharisees or praise the sinners. He simply shows those within the Law that there is a good reason for becoming involved with any one who has gone the wrong way: caring involvement is the only way to bring them back.

This, of course, presented the religious leaders with a challenge, as it challenges all committed Christians. Do we love God enough to get involved with the hurt, diseased, embezzling, crooked, perverted and cruel? If we don't, then however are they to be made whole?

Bidding Prayers

Celebrant   My brothers and sisters, in humility let us pray to our merciful Father.

Reader   For the Church, the Body of Christ;
for each one of its members;
for those who have lapsed or drifted away;
for those who are struggling against doubt and temptation.
Pause
Father, forgive: **and lead us safely home.**

For the many peoples of this earth;
for the spread of justice, respect and goodwill;
for a greater capacity to forgive and restore,
and a weakening of hardened revenge.
Pause
Father, forgive: **and lead us safely home.**

For those who suffer through neglect,
famine, natural disasters or war;
for those who, through their own fault,
now suffer.
Pause
Father, forgive: **and lead us safely home.**

For each other; for those we find
difficult to get on with;
those we envy, admire or despise;
that our love may be open
and generous, wide and strong.
Pause
Father, forgive: **and lead us safely home.**

Celebrant Merciful Father, accept these prayers,
through Christ our Lord. **Amen.**

Ideas for Children

First talk about how we feel if we make a big effort to please someone and

- they don't notice;
- tell us to go away;
- say they don't want what we've made.

Usually we feel SAD and ANGRY.

For example: we make our best picture and someone throws it away; we save a special sweet for someone and they say 'Is that all?' instead of thanking you.

Show the children a large sheet headed:

What had God done for his people?

Water in the desert | Food in the desert
Crossing the Red Sea to be free | Guiding their path

What did they do to God?

Turned their backs on him | Worshipped a golden calf

Put up pictures as you mention each item. No wonder God was sad and angry! He told Moses he was fed up with them, and as they hadn't kept their promise he would punish them.

Moses begged him to forgive them and although he had been very badly let down, God did forgive them.

1 2 3 4 5 6 7 8 9 10 11 12

Let each child make a zig-zag picture to show how turning away from God makes him and us miserable. Turning back to him makes him and us happy.

Each picture is coloured, cut in strips, and pasted on to thin card in the order: 1A 2B 3C etc.

A B C D E F G H I J K L

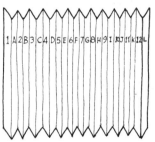

1 A 2 B 3 C 4 D 5 E 6 F 7 G 8 H 9 I 10 J 11 K 12 L

Fold the finished card like a fan, and the two pictures will emerge when viewed from one side or the other.

Music
Recorded Music

Pachelbel – *Canon*

'Live' Music

Alleluia for forgiveness *(SONL, 18)*
Oh the love of my Lord *(ONE, 430)*
The King of love my shepherd is *(ONE, 528)*

25th Sunday in Ordinary Time

Theme
Good stewardship

If we serve God and love him, then we will love and care for all those in need. This means no exploitation of the weak or poor; a real concern in our prayer for the world and those in authority; and a responsible, generous attitude to all money and materials which pass through our hands. Anything less will mean that we attach more value to possessions and power than to God.

Penitential Rite

Use the song If *we only seek peace* (SONL, 76).

Notes on the Readings

Amos 8:4-7

It is no good assuming, because we are religious, or belong to a particular group or nationality, that God will not notice how we behave. He will never excuse meanness, dishonesty or exploitation however much we may protest that 'everybody does it – it's just part of life.' He sees all the surreptitious fiddles, half-truths and false claim forms. He also sees with sorrow the private, individual and national distress and weakness which results.

To be God's people may well mean arousing the ridicule of many; it may well involve standing out from the crowd, and we can expect anger and resentment from colleagues if our behaviour then affirms their guilt or threatens their accepted way of life.

Are we prepared to serve God, rather than money?

1 Timothy 2:1-8

We are encouraged to pray for all those in authority; not merely as a dutiful lip-service, but with the deeply concerned Christian love which supports and is prepared to act and become involved.

There are two reasons for this prayer. One is that, obviously, good government allows us to live peaceful lives, free from terror and violence.

The second reason is that, whether we agree with our leaders or not, whether they are Christian or not, whether they are interested in us or not, they are in God's eyes loved beings whom he has created. God longs for everyone to be saved – that, after all, is why he bothered with the humiliating business of becoming man!

If we live in Christ, we shall start to see all men through his eyes, and that will urge us to pray.

Luke 16:1-13

At first sight Jesus seems to be praising a steward for his dishonest behaviour. In fact he is comparing the shrewd, thorough way in which a dishonest man prepares for himself a settled future, with the vague uncommitted way we often go about preparing ourselves spiritually for our eternal future.

If we gave even a quarter as much attention to the development of our relationship with God as we give to the planning of a holiday, say, or the decorating scheme of the bathroom, we might start to really feel the effect of God's presence in our lives.

Suppose we prepared as carefully for Mass as we do for arranging a dinner party for an important guest? Or spent as much time talking with God as we spend chatting to our friends at the pub or over a cup of tea?

Yet Jesus warns us that if we only use our time and energy pursuing money, material comforts and personal power, we shall not be serving God.

If, on the other hand, we regard all money and possessions as things to be used for good, and for God's glory, then our shrewd, wise handling of material goods may actually help us learn how to be responsible in spiritual matters.

Bidding Prayers

Celebrant We have pledged to commit our lives to Christ; let us then pray in his Spirit.

Reader That all Christians may witness to the value of caring, regardless of race or colour; that they may be maintained in the strength and humility of Christ to serve the world in love.
Pause
Lord, take us: **help us to live.**

For all monarchs, presidents, and those in powerful positions; for those whom they rule, and those with whom they negotiate; that peace and justice may prevail over all our earth.
Pause
Lord, take us: **help us to live.**

For the very poor, the weak and oppressed, the abandoned, rejected and abused; that all obstacles to their healing and wholeness may be removed, all blindness, prejudice and greed transformed through Christ into an outpouring of love and hope.
Pause
Lord, take us: **help us to live.**

For ourselves; that we may see our own faults more clearly, acknowledge our weaknesses as well as our strengths, and give Christ the opportunity to make us new.
Pause
Lord, take us: **help us to live.**

Celebrant Lord God of all creation, accept these prayers through Christ our Lord. **Amen.**

Ideas for Adults

A display about world poverty, particular areas of need, and how we can help will focus attention on possible help. Include in it the good as well as the bad news, and try to borrow some examples of clothes, jewellery, food, musical instruments etc., of the area concerned.

Ideas for Children

Today's readings provide a good opportunity to look at the glaring imbalance between rich and poor countries, and see what is being done to help combat poverty and disease.

Begin with a 'thank you' song, and have a medicine bottle, bread, a coat, model house and glass of clean water on the table.

Talk with the children about how important these things are, and yet how many people have not got them, even though others have more than they need (including us, probably).

To explain the distribution of wealth, cut the bread into ten slices, and ask ten children to stand in the circle. They represent all the people in the world. Divide them into two groups: seven in the South and three in the North.

Have we enough slices for everyone? Count and see.

How is the world's food divided? Give out one plate of seven slices to the three in the North, and one plate of three slices to those in the South.

What would we do to put it right?

When those in the North have given some of theirs away, ask about what will happen next year and so on. Is there a better way than the South always having too little? What is bread made from? (Show some corn on stalks if possible.)

This may be the time to begin sponsoring a child in the Third World, or deciding on a way the children can give help. Some ideas:

- give out small jars filled with sweets to empty, then fill with coins;
- give out sponsor sheets for a sponsored walk/ silence/hop, etc.;
- collect bottle tops, used stamps, etc.

Pray together about the need for us all to be generous and share, so that each person has enough.

Music
Recorded Music

Vaughan Williams – Serenade to Music

'Live' Music

Freely, freely (ONE, 175)
He's got the whole world (ONE, 209)
I give my hands (ONE, 235)
In memory of Jesus (SOS 3, 221)
We shall be one (SONL, 10)

26th Sunday in Ordinary Time

Theme
Inequality and indifference

Wealth leads far more easily to indulgence than generosity, and Jesus forcefully portrays the self-centred blindness which often accompanies luxury and comfort. God cannot be placated with lip service: it is the extent of our caring and sharing which marks our true commitment to him.

Penitential Rite

Our lack of caring cripples the world,
    Lord, have mercy. **Lord, have mercy.**

Our lack of sharing starves the world,
    Christ, have mercy. **Christ, have mercy.**

Our complacency withers the world,
    Lord, have mercy. **Lord, have mercy.**

Notes on the Readings

Amos 6:1, 4-7

The prophet's warning is one which rings unpleasantly true in our own age of affluence. Not that there is anything intrinsically wrong in either ivory beds or videos, finest oil for anointing or expensive suntan lotions and exotic holidays. The crucial point is that 'about the ruin of Joseph they do not care at all.' It is so much harder for us to look inside ourselves when we have the means to be greedy and self-indulgent: it requires an effort of will, for instead of being forced by poverty to go without, we have to choose to do so. It is especially hard when the media bombards us with enticements to spoil ourselves or give ourselves a treat.

Fortunately, the media also does us a service, by bringing into our homes the injustices, poverty, hardships and suffering of our world. So we cannot plead ignorance. We can use the media as Christians, praying through the crises and destruction, and using the information to set about giving, helping, restoring and supporting.

1 Timothy 6:11-16

Nothing short of excellence is expected in Timothy's behaviour. Half-measures, good intentions, easy-going flabbiness are not good enough. The reason for this rigour and full-blooded dedication, is that we and Timothy are working for the most important, powerful being of all time and place, in comparison with whose glory we are as dust. We do well to remember and meditate on the vast, mind-stretching majesty of the God we worship. For we are not dealing with a man-sized creature, but one whose power is so immense that all life and creation bursts from it and is sustained by it. Just imagine how we would feel if this force were evil. That may help us experience some of the awe and vulnerability such almighty power commands. But even more amazing is the fact that God is all goodness. Though he is all-powerful, yet he loves the separate individuals of his immense creation. He is deserving, then, of our complete, abandoned allegiance; if we throw ourselves on him we will be allowed to help in his creative outpouring, so that his Kingdom may be established and all things may be well.

Luke 16:19-31

People often express the view that they do not need to go to church because they are happy as they are and don't do anyone any harm. Dives, the rich man, didn't do anyone any harm. His sin was that he didn't do anyone any good either. Opportunities for helping and caring simply went past unnoticed: he did not realise they existed until it was too late. How can we be sure that we are not also missing opportunities to do good? It is very difficult to look at ourselves objectively but we need to train ourselves to do it regularly if we want to find out in time.

The more closely we live to Jesus, the more enlightened we shall become about where the needs are and how we can help. For we have not only Moses and the prophets to guide us, but also Jesus, risen and glorified, so we cannot say we have not been told. The ball is in our court.

Bidding Prayers

Celebrant   My brothers and sisters, let us pray to our
            heavenly Father who holds us all in his care.

Reader   For the Christian Church,
         that it may truly serve the world,
         and proclaim God's love not only by word
         but also through action.
         Pause
         Yours, Lord, is the power:
         sufficient for all our needs.

         For the world with its areas
         of luxury and deprivation;
         that as we become more aware
         of the problems,
         we may be guided and inspired
         to solve them,
         and as technology brings us closer, we may
         grow in mutual respect and understanding.
         Pause
         Yours, Lord, is the power:
         sufficient for all our needs.

         For an outpouring of God's love
         on the unnoticed, the unloved
         and those for whom no one cares;
         those whose lives are plagued
         with poverty and disease;
         the homeless and the refugees.
         Pause
         Yours, Lord, is the power:
         sufficient for all our needs.

         For the families represented here,
         and all families of every nationality;
         that children may be nurtured
         in love and security,
         and homes may be places
         of peace and joy.
         Pause
         Yours, Lord, is the power:
         sufficient for all our needs.

Celebrant   In silence let us commend our own particular
            needs and thankfulness to the God of
            power and mercy. **Amen.**

Ideas for Adults

Today's Gospel can be dramatised by mime or with speaking parts.

Ideas for Children

Continuing our practical involvement with those in need, make a display board of something like the Clean Water project, or Famine relief, tree planting and mud stoves or a sponsored village.

Supply bright background paper and pictures from newspapers and magazines. Many of the relief organisations are happy to supply excellent material: a selection of addresses is below.

Begin the session with a song of thanks.

Then tell the story that Jesus told about the rich man and Lazarus, and follow up last week's activities for helping before arranging this week's display.

Make it as clear as possible by headings, questions and maps. Coloured wool pinned between areas of the map and relevant information may be helpful.

Display the board where the rest of the congregation can see it, possibly bringing it in at the offertory.

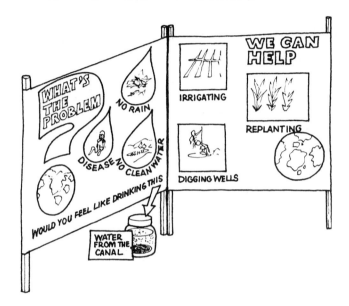

Useful Addresses

Action Aid, Hamlyn House, Archway, London N19 5PG
Christian Aid, P.O. Box 100, London SE1 7RT
CAFOD, 2 Romero Close, Stockwell Road, London SW9 9TY
V.S.O., 317 Putney Bridge Road, London SW15

Music
Recorded Music

One of the folk music funeral songs, such as *The Lyke Wake Dirge*, or an African funeral chant.

'Live' Music

If we only seek peace *(SONL, 76)*
Kum-ba-yah *(ONE, 293)*
Let us break bread together *(ONE, 307)*
Let us talents and tongues employ *(ONE, 308)*

27th Sunday in Ordinary Time

Theme
Steadfast faith

We have been commissioned to hold on to our faith and witness to it throughout all turbulent times in a materialistic and discordant world. Alone we would quickly tire and despair; but we can count on God's power to give us courage and strength.

Penitential Rite

You have never let us down,
Lord, have mercy. **Lord, have mercy.**

You have always kept your word,
Christ, have mercy. **Christ, have mercy.**

You have trusted us with precious gifts,
Lord, have mercy. **Lord, have mercy.**

Notes on the Readings

Habakkuk 1:2-3; 2:2-4

Here we find a man with whom we can readily sympathise when the newspapers and televisions are full of the destructive, evil, aggressive and warped sides of human nature, and we are painfully aware of many, many injustices.

Bitterly, Habakkuk appeals to God. Why ever does he let it all happen? What can it all mean? Why doesn't he do something about it?

God's answer comes as from one who is in full control, but who, unlike us, is not bound by time.

There is no need for anxiety and hysteria, ultimatums or resentment, because in the fullness of time and in God's own way, justice will prevail and everything will be accomplished.

In the meantime we must not allow our impatience and limited human vision to tempt us into giving up our faithfulness. We can trust God; our job is to persevere.

2 Timothy 1:6-8, 13-14

When the Holy Spirit is given to us, we are not suddenly perfect Christians. It is more like the beginning of a flame which needs to be fanned or blown to make a full fire. In the process the first flames are vulnerable as they flicker, but it is through the fanning that they become strong.

We are called to witness to Christ; that is, to act in such a way that people meet Jesus and so are able to experience his love and, being freed from their sinfulness, live in peace and joy.

So we are not witnessing to membership of a weekly club, or an alternative leisure activity; we, through Christ, are inviting them to a completely different life which will make them fulfilled as nothing else ever can. If we do not witness, we deny others the chance of being saved. With such a privilege entrusted to us it is imperative that we are steadfast in our faithfulness, and use every scrap of God's power that we can lay our hands on.

Luke 17:5-10

This witnessing and spreading the news about how people can live in abundance, is not an optional extra when we commit ourselves to Christ. We do not have any choice in the matter, because it is something we are told to do. It is both our privilege and our responsibility. So when we do it, we should not expect great acclaim or admiration: we are simply doing our job. To do it, we need to trust God.

The apostles were aware of how limited their faith was. Jesus' reply must have opened their eyes to see exactly how pitifully small it was – not even as big as the tiny mustard seed!

Faith, or trust, goes against our instincts of independence, of holding on to the control of our lives. It can be hard, painstaking and humiliating as we learn to relinquish our grip and submit to Christ. Yet the more we achieve this, the better witnesses we shall be, and the more lost and bewildered souls there will be who are enabled to share God's peace and joy.

Bidding Prayers

Celebrant   In the Spirit of God our heavenly Father,
let us pray.

Reader   For all Christian witnesses throughout the
whole world, with all their weaknesses,
gifts, victories and disappointments,
that reflecting the brilliant light of Christ
they may direct others to worship him
and know his peace.
Pause
Lord, we believe: **help our unbelief.**

For the inhabitants of this planet in their
daily routines, their work and leisure;
for the silent majorities and those elected to
govern; that all leaders may truly represent
the needs of their peoples, and all may live
in peace with one another.
Pause
Lord, we believe: **help our unbelief.**

For all who are undergoing
long-term or chronic illness,
slow recovery or mental anguish
with no end or hope in sight;
that, holding on to Christ, they may
receive his strength and love
and know that in him they are safe.
Pause
Lord, we believe: **help our unbelief.**

For our own loved ones;
for friends with whom we have lost touch;
for any we have let down;
and for ourselves; that the Spirit
we have been privileged to receive
may burn more and more brightly in us.
Pause
Lord, we believe: **help our unbelief.**

Celebrant   Father, as we dedicate ourselves afresh to
serving you, accept these prayers, through
Christ our Lord. **Amen.**

Ideas for Children

If you have access to some open ground it may be possible to light a small bonfire during the session. If not, use an old, strong metal baking tray and build a miniature bonfire indoors using a few spent matches.

First show some pictures of people in different uniforms (nurses, soldiers, brownies, astronauts, etc.) and ask the children what each person is.

Have the labels ready and stick on the picture as each is names.

Then show an ordinary group of people; they are Christians (put on label), but their uniform is not their clothes – it is the way they behave.

Discuss with the children what marks a Christian. (They worship God, pray, behave lovingly, forgive their enemies, are happy even when they're not being treated well, etc.)

Point out that often we don't behave like this, and then we are letting God down, just as a nurse would let the hospital down if she didn't give the patients their medicine.

Why do we go wrong? We don't use God's strength. God 'lights' us, and as we grow in him, our 'fire' grows bright.

Now light the fire, so they can see it growing, needing a bit of blowing, till it burns brightly.

(Put fire out carefully!)

You may like to give each child a candle lit from the fire.

Sing *Give me love in my heart, keep me burning.*

Music
Recorded Music

Mozart – *Symphony No. 28: Andante*

'Live' Music

Breathe on me, breath of God *(ONE, 70)*
Faith can move mountains *(SONL, 70)*
Give me joy in my heart *(ONE, 159)*
Live in the Spirit *(MSOS, 143; BSOS, 48)*

28th Sunday in Ordinary Time

Theme
To God be the glory

God has the power of healing, spiritual as well as physical. He will take us in the sickness of our sin and make us whole again. So often we only turn to God in deep need: as soon as we are healed we ignore him. Yet thanks and praise should be our response, acknowledging God's power and directing all glory on to him.

Penitential Rite

Our anxiety reveals a lack of trust,
   Lord, have mercy. **Lord, have mercy.**

Our grumbling shows a lack of thankfulness,
   Christ, have mercy. **Christ, have mercy.**

Our vanity reveals begrudging praise,
   Lord, have mercy. **Lord, have mercy.**

Notes on the Readings

2 Kings 5:14-17

Naaman had to swallow his pride in order to obey Elisha's instructions of simply washing seven times in the Jordan. His obedience brought him healing, and he immediately wanted to express his gratitude in a material way to Elisha.

Elisha knows that it was God whose power healed Naaman, and he directs the thanks and praise to its source, so that through his healing Naaman comes to the point of worshipping God.

Whenever God uses us as his instruments of peace, healing or love, there is the possibility that those on the receiving end will enthusiastically give us the credit and praise for what has happened.

Then comes the temptation to enjoy basking in that glory. We may even persuade ourselves that it was indeed our own achievement. We have to be on our guard, and make sure we do direct the praise and glory to its source, so that another soul may be introduced to God's saving love. God entrusted us with his power in order to bring all men to himself. We must not abuse it.

2 Timothy 2:8-13

Though we are all precious individually to our heavenly Father, we are also part of something much larger: of cosmic and eternal significance. This great plan stretches far beyond our understanding, and as individuals we are tiny parts of the complete picture.

It does not matter, then, if we sometimes feel ourselves 'chained', and unable to be as active in working for Christ's Kingdom as we would wish. As Paul says: 'they cannot chain up God's news,' and so long as we remain faithful, alert to God's will and resting in the conviction of his ultimate power of love, then the work of God will certainly continue. In fact, the very way we react to being chained by illness, age or persecution, may itself help to spread the Good News.

It is staying close to Christ which matters. We may not be able to see how he is working or what possible good can come out of our own particular, depressing situation, but if we can't see, then it is a tremendous opportunity to learn to trust God in a more basic, fundamental way. Years later, or at death, we may understand; for one thing is certain: if we do trust him he will never ever let us down or betray our trust.

Luke 17:11-19

The lepers must have had faith in Jesus. They all asked him to take pity on them, and did not hesitate to set off to show themselves to the priest as cleansed men while their bodies were still covered with sores.

It is a mark of Jesus' immense love for us that he never sets our thanks and adoration as a condition of helping us, even though he longs for it. He loves us enough to leave us free to make our own decisions and never forces us to honour him.

Yet how mean and small-minded, how arrogant and discourteous we are if we fail to give God the thanks and credit he deserves, when we have cried to him in distress and he has taken pity on us and healed us.

People pray when they are suddenly aware of their frailty and vulnerability. If we stay with him right through to thankfulness we shall be doubly blessed and the Kingdom of God will be that much closer.

Bidding Prayers

Celebrant Let us approach our heavenly Father in humility as we bring to his love our cares.

Reader Let us bring to him
the divided Christian community
that he may bring wholeness and unity.
Pause
Jesus! Master!: **you alone, can make us whole.**

Let us bring to him
the divided world,
split between wealth and poverty,
complacency and oppression,
that he may break through barriers
with the power of love and reconciliation.
Pause
Jesus! Master!: **you alone, can make us whole.**

Let us bring to him
all lepers and the diseased,
the mentally and physically handicapped
and all whom society prefers to ignore;
that his love may nourish and heal,
restore and accept.
Pause
Jesus! Master!: **you alone, can make us whole.**

Let us bring to him
the wounds and hurts of our own lives
and our families;
all unresolved tensions and sorrows,
all reunions, joys and healing
that he will bless our lives with his presence.
Pause
Jesus! Master!: **you alone, can make us whole.**

Celebrant Heavenly Father, to whom all glory belongs, accept our prayers, through Christ our Lord. **Amen.**

Ideas for Adults

A group could mime the Gospel as it is read.

Ideas for Children

Palm Tree Bible Stories have the story of the ten lepers which can be read aloud to the children today, or the story can be told in your own words. It lends itself well to being acted out, with the help of some sheeting bandages for the lepers which can be flung off as they are healed.

Then talk with the children about when we give presents and enjoy it so much when the person is pleased and thanks us – it draws us closer.

Make a 'thank you' poster by having some pictures of things we want to thank God for, and let each child add to it his own thank you prayer.

Sing: *If I were a butterfly* (ONE, 233),

Music
Recorded Music

Elgar – *Enigma Variations*

'Live' Music

Glorify the Lord *(SONL, 17)*
Lord, when I turn my back on you *(SONL, 40)*
Love divine, all loves excelling *(ONE, 337)*
Majesty *(SOS 3, 232)*
Take, Lord, receive *(SOS 3, 233)*

29th Sunday in Ordinary Time

Theme
Persevere in prayer

We must pray faithfully and not get disheartened if results are not immediate. In time our prayers will be answered, and our persistence will keep us close to God and protect us from all that is evil.

Penitential Rite

Through each moment of each day,
Lord, have mercy. **Lord, have mercy.**

Through the seasons of each year,
Christ, have mercy. **Christ, have mercy.**

Through birth, through life, through death,
Lord, have mercy. **Lord, have mercy.**

Notes on the Readings

Exodus 17:8-13

Moses' uplifted arms in sustained prayer are an outward symbol of the importance of united, persevering prayer which will certainly be answered. In many ways, this constant prayer is for our own benefit, for God knows what we need already.

For our part, we need to make a conscious act of committing ourselves to God and relying on him for our everyday needs. We find this so difficult that, if we stop praying, we are more likely to be back worrying anxiously, busying about in our own strength and ending up exhausted, dissatisfied and restless.

Self control, where prayer is concerned, involves a firm centering of our values, worries and needs on the still source of all being – God himself; it means allowing distractions and jumbled thoughts and ideas to drift past without us losing our anchorage and chasing after them. Drinking deeply from God's well of stillness and peace, we shall be far stronger and more able to cope with the minor irritations and distractions of life.

2 Timothy 3:14 – 4:2

We would not dream of telling someone how to mend a roof or make flaky pastry unless we were thoroughly sure of our facts first, and had tried them out to check that they worked.

Timothy is advised to prepare himself in a similar way before embarking on his task of proclaiming the Christian message and teaching the faith. Perhaps we feel that our learning finished when we were confirmed; perhaps we have stopped reading the Bible regularly over the years. Paul's message to Timothy is a call to us as well: if we are to be useful, effective members of Christ, then we need to be rigorous and constant in our preparation. It is never too late to change!

Luke 18:1-8

The need for persistent prayer is illustrated here by Jesus in his story of the widow nagging a judge to give her justice. The judge is a thoroughly unsympathetic man, who would never help her but for her persistence, which finally drives him to act on her behalf. Jesus couldn't have chosen anyone less likely to grant a request, and yet in the end, justice is done. The contrast between this miserable judge and the all-loving God highlights the certainty of God being prepared to listen to us and see justice done. However long it takes we need never worry that God will turn down our request – it may well be that we are being taught perseverance and gaining a deeper faith in the process.

Bidding Prayers

Celebrant Let us quieten our hearts in the presence of the unchanging and everlasting Father and pray.

Reader For all those involved in the ceaseless
praying on our spinning earth;
for all contemplative orders, and those
whose lives are rooted in prayer;
for those learning to pray and those
who feel they cannot pray.
Pause
Spirit of Jesus: **live in our hearts and minds.**

For the world, for victory of good
over evil in every situation
whether of international
or local significance;
for a deepening of trust and a desire
for truth and peace.
Pause
Spirit of Jesus: **live in our hearts and minds.**

For the disheartened and uninspired;
for those whose lives are frustrating
and endlessly stressful;
for the homeless and the unemployed;
and for those addicted to drugs, alcohol
or gambling.
Pause
Spirit of Jesus: **live in our hearts and minds.**

For the members of our own families,
with their particular needs;
for our local shopkeepers, teachers,
doctors, nurses,
and all who work in this area.
Pause
Spirit of Jesus: **live in our hearts and minds.**

Celebrant God, our heavenly Father,
bless our lives to your constant service.
Through Christ our Lord. **Amen.**

Ideas for Children

Talk with the children about working hard at something until at last it is finished. They may have found it difficult making a model, mixing a cake, tidying their bedroom or learning to swim or skip, for instance.

You could bring to show them something you had to persevere with, such as a knitted jumper, loaf of bread, or piece of music, and tell them you sometimes wanted to stop and give up, but decided not to.

Help them to see that perseverance is not always easy, but it is always worthwhile.

Now tell the story of Moses, using plasticine models or pictures to illustrate it.

Give each child a card to split into days and with a prayer they have made up to say every day. Perhaps their parents might like to say it with them.

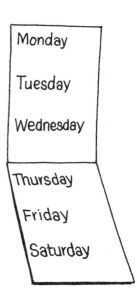

Ask them to bring their cards back next week with a tick drawn each day they remembered to do it.

Music
Recorded Music

Lloyd Webber – Requiem: Libera me – last section

'Live' Music

I am the God who loves you (MSOS, 149)
King of glory, King of peace (ONE, 292)
Lord of all hopefulness (ONE, 329)
On days when much we do goes wrong (SONL, 68)

30th Sunday in Ordinary Time

Theme
Praying with humility

Rank and status are unimportant in God's eyes, since he loves all men equally. God is far more concerned with the openness of a person's heart. If it is closed with hypocrisy or self-righteousness then a relationship with God cannot develop. If it is open in humility, growth is immediately possible, however unpromising the material may seem.

Penitential Rite

Open our hearts to love you more dearly,
Lord, have mercy. **Lord, have mercy.**

Enlighten our minds to know you more clearly,
Christ, have mercy. **Christ, have mercy.**

Strengthen our will to follow you more nearly,
Lord, have mercy. **Lord, have mercy.**

Notes on the Readings

Ecclesiasticus 35:12-14, 16-19

In most societies, however impartial, there is likely to be some bias in the law court. Since we are physical beings we display our characters and pretensions in manner and dress which become signals to other people and evoke certain sympathies or antagonisms. For God, it is different. As Ben Sira says, he is 'no respecter of personages' because he knows us in our entirety and can see intentions as well as actions, realities as well as disguises.

So it is just a waste of time trying to impress God in the same way as we might impress the world. He is never fooled.

2 Timothy 4:6-8, 16-18

Paul is convinced that God will keep his promise of eternal life and joy. He never forgets that he began by persecuting Christ, and is therefore the very least among his followers. Yet in that poverty he prayed and God has answered his prayer magnificently, making him the instrument of bringing the Good News to many pagans.

In one sense Paul remains 'poor': he does not cling on to the successes for himself but passes them all on to the Lord of his life, in whom he has drenched himself. Christ has become his wealth, and since Christ is the ever-present God, he is never alone or rejected, regardless of public opinion, imprisonment or death.

Living in prayer, or communication with Christ, we shall be granted the same freedom and security.

Luke 18:9-14

In this parable Jesus gives us a clear example of how we should approach God.

The self-righteous Pharisee takes God's acceptance of him for granted and assumes an attitude of smug arrogance where all the credit for keeping the law remains firmly in his own pocket.

One of the serious drawbacks of living by rules is that it is possible to keep each rule and imagine we have therefore reached perfection. In reality, of course, perfection transcends all rules, and results from grace freely given, not tactics mechanically worked at. While the Pharisee concentrates on output like this instead of input, Christ is barred from fulfilling and enriching his life.

The Publican is chosen as an exaggerated example of someone most people would regard as beyond the pale as far as God is concerned. His life is no doubt just as grasping, unjust and adulterous as the Pharisee supposes.

Jesus is not suggesting that we need to be more sinful and less religious before we can be at one with God; but he is pointing out the need for an acute sense of sin before we can want God's forgiveness and appreciate his saving power.

At the moment we realise how far short of God's plan we have fallen, God can start to act in us, put things right and remake us. If we never approach him in this way, he will never be able to act.

Bidding Prayers

Celebrant Let us pray to God our Father with wonder and love in our hearts.

Reader For all Christians striving to follow
the Lord of Life;
that they may not fall into the
temptation of complacency,
self-righteous or spiritual pride;
that they may joyfully become the least
important for Christ's sake.
Pause
God, our Father: **be merciful to us sinners.**

For all the worldly struggles for power,
all areas of political unrest,
all decision and policy makers;
that wisdom, common sense and respect
may encourage just and peaceful
government.
Pause
God, our Father: **be merciful to us sinners.**

For the physically blind and their families;
for those who are spiritually blind and
think they can see;
for those whose minds are confused
through accidents, illness or age;
that God's inner sight may bring
enlightenment, order and peace.
Pause
God, our Father: **be merciful to us sinners.**

For ourselves and all those
worshipping in this place;
that we may be increasingly open
to the searing light of Christ
till our darkest corners are lit by his love.
Pause
God, our Father: **be merciful to us sinners.**

Celebrant Lord God, accept these prayers,
through Christ our Lord. **Amen.**

Ideas for Children

Tell the children the story of the Pharisee and the Publican as a puppet show. Simple puppets can be made from wooden spoons with cloth tied round them. Give the Pharisee a snooty expression and make the Publican much more plainly dressed. Their prayers can be based on the Gospel story but including more topical acts of devotion: I go to church three times every Sunday; I collect money for lots of good causes; etc.

Afterwards, help the children to see why the Publican's prayer is better and more likely to bring him closer to Jesus. What was wrong with the Pharisee?

Then give each child a card with the Pharisee drawn in outline one side and the Publican the other. They can be coloured and cut out and their prayers written on the appropriate side.

Music

Recorded Music

Mozart – *Piano Sonata No. 8 in A minor: second movement*

'Live' Music

Build your church *(SONL, 41)*
Make me a channel for your peace *(ONE, 342)*
Song of Simeon *(SONL, 53)*
Walk humbly with your God *(MSOS, 171; BSOS, 68)*

31st Sunday in Ordinary Time

Theme
Tender forgiveness

God cherishes all that he has created; indeed, it is his love which conserves and sustains everything. Tenderly he coaxes and leads us out of our sin to repentance, and, if we allow him full rein in our lives, he will bring all our gifts and good desires to perfection.

Penitential Rite

You know us better than we know ourselves,
   Lord, have mercy. **Lord, have mercy.**

Tenderly you hold us in your love,
   Christ, have mercy. **Christ, have mercy.**

It is our privilege to enjoy your world,
   Lord, have mercy. **Lord, have mercy.**

Notes on the Readings

Wisdom 11:22 – 12:2

This lovely passage captures the essence of the creative God, who delights in what he has made, and cherishes and nurtures it in great tenderness. Viewing the world through God's eyes like this brings an immediate sense of calm and order; for our frantic, anxious lives are suddenly scaled down, and priorities are rebalanced so that there is harmony. Throughout a vast but entirely ordered universe, we are valued and loved. Such a realisation makes us ready to repent and start again, and encourages us to look outwards with love, generosity and forgiveness.

Thessalonians 1:11 – 2:2

Here, as well, we are aware of our Lord taking a great, personal interest in our welfare and our achievements. Like a parent watching a small child take her first steps, God our Father encourages, watches and supports; never in a forceful, interfering way, but quietly delighting in our progress. Since he is right here, now, working in us, we do not need to get steamed up about the many rumours of his second coming.

Saint Francis was once asked what he would do if he were told that God would be coming in an hour's time. He replied that he would carry on doing the gardening.

Luke 19:1-10

Zacchaeus must have presented rather a comic picture to the citizens of Jericho, standing on tiptoe to peer over the crowd and then climbing a sycamore tree in spite of his wealth and status.

Why was he so curious? Perhaps he was a lonely man, for all his riches. Perhaps he already felt vaguely uneasy about his life-style, but hadn't the courage to change without some firm outside incentive.

Whatever his reasons, Jesus' heart goes out to him when he sees him. He senses Zacchaeus' need to be useful and valuable, his longing to be wanted. So he gives him a practical job to do, and then there is no stopping Zacchaeus who cannot wait to get started.

Jesus' outgoing friendship gives him the impetus to respond to others and put right the wrongs Zacchaeus has done. We can almost see the chains of misery dropping off him as he begins his new life of freedom through love. As Christ's ambassadors, we can set other Zacchaeuses free, among our own acquaintances. If we welcome them and value their friendship, look at them instead of through them or past them, we may plant seeds of liberation; for being cherished and valued inspires us to become more loving and giving.

Bidding Prayers

Celebrant My brothers and sisters let us pray at the feet of God our Father, who loves us so dearly.

Reader For the spreading of the Gospel
throughout all countries and cultures;
for all those working to reconcile men
with their creator:
for all involved in counselling,
and spiritual teaching.
Pause
God, our loving Father:
  make us worthy of our calling.

For a deepening spirit
of fellowship and goodwill
among the peoples of this earth;
for a greater willingness to forgive,
negotiate, communicate and support.
Pause
God, our loving Father:
  make us worthy of our calling.

For all victims of violence
and aggression;
for those obsessed with hatred
and retaliation;
for the injured, abused and the dying.
Pause
God, our loving Father:
  make us worthy of our calling.

For God's guidance
and restoration in our own lives;
for more awareness of our faults
and areas of blindness;
for a greater understanding
of God's love for us.
Pause
God, our loving Father:
  make us worthy of our calling.

Celebrant Heavenly Father, trusting in your amazing love, we ask you to accept these prayers. Through Christ our Lord. **Amen.**

Ideas for Adults

The first reading is good to read chorally, using high, medium and low voices.

All:	In your sight, Lord,
High:	the whole world is like a grain of dust that tips the scales,
Medium:	like a drop of morning dew, falling on the ground.
Low:	Yet you are merciful to all,
Low & Medium:	because you can do all things
All:	and overlook men's sins so that they can repent.
One High:	Yes, you love all that exists,
One Low:	you hold nothing of what you have made in abhorrence
Low:	for had you hated anything
Medium:	you would not have formed it.
One Medium:	And how, had you not willed it, could a thing persist;
High:	how be conserved if not called forth by you?
All:	You spare all things because all things are yours, Lord, lover of life.
Low:	You whose imperishable spirit is in all.
High:	Little by little, therefore, you correct those who offend,
Medium:	you admonish
Low:	so that they may abstain from evil and trust in you, Lord.

The Gospel can be acted out by members of the congregation.

Ideas for Children

Children love today's Gospel story. (Palm Tree Bible Stories has a delightful version called *Zacchaeus and Jesus*.) Read or tell the story first, then make a model of the story on a base, such as a baking tray.

Some children can make plasticine or card members of the crowd, some collect twigs to fix in cotton reels as trees, some make box houses and others a sandy road and grass from coloured paper, moss and sand or strip of sandpaper.

The figures could be moved through the main parts of the story again, and left on display with Zacchaeus up the tree and Jesus looking up and seeing him.

Music
Recorded Music

Vaughan Williams – O *taste and see*

'Live' Music

Amazing grace *(ONE, 36)*
Lay your hands *(ONE, 295)*
Oh the love of my Lord *(ONE, 430)*

32nd Sunday in Ordinary Time

Theme
Life beyond death

Resurrection of the dead, which was implicit in many Old Testament writings, has become explicit in the person of Jesus and his teaching. Death is not the end, and life beyond it is not a continuation of the same level of existence. It is a new order, and earthly rules and restrictions will no longer apply. The assurance of God's continuing presence, even through death, will comfort and strengthen us in all earthly distress and danger.

Penitential Rite

In times of temptation,
Lord, have mercy. **Lord, have mercy.**

In times of danger and persecution,
Christ, have mercy. **Christ, have mercy.**

At the time of death,
Lord, have mercy. **Lord, have mercy.**

Notes on the Readings

Maccabees 7:1-2, 9-14

This may not make pleasant reading for the squeamish, even in its abbreviated form, but it is certainly a powerful example of young men whose convictions sustain them even through torture and death.

They were so sure that God would be true to his promise and raise them to everlasting life, that death was preferable to breaking the Law and relinquishing their claim to resurrection. Persecution of any sort and any intensity has the effect of testing the depth of our convictions, measured against our personal safety. It forces us to discover how much we really believe in what we regularly profess; for when threatened, we can no longer sit on the fence.

Standing up for Christian values may well bring us ridicule, ostracism or aggression, but in suffering them we are never alone: Christ will be constantly by our side to give us courage and strength.

2 Thessalonians 2:16 – 3:5

Paul, too, has absolute confidence in Christ's power because he has tried it out frequently and it has never let him down. His experience confirms his belief that the God of love works ceaselessly to bring all good to completion, to encourage and support and to guard his flock from all that is evil.

We shall never have easy, uncomplicated lives if we live as Christians; the mere fact of caring and loving is bound to involve us in heartache and sorrow as well as joy.

But then, Christ never promised us peace in the world's terms, in the first place, so we should not expect it. However,

he did promise to be with us always; and that is no indistinct, flimsy wish, but an absolutely real experience, for it is not his memory which undergoes trouble with us, but his living self.

Luke 20:27-38

The Pharisees and Sadducees were firmly split on the question of life after death, and this is an area where Christ's teaching is quite definite. There is no question of life after death not existing, and Jesus points out that even the ancient personalities of Jewish history were aware of it. The reason for people's scepticism is that they try to explain it in terms of earthly experience, and this makes nonsense of rational thinking: We cannot ever hope to understand eternal matters in a temporal frame of reference, any more than we could explain worldly life to an unborn child in terms of foetal darkness.

Death marks the beginning of a totally new and different existence, which we may sometimes sense in a poetic or spiritual way, and which we actually see in the life of the risen Jesus between Easter morning and the Ascension. We know that life beyond death will encompass all that is good, beautiful and lovely; we know that there we shall meet Jesus face to face at last; we know that within its joy there will be timeless peace. For the rest, should we not simply trust in Jesus and enjoy leaving the details to his good keeping?

Bidding Prayers

Celebrant   Let us pray together, bringing our concerns and cares to the Lord of life.

Reader   We bring before him all
who profess to be Christians,
that in times of trial they may remain faithful
and trust in his everlasting love;
that all who are called upon to witness
at the risk of their lives,
may be given courage and inspiration.
Pause
Lord of the living: **keep us in life everlasting.**

We bring before him all the diverse
societies throughout the world;
that the living Spirit of Christ
may be spread abroad
to purify the corrupt, inspire the apathetic
and unlock the hearts of the bigotted.
Pause
Lord of the living: **keep us in life everlasting.**

We bring before him the weak
and the frightened;
all who suffer from neurosis or phobias,
for the intimidated, the pressurised
and the friendless;
that they may find, in Christ,
courage and hope.
Pause
Lord of the living: **keep us in life everlasting.**

We bring before him our own
circle of friends and family;
all our desires and attempts
to follow Christ;
that he may live within us to protect,
guide and bring us to perfection
at the end of time.
Pause
Lord of the living: **keep us in life everlasting.**

Celebrant   All-powerful God, accept these prayers
through Christ our Lord. **Amen.**

Ideas for Children

Today offers a good opportunity to learn about some of the saints and martyrs who have been prepared to face suffering and death for the sake of remaining faithful to Jesus. The parish saint may be a good example, or the children could be split into groups and each group learn about a different saint.

Pictures of his or her life can be coloured by different members of each group, and arranged on a large sheet of coloured paper.

At the end, all the displays can be shown and the children share what they have learnt with each other.

Possible saints and martyrs are:

- Paul
- Peter
- Stephen
- Lawrence
- Thomas More
- John Ogilvie
- Any local martyr saint

Music
Recorded Music

Beethoven – *Symphony No. 7: final movement, slow section*

'Live' Music

If God is for us *(ONE, 231)*
Jesu, the very thought of thee *(ONE, 287)*
Sing a new song unto the Lord *(SOS 3, 201)*
With you I am secure *(SONL, 50)*

33rd Sunday in Ordinary Time

Theme
Your endurance will win you your lives

From Christ, the first-fruit, leading up to the harvest at the end of time, when all things shall be revealed and judged, there is bound to be much suffering and persecution, as the victory of good over evil is won. Terrifying though it may seem, we need not fear, for Christ will direct our words and actions and see that we are safe: if we, for our part, remain true to him.

Penitential Rite

You see the secrets of our hearts,
    Lord, have mercy. **Lord, have mercy.**

You grieve over our blindness and sin,
    Christ, have mercy. **Christ, have mercy.**

You long to give us your peace,
    Lord, have mercy. **Lord, have mercy,**

Notes on the Readings

Malachi 3:19-20

Speaking to a people who had grown slack, apathetic and cynical, the prophet presents the Day of Atonement or Judgement in stark, black and white terms. The wicked may not appear to be punished at the moment, he says, but they certainly will be then. In contrast, the fire which burns evil will bring healing and wholeness to the righteous.

In the light of Christ, such judgement is seen softened with mercy; but even so, we need to remind ourselves at regular intervals that we are going to be judged at the end of time, and God will not automatically pat us on the back regardless of how we have lived. To believe so is a kind of misguided and sentimental hypocrisy.

God has high standards, based on perfection and excellence, and although he understands our obstacles and difficulties, he is also aware of all the opportunities we ignore and reject.

2 Thessalonians 3:7-12

After an initial flush of enthusiasm for anything new it is usual for things to relax a bit. Partly this is a result of our natural metabolism, and can be beneficial, since we cannot remain on a 'high' indefinitely, and must learn to value the quieter, less exciting times of growth.

But the temptation is to relax standards and values; to be content with the easier, less demanding course; to become lazy and self indulgent. Some of the Christians at Thessalonia seem to have fallen into this trap, and Paul is anxious to halt the decline before it gets any worse.

Reminders of good examples may sometimes help to keep us on our toes. Mutual encouragement and support may even prevent such idleness beginning. It may be that a discreet word is needed by a parish priest or close friend. Whatever is done, it must be done in a spirit of love.

For each of us, a daily check through the day's work during night prayers is a valuable means of keeping ourselves from slipping in this way. We may have hidden our slackness from other people quite well, but in God's light we shall see it clearly.

Luke 21:5-19

It is almost as if the solid beauty of the temple, here, triggers off a glimpse of the world from outside time. Like a speeded-up film we scan the great cosmic cycles and seasons, natural disasters and human agonies, as the earth labours towards its time of accomplishment; and over all God is powerful and fully in control.

Within the terror, distress, upheavals and ructions are scattered the bright lights of individuals who are unperturbed and faithful; those who are not drawn into the panic and confusion but who remain steadfast, strong as rocks in their perseverance.

These are the ones who will win eternal life by their endurance, for when they are tried they are not found wanting. Not just the beginning, but the continuing and completing are vital. And we need not fear; it is, after all, the Father's pleasure to give us the Kingdom, so he will provide us with all the strength we shall need.

Bidding Prayers

Celebrant My sisters and brothers, let us lay at the feet
of God our Father our needs and our cares,
as we pray together in the Spirit of Jesus.

Reader We lay at his feet the need for more priests;
for a firm Christian witness in the face of
materialism and oppression;
for zeal and dedication among all members
of the Body of Christ.

Pause

Lord, we trust you: **hold us safe in your hand.**

We lay at his feet the needs
of our divided fractious world;
its systems and schemes,
fashions and disasters;
that God's Kingdom of love may be
established on earth, as it is in heaven.

Pause

Lord, we trust you: **hold us safe in your hand.**

We lay before him the needs of all
who suffer in earthquakes, floods,
droughts, famine and epidemics,
all who try to supply relief
and medical aid;
that in Christ we may labour
for the good of the world.

Pause

Lord, we trust you: **hold us safe in your hand.**

We lay before him the needs
of this community;
the local problems and injustices;
our Christian usefulness
in this corner of God's world.

Pause

Lord, we trust you: **hold us safe in your hand.**

Celebrant God our Father, trusting in your constant
care and protection we bring you these prayers.
Through Christ our Lord. **Amen.**

Ideas for Children

There is no reason why even quite young children should
not explore the ideas of time ending, judgement and the
second coming, as many of them ask questions about such
matters and are often fobbed off with simplistic answers.

If you can borrow some slides of our planets in the solar
system, stars and space, show these first to an accompani-
ment of music such as *Saturn* from Holst's *Planet Suite*. Or
have a large drawing pad with a series of pictures drawn,
which take us gradually further from earth.

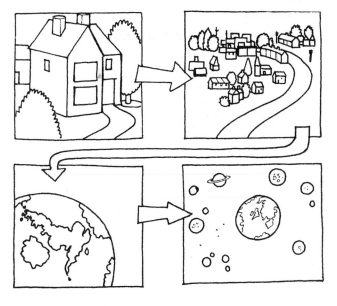

You could sing *There's a seed in a flower* (MWTP) or *He's got the
whole world in his hand*.

Talk with the children about how Jesus promised that at
the end of the world he would come again, only this time not
as a tiny baby, but in all his glory. He will be hoping to find
us ready for him. How can we be ready?

Tell them how Jesus said there would be wars, famines
and earthquakes before the end of the world. Bring a few
newspapers to show he was right.

Explain how we need not be frightened even when really
bad things happen. We can trust Jesus and he holds our
hand and looks after us to keep us safe.

Music
Recorded Music

Luis Milan – *Pavane No. 6*

'Live' Music

I'll send you my Spirit *(MSOS, 147; BSOS, 143)*
In peace and love *(SONL, 91)*
Keep us, ever-living Lord *(SONL, 65)*
Ye choirs of new Jerusalem *(ONE, 623)*

Last Sunday in Ordinary Time
Our Lord Jesus Christ,
Universal King

Theme
In Christ all thing are reconciled

Before anything was created and after the end of created
things, Christ Jesus reigns as Lord and King, and his Kingdom
encompasses all times and peoples universally. Whoever
turns to him will be given his power to persevere joyfully
and know the freedom and peace of his service.

Penitential Rite

Scatter our darkness with your light,
Lord, have mercy. **Lord, have mercy.**

Set us on fire with your love,
Christ, have mercy. **Christ, have mercy.**

Make us strong in your strength,
Lord, have mercy. **Lord, have mercy.**

Notes on the Readings

2 Samuel 5:1-3

Jesus is often referred to as 'the Son of David', and here we
see why. David is appointed King to lead his flock as a
shepherd, and rule over Israel. He is chosen by God and
acclaimed by all the tribes of Israel who pledge themselves
to him.

Jesus was to follow David's line and develop that kingship
to include all peoples with no barriers of time, race or
location.

Colossians 1:12-20

In the resurrection of Christ we are brought into a new understanding of God's cosmic significance. For Christ's actions reveal God's plan to unify, reconcile and overcome all powers of evil and destruction, so that we may no longer be held in their grip.

In Christ we are liberated from any power of the occult, from temporal tyranny and cruelty and even from what grips us most tightly: our own sin.

So we can afford to be filled with joy, laughter, and relaxed peacefulness, because we have just been let out of prison where we were in the condemned cell awaiting death! And the one to thank for it is Jesus Christ, who accomplished it by dying in our place, even though he was innocent. That shows quite a staggering capacity for love.

Luke 23:35-43

If Jesus had been crucified on his own, this valuable opportunity of showing the extent of his compassion would have been missed. As it is, the two thieves crucified with him are representative of all of us, who through rejection of and disloyalty to God, do not deserve his promise of life.

Faced with the realisation that when we suffer Jesus is hanging beside us, also suffering, we can react in two ways. Either we scorn Jesus for what he is doing, demanding that he use his power (if indeed he has any) to do the obvious, sensible thing and save himself and us with him – to intervene and sort things out in the quickest, most dramatic and easiest way; or we can, with the penitent thief, remember with awe that Jesus is God, and if God is prepared to hang beside us and suffer, then that says a great deal about his love for us, and we are humbled into begging his mercy.

Christ's promise to the penitent thief, and to all who turn to him acknowledging their unworthiness, is an indication of all the goodness, truth and love which distinguish God's personality.

Bidding Prayers

Celebrant As sons and daughters of the King, let us ask God's blessing on the Church and on the world

Reader For the work of Christ's Body, the Church;
that all may labour zealously
for the establishment
of God's Kingdom on earth
till the world is drenched
in his peace, joy and love.
Pause
Lord, our heavenly Father:
let your Kingdom come.

For the work of all peacemakers, reformers;
all who work for justice, reconciliation
and harmony;
that the God of peace and love
will bless, support and encourage them.
Pause
Lord, our heavenly Father:
let your Kingdom come.

For the work of those who heal
and tend the injured, sick and dying,
and those in their care;
for all involved in medical research
and those whose lives depend
on drugs, dialysis or radiotherapy.
Pause
Lord, our heavenly Father:
let your Kingdom come.

For our own work in this life;
that we may dedicate our energies
and resources more fully
to establishing Christ's Kingdom;
that we may undertake every task and
activity joyfully in the strength of our King.
Pause
Lord, our heavenly Father:
let your Kingdom come.

Celebrant God our Father we ask you to accept our prayers through Christ our Lord. **Amen.**

Ideas for Children

Although children may not live in a kingdom, they are familiar with kings and queens through fairy tales.

Begin by showing pictures of some earthly royal families, past and present, their crowns and coronations, even including local carnival queens. Talk about what the king or queen does and how the people line the streets and cheer whenever they are in public.

Show them that there are lots of kings and queens all over the world. Their power is limited to one country and their own life time. But there is one king who is king over all the world, all the past, present and future, and all the universe. He must be very powerful. Who do you think it is?

Sing a song to praise and cheer Jesus, the King, such as 'Jesus is Lord' or 'Shout aloud for Jesus!' (both from *Good Morning, Jesus*).

Then remind the children that we are God's sons and daughters. So if the Lord our God is King, what does that make us? Princes and Princesses!

Give out pieces of card cut in crown shapes and let each Prince and Princess make his or her crown. Staple to fit at the end and write 'Jesus is King' round the base of it. Perhaps all the Princes and Princesses can wear their crowns in church.

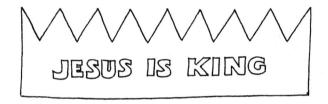

Music
Recorded Music

Beethoven – *Symphony No. 9: third movement*

'Live' Music

A man fully living *(MSOS, 193; BSOS, 5)*
Canticle of David *(SONL, 79)*
Christ is our King *(ONE, 84)*
Come into his presence *(ONE, 101)*
For you and me *(SOS 3, 272)*
Our God reigns *(ONE, 224)*